THE
BOOK OF DISCIPLINE
OF THE
UNITED METHODIST
CHURCH
1988

The United Methodist Publishing House
Nashville, Tennessee

"The Book Editor, the Secretary of the General Conference, the Publisher of The United Methodist Church, and the Committee on Correlation and Editorial Revision shall be charged with editing the Discipline. These editors, in the exercise of their judgment, shall have the authority to make changes in phraseology as may be necessary to harmonize legislation without changing its substance."

—Plan of Organization and Rules of Order of the General Conference, 1988

See Judicial Council Decision 96 which declares the Discipline to be a book of law.

Ronald P. Patterson
Book Editor of The United Methodist Church

C. Faith Richardson
Secretary of the General Conference

Robert K. Feaster
Publisher of The United Methodist Church

The Committee on Correlation and Editorial Revision
Earl W. Riddle, Chairperson
C. Leonard Miller
Naomi G. Bartle
Bruce E. Krause
Gladys M. Fitts

ISBN 0-687-03697-6

Deluxe Edition ISBN 0-687-03700-X

PRINTED IN THE UNITED STATES OF AMERICA

EPISCOPAL GREETINGS

To all people and pastors of United Methodism:
  "Grace and peace to you from God our Father and the Lord
  Jesus Christ."   —I Cor. 1:3

The Discipline is the book of law of The United Methodist
Church. It is the product of the many General Conferences of
historic religious bodies which now form The United Methodist
Church.

The Discipline as the instrument for setting forth the laws,
plan, polity, and process by which United Methodists govern
themselves remains constant. Each General Conference modifies, elaborates, clarifies, and adds its own contribution to the
Discipline. We do not see the Discipline as sacrosanct or infallible,
but we do consider it as a document suitable to our heritage. It
reflects our understanding of the Church and of what is expected
of its ministers and members as they seek to be effective witnesses
in the world as a part of the whole Body of Christ.

The Discipline sets forth the theological grounding of The
United Methodist Church in biblical faith, and affirms that we go
forward as "loyal heirs to all that [is] best in the Christian past."
The Discipline makes clear that The United Methodist Church is
an inclusive society without regard to ethnic origin, economic
condition, sex, or age of its constituents. It calls for the
amenability of bishops, district superintendents, ministers, and
lay members to the Church's faith and order. The Discipline
affirms connectionalism as a distinctive mark of United
Methodist ecclesiology, makes clear the global character of the
Church's mission, and declares interdependence with other
Christian bodies both in spirit and cooperation. The Discipline

affirms with John Wesley that solitary religion is invalid and that Christ lays claim upon the whole life of those who accept him as Lord and Savior.

We therefore commend this Discipline to all in our constituency and to friends beyond our bounds who would seek to understand what it means to be a United Methodist. Communication is essential for understanding what the Church is and does. We expect the Discipline to be found in libraries of local churches, colleges, universities, and seminaries, as well as in the homes of ordained ministers and lay members of The United Methodist Church. We pray that it will enable all persons to celebrate God's grace, exalt the meaning of faithful discipleship, and inspire on the part of many a deeper desire to be more effective witnesses for the Head of the Church, even Jesus Christ our Lord.

The Council of Bishops
Ernest T. Dixon, Jr., President
Jack Marvin Tuell, President-Designate
Paul Andrews Duffey, Secretary
Melvin George Talbert, Secretary-Designate

CONTENTS

Note: The basic unit in the Book of Discipline is the paragraph (¶) rather than page, chapter, section, etc. The paragraphs are numbered consecutively within each chapter or section, but many numbers are skipped between parts, chapters, and sections in order to allow for future enactments and to fit with the following plan:

1- 99	The Constitution, Doctrine and Doctrinal Statements, General Rules, and Social Principles
101- 199	The Mission and Ministry of the Church
201- 299	The Local Church
301- 399	The Diaconal Ministry
401- 499	The Ordained Ministry
501- 599	The Superintendency
601- 799	The Conferences
801-2499	Administrative Order
2501-2599	Church Property
2601-2699	Judicial Administration

Episcopal Greetings.. *page v*
United Methodist Bishops....................................... *page 1*
Historical Statement.. *page 7*

PART I
THE CONSTITUTION
¶¶ 1-64

The Constitution of The United Methodist Church.... *page 19*

PART II
DOCTRINAL STANDARDS AND OUR THEOLOGICAL TASK
¶¶ 66-69

Our Doctrinal Heritage... *page 40*

vii

CONTENTS

Our Doctrinal History... *page 50*
Our Doctrinal Standards and General Rules
  (The Articles of Religion, The Confession of Faith,
  The General Rules)... *page 60*
Our Theological Task.. *page 77*

PART III
SOCIAL PRINCIPLES
¶¶ 70-76

Preface and Preamble.. *page 91*
The Natural World... *page 92*
The Nurturing Community... *page 93*
The Social Community... *page 97*
The Economic Community.. *page 102*
The Political Community... *page 105*
The World Community.. *page 108*
Our Social Creed.. *page 110*

PART IV
THE MINISTRY OF ALL CHRISTIANS

The Mission and Ministry of the Church.......... ¶¶   101-113

PART V
ORGANIZATION AND ADMINISTRATION
¶¶ 201-2626

Chapter One
THE LOCAL CHURCH

   I. The Church and Pastoral Charge............ ¶¶   201-205
  II. Cooperative Parish Ministries.................... ¶   206
 III. Churches in Transitional Communities.... ¶   207
 IV. Church Membership................................. ¶¶   208-243
  V. Organization and Administration............ ¶¶   244-269
 VI. The Method of Organizing a New Local
     Church... ¶   270
 VII. Transfer of a Local Church....................... ¶   271
VIII. Protection of Rights of Congregations...... ¶   272
 IX. Special Sundays... ¶¶   273-276
  X. Lay Speaking... ¶¶   277-279

CONTENTS

Chapter Two
THE DIACONAL MINISTRY

I. Relation to the Ministry of All Christians. ¶ 301
II. The Nature of Diaconal Ministry............. ¶ 302
III. Entrance into Diaconal Ministry............. ¶¶ 303-306
IV. Relationship to the Annual Conference.. ¶¶ 307-313
V. Relationship to the Charge Conference.... ¶ 314
VI. Relationship to the Employing Agency..... ¶ 315-317

Chapter Three
THE ORDAINED MINISTRY

I. Relation of Ordained Ministers to the
    Ministry of All Christians..................... ¶¶ 401-402
II. Entrance Procedures into Ordained
    Ministry.. ¶¶ 403-411
III. Admission and Continuance.................... ¶¶ 412-428
IV. Ordination.. ¶¶ 429-435
V. Appointments to Various Ministries........ ¶¶ 436-443
VI. Evaluation and Continuing Education for
    Full and Associate Members................. ¶¶ 444-446
VII. Changes of Conference Relationship for
    Full, Probationary, and Associate
    Members.. ¶¶ 447-451
VIII. Review of Full and Associate
    Conference Membership......................... ¶¶ 452-453
IX. Readmission to Conference
    Relationship... ¶¶ 454-457

Chapter Four
THE SUPERINTENDENCY

I. Nature of Superintendency...................... ¶¶ 501-502
II. Offices of Bishop and District
    Superintendent..................................... ¶¶ 503-504
III. Election, Assignment, and Termination of
    Bishops.. ¶¶ 505-513
IV. Specific Responsibilities of Bishops......... ¶¶ 514-516
V. Selection, Assignment, and Term of
    District Superintendents........................ ¶¶ 517-518

CONTENTS

VI. Specific Responsibilities of District
   Superintendents...................................... ¶¶   519-525
VII. Expressions of Superintendency.............. ¶¶   526-529
VIII. Appointment-Making............................... ¶¶   530-534

Chapter Five
THE CONFERENCES
   I. The General Conference........................... ¶¶   601-611
  II. The Jurisdictional Conference................. ¶¶   612-635
 III. Central Conferences................................ ¶¶   636-638
 IV. Provisional Central Conferences.............. ¶¶   639-646
  V. Autonomous Methodist Churches,
     Affiliated Autonomous Methodist
     Churches, Affiliated United Churches,
     Covenanting Churches, and Concordat
     Churches.. ¶¶   647-654
 VI. Provisional Annual Conferences.............. ¶¶   655-658
VII. The Missionary Conference...................... ¶¶   659-662
VIII. Missions.. ¶¶   663-664
 IX. The Annual Conference........................... ¶¶   701-745
  X. The District Conference........................... ¶¶   746-756

Chapter Six
ADMINISTRATIVE ORDER
   I. General Provisions.................................... ¶¶   801-824
  II. General Council on Finance and
     Administration...................................... ¶¶   901-932
 III. The General Council on Ministries......... ¶¶ 1001-1007
 IV. General Board of Church and Society.... ¶¶ 1101-1116
  V. General Board of Discipleship................. ¶¶ 1201-1228
 VI. United Methodist National Youth Ministry
     Organization... ¶¶ 1301-1311
VII. General Board of Global Ministries......... ¶¶ 1401-1467
VIII. General Board of Higher Education and
     Ministry... ¶¶ 1501-1532
 IX. General Board of Pensions...................... ¶¶ 1601-1609
  X. General Board of Publication.................. ¶¶ 1701-1743
 XI. General Commission on Archives and
     History... ¶¶ 1801-1812

CONTENTS

XII. General Commission on
Communication...................................... ¶¶ 1901-1909
XIII. General Commission on Christian Unity
and Interreligious Concerns................. ¶¶ 2001-2006
XIV. General Commission on Religion and
Race.. ¶¶ 2101-2108
XV. General Commission on the Status and
Role of Women..................................... ¶¶ 2201-2209
XVI. Commission on Central Conference
Affairs... ¶ 2301
XVII. Interdenominational Agencies................. ¶¶ 2401-2406

Chapter Seven
CHURCH PROPERTY
I. All Titles—in Trust.................................... ¶¶ 2501-2505
II. Compliance with Law.............................. ¶¶ 2506-2509
III. Audits and Bonding of Church Officers.. ¶ 2510
IV. The Methodist Corporation....................... ¶ 2511
V. Annual Conference Property.................. ¶¶ 2512-2516
VI. District Property...................................... ¶¶ 2517-2523
VII. Local Church Property............................ ¶¶ 2524-2552
VIII. Requirements—Trustees of Church
Institutions... ¶ 2553

Chapter Eight
JUDICIAL ADMINISTRATION
I. The Judicial Council................................ ¶¶ 2601-2619
II. Investigations, Trials, and Appeals.......... ¶¶ 2620-2626

Index.. *page 729*

UNITED METHODIST BISHOPS

A List Compiled for
The Book of Discipline
by the Council of Bishops

NAME	ELECTED
Thomas Coke	1784
Francis Asbury	1784
Richard Whatcoat	1800
Phillip William Otterbein	1800
Martin Boehm	1800
Jacob Albright	1807
William M'Kendree	1808
Christian Newcomer	1813
Enoch George	1816
Robert Richford Roberts	1816
Andrew Zeller	1817
Joseph Hoffman	1821
Joshua Soule	1824
Elijah Hedding	1824
Henry Kumler, Sr.	1825
John Emory	1832
James Osgood Andrew	1832
Samuel Heistand	1833
William Brown	1833
Beverly Waugh	1836
Thomas Asbury Morris	1836
Jacob Erb	1837
John Seybert	1839
Henry Kumler, Jr.	1841
John Coons	1841
Joseph Long	1843
Leonidas Lent Hamline	1844
Edmund Storer Janes	1844
John Russel	1845
Jacob John Glossbrenner	1845
William Hanby	1845
William Capers	1846
Robert Paine	1846
David Edwards	1849

NAME	ELECTED
Henry Bidleman Bascom	1850
Levi Scott	1852
Matthew Simpson	1852
Osman Cleander Baker	1852
Edward Raymond Ames	1852
Lewis Davis	1853
George Foster Pierce	1854
John Early	1854
Hubbard Hinde Kavanaugh	1854
Francis Burns	1858
William W. Orwig	1859
Jacob Markwood	1861
Daniel Shuck	1861
John Jacob Esher	1863
Davis Wasgatt Clark	1864
Edward Thomson	1864
Calvin Kingsley	1864
Jonathan Weaver	1865
William May Wightman	1866
Enoch Mather Marvin	1866
David Seth Doggett	1866
Holland Nimmons McTyeire	1866
John Wright Roberts	1866
John Dickson	1869
John Christian Keener	1870
Reuben Yeakel	1871
Thomas Bowman	1872
William Logan Harris	1872
Randolph Sinks Foster	1872
Isaac William Wiley	1872
Stephen Mason Merrill	1872
Edward Gayer Andrews	1872
Gilbert Haven	1872
Jesse Truesdell Peck	1872

1

NAME	ELECTED
Rudolph Dubs	1875
Thomas Bowman	1875
Milton Wright	1877
Nicholas Castle	1877
Henry White Warren	1880
Cyrus David Foss	1880
John Fletcher Hurst	1880
Erastus Otis Haven	1880
Ezekiel Boring Kephart	1881
Alpheus Waters Wilson	1882
Linus Parker	1882
John Cowper Granbery	1882
Robert Kennon Hargrove	1882
William Xavier Ninde	1884
John Morgan Walden	1884
Willard Francis Mallalieu	1884
Charles Henry Fowler	1884
William Taylor	1884
Daniel Kumler Flickinger	1885
William Wallace Duncan	1886
Charles Betts Galloway	1886
Eugene Russell Hendrix	1886
Joseph Stanton Key	1886
John Heyl Vincent	1888
James Newbury FitzGerald	1888
Isaac Wilson Joyce	1888
John Philip Newman	1888
Daniel Ayres Goodsell	1888
James Mills Thoburn	1888
James W. Hott	1889
Atticus Greene Haygood	1890
Oscar Penn Fitzgerald	1890
Wesley Matthias Stanford	1891
Christian S. Haman	1891
Sylvanus C. Breyfogel	1891
William Horn	1891
Job S. Mills	1893
Charles Cardwell McCabe	1896
Joseph Crane Hartzell	1896
Earl Cranston	1896
Warren Akin Candler	1898
Henry Clay Morrison	1898

NAME	ELECTED
David Hastings Moore	1900
John William Hamilton	1900
Edwin Wallace Parker	1900
Francis Wesley Warne	1900
George Martin Mathews	1902
Alexander Coke Smith	1902
Elijah Embree Hoss	1902
Henry Burns Hartzler	1902
William Franklin Heil	1902
Joseph Flintoft Berry	1904
Henry Spellmeyer	1904
William Fraser McDowell	1904
James Whitford Bashford	1904
William Burt	1904
Luther Barton Wilson	1904
Thomas Benjamin Neely	1904
Isaiah Benjamin Scott	1904
William Fitzjames Oldham	1904
John Edward Robinson	1904
Merriman Colbert Harris	1904
William Marion Weekley	1905
William Melvin Bell	1905
Thomas Coke Carter	1905
John James Tigert III	1906
Seth Ward	1906
James Atkins	1906
Samuel P. Spreng	1907
William Franklin Anderson	1908
John Louis Nuelsen	1908
William Alfred Quayle	1908
Charles William Smith	1908
Wilson Seeley Lewis	1908
Edwin Holt Hughes	1908
Robert McIntyre	1908
Frank Milton Bristol	1908
Collins Denny	1910
John Carlisle Kilgo	1910
William Belton Murrah	1910
Walter Russell Lambuth	1910
Richard Green Waterhouse	1910
Edwin DuBose Mouzon	1910
James Henry McCoy	1910
William Hargrave Fouke	1910

NAME	ELECTED
Uriah Frantz Swengel	1910
William Orville Shepard	1912
Theodore Sommers Henderson	1912
Naphtali Luccock	1912
Francis John McConnell	1912
Frederick DeLand Leete	1912
Richard Joseph Cooke	1912
Wilbur Patterson Thirkield	1912
John Wesley Robinson	1912
William Perry Eveland	1912
Henry Harness Fout	1913
Cyrus Jeffries Kephart	1913
Alfred Taylor Howard	1913
Gottlieb Heinmiller	1915
Lawrence Hoover Seager	1915
Herbert Welch	1916
Thomas Nicholson	1916
Adna Wright Leonard	1916
Matthew Simpson Hughes	1916
Charles Bayard Mitchell	1916
Franklin Elmer Ellsworth Hamilton	1916
Alexander Priestly Camphor	1916
Eben Samuel Johnson	1916
William H. Washinger	1917
John Monroe Moore	1918
William Fletcher McMurry	1918
Urban Valentine Williams Darlington	1918
Horace Mellard DuBose	1918
William Newman Ainsworth	1918
James Cannon, Jr	1918
Matthew T. Maze	1918
Lauress John Birney	1920
Frederick Bohn Fisher	1920
Charles Edward Locke	1920
Ernest Lynn Waldorf	1920
Edgar Blake	1920

NAME	ELECTED
Ernest Gladstone Richardson	1920
Charles Wesley Burns	1920
Harry Lester Smith	1920
George Harvey Bickley	1920
Frederick Thomas Keeney	1920
Charles Larew Mead	1920
Anton Bast	1920
Robert Elijah Jones	1920
Matthew Wesley Clair	1920
Arthur R. Clippinger	1921
William Benjamin Beauchamp	1922
James Edward Dickey	1922
Samuel Ross Hay	1922
Hoyt McWhorter Dobbs	1922
Hiram Abiff Boaz	1922
John Francis Dunlap	1922
George Amos Miller	1924
Titus Lowe	1924
George Richmond Grose	1924
Brenton Thoburn Badley	1924
Wallace Elias Brown	1924
Arthur Biggs Statton	1925
John S. Stamm	1926
Samuel J. Umbreit	1926
Raymond J. Wade	1928
James Chamberlain Baker	1928
Edwin Ferdinand Lee	1928
Grant D. Batdorf	1929
Ira David Warner	1929
John W. Gowdy	1930
Chih Ping Wang	1930
Arthur James Moore	1930
Paul Bentley Kern	1930
Angie Frank Smith	1930
George Edward Epp	1930
Juan Ermete Gattinoni	1932
Junius Ralph Magee	1932
Ralph Spaulding Cushman	1932
Elmer Wesley Praetorius	1934
Charles H. Stauffacher	1934

UNITED METHODIST BISHOPS

NAME	ELECTED
Jarrell Waskom Pickett	1935
Roberto Valenzuela Elphick	1936
Wilbur Emery Hammaker	1936
Charles Wesley Flint	1936
Garfield Bromley Oxnam	1936
Alexander Preston Shaw	1936
John McKendree Springer	1936
F. H. Otto Melle	1936
Ralph Ansel Ward	1937
Victor Otterbein Weidler	1938
Ivan Lee Holt	1938
William Walter Peele	1938
Clare Purcell	1938
Charles Claude Selecman	1938
John Lloyd Decell	1938
William Clyde Martin	1938
William Turner Watkins	1938
James Henry Straughn	1939
John Calvin Broomfield	1939
William Alfred Carroll Hughes	1940
Lorenzo Houston King	1940
Bruce Richard Baxter	1940
Shot Kumar Mondol	1940
Clement Daniel Rockey	1941
Enrique Carlos Balloch	1941
Z. T. Kaung	1941
Wen Yuan Chen	1941
George Carleton Lacy	1941
Fred L. Dennis	1941
Dionisio Deista Alejandro	1944
Fred Pierce Corson	1944
Walter Earl Ledden	1944
Lewis Oliver Hartman	1944
Newell Snow Booth	1944
Willis Jefferson King	1944
Robert Nathaniel Brooks	1944
Edward Wendall Kelly	1944
William Angie Smith	1944
Paul Elliott Martin	1944
Costen Jordan Harrell	1944
Paul Neff Garber	1944

NAME	ELECTED
Charles Wesley Brashares	1944
Schuyler Edward Garth	1944
Arthur Frederick Wesley	1944
John Abdus Subhan	1945
John Balmer Showers	1945
August Theodor Arvidson	1946
Johann Wilhelm Ernst Sommer	1946
John Wesley Edward Bowen	1948
Lloyd Christ Wicke	1948
John Wesley Lord	1948
Dana Dawson	1948
Marvin Augustus Franklin	1948
Roy Hunter Short	1948
Richard Campbell Raines	1948
Marshall Russell Reed	1948
Harry Clifford Northcott	1948
Hazen Graff Werner	1948
Glenn Randall Phillips	1948
Gerald Hamilton Kennedy	1948
Donald Harvey Tippett	1948
Jose Labarrete Valencia	1948
Sante Uberto Barbieri	1949
Raymond Leroy Archer	1950
David Thomas Gregory	1950
Frederick Buckley Newell	1952
Edgar Amos Love	1952
Matthew Wesley Clair, Jr.	1952
John Warren Branscomb	1952
Henry Bascom Watts	1952
D. Stanley Coors	1952
Edwin Edgar Voigt	1952
Francis Gerald Ensley	1952
Alsie Raymond Grant	1952
Julio Manuel Sabanes	1952
Friedrich Wunderlich	1953
Odd Arthur Hagen	1953
Ferdinand Sigg	1954
Reuben Herbert Mueller	1954
Harold Rickel Heininger	1954
Lyle Lynden Baughman	1954
Prince Albert Taylor, Jr.	1956

4

NAME	ELECTED	NAME	ELECTED
Eugene Maxwell Frank	1956	Homer Ellis Finger, Jr	1964
Nolan Bailey Harmon	1956	Earl Gladstone Hunt, Jr	1964
Bachman Gladstone Hodge	1956	Francis Enmer Kearns	1964
Hobart Baumann Amstutz	1956	Lance Webb	1964
Ralph Edward Dodge	1956	Escrivao Anglaze Zunguze	1964
Mangal Singh	1956	Robert Fielden Lundy	1964
Gabriel Sundaram	1956	Harry Peter Andreassen	1964
Paul E. V. Shannon	1957	John Wesley Shungu	1964
John Gordon Howard	1957	Alfred Jacob Shaw	1965
Hermann Walter Kaebnick	1958	Prabhakar Christopher	
W. Maynard Sparks	1958	Benjamin Balaram	1965
Paul Murray Herrick	1958	Stephen Trowen Nagbe	1965
Bowman Foster Stockwell	1960	Franz Werner Schäfer	1966
Fred Garrigus Holloway	1960	Benjamin I. Guansing	1967
William Vernon Middleton	1960	Lineunt Scott Allen	1967
William Ralph Ward, Jr	1960	Paul Arthur Washburn	1968
James Kenneth Mathews	1960	Carl Ernst Sommer	1968
Oliver Eugene Slater	1960	David Frederick Wertz	1968
William Kenneth Pope	1960	Alsie Henry Carleton	1968
Paul Vernon Galloway	1960	Roy Calvin Nichols	1968
Aubrey Grey Walton	1960	Arthur James Armstrong	1968
Kenneth Wilford Copeland	1960	William Ragsdale Cannon	1968
Everett Walter Palmer	1960	Abel Tendekayi Muzorewa	1968
Ralph Taylor Alton	1960	Cornelio M. Ferrer	1968
Edwin Ronald Garrison	1960	Paul Locke A. Granadosin	1968
Torney Otto Nall, Jr	1960	Joseph R. Lance	1968
Charles Franklin Golden	1960	Ram Dutt Joshi	1968
Noah Watson Moore, Jr	1960	Eric Algernon Mitchell	1969
Marquis LaFayette Harris	1960	Federico Jose Pagura	1969
James Walton Henley	1960	Armin E. Härtel	1970
Walter Clark Gum	1960	Ole Edvard Borgen	1970
Paul Hardin, Jr	1960	Finis Alonzo	
John Owen Smith	1960	Crutchfield, Jr	1972
Paul William Milhouse	1960	Joseph Hughes Yeakel	1972
Pedro Ricardo Zottele	1962	Robert E. Goodrich, Jr	1972
James Samuel Thomas	1964	Carl Julian Sanders	1972
William McFerrin Stowe	1964	Ernest T. Dixon, Jr	1972
Walter Kenneth Goodson	1964	Don Wendell Holter	1972
Dwight Ellsworth Loder	1964	Wayne K. Clymer	1972
Robert Marvin Stuart	1964	Joel David McDavid	1972
Edward Julian		Edward Gonzalez Carroll	1972
Pendergrass, Jr	1964	Jesse Robert DeWitt	1972
Thomas Marion Pryor	1964	James Mase Ault	1972

UNITED METHODIST BISHOPS

NAME	ELECTED
John B. Warman	1972
Mack B. Stokes	1972
Jack Marvin Tuell	1972
Melvin E. Wheatley, Jr	1972
Edward Lewis Tullis	1972
Frank Lewis Robertson	1972
Wilbur Wong Yan Choy	1972
Robert McGrady Blackburn	1972
Emilio J. M. de Carvalho	1972
Fama Onema	1972
Mamidi Elia Peter	1972
Bennie de Quency Warner	1973
J. Kenneth Shamblin	1976
Alonzo Monk Bryan	1976
Kenneth William Hicks	1976
James Chess Lovern	1976
Leroy Charles Hodapp	1976
Edsel Albert Ammons	1976
C. Dale White	1976
Ngoy Kimba Wakadilo	1976
Almeida Penicela	1976
LaVerne D. Mercado	1976
Hermann Ludwig Sticher	1977
Shantu Kumar A. Parmar	1979
Thomas Syla Bangura	1979
John Alfred Ndoricimpa	1980
William Talbot Handy, Jr.	1980
John Wesley Hardt	1980
Benjamin Ray Oliphint	1980
Louis Wesley Schowengerdt	1980
Melvin George Talbert	1980
Paul Andrews Duffey	1980
Edwin Charles Boulton	1980
John William Russell	1980
Fitz Herbert Skeete	1980
George Willis Bashore	1980
Roy Clyde Clark	1980
William Boyd Grove	1980
Emerson Stephen Colaw	1980
Marjorie Swank Matthews	1980
Carlton Printiss Minnick, Jr.	1980
Calvin Dale McConnell	1980

NAME	ELECTED
Kainda Katembo	1980
Emerito P. Nacpil	1980
Arthur Flumo Kulah	1980
Felton Edwin May	1984
Ernest A. Fitzgerald	1984
R. Kern Eutsler	1984
J. Woodrow Hearn	1984
Walter L. Underwood	1984
Richard B. Wilke	1984
J. Lloyd Knox	1984
Neil L. Irons	1984
Roy I. Sano	1984
L. Bevel Jones III	1984
Forrest C. Stith	1984
Ernest W. Newman	1984
Woodie W. White	1984
Robert Crawley Morgan	1984
David J. Lawson	1984
Elias Gabriel Galvan	1984
Rueben Philip Job	1984
Leontine T. Kelly	1984
Judith Craig	1984
Rüdiger Rainer Minor	1986
Jose Castro Gamboa, Jr	1986
Thomas Barber Stockton	1988
Harold Hasbrouck Hughes, Jr	1988
Richard Carl Looney	1988
Robert Hitchcock Spain	1988
Susan Murch Morrison	1988
R. Sheldon Duecker	1988
Joseph Benjamin Bethea	1988
William B. Oden	1988
Bruce P. Blake	1988
Charles Wilbourne Hancock	1988
Clay Foster Lee, Jr	1988
Sharon A. Brown Christopher	1988
Dan E. Solomon	1988
William B. Lewis	1988
William W. Dew, Jr	1988

HISTORICAL STATEMENT

The Plan of Union proposed to bring together The Methodist Church and the Evangelical United Brethren Church, two churches that share a common historical and spiritual heritage. They hold the same fundamental doctrines of faith. Ecclesiastical organization is similar. They are Protestant churches, whose streams of spiritual life and thought come out of the Protestant Reformation of the sixteenth century.

Since their beginnings they had lived and worked side by side in friendly fellowship. Had it not been for the difference in language—the Methodists working among English-speaking people and the Evangelical and United Brethren working among those speaking German—they might, from the beginning, have been one church. Today the language barrier is gone and the uniting of forces for our common task and calling seems appropriate and timely. Brief historical sketches of the two churches, taken from their respective Disciplines, follow.

The Methodist Church

The Methodist Church is a church of Christ in which "the pure Word of God is preached, and the Sacraments duly administered." This church is a great Protestant body, though it did not come directly out of the Reformation but had its origin within the Church of England. Its founder was John Wesley, a clergyman of that church, as was his father before him. His mother, Susanna Wesley, was a woman of zeal, devotion, and strength of character who was perhaps the greatest single human influence in Wesley's life.

Nurtured in this devout home, educated at Oxford University, the young John Wesley, like a second Paul, sought in vain for religious satisfaction by the strict observance of the rules of religion and the ordinances of the church. The turning point in his life came when, at a prayer meeting in Aldersgate Street, London, on May 24, 1738, he learned what Paul had discovered, that it is not by rules and laws, nor by our own efforts at self-perfection, but by faith in God's mercy as it comes to us in Christ, that one may enter upon life and peace.

The gospel which Wesley thus found for himself he began to proclaim to others, first to companions who sought his counsel, including his brother Charles, then in widening circles that took him throughout the British Isles. His message had a double emphasis, which has remained with Methodism to this day. First was the gospel of God's grace, offered to all and equal to every human need. Second was the moral ideal which this gospel presents. The Bible, he declared, knows no salvation which is not salvation from sin. He called persons to holiness of life, and this holiness, he insisted, is "social holiness," the love and service of others. Methodism meant "Christianity in earnest." The General Rules, which are still found in the Discipline, are the directions which Wesley gave to his followers to enable them to test the sincerity of their purpose and to guide them in this life.

Wesley did not plan to found a new church. In his work he simply followed, like Paul, the clear call of God, first to preach the gospel to the needy who were not being reached by the Established Church and its clergy, second to take care of those who were won to the Christian life. Step by step he was led on until Methodism became a great and transforming movement in the life of England. He gathered his people in groups, in classes and societies. He appointed leaders. He found persons who were ready to carry the gospel to the masses, speaking on the streets, in the open fields, and in private homes. These persons were not ordained ministers but lay preachers, or "local preachers," as they were called. He appointed these preachers, assigned them to various fields of labor, and supervised their work. Once a year he called them together for a conference, just as Methodist preachers meet in their Annual Conference sessions today.

Wesley thus united in extraordinary fashion three notable activities, in all of which he excelled. One was evangelism; "The world is my parish," he declared. His preachers went to the people; they did not wait for the people to come to them, and he

8

himself knew the highways and byways of England as did no other man of his day. The second was organization and administration, by which he conserved the fruits of this preaching and extended its influence. The third was his appreciation of education and his use of the printed page. He made the press a servant of the Church and was the father of the mass circulation of inexpensive books, pamphlets, and periodicals.

From England, Methodism spread to Ireland and then to America. In 1766 Philip Embury, a lay preacher from Ireland, began to preach in the city of New York. At about the same time Robert Strawbridge, another lay preacher from Ireland, settled in Frederick County, Maryland, and began the work there. In 1769 Wesley sent Richard Boardman and Joseph Pilmoor to America, and two years later Francis Asbury, who became the great leader of American Methodism.

Methodism was especially adapted to American life. These itinerant preachers served the people under conditions where a settled ministry was not feasible. They sought out the scattered homes, followed the tide of migration as it moved west, preached the gospel, organized societies, established "preaching places," and formed these into "circuits." Thus by the close of the American Revolution the Methodists numbered some fifteen thousand members and eighty preachers.

In the beginning Wesley had thought of his fellows not as constituting a church but simply as forming so many societies. The preachers were not ordained, and the members were supposed to receive the Sacraments in the Anglican Church. But the Anglican clergy in America were few and far between. The Revolution had severed America from England, and Methodism to all intents and purposes had become an independent church. Wesley responded to appeals for help from America by asking the Bishop of London to ordain some of his preachers. Failing in this, he himself ordained two men and set aside Dr. Thomas Coke, who was a presbyter of the Church of England, to be a superintendent, "to preside over the flock of Christ" in America. Coke was directed to ordain Francis Asbury as a second superintendent.

At the Christmas Conference, which met in Baltimore December 24, 1784, some sixty preachers, with Dr. Coke and his companions, organized the Methodist Episcopal Church in America. Wesley had sent over *The Sunday Service,* a simplified form of the English Book of Common Prayer, with the Articles of Religion reduced in number. This book they adopted, adding to the articles one which recognized the independence of the new nation.

Our present Articles of Religion come from this book and unite us with the historic faith of Christendom. Our Ritual, too, though it has been modified, has this as its source. However, the forms for public worship taken from the Book of Common Prayer were not adapted to the freer religious life of American Methodism and never entered into common use. Instead, Methodism created a book of its own, its Discipline. This contains today the Articles of Religion, Wesley's General Rules, and a large section which deals with the ministry, the various church organizations, and the rules governing the life and work of the Church.

In the history of Methodism two notable divisions occurred. In 1828 a group of earnest and godly persons, largely moved by an insistence on lay representation, separated and became the Methodist Protestant Church. In 1844 there was another division, the cause being construed by some as the question of slavery, by others as a constitutional issue over the powers of the General Conference versus the episcopacy. After years of negotiation a Plan of Union was agreed upon; and on May 10, 1939, the Methodist Episcopal Church, the Methodist Episcopal Church, South, and the Methodist Protestant Church united to form The Methodist Church.

The Methodist Church believes today, as Methodism has from the first, that the only infallible proof of a true church of Christ is its ability to seek and to save the lost, to disseminate the Pentecostal spirit and life, to spread scriptural holiness, and to transform all peoples and nations through the gospel of Christ. The sole object of the rules, regulations, and usages of The Methodist Church is to aid the Church in fulfilling its divine commission. United Methodism thanks God for the new life and strength which have come with reunion, while realizing the new obligations which this brings. At the same time it rejoices in the fact that it is a part of the one Church of our Lord and shares in a common task. Its spirit is still expressed in Wesley's words: "I desire to have a league, offensive and defensive, with every soldier of Christ. We have not only one faith, one hope, one Lord, but are directly engaged in one warfare."

The Evangelical United Brethren Church

The Evangelical United Brethren Church had its roots in the spiritual quickening which emerged in the United States in the late eighteenth and early nineteenth centuries. This movement challenged not only religious indifference, but also the contemporary tendency to substitute "religion" for a vital and experiential relationship with God. In its present form the Evangelical United Brethren Church represents the union, consummated in 1946, of the Church of the United Brethren in Christ and the Evangelical Church.

I. Church of the United Brethren in Christ

The eighteenth century witnessed the eruption of revolutionary ideas and programs in science, industry, and politics. In this agitated world there were marked evidences of religious revitalization. In the English-speaking world it was associated with, though not confined to, Wesleyanism; in the German-speaking world it was associated with pietism. In some places and in some persons, these two movements impinged upon each other.

Philip William Otterbein, an ordained minister of the German Reformed Church who served congregations in Pennsylvania and Maryland, and Martin Boehm, a Pennsynian of Mennonite parentage, were among those who sensed a call to preach the Good News of God's redeeming mercy and love as demonstrated in Jesus Christ, especially among neglected German-speaking settlers of the Middle Colonies. In obedience to this call, they invited others to accept salvation. To be saved, they held, meant both awareness, as real as any sensory awareness, of God's acceptance and personal commitment to Christ. Their labors were blessed, and thriving societies were established which were conceived not so much as alternatives or rivals to established churches as centers for renewal in those churches. This work expanded, and helpers were sought to devote themselves to this evangelistic effort. As persons responded, they were received as fellow laborers.

The gracious work of renewal and reformation spread through Pennsylvania, Maryland, and Virginia. Otterbein's leadership was increasingly acknowledged. In the larger "big meetings" and in more intimate circles, he emphasized the necessity to persuade men to accept the divine invitation to salvation and to lead a new kind of life. To share experiences in this ministry and to seek greater effectiveness in this mission, it was resolved that preachers' meetings be held. One such meeting was held in Baltimore, Maryland, in 1789; another in Paradise Township, York County, Pennsylvania, in 1791.

Beginning with the meeting, September 25, 1800, in Frederick County, Maryland, these ministers' meetings were held annually. They agreed each of them should have liberty as to the mode of baptism, each administering it according to his own conviction. They agreed that Otterbein and Boehm should be their leaders as superintendents or bishops. About this time the name United Brethren in Christ came into use. The work soon extended across the Appalachian Mountains into Ohio, and this prompted the decision to organize a Conference in Ohio in 1810.

Martin Boehm died in 1812; Philip William Otterbein was incapacitated by ill health. Accordingly, in 1813 Christian Newcomer was elected bishop to superintend the concerns of the growing church. Up to this time there was no book of Discipline, so it was determined that a General Conference should be called to provide such a book. The first General Conference of this church convened June 6, 1815, near Mt. Pleasant, Pennsylvania. After deliberation, the conference recommended a book of Discipline containing the doctrines and rules of the church with the exhortation that these together with the Word of God should be strictly observed and admonished the members that "God is a God of order, but where there is no order and no church discipline, the spirit of love and charity will be lost."

The book of Discipline, together with a Constitution which was adopted in 1841, provided regulations under which the Church of the United Brethren in Christ expanded in numbers and mission in the nineteenth and twentieth centuries. The Constitution, with several other factors, was the ground for a division in the denomination in 1889 as the majority, authorized by a referendum in the church, made changes in the Constitution.

II. THE EVANGELICAL CHURCH

Jacob Albright, an unordained Pennsylvania tilemaker-farmer, began preaching that religion was a personal, conscious, experiential relationship with God. About 1800, small groups of people living in three separated communities, impressed by Albright's ideas, covenanted themselves to seek God's grace which would enable them to live holily. Following his experience of salvation in 1791, Albright began to witness in the German language to God's saving grace. He and those associated with him agreed to measures of self-discipline and Christian witness. The number of those inclined to participate in this endeavor increased, and this in turn promoted the enlistment of helpers.

The transition from movement to ecclesiastical organization was marked by the first council of those acknowledging Albright as leader on November 3, 1803. Beginning in 1807, with a meeting at Kleinfeltersville, Lebanon County, Pennsylvania, the preachers gathered in annual meetings. In 1809 a book of Discipline was adopted and printed. In 1816, at the first General Conference of the body, the name, The Evangelical Association, was adopted. For the courageous ministry of this church, conversion was the central theme and purpose, a word which signified the gracious, conscious vitalization of the life of a person by an act of God.

During the nineteenth century the operations of this church enlarged in evangelism, education, and publications. In the latter part of the century differences arose in the Evangelical Association which in 1891 culminated in a division. A considerable number of ministers and laymembers withdrew and took the name the United Evangelical Church, which held its first General Conference in 1894. Both churches continued their activities, side by side, both endeavoring to carry on the work of the Lord with zeal and devotion. Both churches grew in numbers and in missionary enterprise. By 1910 the growing conviction that the two churches should be reunited found articulate expression, and in 1922 the Evangelical Association and the United Evangelical Church were united under the name the Evangelical Church.

III. Union in 1946

Negotiations, beginning in 1933, were consummated in 1946 when the Church of the United Brethren in Christ and the Evangelical Church became the Evangelical United Brethren Church. This church sought to serve its Lord faithfully in the proclamation that salvation is available to any upon the free, personal acceptance of God's offer. Conversion, while personal, is not a private matter and finds its consummation in holy living and in serving as an instrument of God for the redemption of the whole world. In this task, it views itself as one fold, in the one flock, whose Shepherd is our Lord.

Black People and Their United Methodist Heritage

Prior to the organization of the Methodist Episcopal Church in 1784, black people were related to the Methodist societies. On November 29, 1758, John Wesley baptized his first Negro converts at Wandsworth, England. Mr. Wesley claimed that these were the first African Christians he had known.

These African Christians began immediately to "spread scriptural holiness" in the New World. They introduced Methodism in Antigua. By 1786, there were 1,569 Methodists in this country. Only two were white.

Black people embraced the Methodist faith in the United States very early. Two early Methodist societies in America were the John Street Society in New York City and the Log Meeting House in Frederick County, Maryland. Black members are included among the charter members. In the John Street Society, Beatty, a Negro servant of the Heck family, was a charter member. On Sam Creek in Frederick County, Maryland, Anne, a slave of the Schweitzer family, was a charter member. By 1786, there were 1,890 black members in the Methodist Episcopal Church.

Methodism won favor with the black people for two main reasons: (1) its evangelistic appeal; (2) the Church's attitude toward slavery. Later its social concern impressed black people.

The shortest list of early black Methodist evangelists must include Harry Hoosier, Henry Evans, and John Stewart. Harry Hoosier was a traveling companion of Francis Asbury. He accompanied him to preach to the colored people. In alluding to Harry Hoosier, Thomas Coke said: "I believe he is one of the best preachers in the world." A freeborn Negro of Virginia, Henry Evans possessed genius of organization. He organized the Fourth Street Church in Wilmington, Delaware. He is credited also with organizing the first inclusive church in Fayetteville, North Carolina. The Methodist historian Abel Stevens referred to him as the Father of the Methodist Episcopal Church, White and Black in that city. The first home missionary in the Methodist Episcopal Church was John Stewart. He was a freeborn mulatto from Virginia. He became a missionary to the Wyandotte Indians. The arduous labors of John Stewart led directly to the organization of the Home Missionary Society in the Methodist Episcopal Church.

From 1784 to 1864, the black people were included in the membership of the white churches. Black people persuaded the Church to organize them into their own churches. In 1794, the African Zoar Society was organized in Philadelphia. It was the first black society in the Methodist Episcopal Church.

In 1864, the General Conference authorized the organization of Mission Conferences among black people. The first black mission conference to be organized was the Delaware Conference on July 29, 1864. By 1900, nineteen conferences had been organized among the black people. These conferences had 1,705 ministers in full connection and 3,398 organized congregations with an aggregate church membership of 239,274.

Until 1920, these black conferences were supervised by white bishops. On May 19, 1920, Robert Elijah Jones was elected as the first black General Superintendent in the Methodist Episcopal Church. Previously, four black ministers had been elected as missionary bishops for Liberia. By 1975, nineteen other black elders had been consecrated.

On May 10, 1939, the Methodist Episcopal Church, South, the Methodist Protestant Church, and the Methodist Episcopal Church united into The Methodist Church. In order to perfect union, the Jurisdictional System was created. Five regional jurisdictions were created. In addition, the Central Jurisdiction was established to include all the black conferences.

The black conferences did not on the whole approve of the Central Jurisdiction. Most of the conferences opposed it for at least two reasons: (1) the Central Jurisdiction was written into the Constitution of the Church; and (2) it was a segregated unit.

The Central Jurisdiction continued as a segregated structural arrangement in the Constitution of The Methodist Church until 1968. In 1968, The Methodist Church and the Evangelical United Brethren Church united and became The United Methodist Church. The Constitution of the new Church did not provide for the Central Jurisdiction. Black conferences were transferred into the regional jurisdictions. By 1974, all black conferences had merged with the white conferences. United Methodism became inclusive on the associative level.

With the merger of The Methodist Church and the Evangelical United Brethren Church, some Blacks were added to the membership of The United Methodist Church from the former Evangelical United Brethren Church. Perhaps the earliest attempt of the former Evangelical Association in establishing a Negro Mission was in 1822. A Negro named Daniel Wilson opened his home in Orwigsburg, Pennsylvania to the Reverend John Seybert. This church had desultory contacts with American Negroes.

About two decades prior to union of the former Evangelical United Brethren Church and The Methodist Church, the former Evangelical United Brethren Church began to recognize the needs of changing communities in the cities where this denomination was located. Through its Board of National Missions in cooperation with some Annual Conferences, this Church began to minister to the religious needs of black people.

The United Methodist Church

The United Methodist Church brings together two streams of spiritual life with similar emphases which had their beginnings in the evangelistic concerns and passion of John Wesley, Francis Asbury, Philip William Otterbein, Jacob Albright, Martin Boehm, and others who labored with them. These men were

16

dedicated to the task of preaching the gospel to their fellow countrymen.

Since they were men who were deeply moved by a common faith and zeal and held a like emphasis upon personal spiritual experience of salvation, it is no surprise to find instances of fraternity and cooperation among them. They often conferred with each other and sometimes traveled together on their preaching missions. In many communities they shared the same building, with the Methodist preachers conducting services in English at one hour and the Evangelical or United Brethren preachers conducting a German service at another hour. There are many references to the Asbury groups as "English Methodists" and the Otterbein-Boehm-Albright groups as "German Methodists" or "Dutch Methodists."

The firm conviction that Christian faith and experience ought to be expressed in holy living led these early leaders to adopt similar patterns of ecclesiastical organization and discipline to assist Christians in spiritual growth and Christian witness.

When Asbury was ordained and consecrated as bishop in 1784, Otterbein participated with the laying on of hands. When Otterbein ordained Christian Newcomer in 1813, he requested that a Methodist minister participate. William Ryland responded and joined Otterbein in the act of ordination.

There is evidence that Asbury conferred with Otterbein when he was working on the book of Discipline for the Methodists. When this Discipline was later translated into German, it became the basis for the Discipline of the *Evangelische Gemeinschaft* (later known as the Evangelical Church) and—to a lesser degree—the *Vereinigten Bruder* (later known as the United Brethren in Christ).

Over the years there have been many conversations concerning union. Bishop Newcomer's journal records such a conversation as early as April 1, 1803. In 1871 the Evangelical Association voted by a narrow margin of one to join the Methodists, but union was never consummated. During the years these conversations, under the instruction and authorization of the respective General Conferences, led to a plan and basis of union that united the Evangelical United Brethren Church and The Methodist Church into The United Methodist Church. This union embodies the history and traditions of the following churches which are Methodist in name or tradition:

The Methodist Episcopal Church

The Methodist Episcopal Church, South

The Methodist Protestant Church

The Methodist Church (merged into the Protestant Methodist Church in 1877)

United Brethren in Christ

The Evangelical Association

The United Evangelical Church

The Evangelical Church

The Methodist Church

The Evangelical United Brethren Church

Part I
THE CONSTITUTION

PREAMBLE

The Church is a community of all true believers under the Lordship of Christ. It is the redeemed and redeeming fellowship in which the Word of God is preached by persons divinely called, and the Sacraments are duly administered according to Christ's own appointment. Under the discipline of the Holy Spirit the Church seeks to provide for the maintenance of worship, the edification of believers, and the redemption of the world.

The Church of Jesus Christ exists in and for the world, and its very dividedness is a hindrance to its mission in that world.

The prayers and intentions of The Methodist Church and The Evangelical United Brethren Church have been and are for obedience to the will of our Lord that His people be one, in humility for the present brokenness of the Church and in gratitude that opportunities for reunion have been given. In harmony with these prayers and intentions these churches do now propose to unite, in the confident assurance that this act is an expression of the oneness of Christ's people.

Conversations concerning union between the two churches and their constituent members have taken place over a long period of years, and the churches have a long and impressive history of fellowship and cooperation.

Therefore, we, the Commissions on Church Union of The Methodist Church, and of The Evangelical United Brethren Church, holding that these churches are essentially one in origin, in belief, in spirit, and in purpose, and desiring that this essential unity be made actual in organization and administration in the

United States of America and throughout the world, do hereby propose and transmit to our respective General Conferences the following Plan of Union and recommend to the two churches its adoption by the processes which they respectively require.[1]

DIVISION ONE—GENERAL

¶ **1.** *Article I. Declaration of Union.*—The Evangelical United Brethren Church and The Methodist Church shall be united in one Church. The united Church, as thus constituted, is, and shall be, the successor of the two uniting churches.[2]

¶ **2.** *Article II. Name.*—The name of the Church shall be The United Methodist Church. The name of the Church may be translated freely into languages other than English as the General Conference may determine.

¶ **3.** *Article III. Articles of Religion and the Confession of Faith.*—The Articles of Religion and the Confession of Faith shall be those currently held by The Methodist Church and The Evangelical United Brethren Church respectively.

¶ **4.** *Article IV. Inclusiveness of the Church.*—The United Methodist Church is a part of the Church Universal, which is one Body in Christ. Therefore all persons, without regard to race, color, national origin, or economic condition, shall be eligible to attend its worship services, to participate in its programs, and, when they take the appropriate vows, to be admitted into its membership in any local church in the connection. In The United Methodist Church no conference or other organizational unit of the Church shall be structured so as to exclude any member or any constituent body of the Church because of race, color, national origin, or economic condition.[3]

---

[1]The Constitution was adopted in Chicago, Illinois, on Nov. 11, 1966, by the General Conferences of The Evangelical United Brethren Church and The Methodist Church and thereafter by the requisite vote in the Annual Conferences of the two churches. The Plan of Union was made effective by the Uniting Conference in Dallas, Texas, on April 23, 1968.

[2]Amended 1984.

[3]*See* Judicial Council Decisions 242, 246, 340, 351, 362, 377, 398, 594, and Decisions 4 and 5, Interim Judicial Council.

¶ **5.** *Article V. Ecumenical Relations.*—As part of the Church Universal, The United Methodist Church believes that the Lord of the Church is calling Christians everywhere to strive toward unity; and therefore it will seek, and work for, unity at all levels of church life: through world relationships with other Methodist churches and united churches related to The Methodist Church or The Evangelical United Brethren Church, through councils of churches, and through plans of union with churches of Methodist or other denominational traditions.

¶ **6.** *Article VI. Title to Properties.*—Titles to properties in The Evangelical United Brethren Church and The Methodist Church shall, upon consummation of the union, be held and administered in accordance with *The Book of Discipline.*[4] Nothing in the Plan of Union at any time after the union is to be construed so as to require any local church or any other property owner of the former The Evangelical United Brethren Church or the former The Methodist Church to alienate or in any way to change the title to property contained in its deed or deeds at the time of union, and lapse of time or usage shall not affect said title or control.

DIVISION TWO—ORGANIZATION

Section I. Conferences.

¶ **7.** *Article I.*—There shall be a General Conference for the entire Church with such powers, duties, and privileges as are hereinafter set forth.

¶ **8.** *Article II.*—There shall be Jurisdictional Conferences for the Church in the United States of America, with such powers, duties, and privileges as are hereinafter set forth;[5] *provided* that in The United Methodist Church there shall be no jurisdictional or central conference based on any ground other than geographical and regional division.

¶ **9.** *Article III.*—There shall be Central Conferences for

---

[4]Amended 1984.
[5]*See* Judicial Council Decision 128.

the Church outside the United States of America and, if necessary, Provisional Central Conferences, all with such powers, duties, and privileges as are hereinafter set forth.

¶ **10.** *Article IV.*—There shall be Annual Conferences as the fundamental bodies of the Church and, if necessary, Provisional Annual Conferences, with such powers, duties, and privileges as are hereinafter set forth.[6]

¶ **11.** *Article V.*—There shall be a Charge Conference for each church or charge with such powers, duties, and privileges as are hereinafter set forth.[7]

Section II. General Conference.

¶ **12.** *Article I.*—1. The General Conference shall be composed of not less than 600 nor more than 1,000 delegates, one half of whom shall be ministers and one half lay members, to be elected by the Annual Conferences. The Missionary Conferences shall be considered as Annual Conferences for the purpose of this article.[8]

2. Delegates shall be elected by the Annual Conferences except that delegates may be elected by other autonomous Methodist churches if and when the General Conference shall approve concordats with such other autonomous Methodist churches for the mutual election and seating of delegates in each other's highest legislative conferences.

3. In the case of The Methodist Church in Great Britain, mother church of Methodism, upon mutual approval of the concordat now pending, provision shall be made for the reciprocal election and seating of four delegates, two clergy and two lay.[9]

¶ **13. Article II.**—The General Conference shall meet in the month of April or May once in four years at such time and in such place as shall be determined by the General Conference or by its duly authorized committees.

A special session of General Conference, possessing the

---

[6]*See* Judicial Council Decision 354.
[7]*See* Judicial Council Decision 516.
[8]Amended 1976.
[9]Amended 1968; *See* Judicial Council Decisions 333, 402.

authority and exercising all the powers of the General Conference, may be called by the Council of Bishops, or in such other manner as the General Conference may from time to time prescribe, to meet at such time and in such place as may be stated in the call. Such special session of the General Conference shall be composed of the delegates to the preceding General Conference or their lawful successors, except that when a particular Annual Conference or Missionary Conference[10] shall prefer to have a new election it may do so.[11] The purpose of such special session shall be stated in the call, and only such business shall be transacted as is in harmony with the purpose stated in such call unless the General Conference by a two-thirds vote shall determine that other business may be transacted.[12]

¶ 14. *Article III.*—The General Conference shall fix the ratio of representation in the General, Jurisdictional, and Central Conferences from the Annual Conferences, Missionary Conferences,[13] and the Provisional Annual Conferences, computed on a two-factor basis: (1) the number of ministerial members of the Annual Conference and the Missionary Conference,[14] and (2) the number of church members in the Annual Conference and the Missionary Conference;[15] *provided* that each Annual Conference, Missionary Conference,[16] or Provisional Annual Conference shall be entitled to at least one ministerial and one lay delegate in the General Conference and also in the Jurisdictional or Central Conference.[17]

¶ 15. *Article IV.*—The General Conference shall have full legislative power over all matters distinctively connectional, and in the exercise of this power shall have authority as follows:[18]

1. To define and fix the conditions, privileges, and duties

---

[10]Amended 1976.
[11]*See* Judicial Council Decisions 221, 226, 228, 238, 302.
[12]*See* Judicial Council Decision 227.
[13]Amended 1976.
[14]Amended 1976.
[15]Amended 1976.
[16]Amended 1976.
[17]*See* Judicial Council Decision 403.
[18]*See* Judicial Council Decisions 96, 232, 236, 318, 325, 544.

of church membership which shall in every case be without reference to race or status.[19]

2. To define and fix the powers and duties of elders, deacons, supply preachers, local preachers, exhorters, and deaconesses.[20]

3. To define and fix the powers and duties of Annual Conferences, Provisional Annual Conferences, Missionary Conferences and Missions, and of Central Conferences, District Conferences, Charge Conferences, and Congregational Meetings.[21]

4. To provide for the organization, promotion, and administration of the work of the Church outside the United States of America.[22]

5. To define and fix the powers, duties, and privileges of the episcopacy, to adopt a plan for the support of the bishops, to provide a uniform rule for their retirement, and to provide for the discontinuance of a bishop because of inefficiency or unacceptability.[23]

6. To provide and revise the Hymnal and Ritual of the Church and to regulate all matters relating to the form and mode of worship, subject to the limitations of the first and second Restrictive Rules.

7. To provide a judicial system and a method of judicial procedure for the Church, except as herein otherwise prescribed.

8. To initiate and to direct all connectional enterprises of the Church and to provide boards for their promotion and administration.[24]

9. To determine and provide for raising and distributing funds necessary to carry on the work of the Church.[25]

10. To fix a uniform basis upon which bishops shall be elected by the Jurisdictional Conferences and to determine the number of bishops that may be elected by Central Conferences.[26]

---

[19]*See* Judicial Council Decision 558.
[20]*See* Judicial Council Decisions 58, 313.
[21]*See* Judicial Council Decision 411.
[22]*See* Judicial Council Decision 182; amended 1976.
[23]*See* Judicial Council Decisions 35, 114, 312, 365, 413.
[24]*See* Judicial Council Decisions 214, 364, 411.
[25]*See* Judicial Council Decision 30.
[26]*See* Judicial Council Decision 598.

11. To select its presiding officers from the bishops, through a committee; *provided* that the bishops shall select from their own number the presiding officer of the opening session.[27]

12. To change the number and the boundaries of Jurisdictional Conferences upon the consent of a majority of the Annual Conferences in each Jurisdictional Conference involved.[28]

13. To establish such commissions for the general work of the Church as may be deemed advisable.

14. To secure the rights and privileges of membership in all agencies, programs, and institutions in The United Methodist Church regardless of race or status.[29]

15. To enact such other legislation as may be necessary, subject to the limitations and restrictions of the Constitution of the Church.[30]

Section III. Restrictive Rules.

¶ **16. *Article I.*—**The General Conference shall not revoke, alter, or change our Articles of Religion or establish any new standards or rules of doctrine contrary to our present existing and established standards of doctrine.[31]

Article II.—The General Conference shall not revoke, alter, or change our Confession of Faith.

¶ **17. *Article III.*—**The General Conference shall not change or alter any part or rule of our government so as to do away with episcopacy or destroy the plan of our itinerant general superintendency.

¶ **18. *Article IV.*—**The General Conference shall not do away with the privileges of our ministers of right to trial by a committee and of an appeal; neither shall it do away with the privileges of our members of right to trial before the church, or by a committee, and of an appeal.[32]

---

[27]*See* Judicial Council Decision 126.

[28]*See* Judicial Council Decisions 55, 56, 215.

[29]*See* Decisions, 4, 5, Interim Judicial Council, Judicial Council Decisions 427, 433, 442, 451, 540, 558, 567, 588, 594.

[30]*See* Judicial Council Decision 215.

[31]*See* Judicial Council Decisions 86, 142, 243, 358.

[32]*See* Judicial Council Decisions 351, 522, 557, 595.

¶ 19. *Article V.*—The General Conference shall not revoke or change the General Rules of Our United Societies.[33]

¶ 20. *Article VI.*—The General Conference shall not appropriate the net income of the publishing houses, the book concerns, or the Chartered Fund to any purpose other than for the benefit of retired or disabled preachers, their spouses, widows, or widowers, and children or other beneficiaries of the ministerial pension systems.[34]

Section IV. Jurisdictional Conferences.

¶ 21. *Article I.*—The Jurisdictional Conferences shall be composed of as many representatives from the Annual Conferences and Missionary Conferences[35] as shall be determined by a uniform basis established by the General Conference. The Missionary Conferences shall be considered as Annual Conferences for the purpose of this article.[36]

¶ 22. *Article II.*—All Jurisdictional Conferences shall have the same status and the same privileges of action within the limits fixed by the Constitution. The ratio of representation of the Annual Conferences and Missionary Conferences[37] in the General Conference shall be the same for all Jurisdictional Conferences.

¶ 23. *Article III.*—The General Conferences shall fix the basis of representation in the Jurisdictional Conferences; *provided* that the Jurisdictional Conferences shall be composed of an equal number of ministerial and lay delegates to be elected by the Annual Conferences, the Missionary Conferences,[38] and the Provisional Annual Conferences.

¶ 24. *Article IV.*—Each Jurisdictional Conference shall meet at the time determined by the Council of Bishops or its delegated committee, each Jurisdictional Conference convening on the same date as the others and at a place selected by the Jurisdictional Committee on Entertainment, appointed by its

---

[33]*See* Judicial Council Decisions 358, 468.
[34]*See* Judicial Council Decisions 322, 230.
[35]Amended 1976.
[36]Amended 1976.
[37]Amended 1976.
[38]Amended 1976.

College of Bishops unless such a committee has been appointed by the preceding Jurisdictional Conference.

¶ **25.** *Article V.*—The Jurisdictional Conferences shall have the following powers and duties and such others as may be conferred by the General Conferences:

1. To promote the evangelistic, educational, missionary, and benevolent interests of the Church and to provide for interests and institutions within their boundaries.[39]

2. To elect bishops and to cooperate in carrying out such Conference.

3. To establish and constitute Jurisdictional Conference boards as auxiliary to the general boards of the Church as the need may appear and to choose their representatives on the general boards in such manner as the General Conference may determine.[40]

4. To determine the boundaries of their Annual Conferences; *provided* that there shall be no Annual Conference with a membership of fewer than fifty ministers in full connection, except by the consent of the General Conference; and *provided* further that this provision shall not apply to Annual Conferences of the former Evangelical United Brethren Church during the first three quadrenniums after union.[41]

5. To make rules and regulations for the administration of the work of the Church within the jurisdiction, subject to such powers as have been or shall be vested in the General Conference.

6. To appoint a Committee on Appeals to hear and determine the appeal of a traveling preacher of that jurisdiction from the decision of a trial committee.

Section V. Central Conferences.

¶ **26.** *Article I.*—There shall be Central Conferences for the work of the Church outside the United States of America[42] with such duties, powers, and privileges as are hereinafter set forth. The number and boundaries of the Central Conferences shall

---

[39]*See* Judicial Council Decision 67.
[40]*See* Judicial Council Decision 183.
[41]*See* Judicial Council Decision 447.
[42]Amended 1976.

be determined by the Uniting Conference. Subsequently the General Conference shall have authority to change the number and boundaries of Central Conferences. The Central Conferences shall have the duties, powers, and privileges hereinafter set forth.

¶ **27.** *Article II.*—The Central Conferences shall be composed of as many delegates as shall be determined by a basis established by the General Conference. The delegates shall be ministerial and lay in equal numbers.

¶ **28.** *Article III.*—The Central Conferences shall meet within the year succeeding the meeting of the General Conference at such times and places as shall have been determined by the preceding respective Central Conferences or by commissions appointed by them or by the General Conference. The date and place of the first meeting succeeding the Uniting Conference shall be fixed by the bishops of the respective Central Conferences, or in such manner as shall be determined by the General Conference.

¶ **29.** *Article IV.*—The Central Conferences shall have the following powers and duties and such others as may be conferred by the General Conference:

1. To promote the evangelistic, educational, missionary, social-concern, and benevolent interests and institutions of the Church within their own boundaries.

2. To elect the bishops for the respective Central Conferences in number as may be determined from time to time, upon a basis fixed by the General Conference, and to cooperate in carrying out such plans for the support of their bishops as may be determined by the General Conference.[43]

3. To establish and constitute such Central Conference boards as may be required and to elect their administrative officers.[44]

4. To determine the boundaries of the Annual Conferences within their respective areas.

5. To make such rules and regulations for the administration of the work within their boundaries including such changes and adaptations of the General Discipline as the conditions in the

---

[43]*See* Judicial Council Decision 370.
[44]*See* Judicial Council Decision 69.

respective areas may require, subject to the powers that have been or shall be vested in the General Conference.[45]

6. To appoint a Judicial Court to determine legal questions arising on the rules, regulations, and such revised, adapted, or new sections of the Central Conference Discipline enacted by the Central Conference.

7. To appoint a Committee on Appeals to hear and determine the appeal of a traveling preacher of that Central Conference from the decision of a Committee on Trial.[46]

Section VI. Episcopal Administration in Central Conferences.

¶ **30.** *Article I.*—The bishops of the Central Conferences shall be elected by their respective Central Conferences and inducted into office in the historic manner.

¶ **31.** *Article II.*—The bishops of the Central Conferences shall have membership in the Council of Bishops with vote.

¶ **32.** *Article III.*—The bishops of the Central Conferences shall preside in the sessions of their respective Central Conferences.

¶ **33.** *Article IV.*—The bishops of each Central Conference shall arrange the plan of episcopal visitation within their Central Conference.

¶ **34.** *Article V.*—The Council of Bishops may assign one of their number to visit each Central Conference. When so assigned, the bishop shall be recognized as the accredited representative of the general Church and when requested by a majority of the bishops resident in that conference may exercise therein the functions of the episcopacy.

Section VII. Annual Conferences.

¶ **35.** *Article I.*—The Annual Conference shall be composed of ministerial members as defined by the General Conference, together with a lay member elected by each charge, the diaconal ministers, the conference president of United Methodist Women, the conference president of United Methodist Men, the conference lay leader, district lay leaders, the president or

---

[45]*See* Judicial Council Decisions 142, 147, 313.
[46]*See* Judicial Council Decision 595.

equivalent officer of the conference young adult organization, the president of the conference youth organization, and two young persons under twenty-five (25) years of age from each district to be selected in such manner as may be determined by the Annual Conference.[47] Each charge served by more than one minister shall be entitled to as many lay members as there are ministerial members. The lay members shall have been for the two years next preceding their election members of The United Methodist Church[48] and shall have been active participants in The United Methodist Church for at least four years next preceding their election.[49]

If the lay membership should number less than the ministerial members of the Annual Conference, the Annual Conference shall, by its own formula, provide for the election of additional lay members to equalize lay and ministerial membership of the Annual Conference.[50]

¶ **36.** *Article II.*—The Annual Conference is the basic body in the Church and as such shall have reserved to it the right to vote on all constitutional amendments, on the election of ministerial and lay delegates to the General and the Jurisdictional or Central Conferences, on all matters relating to the character and conference relations of its ministerial members, and on the ordination of ministers and such other rights as have not been delegated to the General Conference under the Constitution, with the exception that the lay members may not vote on matters of ordination, character, and conference relations of ministers. It shall discharge such duties and exercise such powers as the General Conference under the Constitution may determine.[51]

¶ **37.** *Article III.*—The Annual Conference shall elect ministerial and lay delegates to the General Conference and to its Jurisdictional or Central Conference in the manner provided in

---

[47]Amended 1968, 1970, 1980, 1984.
[48]Amended 1972.
[49]Amended 1976.
[50]*See* Judicial Council Decisions 24, 113, 129, 349, 378, 479, 495, 511, 553, 561, and Decision 7, Interim Judicial Council.
[51]*See* Judicial Council Decisions 78, 79, 132, 405, 406, 415, 524, 532, 534, 552, 584.

this section, Articles IV and V.[52] The persons first elected up to the number determined by the ratio for representation in the General Conference shall be representatives in that body. Additional delegates shall be elected to complete the number determined by the ratio for representation in the Jurisdictional or Central Conference, who, together with those first elected as above, shall be delegates in the Jurisdictional or Central Conference. The additional delegates to the Jurisdictional or Central Conference shall in the order of their election be the reserve delegates to the General Conference.[53] The Annual Conference shall also elect reserve ministerial and lay delegates to the Jurisdictional or Central Conference as it may deem desirable.

¶ **38.** *Article IV.*—The ministerial delegates to the General Conference and to the Jurisdictional or Central Conference shall be elected by the ministerial members in full connection with the Annual Conference or Provisional Annual Conference; *provided* that such delegates shall have been traveling preachers in The United Methodist Church for at least four years next preceding their election and are in full connection with the Annual Conference or Provisional Annual Conference electing them when elected and at the time of holding the General and Jurisdictional or Central Conferences.[54]

¶ **39.** *Article V.*—The lay delegates to the General and Jurisdictional or Central Conferences shall be elected by the lay members of the Annual Conference or Provisional Annual Conference without regard to age, *provided* such delegates[55] shall have been members of The United Methodist Church for at least two years next preceding their election, and shall have been active participants in The United Methodist Church for at least four years next preceding their election,[56] and are members thereof within the Annual Conference

---

[52]*See* Judicial Council Decision 592.
[53]*See* Judicial Council Decision 352.
[54]*See* Judicial Council Decisions 1, 162, 308, 403, 473, 531, 534, 537.
[55]Amended 1972.
[56]Amended 1976.

electing them at the time of holding the General and Jurisdictional or Central Conferences.[57]

Section VIII. Boundaries.

¶ **40.** *Article I.*—The United Methodist Church shall have Jurisdictional Conferences made up as follows:

Northeastern—Connecticut, Delaware, District of Columbia, Maine, Maryland, Massachusetts, New Hampshire, New Jersey, New York, Pennsylvania, Puerto Rico and the Virgin Islands,[58] Rhode Island, Vermont, West Virginia.[59]

Southeastern—Alabama, Florida, Georgia, Kentucky, Mississippi, North Carolina, South Carolina, Tennessee, Virginia.

North Central—Illinois, Indiana, Iowa, Michigan, Minnesota, North Dakota, Ohio, South Dakota, Wisconsin.

South Central—Arkansas, Kansas, Louisiana, Missouri, Nebraska, New Mexico, Oklahoma, Texas.

Western—Alaska, Arizona, California, Colorado, Hawaii and the territory of the United States in the Pacific region,[60] Idaho, Montana, Nevada, Oregon, Utah, Washington, Wyoming.

¶ **41.** *Article II.*—The work of the Church outside the United States of America[61] may be formed into Central Conferences, the number and boundaries of which shall be determined by the Uniting Conference, the General Conference having authority subsequently to make changes in the number and boundaries.

¶ **42.** *Article III.*—Changes in the number, names, and boundaries of the Jurisdictional Conferences may be effected by the General Conference upon the consent of a majority of the Annual Conferences of each of the Jurisdictional Conferences involved.[62]

¶ **43.** *Article IV.*—Changes in the number, names, and boundaries of the Annual Conferences may be effected by the

---

[57]*See* Judicial Council Decisions 346, 354, 403.
[58]Amended 1980.
[59]Amended 1976.
[60]Amended 1980.
[61]Amended 1976.
[62]*See* Judicial Council Decisions 55, 56, 85, 215.

Jurisdictional Conferences in the United States of America[63] by the Central Conferences outside the United States of America according to the provisions under the respective powers of the Jurisdictional and the Central Conferences.[64]

¶ **44.** *Article V. Transfer of Local Churches.*—1. A local church may be transferred from one Annual Conference to another in which it is geographically located upon approval by a two-thirds vote of those present and voting in each of the following:

 a) The Charge Conference

 b) The Congregational Meeting of the local church

 c) Each of the two Annual Conferences involved

The vote shall be certified by the secretaries of the specified conferences or meetings to the bishops having supervision of the Annual Conferences involved, and upon their announcement of the required majorities the transfer shall immediately be effective.

2. The vote on approval of transfer shall be taken by each Annual Conference at its first session after the matter is submitted to it.

3. Transfers under the provisions of this article shall not be governed or restricted by other provisions of this Constitution relating to changes of boundaries of conferences.

Section IX. District Conferences.

¶ **45.** *Article I.*—There may be organized in an Annual Conference, District Conferences composed of such persons and invested with such powers as the General Conference may determine.

Section X. Charge Conferences.

¶ **46.** *Article I.*—There shall be organized in each charge a Charge Conference composed of such persons and invested with such powers as the General Conference shall provide.

---

[63]Amended 1976.

[64]*See* Judicial Council Decisions 28, 85, 217, 525, 541, and Decisions 1, 2, Interim Judicial Council.

¶ **47.** *Article II.* *Election of Church Officers.*—Unless the General Conference shall order otherwise, the officers of the church or churches constituting a charge shall be elected by the Charge Conference or by the members of said church or churches at a meeting called for that purpose, as may be arranged by the Charge Conference, unless the election is otherwise required by local church charters or state or provincial laws.

DIVISION THREE—EPISCOPAL SUPERVISION

¶ **48.** *Article I.*—There shall be a continuance of an episcopacy in The United Methodist Church of like plan, powers, privileges, and duties as now exist in The Methodist Church and in The Evangelical United Brethren Church in all those matters in which they agree and may be considered identical; and the differences between these historic episcopacies are deemed to be reconciled and harmonized by and in this Plan of Union and Constitution of The United Methodist Church and actions taken pursuant thereto so that a unified superintendency and episcopacy is hereby created and established of, in, and by those who now are and shall be bishops of The United Methodist Church; and the said episcopacy shall further have such powers, privileges, and duties as are herein set forth.[65]

¶ **49.** *Article II.*—The bishops shall be elected by the respective Jurisdictional and Central Conferences and consecrated in the historic manner at such time and place as may be fixed by the General Conference for those elected by the jurisdictions and by each Central Conference for those elected by such Central Conference.[66]

¶ **50.** *Article III.*—There shall be a Council of Bishops composed of all the bishops of The United Methodist Church. The council shall meet at least once a year and plan for the general oversight and promotion of the temporal and spiritual interests of the entire Church and for carrying into effect the

---

[65]*See* Judicial Council Decisions 4, 114, 127, 363.
[66]*See* Judicial Council Decision 21.

rules, regulations, and responsibilities prescribed and enjoined by the General Conference and in accord with the provisions set forth in this Plan of Union.[67]

¶ **51.** *Article IV.*—The bishops of each Jurisdictional and Central Conference shall constitute a College of Bishops and such College of Bishops shall arrange the plan of episcopal supervision of the Annual Conferences, Missionary[68] Conferences, and Missions within their respective territories.[69]

¶ **52.** *Article V.*—The bishops shall have residential and presidential supervision in the Jurisdictional or Central Conferences[70] in which they are elected or to which they are transferred. Bishops may be transferred from one jurisdiction to another jurisdiction for presidential and residential supervision under the following conditions: (1) The transfer of bishops may be on either of two bases: *(a)* a jurisdiction which receives a bishop by transfer from another jurisdiction may transfer to that jurisdiction or to a third jurisdiction one of its own bishops eligible for transfer, so that the number transferred in by each jurisdiction shall be balanced by the number transferred out, or *(b)* a jurisdiction may receive a bishop from another jurisdiction and not transfer out a member of its own College of Bishops. (2) No bishop shall be transferred unless that bishop shall have specifically consented. (3) No bishop shall be eligible for transfer unless the bishop shall have served one quadrennium in the jurisdiction which elected the bishop to the episcopacy. (4) All such transfers shall require the approval by a majority vote of the members, present and voting, of the Jurisdictional Conferences which are involved after consideration by the Committees on Episcopacy. After the above procedures have been followed, the transferring bishop shall become a member of the receiving College of Bishops and shall be subject to residential assignment by that Jurisdictional Conference.

A bishop may be assigned by the Council of Bishops for presidential service or other temporary service in another jurisdiction than that which elected the bishop, provided request

---

[67]*See* Judicial Council Decision 424.
[68]Amended 1976.
[69]*See* Judicial Council Decision 517.
[70]Amended 1980.

is made by a majority of the bishops in the jurisdiction of the proposed service.

In the case of an emergency in any jurisdiction or Central Conference through the death or disability of a bishop or other cause, the Council of Bishops may assign a bishop from another jurisdiction or Central Conference to the work of the said jurisdiction or Central Conference with the consent of a majority of the bishops of that jurisdiction or Central Conference.

¶ **53.** *Article VI.*—The bishops, both active and retired, of The Evangelical United Brethren Church and of The Methodist Church at the time union is consummated, shall be bishops of The United Methodist Church.

The bishops of The Methodist Church elected by the jurisdictions, the active bishops of The Evangelical United Brethren Church at the time of union, and bishops elected by the jurisdictions of The United Methodist Church shall have life tenure. Each bishop elected by a Central Conference of The Methodist Church shall have such tenure as the Central Conference electing him shall have determined.[71]

The Jurisdictional Conference shall elect a standing Committee on Episcopacy, to consist of one ministerial and one lay delegate from each Annual Conference, on nomination of the Annual Conference delegation. The committee shall review the work of the bishops, pass on their character and official administration, and report to the Jurisdictional Conference its findings for such action as the conference may deem appropriate within its constitutional warrant of power. The committee shall recommend the assignments of the bishops to their respective residences for final action by the Jurisdictional Conference.

¶ **54.** *Article VII.*—A bishop presiding over an Annual, Central, or Jurisdictional Conference shall decide all questions of law coming before the bishop in the regular business of a session;[72] *provided* that such questions be presented in writing and that the decisions be recorded in the journal of the conference.

---

[71]*See* Judicial Council Decisions 4, 303, 361.
[72]*See* Judicial Council Decision 33.

Such an episcopal decision shall not be authoritative except for the pending case until it shall have been passed upon by the Judicial Council. All decisions of law made by each bishop shall be reported in writing annually, with a syllabus of the same, to the Judicial Council, which shall affirm, modify, or reverse them.

¶ **55.** *Article VIII.*—The bishops of the several Jurisdictional and Central Conferences shall preside in the sessions of their respective conferences.[73]

¶ **56.** *Article IX.*—In each Annual Conference there shall be one or more district superintendents who shall assist the bishop in the administration of the Annual Conference and shall have such responsibilities and term of office as the General Conference may determine.[74]

¶ **57.** *Article X.*—The bishops shall appoint, after consultation with the district superintendents, ministers to the charges; and they shall have such responsibilities and authorities as the General Conference shall prescribe.

DIVISION FOUR—THE JUDICIARY

¶ **58.** *Article I.*—There shall be a Judicial Council. The General Conference shall determine the number and qualifications of its members, their terms of office, and the method of election and the filling of vacancies.

¶ **59.** *Article II.*—The Judicial Council shall have authority:

1. To determine the constitutionality of any act of the General Conference upon an appeal of a majority of the Council of Bishops or one fifth of the members of the General Conference, and to determine the constitutionality of any act of a Jurisdictional or Central Conference upon an appeal of a majority of the bishops of that Jurisdictional or Central Conference or upon the appeal of one fifth of the members of that Jurisdictional or Central Conference.

2. To hear and determine any appeal from a bishop's decision on a question of law made in the Annual Conference

---

[73]*See* Judicial Council Decision 395.
[74]*See* Judicial Council Decisions 368, 398.

when said appeal has been made by one fifth of that conference present and voting.

3. To pass upon decisions of law made by bishops in Annual Conferences.

4. To hear and determine the legality of any action taken therein by any General Conference board or Jurisdictional or Central Conference board or body, upon appeal by one third of the members thereof, or upon request of the Council of Bishops or a majority of the bishops of a Jurisdictional or a Central Conference.

5. To have such other duties and powers as may be conferred upon it by the General Conference.

6. To provide its own methods of organization and procedure.

¶ **60.** *Article III.*—All decisions of the Judicial Council shall be final. When the Judicial Council shall declare unconstitutional any act of the General Conference then in session, that decision shall be reported back to that General Conference immediately.

¶ **61.** *Article IV.*—The General Conference shall establish for the Church a judicial system which shall guarantee to our ministers a right to trial by a committee and an appeal and to our members a right to trial before the church, or by a committee, and an appeal.[75]

DIVISION FIVE—AMENDMENTS

¶ **62.** *Article I.*—Amendments to the Constitution shall be made upon a two-thirds majority of the General Conference present and voting and a two-thirds affirmative vote of the aggregate number of members of the several Annual Conferences present and voting, except in the case of the first and second Restrictive Rules, which shall require a three-fourths majority of all the members of the Annual Conferences present and voting. The vote, after being completed, shall be canvassed by the Council of Bishops, and the amendment voted upon shall become effective upon their announcement of its having received the required majority.[76]

---

[75]*See* Judicial Council Decision 522.
[76]*See* Judicial Council Decisions 154, 243, 244, 349, 483. Amended 1976.

¶ **63.** *Article II.*—Amendments to the Constitution may originate in either the General Conference or the Annual Conferences.

¶ **64.** *Article III.*—A Jurisdictional or Central Conference[77] may by a majority vote propose changes in the Constitution of the Church, and such proposed changes shall be submitted to the next General Conference. If the General Conference adopts the measure by a two-thirds vote, it shall be submitted to the Annual Conferences according to the provision for amendments.

---

[77]Amended 1980.

Part II
DOCTRINAL STANDARDS AND OUR THEOLOGICAL TASK[1]

¶ 66. SECTION 1—OUR DOCTRINAL HERITAGE

United Methodists profess the historic Christian faith in God, incarnate in Jesus Christ for our salvation and ever at work in human history in the Holy Spirit. Living in a covenant of grace under the Lordship of Jesus Christ, we participate in the first fruits of God's coming reign and pray in hope for its full realization on earth as in heaven.

Our heritage in doctrine and our present theological task focus upon a renewed grasp of the sovereignty of God and of God's love in Christ amid the continuing crises of human existence.

Our forebears in the faith reaffirmed the ancient Christian message as found in the apostolic witness, even as they applied it anew in their own circumstances.

Their preaching and teaching were grounded in Scripture, informed by Christian tradition, enlivened in experience, and tested by reason.

Their labors inspire and inform our attempts to convey the saving gospel to our world with its needs and aspirations.

---

[1]The Judicial Council ruled in 1972 that all sections of Part II except ¶ 68 were "legislative enactments and neither part of the Constitution nor under the Restrictive Rules" (*See* Judicial Council Decision 358).

Our Common Heritage as Christians

United Methodists share a common heritage with Christians of every age and nation. This heritage is grounded in the apostolic witness to Jesus Christ as Savior and Lord, which is the source and measure of all valid Christian teaching.

Faced with diverse interpretations of the apostolic message, leaders of the early church sought to specify the core of Christian belief in order to ensure the soundness of Christian teaching.

The determination of the canon of Christian Scripture and the adoption of ecumenical creeds, such as the formulations of Nicaea and Chalcedon, were of central importance to this consensual process. Such creeds helped preserve the integrity of the Church's witness, set boundaries for acceptable Christian doctrine, and proclaimed the basic elements of the enduring Christian message. These statements of faith, along with the Apostles' Creed, contain the most prominent features of our ecumenical heritage.

The Protestant reformers of the sixteenth and seventeenth centuries devised new confessional statements that reiterated classical Christian teaching in an attempt to recover the authentic biblical witness. These documents affirmed the primacy of Scripture and provided formal doctrinal standards through their statements of essential beliefs on matters such as the way of salvation, the Christian life, and the nature of the Church.

Many distinctively Protestant teachings were transmitted into United Methodist understandings through doctrinal formulations such as the Articles of Religion of the Church of England and the Heidelberg Catechism of the Reformed tradition.

Various doctrinal statements in the form of creeds, confessions of belief, and articles of faith were officially adopted by churches as standards of Christian teaching. Notwithstanding their importance, these formal doctrinal standards by no means exhausted authoritative Christian teaching.

The standards themselves initially emerged from a much wider body of Christian thought and practice, and their fuller significance unfolded in the writings of the Church's teachers.

Some writings have proved simply to be dated benchmarks in the story of the Church's continuing maturation.

By contrast, some sermons, treatises, liturgies, and hymns have gained considerable practical authority in the life and thought of the Church by virtue of their wide and continuing acceptance as faithful expositions of Christian teaching. Nonetheless, the basic measure of authenticity in doctrinal standards, whether formally established or received by tradition, has been their fidelity to the apostolic faith grounded in Scripture and evidenced in the life of the Church through the centuries.

Basic Christian Affirmations

With Christians of other communions we confess belief in the triune God—Father, Son, and Holy Spirit. This confession embraces the biblical witness to God's activity in creation, encompasses God's gracious self-involvement in the dramas of history, and anticipates the consummation of God's reign.

The created order is designed for the well-being of all creatures and as the place of human dwelling in covenant with God. As sinful creatures, however, we have broken that covenant, become estranged from God, wounded ourselves and one another, and wreaked havoc throughout the natural order. We stand in need of redemption.

We hold in common with all Christians a faith in the mystery of salvation in and through Jesus Christ. At the heart of the gospel of salvation is God's incarnation in Jesus of Nazareth. Scripture witnesses to the redeeming love of God in Jesus' life and teachings, his atoning death, his resurrection, his sovereign presence in history, his triumph over the powers of evil and death, and his promised return. Because God truly loves us in spite of our willful sin, God judges us, summons us to repentance, pardons us, receives us by that grace given to us in Jesus Christ, and gives us hope of life eternal.

We share the Christian belief that God's redemptive love is realized in human life by the activity of the Holy Spirit, both in personal experience and in the community of believers. This community is the Church, which the Spirit has brought into existence for the healing of the nations.

Through faith in Jesus Christ we are forgiven, reconciled to God, and transformed as people of the new covenant.

"Life in the Spirit" involves diligent use of the means of grace such as praying, fasting, attending upon the Sacraments, and inward searching in solitude. It also encompasses the communal life of the Church in worship, mission, evangelism, service, and social witness.

We understand ourselves to be part of Christ's universal Church when by adoration, proclamation, and service we become conformed to Christ. We are initiated and incorporated into this community of faith by Baptism, receiving the promise of the Spirit that re-creates and transforms us. Through the regular celebration of Holy Communion, we participate in the risen presence of Jesus Christ and are thereby nourished for faithful discipleship.

We pray and work for the coming of God's realm and reign to the world and rejoice in the promise of everlasting life that overcomes death and the forces of evil.

With other Christians we recognize that the reign of God is both a present and future reality. The Church is called to be that place where the first signs of the reign of God are identified and acknowledged in the world. Wherever persons are being made new creatures in Christ, wherever the insights and resources of the gospel are brought to bear on the life of the world, God's reign is already effective in its healing and renewing power.

We also look to the end time in which God's work will be fulfilled. This prospect gives us hope in our present actions, as individuals and as the Church. This expectation saves us from resignation and motivates our continuing witness and service.

We share with many Christian communions a recognition of the authority of Scripture in matters of faith, the confession that our justification as sinners is by grace through faith, and the sober realization that the Church is in need of continual reformation and renewal.

We affirm the general ministry of all baptized Christians who share responsibility for building up the Church and reaching out in mission and service to the world.

With other Christians, we declare the essential oneness of the Church in Christ Jesus. This rich heritage of shared Christian belief finds expression in our hymnody and liturgies. Our unity is affirmed in the historic creeds as we confess one holy, catholic, and apostolic Church. It is also experienced in joint ventures of ministry and in various forms of ecumenical cooperation.

Nourished by common roots of this shared Christian heritage, the branches of Christ's Church have developed diverse traditions that enlarge our store of shared understandings. Our avowed ecumenical commitment as United Methodists is to gather our own doctrinal emphases into the larger Christian unity, there to be made more meaningful in a richer whole.

If we are to offer our best gifts to the common Christian treasury, we must make a deliberate effort as a church to strive for critical self-understanding. It is as Christians involved in ecumenical partnership that we embrace and examine our distinctive heritage.

Our Distinctive Heritage as United Methodists

The underlying energy of the Wesleyan theological heritage stems from an emphasis upon practical divinity, the implementation of genuine Christianity in the lives of believers.

Methodism did not arise in response to a specific doctrinal dispute, though there was no lack of theological controversy. Early Methodists claimed to preach the scriptural doctrines of the Church of England as contained in the Articles of Religion, the Homilies, and the Book of Common Prayer.

Their task was not to reformulate doctrine. Their tasks were to summon people to experience the justifying and sanctifying grace of God and encourage people to grow in the knowledge and love of God through the personal and corporate disciplines of the Christian life.

The thrust of the Wesleyan movement and of the United Brethren and Evangelical Association was "to reform the nation, particularly the Church, and to spread scriptural holiness over the land."

Wesley's orientation toward the practical is evident in his focus upon the "scripture way of salvation." He considered doctrinal matters primarily in terms of their significance for Christian discipleship.

The Wesleyan emphasis upon the Christian life—faith and love put into practice—has been the hallmark of those traditions now incorporated into The United Methodist Church. The distinctive shape of the Wesleyan theological heritage can be seen in a constellation of doctrinal emphases that display the creating, redeeming, and sanctifying activity of God.

Distinctive Wesleyan Emphases

Although Wesley shared with many other Christians a belief in grace, justification, assurance, and sanctification, he combined them in a powerful manner to create distinctive emphases for living the full Christian life. The Evangelical United Brethren tradition, particularly as expressed by Phillip William Otterbein, from a Reformed background, gave similar distinctive emphases.

Grace pervades our understanding of Christian faith and life. By grace we mean the undeserved, unmerited, and loving action of God in human existence through the ever-present Holy Spirit. While the grace of God is undivided, it precedes salvation as "prevenient grace," continues in "justifying grace," and is brought to fruition in "sanctifying grace."

We assert that God's grace is manifest in all creation even though suffering, violence, and evil are everywhere present. The goodness of creation is fulfilled in human beings, who are called to covenant partnership with God. God has endowed us with dignity and freedom and has summoned us to responsibility for our lives and the life of the world.

In God's self-revelation, Jesus Christ, we see the splendor of our true humanity. Even our sin, with its destructive consequences for all creation, does not alter God's intention for us—holiness and happiness of heart. Nor does it diminish our accountability for the way we live.

Despite our brokenness, we remain creatures brought into being by a just and merciful God. The restoration of God's image in our lives requires divine grace to renew our fallen nature.

Prevenient Grace.—We acknowledge God's prevenient grace, the divine love that surrounds all humanity and precedes any and all of our conscious impulses. This grace prompts our first wish to please God, our first glimmer of understanding concerning God's will, and our "first slight transient conviction" of having sinned against God.

God's grace also awakens in us an earnest longing for deliverance from sin and death and moves us toward repentance and faith.

Justification and Assurance.—We believe God reaches out to the repentant believer in justifying grace with accepting and pardoning love. Wesleyan theology stresses that a decisive change in the human heart can and does occur under the prompting of grace and the guidance of the Holy Spirit.

In justification we are, through faith, forgiven our sin and restored to God's favor. This righting of relationships by God through Christ calls forth our faith and trust as we experience regeneration, by which we are made new creatures in Christ.

This process of justification and new birth is often referred to as conversion. Such a change may be sudden and dramatic, or gradual and cumulative. It marks a new beginning, yet it is part of an ongoing process. Christian experience as personal transformation always expresses itself as faith working by love.

Our Wesleyan theology also embraces the scriptural promise that we can expect to receive assurance of our present salvation, as the Spirit "bears witness with our spirit that we are children of God."

Sanctification and Perfection.—We hold that the wonder of God's acceptance and pardon does not end God's saving work, which continues to nurture our growth in grace. Through the power of the Holy Spirit we are enabled to increase in the knowledge and love of God and in love for our neighbor.

New birth is the first step in this process of sanctification. Sanctifying grace draws us toward the gift of Christian perfection, which Wesley described as a heart "habitually filled with the love of God and neighbor" and as "having the mind of Christ and walking as he walked."

This gracious gift of God's power and love, the hope and expectation of the faithful, is neither warranted by our efforts nor limited by our frailties.

Faith and Good Works.—We see God's grace and human activity working together in the relationship of faith and good works. God's grace calls forth human response and discipline.

Faith is the only response essential for salvation. However, the General Rules remind us that salvation evidences itself in good works. For Wesley, even repentance should be accompanied by "fruits meet for repentance," or works of piety and mercy.

Both faith and good works belong within an all-encompassing theology of grace, since they stem from God's gracious love "shed abroad in our hearts by the Holy Spirit."

Mission and Service.—We insist that personal salvation always involves Christian mission and service to the world. By joining heart and hand we assert that personal religion, evangelical witness, and Christian social action are reciprocal and mutually reinforcing.

Scriptural holiness entails more than personal piety; love of God is always linked with love of neighbor, a passion for justice and renewal in the life of the world.

The General Rules represent one traditional expression of the intrinsic relationship between Christian life and thought as understood within the Wesleyan tradition. Theology is the servant of piety, which in turn is the ground of social conscience and the impetus for social action and global interaction, always in the empowering context of the reign of God.

Nurture and Mission of the Church.—Finally, we emphasize the nurturing and serving function of Christian fellowship in the

Church. The personal experience of faith is nourished by the worshiping community.

For Wesley there is no religion but social religion, no holiness but social holiness. The communal forms of faith in the Wesleyan tradition not only promote personal growth; they also equip and mobilize us for mission and service to the world.

The outreach of the Church springs from the working of the Spirit. As United Methodists, we respond to that working through a connectional polity based upon mutual responsiveness and accountability. Connectional ties bind us together in faith and service in our global witness, enabling faith to become active in love and intensifying our desire for peace and justice in the world.

Doctrine and Discipline in the Christian Life

No motif in the Wesleyan tradition has been more constant than the link between Christian doctrine and Christian living. Methodists have always been strictly enjoined to maintain the unity of faith and good works through the means of grace, as seen in John Wesley's *The Nature, Design, and General Rules of the United Societies* (1743). The coherence of faith with ministries of love forms the discipline of Wesleyan spirituality and Christian discipleship.

The General Rules were originally designed for members of Methodist societies, who participated in the sacramental life of the Church of England. The terms of membership in these societies were simple: "a desire to flee from the wrath to come and to be saved from their sins."

Wesley insisted, however, that evangelical faith should manifest itself in evangelical living. He spelled out this expectation in the three-part formula of the Rules:

> It is therefore expected of all who continue therein that they should continue to evidence their desire of salvation,
> *First:* By doing no harm, by avoiding evil of every kind . . . ;
> *Secondly:* By . . . doing good of every possible sort, and, as far as possible, to all . . . ;
> *Thirdly:* By attending upon all the ordinances of God (*See* ¶ 68).

Wesley's illustrative cases under each of these three rules show how the Christian conscience might move from general principles to specific actions. Their explicit combination highlights the spiritual spring of moral action.

Wesley rejected undue reliance upon these rules. Discipline was not church law; it was a way of discipleship. Wesley insisted that true religion is "the knowledge of God in Christ Jesus," "the life which is hid with Christ in God," and "the righteousness that [the true believer] thirsts after."

General Rules and Social Principles

Upon such evangelical premises, Methodists in every age have sought to exercise their responsibility for the moral and spiritual quality of society. In asserting the connection between doctrine and ethics, the General Rules provide an early signal of Methodist social consciousness.

The Social Principles (¶¶ 70-76) provide our most recent official summary of stated convictions that seek to apply the Christian vision of righteousness to social, economic, and political issues. Our historic opposition to evils such as smuggling, inhumane prison conditions, slavery, drunkenness, and child labor was founded upon a vivid sense of God's wrath against human injustice and wastage.

Our struggles for human dignity and social reform have been a response to God's demand for love, mercy, and justice in the light of the Kingdom. We proclaim no *personal gospel* that fails to express itself in relevant social concerns; we proclaim no *social gospel* that does not include the personal transformation of sinners.

It is our conviction that the good news of the Kingdom must judge, redeem, and reform the sinful social structures of our time.

The Book of Discipline and the General Rules convey the expectation of discipline within the experience of individuals and the life of the Church. Such discipline assumes accountability to the community of faith by those who claim that community's support.

Support without accountability promotes moral weakness; accountability without support is a form of cruelty.

A church that rushes to punishment is not open to God's mercy, but a church lacking the courage to act decisively on personal and social issues loses its claim to moral authority. The Church exercises its discipline as a community through which God continues to "reconcile the world to himself."

Conclusion

These distinctive emphases of United Methodists provide the basis for "practical divinity," the experiential realization of the gospel of Jesus Christ in the lives of Christian people. These emphases have been preserved not so much through formal doctrinal declarations as through the vital movement of faith and practice as seen in converted lives and within the disciplined life of the Church.

Devising formal definitions of doctrine has been less pressing for United Methodists than summoning people to faith and nurturing them in the knowledge and love of God. The core of Wesleyan doctrine that informed our past rightly belongs to our common heritage as Christians and remains a prime component within our continuing theological task.

¶ 67. SECTION 2—OUR DOCTRINAL HISTORY

The pioneers in the traditions that flowed together into The United Methodist Church understood themselves as standing in the central stream of Christian spirituality and doctrine, loyal heirs of the authentic Christian tradition. In John Wesley's words, theirs was "the old religion, the religion of the Bible, the religion . . . of the whole church in the purest ages." Their gospel was grounded in the biblical message of God's self-giving love revealed in Jesus Christ.

Wesley's portrayal of the spiritual pilgrimage in terms of "the scripture way of salvation" provided their model for experiential Christianity. They assumed and insisted upon the integrity of basic Christian truth and emphasized its practical application in the lives of believers.

This perspective is apparent in the Wesleyan understanding of "catholic spirit." While it is true that United Methodists are fixed upon certain religious affirmations, grounded in the gospel and confirmed in their experience, they also recognize the right of Christians to disagree on matters such as forms of worship, structures of church government, modes of Baptism, or theological explorations. They believe such differences do not break the bond of fellowship that ties Christians together in Jesus Christ. Wesley's familiar dictum was, "As to all opinions which do not strike at the root of Christianity, we think and let think."

But, even as they were fully committed to the principles of religious toleration and theological diversity they were equally confident that there is a "marrow" of Christian truth that can be identified and that must be conserved. This living core, as they believed, stands revealed in Scripture, illumined by tradition, vivified in personal and corporate experience, and confirmed by reason. They were very much aware, of course, that God's eternal Word never has been, nor can be, exhaustively expressed in any single form of words.

They were also prepared, as a matter of course, to reaffirm the ancient creeds and confessions as valid summaries of Christian truth. But they were careful not to set them apart as absolute standards for doctrinal truth and error.

Beyond the essentials of vital religion, United Methodists respect the diversity of opinions held by conscientious persons of faith. Wesley followed a time-tested approach: "In essentials, unity; in non-essentials, liberty; and in all things, charity."

The spirit of charity takes into consideration the limits of human understanding. "To be ignorant of many things and to be mistaken in some," Wesley observed, "is the necessary condition of humanity." The crucial matter in religion is steadfast love for God and neighbor, empowered by the redeeming and sanctifying work of the Holy Spirit.

The Wesleyan "Standards" in Great Britain

In this spirit, the British Methodists under the Wesleys never reduced their theology to a confessional formula as a doctrinal test. Methodism was a movement within the Church of England, and John Wesley constantly maintained that he taught the scriptural doctrines contained in the Thirty-Nine Articles, the Homilies, and the Book of Common Prayer of his national church. The Bible, of course, constituted for him the final authority in all doctrinal matters.

As the movement grew, Wesley provided his people with published sermons and a Bible commentary for their doctrinal instruction. His *Sermons on Several Occasions* (1746–60) set forth those doctrines which, he said, "I embrace and teach as the essentials of true religion." In 1755, he published *Explanatory Notes Upon the New Testament* as a guide for Methodist biblical exegesis and doctrinal interpretation.

As occasional controversies arose, the need for a standard measure of Methodist preaching became evident. In 1763, Wesley produced a "Model Deed" for Methodist properties, which stipulated that the trustees for each preaching house were responsible for ensuring that the preachers in their pulpits "preach no other doctrine than is contained in Mr. Wesley's *Notes Upon the New Testament* and four volumes of *Sermons.*"

These writings, then, contained the standard exposition of Methodist teaching. They provide a model and measure for adequate preaching in the Wesleyan tradition. The primary norm for Wesley's writings was Scripture, as illumined by historic traditions and vital faith. Wesley put forth no summary of biblical revelation for the British Methodists because the Thirty-Nine Articles of the Church of England were already available.

The Wesley brothers also composed hymns that were rich in doctrinal and experiential content. The hymns, especially those of Charles Wesley, not only are among the best-loved within Methodism but also are major resources for doctrinal instruction.

Furthermore, John Wesley specified various disciplines and rules, such as the General Rules, to implement in personal and communal life the practical divinity he proclaimed.

In addition to these writings, Wesley established the conference to instruct and supervise the Methodist preachers. He produced Minutes to ensure their fidelity to the doctrines and disciplines of the Methodist movement. These writings and structures filled out the Wesleyan understanding of the Church and the Christian life.

Doctrinal Standards in American Methodism

As long as the American colonies were primarily under British control, the Methodists could continue as part of the sacramental community of the Church of England. The early conferences, under the leadership of British preachers, declared their allegiance to the Wesleyan principles of organization and doctrine. They stipulated that the Minutes of the British and American conferences, along with the *Sermons* and *Notes* of Wesley, contained their basic doctrine and discipline.

After the formal recognition of American independence in 1783, Wesley realized that the Methodists in America were free of English control, religious as well as civil, and should become an independent Methodist church. Wesley then furnished the American Methodists with a liturgy *(The Sunday Service of the Methodists in North America)* and a doctrinal statement *(The Articles of Religion)*. The Sunday Service was Wesley's abridgment of the Book of Common Prayer; the Articles of Religion were his revision of the Thirty-Nine Articles.

The American Methodist preachers, gathered at Baltimore in December 1784, adopted the Sunday Service and the Articles of Religion as part of their actions in forming the new Methodist Episcopal Church. This "Christmas Conference" also accepted a hymnbook that Wesley had prepared (1784) and adopted a slightly modified version of the General Rules as a statement of the Church's nature and discipline. The conference spent most of its time adapting the British "Large Minutes" to American conditions. Subsequent editions of this document came to be known as the *Doctrines and Discipline of the Methodist Episcopal Church* (the Book of Discipline).

The shift from "movement" to "church" had changed the function of doctrinal norms within American Methodism. Rather than prescribing doctrinal emphases for preaching within a movement, the Articles outlined basic norms for Christian belief within a church, following the traditional Anglican fashion.

The preface to the first separate publication of the Articles states, "These are the doctrines taught among the people called Methodists. Nor is there any doctrine whatever, generally

53

received among that people, contrary to the articles now before you."

American Methodists were not required to subscribe to the Articles after the Anglican manner, but they were accountable (under threat of trial) for keeping their proclamation of the gospel within the boundaries outlined therein. For generations, the *Doctrines and Discipline* cited only the Articles as the basis for testing correct doctrine in the newly formed Church: the charge of doctrinal irregularity against preachers or members was for "disseminating doctrines contrary to our Articles of Religion." In this manner, the Church protected its doctrinal integrity against the heresies that were prevalent at the time—Socinianism, Arianism, and Pelagianism (*see* Articles I, II, and IX).

The Articles of Religion, however, did not guarantee adequate Methodist preaching; they lacked several Wesleyan emphases, such as assurance and Christian perfection. Wesley's *Sermons* and *Notes,* therefore, continued to function as the traditional standard exposition of distinctive Methodist teaching.

The General Conference of 1808, which provided the first Constitution of the Methodist Episcopal Church, established the Articles of Religion as the Church's explicit doctrinal standards. The first Restrictive Rule of the Constitution prohibited any change, alteration, or addition to the Articles themselves, and it stipulated that no new standards or rules of doctrine could be adopted that were contrary to the "present existing and established standards of doctrine."

Within the Wesleyan tradition, then as now, the *Sermons* and *Notes* furnished models of doctrinal exposition. Other documents have also served American Methodism as vital expressions of Methodist teaching and preaching. Lists of recommended doctrinal resources vary from generation to generation but generally acknowledge the importance of the hymnbook, the ecumenical creeds, and the General Rules. Lists of such writings in the early nineteenth century usually included John Fletcher's *Checks Against Antinomianism* and Richard Watson's *Theological Institutes.*

The doctrinal emphases of these statements were carried forward by the weight of tradition rather than the force of law.

They became part of the heritage of American Methodism to the degree that they remained useful to continuing generations.

During the great frontier revivals of the nineteenth century, the influence of European theological traditions waned in America. Preaching focused on "Christian experience," understood chiefly as "saving faith in Christ." Among the Methodists there was a consistent stress on free will, infant baptism, and informal worship, which led to protracted controversies with the Presbyterians, Baptists, and Episcopalians, respectively.

Methodist interest in formal doctrinal standards remained secondary to evangelism, nurture, and mission. The Wesleyan hymnody served in practice as the most important single means of communicating and preserving the doctrinal substance of the gospel.

By the end of the nineteenth century, Methodist theology in America had become decidedly eclectic, with less specific attention paid to its Wesleyan sources.

The force of the Articles of Religion underwent several shifts. For a time, the first Restrictive Rule was exempted from the process of constitutional amendment, thus allowing no consideration of change in doctrinal standards. Mention of the Articles of Religion was included in the membership vows of the Methodist Episcopal Church, South.

At the beginning of the twentieth century, however, the waning force of doctrinal discipline and the decreasing influence of the Wesleyan theological heritage among the American Methodists, along with minor but significant changes in the wording of the Book of Discipline regarding doctrinal standards, led to a steady dilution of the force of the Articles of Religion as the Church's constitutional standards of doctrine.

During this same period, theologians and church leaders began to explore ways of expressing the gospel that were in keeping with developing intellectual currents. These leaders also began to rethink the historical social compassion of the Wesleyan tradition in the midst of the emerging industrial, urban civilization. They deepened our awareness of the systemic nature of evil and the urgency to proclaim the gospel promise of social redemption. Consequently, theologies supportive of the social gospel found fertile soil within the Methodist traditions.

These years were times of theological and ethical controversy within Methodism as new patterns of thought clashed with the more familiar themes and styles of the previous two centuries.

In recent decades there has been a strong recovery of interest in Wesley and in the more classic traditions of Christian thought. This recovery has been part of a broad resurgence of Reformation theology and practice in Europe and America, renewing the historical legacy of Protestantism in the context of the modern world. These trends have been reinforced in North America by the reaffirmation of evangelical piety.

The ecumenical movement has brought new appreciation for the unity as well as the richness and diversity of the Church catholic.

Currents of theology have developed out of black people's struggle for freedom, the movement for the full equality of women in Church and society, and the quest for liberation and for indigenous forms of Christian existence in churches around the world.

The challenge to United Methodists is to discern the various strands of these vital movements of faith that are coherent, faithful understandings of the gospel and the Christian mission for our times.

The task of defining the scope of our Wesleyan tradition in the context of the contemporary world includes much more than formally reaffirming or redefining standards of doctrine, although these tasks may also be involved. The heart of our task is to reclaim and renew the distinctive United Methodist doctrinal heritage, which rightly belongs to our common heritage as Christians, for the life and mission of the whole Church today.

Doctrinal Traditions in the Evangelical Church and the United Brethren Church

The unfolding of doctrinal concerns among Jacob Albright's Evangelical Association and Phillip William Otterbein's United Brethren in Christ roughly parallels Methodist developments. Differences emerged largely from differing ecclesiastical traditions brought from Germany and Holland, together with the modified Calvinism of the Heidelberg Catechism.

In the German-speaking communities of America, Albright and Otterbein considered evangelism more important than theological speculation. Although they were not doctrinally indifferent, they stressed conversion, "justification by faith confirmed by a sensible assurance thereof," Christian nurture, the priesthood of all believers in a shared ministry of Christian witness and service, and entire sanctification as the goal of Christian life.

As with Wesley, their primary source and norm for Christian teaching was Scripture. Otterbein enjoined his followers "to be careful to preach no other doctrine than what is plainly laid down in the Bible." Each new member was asked "to confess that he received the Bible as the Word of God." Ordinands were required to affirm without reserve the plenary authority of Scripture.

Matched with these affirmations was the conviction that converted Christians are enabled by the Holy Spirit to read Scripture with a special Christian consciousness. They prized this principle as the supreme guide in biblical interpretation.

Jacob Albright was directed by the Conference of 1807 to prepare a list of Articles of Religion. He died before he could attempt the task.

George Miller then assumed the responsibility. He recommended to the Conference of 1809 the adoption of the German translation of the Methodist Articles of Religion, with the addition of a new one, "Of the Last Judgment." The recommendation was adopted. This action affirms a conscious choice of the Methodist Articles as normative. The added article was from the Augsburg Confession, on a theme omitted in the Anglican Articles.

In 1816, the original twenty-six Articles were reduced to twenty-one by omitting five polemical articles aimed at Roman Catholics, Anabaptists, and sixteenth-century sectaries. This act of deletion reflected a conciliatory spirit in a time of bitter controversy.

In 1839, a few slight changes were made in the text of 1816. It was then stipulated that "the Articles of Faith . . . should be constitutionally unchangeable among us."

In the 1870s, a proposal to revise the Articles touched off a flurry of debate, but the Conference of 1875 decisively rejected the proposal.

In later action the twenty-one Articles were reduced to nineteen by combining several, but without omitting any of their original content.

These nineteen were brought intact into the Evangelical United Brethren union of 1946.

Among the United Brethren in Christ, a summary of normative teaching was formulated in 1813 by Christian Newcomer and Christopher Grosch, colleagues of Otterbein. Its first three paragraphs follow the order of the Apostles' Creed. Paragraphs four and five affirm the primacy of Scripture and the universal proclamation of "the biblical doctrine . . . of man's fall in Adam and his deliverance through Jesus Christ." An added section commends "the ordinances of baptism and the remembrance of the Lord" and approves foot washing as optional.

The first General Conference of the United Brethren in Christ (1815) adopted a slight revision of this earlier statement as the denomination's Confession of Faith. A further revision was made in 1841, with the stipulation that there be no further changes: "No rule or ordinance shall at any time be passed to change or do away with the Confession of Faith as it now stands." Even so, agitation for change continued.

In 1885, a church commission was appointed to "prepare such a form of belief and such amended fundamental rules for the government of this church in the future as will, in their judgment, be best adapted to secure its growth and efficiency in the work of evangelizing the world."

The resulting proposal for a new Confession of Faith and Constitution was submitted to the general membership of the Church, the first such referendum on a Confession of Faith in United Brethren history, and was then placed before the General Conference of 1889. Both the general membership and the Conference approved the Confession by preponderant majorities. It was thereupon enacted by episcopal "proclamation." However, this action was protested by a minority as a violation of the Restrictive Rule of 1841 and became a basic cause for a consequent schism, resulting in the formation of The United Brethren Church (Old Constitution).

The Confession of Faith of 1889 was more comprehensive than any of its antecedents, with articles on depravity, justification, regeneration and adoption, sanctification, the Christian Sabbath, and the future state. The article on sanctification, though brief, is significant in its reflection of the doctrine of holiness of the Heidelberg Catechism. The 1889 Confession was brought by the United Brethren into the union with the Evangelicals in 1946.

The Evangelical United Brethren Confession of Faith

The Discipline of the new Evangelical United Brethren Church (1946) contained both the Evangelical Articles and the United Brethren Confession. Twelve years later the General Conference of the united church authorized its Board of Bishops to prepare a new Confession of Faith.

A new Confession, with sixteen articles, of a somewhat more modern character than any of its antecedents, was presented to the General Conference of 1962 and adopted without amendment. The Evangelical article, "Entire Sanctification and Christian Perfection," is reflected in this confession as a distinctive emphasis. The Confession of Faith replaced both former Articles and Confession and was brought over intact into the Discipline of The United Methodist Church (1968).

Doctrinal Standards in The United Methodist Church

In the Plan of Union for The United Methodist Church, the preface to the Methodist Articles of Religion and the Evangelical United Brethren Confession of Faith explains that both were accepted as doctrinal standards for the new Church. Additionally, it stated that although the language of the first Restrictive Rule never has been formally defined, Wesley's *Sermons* and *Notes* were understood specifically to be included in our present existing and established standards of doctrine. It also stated that the Articles, the Confession, and the Wesleyan "standards" were "thus deemed congruent if not identical in their doctrinal perspectives and not in conflict." This declaration was accepted by subsequent rulings of the Judicial Council.[2]

The Constitution of The United Methodist Church, in its Restrictive Rules (*see* ¶¶ 16-20), protects both the Articles of Religion and the Confession of Faith as doctrinal standards that shall not be revoked, altered, or changed. The process of creating new "standards or rules of doctrine" thus continues to be restricted, requiring either that they be declared "not contrary to" the present standards or that they go through the difficult process of constitutional amendment.

The United Methodist Church stands continually in need of doctrinal reinvigoration for the sake of authentic renewal, fruitful evangelism, and ecumenical dialogue. In this light, the recovery and updating of our distinctive doctrinal heritage—catholic, evangelical, and reformed—is essential.[3]

This task calls for the repossession of our traditions as well as the promotion of theological inquiry both within the denomination and in our ecumenical efforts. All are invited to share in this endeavor to stimulate an active interest in doctrinal understanding in order to claim our legacy and to shape that legacy for the Church we aspire to be.

¶ 68. SECTION 3—OUR DOCTRINAL STANDARDS AND GENERAL RULES

THE ARTICLES OF RELIGION OF THE METHODIST CHURCH[4]

[Bibliographical Note: The Articles of Religion are here reprinted from the *Discipline* of 1808 (when the first Restrictive Rule took effect), collated against Wesely's original text in *The Sunday Service of the Methodists* (1784). To these are added two Articles: "Of Sanctification" and "Of the Duty of Christians to the Civil Authority," which are legislative enactments and not integral parts of the document as protected by the Constitution (*see* Judicial Council Decisions 41, 176).]

---

[2]*See* Judicial Council Decision 358.
[3]The need to interpret the Articles in the light of their historical context and biases is reflected in the Resolution of Intent (1970), found in the Book of Resolutions.
[4]Protected by Restrictive Rule 1 (¶ 16).

Article I.—Of Faith in the Holy Trinity

There is but one living and true God, everlasting, without body or parts, of infinite power, wisdom, and goodness; the maker and preserver of all things, both visible and invisible. And in unity of this Godhead there are three persons, of one substance, power, and eternity—the Father, the Son, and the Holy Ghost.

Article II.—Of the Word, or Son of God, Who Was Made Very Man

The Son, who is the Word of the Father, the very and eternal God, of one substance with the Father, took man's nature in the womb of the blessed Virgin; so that two whole and perfect natures, that is to say, the Godhead and Manhood, were joined together in one person, never to be divided; whereof is one Christ, very God and very Man, who truly suffered, was crucified, dead, and buried, to reconcile his Father to us, and to be a sacrifice, not only for original guilt, but also for actual sins of men.

Article III.—Of the Resurrection of Christ

Christ did truly rise again from the dead, and took again his body, with all things appertaining to the perfection of man's nature, wherewith he ascended into heaven, and there sitteth until he return to judge all men at the last day.

Article IV.—Of the Holy Ghost

The Holy Ghost, proceeding from the Father and the Son, is of one substance, majesty, and glory with the Father and the Son, very and eternal God.

Article V.—Of the Sufficiency of the Holy Scriptures for Salvation

The Holy Scripture containeth all things necessary to salvation; so that whatsoever is not read therein, nor may be

61

proved thereby, is not to be required of any man that it should be believed as an article of faith, or be thought requisite or necessary to salvation. In the name of the Holy Scripture we do understand those canonical books of the Old and New Testament of whose authority was never any doubt in the Church. The names of the canonical books are:

Genesis, Exodus, Leviticus, Numbers, Deuteronomy, Joshua, Judges, Ruth, The First Book of Samuel, The Second Book of Samuel, The First Book of Kings, The Second Book of Kings, The First Book of Chronicles, The Second Book of Chronicles, The Book of Ezra, The Book of Nehemiah, The Book of Esther, The Book of Job, The Psalms, The Proverbs, Ecclesiastes or the Preacher, Cantica or Songs of Solomon, Four Prophets the Greater, Twelve Prophets the Less.

All the books of the New Testament, as they are commonly received, we do receive and account canonical.

Article VI.—Of the Old Testament

The Old Testament is not contrary to the New; for both in the Old and New Testament everlasting life is offered to mankind by Christ, who is the only Mediator between God and man, being both God and Man. Wherefore they are not to be heard who feign that the old fathers did look only for transitory promises. Although the law given from God by Moses as touching ceremonies and rites doth not bind Christians, nor ought the civil precepts thereof of necessity be received in any commonwealth; yet notwithstanding, no Christian whatsoever is free from the obedience of the commandments which are called moral.

Article VII.—Of Original or Birth Sin

Original sin standeth not in the following of Adam (as the Pelagians do vainly talk), but it is the corruption of the nature of every man, that naturally is engendered of the offspring of Adam, whereby man is very far gone from original righteousness, and of his own nature inclined to evil, and that continually.

Article VIII.—Of Free Will

The condition of man after the fall of Adam is such that he cannot turn and prepare himself, by his own natural strength and works, to faith, and calling upon God; wherefore we have no power to do good works, pleasant and acceptable to God, without the grace of God by Christ preventing us, that we may have a good will, and working with us, when we have that good will.

Article IX.—Of the Justification of Man

We are accounted righteous before God only for the merit of our Lord and Saviour Jesus Christ, by faith, and not for our own works or deservings. Wherefore, that we are justified by faith, only, is a most wholesome doctrine, and very full of comfort.

Article X.—Of Good Works

Although good works, which are the fruits of faith, and follow after justification, cannot put away our sins, and endure the severity of God's judgment; yet are they pleasing and acceptable to God in Christ, and spring out of a true and lively faith, insomuch that by them a lively faith may be as evidently known as a tree is discerned by its fruit.

Article XI.—Of Works of Supererogation

Voluntary works—besides, over and above God's commandments—which they call works of supererogation, cannot be taught without arrogancy and impiety. For by them men do declare that they do not only render unto God as much as they are bound to do, but that they do more for his sake than of bounden duty is required; whereas Christ saith plainly: When you have done all that is commanded you, say, We are unprofitable servants.

Article XII.—Of Sin After Justification

Not every sin willingly committed after justification is the sin against the Holy Ghost, and unpardonable. Wherefore, the grant of repentance is not to be denied to such as fall into sin after justification. After we have received the Holy Ghost, we may depart from grace given, and fall into sin, and, by the grace of God, rise again and amend our lives. And therefore they are to be condemned who say they can no more sin as long as they live here; or deny the place of forgiveness to such as truly repent.

Article XIII.—Of the Church

The visible Church of Christ is a congregation of faithful men in which the pure Word of God is preached, and the Sacraments duly administered according to Christ's ordinance, in all those things that of necessity are requisite to the same.

Article XIV.—Of Purgatory[5]

The Romish doctrine concerning purgatory, pardon, worshiping, and adoration, as well of images as of relics, and also invocation of saints, is a fond thing, vainly invented, and grounded upon no warrant of Scripture, but repugnant to the Word of God.

Article XV.—Of Speaking in the Congregation in Such a Tongue as the People Understand

It is a thing plainly repugnant to the Word of God, and the custom of the primitive Church, to have public prayer in the church, or to minister the Sacraments, in a tongue not understood by the people.

Article XVI.—Of the Sacraments

Sacraments ordained of Christ are not only badges or tokens of Christian men's profession, but rather they are certain signs of grace, and God's good will toward us, by which he doth work

---

[5]For the contemporary interpretation of this and similar articles (i.e., Articles XIV, XV, XVI, XVIII, XIX, XX and XXI), *see* A Resolution of Intent of the General Conference of 1970 (*Journal,* pp. 254-55) and The Book of Resolutions (1968, pp. 65-72).

invisibly in us, and doth not only quicken, but also strengthen and confirm, our faith in him.

There are two Sacraments ordained of Christ our Lord in the Gospel; that is to say, Baptism and the Supper of the Lord.

Those five commonly called sacraments, that is to say, confirmation, penance, orders, matrimony, and extreme unction, are not to be counted for Sacraments of the Gospel; being such as have partly grown out of the *corrupt* following of the apostles, and partly are states of life allowed in the Scriptures, but yet have not the like nature of Baptism and the Lord's Supper, because they have not any visible sign or ceremony ordained of God.

The Sacraments were not ordained of Christ to be gazed upon, or to be carried about; but that we should duly use them. And in such only as worthily receive the same, they have a wholesome effect or operation; but they that receive them unworthily, purchase to themselves condemnation, as St. Paul saith.

Article XVII.—Of Baptism

Baptism is not only a sign of profession and mark of difference whereby Christians are distinguished from others that are not baptized; but it is also a sign of regeneration or the new birth. The baptism of young children is to be retained in the church.[6]

Article XVIII.—Of the Lord's Supper

The Supper of the Lord is not only a sign of the love that Christians ought to have among themselves one to another, but rather is a sacrament of our redemption by Christ's death; insomuch that, to such as rightly, worthily, and with faith receive the same, the bread which we break is a partaking of the body of Christ; and likewise the cup of blessing is a partaking of the blood of Christ.

---

[6]*See* Judicial Council Decision 142.

Transubstantiation, or the change of the substance of bread and wine in the Supper of our Lord, cannot be proved by Holy Writ, but is repugnant to the plain words of Scripture, overthroweth the nature of a sacrament, and hath given occasion to many superstitions.

The body of Christ is given, taken, and eaten in the Supper, only after a heavenly and spiritual manner. And the mean whereby the body of Christ is received and eaten in the Supper is faith.

The Sacrament of the Lord's Supper was not by Christ's ordinance reserved, carried about, lifted up, or worshiped.

Article XIX.—Of Both Kinds

The cup of the Lord is not to be denied to the lay people; for both the parts of the Lord's Supper, by Christ's ordinance and commandment, ought to be administered to all Christians alike.

Article XX.—Of the One Oblation of Christ, Finished upon the Cross

The offering of Christ, once made, is that perfect redemption, propitiation, and satisfaction for all the sins of the whole world, both original and actual; and there is none other satisfaction for sin but that alone. Wherefore the sacrifice of masses, in the which it is commonly said that the priest doth offer Christ for the quick and the dead, to have remission of pain or guilt, is a blasphemous fable and dangerous deceit.

Article XXI.—Of the Marriage of Ministers

The ministers of Christ are not commanded by God's law either to vow the estate of single life, or to abstain from marriage; therefore it is lawful for them, as for all other Christians, to marry at their own discretion, as they shall judge the same to serve best to godliness.

Article XXII.—Of the Rites and Ceremonies of Churches

It is not necessary that rites and ceremonies should in all places be the same, or exactly alike; for they have been always different, and may be changed according to the diversity of countries, times, and men's manners, so that nothing be ordained against God's Word. Whosoever, through his private judgment, willingly and purposely doth openly break the rites and ceremonies of the church to which he belongs, which are not repugnant to the Word of God, and are ordained and approved by common authority, ought to be rebuked openly, that others may fear to do the like, as one that offendeth against the common order of the church, and woundeth the consciences of weak brethren.

Every particular church may ordain, change, or abolish rites and ceremonies, so that all things may be done to edification.

Article XXIII.—Of the Rulers of the United States of America

The President, the Congress, the general assemblies, the governors, and the councils of state, *as the delegates of the people,* are the rulers of the United States of America, according to the division of power made to them by the Constitution of the United States and by the constitutions of their respective states. And the said states are a sovereign and independent nation, and ought not to be subject to any foreign jurisdiction.

Article XXIV.—Of Christian Men's Goods

The riches and goods of Christians are not common as touching the right, title, and possession of the same, as some do falsely boast. Notwithstanding, every man ought, of such things as he possesseth, liberally to give alms to the poor, according to his ability.

Article XXV.—Of a Christian Man's Oath

As we confess that vain and rash swearing is forbidden Christian men by our Lord Jesus Christ and James his apostle, so we judge that the Christian religion doth not prohibit, but that a man may swear when the magistrate requireth, in a cause of faith and charity, so it be done according to the prophet's teaching, in justice, judgment, and truth.

[The following Article from the Methodist Protestant *Discipline* is placed here by the Uniting Conference (1939). It was not one of the Articles of Religion voted upon by the three churches.]

Of Sanctification

Sanctification is that renewal of our fallen nature by the Holy Ghost, received through faith in Jesus Christ, whose blood of atonement cleanseth from all sin; whereby we are not only delivered from the guilt of sin, but are washed from its pollution, saved from its power, and are enabled, through grace, to love God with all our hearts and to walk in his holy commandments blameless.

[The following provision was adopted by the Uniting Conference (1939). This statement seeks to interpret to our churches in foreign lands Article XXIII of the Articles of Religion. It is a legislative enactment but is not a part of the Constitution. (*See* Judicial Council Decisions 41, 176, and Decision 6, Interim Judicial Council.)]

Of the Duty of Christians to the Civil Authority

It is the duty of all Christians, and especially of all Christian ministers, to observe and obey the laws and commands of the governing or supreme authority of the country of which they are citizens or subjects or in which they reside, and to use all laudable means to encourage and enjoin obedience to the powers that be.

THE CONFESSION OF FAITH
OF THE EVANGELICAL UNITED BRETHREN CHURCH[7]

[Bibliographical Note: The text of the Confession of Faith is identical with that of its original in *The Discipline of The Evangelical United Brethren Church* (1963).]

Article I.—God

We believe in the one true, holy and living God, Eternal Spirit, who is Creator, Sovereign and Preserver of all things

---

[7]Protected by Restrictive Rule 2 (¶ 16).

visible and invisible. He is infinite in power, wisdom, justice, goodness and love, and rules with gracious regard for the well-being and salvation of men, to the glory of his name. We believe the one God reveals himself as the Trinity: Father, Son and Holy Spirit, distinct but inseparable, eternally one in essence and power.

Article II.—Jesus Christ

We believe in Jesus Christ, truly God and truly man, in whom the divine and human natures are perfectly and inseparably united. He is the eternal Word made flesh, the only begotten Son of the Father, born of the Virgin Mary by the power of the Holy Spirit. As ministering Servant he lived, suffered and died on the cross. He was buried, rose from the dead and ascended into heaven to be with the Father, from whence he shall return. He is eternal Savior and Mediator, who intercedes for us, and by him all men will be judged.

Article III.—The Holy Spirit

We believe in the Holy Spirit who proceeds from and is one in being with the Father and the Son. He convinces the world of sin, of righteousness and of judgment. He leads men through faithful response to the gospel into the fellowship of the Church. He comforts, sustains and empowers the faithful and guides them into all truth.

Article IV.—The Holy Bible

We believe the Holy Bible, Old and New Testaments, reveals the Word of God so far as it is necessary for our salvation. It is to be received through the Holy Spirit as the true rule and guide for faith and practice. Whatever is not revealed in or established by the Holy Scriptures is not to be made an article of faith nor is it to be taught as essential to salvation.

Article V.—The Church

We believe the Christian Church is the community of all true believers under the Lordship of Christ. We believe it is one, holy, apostolic and catholic. It is the redemptive fellowship in which the Word of God is preached by men divinely called, and the sacraments are duly administered according to Christ's own appointment. Under the discipline of the Holy Spirit the Church exists for the maintenance of worship, the edification of believers and the redemption of the world.

Article VI.—The Sacraments

We believe the sacraments, ordained by Christ, are symbols and pledges of the Christian's profession and of God's love toward us. They are means of grace by which God works invisibly in us, quickening, strengthening and confirming our faith in him. Two sacraments are ordained by Christ our Lord, namely Baptism and the Lord's Supper.

We believe Baptism signifies entrance into the household of faith, and is a symbol of repentance and inner cleansing from sin, a representation of the new birth in Christ Jesus and a mark of Christian discipleship.

We believe children are under the atonement of Christ and as heirs of the Kingdom of God are acceptable subjects for Christian baptism. Children of believing parents through baptism become the special responsibility of the Church. They should be nurtured and led to personal acceptance of Christ, and by profession of faith confirm their baptism.

We believe the Lord's Supper is a representation of our redemption, a memorial of the sufferings and death of Christ, and a token of love and union which Christians have with Christ and with one another. Those who rightly, worthily and in faith eat the broken bread and drink the blessed cup partake of the body and blood of Christ in a spiritual manner until he comes.

Article VII.—Sin and Free Will

We believe man is fallen from righteousness and, apart from the grace of our Lord Jesus Christ, is destitute of holiness and inclined to evil. Except a man be born again, he cannot see the Kingdom of God. In his own strength, without divine grace, man cannot do good works pleasing and acceptable to God. We believe, however, man influenced and empowered by the Holy Spirit is responsible in freedom to exercise his will for good.

Article VIII.—Reconciliation Through Christ

We believe God was in Christ reconciling the world to himself. The offering Christ freely made on the cross is the perfect and sufficient sacrifice for the sins of the whole world, redeeming man from all sin, so that no other satisfaction is required.

Article IX.—Justification and Regeneration

We believe we are never accounted righteous before God through our works or merit, but that penitent sinners are justified or accounted righteous before God only by faith in our Lord Jesus Christ.

We believe regeneration is the renewal of man in righteousness through Jesus Christ, by the power of the Holy Spirit, whereby we are made partakers of the divine nature and experience newness of life. By this new birth the believer becomes reconciled to God and is enabled to serve him with the will and the affections.

We believe, although we have experienced regeneration, it is possible to depart from grace and fall into sin; and we may even then, by the grace of God, be renewed in righteousness.

Article X.—Good Works

We believe good works are the necessary fruits of faith and follow regeneration but they do not have the virtue to remove our sins or to avert divine judgment. We believe good works, pleasing and acceptable to God in Christ, spring from a true and living faith, for through and by them faith is made evident.

Article XI.—Sanctification and Christian Perfection

We believe sanctification is the work of God's grace through the Word and the Spirit, by which those who have been born again are cleansed from sin in their thoughts, words and acts, and are enabled to live in accordance with God's will, and to strive for holiness without which no one will see the Lord.

Entire sanctification is a state of perfect love, righteousness and true holiness which every regenerate believer may obtain by being delivered from the power of sin, by loving God with all the heart, soul, mind and strength, and by loving one's neighbor as one's self. Through faith in Jesus Christ this gracious gift may be received in this life both gradually and instantaneously, and should be sought earnestly by every child of God.

We believe this experience does not deliver us from the infirmities, ignorance, and mistakes common to man, nor from the possibilities of further sin. The Christian must continue on guard against spiritual pride and seek to gain victory over every temptation to sin. He must respond wholly to the will of God so that sin will lose its power over him; and the world, the flesh, and the devil are put under his feet. Thus he rules over these enemies with watchfulness through the power of the Holy Spirit.

Article XII.—The Judgment and the Future State

We believe all men stand under the righteous judgment of Jesus Christ, both now and in the last day. We believe in the resurrection of the dead; the righteous to life eternal and the wicked to endless condemnation.

Article XIII.—Public Worship

We believe divine worship is the duty and privilege of man who, in the presence of God, bows in adoration, humility and dedication. We believe divine worship is essential to the life of the Church, and that the assembling of the people of God for such worship is necessary to Christian fellowship and spiritual growth.

We believe the order of public worship need not be the same in all places but may be modified by the Church according to circumstances and the needs of men. It should be in a language and form understood by the people, consistent with the Holy Scriptures to the edification of all, and in accordance with the order and *Discipline* of the Church.

Article XIV.—The Lord's Day

We believe the Lord's Day is divinely ordained for private and public worship, for rest from unnecessary work, and should be devoted to spiritual improvement, Christian fellowship and service. It is commemorative of our Lord's resurrection and is an emblem of our eternal rest. It is essential to the permanence and growth of the Christian Church, and important to the welfare of the civil community.

Article XV.—The Christian and Property

We believe God is the owner of all things and that the individual holding of property is lawful and is a sacred trust under God. Private property is to be used for the manifestation of Christian love and liberality, and to support the Church's mission in the world. All forms of property, whether private, corporate or public, are to be held in solemn trust and used responsibly for human good under the sovereignty of God.

Article XVI.—Civil Government

We believe civil government derives its just powers from the sovereign God. As Christians we recognize the governments under whose protection we reside and believe such governments should be based on, and be responsible for, the recognition of human rights under God. We believe war and bloodshed are contrary to the gospel and spirit of Christ. We believe it is the duty of Christian citizens to give moral strength and purpose to their respective governments through sober, righteous and godly living.

THE STANDARD SERMONS OF WESLEY

[Bibliographical Note: The Wesleyan "standards" have been reprinted frequently. The critical edition of Wesley's *Sermons* is included in *The Works of John Wesley*, vols. 1–4 (Nashville: Abingdon Press, 1984-87).]

THE EXPLANATORY NOTES UPON
THE NEW TESTAMENT

[Bibliographical Note: *The Explanatory Notes Upon the New Testament* (1755) is currently in print (Ward's 1976 edition) and is forthcoming as vols. 5–6 of *The Works of John Wesley*.]

THE GENERAL RULES
OF THE METHODIST CHURCH[8]

[Bibliographical Note: The General Rules are printed here in the text of 1808 (when the fifth Restrictive Rule took effect), as subsequently amended by constitutional actions in 1848 and 1868.]

The Nature, Design, and General Rules of Our United Societies

In the latter end of the year 1739 eight or ten persons came to Mr. Wesley, in London, who appeared to be deeply convinced of sin, and earnestly groaning for redemption. They desired, as did two or three more the next day, that he would spend some time with them in prayer, and advise them how to flee from the wrath to come, which they saw continually hanging over their heads. That he might have more time for this great work, he appointed a day when they might all come together, which from thenceforward they did every week, namely, on Thursday in the evening. To these, and as many more as desired to join with them (for their number increased daily), he gave those advices from time to time which he judged most needful for them, and they

---

[8]Protected by Restrictive Rule 5 (¶ 19).

always concluded their meeting with prayer suited to their several necessities.

This was the rise of the **United Society,** first in Europe, and then in America. Such a society is no other than "a company of men having the *form* and seeking the *power* of godliness, united in order to pray together, to receive the word of exhortation, and to watch over one another in love, that they may help each other to work out their salvation."

That it may the more easily be discerned whether they are indeed working out their own salvation, each society is divided into smaller companies, called **classes,** according to their respective places of abode. There are about twelve persons in a class, one of whom is styled the **leader.** It is his duty:

1. To see each person in his class once a week at least, in order: (1) to inquire how their souls prosper; (2) to advise, reprove, comfort or exhort, as occasion may require; (3) to receive what they are willing to give toward the relief of the preachers, church, and poor.

2. To meet the ministers and the stewards of the society once a week, in order: (1) to inform the minister of any that are sick, or of any that walk disorderly and will not be reproved; (2) to pay the stewards what they have received of their several classes in the week preceding.

There is only one condition previously required of those who desire admission into these societies: "a desire to flee from the wrath to come, and to be saved from their sins." But wherever this is really fixed in the soul it will be shown by its fruits.

It is therefore expected of all who continue therein that they should continue to evidence their desire of salvation,

First: By doing no harm, by avoiding evil of every kind, especially that which is most generally practiced, such as:

The taking of the name of God in vain.

The profaning the day of the Lord, either by doing ordinary work therein or by buying or selling.

Drunkenness: buying or selling spirituous liquors, or drinking them, unless in cases of extreme necessity.

Slaveholding; buying or selling slaves.

Fighting, quarreling, brawling, brother going to law with brother; returning evil for evil, or railing for railing; the using many words in buying or selling.

The buying or selling goods that have not paid the duty.

The giving or taking things on usury—i.e., unlawful interest.

Uncharitable or unprofitable conversation; particularly speaking evil of magistrates or of ministers.

Doing to others as we would not they should do unto us.

Doing what we know is not for the glory of God, as:

The putting on of gold and costly apparel.

The taking such diversions as cannot be used in the name of the Lord Jesus.

The singing those songs, or reading those books, which do not tend to the knowledge or love of God.

Softness and needless self-indulgence.

Laying up treasure upon earth.

Borrowing without a probability of paying; or taking up goods without a probability of paying for them.

It is expected of all who continue in these societies that they should continue to evidence their desire of salvation,

Secondly: By doing good; by being in every kind merciful after their power; as they have opportunity, doing good of every possible sort, and, as far as possible, to all men:

To their bodies, of the ability which God giveth, by giving food to the hungry, by clothing the naked, by visiting or helping them that are sick or in prison.

To their souls, by instructing, reproving, or exhorting all we have any intercourse with; trampling under foot that enthusiastic doctrine that "we are not to do good unless *our hearts be free to it.*"

By doing good, especially to them that are of the household of faith or groaning so to be; employing them preferably to others; buying one of another, helping each other in business, and so much the more because the world will love its own and them only.

By all possible diligence and frugality, that the gospel be not blamed.

By running with patience the race which is set before them, denying themselves, and taking up their cross daily; submitting to bear the reproach of Christ, to be as the filth and offscouring of the world; and looking that men should say all manner of evil of them *falsely,* for the Lord's sake.

It is expected of all who desire to continue in these societies that they should continue to evidence their desire of salvation,
Thirdly: By attending upon all the ordinances of God; such are:
The public worship of God.
The ministry of the Word, either read or expounded.
The Supper of the Lord.
Family and private prayer.
Searching the Scriptures.
Fasting or abstinence.

These are the General Rules of our societies; all of which we are taught of God to observe, even in his written Word, which is the only rule, and the sufficient rule, both of our faith and practice. And all these we know his Spirit writes on truly awakened hearts. If there be any among us who observe them not, who habitually break any of them, let it be known unto them who watch over that soul as they who must give an account. We will admonish him of the error of his ways. We will bear with him for a season. But then, if he repent not, he hath no more place among us. We have delivered our own souls.

¶ 69. SECTION 4—OUR THEOLOGICAL TASK

Theology is our effort to reflect upon God's gracious action in our lives. In response to the love of Christ, we desire to be drawn into a deeper relationship with the "author and perfecter of our faith." Our theological explorations seek to give expression to the mysterious reality of God's presence, peace, and power in the world. By so doing, we attempt to articulate more clearly our understanding of the divine–human encounter and are thereby more fully prepared to participate in God's work in the world.

The theological task, though related to the Church's doctrinal expressions, serves a different function. Our doctrinal affirmations assist us in the discernment of Christian truth in ever-changing contexts. Our theological task includes the testing, renewal, elaboration, and application of our doctrinal perspective in carrying out our calling "to spread scriptural holiness over these lands."

While the Church considers its doctrinal affirmations a central feature of its identity and restricts official changes to a constitutional process, the Church encourages serious reflection across the theological spectrum.

As United Methodists, we are called to identify the needs both of individuals and of society and to address those needs out of the resources of Christian faith in a way that is clear, convincing, and effective. Theology serves the Church by interpreting the world's needs and challenges to the Church and by interpreting the gospel to the world.

The Nature of Our Theological Task

Our theological task is both critical and constructive. It is *critical* in that we test various expressions of faith by asking, Are they true? Appropriate? Clear? Cogent? Credible? Are they based on love? Do they provide the Church and its members with a witness that is faithful to the gospel as reflected in our living heritage and that is authentic and convincing in the light of human experience and the present state of human knowledge?

Our theological task is *constructive* in that every generation must appropriate creatively the wisdom of the past and seek God in their midst in order to think afresh about God, revelation, sin, redemption, worship, the Church, freedom, justice, moral responsibility, and other significant theological concerns. Our summons is to understand and receive the gospel promises in our troubled and uncertain times.

Our theological task is both individual and communal. It is a feature in the ministry of *individual* Christians. It requires the participation of all who are in our Church, lay and ordained, because the mission of the Church is to be carried out by everyone who is called to discipleship. To be persons of faith is to hunger to understand the truth given to us in Jesus Christ.

Theological inquiry is by no means a casual undertaking. It requires sustained disciplines of study, reflection, and prayer.

Yet the discernment of "plain truth for plain people" is not limited to theological specialists. Scholars have their role to play in assisting the people of God to fulfill this calling, but all Christians are called to theological reflection.

Our theological task is *communal*. It unfolds in conversations open to the experiences, insights, and traditions of all constituencies that make up United Methodism.

This dialogue belongs to the life of every congregation. It is fostered by laity and clergy, by the bishops, by the boards, agencies, and theological schools of the Church.

Conferences speak and act for United Methodists in their official decisions at appropriate levels. Our conciliar and representative forms of decision-making do not release United Methodists as individuals from the responsibility to develop sound theological judgment.

Our theological task is contextual and incarnational. It is grounded upon God's supreme mode of self-revelation—the incarnation in Jesus Christ. God's eternal Word comes to us in flesh and blood in a given time and place, and in full identification with humanity. Therefore, theological reflection is energized by our incarnational involvement in the daily life of the Church and the world, as we participate in God's liberating and saving action.

Our theological task is essentially practical. It informs the individual's daily decisions and serves the Church's life and work. While highly theoretical constructions of Christian thought make important contributions to theological understanding, we finally measure the truth of such statements in relation to their practical significance. Our interest is to incorporate the promises and demands of the gospel into our daily lives.

Theological inquiry can clarify our thinking about what we are to say and do. It presses us to pay attention to the world around us.

Realities of intense human suffering, threats to the survival of life, and challenges to human dignity confront us afresh with fundamental theological issues: the nature and purposes of God, the relations of human beings to one another, the nature of human freedom and responsibility, and the care and proper use of all creation.

Theological Guidelines: Sources and Criteria

As United Methodists, we have an obligation to bear a faithful Christian witness to Jesus Christ, the living reality at the center of the Church's life and witness. To fulfill this obligation, we reflect critically on our biblical and theological inheritance, striving to express faithfully the witness we make in our own time.

Two considerations are central to this endeavor: the sources from which we derive our theological affirmations and the criteria by which we assess the adequacy of our understanding and witness.

Wesley believed that the living core of the Christian faith was revealed in Scripture, illumined by tradition, vivified in personal experience, and confirmed by reason.

Scripture is primary, revealing the Word of God "so far as it is necessary for our salvation." Therefore, our theological task, in both its critical and constructive aspects, focuses on disciplined study of the Bible.

To aid his study of the Bible and deepen his understanding of faith, Wesley drew on Christian tradition, in particular the Patristic writings, the ecumenical creeds, the teachings of the Reformers, and the literature of contemporary spirituality.

Thus, tradition provides both a source and a measure of authentic Christian witness, though its authority derives from its faithfulness to the biblical message.

The Christian witness, even when grounded in Scripture and mediated by tradition, is ineffectual unless understood and appropriated by the individual. To become our witness, it must make sense in terms of our own reason and experience.

For Wesley, a cogent account of the Christian faith required the use of reason, both to understand Scripture and to relate the biblical message to wider fields of knowledge. He looked for confirmations of the biblical witness in human experience, especially the experiences of regeneration and sanctification, but also in the "common sense" knowledge of everyday experience.

The interaction of these sources and criteria in Wesley's own theology furnishes a guide for our continuing theological task as United Methodists. In that task Scripture, as the constitutive witness to the wellsprings of our faith, occupies a place of primary authority among these theological sources.

In practice, theological reflection may also find its point of departure in tradition, experience, or rational analysis. What matters most is that all four guidelines be brought to bear in faithful, serious, theological consideration. Insights arising from serious study of the Scriptures and tradition enrich contemporary experience. Imaginative and critical thought enables us to understand better the Bible and our common Christian history.

Scripture

United Methodists share with other Christians the conviction that Scripture is the primary source and criterion for Christian doctrine. Through Scripture the living Christ meets us in the experience of redeeming grace. We are convinced that Jesus Christ is the living Word of God in our midst whom we trust in life and death.

The biblical authors, illumined by the Holy Spirit, bear witness that in Christ the world is reconciled to God. The Bible bears authentic testimony to God's self-disclosure in the life, death, and resurrection of Jesus Christ as well as in God's work of creation, in the pilgrimage of Israel, and in the Holy Spirit's ongoing activity in human history.

As we open our minds and hearts to the Word of God through the words of human beings inspired by the Holy Spirit, faith is born and nourished, our understanding is deepened, and the possibilities for transforming the world become apparent to us.

The Bible is sacred canon for Christian people, formally acknowledged as such by historic ecumenical councils of the Church. Our doctrinal standards identify as canonical thirty-nine books of the Old Testament and the twenty-seven books of the New Testament.

Our standards affirm the Bible as the source of all that is "necessary" and "sufficient" unto salvation (Articles of Religion) and "is to be received through the Holy Spirit as the true rule and guide for faith and practice" (Confession of Faith).

We properly read Scripture within the believing community, informed by the tradition of that community. We interpret individual texts in light of their place in the Bible as a whole.

We are aided by scholarly inquiry and personal insight, under the guidance of the Holy Spirit. As we work with each text, we take into account what we have been able to learn about the original context and intention of that text. In this understanding we draw upon the careful historical, literary, and textual studies of recent years, which have enriched our understanding of the Bible.

Through this faithful reading of Scripture, we may come to know the truth of the biblical message in its bearing on our own lives and the life of the world. Thus the Bible serves both as a source of our faith and as the basic criterion by which the truth and fidelity of any interpretation of faith is measured.

While we acknowledge the primacy of Scripture in theological reflection, our attempts to grasp its meaning always involve tradition, experience, and reason. Like Scripture, these may become creative vehicles of the Holy Spirit as they function within the Church. They quicken our faith, open our eyes to the wonder of God's love, and clarify our understanding.

The Wesleyan heritage, reflecting its origins in the catholic and reformed ethos of English Christianity, directs us to a self-conscious use of these three sources in interpreting Scripture and in formulating faith statements based on the biblical witness. These sources are, along with Scripture, indispensable to our theological task.

The close relationship of tradition, experience, and reason appears in the Bible itself. Scripture witnesses to a variety of diverse traditions, some of which reflect tensions in interpretation within the early Judeo-Christian heritage. However, these traditions are woven together in the Bible in a manner that expresses the fundamental unity of God's revelation as received and experienced by people in the diversity of their own lives.

The developing communities of faith judged them, therefore, to be an authoritative witness to that revelation. In recognizing the interrelationship and inseparability of the four basic resources for theological understanding, we are following a model which is present in the biblical text itself.

Tradition

The theological task does not start anew in each age or each person. Christianity does not leap from New Testament times to the present as though nothing were to be learned from that great cloud of witnesses in between. For centuries Christians have sought to interpret the truth of the gospel for their time.

In these attempts, tradition, understood both in terms of process and form, has played an important role. The passing on and receiving of the gospel among persons, regions, and generations constitutes a dynamic element of Christian history. The formulations and practices that grew out of specific circumstances constitute the legacy of the corporate experience of earlier Christian communities.

These traditions are found in many cultures around the globe. But the history of Christianity includes a mixture of ignorance, misguided zeal, and sin. Scripture remains the norm by which all traditions are judged.

The story of the Church reflects the most basic sense of tradition, the continuing activity of God's Spirit transforming human life. Tradition is the history of that continuing environment of grace in and by which all Christians live, God's self-giving love in Jesus Christ. As such, tradition transcends the story of particular traditions.

In this deeper sense of tradition, all Christians share a common history. Within that history, Christian tradition precedes Scripture, and yet Scripture comes to be the focal expression of the tradition. As United Methodists, we pursue our theological task in openness to the richness of both the form and power of tradition.

The multiplicity of traditions furnishes a richly varied source for theological reflection and construction. For United Methodists, certain strands of tradition have special importance as the historic foundation of our doctrinal heritage and the distinctive expressions of our communal existence.

We are now challenged by traditions from around the world which accent dimensions of Christian understanding that grow out of the sufferings and victories of the downtrodden. These traditions help us rediscover the biblical witness to God's special commitment to the poor, the disabled, the imprisoned, the oppressed, the outcast. In these persons we encounter the living presence of Jesus Christ.

These traditions underscore the equality of all persons in Jesus Christ. They display the capacity of the gospel to free us to embrace the diversity of human cultures and appreciate their values. They reinforce our traditional understanding of the inseparability of personal salvation and social justice. They deepen our commitment to global peace.

A critical appreciation of these traditions can compel us to think about God in new ways, enlarge our vision of shalom, and enhance our confidence in God's provident love.

Tradition acts as a measure of validity and propriety for a community's faith insofar as it represents a consensus of faith. The various traditions that presently make claims upon us may contain conflicting images and insights of truth and validity. We examine such conflicts in light of Scripture, reflecting critically upon the doctrinal stance of our Church.

It is by the discerning use of our standards and in openness to emerging forms of Christian identity that we attempt to maintain fidelity to the apostolic faith.

At the same time, we continue to draw on the broader Christian tradition as an expression of the history of divine grace within which Christians are able to recognize and welcome one another in love.

Experience

In our theological task, we follow Wesley's practice of examining experience, both individual and corporate, for confirmations of the realities of God's grace attested in Scripture.

Our experience interacts with Scripture. We read Scripture in light of the conditions and events that help shape who we are, and we interpret our experience in terms of Scripture.

All religious experience affects all human experience; all human experience affects our understanding of religious experience.

On the personal level, experience is to the individual as tradition is to the Church: it is the personal appropriation of God's forgiving and empowering grace. Experience authenticates in our own lives the truths revealed in Scripture and illumined in tradition, enabling us to claim the Christian witness as our own.

Wesley described faith and its assurance as "a sure trust and confidence" in the mercy of God through our Lord Jesus Christ, and a steadfast hope of all good things to be received at God's hand. Such assurance is God's gracious gift through the witness of the Holy Spirit.

This "new life in Christ" is what we as United Methodists mean when we speak of "Christian experience." Christian experience gives us new eyes to see the living youth in Scripture. It confirms the biblical message for our present. It illumines our understanding of God and creation, and motivates us to make sensitive moral judgments.

Although profoundly personal, Christian experience is also corporate; our theological task is informed by the experience of the Church and by the common experiences of all humanity. In our attempts to understand the biblical message, we recognize that God's gift of liberating love embraces the whole of creation.

Some facets of human experience tax our theological understanding. Many of God's people live in terror, hunger, loneliness, and degradation. Everyday experiences of birth and death, of growth and life in the created world, and an awareness of wider social relations also belong to serious theological reflection.

A new awareness of such experiences can inform our appropriation of scriptural truths and sharpen our appreciation of the good news of the Kingdom of God.

As a source for theological reflection, experience, like tradition, is richly varied, challenging our efforts to put into words the totality of the promises of the gospel. We interpret experience in the light of scriptural norms, just as our experience informs our reading of the biblical message. In this respect,

Scripture remains central in our efforts to be faithful in making our Christian witness.

Reason

Although we recognize that God's revelation and our experiences of God's grace continually surpass the scope of human language and reason, we also believe that any disciplined theological work calls for the careful use of reason.

By reason we read and interpret Scripture.

By reason we determine whether our Christian witness is clear.

By reason we ask questions of faith and seek to understand God's action and will.

By reason we organize the understandings that compose our witness and render them internally coherent.

By reason we test the congruence of our witness to the biblical testimony and to the traditions which mediate that testimony to us.

By reason we relate our witness to the full range of human knowledge, experience, and service.

Since all truth is from God, efforts to discern the connections between revelation and reason, faith and science, grace and nature, are useful endeavors in developing credible and communicable doctrine. We seek nothing less than a total view of reality that is decisively informed by the promises and imperatives of the Christian gospel, though we know well that such an attempt will always be marred by the limits and distortions characteristic of human knowledge.

Nevertheless, by our quest for reasoned understandings of Christian faith we seek to grasp, express, and live out the gospel in a way that will commend itself to thoughtful persons who are seeking to know and follow God's ways.

In theological reflection, the resources of tradition, experience, and reason are integral to our study of Scripture without displacing Scripture's primacy for faith and practice. These four sources—each making distinctive contributions, yet all finally working together—guide our quest as United Methodists for a vital and appropriate Christian witness.

The Present Challenge to Theology in the Church

In addition to historic tensions and conflicts that still require resolution, new issues continually arise that summon us to fresh theological inquiry. Daily we are presented with an array of concerns that challenge our proclamation of God's reign over all of human existence.

Of crucial importance are concerns generated by great human struggles for dignity, liberation, and fulfillment—aspirations that are inherent elements in God's design for creation. These concerns are borne by theologies that express the heart cries of the downtrodden and the aroused indignation of the compassionate.

The perils of nuclear destruction, terrorism, war, poverty, violence, and injustice confront us. Injustices linked to race, gender, class, and age are widespread in our times. Misuse of natural resources and disregard for the fragile balances in our environment contradict our calling to care for God's creation. Secularism pervades high-technology civilizations, hindering human awareness of the spiritual depths of existence.

We seek an authentic Christian response to these realities, that the healing and redeeming work of God might be present in our words and deeds. Too often, theology is used to support practices that are unjust. We look for answers that are in harmony with the gospel and do not claim exemption from critical assessment.

A rich quality of our Church, especially as it has developed in the last century, is its global character. We are a church with a distinctive theological heritage, but that heritage is lived out in a global community, resulting in understandings of our faith enriched by indigenous experiences and manners of expression.

We affirm the contributions which United Methodists of varying ethnic, language, cultural, and national groups make to one another and to our Church as a whole. We celebrate our shared commitment to clear theological understanding and vital missional expression.

United Methodists as a diverse people continue to strive for consensus in understanding the gospel. In our diversity, we are held together by a shared inheritance and a common desire to participate in the creative and redemptive activity of God.

Our task is to articulate our vision in a way that will draw us together as a people in mission.

In the name of Jesus Christ we are called to work within our diversity while exercising patience and forbearance with one another. Such patience stems neither from indifference toward truth nor from an indulgent tolerance of error but from an awareness that we know only in part and that none of us is able to search the mysteries of God except by the Spirit of God. We proceed with our theological task, trusting that the Spirit will grant us wisdom to continue our journey with the whole people of God.

Ecumenical Commitment

Christian unity is founded on the theological understanding that in our Baptism, we are made members-in-common of the one Body of Christ. Christian unity is not an option; it is a gift to be received and expressed.

United Methodists respond to the theological, biblical, and practical mandates for Christian unity by firmly committing ourselves to the cause of Christian unity at local, national, and world levels. We invest ourselves in many way by which mutual recognition of churches, of members, and of ministries may lead us to sharing in Holy Communion with all of God's people.

Knowing that denominational loyalty is always subsumed in our life in the Church of Jesus Christ, we welcome and celebrate the rich experience of United Methodist leadership in church councils and consultations, in multilateral and bilateral dialogues, as well as in other forms of ecumenical convergence that have led to the healing of churches and nations.

We see the Holy Spirit at work in making the unity among us more visible.

Concurrently, we have entered into serious interfaith encounters and explorations between Christians and adherents of other living faiths of the world. Scripture calls us to be both neighbors and witnesses to all peoples. Such encounters require us to reflect anew on our faith and seek guidance for our witness among neighbors of other faiths. We then rediscover that the God who has acted in Jesus Christ for the salvation of the whole world is also the Creator of all humankind, the One who is "above all and through all and in all" (Ephesians 4:6).

As people bound together on one planet, we see the need for a self-critical view of our own tradition and accurate appreciation of other traditions. In these encounters, our aim is not to reduce doctrinal differences to some lowest common denominator of religious agreement but to raise all such relationships to the highest possible level of human fellowship and understanding.

We labor together with the help of God toward the salvation, health, and peace of all people. In respectful conversations and in practical cooperation, we confess our Christian faith and strive to display the manner in which Jesus Christ is the life and hope of the world.

Conclusion

Doctrine arises out of the life of the Church—its faith, its worship, its discipline, its conflicts, its challenges from the world it would serve.

Evangelism, nurture, and mission require a constant effort to integrate authentic experience, rational thought, and purposeful action with theological integrity.

A convincing witness to our Lord and Savior Jesus Christ can contribute to the renewal of our faith, bring persons to that faith, and strengthen the Church as an agent of healing and reconciliation.

This witness, however, cannot fully describe or encompass the mystery of God. Though we experience the wonder of God's grace at work with us and among us, and though we know the joy of the present signs of God's kingdom, each new step makes us more aware of the ultimate mystery of God, from which arises a heart of wonder and an attitude of humility. Yet we trust that we can know more fully what is essential for our participation in God's saving work in the world, and we are confident in the ultimate unfolding of God's justice and mercy.

In this spirit we take up our theological task, endeavoring to understand the love of God given in Jesus Christ and to spread this love abroad. As we see more clearly who we have been, as we understand more fully the needs of the world, as we draw more effectively upon our theological heritage, we will become better equipped to fulfill our calling as the people of God.

> Now to God
> who by the power at work within us
> is able to do far more abundantly
> than all that we ask or think,
> to God be glory in the church
> and in Christ Jesus to all generations,
> for ever and ever. Amen.
>   —Ephesians 3:20-21 (based on RSV)

Part III
SOCIAL PRINCIPLES

PREFACE

The United Methodist Church has a long history of concern for social justice. Its members have often taken forthright positions on controversial issues involving Christian principles. Early Methodists expressed their opposition to the slave trade, to smuggling, and to the cruel treatment of prisoners.

A social creed was adopted by the Methodist Episcopal Church (North) in 1908. Within the next decade similar statements were adopted by the Methodist Episcopal Church, South, and by the Methodist Protestant Church. The Evangelical United Brethren Church adopted a statement of social principles in 1946 at the time of the uniting of the United Brethren and The Evangelical Church. In 1972, four years after the uniting in 1968 of The Methodist Church and The Evangelical United Brethren Church, the General Conference of The United Methodist Church adopted a new statement of Social Principles, which was revised in 1976.

The Social Principles are a prayerful and thoughtful effort on the part of the General Conference to speak to the human issues in the contemporary world from a sound biblical and theological foundation as historically demonstrated in United Methodist traditions. They are intended to be instructive and persuasive in the best of the prophetic spirit. The Social Principles are a call to all members of The United Methodist Church to a prayerful, studied dialogue of faith and practice. (*See* ¶ 610.)

PREAMBLE

We, the people called United Methodists, affirm our faith in God our Father, in Jesus Christ our Savior, and in the Holy Spirit, our Guide and Guard.

We acknowledge our complete dependence upon God in birth, in life, in death, and in life eternal. Secure in God's love, we affirm the goodness of life and confess our many sins against God's will for us as we find it in Jesus Christ. We have not always been faithful stewards of all that has been committed to us by God the Creator. We have been reluctant followers of Jesus Christ in his mission to bring all persons into a community of love. Though called by the Holy Spirit to become new creatures in Christ, we have resisted the further call to become the people of God in our dealings with each other and the earth on which we live.

Grateful for God's forgiving love, in which we live and by which we are judged, and affirming our belief in the inestimable worth of each individual, we renew our commitment to become faithful witnesses to the gospel, not alone to the ends of earth, but also to the depths of our common life and work.

¶ 70.   I. THE NATURAL WORLD

All creation is the Lord's and we are responsible for the ways in which we use and abuse it. Water, air, soil, minerals, energy resources, plants, animal life, and space are to be valued and conserved because they are God's creation and not solely because they are useful to human beings. Therefore, we repent of our devastation of the physical and nonhuman world. Further, we recognize the responsibility of the Church toward life-style and systemic changes in society that will promote a more ecologically just world and a better quality of life for all creation.

A) Water, Air, Soil, Minerals, Plants.—We support and encourage social policies that serve to reduce and control the creation of industrial by-products and waste; facilitate the safe processing and disposal of toxic and nuclear waste; provide for appropriate disposal of municipal waste; and enhance the rejuvenation of polluted air, water, and soil. We support measures which will halt the spread of deserts into formerly productive lands. We support regulations designed to protect plant life, including those that provide for reforestation and for conservation of grasslands. We support policies that retard the *indiscriminate* use of chemicals, including those used for growing, processing, and preserving food, and encourage adequate research into their effects upon God's creation prior to utilization. We urge development of international agreements concerning equitable utilization of the ocean's resources for human benefit so long as the integrity of the seas is maintained. Moreover, we support policies on the part of governments and industries that conserve fossil and other fuels, and that eliminate methods of securing minerals that destroy plants, animals, and soil. We encourage creation of new sources for food and power, while maintaining the goodness of the earth.

B) Energy Resources Utilization.—We support and encourage social policies that are directed toward rational and restrained transformation of parts of the nonhuman world into energy for human usage, and which de-emphasize or eliminate energy-producing technologies that endanger the health, safety, and even existence of the present and future human and nonhuman creation. Further, we urge wholehearted support of the conservation of energy and responsible development of all energy resources, with special concern for the development of renewable energy sources, that the goodness of the earth may be affirmed.

C) Animal Life.—We support regulations that protect the life and health of animals, including those ensuring the humane treatment of pets and other domestic animals, and the painless slaughtering of meat animals, fish, and fowl. Furthermore, we encourage the preservation of animal species now threatened with extinction.

D) Space.—The moon, planets, stars, and the space between and among them are the creation of God and are due the respect we are called to give the earth. We support the extension of knowledge through space exploration, but only when that knowledge is used for the welfare of humanity.

¶ 71. II. THE NURTURING COMMUNITY

The community provides the potential for nurturing human beings into the fullness of their humanity. We believe we have a responsibility to innovate, sponsor, and evaluate new forms of community that will encourage development of the fullest potential in individuals. Primary for us is the gospel understanding that all persons are important—because they are human beings created by God and loved through and by Jesus Christ and not because they have merited significance. We therefore support social climates in which human communities are maintained and strengthened for the sake of every person.

A) The Family.—We believe the family to be the basic human community through which persons are nurtured and sustained in mutual love, responsibility, respect, and fidelity. We understand the family as encompassing a wider range of options than that of the two-generational unit of parents and children (the nuclear family), including the extended family, families with adopted children, single parents, stepfamilies, couples without children. We affirm shared responsibility for parenting by men and women and encourage social, economic, and religious efforts to maintain and strengthen relationships within families in order that every member may be assisted toward complete personhood.

B) Other Christian Communities.—We further recognize the movement to find new patterns of Christian nurturing communities such as Koinonia Farms, certain monastic and other religious orders, and some types of corporate church life. We urge the Church to seek ways of understanding the needs and concerns of such Christian groups and to find ways of ministering to them and through them.

C) Marriage.—We affirm the sanctity of the marriage covenant which is expressed in love, mutual support, personal commitment, and shared fidelity between a man and a woman. We believe that God's blessing rests upon such marriage, whether or not there are children of the union. We reject social norms that assume different standards for women than for men in marriage.

D) Divorce.—Where marriage partners, even after thoughtful consideration and counsel, are estranged beyond reconciliation, we recognize divorce as regrettable but recognize the right of divorced persons to remarry. We express our deep concern for the care and nurture of the children of divorced and/or remarried persons. We encourage that either or both of the divorced parents be considered for custody of the minor children of the marriage. We encourage an active, accepting, and enabling commitment of the church and our society to minister to the members of divorced and remarried families.

E) Single Persons.—We affirm the integrity of single persons, and we reject all social practices that discriminate or social attitudes that are prejudicial against persons because they are unmarried.

F) Human Sexuality.—We recognize that sexuality is God's good gift to all persons. We believe persons may be fully human only when that gift is acknowledged and affirmed by themselves, the Church, and society. We call all persons to the disciplined, responsible fulfillment of themselves, others, and society in the stewardship of this gift. We also recognize our limited understanding of this complex gift and encourage the medical, theological, and social science disciplines to combine in a determined effort to understand human sexuality more completely. We call the Church to take the leadership role in bringing together these disciplines to address this most complex issue. Further, within the context of our understanding of this gift of God, we recognize that God challenges us to find responsible, committed, and loving forms of expression.

Although all persons are sexual beings whether or not they are married, sexual relations are only clearly affirmed in the marriage bond. Sex may become exploitative within as well as outside marriage. We reject all sexual expressions which damage or destroy the humanity God has given us as birthright, and we affirm only that sexual expression which enhances that same humanity, in the midst of diverse opinion as to what constitutes that enhancement.

We deplore all forms of the commercialization and exploitation of sex with their consequent cheapening and degradation of human personality. We call for strict enforcement of laws prohibiting the sexual exploitation or use of children by adults. We call for the establishment of adequate protective services, guidance, and counseling opportunities for children thus abused. We insist that all persons, regardless of age, gender, marital status, or sexual orientation, are entitled to have their human and civil rights ensured.

We recognize the continuing need for full, positive, and

factual sex education opportunities for children, youth, and adults. The Church offers a unique opportunity to give quality guidance/education in this area.

Homosexual persons no less than heterosexual persons are individuals of sacred worth. All persons need the ministry and guidance of the Church in their struggles for human fulfillment, as well as the spiritual and emotional care of a fellowship which enables reconciling relationships with God, with others, and with self. Although we do not condone the practice of homosexuality and consider this practice incompatible with Christian teaching, we affirm that God's grace is available to all. We commit ourselves to be in ministry for and with all persons.

G) Abortion.—The beginning of life and the ending of life are the God-given boundaries of human existence. While individuals have always had some degree of control over when they would die, they now have the awesome power to determine when and even whether new individuals will be born. Our belief in the sanctity of unborn human life makes us reluctant to approve abortion. But we are equally bound to respect the sacredness of the life and well-being of the mother, for whom devastating damage may result from an unacceptable pregnancy. In continuity with past Christian teaching, we recognize tragic conflicts of life with life that may justify abortion, and in such cases support the legal option of abortion under proper medical procedures. We cannot affirm abortion as an acceptable means of birth control, and we unconditionally reject it as a means of gender selection. We call all Christians to a searching and prayerful inquiry into the sorts of conditions that may warrant abortion. Governmental laws and regulations do not provide all the guidance required by the informed Christian conscience. Therefore, a decision concerning abortion should be made only after thoughtful and prayerful consideration by the parties involved, with medical, pastoral, and other appropriate counsel.

H) Death with Dignity.—We applaud medical science for efforts to prevent disease and illness and for advances in treatment that extend the meaningful life of human beings. At the same time, in the varying stages of death and life that advances in medical science have occasioned, we recognize the agonizing personal and moral decisions faced by the dying, their physicians, their families, and their friends. Therefore, we assert the right of every person to die in dignity, with loving personal care and without efforts to prolong terminal illnesses merely because the technology is available to do so.

¶ 72.   III. THE SOCIAL COMMUNITY

The rights and privileges a society bestows upon or withholds from those who comprise it indicate the relative esteem in which that society holds particular persons and groups of persons. We affirm all persons as equally valuable in the sight of God. We therefore work toward societies in which each person's value is recognized, maintained, and strengthened.

A) Rights of Racial and Ethnic Persons.—Racism is the combination of the power to dominate by one race over other races and a value system which assumes that the dominant race is innately superior to the others. Racism includes both personal and institutional racism. Personal racism is manifested through the individual expressions, attitudes, and/or behaviors which accept the assumptions of a racist value system and which maintain the benefits of this system. Institutional racism is the established social patterns which support implicitly or explicitly the racist value system. Racism plagues and cripples our growth in Christ, inasmuch as it is antithetical to the gospel itself. Therefore, we recognize racism as sin and affirm the ultimate and temporal worth of all persons. We rejoice in the gifts which particular ethnic histories and cultures bring to our total life. We commend and encourage the self-awareness of all racial and ethnic groups and oppressed people which leads them to demand their just and equal rights as members of society. We assert the obligation of society, and groups within the society, to implement compensatory programs that redress long-standing systemic social deprivation of racial and ethnic people. We further assert the right of members of racial and ethnic groups to equal opportunities in employment and promotion; to education and training of the highest quality; to nondiscrimination in voting, in access to public accommodations, and in housing purchase or rental; and positions of leadership and power in all elements of our life together. We support affirmative action as one method of addressing the inequalities and discriminatory practices within our Church and society.

B) Rights of Religious Minorities.—Religious persecution has been common in the history of civilization. We urge policies and practices that ensure the right of every religious group to exercise its faith free from legal, political, or economic restrictions. In particular, we condemn anti-Semitic, anti-Muslim, and anti-Christian attitudes and policies in both their overt and covert forms, being especially sensitive to their expression in media stereotyping, and assert the right of all religions and their adherents to freedom from legal, economic, and social discrimination.

C) Rights of Children.—Once considered the property of their parents, children are now acknowledged to be full human beings in their own right, but beings to whom adults and society in general have special obligations. Thus, we support the development of school systems and innovative methods of education designed to assist every child toward complete fulfillment as individual persons of worth. All children have the right to quality education, including a full sexual education appropriate to their stage of development that utilizes the best educational techniques and insights. Moreover, children have the rights to food, shelter, clothing, health care, and emotional well-being as do adults, and these rights we affirm as theirs regardless of actions or inactions of their parents or guardians. In particular, children must be protected from economic and sexual exploitation.

D) Rights of Youth and Young Adults.—Our society is characterized by a large population of youth and young adults who frequently find full participation in society difficult. Therefore, we urge development of policies that encourage inclusion of youth and young adults in decision-making processes and that eliminate discrimination and exploitation. Creative and appropriate employment opportunities should be legally and socially available for youth and young adults.

E) Rights of the Aging.—In a society that places primary emphasis upon youth, those growing old in years are frequently isolated from the mainstream of social existence. We support social policies that integrate the aging into the life of the total community, including sufficient incomes, increased and nondiscriminatory employment opportunities, educational and service opportunities, and adequate medical care and housing within existing communities. We urge social policies and programs, with emphasis on the unique concerns of older women and ethnic persons, that ensure to the aging the respect and dignity that is their right as senior members of the human community. Further, we urge increased consideration for adequate pension systems by employers with provisions for the surviving spouse.

F) Rights of Women.—We affirm women and men to be equal in every aspect of their common life. We therefore urge that every effort be made to eliminate sex role stereotypes in activity and portrayal of family life and in all aspects of voluntary and compensatory participation in the Church and society. We affirm the right of women to equal treatment in employment, responsibility, promotion, and compensation. We affirm the importance of women in decision-making positions at all levels of church life and urge such bodies to guarantee their presence through policies of employment and recruitment. We support affirmative action as one method of addressing the inequalities and discriminatory practices within our Church and society. We urge employers of persons in dual career families, both in the Church and society, to apply proper consideration of both parties when relocation is considered.

G) Rights of Persons with Handicapping Conditions.—We recognize and affirm the full humanity and personhood of all individuals as members of the family of God. We affirm the responsibility of the Church and society to be in ministry with all persons, including those persons with mentally, physically, and/or psychologically handicapping conditions whose disabilities or differences in appearance or behavior create a problem in mobility, communication, intellectual comprehension, or personal relationships, which interfere with their participation or that of their families in the life of the Church and the community. We urge the Church and society to receive the gifts of persons with handicapping conditions to enable them to be full participants in the community of faith. We call the Church and society to be sensitive to, and advocate programs of rehabilitation, services, employment, education, appropriate housing, and transportation.

H) Population.—Since growing populations will increasingly strain the world's supply of food, minerals, and water, and sharpen international tensions, the reduction of the rate of consumption of resources by the affluent and the reduction of current population growth rates in some regions of the world have become imperative. People have the duty to consider the impact on the total society of their decisions regarding childbearing, and should have access to information and appropriate means to limit their fertility, including voluntary sterilization. We affirm that programs to achieve a stabilized population should be placed in a context of total economic and social development, including an equitable use and control of resources; improvement in the status of women in all cultures; a human level of economic security, health care, and literacy for all.

I) Alcohol and Other Drugs.—We affirm our long-standing support of abstinence from alcohol as a faithful witness to God's liberating and redeeming love for persons. We also recommend abstinence from the use of marijuana and any illegal drugs. As the use of alcohol is a major factor in both disease and death, we support educational programs encouraging abstinence from such use.

Millions of living human beings are testimony to the beneficial consequences of therapeutic drug use, and millions of others are testimony to the detrimental consequences of drug misuse. We encourage wise policies relating to the availability of potentially beneficial or potentially damaging prescription and over-the-counter drugs; we urge that complete information about their use and misuse be readily available to both doctor and patient. We support the strict administration of laws regulating the sale and distribution of all opiates. We support regulations that protect society from users of drugs of any kind where it can be shown that a clear and present social danger exists. The drug dependent person is an individual of infinite human worth in need of treatment and rehabilitation, and misuse should be viewed as a symptom of underlying disorders for which remedies should be sought.

J) Tobacco.—We affirm our historic tradition of high standards of personal discipline and social responsibility. In light of the overwhelming evidence that tobacco smoking and the use of smokeless tobacco are hazardous to the health of persons of all ages, we recommend total abstinence from the use of tobacco. We urge that our educational and communication resources be utilized to support and encourage such abstinence.

K) Medical Experimentation.—Physical and mental health has been greatly enhanced through discoveries by medical science. It is imperative, however, that governments and the medical profession carefully enforce the requirements of the prevailing medical research standard, maintaining rigid controls in testing new technologies and drugs utilizing human beings. The standard requires that those engaged in research shall use human beings as research subjects only after obtaining full, rational, and uncoerced consent.

L) Genetic Technology.—The responsibility of humankind for the whole creation challenges us to deal carefully with the possibilities of genetic research and gene-technology. We welcome the development and application of gene-technological methods for battling hunger through new sorts of plants and improved crops as well as for healing diseases by new, more effective, and cheaper medicine.

Because of the deep effects on the genotype of present and future generations as well as on the whole creation, we call for legal control of both research and application, in order to prevent any action which might lead to loss of control over these technologies and their consequences or to abuse for economic, political, or military ends.

Changes of human chromosomes are justified only for therapeutic reasons, and only if they do not include experiments which produce waste embryos or changes in germ cells. All kinds of positive eugenics, of cell-clones and hybridization must be prevented, if necessary by suitable legal action. The knowledge of the chromosomes of any individual must in no case be used to his or her disadvantage. Such knowledge shall be liable to medical secrecy, to strict privacy and data protection.

M) Rural Life.—We support the right of persons and families to live and prosper as farmers, farm workers, merchants, professionals, and others outside of the cities and metropolitan centers. We believe our culture is impoverished and our people deprived of a meaningful way of life when rural and small-town living becomes difficult or impossible. We recognize that the improvement of this way of life may sometimes necessitate the use of some lands for nonagricultural purposes. We oppose the indiscriminate diversion of agricultural land for nonagricultural uses when nonagricultural land is available. Further, we encourage the preservation of appropriate lands for agriculture and open space uses through thoughtful land use programs. We support governmental and private programs designed to benefit the resident farmer rather than the factory farm, and programs that encourage industry to locate in nonurban areas.

N) Urban-Suburban Life.—Urban-suburban living has become a dominant style of life for more and more persons. For many it furnishes economic, educational, social, and cultural opportunities. For others, it has brought alienation, poverty, and depersonalization. We in the Church have an opportunity and responsibility to help shape the future of urban-suburban life. Massive programs of renewal and social planning are needed to bring a greater degree of humanization into urban-suburban life-styles. Christians must judge all programs, including economic and community development, new towns, and urban renewal by the extent to which they protect and enhance human values, permit personal and political involvement, and make possible neighborhoods open to persons of all races, ages, and income levels. We affirm the efforts of all developers who place human values at the heart of their planning. We must help shape urban-suburban development so it provides for the human need to identify with and find meaning in smaller social communities. At the same time such smaller communities must be encouraged to assume responsibilities for the total urban-suburban community instead of isolating themselves from it.

¶ 73.   IV. THE ECONOMIC COMMUNITY

We claim all economic systems to be under the judgment of God no less than other facets of the created order. Therefore, we recognize the responsibility of governments to develop and implement sound fiscal and monetary policies that provide for the economic life of individuals and corporate entities, and that ensure full employment and adequate incomes with a minimum of inflation. We believe private and public economic enterprises are responsible for the social costs of doing business, such as unemployment and environmental pollution, and that they should be held accountable for these costs. We support measures that would reduce the concentration of wealth in the hands of a few. We further support efforts to revise tax structures and eliminate governmental support programs that now benefit the wealthy at the expense of other persons.

A) Property.—We believe private ownership of property is a trusteeship under God, both in those societies where it is encouraged and where it is discouraged, but is limited by the overriding needs of society. We believe that Christian faith denies to any person or group of persons exclusive and arbitrary control of any other part of the created universe. Socially and culturally conditioned ownership of property is, therefore, to be considered a responsibility to God. We believe, therefore, governments have the responsibility, in the pursuit of justice and order under law, to provide procedures that protect the rights of the whole society, as well as those of private ownership.

B) Collective Bargaining.—We support the right of public and private (including farm, government, institutional, and domestic) employees and employers to organize for collective bargaining into unions and other groups of their own choosing. Further, we support the right of both parties to protection in so doing, and their responsibility to bargain in good faith within the framework of the public interest. In order that the rights of all members of the society may be maintained and promoted, we support innovative bargaining procedures that include representatives of the public interest in negotiation and settlement of labor-management contracts including some that may lead to forms of judicial resolution of issues.

C) Work and Leisure.—Every person has the right and responsibility to work for the benefit of himself or herself and the enhancement of human life and community and to receive adequate remuneration. We support social measures that ensure the physical and mental safety of workers, that provide for the equitable division of products and services and that encourage an increasing freedom in the way individuals may use their leisure time. We recognize the opportunity leisure provides for creative contributions to society and encourage methods that allow workers additional blocks of discretionary time. We support educational, cultural, and recreational outlets that enhance the use of such time. We believe that persons come before profits. We deplore the selfish spirit which often pervades our economic life. We support policies which encourage workplace democracy, cooperative and collective work arrangements. We support rights of workers to refuse to work in situations that endanger health and/or life, without jeopardy to their jobs. We support policies which would reverse the increasing concentration of business and industry into monopolies.

D) Consumption.—We support efforts to ensure truth in pricing, packaging, lending, and advertising. We assert that the consumers' primary responsibility is to provide themselves with needed goods and services of high quality at the lowest cost consistent with economic practices. They should exercise their economic power to encourage the manufacture of goods that are necessary and beneficial to humanity while avoiding the desecration of the environment in either production or consumption. Those who manufacture goods and offer services serve society best when they aid consumers in fulfilling these responsibilities. Consumers should evaluate their consumption of goods and services in the light of the need for enhanced quality of life rather than unlimited production of material goods. We call upon consumers to organize to achieve these goals.

E) Poverty.—In spite of general affluence in the industrialized nations, the majority of persons in the world live in poverty. In order to provide basic needs such as food, clothing, shelter, education, health care, and other necessities, ways must be found to share more equitably the resources of the world. Increasing technology and exploitative economic practices impoverish many persons and make poverty self-perpetuating. Therefore, we do not hold poor people morally responsible for their economic state. To begin to alleviate poverty, we support such policies as: adequate income maintenance, quality education, decent housing, job training, meaningful employment opportunities, adequate medical and hospital care, and humanization and radical revisions of welfare programs.

F) Migrant Workers.—Migratory and other farm workers, who

have long been a special concern of the Church's ministry, are by the nature of their way of life excluded from many of the economic and social benefits enjoyed by other workers. We advocate their right to, and applaud their efforts toward, responsible self-organization and self-determination. We call upon governments and all employers to ensure for migratory workers the same economic, educational, and social benefits enjoyed by other citizens. We call upon our churches to seek to develop programs of service to such migrant people as come within their parish.

G) Gambling.—Gambling is a menace to society, deadly to the best interests of moral, social, economic, and spiritual life, and destructive of good government. As an act of faith and love, Christians should abstain from gambling, and should strive to minister to those victimized by the practice. Where gambling has become addictive, the Church will encourage such individuals to receive therapeutic assistance so that the individual's energies may be redirected into positive and constructive ends. Community standards and personal life styles should be such as would make unnecessary and undesirable the resort to commercial gambling, including public lotteries, as a recreation, as an escape, or as a means of producing public revenue or funds for support of charities or government.

¶ 74.   V. THE POLITICAL COMMUNITY

While our allegiance to God takes precedence over our allegiance to any state, we acknowledge the vital function of government as a principal vehicle for the ordering of society. Because we know ourselves to be responsible to God for social and political life, we declare the following relative to governments:

A) Basic Freedoms.—We hold governments responsible for the protection of the rights of the people to free and fair elections and to the freedoms of speech, religion, assembly, and communications media, and petition for redress of grievances without fear of reprisal; to the right to privacy; and to the guarantee of the rights to adequate food, clothing, shelter, education, and health care. We also strongly reject domestic surveillance and intimidation of political opponents by governments in power, and all other misuses of elective or appointive offices. The use of detention and imprisonment for the harassment and elimination of political opponents or other dissidents violates fundamental human rights. Furthermore, the mistreatment or torture of persons by governments for any purpose violates Christian teaching and must be condemned and/or opposed by Christians and churches wherever and whenever it occurs.

The Church regards the institution of slavery as an infamous evil. All forms of enslavement are totally prohibited and shall in no way be tolerated by the Church.

B) Political Responsibility.—The strength of a political system depends upon the full and willing participation of its citizens. We believe that the state should not attempt to control the Church, nor should the Church seek to dominate the state. "Separation of church and state" means no organic union of the two, but does permit interaction. The Church should continually exert a strong ethical influence upon the state, supporting policies and programs deemed to be just and compassionate and opposing policies and programs which are not.

C) Freedom of Information.—Citizens of all countries should have access to all essential information regarding their government and its policies. Illegal and unconscionable activities directed against persons or groups by their own governments must not be justified or kept secret even under the guise of national security.

D) Education.—We believe responsibility for education of the young rests with the family, the Church, and the government. In our society this function can best be fulfilled through public policies which ensure access for all persons to free public elementary and secondary schools and to post-secondary schools of their choice. Persons in our society should not be precluded by financial barriers from access to church-related and other independent institutions of higher education. We affirm the right of public and independent colleges and universities to exist, and we endorse public policies which ensure access and choice and which do not create unconstitutional entanglements between Church and state. The state should not use its authority to inculcate particular religious beliefs (including atheism) nor should it require prayer or worship in the public schools, but should leave students free to practice their own religious convictions.

E) Civil Obedience and Civil Disobedience.—Governments and laws should be servants of God and of human beings. Citizens have a duty to abide by laws duly adopted by orderly and just process of government. But governments, no less than individuals, are subject to the judgment of God. Therefore, we recognize the right of individuals to dissent when acting under the constraint of conscience and after exhausting all legal recourse, to disobey laws deemed to be unjust. Even then, respect for law should be shown by refraining from violence and by accepting the costs of disobedience. We offer our prayers for those in rightful authority who serve the public and we support their efforts to afford justice and equal opportunity for all people. We assert the duty of churches to support everyone who suffers for the cause of conscience, and urge governments seriously to consider restoration of rights to such persons while also maintaining respect for those who obey.

F) Criminal Justice.—To protect all citizens from those who would encroach upon personal and property rights, it is the duty of governments to establish police forces, courts, and facilities for the confinement, punishment, and rehabilitation of offenders. We support governmental measures designed to reduce and eliminate crime, consistent with respect for the basic freedom of persons. We reject all misuse of these necessary mechanisms, including their use for the purpose of persecuting or intimidating those whose race, appearance, life-style, economic condition, or beliefs differ from those in authority, and we reject all careless, callous, or discriminatory enforcement of law. We further support measures designed to remove the social conditions that lead to crime, and we encourage continued positive interaction between law enforcement officials and members of the community at large. In the love of Christ who came to save those who are lost and vulnerable, we urge the creation of genuinely new systems for the care and support of the victims of crime, and for rehabilitation that will restore, preserve, and nurture the humanity of the imprisoned. For the same reason, we oppose capital punishment and urge its elimination from all criminal codes.

G) Military Service.—Though coercion, violence, and war are presently the ultimate sanctions in international relations, we reject them as incompatible with the gospel and spirit of Christ. We therefore urge the establishment of the rule of law in international affairs as a means of elimination of war, violence, and coercion in those affairs.

We reject national policies of enforced military service as incompatible with the gospel. We acknowledge the agonizing tension created by the demand for military service by national Church as they reach a conscientious decision concerning the nature of their responsibility as citizens. Pastors are called upon to be available for counseling with all young adults who face conscription, including those who conscientiously refuse to cooperate with a system of conscription.

We support and extend the ministry of the Church to those persons who conscientiously oppose all war, or any particular war, and who therefore refuse to serve in the armed forces or to cooperate with systems of military conscription. We also support and extend the Church's ministry to those persons who conscientiously choose to serve in the armed forces or to accept alternative service.

¶ 75.   VI. THE WORLD COMMUNITY

God's world is one world. The unity now being thrust upon us by technological revolution has far outrun our moral and spiritual capacity to achieve a stable world. The enforced unity of humanity, increasingly evident on all levels of life, presents the Church as well as all people with problems that will not wait for answer: injustice, war, exploitation, privilege, population, international ecological crisis, proliferation of arsenals of nuclear weapons, development of transnational business organizations that operate beyond the effective control of any governmental structure, and the increase of tyranny in all its forms. This generation must find viable answers to these and related questions if humanity is to continue on this earth. We commit ourselves, as a Church, to the achievement of a world community that is a fellowship of persons who honestly love one another. We pledge ourselves to seek the meaning of the gospel in all issues that divide people and threaten the growth of world community.

A) Nations and Cultures.—As individuals are affirmed by God in their diversity, so are nations and cultures. We recognize that no nation or culture is absolutely just and right in its treatment of its own people, nor is any nation totally without regard for the welfare of its citizens. The Church must regard nations as accountable for unjust treatment of their citizens and others living within their borders. While recognizing valid differences in culture and political philosophy, we stand for justice and peace in every nation.

B) National Power and Responsibility.—Some nations possess more military and economic power than do others. Upon the powerful rests responsibility to exercise their wealth and influence with restraint. We affirm the right and duty of people of all nations to determine their own destiny. We urge the major political powers to use their nonviolent power to maximize the political, social, and economic self-determination of other nations, rather than to further their own special interests. We applaud international efforts to develop a more just international economic order, in which the limited resources of the earth will be used to the maximum benefit of all nations and peoples. We urge Christians, in every society, to encourage the governments under which they live, and the economic entities within their societies, to aid and to work for the development of more just economic orders.

C) War and Peace.—We believe war is incompatible with the teachings and example of Christ. We therefore reject war as an instrument of national foreign policy and insist that the first moral duty of all nations is to resolve by peaceful means every dispute that arises between or among them; that human values must outweigh military claims as governments determine their priorities; that the militarization of society must be challenged and stopped; that the manufacture, sale, and deployment of armaments must be reduced and controlled; and that the production, possession, or use of nuclear weapons be condemned.

D) Justice and Law.—Persons and groups must feel secure in their life and right to live within a society if order is to be achieved

109

and maintained by law. We denounce as immoral an ordering of life that perpetuates injustice. Nations, too, must feel secure in the world if world community is to become a fact.

Believing that international justice requires the participation of all peoples, we endorse the United Nations and its related bodies and the International Court of Justice as the best instruments now in existence to achieve a world of justice and law. We commend the efforts of all people in all countries who pursue world peace through law. We endorse international aid and cooperation on all matters of need and conflict. We urge acceptance for membership in the United Nations of all nations who wish such membership and who accept United Nations responsibility. We urge the United Nations to take a more aggressive role in the development of international arbitration of disputes and actual conflicts among nations by developing binding third-party arbitration. Bilateral or multilateral efforts outside of the United Nations should work in concert with, and not contrary to, its purposes. We reaffirm our historic concern for the world as our parish and seek for all persons and peoples full and equal membership in a truly world community.

¶ 76.   VII. OUR SOCIAL CREED

We believe in God, Creator of the world; and in Jesus Christ the Redeemer of creation. We believe in the Holy Spirit, through whom we acknowledge God's gifts, and we repent of our sin in misusing these gifts to idolatrous ends.

We affirm the natural world as God's handiwork and dedicate ourselves to its preservation, enhancement, and faithful use by humankind.

We joyfully receive, for ourselves and others, the blessings of community, sexuality, marriage, and the family.

We commit ourselves to the rights of men, women, children, youth, young adults, the aging, and those with handicapping conditions; to improvement of the quality of life; and to the rights and dignity of racial, ethnic, and religious minorities.

We believe in the right and duty of persons to work for the good of themselves and others, and in the protection of their welfare in so doing; in the rights to property as a trust from God, collective bargaining, and responsible consumption; and in the elimination of economic and social distress.

We dedicate ourselves to peace throughout the world, to freedom for all peoples, and to the rule of justice and law among nations.

We believe in the present and final triumph of God's Word in human affairs, and gladly accept our commission to manifest the life of the gospel in the world. Amen.

(It is recommended that this statement of Social Principles be continually available to United Methodist Christians and that it be emphasized regularly in every congregation. It is further recommended that our Social Creed be frequently used in Sunday worship.)

Part IV

THE MINISTRY
OF ALL CHRISTIANS

THE MISSION AND MINISTRY OF THE CHURCH

Section I. The Churches.

¶ 101. From the beginning, God has dealt with the human family through covenants: with Adam and Eve, Noah, Abraham, Sarah and Hagar, Moses; with Deborah, Ruth, and Jeremiah and other prophets. In each covenant, God offered the chosen people the blessings of providence and commanded of them obedience to the divine will and way, that through them all the world should be blessed (Genesis 18:18; 22:18). In the new covenant in Christ, yet another community of hope was called out and gathered up, with the same promise and condition renewed that all who believe and obey shall be saved and made ministers of Christ's righteousness. John Wesley and our other spiritual forebears stressed this biblical theme of covenant-making and covenant-keeping as central in Christian experience.

¶ 102. The biblical story is marred by disregarded covenants and disrupted moral order, by sin and rebellion, with the resulting tragedies of alienation, oppression, and disorder. In the gospel of the new covenant, God in Christ has provided a new basis for reconciliation—justification by faith and birth into a new life in the Spirit, which is marked by growth toward wholeness. This wholeness of life is a gift revealed in Christ who came not to be served but to serve (Mark 10:45) and to give his life for the world. Christ freely took the nature of a servant, carrying this servanthood to its utmost limits (Philippians 2:7).

¶ **103.** God's self-revelation in the life, death, and resurrection of Jesus Christ summons the Church to ministry in the world through witness by word and deed in light of the Church's mission. The visible Church of Christ as a faithful community of persons affirms the worth of all humanity and the value of interrelationship in all of God's creation.

In the midst of a sinful world, through the grace of God, we are brought to repentance and faith in Jesus Christ. We become aware of the presence and life-giving power of God's Holy Spirit. We live in confident expectation of the ultimate fulfillment of God's purpose.

We are called together for worship and fellowship and for the upbuilding of the Christian community. We advocate and work for the unity of the Christian church. We call persons into discipleship.

As servants of Christ we are sent into the world to engage in the struggle for justice and reconciliation. We seek to reveal the love of God for men, women, and children of all ethnic, racial, cultural, and national backgrounds and to demonstrate the healing of the gospel with those who suffer.

Section II. The Heart of the Christian Ministry.

¶ **104.** The heart of Christian ministry is Christ's ministry of outreaching love. Christian ministry is the expression of the mind and mission of Christ by a community of Christians that demonstrates a common life of gratitude and devotion, witness and service, celebration and discipleship. All Christians are called to this ministry of servanthood in the world to the glory of God and for human fulfillment. The forms of this ministry are diverse in locale, in interest, and in denominational accent, yet always catholic in spirit and outreach.

Section III. The General Ministry of All Christian Believers.

¶ **105.** The Church as the community of the new covenant has participated in Christ's ministry of grace across the years and around the world. It stretches out to human needs wherever love and service may convey God's love and ours. The outreach of such ministries knows no limits. Beyond the diverse forms of ministry is this ultimate concern: that men and women may be renewed after the image of their creator (Colossians 3:10). This means that all Christians are called to minister wherever Christ would have them serve and witness in deeds and words that heal and free.

¶ **106.** This general ministry of all Christians in Christ's name and spirit is both a gift and a task. The gift is God's unmerited grace; the task is unstinting service. Entrance into the Church is acknowledged in Baptism and may include persons of all ages. In this Sacrament the Church claims God's promise, "the seal of the Spirit" (Ephesians 1:13). Baptism is followed by nurture and the consequent awareness by the baptized of the claim to ministry in Christ placed upon their lives by the Church. Such a ministry is ratified in confirmation, where the pledges of Baptism are accepted and renewed for life and mission. Entrance into and acceptance of ministry begin in a local church, but the impulse to minister always moves one beyond the congregation toward the whole human community. God's gifts are richly diverse for a variety of services; yet all have dignity and worth.

¶ **107.** The people of God are the Church made visible in the world. It is they who must convince the world of the reality of the gospel or leave it unconvinced. There can be no evasion or delegation of this responsibility; the Church is either faithful as a witnessing and serving community, or it loses its vitality and its impact on an unbelieving world.

Section IV. Representative Ministry.

¶ **108.** Within the people of God, there are those called to the representative ministry—ordained and diaconal. Such callings are evidenced by special gifts, evidence of God's grace, and promise of usefulness. God's call to representative ministry is inward as it comes to the individual and outward through the judgment and validation of the Church. When inner and outer call agree and are affirmed through election by an Annual Conference, the candidate may then be ordained or consecrated, according to such election, through symbolic acts which confer special roles of responsibility.

¶ **109.** *Diaconal Ministry.*—The diaconal ministers are called to specialized ministries of service, justice, and love within local congregations and in the wider world. Servant ministry must always involve a concern for justice as well as a love for persons. Diaconal ministers focus their service through a variety of ministries, such as, administration, education, evangelism, music, health ministries, and community development—to the local congregation and the wider community. Christ's service to humankind and the Church's responsibility for continuing that service in the world are both symbolized and enabled especially, but not exclusively, in diaconal ministry. Diaconal ministry exists to intensify and make more effective the self-understanding of the whole people of God as servants in Christ's name.

¶ **110.** *Ordained Ministry.*—The ordained ministers are called to specialized ministries of Word, Sacrament, and order. Through these distinctive functions ordained ministers devote themselves wholly to the work of the Church and to the upbuilding of the general ministry. They do this through careful study of the Scripture and its faithful interpretation, through effective proclamation of the gospel and responsible administration of the Sacraments, through diligent pastoral leadership of their congregations for fruitful discipleship, and by following the guidance of the Holy Spirit in witnessing beyond the congregation in the local community and to the ends of the earth. The ordained ministry is defined by its intentionally representative character, by its passion for the hallowing of life, and by its concern to link all local ministries with the widest boundaries of the Christian community.

Section V. The Unity of Ministry in Christ.

¶ **111.** There is but one ministry in Christ, but there are diverse gifts and evidence of God's grace in the Body of Christ (Ephesians 4:4-16). The general and representative ministries in The United Methodist Church are complementary. Neither is subservient to the other. Both are summoned and sent by Christ to live and work together in mutual interdependence and to be guided by the Spirit into the truth that frees and the love that reconciles.

Section VI. The Journey of a Connectional People.

¶ **112.** 1. *Introduction.*—Ever since John Wesley began to refer to the scattered Methodist classes, bands and societies throughout eighteenth-century England as "the connexion," Methodists everywhere have embraced the idea that as a people of faith we journey together in connection and in covenant with one another. Expressing the high degree of cohesiveness and centralized organization among Methodists, the connectional principle became the distinguishing mark which set them apart from the normal patterns of Anglican ecclesiastical organization as well as the more loosely organized Protestant bodies of the day.

2. *Roots.*—This acceptance of strong covenantal bonds among the Methodists was no accident. There were deep theological roots, including the concept and experience of covenant and the resulting emphasis on faith journeying in covenant with God and one another. The connectional idea is a style of relationship rather than simply an organizational or structural framework. As Bishop Paul Washburn once said, it is made up of "living, interdependent and interacting relationships . . . born in covenant-making events."

There were deep biblical roots as well. Images of the Church, especially in the New Testament—the vine and the branches, the wedding feast, the household or commonwealth of God, the new humanity with cosmic and kingdom dimensions, the fellowship of the saints, the Body of Christ, and a host of others—supplemented the covenant concept. The very structure of the Apostolic Church was connectional and covenantal. Paul realized very early the importance of superintending scattered congregations.

It is important to note that we are not a connectional people because of biblical or theological or even historical mandates. The evolution of our polity has, however, been a natural response to these elements in our background and they continue to inform and direct our efforts.

3. *The Principle Itself.*—Let us simply state the **connectional principle** and its essential ingredients:

The United Methodist connectional principle, born out of
our historical tradition, many biblical roots, and accepted
theological ideas,

is the basic form of our polity, the way in which we carry out
God's mission as a people.

It is in essence a network of interdependent relationships
among persons and groups throughout the life of the
whole denomination.

It declares that our identity is in our wholeness together in
Christ that each part is vital to the whole, that our mission
is more effectively carried out by a connectional life
which incorporates Wesleyan zeal into the life of the
people.

a) Shared Vision.—The principle provides a way to identify
the gospel alive in today's world as a shared vision that inspires
our actions on behalf of Christ. The lonely witness for salvation
in Christ has its place but only when sustained and inspired by
others sharing that vision.

b) Memory.—The principle provides continued remembrance of the story of our heritage as United Methodist
Christians in order that we might share more meaningfully in
the experience and the mission of the universal Church. As we
know and share the common story of our faith journey, our
witness to the world is strengthened.

c) Community.—The principle provides for relationships of
Holy Spirit–empowered community wherein support, supervision, healing, accountability, and growth can take place for
persons and groups across the denomination. Our life together,
with its mutual accountability and relationships, keeps us ever
alert to being faithful to the gospel in all our efforts. Through
it the whole system may be fueled with life-giving Spirit
energy.

d) Discipline.—The principle provides a life of voluntary
compliance to a discipline which includes rights and privileges
as well as responsibilities and obligations. Our mutual acceptance of a disciplined life together enables more effective
ministry to the world.

e) Leadership.—The principle provides a sharing of resources and resource persons for mission and ministry—for

pastors and lay people in local settings or beyond local settings. This is done through superintending pastors, boards, and agencies that serve the denomination in ways it may determine.

f) Mobilization.—The principle provides coordinated missional mobilization and deployment in response to the gospel call. The intentional work of the entire body has the potential of greater influence on human life—in response to great social issues, in extending the gospel to new fields, in deploying the ordained in the most effective way. All parts of the Church are vessels of mission, bound together by a form, so an effective whole is developed.

g) Linkage.—The principle provides an interdependent network of gathering points which brings us together in various ways to carry out our shared mission. In these "conferring" experiences we all celebrate together and together lay out our strategy for sharing the good news of Jesus Christ. In this way corporate, compassionate power is released.

4. *Affirmation and Stress.*—As United Methodist people we celebrate the fact that connectionalism has served us well in our mission and ministry, and we affirm its central place in our life together. At the same time we recognize there are stresses that must be addressed if the connectional principle is to continue to serve us well in the future. The stresses include issues surrounding clergy itineracy and the appointment process, decision-making, apportionments and designated giving, episcopal leadership, and mutual accountability. It is important for connectionalism to bend, to have tolerance in a changing world, to be able to live in the new days ahead of us with freshness and new commitment.

5. *The Challenge.*—Now we have the special opportunity to take this way of doing mission and ministry and to use it effectively in accomplishing our goals as a Church. We have a unique avenue for witnessing and reaching out with the good news of salvation in Jesus Christ to the end that the world will indeed be reformed. The connectional principle should be interpreted to all our people in new and fresh ways and lifted up with enthusiasm as an effective instrument in our efforts to bring the world as we know it closer in harmony with the will and purpose of God as revealed in Jesus Christ.

Section VII. The Fulfillment of Ministry Through The United Methodist Church.

¶ **113.** Affirming the spiritual dimensions of the ministry of all Christians, as proclaimed in ¶¶ 101-112 of this Book of Discipline, it is recognized that this ministry exists in the secular world, and that civil authorities may seek legal definition predicated on the nature of The United Methodist Church in seeking fulfillment of this ministry. Accordingly, it is appropriate that the meaning of "The United Methodist Church," the "general Church," the "entire Church," and "the Church" as used in the Book of Discipline should now be stated consistently with the traditional self-understanding of United Methodists as to the meaning of these words.

These terms refer to the overall denomination and connectional relation and identity of its many local churches, the various conferences and their respective councils, boards, and agencies, and other church units, which collectively constitute the religious system known as United Methodism. Under the Constitution and disciplinary procedures set forth in this Book of Discipline "The United Methodist Church" as a denominational whole is not an entity, nor does it possess legal capacities and attributes. It does not and cannot hold title to property, nor does it have any officer, agent, employee, office, or location. Conferences, councils, boards, agencies, local churches, and other units bearing the name "United Methodist" are, for the most part, legal entities capable of suing and being sued and possessed of legal capacities.

Part V

ORGANIZATION
AND ADMINISTRATION

Chapter One
THE LOCAL CHURCH

Section I. The Church and Pastoral Charge.

¶ **201. A local church** is a community of true believers under the Lordship of Christ. It is the redemptive fellowship in which the Word of God is preached by persons divinely called, and the Sacraments are duly administered according to Christ's own appointment. Under the discipline of the Holy Spirit the Church exists for the maintenance of worship, the edification of believers, and the redemption of the world.

¶ **202.** The Church of Jesus Christ exists in and for the world. It is primarily at the level of the local church that the Church encounters the world. The local church is a strategic base from which Christians move out to the structures of society. It is the function of the local church to minister to the needs of persons in the community where the church is located, to provide appropriate training and nurture to all age groups, cultural groups, racial groups, ethnic groups, and groups with handicapping conditions, to cooperate in ministry with other local churches, and to participate in the worldwide mission of the Church, as minimal expectations of an authentic church.

¶ **203.** The local church is a connectional society of persons who have professed their faith in Christ, have been baptized, have assumed the vows of membership in The United Methodist Church, and are associated in fellowship as a local United

Methodist church in order that they may hear the Word of God, receive the Sacraments, and carry forward the work which Christ has committed to his Church. Such a society of believers, being within The United Methodist Church and subject to its Discipline, is also an inherent part of the Church Universal, which is composed of all who accept Jesus Christ as Lord and Savior, and which in the Apostles' Creed we declare to be the holy catholic Church.

¶ **204.** Each local church shall have a definite nurturing and evangelistic responsibility to its members and the surrounding area, and a missional outreach responsibility to the local and global community. It shall be responsible for ministering to all its members, wherever they live, and for persons who choose it as their church.

¶ **205.** 1. A **pastoral charge** shall consist of one or more churches which are organized under, and subject to, the Discipline of The United Methodist Church, with a Charge Conference, and to which an ordained or licensed minister is or may be duly appointed or appointable as pastor in charge or co-pastor. Where co-pastors are appointed, the bishop shall designate for administrative purposes one as pastor in charge.[1]

2. A pastoral charge of two or more churches may be designated a **circuit** or a cooperative parish.

Section II. Cooperative Parish Ministries.

¶ **206.** 1. Local churches, with the guidance of the Holy Spirit, may enhance their witness to each other and to the world by showing forth the love of Jesus Christ through forms of mutual cooperation.

2. Annual Conferences shall consider a process of cooperative parish development through which **cooperative parish ministries** are initiated and developed, in both urban and town-and-country situations. Where cooperative parish ministries already exist in Annual Conferences, care and support shall be given in the ongoing development of such ministries, and the Annual Conference shall consider adopting a formal written policy concerning cooperative parish ministries, including a plan

---

[1]*See* Judicial Council Decisions 113, 319.

for finanical support. Parish development is an intentional plan of enabling congregations, church-related agencies, and pastors in a defined geographic area to develop a relationship of trust and mutuality which results in coordinated church programs and ministry, supported by appropriate organizational structures and policy. A superintendent or director of parish development may be appointed to work with the Cabinet(s) in the implementation of these ministries in a conference or an area.

3. Cooperative parish ministries may be expressed in forms such as the following: *(a)* Larger parish—a number of congregations working together using a parish-wide Administrative Council, or Administrative Board and Council on Ministries, and other committees and work groups as the parish may determine; providing representation on boards and committees from all churches; guided by a constitution or covenant; and served by a staff appointed to the parish and involving a director. *(b)* Multiple charge parish—an intentionally organized group of two or more pastoral charges in which each church continues to relate to its Charge Conference on the organizational level and also participates in a parish-wide council. The ordained ministers are appointed to the charges and also to the parish, and a director or coordinator is appointed by the bishop.[2] *(c)* Group ministry—a loosely organized group of two or more pastoral charges in which ordained ministers are appointed to charges. The ordained ministers and/or lay council, representing all churches, may designate a coordinator. *(d)* Enlarged charge—two or more congregations, usually on the same circuit and of relatively equal size, that work as a unit with the leadership of one or more pastors. There may be a charge Administrative Council, or Administrative Board and Council on Ministries, and necessary committees. *(e)* Extended or shared ministry—a larger membership church sharing ministry with a smaller membership church usually served by one pastor. *(f)* Cluster groups—a group of churches located in the same geographic area with a loosely knit organization which allows the participating congregations and pastoral charges to engage in cooperative programs in varying degree. A district may be divided into cluster groups for

---

[2]*See* Judicial Council Decision 556.

administrative purposes. *(g)* Probe staff—composed of ordained ministers and other staff assigned to a geographic region to explore possibilities for cooperation and developing strategy for improved ministries to persons. *(h)* Ecumenical parish—a group of United Methodist churches and churches of other Christian traditions joined in a common shared ministry. *(i)* Shared facilities—two or more United Methodist congregations sharing a building such as those performing ministries in different languages and/or with different racial and ethnic groups. The congregations may enter into a covenant which ensures mutual representation on such bodies as Administrative Council, Administrative Board, Council on Ministries, Board of Trustees, and other committees and work groups.

Section III. Churches in Transitional Communities.

¶ **207.** Since many of the communities in which the local church is located are experiencing transition, special attention must be given to forms of ministry required in such communities. The local church is required to respond to the changes which are occurring in its surrounding community and to organize its mission and ministry accordingly.

1. When the communities where the church is located experience transition especially identified as economic and or ethnic, the local church shall engage in deliberate analysis of the neighborhood change and alter its program to meet the needs and cultural patterns of the new residents. The local church shall make every effort to remain in the neighborhood and develop effective ministries to those who are newcomers, whether of a cultural, economic, or ethnic group different from the original or present members.

2. In communities in transition the local church shall be regarded as a principal base of mission from which structures of society shall be confronted, evangelization shall occur, and a principal witness to the changing community shall be realized.

3. It is recommended that decisions concerning ministry in transitional communities be made after thorough consultation has taken place between structures and agencies in the connection.

4. It is recommended that the commitment of resources in terms of money and personnel to ministries in transitional communities be of sufficient longevity to allow for experimentation, evaluation, and mid-course corrections to ensure an adequate effort in ministry in those situations. Evaluations shall involve those on the local level, as well as those at the funding level.

5. The ministry of the local church in transitional areas may be enhanced by review of, and possible development of, some form of cooperative parish ministry.

Section IV. Church Membership.

¶ **208.** The United Methodist Church, a fellowship of believers, is a part of the Church Universal. Therefore all persons, without regard to race, color, national origin, or economic condition, shall be eligible to attend its worship services, to participate in its programs, and, when they take the appropriate vows, to be admitted into its membership in any local church in the connection.

¶ **209.** The membership of a local United Methodist church shall include all baptized persons who have come into membership by confession of faith or transfer and whose names have not been removed from the membership rolls by reason of death, transfer, withdrawal, or removal for cause. (*See* ¶¶ 230, 232, 236-243.)

¶ **210.** A member of any local United Methodist church is a member of the total United Methodist connection.

THE MEANING OF MEMBERSHIP

¶ **211.** When persons unite with a local United Methodist church, they profess their faith in God, the Father Almighty, maker of heaven and earth, and in Jesus Christ his only Son, and in the Holy Spirit. They covenant together with God and with the members of the local church to keep the vows which are a part of the order of confirmation and reception into the Church:

1. To confess Jesus Christ as Lord and Savior and pledge their allegiance to his kingdom,

2. To receive and profess the Christian faith as contained in the Scriptures of the Old and New Testaments,

3. To promise according to the grace given them to live a Christian life and always remain faithful members of Christ's holy Church,

4. And to be loyal to The United Methodist Church and uphold it by their prayers, their presence, their gifts, and their service.

¶ **212.** Faithful membership in the local church is essential for personal growth and for developing an increasing sensitivity to the will and grace of God. As members involve themselves in private and public prayer, worship, the Sacraments, study, Christian action, systematic giving, and holy discipline, they grow in their appreciation of Christ, understanding of God at work in history and the natural order, and an understanding of themselves.

¶ **213.** Faithful participation in the corporate life of the congregation is an obligation of the Christian to fellow members of the Body of Christ. A member is bound in sacred covenant to shoulder the burdens, share the risks, and celebrate the joys of fellow members. A Christian is called to speak the truth in love, always ready to confront conflict in the spirit of forgiveness and reconciliation.

¶ **214.** A member of The United Methodist Church is to be a servant of Christ on mission in the local and worldwide community. This servanthood is performed in family life, daily work, recreation and social activities, responsible citizenship, the stewardship of property and accumulated resources, the issues of corporate life, and all attitudes toward other persons. Participation in disciplined groups is an expected part of personal mission involvement. Each member is called upon to be a witness for Christ in the world, a light and leaven in society, and a reconciler in a culture of conflict. Each member is to identify with the agony and suffering of the world and to radiate and exemplify the Christ of hope. The standards of attitude and conduct set forth in the Social Principles (Part III) shall be considered as an essential resource for guiding each member of the Church in being a servant of Christ on mission.

¶ **215.** Should any member give evidence of a lack of commitment to the faith, it shall be the responsibility of the local church, working through its Council on Ministries or Administrative Council, to minister to that person to the end that that person may reaffirm faith and commitment to the Church and its ministry of loving service.

ADMISSION INTO THE CHURCH

¶ 216. 1. All persons seeking to be saved from their sins and sincerely desiring to be Christian in faith and practice are proper candidates for full membership in The United Methodist Church. When such persons offer themselves for membership, it shall be the duty of the pastor, or of proper persons appointed by the pastor, to instruct them in the meaning of the Christian faith and the history, organization, and teaching of The United Methodist Church, using materials approved by The United Methodist Church to explain to them the baptismal and membership vows, and to lead them to commit themselves to Jesus Christ as Lord and Savior. When they shall have confessed their faith in Christ and have made known their desire to assume the obligations and become faithful members of The United Methodist Church, after the completion of a reasonable period of training, and after the Sacrament of Baptism has been administered to those who have not been previously baptized, the pastor shall bring them before the congregation, administer the vows, receive them into the fellowship of the Church, and duly enroll them as full members.

2. Membership training is a lifelong process and is carried on through all the activities which may have educational value. The instruction for which the pastor is specifically responsible is confirmation preparation and is a part of the fuller work of membership training. Confirmation preparation focuses attention upon the meaning of full membership and the need for church members to be in mission in all of life's relationships.

3. Preparation for the experience of confirmation shall be provided for all candidates for full membership, including adults, but youth who are completing the sixth grade shall normally be the youngest persons recruited for confirmation preparation and full membership. When younger persons, of their own volition, seek enrollment in confirmation preparation, such preparation shall be at the discretion of the pastor.

4. Persons in preparation for full membership make up the preparatory roll of the church. All baptized children shall be listed on the preparatory membership roll, and other persons who have declared their interest in church membership and have been enrolled in confirmation preparation may be listed as preparatory members. (*See also* ¶¶ 223, 232.2.)

¶ **217.** A duly authorized ordained minister of The United Methodist Church while serving as chaplain of any organization, institution, or military unit, or as a campus pastor, or while otherwise present where a local church is not available, may receive a person into the membership of The United Methodist Church when such person shall have confessed faith in Christ and expressed a desire to assume the obligations and become a faithful member of the Church. After the vows of membership have been administered, such ordained minister shall issue a statement of membership to the local church of the choice of the person concerned, and the pastor thereof on receiving such statement shall duly enroll that person as a member.

¶ **218.** When a person in military service or a member of the family of such person is received into the Church by a chaplain and has no local church to which the membership and records may be sent, the chaplain shall send the name, address, and related facts to the General Board of Discipleship for recording on the general roll of military service personnel and families. When a child of such a member is baptized by a chaplain, that record may be handled in the same manner. It is desirable that as soon as possible these persons be transferred to a local United Methodist church of their choice.

¶ **219.** Any candidate for church membership who for good reason is unable to appear before the congregation may, at the discretion of the pastor, be received elsewhere in accordance with the Ritual of The United Methodist Church. In any such case lay members should be present to represent the congregation. Names of such persons shall be placed on the church roll, and announcement of their reception shall be made to the congregation.

¶ **220.** A member in good standing in any Christian denomination who has been baptized and who desires to unite with The United Methodist Church may be received into membership by a proper certificate of transfer from that person's former church, or by a declaration of Christian faith, and upon affirming willingness to be loyal to The United Methodist Church. The pastor will report to the sending church the date of reception of such a member. It is recommended that instruction in the faith and work of the Church be provided for all such persons. Persons received from churches which do not issue certificates of transfer or letters of recommendation shall be listed as "Received from other denominations."

CHILDREN AND THE CHURCH

¶ **221.** Because the redeeming love of God, revealed in Jesus Christ, extends to all persons and because Jesus explicitly included the children in his kingdom, the pastor of each charge shall earnestly exhort all Christian parents or guardians to present their children to the Lord in Baptism at an early age. Before Baptism is administered, the pastor shall diligently instruct the parents or guardians regarding the meaning of this Sacrament and the vows which they assume. It is expected of parents or guardians who present their children for Baptism that they shall use all diligence in bringing them up in conformity to the Word of God and in the fellowship of the Church. It is desired that one or both parents or guardians shall be members of a Christian church or that sponsors who are members shall assume the baptismal vows. They shall be admonished of this obligation and be earnestly exhorted to faithfulness therein. At the time of Baptism they shall be informed that the Church, with its church school program, will aid them in the Christian nurture of their children.

¶ **222.** The pastor of the church shall, at the time of administering the Sacrament of Baptism, furnish the parents or guardians of the child who is baptized with a certificate of Baptism, which shall also clearly state that the child is now enrolled as a preparatory member in The United Methodist Church. The pastor shall also admonish members of the congregation of their responsibility for the Christian nurture of the child. The pastor shall be responsible for seeing that the membership secretary adds the full name of the baptized child to the preparatory membership roll of the church. When the baptized child lives in a community not served by the pastor who administers the Sacrament of Baptism, the pastor is responsible for reporting the baptism to a pastor or district superintendent who serves in the area where the baptized child lives in order that the child's name might be properly entered on the preparatory membership roll. (*See* ¶ 223.)

¶ **223.** The pastor shall keep and transmit to the succeeding pastor an accurate register of the names of all baptized children in the charge, including both those who have been baptized there and those who have been baptized elsewhere. This register of baptized children, along with a list of other preparatory members (¶ 216.4), shall constitute the preparatory membership roll of the church. It shall give the full name of the child, the date of birth, the date and place of Baptism, and the names of the parents or guardians and their place of residence.

¶ **224.** All baptized children under the care of a United Methodist church shall be retained as preparatory members in the church until this status is terminated by: confirmation and reception into full membership after a proper course of training both in the church school and in the pastor's class, transfer with their families to another United Methodist church, transfer with their families to a church of another Christian denomination, death, withdrawal, or transfer to the constituency roll of the church at the age of nineteen. The preparatory membership roll shall be corrected each year by adding and subtracting the names received and removed during the year, using the forms provided for this purpose.

¶ **225.** It shall be the duty of the pastor, the parents or guardians, and the officers and teachers of the church school to provide training for the children of the church throughout their childhood that will lead to an understanding of the Christian faith, to an appreciation of the privileges and obligations of Church membership, and to a personal commitment to Jesus Christ as Lord and Savior. The pastor shall, at least annually, building on the preparation which boys and girls have received throughout their childhood, organize into classes for confirmation the youth who, preferably, are completing the sixth grade. This instruction shall be based on materials which the boys and girls have already used and on other resources produced by

The United Methodist Church for the purpose of confirmation preparation. Wherever boys and girls so prepared shall give evidence of their own Christian faith and purpose and understanding of the privileges and obligations of Church membership, they may be received into full membership.

Youth

¶ **226.** Youth who are full members of the church have all rights and responsibilities of church membership. (*See* ¶ 263.2.) It is strongly recommended that each local church offer for senior high youth who are full members of the Church an advanced class of instruction in the meaning of the Christian life and Church membership. It is further recommended that this course, taught by the pastor, emphasize the doctrines of The United Methodist Church and the nature and mission of the Church, leading to continued growth in the knowledge, grace, and service of our Lord Jesus Christ.

Affiliate and Associate Membership

¶ **227.** A member of The United Methodist Church, of an Affiliated Autonomous Methodist or United Church, or of a Methodist church which has a concordat agreement with The United Methodist Church, residing for an extended period in a city or community at a distance from the member's home church, may on request be enrolled as an **affiliate member** of a United Methodist church located in the vicinity of the temporary residence. The home pastor shall be notified of the affiliate membership. Such membership shall entitle the person to the fellowship of that church, to its pastoral care and oversight, and to participation in its activities, including the holding of office, except such office which would place one on the Administrative Council or Administrative Board, but that person shall be counted and reported only as a member of the home church. A member of another denomination may become an **associate member** under the same conditions.[3] This relationship may be

---

[3]*See* Judicial Council Decision 372.

terminated at the discretion of the United Methodist church in which the affiliate or associate membership is held whenever the affiliate or associate member shall move from the vicinity of the United Methodist church in which the affiliate or associate membership is held.

Care of Members

¶ **228.** The local church shall endeavor to enlist each member in activities for spiritual growth and in participation in the services and ministries of the Church and its organizations. It shall be the duty of the pastor and of the Administrative Council or the Council on Ministries by regular visitation, care, and spiritual oversight, to provide necessary activities and opportunities for spiritual growth through individual and family worship and individual and group study, and continually to aid the members to keep their vows to uphold the Church by attendance, prayers, gifts, and service. The Church has a moral and spiritual obligation to nurture its nonparticipating and indifferent members and to lead them into a full and active church relationship.

¶ **229.** The pastor in cooperation with the Administrative Council or the Council on Ministries may arrange the membership in groups—with a leader for each group—designed to involve the membership of the church in its ministry to the community. These groups shall be of such size, usually not larger than eight or ten families, as to be convenient and effective for service. Such groups may be especially helpful in evangelistic outreach by contacting newcomers and unreached persons, by visitation, by mobilizing neighbors to meet social issues in the community, by responding to personal and family crises, by holding prayer meetings in the homes, by distributing Christian literature, and by other means. Nonresident members should constitute a special group to be served by correspondence. The groups shall be formed and the leaders appointed by the Administrative Council or the Council on Ministries upon recommendation of the pastor.

¶ **230.** While primary responsibility and initiative rests with each individual member faithfully to perform the vows of membership which have been solemnly assumed, if the member should be neglectful of that responsibility, these procedures shall be followed:

1. If a member residing in the community is negligent of the vows, or is regularly absent from the worship of the church without valid reason, the pastor and the membership secretary shall report that member's name to the Administrative Council or the Council on Ministries, which shall do all in its power to reenlist the member in the active fellowship of the Church. It shall visit the member and make clear that, while the member's name is on the roll of a particular local church, one is a member of The United Methodist Church as a whole, and that, since the member is not attending the church where enrolled, the member is requested to do one of four things: *(a)* renew the vows and become a regular worshiper in the church where the member's name is recorded, *(b)* request transfer to another United Methodist church where the member will be a regular worshiper, *(c)* arrange transfer to a particular church of another denomination, or *(d)* request withdrawal. If the member does not comply with any of the available alternatives over a period of three years, the member's name may be removed. *(See* § 4.)

2. If a member whose address is known is residing outside the community and is not participating in the worship or activity of the church, the directives to encourage a transfer of membership shall be followed each year until that member joins another church or requests in writing that the name be removed from the membership roll; *provided,* however, that if after three years the council has not been able to relate that member to the church at the new place of residence, the name may be removed by the procedure of § 4 below.

3. If the address of a member is no longer known to the pastor, the membership secretary and the evangelism work area chairperson or the Commission on Evangelism shall make every effort to locate the member, including listing the name in the church bulletin, circularizing it throughout the parish, and reading it from the pulpit. If the member can be located, the directives of either § 1 or § 2 above shall be followed, but if after three years of such efforts the address is still unknown, the member's name may be removed from the membership roll by the procedure of § 4 below.

4. If the directives of §§ 1, 2, or 3 above have been followed for the specified number of years without success, the member's name may be removed from the membership roll by vote of the Charge Conference on recommendation of the pastor and the evangelism work area chairperson or the Commission on Evangelism, each name being considered individually; *provided* that the member's name shall have been entered in the minutes of the annual Charge Conference for three consecutive years preceding removal. On the roll there shall be entered after the name: "Removed by order of the Charge Conference"; and if the action is on the basis of § 3, there shall be added: "Reason: address unknown." The membership of the person shall thereby be terminated, and the record thereof shall be retained;[4] *provided* that upon request the member may be restored to membership by recommendation of the pastor; and *provided* further, that should a transfer of membership be requested, the pastor may restore the person's membership for this purpose and issue the certificate of transfer.

5. Recognizing that the Church has a continuing moral and spiritual obligation to nurture all persons, even those whose names have been removed from the membership roll, it is recommended that a roll of persons thus removed shall be maintained. It shall then become the responsibility of the Administrative Council or Administrative Board to provide for the review of this roll at least once a year. (*See also* ¶ 235.) After the review has been made, it is recommended that the pastor and/or the Commission on Evangelism contact those whose names appear on this roll, either in person or by other means, in the most effective and practical manner. The names and addresses of those who have moved outside the local church's area should be sent to local churches in their new communities, that those churches may visit and minister to them.

¶ **231.** If a local church is discontinued, the district superintendent shall select another United Methodist church and transfer its members thereto, or to such other churches as the members may select. (*See* ¶ 2548.1.)

---

[4]*See* Judicial Council Decision 207.

¶ **232.** Each local church shall accurately maintain the following membership rolls:

1. **Full Membership Roll** (¶ 209).

2. **Preparatory Membership Roll** (¶ 216.4), containing the names and pertinent information of baptized children and youth of the church eighteen years of age and under who are not full members, and other persons who have been enrolled in confirmation preparation.

3. **Members Removed by Charge Conference Action** (¶ 230.4).

4. **Constituency Roll,** containing the names and addresses of such persons as are not members of the church concerned, including unbaptized children, dedicated children, church school members, preparatory members who have reached the age of nineteen who have not been received into full membership, and other nonmembers for whom the local church has pastoral responsibility.

5. **Affiliate Membership Roll** (¶ 227).

6. **Associate Membership Roll** (¶ 227).

7. In the case of a Union or Federated Church with a church of another denomination, the governing body of such a church may report an equal share of the total membership to each judicatory, and such membership shall be published in the minutes of each church with a note to the effect that the report is that of a Union or Federated Church and with an indication of the total actual membership.

¶ **233.** The pastor shall report to each Charge Conference the names of persons received into the membership of the church or churches of the pastoral charge and the names of persons whose membership in the church or churches of the pastoral charge has been terminated since the last Charge Conference, indicating how each was received or how the membership was terminated. The Administrative Council or Administrative Board shall appoint a committee to audit the membership rolls, submitting the report annually to the Charge Conference.

¶ **234.** The basic membership records in each local church shall consist of: a permanent church register and a card index, a loose-leaf book, or a membership record on an electronic information system.

1. The **permanent church register** shall be a bound volume of durable material prepared by The United Methodist Publishing House in the form approved by the General Council on Finance and Administration. The names shall be recorded chronologically as each person is received into the fellowship of that church, and without reference to alphabetical order. The names shall be numbered in regular numerical order, and the number of each shall appear on the corresponding card, page, or record in the card index, loose-leaf book, or electronic system membership record.

2. The **card index, loose-leaf book, or electronic system membership record** shall be kept on a form approved by the General Council on Finance and Administration or, in the case of electronically maintained records, shall contain the same information as required in the approved form. This record of membership shall be filed in alphabetical order and shall show the number appearing opposite each name on the permanent register. The pastor shall report annually to the Annual Conference the total membership of the charge as shown on the membership records.

3. When an electronic information system is used for record-keeping, print-out copies of the membership records and back-up electronic media shall be retained in a secure off-site place.

¶ **235.** The **membership secretary** shall, under the direction of the pastor, keep accurate records of all membership rolls (*see* ¶ 232), shall be a member of the work area on evangelism (if it exists), and shall report regularly to the Administrative Council or the Administrative Board and the Council on Ministries through the chairperson of evangelism.

TRANSFER AND TERMINATION OF MEMBERSHIP

¶ **236.** Membership in a local church may be terminated by death, transfer, withdrawal, expulsion, or action of the Charge Conference. It shall be the duty of the pastor of the charge or of the membership secretary to keep an accurate record of all terminations of membership and to report to each Charge

Conference the names of all persons whose membership has been terminated since the conference preceding, in each instance indicating the reason for such termination.

¶ 237. If a member of a United Methodist church shall move to another community so far removed from the home church that the member cannot participate regularly in its worship and activity, this member shall be encouraged to transfer membership to a United Methodist church in the community of the newly established residence. As soon as the pastor is reliably informed of this change of residence, actual or contemplated, it shall be the pastor's duty and obligation to assist the member to become established in the fellowship of a church in the community of the future home and to send to a United Methodist pastor in such community, or to the district superintendent, or (if neither is known) to the General Board of Discipleship, a letter of notification, giving the latest known address of the person or persons concerned and requesting local pastoral oversight.

¶ 238. Lay persons in service outside the United States under the World Division of the General Board of Global Ministries and assigned to churches other than United Methodist may accept all the rights and privileges, including associate membership, offered them by a local church in their place of residence without impairing their relationship to their home local church.

¶ 239. When a pastor discovers a member of The United Methodist Church residing in the community whose membership is in a church so far removed from the place of residence that the member cannot participate regularly in its worship and activity, it shall be the duty and obligation of the pastor to give pastoral oversight to such person and to encourage transfer of membership to a United Methodist church in the community where the member resides.

¶ 240. When a pastor receives a request for a transfer of membership from the pastor of another United Methodist church, or a district superintendent, that pastor shall send the proper certificate directly to the pastor of the United Methodist church to which the member is transferring, or if there is no pastor, to the district superintendent. On receipt of such a **certificate of transfer,** the pastor or district superintendent shall enroll the name of the person so transferring after public reception in a regular service of worship, or if circumstances demand, public announcement in such a service. The pastor of the church issuing the certificate shall then be notified, whereupon said pastor shall remove the member from the roll.

Certificates of transfer shall be accompanied by two official forms. A "Notice of Transfer of Membership" is to be sent to the member by the pastor who transfers the membership. An "Acknowledgment of Transfer of Membership" is to be sent to the former pastor by the pastor who receives the transferred member.

In case the transfer is not made effective, the pastor shall return the certificate to the pastor of the sending church.

¶ **241.** A pastor upon receiving a request from a member to transfer to a church of another denomination, or upon receiving such request from a pastor or duly authorized official of another denomination, shall (with the approval of the member) issue a certificate of transfer and, upon receiving confirmation of said member's reception into another congregation, shall properly record the transfer of such person on the membership roll of the local church; and the membership shall thereby be terminated. For the transfer of a member of The United Methodist Church to a church of another denomination, an official "Transfer of Membership to Another Denomination" form shall be used.

¶ **242.** If a pastor is informed that a member has without notice united with a church of another denomination, the pastor shall make diligent inquiry and, if the report is confirmed, shall enter "Withdrawn" after the person's name on the membership roll and shall report the same to the next Charge Conference.

¶ **243.** If a member proposes to withdraw from The United Methodist Church, that member shall communicate the purpose in writing to the pastor of the local church in which membership is held. On receiving such notice of withdrawal, the pastor shall properly record the fact of withdrawal on the membership roll. If requested, the pastor shall give a statement of withdrawal to such member. Such person, upon written request, may be restored to membership on recommendation of the pastor.

Section V. Organization and Administration.

¶ **244.** The local church shall be organized so that adequate provision is made for these basic responsibilities: (1) planning and implementing a program of nurture, outreach, and witness for persons and families within and without the congregation; (2) providing for effective pastoral and lay leadership; (3) providing for financial support, physical facilities, and the legal obligations of the church; (4) ensuring relationships of the local church organizations to appropriate district and Annual Conference structures and programs, and (5) providing for the proper creation, maintenance, and disposition of documentary record material of the local church. (*See* ¶ 1811.1*b*.) Every local church shall choose from one of two plans for organizing its administrative and programmatic responsibilities.

1. Local churches may establish an Administrative Council, which shall be both the administrative body to which the members, organizations, and agencies are amenable, and the programmatic body which shall consider, develop, and coordinate goals and program proposals for the church's mission in accordance with the mission of The United Methodist Church.

2. Or local churches may establish an Administrative Board to which its members, organizations, and agencies are amenable, and a Council on Ministries which shall consider, develop, and coordinate goals and program proposals for the church's mission in accordance with the mission of The United Methodist Church (¶ 113). The Administrative Council or Administrative Board shall be amenable to and function as the executive agency of the Charge Conference. (*See* ¶ 246.)

¶ **245.** The basic organizational plan for the local church shall include provision for the following units: a Charge Conference, an Administrative Council or Administrative Board and Council on Ministries, a Committee on Pastor-Parish Relations, a Board of Trustees, a Committee on Finance, a Committee on Nominations and Personnel, and such other elected leaders, commissions, councils, committees, and task forces as the Charge Conference may determine.

The Charge Conference

¶ **246.** *General Provisions.*—1. Within the pastoral charge the basic unit in the connectional system of The United Methodist Church is the **Charge Conference.** The Charge Conference shall therefore be organized from the church or churches in every pastoral charge as set forth in the Constitution (¶ 46). It shall meet annually for the purposes set forth in ¶ 247. It may meet at other times as indicated in § 7 below.

2. The membership of the Charge Conference shall be all members of the Administrative Council or Administrative Board named in ¶ 254, together with retired ordained ministers who elect to hold their membership in said Charge Conference and any others as may be designated in the Discipline. If more than one church is on the pastoral charge, all members of each Administrative Council or Administrative Board shall be members of the Charge Conference.

3. The Charge Conference may make provision for recognition of the faithful service of those members of the Administrative Council or Administrative Board who have reached the age of seventy-two, or who have become physically incapacitated, by electing them honorary members. An honorary member shall be entitled to all the privileges of a member, except the right to vote.

4. The district superintendent shall fix the time of meetings of the Charge Conference. The Charge Conference shall determine the place of meeting.

5. The district superintendent shall preside at the meetings of the Charge Conference or may designate an elder to preside.

6. The members present and voting at any duly announced meeting shall constitute a quorum.

7. Special sessions may be called by the district superintendent after consultation with the pastor of the charge, or by the pastor with the written consent of the district superintendent. The purpose of such special session shall be stated in the call, and only such business shall be transacted as is in harmony with the purposes stated in the call. Any such special session may be convened as a Church Conference in accordance with ¶ 248.

8. Notice of time and place of a regular or special session of the Charge Conference shall be given at least ten days in advance.

9. A Charge Conference shall be conducted in the language of the majority with adequate provision being made for translation.

10. A **Joint Charge Conference** for two or more pastoral

charges may be held at the same time and place, as the district superintendent may determine.

¶ **247.** *Powers and Duties*—1. The Charge Conference shall be the connecting link between the local church and the general Church and shall have general oversight of the Administrative Council(s) or Administrative Board(s).

2. The Charge Conference, the district superintendent, and the pastor shall organize and administer the pastoral charge and churches according to the policies and plans herein set forth. When the membership size, program scope, mission resources, or other circumstances so require, the Charge Conference may, in consultation with and upon the approval of the district superintendent, modify the organizational plans; *provided* that the provisions of ¶ 244 are observed.

3. The primary responsibilities of the Charge Conference in the annual meeting shall be to review and evaluate the total mission and ministry of the church (¶¶ 201-204), receive reports, and adopt objectives and goals recommended by the Administrative Council or Administrative Board which are in keeping with the objectives of The United Methodist Church.

4. The Charge Conference shall elect a **recording secretary** who shall keep an accurate record of the proceedings and shall be the custodian of all records and reports, and with the presiding officer shall sign the minutes. A copy of the minutes shall be provided for the district superintendent. When there is only one local church on a charge, the secretary of the Administrative Council or Administrative Board shall be the secretary of the Charge Conference. When there is more than one church on a charge, one of the secretaries of the Administrative Councils or Administrative Boards shall be elected to serve as secretary of the Charge Conference.

5.*a)* The Charge Conference should elect a **church historian,** who shall keep the **historical records** up to date, shall serve as chairperson of the Committee on Records and History; shall cooperate with the Annual Conference Commission on Archives and History; shall provide an annual report on the care of church records and historical materials to the Charge Conference; and shall provide, with the pastor and the Committee on Records and History, for the preservation of all local church records and historical materials no longer in current use. Records and historical materials include all documents, minutes, journals, diaries, reports, letters, pamphlets, papers, manuscripts, maps, photographs, books, audiovisuals, sound recordings, magnetic or other tapes, or any other documentary material, regardless of form or characteristics, made or received pursuant to any provisions of the Discipline in connection with the transaction of church business by any local church of The United Methodist Church or any of its constituent predecessors. The church historian shall be a member of the Administrative Council or Administrative Board. This person may also hold another elected position on the council or board.

b) There may be a local church **Committee on Records and History,** chaired by the church historian, to assist in fulfilling these responsibilities.

6. The Charge Conference shall determine the number of members at large to serve on the Administrative Council or Administrative Board in keeping with the following provisions. Churches of five hundred members or less may include at least four but not more than thirty-five members at large, exclusive of ex officio members. In churches of more than five hundred members, there may be elected additional members at large not to exceed the ratio of one for each thirty additional members. The members at large, if elected, shall include at least two young adults between the ages of nineteen and thirty, at least two older adults over sixty-five years of age, and at least two youth nominated by the youth coordinator or Youth Council.

7. The Charge Conference may establish a limit to the consecutive terms of office for any or all of the elected or appointed officers of the local church except where otherwise mandated. It is recommended that no officer serve more than three consecutive years in the same office.

8. The Charge Conference shall examine and recommend to the district Committee on Ordained Ministry, faithfully adhering to the provisions of ¶ 404.3(*b*), candidates for the ordained ministry who have been members in good standing of the local church for at least one year; whose gifts, evidence of God's grace, and call to the ministry clearly establish them as candidates; and who have met the educational requirements.

9. It shall examine and recommend, faithfully adhering to the provisions of ¶ 405, renewal of candidacy of candidates for the ordained ministry.

10. The Charge Conference shall examine and recommend to the responsible church agency any candidates for church-related vocations.

11. The Charge Conference shall affirm the good standing in the congregation of the persons seeking the diaconal minister relationship in the Annual Conference and shall transmit this information to the conference Board of Diaconal Ministry.

12. It shall inquire annually into the gifts, labors, and usefulness of the lay speakers related to the charge, and recommend to the district and/or conference Committee on Lay Speaking those persons who have met the standards set forth for a Local Church Lay Speaker and/or for Certified Lay Speaker (¶¶ 277-279).

13. The Charge Conference shall in consultation with the district superintendent set the salary and other remuneration of the pastor and other staff appointed by the bishop.[5]

14. As soon as practicable after the session of Annual Conference, each district superintendent or designated agent shall notify each local church in the district what amounts have been apportioned to it for World Service and Conference Benevolences. Following the Annual Conference, it shall be the responsibility of the pastor and the lay member(s) of the Annual Conference and/or the church lay leader(s) to present to a meeting of each Charge Conference a statement of the apportionments for World Service and Conference Benevolences, explaining the causes supported by each of these funds and their place in the total program of the Church. The district superintendent or designated agent shall also notify each Charge Conference of all other amounts properly apportioned to it. (*See* ¶ 719.)

15. The Charge Conference shall receive and act on the annual report from the pastor concerning all membership rolls. (*See* ¶ 233.)

16. In those instances where there are two or more churches on a pastoral charge, the Charge Conference may provide for a

---

[5]*See* Judicial Council Decisions 213, 252, 461.

chargewide or parish Administrative Council or Administrative Board and Council on Ministries, a chargewide or parish treasurer, and such other officers, commissions, committees, and task groups as necessary to carry on the work of the charge.

17. In those instances where there are two or more churches on a pastoral charge, the Charge Conference may elect a chargewide or parish Committee on Nominations and Personnel, a chargewide or parish Committee on Pastor-Parish Relations, a chargewide or parish Committee on Finance, and a chargewide or parish Board of Trustees in such instances where property is held in common by two or more churches of the charge. All churches of the charge shall be represented on such chargewide or parish committees or boards. Chargewide or parish organization shall be consistent with disciplinary provisions for the local church.

18. In instances of multiple church charges, the Charge Conference shall provide for an equitable distribution of parsonage maintenance and upkeep expense or adequate housing allowance (if Annual Conference policy permits) among the several churches.

19. If any Charge Conference initiates, joins, monitors, or terminates a boycott, the guidelines in the Book of Resolutions 1988 should be followed. The General Conference is the only body that can initiate, empower, or join a boycott in the name of The United Methodist Church.

20. Such other duties and responsibilities as the General, Jurisdictional, or Annual Conference may duly commit to it.

¶ **248.** *The Church Conference.*—To encourage broader participation by members of the church, the Charge Conference may be convened as the **Church Conference,** extending the vote to all local church members present at such meetings. The Church Conference may be authorized by the district superintendent on written request of the pastor or the Administrative Council or Administrative Board or 10 percent of the membership of the local church to the district superintendent, with a copy to the pastor, or at the discretion of the district superintendent. Additional regulations governing the call and conduct of the Charge Conference as set forth in ¶¶ 246-247 shall apply also to the Church Conference. A joint

Church Conference for two or more churches may be held at the same time and place as the district superintendent may determine. A Church Conference shall be conducted in the language of the majority with adequate provision being made for translation. (For Church Local Conference *see* ¶ 2526.)

¶ **249.** The Charge Conference, or Church Conference authorized by the district superintendent, shall elect upon nomination of the Committee on Nominations and Personnel of each local church on the pastoral charge or by nomination from the floor and by vote of each such local church, at least the following leaders for the four basic responsibilities (¶ 244):

1. Chairperson of the Administrative Council or chairpersons of the Administrative Board and the Council on Ministries.

2. The Committee on Nominations and Personnel.

3. The Committee on Pastor-Parish Relations and its chairperson.

4. A chairperson and additional members of the Committee on Finance; the financial secretary and the church treasurer(s) if not paid employees of the local church; and the trustees as provided in ¶¶ 2525-2527, unless otherwise required by state law.

5. The lay member(s) of the Annual Conference and lay leader(s).

6. A recording secretary. (*See* ¶ 247.4.)

7. Special attention shall be given to the inclusion of women, men, youth, young adults, persons over sixty-five years of age, persons with a handicapping condition, and racial and ethnic persons.

¶ **250.** The Charge Conference, or Church Conference authorized by the district superintendent, may elect, upon nomination of the Committee on Nominations and Personnel of each local church on the pastoral charge or by nomination from the floor and by vote of each such church, such leaders and officers of the local church(es) as it may choose from among the following, who may be known as stewards. Stewards are lay persons who are entrusted, along with the pastor(s), with leadership responsibilities for the spiritual and temporal life of the local church.

1. Chairpersons of work areas (*see* ¶¶ 252.1 and 260),

age-level coordinators (family, children, youth, adult), superintendent of the church school, health and welfare ministries representative, coordinator of communications, district steward, church historian, and membership secretary.

2. Members at large of the Administrative Council or Administrative Board.

3. Such other personnel and committees as it may choose or as may elsewhere be ordered by the Discipline.

4. Special attention shall be given to the inclusion of women, men, youth, young adults, persons over sixty-five years of age, persons with a handicapping condition, and racial and ethnic persons.

¶ **251.** 1. Out of the general ministry of each local church (¶ 105) there shall be elected by the Charge Conference a **lay leader** who shall function as the primary lay representative of the laity in that local church and shall have the following responsibilities:

a) Fostering awareness of the role of laity both within the congregation and through their ministries in the home, work place, community, and world and finding ways within the community of faith to recognize all these ministries.

b) meeting regularly with the pastor to discuss the state of the church and the needs for ministry.

c) membership in the Charge Conference and the Administrative Council (or the Administrative Board and the Council on Ministries), the Committee on Finance, and the Committee on Nominations and Personnel, where, along with the pastor, the lay leader shall serve as an interpreter of the actions and programs of the Annual Conference and the general Church;

d) continuing involvement in study and training opportunities to develop a growing understanding of the Church's reason for existence and the types of ministry that will most effectively fulfill the Church's mission;

e) assisting in advising the Administrative Council (or the Administrative Board and the Council on Ministries) of opportunities available and the needs expressed for a more effective ministry of the church through its laity in the community;

f) informing the laity of training opportunities provided by the Annual Conference. Where possible, the lay leader shall attend training opportunities in order to strengthen his/her work.

In instances where more than one church is on a charge, the Charge Conference shall elect additional lay leaders so that there will be one lay leader in each church. Associate lay leaders may be elected, to work with the lay leader, in any local church.

2. The **lay member(s)** of the Annual Conference and one or more alternates shall be elected annually or quadrennially as the Annual Conference directs. If the charge's lay representative to the Annual Conference shall cease to be a member of the charge or shall for any reason fail to serve, an alternate member in the order of election shall serve in place.

Both the lay members and the alternates shall have been members in good standing of The United Methodist Church and of the local church from which they are elected for at least two years (*see* ¶ 35), except in a newly organized church, which shall have the privilege of representation at the Annual Conference session.[6] No local pastor shall be eligible as a lay member or alternate.[7] United Methodist churches which become part of an ecumenical ministry of which The United Methodist Church is a sponsor shall not be deprived of their right of representation by a lay member in the Annual Conference. The lay member(s) of the Annual Conference, along with the pastor, shall serve as an interpreter of the actions of the Annual Conference session. These persons shall report to the local church Administrative Council or Administrative Board on actions of the Annual Conference as soon as possible, but not later than three months after the close of the conference.

THE ADMINISTRATIVE COUNCIL

¶ **252.** 1. The **Administrative Council** shall provide for the planning and implementing of the program of nurture and outreach of the church, and for the administration of its organizational and temporal life. The Administrative Council shall have all of the responsibilities of the Administrative Board

---

[6]*See* Judicial Council Decision 495.
[7]*See* Judicial Council Decisions 170, 305, 328, 342, 469.

(¶ 256) and the Council on Ministries (¶ 257). Its membership shall include the combined membership of those named to the Administrative Board and the Council on Ministries insofar as the offices listed in ¶ 254 and ¶ 258 exist within the local church. Since a majority of United Methodist churches are of smaller membership (approximately two hundred members or less) and may differ as to numbers of leaders, program scope, missional resources, and other ways, the program responsibilities of the Administrative Council can be carried out by chairpersons of nurture, evangelism, outreach, and a coordinator of age-level and family ministries.

a) The work area **chairperson of nurture** is responsible for the planning and implementation of programs related to the spiritual growth of persons through Christian education, worship, and stewardship, and the development of the fellowship of the congregation. The chairperson should relate to district and Annual Conference agencies dealing with education, higher education and campus ministry, worship and stewardship.

b) The work area **chairperson of outreach** is responsible for the planning and implementation of programs to deal with the needs and concerns of persons beyond the congregation, relating the ministry of the local church to the needs of the world. This chairperson should relate to district and Annual Conference agencies dealing with Christian unity and interreligious concerns, Church and society, missions, religion and race, status and role of women, and health and welfare ministries. He/she shall report to the Administrative Council regularly on the stewardship and missional use of church-owned property, land, and investments.

c) The work area on evangelism shall respond to the mandate of the gospel to "go and make disciples of Jesus Christ." The work area shall develop programs to proclaim the gospel to those outside the Church, to invite persons to faith in Christ and to receive them into Christian fellowship. The work area will also develop programs to aid the spiritual growth of those new persons. It would relate to district and Annual Conference evangelism structures.

d) The **coordinator of age-level and family ministries** is responsible for the coordination of ministry to each age level and to the family as outlined in ¶ 259. The coordinator should relate to district and Annual Conference agencies dealing with children's, youth, adult, and family ministries.

e) The chairperson of the Administrative Council may fulfill the responsibilities of lay leader and lay member of the Annual Conference.

2. Churches which desire a more extensive program may establish commissions in one or more of the work areas, and/or councils in one or more of the age-level and family ministries, and/or they may elect other committees and task forces as may be advisable.

3. *Meetings.*—The Administrative Council shall meet at least quarterly. Special meetings may be ordered by the Administrative Council or called by the chairperson or pastor.

4. *Quorum.*—The members present and voting at any duly announced meeting shall constitute a quorum.

The Administrative Board

¶ **253.** 1. *Purpose.*—The **Administrative Board** shall have general oversight of the administration and program of the local church. (*See* ¶ 244.2.)

2. *Meetings.*—The Administrative Board shall meet at least quarterly. Special meetings may be ordered by the Administrative Board or called by the chairperson or the pastor.

3. *Quorum.*—The members present and voting at any duly announced meeting shall constitute a quorum.

4. *Minutes.*—Minutes of all Administrative Board meetings shall be kept on record and made available to any member of the Administrative Board and to any full member of the congregation.

¶ **254.** *Membership.*—The membership of the Administrative Board shall consist of the following insofar as the offices and relationships exist within the local church:

The pastor and the associate pastor or pastors; diaconal ministers, deaconesses, and home missionaries appointed to serve therein; church and community workers under appointment by and certified by the National Division of the General Board of Global Ministries, providing their memberships are in said local church, with an advisory relationship in all other churches to which they are assigned; the lay leader(s); the lay member(s) of the Annual Conference; chairperson of the trustees; the church administrator (business manager); the chairperson of the Committee on Finance; the chairperson of the Committee on Pastor-Parish Relations or one of the church's representatives on the Committee on Pastor-Parish Relations, if chairperson of the committee is from one of the other churches; the secretary of the Committee on Nominations and Personnel; the church treasurer(s); the financial secretary; the church historian; the director or the associate of Christian education or the educational assistant; the director or the associate of evangelism; the director or the associate of music or the music assistant; the chairperson of the Council on Ministries; the work area chairpersons; the age-level and family coordinators; the superintendent of the church school; the health and welfare ministries representative; the coordinator of communications; the membership secretary; the president of United Methodist Women; the president of United Methodist Men; the president of the United Methodist Youth Council; members at large (¶ 250.2). The employed professional staff who are members of the Administrative Board shall not vote on matters pertaining to their employee relationship.

Members of the Administrative Board shall be persons of genuine Christian character who love the Church, are morally disciplined, are committed to the mandate of inclusiveness in the life of the Church, are loyal to the ethical standards of The United Methodist Church set forth in the Social Principles, and are competent to administer its affairs. It shall include youth members chosen according to the same standards as adults. All shall be members of the local church, except where Central Conference legislation provides otherwise. The pastor shall be the administrative officer, and as such shall be an ex officio member of all conferences, boards, councils, commissions, committees, and task forces, unless restricted by the Discipline.[8]

¶ **255.** *Organization.*—The Administrative Board shall be organized annually by the election of a chairperson, a vice-chairperson, and a recording secretary. These officers shall be

---

[8]*See* Judicial Council Decisions 469, 500.

lay persons nominated by the Committee on Nominations and Personnel. The chairperson shall be elected by the Charge Conference. The vice-chairperson and recording secretary shall be elected by the Administrative Board at the first meeting of the new year. Additional nominations may be made from the floor.

¶ **256.** *Responsibilities.*—As the executive agency of the Charge Conference, the Administrative Board shall have general oversight of the administration and program of the local church (¶ 253). The pastor in charge shall be the administrative officer. The Administrative Board shall initiate planning, establish objectives, adopt goals, authorize action, determine policy, receive reports, evaluate the church's ministries, and review the mission and ministry of the church.

1. The Administrative Board shall be responsible for administering the organization of the local church which shall include: the Council on Ministries (¶ 257), the Committee on Nominations and Personnel (¶ 269.1), the Committee on Pastor-Parish Relations (¶ 269.2),[9] the Committee on Finance (¶ 269.3), and the Board of Trustees (¶ 2524). The Administrative Board may co-opt additional persons from time to time to assist the local church in fulfilling its mission.

2. The Administrative Board may adjust the local church's program year to correspond with the Annual Conference fiscal year. The Administrative Board shall determine the date when all elected personnel shall take office and establish their tenure except when the General Conference or the Annual Conference orders otherwise.

3. The Administrative Board shall:

a) Initiate planning, establish objectives, adopt goals and program plans for the ministries and the mission of the local church and evaluate their effectiveness. To fulfill this responsibility the board shall receive and act on recommendations from the Council on Ministries and other groups amenable to it. It shall submit an annual report to the Charge Conference.

b) Review the membership of the local church. To fulfill this responsibility the board shall receive reports from the pastor/membership secretary on membership changes, review practices

---

[9]*See* Judicial Council Decisions 509, 550.

of membership enlistment, training, and care with the pastor and evangelism work area, and act on the goals and plans for membership growth recommended by the Council on Ministries.

c) Upon nomination by the Committee on Nominations and Personnel or from the floor, fill vacancies occurring among the lay officers listed in ¶ 250.1 between sessions of the Charge Conference.

d) Establish the budget on recommendation of the Committee on Finance.

e) Recommend to the Charge Conference the salary and other remuneration for the pastor(s) after receiving recommendations from the Committee on Pastor-Parish Relations.

f) Review the recommendation of the Committee on Pastor-Parish Relations regarding the provision of adequate housing for the pastor(s), with attention to Annual Conference parsonage standards, and report the same to the Charge Conference for approval. It is the responsibility of the Administrative Board to provide for adequate housing for the pastor(s). Housing shall not be considered as part of compensation or remuneration, but shall be considered as a means provided by the local church, and for the convenience of the local church, to enable its ministry and the itinerant ministry of the Annual Conference.[10]

4. The Administrative Board shall ensure the promotion of all the benevolent causes authorized by the General, Jurisdictional, Central, Annual, and District Conferences, and encourage the support of World Service, conference, and other benevolences. The board shall coordinate all financial promotion that takes place within the local church. It shall assure that there is an adequate promotion and interpretation of the benevolent ministries of the church by working with such persons and units as the pastor (¶ 247.14), Committee on Finance (¶ 269.4), Council on Ministries (¶ 257), coordinator of communications (¶ 262.3), work area chairperson of missions (¶ 261.6), work area chairperson of education (¶ 261.3), and work area chairperson of stewardship (¶ 261.9). In the promotion of special days with offering (¶¶ 273, 274, 276) the Administrative Board shall assign

---

[10]*See* Judicial Council Decisions 510, 547, 550, 562, 568, 588.

responsibility to the local church program unit most closely related to the purpose of the offering.

5. It shall make proper and adequate provision for the financial needs of the church, including ministerial support (i.e., for the pastor or pastors, district superintendent, conference claimants, and bishops); approved items of local expense; World Service, conference, and other benevolences; other items apportioned to the church by the proper authorities; and all obligations assumed by the local church.

6. It shall discharge faithfully any and all duties and responsibilities committed to it by the Charge Conference or by law of the Church.

7. It shall develop in the members of the congregation a concern for and responsibility in the establishment of new churches, new church schools, and other forms of ministry, and when specifically authorized by the district superintendent and the district Board of Church Location and Building (¶ 2518), it shall organize and sponsor new churches, church schools, and other forms of ministry needed in the community.

8. It shall foster understanding of the unity of the Church and shall initiate responsible participation in the ministries of the ecumenical community.[11]

9. It shall encourage understanding of and commitment to inclusiveness in the life of the Church.

THE COUNCIL ON MINISTRIES

¶ **257.** The **Council on Ministries** shall draw upon the local and connectional program suggestions as it prepares its recommendation regarding the ministries to be implemented in fulfilling the congregation's responsibility in the local and worldwide community. It shall furnish the Committee on Finance with the recommended level of funding needed to implement each area of ministry.

The local church Council on Ministries shall consider, develop, and coordinate goals and program proposals for the church's mission. It shall receive and, where possible, utilize

---

[11]*See* Judicial Council Decision 516.

resources for missions provided by the District, Annual, Jurisdictional, Central, and General Councils on Ministries, boards, and agencies, and shall coordinate these resources with the church's plan for ministries. The council shall be amenable to the Administrative Board, to which it shall submit its goals and program plans for revision and appropriate action. Upon adoption of the goals and program plans by the Administrative Board, the council shall implement and evaluate the goals and program plans which are assigned.

The Council on Ministries shall elect teachers, counselors, and officers for the church school except where these are subject to election by the Charge Conference. In local churches when size and organization permit, and where the educational program can be enhanced by division superintendents, the council may elect such person(s). Nominations for these positions shall be made by the work area chairperson of education upon the recommendation of the superintendent of the church school and after consultation with the pastor, the division superintendents, and such other groups or persons as the Council on Ministries may designate. It is recommended that the Committee on Nominations and Personnel be a resource in this process (¶ 268.1).

The Council on Ministries shall make recommendations to the Committee on Finance requesting the financial resources needed to undergird the ministries which it has developed, using local and connectional program suggestions, and which the council recommends to the Administrative Board.

The Council on Ministries, in consultation with the pastor, may make recommendations to the Committee on Pastor-Parish Relations regarding the professional and other staff positions needed to carry out the program projected by the council.

Since local churches vary greatly in needs and size, the structure and organization required will differ. The Council on Ministries with its several elected representatives is the minimum structure for the development and administration of the local church program. The Council on Ministries, in order to implement the church's mission, may request expansion of the structure to include councils, commissions, task groups, committees, and other groups as needed. Where the committees, councils, task groups, commissions, etc., are not organized, the duties assigned to each become the responsibility of the Council on Ministries.

¶ **258.** The basic membership of the Council on Ministries shall include the following insofar as the offices and relationships exist within the local church: the pastor and other staff persons who are engaged in program work; the chairperson of the Administrative Board; the lay leader; the president of United Methodist Women; the president of United Methodist Men; the superintendent of the church school; the coordinators of age levels: children, youth, and adult; a coordinator of family ministry; the chairperson of each work area: Christian unity and interreligious concerns, Church and society, education, evangelism, higher education and campus ministry, missions, religion and race, status and role of women, stewardship, and worship; the coordinator of communications; the local church health and welfare ministries representative; a lay member of Annual Conference; two youth members (twelve through eighteen), two young adult members (nineteen through thirty), and two older adult members (over sixty-five years of age) of the congregation if not otherwise provided for.

The Charge Conference may elect to the Council on Ministries upon nomination of the Committee on Nominations and Personnel: a representative of United Methodist Youth Ministry, coordinator of young adult ministries, coordinator of older adult ministries, coordinator of single adult ministries, persons in ministry with persons who have handicapping conditions, and other persons on the basis of their competency in program planning.

The officers of the Council on Ministries shall be a chairperson, a vice-chairperson, and a secretary. All officers shall be lay persons or clergypersons who are not members of the local staff. The chairperson shall be elected by the Charge Conference; the vice-chairperson and secretary shall be elected by the council from its own membership.

¶ **259.** *Age-Level, Family, and Specialized-Ministries Coordinators (see also ¶ 252).*—1. The Charge Conference may elect annually a **coordinator of children's ministries,** a **coordinator of youth ministries,** a **coordinator of adult ministries,** and a **co-**

ordinator of family ministries. Where young adult and specific age-level ministries would be enhanced, **coordinators of young adult and/or older adult ministries** may be elected. Where needs for specialized areas of ministry arise (for example, single adults or persons with handicapping conditions), coordinators of these areas of ministry may be elected. Each of the coordinators shall, under the guidance of the pastor or a representative from the employed professional staff and the chairperson of the Council on Ministries or Administrative Council, study the needs of the age group and the goals of the congregation's ministry and coordinate the planning and implementation of a unified and comprehensive ministry with the age group. Each coordinator shall serve as liaison with organizations, persons, and resources in and beyond the local church which relate to the particular age level. The coordinator shall represent on the Council on Ministries or Administrative Council the concerns of age-level organizations when they are not otherwise represented. Youth and adult ministry coordinators, in cooperation with others holding related responsibilities, will bring before the congregation Christian vocation as a calling to ministry in all spheres of life.

2. The **coordinator of family ministries** shall work with the age-level coordinators and the Council on Ministries or Administrative Council to develop a family ministry for the local church, taking into consideration the suggestions of the general church agency and the Annual Conference agency responsible for family life. This coordinator shall keep the Council on Ministries or Administrative Council aware of resources and activities to be used in planning family activities in the church and home, in the guidance of families in Christian living in the home, in the preparation of youth for marriage, and in helping families find opportunities for service in the community and the world.

¶ **260.** *Work Areas (See also* ¶ 252).—Major concerns of the Church Universal and local church include Christian unity and interreligious concerns, Church and society, education, evangelism, higher education and campus ministry, missions, religion and race, the status and role of women, stewardship, and worship. Therefore the Charge Conference may elect annually the **chairperson of Christian unity and interreligious concerns,** the **chairperson of Church and society,** the **chairperson of** education, the **chairperson of evangelism,** the **chairperson of higher education and campus ministry,** the **chairperson of missions,** the **chairperson of religion and race,** the **chairperson of the status and role of women,** the **chairperson of stewardship,** and the **chairperson of worship.** Where desirable, the Charge Conference may combine coordinators' and work area chairpersons' assignments.

Each work area chairperson, with the guidance of the pastor or a representative from the employed staff and the chairperson of the Council on Ministries or Administrative Council, shall contact the program agencies, obtain guidance material, and study the implications for the work area in the total mission of the Church; shall interpret and recommend to the Council on Ministries or Administrative Council ways of implementing the mission of the Church represented by the area; shall make specific recommendations of the work area for different age groups; shall serve as liaison within and beyond the local church. When an activity in the area of work is planned by the Council on Ministries or Administrative Council to include two or more age levels, the chairperson of the work area may serve, when designated by the Council on Ministries or Administrative Council, as chairperson of a group from the age levels to carry out the activity.

¶ **261.** 1. The work area **chairperson of Christian unity and interreligious concerns** shall encourage awareness and understanding of ecumenism at all levels, including furthering dialogue and fellowship with other Christians and with persons of other faiths, cultures, and ideologies, participation in councils of churches, interfaith councils, and consulting on church unions. In keeping with standards and guidance materials supplied by the General Commission on Christian Unity and Interreligious Concerns and the Annual Conference commission (or comparable organization), the chairperson shall stimulate studies, plan programs, and cooperate in specific Christian unity and interreligious endeavors. It shall be the responsibility of the work area chairperson to interpret ecumenical structures and agencies, such as the Interdenominational Cooperation Fund, the World Council of Churches, the National Council of the Churches of Christ in the U.S.A., the World Methodist

Council, and the Consultation on Church Union to the local church.

2. The work area **chairperson of Church and society** shall keep the Council on Ministries or Administrative Council aware of the need for study and action in the areas of peace and world order, human welfare, political and human rights, social and economic justice, environmental justice and survival. In keeping with standards and guidance materials supplied by the General Board of Church and Society and the Annual Conference Board of Church and Society (or comparable organization), the chairperson shall recommend to the Council on Ministries or Administrative Council study/action projects in the field of social concerns. He/she shall cooperate with other commissions in surveying the needs of the local community and in making program recommendations for responding to local, community, state, national, and international needs to which the Church ministers by its service, education, witness, and action.

3. The work area **chairperson of education** shall design and recommend to the Council on Ministries or Administrative Council an organization of the educational program of the church in keeping with the standards and policies developed by the General Board of Discipleship and shall keep the Council on Ministries or Administrative Council aware of sound educational procedures. The chairperson shall nominate persons to the Council on Ministries or Administrative Council for election as division superintendents (as needed), teachers, counselors, and officers of the church school.

The work area chairperson of education shall assure that persons of all ages are provided with opportunities to study the Bible and the Christian faith and life, and facilitate the use of resources which are based on curriculum plans which have been approved by the General Board of Discipleship.

The work area chairperson shall assure that persons of all ages are provided with opportunities to consider their vocation as Christians and particular opportunities to express vocation of ministry in their chosen careers and occupations. The chairperson in cooperation with the pastor shall assure that opportunities for professional church-related ministries are interpreted within the congregation.

The work area chairperson of education shall assure that supervision is provided for week-day nursery and kindergarten programs where these are included as a part of the church's educational program. This supervision shall include selection, guidance, and training of leaders, resources, and budget.

The chairperson shall promote the local observance of Christian Education Sunday to emphasize the importance of Christian education and to receive an offering to strengthen Christian education in areas of greatest need. The offerings shall be sent to the treasurer of the conference, who shall distribute the funds in accordance with ¶ 276.1.

The chairperson shall encourage certification of educational assistants as directors or ministers of Christian education or as associates in Christian education.

4. The work area **chairperson of evangelism,** with his/her work-area members, shall work with the pastor, the Administrative Council, or the Administrative Board and Council on Ministries to make evangelism an ongoing priority ministry of the congregation to win people to a profession or a renewal of faith in Jesus Christ. The chairperson shall recommend activities and structure to respond to the evangelistic mission of the local church in keeping with the standards and guidance material supplied by the General Board of Discipleship and the Annual Conference Board of Discipleship, or its counterpart. The concerns of the work area on evangelism shall include the people who are not members in any local church, the church's own inactive members, and the care of all its members. The responsibilities and opportunities of the work area on evangelism shall include, but not be limited to, working with all organizations of the church to identify and reach out to persons who are neither members nor active in a church, helping persons share the good news of Jesus Christ, keeping a current prospect file, providing for visitation programs, setting growth goals, inviting persons to Christian discipleship in the worship services, planning specific evangelism events and missions, incorporating new members, and assisting in the possibilities of starting new congregations. In cooperation with the pastor and the Council on Ministries/ Administrative Council the chairperson shall develop and implement ministries of membership care, growth in disciple-

ship, and spiritual formation including distribution of *The Upper Room* and other devotional resources.

5.*a*) The work area **chairperson of higher education and campus ministry** shall keep the Council on Ministries or Administrative Council aware of higher education concerns and provide locally for the promotion and support of the interest of higher education and campus ministry in accordance with the programs of the Annual Conference and the Division of Higher Education of the General Board of Higher Education and Ministry. This shall include plans for the ministry to college and university students, staff, faculty, and administrators related to the local church; recruitment of students for United Methodist institutions; relating students to United Methodist–supported campus ministries; encouraging local support of United Methodist colleges, universities, and campus ministries in the Annual Conference through scholarships, special grants, and interpretive programs. The chairperson shall also interpret and promote these programs of the general Church: the Black College Fund; Hispanic, Asian, and Native American (HANA) Educational Ministries; World Communion Sunday offering for Ethnic Minority Scholarships, Minority In-Service Training Program, and Crusade Scholarships; United Methodist Student Day; and the receiving of an offering for the support of United Methodist scholarships and the United Methodist Student Loan Fund (¶ 274.4).

b) The work area chairperson of higher education and campus ministry shall coordinate and guide, with the pastor and related interests of the local church, a program of interpretation and counseling which will assist persons in their vocational decisions related to the church.

c) The work area chairperson of higher education and campus ministry shall maintain contact with persons who attend schools, colleges, and universities, who join the military, or are in other educational situations which require their moving temporarily from the local church. The chairperson shall forward the name and address of each person to the appropriate college/university/military chaplain or campus minister.

The chairperson shall forward to United Methodist colleges and universities related to the Annual Conference the names and addresses of high school juniors and seniors in the local church and shall send the names and addresses of college students to the chaplain or campus minister of the college they are attending. The chairperson shall develop a program enabling the local church to maintain contact with persons attending colleges and universities, and especially those away from home.

6. The work area **chairperson of missions** shall keep the Council on Ministries or Administrative Council aware of the purpose and needs of programs and institutions supported by the Church in the nation and around the world. In keeping with the standards and guidance material supplied by the General Board of Global Ministries and the Annual Conference Board of Global Ministries (or comparable organization), the chairperson shall provide resources to be used in the study program of the church. Through the council he/she shall cooperate with other commissions in surveying the needs of the local community and recommend to the Council on Ministries or Administrative Council plans for local mission and service projects and for participation in enterprises related to the National Division or the Health and Welfare Ministries Department of the General Board of Global Ministries in the geographic area of the local church. The chairperson shall recommend means of keeping the church informed of the qualifications and current needs for personnel to serve through the Church around the world. He/she shall develop a benevolence budget and submit it to the Council on Ministries for its recommendation to the Committee on Finance. The chairperson shall recommend Advance specials on behalf of the entire Church and in addition shall promote acceptance of Advance specials by individuals and groups.

7. The work area **chairperson of religion and race** or outreach work area chairperson shall keep the Council on Ministries or the Administrative Council and the congregation aware of the meaning of a racial and ethnic pluralistic United Methodist Church. In keeping with the standards and guidance material supplied by the General Commission on Religion and Race and the Annual Conference Commission on Religion and Race (or comparable organization), he/she shall recommend to the Council on Ministries or the Administrative Council program opportunities for worship, fellowship, witness, study, nurture,

and service with persons, groups, and congregations across racial and ethnic lines.

8. The work area **chairperson of the status and role of women** shall keep the Council on Ministries or Administrative Council and the congregation aware of the meaning of the church's continuing commitment to the full and equal responsibility and participation of women in the total life and mission of the Church. The chairperson shall be a woman. She shall maintain contact with the Annual Conference Commission on the Status and Role of Women and the district Council on Ministries and shall cooperate with United Methodist Women in recommending to the Council on Ministries or Administrative Council program opportunities for worship, fellowship, witness, study, nurture, and service with persons and groups which confirm anew the liberating message of Jesus Christ that recognizes every person, woman or man, as full and equal part of God's human family.

9. *a)* The work area **chairperson of stewardship** shall interpret and encourage stewardship consistent with the historic standards of The United Methodist Church. The chairperson shall encourage both individual and corporate stewardship, informing them that tithing is the minimum goal of giving in The United Methodist Church. Using as a basis Scripture, tradition, reason, and experience, stewardship shall have five components: (1) the use of God-given talents, (2) personal financial management and life commitments, (3) personal giving through the church, (4) local church management of resources, and (5) the Christian steward's responsibility in God's world. The chairperson of stewardship shall work with others on the Council on Ministries or Administrative Council to formulate plans and recommend resources to encourage growth in each of these areas. In churches where a Commission on Stewardship is organized, the Council on Ministries or Administrative Council shall elect representatives of the Committee on Finance to serve on the commission. The chairperson of the work area of stewardship shall be a member of the Committee on Finance and the Council on Ministries or Administrative Council.

b) The chairperson of stewardship in cooperation with the Council on Ministries or Administrative Council may (1) organize a **Wills and Estate Planning Task Force** which shall have the responsibility to *(a)* emphasize the need for adults of all ages to have a will and an estate plan and provide information on the preparation of these to the members of the congregation; *(b)* stress the opportunities for church members and constituents to make provisions for giving through United Methodist churches, institutions, agencies, and causes by means of wills, annuities, trusts, life insurance, memorials, and various types of property; (2) arrange for the dissemination of information that will be helpful in preretirement planning, including such considerations as establishing a living will and a living trust; (3) recommend an educational design to stress the need for each person to designate someone to serve as a responsible advocate should independent decision-making ability be lost. Resources for these tasks may be secured from the General Board of Discipleship and other appropriate sources for program assistance and direction.

10. The work area **chairperson of worship** shall aid the congregation to become increasingly aware of the meaning, purpose, and practice of worship. In keeping with the standards and guidance material supplied by the General Board of Discipleship, the chairperson shall recommend plans for the study by individuals and groups of the art of worship; shall cooperate with the pastor in planning and caring for worship, music, and the other arts, ushering, furnishings, appointments, and sacramental elements for congregational worship; shall enable the congregation to experience the worship styles and contributions of the various racial and ethnic groups; shall recommend standards for the placement in the church of memorial gifts as aids to worship. To the end that music and other arts may contribute largely to the communication and celebration of the gospel, the work area chairperson shall promote adequate musical leadership in the church; cooperate with other educational enterprises of the church in teaching persons of all ages our heritage of song and the meaning of worship as it uses music and other arts both traditional and contemporary; encourage certification of music leaders as directors and ministers of music and music associates; encourage wider use and understanding of visual arts, dramatic arts, and architectural design as expressions of faith and means of

proclamation of the gospel; seek guidance and resources from appropriate general agencies, commissions, or task groups.

¶ **262.** *Program Support Personnel.*—1. The Charge Conference may elect a **superintendent of the church school** or Sunday School who shall be responsible, under the guidance of the education work area chairperson or commission and the pastor or representative of the employed staff, for the supervision of the total program of education in the church. Responsibilities may include: *(a)* serving as the administrator of the church school; *(b)* working with the Christian education or nurture work area in the selection of church school teachers and leaders for approval by the Council on Ministries or Administrative Council; *(c)* identifying the needs for various kinds of study opportunities and recommending plans for a study program in accordance with those needs; *(d)* serving as an educational consultant to persons responsible for the Christian education of children, the Christian education of youth, the Christian education of adults, and Christian education for marriage and family life; *(e)* developing and implementing programs to promote church school attendance and participation; and *(f)* evaluating the effectiveness of the study program of the church. When desirable, in churches with small membership, the Charge Conference may combine responsibilities of the superintendent of the church school and the chairperson of the work area on education.

2. The **health and welfare ministries representative,** if elected, shall assist the local church and its people to be involved in direct service to persons in need, especially in the areas of child care, aging, health care, and handicapping conditions, and shall help coordinate these ministries. The representative shall serve as the chairperson of the Committee on Health and Welfare Ministries, if it is organized, or may serve as a member of the work areas on missions and church and society.

The responsibilities of this representative shall be: *(a)* to act as liaison between the local church and district and Annual Conference Health and Welfare Ministries units; to act as liaison between the local church and the Health and Welfare Ministries Department of the General Board of Global Ministries; and to make use of guidance materials and leadership training from these units; *(b)* to help the local church to know about, to support and to make use of services through health and welfare institutions and programs within the Annual Conference that are related to a connectional unit of The United Methodist Church; *(c)* to promote within the local church the observance of the Golden Cross offering and other means of giving for health and welfare ministries; *(d)* to work through the Council on Ministries or Administrative Council and with other groups in the church and community to locate human need in the church and community, to support existing programs or to initiate new programs, including local church direct service ministries, and to advocate needed social change; *(e)* to encourage the local church to be aware of the gifts and needs of persons with handicapping conditions, as well as the need for the local church to be structurally accessible.

3. The **coordinator of communications,** if elected, shall assist church members with communication tasks, which are a responsibility of all Christians, making available ideas, resources, and skills. The coordinator shall advise and assist work areas, committees and organizations of the local church with their communications. She/he shall help to accomplish effective communications throughout the congregation and make resources available, utilizing district, conference, and general church agencies. Major areas of responsibility are: *(a)* external communications, to the community; *(b)* internal communications, within the congregation, including devices to aid communications for persons with vision and hearing handicapping conditions; and *(c)* promotion of local, district, conference, and churchwide program and benevolences.

¶ **263.** *Program Agencies.*—The ministries of the local church are implemented through the encounter of persons with God's redeeming love for the world and with his action in the world. To achieve this ministry persons are involved in age-level or family groupings. Usually a variety of settings is essential. Some will be formed by the Administrative Council or the Council on Ministries. Others will emerge with the approval of these bodies. Another type is historical, expressing itself in organizational structures that are related to counterparts in Annual Conferences and the general Church. These are referred to as **program agencies** and are related to the Administrative Council or the

Council on Ministries through age-level and family coordinators, work area chairpersons, and councils or commissions.

1. *The Church School.*—In each local church there shall be a **church school** for the purpose of accomplishing the church's educational ministry in accordance with ¶ 1208.

a) The church school provides a variety of settings and resources for all persons—children, youth, and adults—to explore the meanings of the Christian faith in all its dimensions, to discover and appropriate to themselves those meanings which are relevant for their lives and for society, and to assume personal responsibility for expressing those meanings in all their relationships. Through such experiences persons will be encouraged to commit themselves to Christ and to unite with the Christian community through membership in a local church. The General Board of Discipleship sets standards and provides guidance resources and plans for the organization, administration, grouping, and leadership of the church school (¶ 1209.2).

b) All the concerns of the church will be present in the church school's educational ministry: Christian unity and interreligious concerns, Church and society, evangelism, higher education and campus ministry, missions, religion and race, the status and role of women, stewardship, and worship. The curriculum of the church school will include the meanings and experiences of the Christian faith as found in the Bible, in history, and in human encounter with the natural world and contemporary society. The resources shall be based on curriculum plans approved by the General Board of Discipleship (¶ 1224).

c) The church school shall be administratively related to the Commission on Education, if organized, or the unit responsible for Christian education. The superintendent of the church school, who is the administrator of the church school, shall be responsible for relating the church school to the total ministry of the church through the Commission on Education, if organized, and the Administrative Council or Council on Ministries.

d) To further the church's educational and nurturing ministry, a church library should be established wherever possible.

e) Church school settings include the Sunday church school and all other ongoing and short-term classes and learning groups

165

for persons of all ages. The church school may be organized with three divisions if desired: children's division for persons from birth through the sixth grade; youth division for persons from the seventh grade through the twelfth grade; and adult division for persons beyond the twelfth grade. Division superintendents, teachers, counselors, church school secretary, curriculum resources secretary, librarian, and such other officers as needed to administer and operate the church school shall be nominated by the work area chairperson on education upon the recommendation of the superintendent of the church school in consultation with the pastor or representative of the employed staff and elected by the Council on Ministries or Administrative Council.

f) The chairperson of the work area on education may suggest to the Administrative Council or to the Council on Ministries of the local church to recommend to the Administrative Board or Administrative Council that the Fourth Sunday's church school offerings be set aside for World Service.

g) Mission education shall be a part of the church school education for children. The chairperson of the work area on education and the children's division superintendent (if elected) or the coordinator of children's ministries shall interpret the Children's Fund for Christian Mission (to be referred to as the United Methodist Children's Fund for Christian Mission) as a means of mission education for children. This fund is established in accordance with ¶¶ 1206.5, 1210.3*e.*

2. *Youth Ministry.*—The term "youth ministry" is an inclusive title, encompassing all the concerns of the church and all activities by, with, and for youth. The youth ministry of The United Methodist Church shall include all persons from approximately twelve through eighteen years of age (generally persons in the seventh grade through the twelfth grade, taking into account the grouping of youth in the public schools), who are currently or potentially associated with the church or any of its activities.

Youth who are full members of the church have all rights and responsibilities of church membership except voting on matters prohibited by state law. (*See* ¶ 226.) The coordinator of youth ministries and the Youth Council, when organized, shall be responsible for recommending to the Administrative Council or Council on Ministries activities, program emphases, and settings for youth. The local church may designate one of its settings as the United Methodist Youth Fellowship. The coordinator and council shall use available resources and means to inform youth concerning the Youth Service Fund and shall cultivate its support; *provided* that prior to this cultivation or as a part of it, the youth shall have been challenged to assume their financial responsibilities in connection with the total program and budget of the local church.

3. *Young Adult Ministry.*—The ministry of the local church shall include and be extended to persons out of high school (approximately nineteen through thirty years of age). Such ministry shall seek to meet the needs of young adults and bring them to a knowledge of Jesus Christ. Such ministry shall be the responsibility of the Administrative Council or Council on Ministries, working through its adult coordinator or young adult coordinator, if elected, or the Adult/Young Adult Council, if organized. A cooperative approach to young adult ministries with other churches, denominations, community organizations and groups shall be encouraged as a valid outreach ministry of the local United Methodist church.

4. *Single Adult Ministry.*—The ministry of the local church shall include and be extended to persons of all ages who are single, widowed, divorced, never married, or married and spouse-absent. These persons share unique needs and life situations toward which the church can direct its support, love, and Christian responsibility. Such a ministry shall be the responsibility of the Administrative Council or Council on Ministries, working through its adult coordinator or single adult coordinator. If elected, its coordinator of age-level and family ministries, or the Adult/Single Adult/Older Adult Council if organized. A cooperative approach to single adult ministries with other churches, denominations, community organizations, and groups shall be encouraged as valid outreach ministry of the local United Methodist church.

5. *Older Adult Ministry.*—A ministry by, with, and for older adults shall serve the twofold purpose of meeting the needs of such persons in the church and community and recognizing the valuable contribution they can make to the ministry and mission of the church in the community and world. Older adults in the

church shall be recognized as full participants in the fellowship, ministry, and service of the congregation.

6. *United Methodist Women.*—In every local church there shall be an organized unit of **United Methodist Women.** The following is the authorized constitution:

Article 1. Name.—The name of this organization shall be United Methodist Women.

Article 2. Relationships.—The unit of United Methodist Women in the local church is directly related to the district and conference organizations of United Methodist Women and to the Women's Division of the General Board of Global Ministries of The United Methodist Church.

Article 3. Purpose.—The organized unit of United Methodist Women shall be a community of women whose purpose is to know God and to experience freedom as whole persons through Jesus Christ; to develop a creative, supportive fellowship; and to expand concepts of mission through participation in the global ministries of the church.

Article 4. Membership.—Membership shall be open to any woman who indicates her desire to belong and to participate in the global mission of the church through United Methodist Women. The pastor(s) shall be an ex officio member of the local unit and of its executive committee.

Article 5. Officers and Committees.—The local unit shall elect a president, a vice-president, a secretary, a treasurer, and a Committee on Nominations. Additional officers and committees shall be elected or appointed as needed, in accordance with the plans of the Women's Division as set forth in the bylaws for the local unit of United Methodist Women.

Article 6. Funds.—*a)* The organized unit of United Methodist Women shall secure funds for the fulfillment of its purpose.

b) All funds, from whatever source secured by the unit of United Methodist Women, belong to the organization and shall be disbursed only in accordance with its constitution and by its order.

c) The total budget secured and administered by the organized unit in the local church shall include (1) pledges and other money for the programs and responsibilities of the Women's Division to be directed through regular channels of finance of United Methodist Women; and (2) funds to be used in mission locally, which shall include amounts for administration and membership development.

d) The organized unit in the local church shall make an annual pledge to the total budget of the district or conference organization of United Methodist Women.

e) All undesignated funds channeled to the Women's Division shall be appropriated by the division.

Article 7. Meetings.—The organized unit in the local church shall hold such meetings for implementing the purpose and transacting its business as the unit itself shall decide.

Article 8. Relationship in the Local Church.—The organized unit of United Methodist Women shall encourage all women to participate in the total life and work of the church and shall support them in assuming positions of responsibility and leadership.

Article 9. Amendments.—Proposed amendments to this constitution may be sent to the recording secretary of the Women's Division of the General Board of Global Ministries before the last annual meeting of the division in the quadrennium.

Note: For a description of the Women's Division of the General Board of Global Ministries and its subsidiary organizations, *see* ¶¶ 1422-30.

¶ **264.** *United Methodist Men.*—Each church or charge shall have an organized unit of **United Methodist Men** chartered and annually recertified through the General Board of Discipleship to provide another channel for involving men in the total ministry of the church.

1. Resources for organization and implementation of the ministry of men at the local church, district, conference, and jurisdictional levels shall be provided by the General Board of Discipleship.

2. United Methodist Men shall be a creative supportive fellowship of men who seek to know Jesus Christ, to grow spiritually, and to seek daily his will. Its primary purpose is to declare the centrality of Christ in the lives of men and in all their relationships. The major concerns are:

a) To encourage knowledge of and support for the total mission of The United Methodist Church.

b) To engage in evangelism by sharing the fullness of the gospel in its personal and social dimensions.

c) To clarify and speak to the identity and role of the man in contemporary society.

d) To seek commitment to discipleship.

e) To study and become familiar with The United Methodist Church, its organization, doctrines, and belief.

f) To cooperate with all units of United Methodist Men in obtaining these objectives through district, conference, and churchwide goals.

3. Men seeking membership in a local unit of United Methodist Men will be asked to subscribe to the major concerns listed in §2 above and to these personal objectives:

a) To engage daily in Bible study and prayer.

b) To bear witness to Christ's way in daily work and in all personal contacts through words and actions.

c) To engage in Christian service.

4. Units of United Methodist Men may be formed in clusters and in other groupings of local churches as needed.

5. The duly appointed pastor(s) of the church shall be ex officio member(s) of the unit and its executive committee.

¶ **265.** *Age-Level and Family Councils.*—Where the size of the church and the extent of the program indicate the need, the work of the Council on Ministries or Administrative Council may be facilitated by one or more **age-level councils** and/or a **family council,** or such other means as fit the needs of the congregation. The age-level councils shall work under the leadership of the age-level coordinators to expedite the work of the Council on Ministries or Administrative Council in adapting the program to the age level.

The membership of these councils, except for ex officio members, shall be elected by the Council on Ministries or Administrative Council and may include the following:

1. *Children's Council.*—Representative teachers and leaders of children's activities of the church (including its activities in music and the other arts), representative parents, and representatives of work areas (Christian unity and interreligious concerns, Church and society, education, evangelism, higher education and campus ministry, missions, religion and race, status and role of women, stewardship, and worship) related to the church's ministry with children. The council may also include the director

170

of the weekday nursery school or day care center (if such is provided), when the nursery school or day care center is sponsored by the local church.

2. *Youth Council.*—Representatives of adult leaders and counselors of youth, representative parents, representatives of work areas (Christian unity and interreligious concerns, Church and society, education, evangelism, higher education and campus ministry, missions, religion and race, status and role of women, stewardship, and worship) related to the church's ministry with youth, representatives of the church's activities in music and the other arts, a youth and an adult from each youth-serving organization sponsored by the church, and in a number that is at least one youth for each adult on the council.

3. *Adult Council.*—Representatives of adult study/action groups, fellowship groups, administrative groups, and service organizations such as United Methodist Women, United Methodist Men, and special adult ministries; and representatives of work areas (Christian unity and interreligious concerns, Church and society, education, evangelism, higher education and campus ministry, missions, religion and race, status and role of women, stewardship, and worship) related to the church's ministry with adults. Where special adult ministries would be enhanced, a **Young Adult,** a **Single Adult,** and/or an **Older Adult Council** may be organized.

4. *Family Council.*—When the size of the church and the extent of the program indicate the need, the Council on Ministries or Administrative Council may designate a group including representatives of the age-group councils and work areas to work with the coordinator in planning program suggestions to be submitted to the Council on Ministries or Administrative Council.

The pastor or a member of the professional staff of the church appointed by the pastor shall be an ex officio member of each council. Additional members, such as representatives of community agencies, may be elected to each council on the basis of their interest and competency.

The coordinators shall serve as the chairpersons of their respective councils except that the Council on Ministries or Administrative Council may authorize the Youth Council to elect its own chairperson.

171

¶ **266.** *Work Area Commissions.*—When the size of the church and the extent of the program indicate the need, the Council on Ministries or Administrative Council may choose to establish one or more **work area commissions** (Christian unity and interreligious concerns, Church and society, education, evangelism, higher education and campus ministry, missions, religion and race, status and role of women, stewardship, and worship). Where a commission is established, it shall work under the leadership of the work area chairperson and shall assume the responsibilities assigned to that chairperson. The representative of the work area serving on each age-level council shall be a member of the commission. At least two youths shall be included in the membership of all commissions. The Council on Ministries or Administrative Council may elect other persons to the commission because of particular interest and competency in the area. The pastor or a member of the professional staff of the church designated by the pastor shall serve as an ex officio member of each commission.

¶ **267.** **Task groups** may be formed by the Council on Ministries or Administrative Council, its councils or commissions, for the purpose of accomplishing specific and particular goals of the Church's mission to the world. These groups shall be oriented to immediate tasks. They shall prepare for their mission by the study of the Scriptures' mandates in the light of the community's immediate needs. They shall meet regularly for study and for planning their strategy in mission. They shall be disciplined to individual and corporate action and shall be amenable to the Council on Ministries or Administrative Council and report to it.

¶ **268.** *Class Meetings.*—A structure for the **Class Meetings** may be organized within the Council on Ministries or Administrative Council with the following responsibilities and programs:

1. Class Meetings may be organized within the church by the Council on Ministries or Administrative Council by region, interest group, or age-level groups consisting of ten to fifteen families to each class (or as designed by the council) for the purpose of spiritual nurture, prayer support, growth in evangelism, and accountable discipleship.

2. Class leaders shall be elected by the Charge Conference to

lead and coordinate the classes under the direct supervision of the pastor.

3. Classes shall meet regularly as designated by the council for the purpose of:

Bible study and prayer; spiritual fellowship at homes; accountable discipleship through small groups; outreach and involvement of new members; care and support of the members.

4. Class leaders may be members of the Council on Ministries or Administrative Council.

ADMINISTRATIVE COMMITTEES

¶ **269.** 1. There shall be elected annually by the Charge Conference in each local church a **Committee on Nominations and Personnel** who are members of the local church. This committee is to be composed of not more than nine persons, in addition to the pastor and the lay leader. The pastor shall be the chairperson. The committee shall nominate to the Charge Conference or Church Conference in its annual session such officers and members of the Administrative Council or Administrative Board and Charge Conference and committees as the law of the Church requires or as the conference may determine as necessary to its work; *provided* that to secure experience and stability the membership shall be divided into three classes, one of which shall be elected each year for a three-year term; *provided* further, that to begin the process of rotation on the first year one class be elected for one year, one class for two years, and one for three years; *provided* further, that each year the new class of members to serve on the Committee on Nominations and Personnel, and vacancies as they occur, shall be elected from nominees from the floor. At least one youth and one young adult, elected by the Charge Conference or Church Conference, shall serve as members of the Committee on Nominations and Personnel. Churches are encouraged to establish a policy that retiring members of the Committee on Nominations and Personnel not succeed themselves.

The Committee on Nominations and Personnel shall serve throughout the year to guide the Administrative Council or Administrative Board on personnel matters (other than employed staff) and recruit, support, and recognize leaders and provide for their training so as to coordinate the leadership and service needs with personnel of the congregation, working in relationship to the committees and work areas of the Administrative Council or the Administrative Board and Council on Ministries in both its nominations and personnel guidance.

In the nomination process, care shall be given that each board, committee, council, and work area, as well as the total nominated personnel shall, insofar as possible, be representative of the age level, sexual, cultural, racial/ethnic membership, as well as economic, social, and theological orientation of the congregation.

2. There shall be a **Committee on Pastor-Parish Relations (Staff-Parish Relations)** of not fewer than five nor more than nine lay persons representative of the total charge. One of the five to nine persons shall be a young adult. One of the five to nine persons may be a senior high youth. In addition to the five to nine persons, a lay member to Annual Conference shall also be a member. All shall be members of the local church or charge except where Central Conference legislation provides otherwise. No staff member or immediate family member of a pastor or staff member may serve on the committee. If a person ineligible to serve on the committee is elected as a lay member to Annual Conference and there is no other elected lay member to the Annual Conference available to serve, the vacancy will be filled upon election by the Charge Conference following the nomination of the Committee on Nominations and Personnel.[12]

a) The members, including the chairperson, shall be elected by the Charge Conference upon nomination by the Committee on Nominations and Personnel. In order to secure experience and stability, the membership shall be divided into three classes, one of which shall be elected each year for a three-year term. Where there is more than one church on a charge, the committee shall include at least one representative from each congregation with a representative of each church to be a member of that church's Administrative Council or Administrative Board.

b) In those charges where there is a multiple staff, full or part time, the committee shall relate to the entire staff, clergy

---

[12]*See* Judicial Council Decisions 500, 509, 550.

and lay, providing to all staff members direct personal and professional access to the Committee on Pastor-Parish Relations as well as to the pastor, the district superintendent, and the bishop. In such cases the committee may be known as the Committee on Staff-Parish Relations.

c) In those charges where there is more than one church, the committee shall include at least one representative from each local church. The Charge Conference may appoint a local church **pastoral advisory committee** for those churches desiring such a committee. The advisory committee shall consist of three persons placed in three classes with the chairperson serving as a member of the charge committee. The committee shall meet upon request of the pastor or of the chairperson, and its duties shall be those outlined in ¶ 269.2*f*(1) and (2). The committee shall meet only with the knowledge of the pastor.

d) The Committees on Pastor-Parish Relations of charges which are in cooperative parish ministries shall meet together to consider the professional leadership needs of the cooperative parish ministry as a whole. Where churches are organized as a larger parish the Committee on Pastor-Parish Relations shall consist of at least one representative from each church. Individual churches may form pastoral advisory committees as needed.

e) The committee shall meet at least quarterly. It shall meet additionally at the request of the bishop, the district superintendent, the pastor, any member of the professional staff, or the chairperson of the committee. The committee shall meet only with the knowledge of the pastor and/or the district superintendent. It may meet with the district superintendent without the pastor being present; however, when the pastor is not present, the pastor, or any member of the staff under consideration, shall be informed prior to such a meeting and immediately thereafter be brought into consultation either by the committee or by the district superintendent. In the event that only one congregation on a charge containing more than one church has concerns which it wishes to share, its member(s) in the committee may meet separately with the pastor or any member of the professional staff or the district superintendent, but only with the knowledge of the pastor and/or district superintendent. The committee may meet in closed session upon recommendation of the pastor, or any other person accountable to the committee, or the chairperson of the committee, or the district superintendent.

f) The duties of the committee shall include the following:

(1) To confer and counsel with the pastor and staff in making an effective ministry by being available for counsel, keeping the pastor and staff advised concerning conditions within the congregation as they affect relations between the pastor/staff and the people, and continually interpreting to the people the nature and function of the ministry, including cross-racial appointments and sensitivity to open itineracy.

(2) To counsel with the pastor and staff on matters pertaining to their relationship with the congregation, including priorities to be given in the use of their time and skill in relation to the goals and objectives set for the congregation's mission and the demands upon the ministry.

(3) Provide evaluation annually for the pastor's and staff's use in an ongoing effective ministry and for identifying continuing education needs and plans. The criteria, processes, and training for evaluation and continuing education shall be developed by the conference Board of Ordained Ministry and Cabinet (¶ 445), and, where applicable, the conference Board of Diaconal Ministry.

(4) To consult on matters pertaining to pulpit supply, proposals for salary, travel expense, vacation, health and life insurance, pension, housing (which may be a church-owned parsonage or housing allowance in lieu of parsonage if in compliance with the policy of the Annual Conference), and other practical matters affecting the work and families of the pastor and staff, and to make annual recommendations regarding such matters to the Administrative Council or Administrative Board, reporting budget items to the Committee on Finance. The parsonage is to be mutually respected by the pastor's family as the property of the church and by the church as a place of privacy for the pastor's family. The chairperson of the Committee on Pastor-Parish Relations, the chairperson of the Board of Trustees, and pastor shall make an annual review of the church-owned parsonage to assure proper maintenance.

(5) To consult with the pastor and staff concerning continuing education and to arrange with the Administrative

Council or Administrative Board for the necessary time and financial assistance for the attendance of the pastor and/or staff at such continuing education events as may serve their professional and spiritual growth.

(6) To enlist, interview, evaluate, review, and recommend annually to the Charge Conference persons for candidacy for ministry, recognizing that The United Methodist Church affirms the biblical and theological support of women and men of all races and ethnic origin for ministry. The committee shall provide to the Charge Conference a list of ministerial students from the charge and shall maintain contact with these students, supplying the Charge Conference with a progress report on each student.

(7) To interpret preparation for ordained ministry and the Ministerial Education Fund to the congregation.

(8) To confer with the pastor and/or other appointed members of the staff if it should become evident that the best interests of the charge and pastor(s) will be served by a change of pastor(s). The committee shall cooperate with the pastor(s), the district superintendent, and the bishop in securing clergy leadership. Its relationship to the district superintendent and the bishop shall be advisory only. (*See* ¶¶ 530-533.)

(9) To recommend to the Administrative Council or Administrative Board, after consultation with the pastor and the Council on Ministries (where such exists), the professional and other staff positions needed to carry out the work of the church or charge. The committee and the pastor shall recommend to the Administrative Board or Council a written statement of policy and procedures regarding the process for hiring, evaluating, promoting, retiring, and dismissing staff personnel who are not subject to episcopal appointment as ordained clergy. Until such a policy has been adopted, the committee and the pastor shall have the authority to hire, evaluate, promote, retire, and dismiss nonappointed personnel. When persons are hired, consideration shall be given to the training qualifications and certification standards set forth by the general church agency to which such positions are related. The committee shall further recommend to the Administrative Council or Administrative Board a provision for adequate health and life insurance, pension benefits, and severance pay for all lay employees.

(10) To recommend to the Charge Conference, when the size of the employed staff of the charge makes it desirable, the establishment of a Personnel Committee. This committee shall be composed of such members of the Committee on Pastor-Parish Relations as it may designate and such additional members as the Charge Conference may determine.

3. There shall be a Board of Trustees whose membership and duties are detailed in ¶¶ 2524-2549.

4. There shall be a **Committee on Finance,** elected annually by the Charge Conference upon nomination by the Committee on Nominations and Personnel, composed of the chairperson; the pastor(s); a lay member of the Annual Conference; the chairperson of the Administrative Council, or the chairpersons of the Administrative Board and Council on Ministries; a representative of the trustees to be selected by the trustees; the chairperson of the work area on stewardship; the lay leader; the financial secretary; the treasurer; the church business administrator; and other members to be added as the Charge Conference may determine. It is recommended that the chairperson of the Committee on Finance shall be a member of the Administrative Council or Administrative Board. The financial secretary, treasurer, and church business administrator, if paid employees, shall be members without vote.

Inasmuch as giving is clearly an integral part of Christian life, a program should be developed within every local church to engage in a stewardship education program which reflects a biblical understanding of wholistic stewardship and proportionate giving and tithing. This program should be auxiliary to the area of stewardship in the General Board of Discipleship (¶ 1215; *see* ¶ 261.9).

All financial askings to be included in the annual budget of the local church shall be submitted to the Committee on Finance. The Committee on Finance shall compile annually a complete budget for the local church and submit it to the Administrative Council or Administrative Board for review and adoption. The Committee on Finance shall be charged with responsibility for developing and implementing plans which will raise sufficient income to meet the budget adopted by the Administrative Council or Administrative Board. It shall administer the funds received according to instructions from the Administrative Council or Administrative Board.

The committee shall carry out the Administrative Council's or Administrative Board's directions in guiding the treasurer(s) and financial secretary.

a) The committee shall designate at least two persons (preferably not of the same family) to count the offering, giving a record of funds received to both the financial secretary and church treasurer. Funds received shall be deposited promptly in accordance with procedures established by the Committee on Finance. The financial secretary shall keep records of the contributions and payments.

b) The **church treasurer(s)** shall disburse all money contributed to causes represented in the local church budget, and such other funds and contributions as the Administrative Council or Administrative Board may determine. The treasurer(s) shall remit each month to the conference treasurer all World Service and Conference Benevolence funds then on hand. Contributions to benevolence shall not be used for any cause other than that to which they have been given. The church treasurer shall make regular and detailed reports on funds received and expended to the Committee on Finance and the Administrative Council or Administrative Board.[13] The treasurer(s) shall be adequately bonded.

c) The committee shall make provision for an annual audit of the records of the financial officers of the local church and all its organizations and shall report to the Charge Conference.

d) The committee shall recommend to the Administrative Council or Administrative Board proper depositories for the church's funds. Funds received shall be deposited promptly in the name of the local church.

e) Contributions designated for specific causes and objects shall be promptly forwarded according to the intent of the donor and shall not be used for any other purpose.

f) After the budget of the local church has been approved, additional appropriations or changes in the budget must be approved by the Administrative Council or Administrative Board.

----

[13]*See* Judicial Council Decisions 63, 320, 539.

g) The committee shall prepare annually a report to the Administrative Council or Administrative Board of all designated funds which are separate from the current expense budget.

5. The Administrative Council or Administrative Board may appoint such other committees as it deems advisable, including: Committee on Communications, Committee on Records and History, Committee on Health and Welfare, and Committee on Memorial Gifts.

Section VI. The Method of Organizing a New Local Church.

¶ **270.** 1. **A new local church** or **mission** shall be established only with the consent of the bishop in charge and his Cabinet and with due consideration of the conference Board of Global Ministries' programs of home missions and church extension (if any; *see* ¶ 731). The bishop shall designate the district within whose bounds the church shall be organized. The district superintendent of that district shall be the agent in charge of the project and shall recommend to the district Board of Church Location and Building (¶ 2518) the site for the proposed new congregation, or shall recommend to the Board of Trustees of a selected local church that they share their facility with the proposed congregation. If there is a city or district missionary organization, that body shall also be asked to approve this site (¶ 1415.7).

2. The district superintendent shall call the persons interested in the proposed church to meet at an appointed time and place, or may by written authorization designate any pastor in the district to call such a meeting.

3. The district superintendent or the pastor to whom authority is designated shall preside and shall appoint a secretary to keep a record of the meeting. Following a period of worship, opportunity shall be given those in attendance to present themselves for membership by proper certificates of transfer. Pastors issuing such certificates to a church not yet organized shall describe therein the proposed new church to which it is issued, as, for instance, "the proposed new church on Boston Avenue."

4. Persons desiring to become members on profession of their faith in Christ shall also be given opportunity to present themselves for membership. When the presiding pastor is

satisfied as to the genuineness of their faith and purpose, they shall be received into the membership of the Church.

5. A list shall be made of all the persons received into the membership of the proposed church, by transfer and on profession. Those persons shall be members of the **Constituting Church Conference,** and each shall be entitled to vote.

6. The Constituting Church Conference shall then be called to order. A committee on nominations, appointed by the presiding pastor or elected on nominations from the floor as the conference may determine, shall nominate members at large of the proposed Administrative Council or Administrative Board. The presiding pastor shall be the chairperson of the committee on nominations. When the members at large have been chosen in proper number, the presiding pastor shall declare the church properly constituted.

7. The presiding pastor shall then adjourn the Constituting Church Conference and call to order the Charge Conference of the pastoral charge. The membership of the Charge Conference shall be those newly elected and any others entitled to membership. The Charge Conference shall then elect such officers of the church as the Discipline requires, including trustees of church property, and shall set up commissions and committees as provided in the Discipline. When such officers have been duly elected and the proper commissions and committees constituted, the church is duly organized, and from this point its work shall proceed as described in the Discipline; *provided* that when a newly organized church is attached to a circuit, the Charge Conference shall not be held until such time as representatives from all the churches of the charge can be properly assembled for that purpose.

8. The Charge Conference may take action at its discretion, authorizing and directing the newly elected trustees to incorporate the newly organized church in accordance with local laws and the provisions of the Discipline.

Section VII. Transfer of a Local Church.

¶ **271.** A local church may be transferred from one Annual Conference to another in which it is geographically located by a two-thirds vote of those present and voting in each of the following: (1) the Charge Conference, (2) a congregational meeting of the local church, and (3) each of the two Annual Conferences involved. Upon announcement of the required majorities by the bishop or bishops involved, the transfer shall immediately be effective. The votes required may originate in the local church or either of the Annual Conferences involved and shall be effective regardless of the order in which taken. In each case a two-thirds vote of those present and voting shall remain effective unless and until rescinded prior to the completion of the transfer by a vote of a majority of those present and voting.

Section VIII. Protection of Rights of Congregations.

¶ **272.** Nothing in the Plan and Basis of Union at any time after the union is to be construed so as to require any local church of the former Church of the United Brethren in Christ, or of the former The Evangelical Church, or of the former The Evangelical United Brethren Church, or of the former The Methodist Church to alienate or in any way to change the title to property contained in its deed or deeds at the time of union; and lapse of time or usage shall not affect said title or control.

Section IX. Special Sundays.

¶ **273.** The special Sundays in The United Methodist Church are intended to be illustrative of the nature and calling of the Church and are celebrated annually. The special Sundays are placed on the calendar in the context of the Christian year, which is designed to make clear the calling of the Church as the people of God, and to give persons the opportunity of contributing offerings to special programs.

Six special churchwide Sundays provide for churchwide offerings to do deeds expressive of our commitment: Human Relations Day, One Great Hour of Sharing, World Communion Sunday, United Methodist Student Day, Peace with Justice Sunday, and Native American Awareness Sunday. Three special Sundays without offering: Heritage Sunday, Laity Sunday, and Rural Life Sunday. One churchwide Sunday, Christian Education Sunday, and one Annual Conference Sunday, Golden

Cross Sunday, provide opportunities for Annual Conference offerings.

The special Sundays approved by General Conference shall be the only Sundays of churchwide emphasis. The program calendar of the denomination shall include only the special Sundays approved by General Conference, special Sundays approved by ecumenical agencies to which The United Methodist Church is officially related, and the days and seasons of the Christian year.

GENERAL PROVISIONS
REGARDING CHURCHWIDE SPECIAL SUNDAYS WITH OFFERINGS

¶ 274. Six special churchwide Sundays provide for church-wide offerings to express our commitment.

Purpose.—The purpose of the churchwide offerings shall be determined by General Conference upon recommendation of the General Council on Finance and Administration, after consultation with the Council of Bishops and the General Council on Ministries. The purpose of these funds shall remain constant for the quadrennium. The funds shall be promoted by the General Commission on Communication in cooperation with the agencies responsible for the administration of these funds. (*See* ¶ 1906.12.)

Each offering shall be promptly remitted in full by the local church treasurer to the Annual Conference treasurer, who shall transmit the funds in full to the General Council on Finance and Administration within thirty (30) days of receipt in the office of the Annual Conference treasurer.

1. *Human Relations Day*—Human Relations Day shall be observed during the Season of Epiphany on the Sunday before the observance of Martin Luther King, Jr.'s birthday with an offering recommended by the General Council on Finance and Administration and adopted by the General Conference. Epiphany is the season of manifesting God's light to the world. Human Relations Day calls the Church to recognize the right of all God's children in realizing their potential as human beings in relationship with each other. The purpose of the day is to further the development of better human relations through

183

funding programs determined by the General Conference upon recommendation of the General Council on Finance and Administration after consultation with the General Council on Ministries.

For the 1989–1992 quadrennium the offering receipts will be allocated and administered as follows:

a) Community Developers Program: 57 percent (administered by the National Division, General Board of Global Ministries).

b) United Methodist Voluntary Services Program: 33 percent (administered by the National Division, General Board of Global Ministries).

c) Youth Offender Rehabilitation Program: 10 percent (administered by the General Board of Church and Society).

Net receipts of the Human Relations Day Offering shall be distributed on ratio to the administering agencies.

2. *One Great Hour of Sharing*—One Great Hour of Sharing shall be observed on the fourth Sunday of Lent. Lent is the season of repentance, self-examination, and awareness of the hurts of the peoples of the world. One Great Hour of Sharing calls the Church to share the goodness of life with those who hurt. All local churches shall be fully informed and encouraged to receive a freewill offering in behalf of the relief program. The observance shall be under the general supervision of the General Commission on Communication. Insofar as possible, the planning and promotion of the One Great Hour of Sharing shall be done cooperatively with other denominations through the National Council of the Churches of Christ in the U.S.A., it being understood, however, that receipts shall be administered by The United Methodist Church. Net receipts from the offering, after payment of the expenses of promotion, shall be remitted by the treasurer of the General Council on Finance and Administration to the United Methodist Committee on Relief Department of the General Board of Global Ministries, to be administered by that department.

3. *World Communion Sunday*—World Communion Sunday shall be observed the first Sunday of October. World Communion Sunday calls the Church to be the catholic inclusive Church. In connection with World Communion Sunday there shall be a

churchwide appeal conducted by the General Commission on Communication in accord with the following directives: Each local church shall be requested to remit as provided in ¶ 916.7 all the communion offering received on World Communion Sunday and such portion of the communion offering received at other observances of the Sacrament of the Lord's Supper as the local church may designate.

The net receipts, after payment of promotional costs, shall be divided as follows: 50 percent for Crusade Scholarships, to be administered by the Crusade Scholarship Committee; 35 percent for the Ethnic Scholarship Program; and 15 percent for the Ethnic In-Service Training Program; the last two to be administered by the General Board of Higher Education and Ministry. Over one-half must go to ministries beyond the United States of America.

4. *United Methodist Student Day*—United Methodist Student Day shall be observed on the Sunday after Thanksgiving. United Methodist Student Day calls the Church to support students as they prepare for life in uniting faith with knowledge. The United Methodist Student Day offering, taken annually on the Sunday after Thanksgiving, shall be received for the support of the United Methodist Scholarships and the United Methodist Student Loan Fund. (The changes in ¶ 274.4 become effective upon the adjournment of the 1988 General Conference.) Net receipts from the offering, after payment of the expenses of promotion, shall be remitted by the treasurer of the General Council on Finance and Administration to the General Board of Higher Education and Ministry, to be administered by that board.

5. *Peace with Justice Sunday*—Peace with Justice Sunday shall be observed on the Second Sunday after Pentecost. Peace with Justice witnesses to God's demand for a faithful, just, disarmed, and secure world. The observance of Peace with Justice Sunday shall be under the general supervision of the General Board of Church and Society. Net receipts from the offering will be distributed as follows:

a) There shall be a churchwide appeal and offering. All receipts shall be remitted by the local church treasurer to the Annual Conference treasurer.

b) The Annual Conference treasurer shall retain 50 percent of the moneys for Peace with Justice Ministries in the Annual Conference, to be administered by the Annual Conference Board of Church and Society or equivalent structure.

c) The Annual Conference treasurer shall remit the remaining 50 percent of the moneys to the General Council on Finance and Administration. Net receipts from the offering after payment of the expenses of promotion shall be remitted by the treasurer of the General Council on Finance and Administration to the General Board of Church and Society for Peace with Justice Ministries.

6. *Native American Awareness Sunday*—Native American Awareness Sunday shall be observed annually on a day to be determined by the General Council on Ministries. This Sunday serves to remind the Church of the gifts and contributions made by Native Americans to our society. The observance of Native American Awareness Sunday will be under the general supervision of the General Board of Global Ministries.

a) There shall be a churchwide appeal and offering. All receipts shall be remitted by the local church treasurer to the Annual Conference treasurer.

b) The Annual Conference treasurer shall retain 50 percent of the moneys for the developing and strengthening of Native American ministries within the Annual Conference, to be administered by the Conference Board of Global Ministries.

Should there be no Native American Ministries within the Annual Conference, the Annual Conference Treasurer shall remit this 50 percent to the General Council on Finance and Administration to be used by the General Board of Global Ministries to expand the number of target cities in their Native American Urban Initiative.

c) The Annual Conference Treasurer shall remit the remaining 50 percent of the moneys to the General Council on Finance and Administration. Net receipts from the offering after the payment of the expenses of promotion shall be remitted by the treasurer of the General Council on Finance and Administration to the General Board of Higher Education and Ministries for use to provide scholarships for Native Americans attending United Methodist schools of theology.

¶ 275. Three special Sundays, without churchwide offering shall be approved by General Conference upon recommendation of the General Council on Ministries after consultation with the Council of Bishops. The program functions assigned to the general agencies are carried out by the respective agencies through normal programmatic channels. Special Sundays are not needed for these program functions to be implemented.

1. *Heritage Sunday*—Heritage Sunday shall be observed on April 23, the day in 1968 when The United Methodist Church was created by the union of The Evangelical United Brethren Church and The Methodist Church, or the Sunday following that date. It falls during Eastertide, the season in which we remember the Resurrection and triumph of our Lord. Heritage Sunday calls the Church to remember the past by committing itself to the continuing call of God. The observance of Heritage Sunday shall be under the general supervision of the General Commission on Archives and History. Any general agency of the Church which desires to recommend a theme for a given year for this Sunday may do so one year prior to the observance for which the recommendation is made. This recommendation is to be made to the General Commission on Archives and History, and the decision of the annual theme of this Sunday shall be made by the voting members of the General Commission on Archives and History.

2. *Laity Sunday*—Laity Sunday shall be observed on the third Sunday in October. Laity Sunday calls the Church to celebrate the ministry of all lay Christians, as their lives are empowered for ministry by the Holy Spirit. The observance of Laity Sunday shall be under the general supervision of the General Board of Discipleship. Any general agency of the Church which desires to recommend a theme for a given year for this Sunday may do so two years prior to the observance for which the recommendation is made. This recommendation is to be made to the General Board of Discipleship, and the decision of the annual theme of this Sunday shall be made by the voting members of the General Board of Discipleship.

3. *Rural Life Sunday*—Rural Life Sunday shall be observed annually on a Sunday determined by each Annual Conference. Rural Life Sunday calls the Church to celebrate the rural roots of The United Methodist Church and to affirm worldwide the people and communities who work with and on the land raising food and fiber for the world's people. The observance of Rural Life Sunday shall be under the general supervision of the General Board of Global Ministries. Any general agency of the Church which desires to recommend a theme for a given year for this Sunday may do so one year prior to the observance for which the recommendation is made. This recommendation is to be made to the General Board of Global Ministries, and the decision of the annual theme of this Sunday shall be made by the voting members of the General Board of Global Ministries.

¶ **276.** Two special Sundays, approved by General Conference, provide opportunities for Annual Conference offerings.

1. *Christian Education Sunday*—Christian Education Sunday shall be observed on a date determined by the Annual Conference. It calls the Church as the people of God to be open to growth and learning as disciples of Jesus Christ. If the Annual Conference so directs, an offering may be received for the work of Christian education within the Annual Conference. Local church treasurers shall remit the receipts of the offering to the Annual Conference treasurer, and receipts will be acknowledged in accordance with the procedure of the Annual Conference. Local churches shall report the amount of the offering in the manner indicated in the Local Church Report to the Annual Conference.

2. *Golden Cross Sunday*—Golden Cross Sunday shall be observed annually on the first Sunday in May. If the Annual Conference so directs, an offering may be received for the work of health and welfare ministries in the Annual Conference. Local church treasurers shall remit the receipts of the offering to the Annual Conference treasurer, and receipts will be acknowledged in accordance with the procedure of the Annual Conference. Local churches shall report the amount of the offering in the manner indicated on the Local Church Report to the Annual Conference.

Annual Conferences may determine other special Sundays

with or without offering. Special Sundays with offering shall be approved by the Annual Conference upon recommendation of the Annual Conference Council on Ministries in consultation with Annual Conference Council on Finance and Administration. Special Sundays without offering shall be approved by the Annual Conference upon recommendation of the Annual Conference Council on Ministries.

Section X. Lay Speaking.

¶ **277.** *Local Church Lay Speaker.*—1. A **lay speaker** is a member of a local church or charge who is ready and desirous to serve the Church and who is well informed on the Scriptures and the doctrine, heritage, organization, and life of The United Methodist Church and who has received specific training to develop skills in witnessing to the Christian faith through spoken communication, church and community leadership, and care-giving ministries. An applicant must be active in the support of his/her local church or charge.

2. Lay speakers are to serve the local church or charge in any way in which their witness of leadership and service inspires the laity to deeper commitment to Christ and more effective discipleship, including the interpretation of the Scriptures, doctrine, organization, and ministries of the Church.

3. The applicant shall apply in writing with a recommendation from the pastor and the Administrative Council or Administrative Board or Charge Conference of the church or charge in which he/she holds membership to the appropriate district or conference committee. The pastor shall be responsible for reporting the names of applicants to the district director of lay speaking. The applicant shall then complete a basic training course for lay speakers recommended by the General Board of Discipleship or an alternate approved by appropriate committee. Such training should enable ministries with all language and cultural groups as appropriate. To maintain status, a report and re-application must be submitted annually. (*See* ¶ 247.12.)

4. Through continued study and training, a lay speaker should prepare to undertake one or more of the following functions, giving primary attention to service within the local church or charge.

a) To take initiative in giving assistance and support to the program emphases of the Church and to assist in giving vital leadership to the total work of the Church.

b) To assist in the conduct of worship services and to lead meetings for prayer, study, and discussion when requested by the pastor.

c) To conduct services of worship, present sermons and addresses, and lead meetings for study and training in the local church or charge in which the lay speaker holds membership, when requested by the pastor.

d) To relate to appropriate committees and work areas in the local church in providing leadership for congregational and community life and fostering care-giving ministries.

¶ **278.** *Certified Lay Speaker.*—1. A candidate may be certified as a lay speaker by the district or conference Committee on Lay Speaking (or other responsible group as the district or conference may determine) after the candidate has:

a) Made application in writing to the appropriate committee and has been recommended by the pastor and the Administrative Council or Administrative Board or the Charge Conference of the local church in which he or she holds membership.

b) Completed both basic and one advanced training courses for lay speakers that have been recommended by the General Board of Discipleship or an alternate approved by the appropriate committee.

c) Appeared before the appropriate committee for a review of his/her application and a consideration of the responsibilities of a lay speaker. (*See* ¶ 277.4.)

2. The certified lay speaker shall continue to serve the local church in the witness of the spoken word and vital leadership service and care-giving ministry.

a) By taking initiative in giving assistance and support to the program emphases of the Church.

b) By helping in the conduct of worship services and by leading meetings for prayer, study, and discussion when requested by the pastor.

c) By conducting services of worship, presenting sermons and addresses, and leading meetings for study and training in settings other than those in the local church in which the certified lay speaker holds membership, when recommended or requested by a pastor or district superintendent.

d) By relating to appropriate committees and work areas in the local church, district, and conference in providing leadership for congregational and community life and fostering care-giving ministries.

3. It is recommended that a consecration service planned by the district Committee on Lay Speaking be held in the district for persons certified as lay speakers.

¶ 279. *Renewal of Certification of a Certified Lay Speaker.*— The certification of a certified lay speaker shall be reviewed annually by the district or conference Committee on Lay Speaking (or other responsible group as the district or conference may determine), after the certified lay speaker has:

a) Requested in writing the renewal of certification.

b) Submitted an annual report to his/her Charge Conference and the appropriate committee, giving evidence of the satisfactory performance of activities related to the office of certified lay speaker.

c) Been recommended by the pastor and the Administrative Council or Administrative Board or Charge Conference.

d) Completed at least once in every three years an advanced course for lay speakers, which may be one recommended by the General Board of Discipleship or an alternate approved by the appropriate committee. These advanced courses should enable ministries with all language and cultural groups as appropriate.

Chapter Two

THE DIACONAL MINISTRY

Section I. Relation to the Ministry of All Christians.

¶ **301.** The New Testament witness to Jesus Christ makes clear that the primary form of his ministry, in God's name, was that of service (diakonia) in the world. Very early in its history the Church came to understand that all of its members were commissioned, in baptism, to ministries of love, justice, and service, within local congregations and the larger communities in which they lived; all who follow Jesus have a share in the ministry of Jesus, who came not to be served, but to serve. There is thus a general ministry of all baptized Christians (¶¶ 105-107).

The Church also affirms that particular persons are called and set apart for representative ministries of leadership within the body, to help the whole of the membership of the Church be engaged in and fulfill its ministry of service (¶ 109). The purpose of such leadership is the equipping of the general ministry of the Church, to the end that the whole Church may be built up as the Body of Christ for the work of ministry. This set-apart ministry is not a substitute for the diaconal responsibility of all members of the general ministry. Rather, it exists to intensify and make more effective the self-understanding of the whole People of God as servants in Christ's name.

Section II. The Nature of Diaconal Ministry.

¶ **302.** The words *deacon, deaconess, diaconate,* and *diaconal* all spring from a common Greek root—*diakonia,* or "service." Very early in its history the Church instituted an order of ordained ministers to personify or focus the servanthood to which all Christians are called. These people were named deacons.

Those who are called to this representative ministry of service in the Church and world may be set apart to the office of diaconal minister. This ministry exemplifies the servanthood every Christian is called to live in both Church and world. Participating with the elder in the leadership of worship, working in a serving-profession in the Church, and serving the needs of the poor, the sick, or oppressed, the diaconal minister embodies the unity of the congregation's worship with its life in the world.

Section III.   Entrance into Diaconal Ministry.

¶ **303.** The diaconal ministry is recognized by The United Methodist Church as a called-out and set-apart ministry. Therefore, it is appropriate that those persons who present themselves as candidates for diaconal ministry be examined regarding the authenticity of their call by God to this office. Accordingly, let those who consider recommending such persons for candidacy as diaconal ministers in The United Methodist Church prayerfully and earnestly ask themselves these historic questions, as applied to the nature of diaconal ministry:

1. Do they know God as a pardoning God? Do they desire nothing but God? Are they holy in all manner of conversation?

2. Have they gifts, as well as evidence of God's grace, for the work of diaconal ministry? Have they the love of God abiding in them? Do they show forth that love in service to others? Have they an abiding sense of the urgency for justice in the world?

3. Have they fruit? Are others edified by their service?

As long as these signs are visible in them, we believe they are called of God to serve. These we receive as sufficient proof that they are moved by the Holy Spirit.[1]

¶ **304.** *Candidacy for Diaconal Ministry.*—A person seeking to enter the diaconal ministry of The United Methodist Church, upon hearing and heeding the call to serve, shall initiate the process toward the diaconal ministry by contacting the conference Board of Diaconal Ministry to take the first step to qualify as a candidate. The person thus is under the care and supervision of the conference Board of Diaconal Ministry. (Where appropriate, the candidates may also be related to a district committee on diaconal ministry.) A certificate of candidacy may be issued by the conference Board of Diaconal Ministry after the person has met the following conditions.

---

[1] These questions were first asked by John Wesley at the third conference of Methodist preachers in 1746. They have been retained ever since, in substantially the same words, as the standards by which prospective Methodist ordained ministers have been judged. Here they have been edited for the office of diaconal minister.

1. Each person seeking to enter the diaconal ministry must have agreed for the sake of the mission of Jesus Christ in the world and the most effective witness to the Christian gospel, and in consideration of his/her influence as a minister, to make a complete dedication of himself/herself to the highest ideals of the Christian life as set forth in ¶¶ 66-76 and to this end agree to exercise responsible self-control by personal habits conducive to the bodily health, mental and emotional maturity, fidelity in marriage and celibacy in singleness, social responsibility, and growth in grace and the knowledge and love of God.

2. Each person must have been a member in good standing of a local United Methodist congregation for at least one year immediately preceding the application for candidacy.

3. Each person must have been graduated from an accredited high school or its equivalent. He/she must have completed the exploration phase preceeding the candidacy process as prescribed by the Division of Diaconal Ministry.

4. Each person must have met with the Committee on Pastor-Parish (Staff-Parish) Relations and the pastor of his/her local congregation for consultation after submitting a written request and statement; the committee shall use the questions in ¶ 303 as a guide in examination of the person and shall make its recommendation to the Charge Conference.

5. Each person must have secured the recommendation of the Charge Conference of the local church in which he/she holds membership in the following way: A Charge Conference for the purpose of recommending a person for diaconal candidacy must be preceded by at least two public announcements. The authorized presiding elder shall counsel with those present regarding the ability and qualifications of the applicant and make plain the importance of such recommendation to the diaconal candidacy; to be valid, such a recommendation must be voted by written ballot by two-thirds of the members of the Charge Conference present at this meeting. An affiliate member can be recommended by the Charge Conference provided he/she has been an affiliate member of that local congregation for one year, has been in consultation and has received the support of the Charge Conference of the home church where membership is held.

6. Each person must have applied to the conference Board

of Diaconal Ministry in writing and be interviewed for candidacy. The conference board will then determine whether or not the person will be approved as an official candidate before a candidacy certificate may be issued.

7. The conference Board of Diaconal Ministry shall require psychological assessment to provide additional information on each person's gifts for diaconal ministry following the criteria established by the Division of Diaconal Ministry. This assessment shall occur during the first year of candidacy and prior to the first renewal of candidacy. He/she must complete the studies exploring his/her spiritual, professional, academic, and personal potentialities as recommended by the Division of Diaconal Ministry and provide such other information as the board may require for determining his/her gifts and promise for ministry.

¶ **305.** *Continuation of Candidacy.*—The progress of candidates must be reviewed and candidacy renewed annually. On recommendation of the Charge Conference, continuing evidence of the candidate's gifts, evidence of God's grace, and fruits, and satisfactory progress in the required studies, candidacy shall be renewed by the conference Board of Diaconal Ministry.

1. A candidate who is preparing to become a diaconal minister and is enrolled in a school, college, university, or school of theology listed by the University Senate or approved by a regional or state accrediting agency shall present annually to the conference Board of Diaconal Ministry a statement of academic progress from the school the person is attending. This statement shall take the place of any formal examination, providing academic progress and character are satisfactory.

2. A candidate who is already certified in a professional career shall complete the foundational studies for diaconal ministers.

3. When a candidate for diaconal ministry desires to transfer to another Annual Conference, the candidate shall notify the receiving conference board to request the files from the sending conference board. The receiving conference board shall acknowledge the candidacy, interview the candidate, and inform the candidate of the board's procedures and expectations, which include local church membership in that Annual Conference.

4. When candidacy has lapsed, it may be reinstated by action of the conference Board of Diaconal Ministry only when the

candidate has completed satisfactorily the current candidacy requirements.

¶ **306.** *Completion of Candidacy.*—A person shall be eligible for consecration as a diaconal minister in the Annual Conference by vote of the Annual Conference on recommendation of its Board of Diaconal Ministry after meeting the following qualifications:

1. Each candidate must have been in candidacy for diaconal ministry for at least one year and no more than eight years.

2. Each candidate must have been employed for a minimum of one year immediately preceding consecration and be currently employed in a position approved by the board in the conference where he/she is employed; such position should be consistent with ¶ 310.1.

3. Each candidate must have met the following educational requirements:

a) Must have received a bachelor's degree, or demonstrate competency equivalence, through an external degree program from a college or university listed by the University Senate or approved by a regional or state accrediting agency. Exceptions to the undergraduate degree requirement may be made in consultation with the Division of Diaconal Ministry in rare instances for persons who (1) have been prevented from pursuit of the normal course of baccalaureate education, or who (2) are members of groups whose cultural practices and training enhance insight and skills for effective ministry not available through conventional formal education.

b) Must have: (1) received a graduate theological degree from a school approved by the University Senate; or (2) received a master's degree from a graduate school listed by the University Senate or approved by a regional or state accrediting agency; or (3) completed the academic requirements for professional certification; or (4) been commissioned by the General Board of Global Ministries for service either in the United States or in other countries.

c) Must have completed the basic studies of the Christian faith: Bible—Old Testament, New Testament, theology, church history (including United Methodist history), mission of the Church in the world, United Methodist doctrine and polity—

196

either through a graduate degree program or through the Foundational Course of Study for Diaconal Ministers under the supervision and verification of the Division of Diaconal Ministry of the General Board of Higher Education and Ministry. Each course must be taken for no less than two semester or equivalent quarter hours of graduate academic credit.

The Board of Diaconal Ministry shall require an official transcript of credits from each applicant before recognizing any of the applicant's educational claims. In case of doubt, the board may submit a transcript to the Division of Diaconal Ministry for evaluation.

4. Each candidate must present a satisfactory certificate of good health by a physician on the prescribed form. Handicapping conditions are not to be construed as unfavorable health factors when such a person is capable of meeting the professional standards and is physically able to render effective service in the office of diaconal minister.

5. Each candidate must have responded to a written and/or oral doctrinal examination administered by the conference Board of Diaconal Ministry. The examination must cover the following:

a) Describe your personal experience of God and the understanding of God you derive from biblical, theological, and historical sources.

b) What is the Christian understanding of humanity, and the human need for divine grace?

c) How do you interpret the statement "Jesus Christ is Lord"?

d) What is your conception of the activity of the Holy Spirit in personal faith, in the community of believers, and in responsible living in the world?

e) The United Methodist Church holds that Scripture, tradition, experience, and reason are sources and norms for belief and practice, but that the Bible is primary among them. What is your understanding of this theological position of the Church?

f) What are the marks of the Christian life? What is your understanding of the Christian life as set forth in the Articles of Religion, the statement of Our Theological Task, and the Social

Principles in the Book of Discipline of The United Methodist Church?

g) Describe the nature and mission of the Church. What are its primary tasks today?

h) What is your understanding of (1) the Kingdom of God, (2) the Resurrection, (3) eternal life?

i) How do you perceive yourself, your gifts, your motives, your role, and your commitment as a diaconal minister?

j) What is the meaning and significance of diakonia?

k) What is the meaning of consecration and ordination, especially in the context of the general ministry of the Church?

l) What is your understanding of the organization, structure, and function of The United Methodist Church?

m) What is your understanding of the relationship of the diaconal minister to the Annual Conference and The United Methodist Church?

n) Describe your understanding of and appreciation for persons of different racial/ethnic heritages.

o) Are you willing to relate to and serve all persons without regard to race, color, national origin, or social status?

6. Each candidate must have a personal interview with the conference Board of Diaconal Ministry to complete his/her candidacy.

Section IV.   Relationship to the Annual Conference.

¶ **307.** *Consecration.*—The diaconal minister's relationship to the Annual Conference of The United Methodist Church shall be conferred by the act of consecration. Consecration should take place in the Annual Conference where local membership is held. Consecration to the office of diaconal minister shall be at the Annual Conference session following the guidelines established by the Division of Diaconal Ministry. The Service for Consecration and the Service for Ordination may be incorporated into one service. The bishop and secretary of the Annual Conference shall provide credentials to the diaconal minister upon consecration.

¶ **308.** *General Provisions.*—Diaconal ministers shall be amenable to the Annual Conference in the performance of their duties as diaconal ministers.

¶ **309.** *Rights of Diaconal Ministers.*—1. The diaconal minister shall have the rights of voice and vote in the Annual Conference where church membership is held; shall be eligible to serve as a lay person on boards, commissions, or committees of the Annual Conference and hold office on the same; shall be eligible for election as a lay delegate to the General or Jurisdictional Conference. The diaconal minister shall attend the sessions of the Annual Conference. Any diaconal minister unable to attend shall report by letter to the bishop setting forth the reason for the absence.[2]

2. The bishop, representatives of the Cabinet and conference Board of Diaconal Ministry shall provide an opportunity to meet annually with the diaconal ministers of the conference. The bishop shall convene the meeting which is to be planned by the Cabinet and the Board of Diaconal Ministry. The purpose of this meeting is to gain understanding of one another's role and function in ministry.

¶ **310.** *Service Appointment of Diaconal Ministers.*—1. Diaconal ministers may serve:

a) Within a local congregation, charge, or cooperative parish,

b) Through United Methodist Church–related agencies, ecumenical agencies, or

c) Through other ministries which extend the witness and service of Christ's love and justice in the world through equipping persons to fulfill their own calls to Christian service.

2. This service shall be in a setting which allows one to fulfill the call to specialized ministry and provides supervision with goals, evaluation, and accountability acceptable to the Board of Diaconal Ministry, Cabinet, and the bishop.

3. Service shall mean that the majority of the person's vocational time is devoted to the work of ministry in the field of service approved by the bishop.

4. Diaconal ministers serve in a nonitinerating ministry. A district superintendent or bishop may initiate or recommend an appointment, but they have no responsibility to do so.

5. The service appointment of the diaconal minister shall be:

---

[2]*See* Judicial Council Decisions 391, 464.

a) Initiated by the individual diaconal minister or agency seeking his/her service;

b) Clarified by a written statement of intentionality of diakonia in order to establish a clear distinction between the work to which all Christians are called and the work for which diaconal ministers are appropriately prepared and authorized;

c) Recommended by the conference Board of Diaconal Ministry;

d) Reviewed by the Cabinet and approved by the bishop of the Annual Conference.

6. A diaconal minister may serve less than full-time. This shall mean that a specified amount of time, agreed upon by the bishop and the Cabinet, the diaconal minister, and the Annual Conference Board of Diaconal Ministry, is devoted to the work of ministry in the field of service to which the person is appointed by the bishop. At his/her own initiative, a diaconal minister may request, and the bishop may approve, a service appointment to less than full-time service; *provided* that the following conditions are met:

a) The diaconal minister shall present a written request to the bishop and the conference Board of Diaconal Ministry, giving rationale for the request at least six months prior to the Annual Conference at which the service appointment is to be made.

b) Reappointment to less than full-time service shall be requested of the bishop by the diaconal minister annually and shall be approved annually by the conference Board of Diaconal Ministry.

c) The bishop may make an ad-interim service appointment of less than full-time service upon request of a diaconal minister with the recommendation of the executive committee of the conference Board of Diaconal Ministry. Action by the entire board shall be taken on the appointment prior to the next Annual Conference.

¶ **311.** *Credentials and Records.*—The diaconal ministers' credentials and records shall be maintained by the conference Board of Diaconal Ministry in the conference to which they relate. The diaconal ministers' credentials and records shall be transferred from one Annual Conference to another on recommendation of the conference Boards of Diaconal Ministry and the approval of the Annual Conferences involved.

¶ **312.** *Transfers.*—Diaconal ministers moving from one Annual Conference to another conference in The United Methodist Church may be received by transfer with the approval of the receiving bishop following that bishop's consultation with the chairperson or executive committee of the receiving conference Board of Diaconal Ministry. The place of service appointment shall have been approved by the receiving bishop.

¶ **313.** *Change in Conference Relationship.*—Diaconal ministers seeking a change in conference relationship shall make written request to their conference Board of Diaconal Ministry stating the reasons for the requested change in status. In addition, the Board of Diaconal Ministry may request personal interviews with diaconal ministers requesting the change in status. The conference Board of Diaconal Ministry will be in consultation with the Cabinet.

1. *Leaves of Absence.*—Each leave or return to active status granted by the Annual Conference shall be recorded in the conference journal. When a diaconal minister requests a leave or return to active status between sessions of the Annual Conference, the executive committee of the conference Board of Diaconal Ministry, in consultation with the diaconal minister, the district superintendent, and the employing agency, may recommend the leave of absence or return to active status for approval by the bishop for the remainder of the conference year. Any such leave or return granted between sessions of the Annual Conference, with the effective date of such leave, shall be entered in the conference journal of the next regular session of the conference.

a) Disability Leave.—When diaconal ministers are forced to give up their ministry because of their physical or emotional disability, upon recommendation of the conference Board of Diaconal Ministry and by a majority vote of the members of the Annual Conference, they may be granted annual disability leave without losing their relationship to the Annual Conference. When diaconal ministers on disability leave recover sufficiently to resume their ministry, they may return to an active relationship to the Annual Conference through the process described for a service appointment (¶ 310).

b) Maternity/Paternity Leave.—Maternity/paternity leave up to one-fourth of a year will be available to any diaconal minister who so requests it at the birth or arrival into the home for purposes of adoption of a child. During the leave, the diaconal minister's Annual Conference relations shall remain unchanged, and the insurance coverage will remain in force. It is recommended that salary be maintained for no less than the first six weeks of the leave. Persons desiring maternity/paternity leave should file their request with the personnel committee of the employing agency and the conference Board of Diaconal Ministry prior to its beginning.

c) Study/Sabbatical Leave.—Diaconal ministers shall be encouraged to continue their education throughout their careers, including pursuit of carefully developed personal programs of study augmented periodically by involvement in organized educational activities. A study leave of up to one year negotiated by a diaconal minister, his/her employing agency, and the conference Board of Diaconal Ministry shall not affect the relationship to the Annual Conference. The leave may be renewed annually up to five years if the diaconal minister is enrolled in a degree program. The diaconal minister's continuing education program should allow for leaves of absence for study at least one week each year and at least one month during one year of each quadrennium. Such leaves shall not be considered as part of the diaconal minister's vacation and should be planned in consultation with his/her employing agency. Diaconal ministers shall be asked by the district superintendent in the Charge Conference to outline their programs of continuing education for the year.

d) Personal Leave.—When a diaconal minister is temporarily unable or unwilling to perform the work of his/her ministry, a personal leave of absence may be granted upon recommendation of the conference Board of Diaconal Ministry. This relationship shall be approved annually and shall not exceed five consecutive years.

e) In exceptional circumstances, an extended leave, beyond that described in ¶ 312.1(*d*), may be granted upon the approval of the conference Board of Diaconal Ministry. When a diaconal minister is on extended leave, he/she shall not have voice or vote in the Annual Conference. He/she may request reinstatement upon recommendation of the conference Board of Diaconal Ministry and vote of the Annual Conference.

2. *Retired Relationship.*—Retired diaconal ministers are those who at their own request or by action of the members of the Annual Conference, on recommendation of the conference Board of Diaconal Ministry, have been placed in the retired relationship.

a) A diaconal minister may take retired relationship in the Annual Conference upon reaching age sixty-two by July 1 in the year of retirement or after twenty years of service.

b) By a two-thirds vote of those present and voting, the Annual Conference may place diaconal ministers in the retired relation with or without their consent and irrespective of their age if such relation is recommended by the conference Board of Diaconal Ministry. The conference Board of Diaconal Ministry shall provide guidance and counseling to the retiring member.

c) Every diaconal minister whose seventieth birthday is on or before July 1 shall automatically be retired from the active relationship at the conference session closest to that date.

d) Retired diaconal ministers shall be listed annually in the journal of the Annual Conference in which their retired relationship is held.

3. *Termination of Conference Relationship.—a) Voluntary Termination.*—A diaconal minister who desires to withdraw from the Annual Conference may, after consultation with the conference Board of Diaconal Ministry, deposit his/her credentials with the bishop between sessions of the Annual Conference. When this action is taken between sessions of the Annual Conference, it shall be reported by the conference Board of Diaconal Ministry for confirmation by the Annual Conference at its next regular session.

b) Involuntary Termination.—A diaconal minister's relationship to the Annual Conference may be terminated by a two-thirds vote of the members of the Annual Conference on recommendation of the conference Board of Diaconal Ministry. Termination may be recommended, in consultation with the diaconal minister in question, on the basis of incompetence in professional function, indifference to the work of the ministry, or personal conduct which is deemed seriously to impair usefulness as a diaconal minister (Chapter Eight, Section II).

c) A diaconal minister's relationship to the Annual Conference may be reinstated if the following conditions are met: (1) Satisfactory report and recommendation by the Charge Conference and pastor of the local church in which his/her membership is held; (2) recommendation of the conference Board of Diaconal Ministry following a review of his/her qualifications and circumstances related to his/her determination; (3) majority vote of the members of the Annual Conference.

Section V.   Relationship to the Charge Conference.

¶ **314.** 1. A person appointed as a diaconal minister to a local congregation, charge, or cooperative parish shall be a member of a local church within the community where she/he resides and/or works, and a voting member of its Charge Conference.

2. A person appointed as a diaconal minister in a church-related agency within his/her Annual Conference shall be a member of a local church and be a voting member of its Charge Conference in the community where he/she resides, or in a neighboring community.

3. A person appointed as a diaconal minister in a church-related agency outside his/her Annual Conference shall be a member of a local church and be a voting member of its Charge Conference in the community where he/she resides or shall have membership in a local church within his/her home Annual Conference, in which case he/she shall have an affiliate membership in the Charge Conference of a local church in the community in which he/she resides, or in a neighboring community.

4. A person appointed as a diaconal minister to a ministry which extends the witness and service of Christ's love and justice in the world other than a church-related agency shall be a member of a local church and be a voting member of its Charge Conference, after consultation with the pastor, in the community where he/she resides, or in a neighboring community.

5. The diaconal minister shall make a report to the Charge Conference of which he/she is a member.

Section VI. Relationship to the Employing Agency.

¶ **315.** The employing agency in which a full-time diaconal minister is serving shall provide:

1. Adequate salaries plus pension benefits, with an opportunity to participate in the United Methodist pension and benefit funds, health-care insurance, and continuing education. It is expected that these will be guided by the Annual Conference standards for ordained elders.

2. Social Security benefits as required by Federal legislation.

3. The local United Methodist church which employs a full-time diaconal minister shall provide the above-mentioned benefits in entirety as part of compensatory consideration.

4. When a diaconal minister is employed by a local church, it is the responsibility of the Committee on Pastor-Parish (Staff-Parish) Relations to act as the employing agent for the Administrative Board. This committee, in consultation with the pastor in charge, shall interview, employ, issue job descriptions and contracts (which clearly state employment practices, including procedures for dismissal, vacation, and leave policies), and evaluate and terminate employment (269.2*f*[8]). The diaconal minister shall have full access to the entire committee (269.2*b*).

¶ **316.** In United Methodist churches and other employing agencies there shall be an annual review of the diaconal minister's performance no later than ninety (90) days prior to Annual Conference.

¶ **317.** Since diaconal ministers are not guaranteed a place of employment in the Church, special attention shall be given to termination procedures which allow time for seeking another service appointment. Notification of dismissal shall provide a ninety-day period prior to final termination of employment. The date for termination of employment shall coincide with the date of the Annual Conference or the date stipulated in the contract, except for causes as listed in ¶ 2621.

In turn, the diaconal minister shall give the employing agency ninety days notice regarding resignation unless the contract states otherwise.

The employing agency shall bear sole responsibility for meeting salary obligations and the Annual Conference shall not bear any fiscal responsibility for guaranteeing salary continuance.

Chapter Three

THE ORDAINED MINISTRY

Section I. Relation of Ordained Ministers to the Ministry of All Christians.

¶ **401.** Ministry in the Christian church is derived from the ministry of Christ, the ministry of the Father through the Incarnate Son by the Holy Spirit. It is a ministry bestowed upon and required of the entire Church. All Christians are called to ministry, and theirs is a ministry of the people of God within the community of faith and in the world. Members of The United Methodist Church receive this gift of ministry in company with all Christians and sincerely hope to continue and extend it in the world for which Christ lived, died, and lives again. The United Methodist Church believes that Baptism, confirmation, and responsible membership in the Church are visible signs of acceptance of this ministry. (*See* Part IV, "The Ministry of All Christians," ¶¶ 101-113.)

¶ **402.** 1. There are persons within the ministry of the baptized who are called of God and set apart by the Church for the specialized ministry of Word, Sacrament, and Order (¶¶ 429-436).

2. While such persons set apart by the Church for the ministry of Word, Sacrament, and Order are subject to all the frailties of the human condition and pressures of society, they are required to maintain the highest standards represented by the practice of fidelity in marriage and celibacy in singleness.[1] Since the practice of homosexuality is incompatible with Christian teaching, self-avowed practicing homosexuals are not to be accepted as candidates, ordained as ministers, or appointed to serve in The United Methodist Church.[2]

---

[1]*See* Judicial Council Decision 542.
[2]*See* Judicial Council Decision 544.

Section II.   Entrance Procedures into Ordained Ministry.

¶ **403.** *Wesley's Questions for the Examiners.*—In order that The United Methodist Church may be assured that those persons who present themselves as candidates for ministry are truly called of God to this office, let those who consider recommending such persons for candidacy as ordained ministers in The United Methodist Church prayerfully and earnestly ask themselves these questions:

1. Do they know God as a pardoning God? Have they the love of God abiding in them? Do they desire nothing but God? Are they holy in all manner of conversation?

2. Have they gifts, as well as evidence of God's grace, for the work? Have they a clear, sound understanding; a right judgment in the things of God; a just conception of salvation by faith? Do they speak justly, readily, clearly?

3. Have they fruit? Have any been truly convinced of sin and converted to God, and are believers edified by their preaching?

As long as these marks concur in them, we believe they are called of God to preach. These we receive as sufficient proof that they are moved by the Holy Spirit.[3]

CANDIDACY FOR ORDAINED MINISTRY

¶ **404.** Candidacy for ordained ministry through a process prescribed by the Division of Ordained Ministry of the General Board of Higher Education and Ministry is the first set of formal steps through which a person moves toward ordination and Annual Conference membership.

1. *The Inquiring Candidate.*—Upon hearing a call to ministry the candidate should read the vocational guide *The Christian As Minister.* This book should be discussed in consultation with the candidate's pastor or another United Methodist minister.

---

[3]These questions were first asked by John Wesley at the third conference of Methodist preachers in 1746. They have been retained ever since, in substantially the same words, as the standards by which prospective Methodist preachers have been judged.

2. *The Exploring Candidate.*—Those seeking to explore candidacy for ordained ministry shall *(a)* apply to the district superintendent in writing for admission to candidacy studies as defined by the Division of Ordained Ministry, and *(b)* be assigned as an exploring candidate to a supervising pastor by the district committee and complete appropriate candidacy studies after proper registration through the Annual Conference candidacy registrar and the Division of Ordained Ministry.

3. *The Declared Candidate.*—Those seeking to become certified candidates for ordained ministry shall *(a)* consult with the pastor and Committee on Pastor-Parish Relations after formulating a written statement reflecting their call to ordained ministry and requesting recommendation for certification. The candidate shall be interviewed by the committee on his/her statement and Wesley's historic questions in ¶ 403: and *(b)* be recommended by the Charge Conference in accordance with the following method. A meeting for the purpose of recommending a candidate for the ministry must be preceded by at least two public announcements and must be held in the presence of the bishop, district superintendent, or an authorized elder, who shall counsel with those present regarding the ability and qualifications of the applicant and make plain the importance of such recommendation to the ordained ministry. To be valid such a recommendation must be (i) voted by written ballot by two-thirds of the Charge Conference present at this meeting; (ii) the candidate must have been a member or affiliate member of the congregation for one year; *provided* that in the case of an affiliate member there has been consultation with and approval by the Charge Conference of the home church; and (iii) have been graduated from an accredited high school or received a certificate of equivalency.

4. *The Certified Candidate.*—Candidates who have completed the requirements of ¶ 404.2, .3 and desire to be certified as candidates for ordained ministry shall *(a)* appear before the district Committee on Ordained Ministry for examination; *(b)* make themselves available for any psychological and aptitude tests it may require; submit a written response providing evidence of understanding and expectation to the following: (i) Describe the most important experiences of your Christian life

including your call to ministry; (ii) How do you describe and interpret your response to God's call as you understand it? (iii) What are your future plans for ministry in The United Methodist Church? (iv) Describe your personal beliefs as a Christian; (v) Describe and evaluate your personal gifts for ministry; (vi) Indicate in some detail how your close personal relationships may affect your future ministry; *(c)* submit a written response providing evidence of understanding the expectations and obligations of the itinerant system; *(d)* provide and supply such other information as it may require for determining their gifts, evidence of God's grace, fruits, and demonstration of the call; and *(e)* agree for the sake of the mission of Jesus Christ in the world and the most effective witness of the gospel, and in consideration of their influence as ministers, to make a complete dedication of themselves to the highest ideals of the Christian life as set forth in ¶¶ 66-76, and to this end agree to exercise responsible self-control by personal habits conducive to bodily health, mental and emotional maturity, fidelity in marriage and celibacy in singleness, social responsibility, and growth in grace and the knowledge and love of God.[4]

---

[4]In adopting the statements in ¶¶ 404.4*(e)* and 414.8 on the moral and social responsibility of ordained ministers, the General Conference seeks to elevate the standards by calling for a more thoroughgoing moral commitment by the candidate and for a more careful and thorough examination of candidates by district committees and boards of the ministry.

The legislation in no way implies that the use of tobacco is a morally indifferent question. In the light of the developing evidence against the use of tobacco, the burden of proof would be upon all users to show that their use of it is consistent with the highest ideals of the Christian life. Similarly, regarding beverage alcohol, the burden of proof would be upon users to show that their action is consistent with the ideals of excellence of mind, purity of body, and responsible social behavior.

Therefore, the changes here do not relax the traditional view concerning the use of tobacco and beverage alcohol by ordained ministers in The United Methodist Church. Rather they call for higher standards of self-discipline and habit formation in all personal and social relationships. They call for dimensions of moral commitment that go far beyond any specific practices which might be listed. *See* Judicial Council Decision 318.

The General Conference, in response to expressions throughout the Church regarding homosexuality and ordination, reaffirms the present language of the Discipline regarding the character and commitment of persons seeking ordination, and affirms its high standards.

For more than 200 years candidates for ordination have been asked Wesley's Questions, including ". . . Have they a clear, sound understanding; right

¶ **405.** *Continuation of Candidacy.*—The progress of candidates must be reviewed and candidacy renewed annually. Candidacy may be renewed by the district Committee on Ordained Ministry (¶ 751) on recommendation of the Charge Conference and on evidence that the candidate's gifts, fruits, and evidence of God's grace continue to be satisfactory and that the candidate is making satisfactory progress in the required studies.

1. A candidate preparing to become a probationary member who is enrolled as a student in a school, college, university, or school of theology listed by the University Senate shall present annually to the district Committee on Ordained Ministry an official transcript from the school the person is attending.

The transcript shall be considered by the district Committee on Ordained Ministry along with other evidence that the candidate's gifts, evidence of God's grace, and fruits continue to be satisfactory. An annual personal interview with the candidate is recommended.

2. A candidate who is not a student as defined in ¶ 405.1 shall complete the studies for the license for the local pastor after being accepted as a candidate and shall continue preparation through the five-year course of study under the Division of

---

judgment in the things of God; a just conception of salvation by faith? . . ." (¶ 403).

All candidates agree to make a complete dedication of themselves to the highest ideals of the Christian life, and to this end agree "to exercise responsible self-control, by personal habits conducive to bodily health, mental and emotional maturity, fidelity in marriage and celibacy in singleness, social responsibility, and growth in grace and the knowledge and love of God" (¶ 404).

The character and commitment of candidates for the ordained ministry is described or examined in six places in the Book of Discipline. (¶ 403, 404.4, 414, 421, 424, and 430.) These say in part: "Only those shall be elected to full membership who are of unquestionable moral character and genuine piety, sound in the fundamental doctrines of Christianity and faithful in the discharge of their duties" (¶ 421).

The statement on ordination (¶ 430) states: *It is expected that persons to be ordained shall:*

6. . . . be willing to make a complete dedication of himself/herself to the highest ideals of the Christian life; . . . and agree to exercise responsible self-control by personal habits. . . .

7. Be persons in whom the community can place trust and confidence."

There are eight crucial steps in the examination of candidates. They are:

Ordained Ministry. The course must be completed within eight years after the issuance of the license for the local pastor, except as provided in ¶ 408.2. An Annual Conference Board of Ordained Ministry may require one year in candidacy before application for licensing as a local pastor.

3. When candidacy has lapsed, it may be reinstated at the discretion of the district Committee on Ordained Ministry.

4. A person who is a certified candidate or who is in the candidacy process may have his/her status or studies accepted by another district committee in the same or another Annual Conference.

LOCAL PASTOR

¶ 406. *Authority and Duties.*—1. A **local pastor** is a lay person approved annually by the district Committee on Ordained Ministry and licensed by the bishop to perform all the duties of a pastor (¶ 439) including the Sacraments of Baptism and Holy Communion as well as the service of marriage (where state laws allow), burial, confirmation, and membership reception, while assigned to a particular charge.

2. Such authorization granted by the license may be renewed annually by the district Committee on Ordained Ministry and extends only within the charge to which the local pastor is appointed.

---

(1) The self-examination of the individual seeking ordination as he or she responds to God's call in personal commitment to Christ and his Church.

(2) The decision of the Committee on Pastor-Parish Relations which makes the first recommendation to the Charge Conference when a member seeks to become a candidate for ordained ministry.

(3) The decision of the Charge Conference which must recommend the candidate.

(4) The decision of the district Committee on Ordained Ministry which must recommend the candidate to the conference Board of Ordained Ministry and, where applicable, the decision of the District Conference.

(5) The decision of the Board of Ordained Ministry which must recommend deacon's ordination and probationary membership. *See* Judicial Council Decisions 513, 536, 542.

(6) The decision of the clergy members of the Annual Conference who must elect candidates to deacon's ordination probationary membership.

(7) The recommendation of the Board of Ordained Ministry for elder's ordination and full membership.

3. The license shall remain valid only so long as the appointment continues and must be recertified by the bishop when assignments change between sessions of the Annual Conference.[5]

4. A local pastor shall be under the supervision of a district superintendent and a counseling elder who shall supervise the local pastor's work in the course of study for ordained ministry and give counsel on matters of pastoral responsibility (¶ 411).

5. Local pastors shall be amenable to the Annual Conference in the performance of their pastoral duties and shall attend the sessions of the Annual Conference.

6. The church membership of part-time local pastors (¶ 408.2) shall be in the charge to which they are appointed, and they shall be members of the Charge Conference subject to the annual authorization of the Annual Conference.

7. Student local pastors (¶ 408.3) may retain their membership in their home church and Charge conference, but in the

---

(8) The election to elder's ordination and full membership by the clergy members of the Annual Conference.

All pastors are accountable as to character and effectiveness to the Annual Conference throughout their entire ministry.

The General Conference has made it clear in the "Doctrinal Standards and Our Theological Task" (Part II of the Discipline) that Scripture, tradition, experience, and reason are our guidelines. "United Methodists share with all other Christians the conviction that Scripture is the primary source and guideline for doctrine."

In the Social Principles, the General Conference has said that "we do not condone the practice of homosexuality and consider this practice incompatible with Christian teaching." Furthermore, the Principles state that "we affirm the sanctity of the marriage covenant which is expressed in love, mutual support, personal commitment, and shared fidelity between a man and a woman. We believe that God's blessing rests upon such marriage, whether or not there are women than for men in marriage." Also, "we affirm the integrity of single persons and we reject all social practices that discriminate, or social attitudes that are prejudicial against persons because they are unmarried."

The General Conference affirms the wisdom of our heritage expressed in the Disciplinary provisions relating to the character and commitment of ordained ministers. The United Methodist Church has moved away from prohibitions of specific acts, for such prohibitions can be endless. We affirm our trust in the covenant community and the process by which we ordain ministers.

In our covenant we are called to trust one another as we recommend, examine, and elect candidates for the ordained ministry and conference membership. *See* Judicial Council Decision 480.

[5]*See* Judicial Council Decision 112.

discharge of their ministerial functions they shall be amenable to the district superintendent under whom they serve.

¶ **407.** *License As a Local Pastor.*—All persons not ordained as deacons or elders who preach and conduct divine worship and perform the duties of a pastor under pastoral appointment shall have a license as a local pastor. The district Committee on Ordained Ministry may authorize the licensing of those persons who have:

1. Completed the conditions for candidacy certification in ¶ 404;

2. Completed the studies for the license as a local pastor as prescribed and supervised by the Division of Ordained Ministry, or one-half of their work for a Master of Divinity degree at a school of theology listed by the University Senate;

3. Been examined by the district Committee on Ordained Ministry; and

4. If they are applying for license as a local pastor, been approved by the Board of Ordained Ministry (¶ 732.2*g*) and provided the board with a satisfactory certificate of good health on a prescribed form from a physician approved by that board if they are to be participants in the Comprehensive Protection Plan. The conference may require psychological and/or psychiatric tests and evaluations to provide additional information to qualify for such coverage.

¶ **408.** *Categories of Local Pastor.*—Upon satisfactory completion of the requirements of ¶ 407, the district Committee on Ordained Ministry shall certify the completion of the prescribed studies to the candidates and the Board of Ordained Ministry, and they shall be listed in the journal as eligible to be appointed as local pastors. Award of the license shall not be made until an appointment to a pastoral charge is made in accordance with ¶ 437. In recommending to the Annual Conference those who have met the requirements to serve as local pastors for the ensuing year, the Board of Ordained Ministry shall classify them in three categories with educational and other requirements of their category. Any person who fails to meet these requirements shall be discontinued as a local pastor. The categories shall be defined as follows:

1. *Full-time Local Pastors.*—Those eligible to be appointed full-time local pastors are lay persons *(a)* who have met the provisions for the license as a local pastor (¶ 407); *(b)* who may devote their entire time to the church in the charge to which they are appointed and its outreach in ministry and mission to the community; *(c)* who receive in cash support per annum from all church sources a sum equal to or larger than the minimum salary established by the Annual Conference for full-time local pastors; *(d)* who, unless they have completed the course of study for ordained ministry, shall complete one full year of work per year in a course of study school under the Division of Ordained Ministry (¶ 1529.2); *provided,* however, that in a case of emergency or unusual circumstances, on approval by the board, they may be authorized to pursue not more than one year of studies by correspondence; *(e)* who, when they have completed educational requirements for associate membership, are involved in continuing education (¶ 445);[6] *(f)* who shall not be enrolled as a full-time student in any school.

2. *Part-time Local Pastors.*—Those eligible to be appointed as part-time local pastors are lay persons *(a)* who have met the provisions of ¶ 407; *(b)* who do not devote their entire time to the charge to which they are appointed; or *(c)* do not receive in cash support per annum from all church sources a sum equal to or larger than the minimum salary established by the Annual Conference for full-time local pastors; and *(d)* who, unless they have completed the course of study for ordained ministry, shall complete a minimum of one-half a year's work in the course of study for ordained ministry; *provided,* however, that in a case of emergency or unusual circumstances, on approval by the board, they may be authorized to pursue the course for the current year by correspondence.

3. *Student Local Pastors.*—Those eligible to be appointed as student local pastors shall be enrolled as pretheological or theological students in a college, university, or school of theology listed by the University Senate *(a)* who have met the provisions of ¶ 407; and *(b)* who shall make appropriate progress in their educational program as determined by the Board of Ordained Ministry.

---

[6]*See* Judicial Council Decisions 343, 572.

4. Upon recommendation of the Board of Ordained Ministry, the clergy members in full connection may vote approval annually for students of other denominations enrolled in a school of theology listed by the University Senate to serve as local pastors for the ensuing year under the direction of the district superintendent; *provided* that they shall indicate to the satisfaction of the Board of Ordained Ministry their agreement to support and maintain the doctrine and polity of The United Methodist Church while under appointment.

5. Full-time local pastors may serve on any board, commission, or committee except the Board of Ordained Ministry and Board of Trustees (¶¶ 733.1, 2512.1). They shall not be eligible for election as delegates to the General, Jurisdictional, or Central Conference.

¶ **409.** *Continuance as a Local Pastor.*—1. Persons licensed as local pastors shall continue in the course of study for ordained ministry, in college or in seminary as outlined in ¶ 408, until they have completed the educational requirements for associate or probationary membership.

2. Upon completing each year's education and other qualifications, a local pastor may be recommended for continuance by the district Committee on Ordained Ministry. The clergy members in full connection of the Annual Conference may approve continuance of a local pastor after reference to and recommendation by its Board of Ordained Ministry.

3. A full-time local pastor shall complete the educational requirements within eight years and a part-time local pastor within ten unless a family situation or other circumstance precludes the local pastor's opportunity to meet said requirements. The local pastor may be granted an annual extension beyond the prescribed limit upon a three-fourths vote of the district Committee on Ordained Ministry, recommendation by the conference Board of Ordained Ministry, and the vote of the clergy members in full connection.[7]

4. A local pastor may choose to remain in a local relationship with the Annual Conference upon having completed a minimum of sixty (60) semester hours toward the Bachelor of Arts or an

---

[7]*See* Judicial Council Decisions 436, 439.

equivalent degree in a college or university listed by the University Senate, or competency equivalence through an external degree program at a college or university listed by the University Senate, and the five-year course of study for ordained ministry.

5. An Annual Conference may permit a local pastor to move from associate to full conference membership under the provisions of ¶¶ 416 and 424.

6. None of the provisions in this legislation shall be interpreted to change or limit authorizations to local pastors ordained as deacon and elder prior to 1976 or enrolled in the second year of the ministerial course of study prior to January 1, 1977.[8]

¶ **410.** *Exiting, Reinstatement, and Retirement of Local Pastors.*— 1. *Discontinuance of Local Pastor.*—Whenever a local pastor is no longer approved for appointment by the Annual Conference as required in ¶ 408, or whenever any local pastor severs relationship with The United Methodist Church, or whenever the appointment of a local pastor is discontinued by the bishop, license and credentials shall be surrendered to the district superintendent for deposit with the secretary of the conference. This does not apply to persons who were licensed to preach prior to 1950. After consultation with the pastor, the former local pastor shall designate the local church in which membership shall be held. The Board of Ordained Ministry shall file with the resident bishop a permanent record of the circumstances relating to the discontinuance of local pastor status as required in ¶ 732.3d.

2. *Withdrawal Under Complaints and Charges.*—When a local pastor is accused of an offense under ¶ 2621 and desires to withdraw from the Church, the procedures described in ¶ 2626.2 shall apply.

3. *Trial of Local Pastor.*—When a local pastor is accused of an offense under ¶ 2621, the procedures described in ¶¶ 2623-2624 shall apply.

4. *Reinstatement of Local Pastor Status.*—Local pastors whose approved status has been discontinued from an Annual

---

[8]*See* Judicial Council Decisions 436, 439.

Conference of The United Methodist Church or one of its legal predecessors may be reinstated by the Annual Conference which previously approved them, or its legal successor, or the Annual Conference of which the major portion of their former conference is a part, only upon recommendation by the district Committee on Ordained Ministry from which their license was discontinued, the Board of Ordained Ministry, and the Cabinet. When approved by the clergy members in full connection as provided in ¶ 436, their license and credentials shall be restored, and they shall be eligible for appointment as pastors of a charge. They shall complete current studies and meet requirements as provided in ¶¶ 407, 408.

Whenever persons whose approval as local pastors has been discontinued by an Annual Conference are being considered for appointment or temporary employment in another Annual Conference, the Board of Ordained Ministry where these persons are being considered shall obtain from the Board of Ordained Ministry of the conference where approval has been discontinued certification of their qualifications and information about the circumstances relating to the termination of their approval as local pastors. Before such persons shall be appointed, they shall be recommended by the board and approved by the Annual Conference. A district superintendent may arrange for them to serve temporarily when the board and the Cabinet agree and when the board certifies that they are enrolled for those studies which they have not completed previously.[9]

5. *Retirement of Local Pastor.*—On recommendation of the Board of Ordained Ministry and by vote of the clergy members in full connection, a local pastor who has completed the course of study and served not less than four years as a local pastor may be recognized as a retired local pastor. Retirement provisions for local pastors shall be the same as those for clergy members in ¶ 451.1, .2, .4, .6 with pensions payable in accordance with ¶ 1606.5*a*.

¶ **411.** *Counseling Elders.*—Counseling elders are clergy members in full connection in an Annual Conference recommended by the Cabinet, approved, trained, and assigned by the

---

[9]*See* Judicial Council Decision 412.

Board of Ordained Ministry to provide supervision and counsel for certified candidates for ordained ministry, local pastors, probationers, and associate members seeking probationary membership under ¶ 416.2. Such assignments should be done after consultation with the candidates involved. The counseling elder shall:

1. Work specifically in the development of vocational goals which shall be reviewed annually and reported to the district Committee and/or Board of Ordained Ministry.

2. Develop a covenant of supportive accountability for growth and decision making in the pursuit of effective ministry.

3. Work specifically in supervision and counsel regarding preaching and teaching the Scriptures, celebration of the Sacraments and other services of worship, ordering the life of the congregation for nurture and care, and all other aspects of the practice of ministry.

4. Work under the direction of the Board of Ordained Ministry in consultation with the district superintendent, making an annual report of their activities to the board. The Board of Ordained Ministry may consider assigning one counseling elder to supervise several local pastors or other ministerial candidates preparing for full conference membership.

Section III. Admission and Continuance.

¶ **412.** *General Provisions.*—1. The Annual Conference is the basic body of The United Methodist Church. The clergy membership of an Annual Conference shall consist of members in full connection (¶ 422), probationary members (¶ 413), associate members (¶ 419), affiliate members (¶ 1431.5a), and local pastors under full-time appointment to a pastoral charge (¶ 408.1). All ordained ministers are amenable to the Annual Conference in the performance of their duties in the positions to which they are appointed.[10]

2. Both men and women are included in all provisions of the Discipline which refer to the ordained ministry.[11]

---

[10]*See* Judicial Council Decisions 327, 371.
[11]*See* Judicial Council Decisions 317, 155.

¶ **413.** *Eligibility and Rights of Probationary Membership.*—Probationary members are on trial in preparation for membership in full connection with the Annual Conference. They are on probation as to character, preaching, and effectiveness as pastors. The Annual Conference has jurisdiction over probationary members. Annually the Board of Ordained Ministry shall review and evaluate their relationship and make recommendation to the clergy members in full connection regarding their continuance. Probationary members may request discontinuance of this relationship or may be discontinued by the Annual Conference, upon recommendation of the Board of Ordained Ministry (¶ 418), without reflection upon their character.

1. Probationary members are eligible for ordination as deacons but may not be ordained elders until they qualify for membership in full connection in the Annual Conference.

2. Probationary members shall have the right to vote in the Annual Conference on all matters except the following: *(a)* constitutional amendments; *(b)* election of delegates to the General and Jurisdictional or Central Conferences; *(c)* all matters of ordination, character, and conference relations of clergy.

3. Probationary members may serve on any board, commission, or committee of the Annual Conference except the Board of Ordained Ministry and Board of Trustees (¶¶ 732.1, 2512.1). They shall not be eligible for election as delegates to the General or Jurisdictional Conferences.

4. Probationary members shall be amenable to the Annual Conference in the performance of their ministry and shall be granted the same security of appointment as associate members and members in full connection as long as they are probationary members.

5. Probationary members who are regularly appointed to a pastoral charge are subject to the provisions of the Discipline in the performance of their pastoral duties. The district superintendent under whom they are appointed shall provide guidance through the Board of Ordained Ministry and the educational institution in performance of work.

6. Probationary members in appointments beyond the local church shall relate themselves to the district superintendent in the area where their work is done. The district superintendent shall give them supervision and report annually to their Board of Ordained Ministry.

¶ **414.** *Qualifications for Election to Probationary Membership.*— Candidates may be elected to probationary membership by vote of the clergy members in full connection on recommendation of the Board of Ordained Ministry after meeting the following conditions:

1. Each candidate must have been certified as a candidate for ministry for at least one year.

2. Each must have met the educational requirements (¶¶ 415, 416).

3. Each candidate must have been recommended in writing on the basis of a three-fourths majority vote of the district Committee on Ordained Ministry.

4. Each must present a satisfactory certificate of good health on the prescribed form from a physician approved by the board. Handicapping conditions are not to be construed as unfavorable health factors when such a person is capable of meeting the professional standards and is physically able to render effective service in the office of ordained minister. The conference may require psychological and/or psychiatric tests and evaluations to provide additional information on the candidate's fitness for the ministry.

5. Each must file with the board, in duplicate on the prescribed form, a satisfactory written, concise autobiographical statement concerning age, health, family, Christian experience, call to the ministry, educational record, formative Christian experiences, and plans for service in the Church.

6. Each must prepare and preach at least one written sermon on a biblical passage specified by the Board of Ordained Ministry.

7. Each must present a plan and outline for teaching a book or books of the Bible.

8. Each must have been examined in written form covering the areas indicated and approved by the Board of Ordained Ministry with respect to the following questions:

a) Describe your personal experience of God and the understanding of God you derive from biblical, theological, and historical sources.

b) What is your understanding of humanity and the human need for divine grace?

c) How do you interpret the statement "Jesus Christ is Lord"?

d) What is your conception of the activity of the Holy Spirit in personal faith, in the community of believers, and in responsible living in the world?

e) How do you understand the theological tasks of an ordained United Methodist minister, with special reference to Part II of the Book of Discipline?

f) What is your understanding of the expectations and obligations of the itinerant system?

g) For the sake of the mission of Jesus Christ in the world and the most effective witness to the Christian gospel, and in consideration of your influence as an ordained minister, are you willing to make a complete dedication of yourself to the highest ideals of the Christian life; and to this end will you agree to exercise responsible self-control by personal habits conducive to physical health, intentional intellectual development, fidelity in marriage and celibacy in singleness,[12] social responsibility, and growth in grace and the knowledge and love of God?

h) What is your understanding of the teaching office of the ordained ministry, particularly the teaching of the Bible?

i) What is the meaning of ordination, especially in the context of the general ministry of the Church?

j) What is the role and significance of the Sacraments in your ministry?

k) Do you believe in and will you practice infant Baptism?

l) Describe the nature and purpose of your ministry as an expression of the mission of the Church.

m) Describe your understanding of an inclusive Church and ministry.

n) Are you presently convinced that the ordained ministry is the best way to fulfill your response to God? Explain.

---

[12]*See* Judicial Council Decision 542.

o) Indicate in some detail how your close personal relationships affect your ministry.

p) Describe your understanding of and appreciation for persons of different racial/ethnic heritages.

q) Mismanagement of personal finances may detract from your effectiveness as a minister. Are you presently in debt so as to interfere with your work, or have you obligations to others which will make it difficult for you to live on the salary you may receive?

¶ **415.** *Educational Requirements.*—A candidate for probationary membership must (1) have been graduated with a Bachelor of Arts in liberal education or equivalent degree in a college or university listed by the University Senate or competency equivalence through an external degree program at a college or university listed by the University Senate; (2) have completed at least one-half of the work required for a Master of Divinity or equivalent first professional degree in a school of theology listed by the University Senate except under the special conditions of ¶ 416.2; (3) an Annual Conference may designate a Master of Divinity or equivalent first professional degree from a school of theology listed by the University Senate as the minimum educational requirement for probationary membership; and (4) the educational standards and other requirements for admission and ordination shall be set by the Central and Provisional Central Conferences for the Annual and Provisional Annual Conferences within their territories, and outside such territories by the Annual or Provisional Annual Conference itself.[13]

¶ **416.** *Special Conditions.*—Under special conditions an Annual Conference may, by a three-fourths majority vote of the clergy members in full connection, present and voting, admit to probationary membership a candidate who exhibits promise for effective ministry in the following cases:

1. If the candidate is a graduate with a Bachelor of Arts in liberal education from a college not listed by the University Senate or competency equivalence through an external degree program at a college or university listed by the University Senate, who has completed one-half of the work required for the Master

---

[13]*See* Judicial Council Decision 187.

of Divinity or equivalent first professional degree in a school of theology listed by the University Senate.

2. If the candidate has *(a)* reached thirty-five years of age; *(b)* served as an associate member for a minimum of two years under full-time appointment; *(c)* completed a Bachelor of Arts or its equivalent degree in a college or university listed by the University Senate or competency equivalence determined by an external degree program at a school, college, or university approved by the University Senate (exceptions to the undergraduate degree requirement may be made in rare instances for persons who (i) have been prevented from pursuit of the normal course of baccalaureate education and/or (ii) are members of groups whose cultural practices and training enhance insight and skills for effective ministry not available through conventional formal education, in consultation with the Division of Ordained Ministry); *(d)* completed two years of advanced study prescribed by the Division of Ordained Ministry through an advanced course of study at a school or theological school approved by the University Senate; and *(e)* been recommended by a three-fourths vote of the Cabinet and a three-fourths vote of the Board of Ordained Ministry, written statements of such recommendations having been read to the conference before the vote is taken, setting forth the particular ways the candidate's ministry is exceptional and, the special reasons this person should be received into probationary membership.

¶ **417.** *Continuation in Probationary Membership.*—To be continued as probationary members, candidates shall make regular progress in their studies for ordained ministry. In case of failure or delay, the Board of Ordained Ministry shall investigate the circumstances and judge whether to extend the time within the following limits: (1) for completing the theological course for the Master of Divinity or equivalent first professional degree, a total of eight years; (2) for completing the advanced studies in the ministerial course of study, a total of four years. In a case clearly recognized as exceptional the board, by a three-fourths vote, may recommend an extension beyond these limits, which may be approved by a three-fourths vote of the clergy members in full connection, present and voting; *provided,* however, that no candidates shall be continued on probation beyond the eighth regular conference session following their admission to probationary membership; (3) each probationary member shall have an elder in full connection assigned by the Board of Ordained Ministry as counselor during the period of probation. The counselor is to advise and counsel the probationer in light of the expectations for United Methodist ministry reflected in ¶¶ 423-424; (4) probationary members in appointments beyond the local church shall relate themselves to the district superintendent in the area where their work is done. The district superintendent shall give them supervision and report annually to their Board of Ordained Ministry; and (5) whenever probationary members find it necessary to discontinue their theological education, the Board of Ordained Ministry shall review their relation to the Annual Conference. If they desire to continue in the ordained ministry, they shall receive credit in the course of study for their theological work as the Division of Ordained Ministry shall determine.

¶ **418.** *Discontinuance from Probationary Membership.*—Probationary members may request discontinuance of this relationship or may be discontinued by the Annual Conference, upon recommendation of the Board of Ordained Ministry, without reflection upon their character. When this relationship is discontinued, they shall no longer be permitted to exercise ministerial functions and shall surrender their credentials to the district superintendent for deposit with the secretary of the conference, and their membership transferred by the district superintendent to the local church which they designate after consultation with the pastor. The Board of Ordained Ministry shall file with the resident bishop and the secretary of the conference a permanent record of the circumstances relating to discontinuance as a probationary member as required in ¶ 732.3*d*. If after discontinuance, probationary members are classified and approved as local pastors in accordance with the provision of ¶ 408 and under the conditions outlined in ¶ 409, they may be permitted to retain their credentials of ordination and shall receive credit in the course of study for their theological work as the Division of Ordained Ministry shall determine.[14]

---

[14]*See* Judicial Council Decision 522.

¶ **419.** *Eligibility and Rights of Associate Members.*—Associate members of an Annual Conference are in the itinerant ministry of the Church and are available on a continuing basis for appointment by the bishop. They offer themselves without reserve to be appointed and to serve as their superiors in office shall direct. They shall be amenable to the Annual Conference in the performance of their ministry and shall be granted the same security of appointment as probationary members and members in full connection.[15]

1. Associate members are eligible for ordination as deacons but may not be ordained elders unless they qualify through probationary membership for membership in full connection in the Annual Conference (¶ 424).

2. Associate members shall have the right to vote in the Annual Conference on all matters except the following: *(a)* constitutional amendments; *(b)* election of delegates to the General and Jurisdictional or Central Conferences; *(c)* all matters of ordination, character, and conference relations of ministers.

3. Associate members may serve on any board, commission, or committee of an Annual Conference except the Board of Ordained Ministry and the Board of Trustees (¶¶ 733.1, 2512.1). They shall not be eligible for election as delegates to the General or Jurisdictional or Central Conferences.

4. Ordained ministers of Methodist or United Churches from nations other than the United States serving as missionaries certified by the General Board of Global Ministries within the bounds of an Annual Conference may be **affiliate members** of the conference, without prejudice to their relationship to their churches of origin (¶ 1431.5*a*).

5. Associate members shall be subject to the provisions governing sabbatical leave, leave of absence, location, retirement, minimum salary, and pension.

¶ **420.** 1. *Requirements for Election as Associate Members.*—Candidates may be elected to associate membership by vote of the

---

[15]*See* Judicial Council Decision 554.

clergy members in full connection, upon recommendation of the Board of Ordained Ministry, when they have met the following conditions. They shall have (1) reached age thirty-five; (2) served four years as full-time local pastors; (3) completed the five-year course of study for ordained ministry in addition to the studies for license as a local pastor, no more than one year of which may be taken by correspondence; (4) completed a minimum of sixty (60) semester hours toward the Bachelor of Arts or an equivalent degree in a college or university listed by the University Senate or competency equivalence through an external degree program at a college or university listed by the University Senate; (5) been recommended by the district Committee on Ordained Ministry and the Board of Ordained Ministry; (6) declared their willingness to accept continuing full-time appointment; (7) satisfied the board regarding their physical, mental, and emotional health (the Annual Conference may require psychological tests to provide additional information on the candidate's fitness for the ministry); (8) for the sake of the mission of Jesus Christ in the world and the most effective witness to the Christian gospel, and in consideration of his/her influence as an ordained minister, be willing to make a complete dedication of himself/herself to the highest ideals of the Christian life; and to this end agree to exercise responsible self-control by personal habits conducive to bodily health, mental and emotional maturity, fidelity in marriage and celibacy in singleness, social responsibility, and growth in grace and the knowledge and love of God; and (9) prepared at least one written sermon on a biblical passage specified by the Board of Ordained Ministry and given satisfactory answers in a written doctrinal examination administered by the Board of Ordained Ministry. (Consideration shall be given to the questions listed in ¶ 414.8.)[16]

2. Upon recommendation of the Board of Ordained Ministry, an Annual Conference may equate part-time service to the requirement of full-time service. Such equivalence is to be determined in light of the years of service involved, the quality of that service, the maturity of the applicant, and other relevant factors.

---

[16]*See* Judicial Council Decisions 343, 542, 544.

¶ **421.** *Progression into Full Membership.*—Associate members who exhibit exceptional promise for the ordained ministry may qualify for probationary membership in the Annual Conference under special conditions as set forth in ¶ 416.2 upon receiving a three-fourths majority vote of the clergy members of the conference in full connection, present and voting.

ADMISSION AND CONTINUANCE OF FULL
MEMBERSHIP IN THE ANNUAL CONFERENCE

¶ **422.** *Members in Full Connection.*—Members in full connection with an Annual Conference by virtue of their election and ordination are bound in special covenant with all the ordained ministers of the Annual Conference. In the keeping of this covenant they perform the ministerial duties and maintain the ministerial standards established by those in the covenant. They offer themselves without reserve to be appointed and to serve, after consultation, as the appointive authority may determine. They live with their fellow ordained ministers in mutual trust and concern and seek with them the sanctification of the fellowship. Only those shall be elected to full membership who are of unquestionable moral character and genuine piety, sound in the fundamental doctrines of Christianity and faithful in the discharge of their duties.[17] There shall be an annual meeting of this covenant body in executive session at the site of the regular session of the Annual Conference to consider questions relating to matters of ordination, character, and conference relations (¶ 704.6).[18]

A full member of an Annual Conference shall be eligible for ordination as elder by a bishop and such other elders as the ordaining bishop may determine.

¶ **423.** *Rights and Responsibilities.*—*1. Of Full Members.*—Members in full connection shall have the right to vote on all matters in the Annual Conference except in the election of lay delegates to the General and Jurisdictional or Central Conferences (¶ 701.1*a*) and shall have sole responsibility for all matters of ordination, character, and conference relations of ordained

---

[17]*See* Judicial Council Decisions 406, 534, 552, 555.
[18]*See* Judicial Council Decisions 42, 406, 534, 555.

ministers, which responsibility shall not be limited by the recommendation or lack of recommendation by the Board of Ordained Ministry, notwithstanding provisions of Chapter 3 which grant to the Board of Ordained Ministry the right of recommendation. They shall be eligible to hold office in the Annual Conference and to be elected delegates to the General and Jurisdictional or Central Conferences under the provision of the Constitution (¶ 38, Art. IV). Every effective member in full connection who is in good standing shall receive an annual appointment by the bishop.[19]

2. There are professional responsibilities which clergy members are expected to fulfill and which represent a fundamental part of their accountability and a primary basis of their guaranteed appointment. These shall include:

a) Continuing availability for appointment.

b) Annual participation in evaluation with Committees on Pastor-Parish Relations for use in an ongoing effective ministry and for identifying continuing education needs and plans.

c) Annual participation in evaluation with district superintendents to determine the pastor's gifts, health, and effectiveness for ministry (269.2*f*, 520.2, 732.2*n*, *o*,) both within the current appointment and for future appointments.

d) Growth in competence and effectiveness through continuing education is expected of conference members. The Board of Ordained Ministry (¶ 733.2*n*) shall set minimal standards and specific guidelines for continuing education programs for members of their conference and ensure their availability.

¶ **424.** *Requirements for Admission.*—Candidates who have been probationary members for at least two years may be admitted into membership in full connection in an Annual Conference by vote of the clergy members in full connection, on recommendation of the Board of Ordained Ministry,[20] after they have qualified as follows. They shall have: (1) served full time under episcopal appointment for at least two full Annual Conference years following the completion of the educational requirements specified in 3 *(b)* below. Upon recommendation of

[19]*See* Judicial Council Decisions 462, 473, 492, 534, 552, 555.
[20]*See* Judicial Council Decisions 157, 344.

the Board of Ordained Ministry, an Annual Conference may equate less than full-time to the requirement of full-time service. Such equivalence is to be determined in light of the years of service involved, the quality of that service, the maturity of the applicant, and other relevant factors. Supervision is to be *(a)* personally assumed or delegated by the district superintendent, and *(b)* assumed by a counseling elder assigned by the Board of Ordained Ministry. Their service must be evaluated by the Board of Ordained Ministry as effective according to guidelines developed by the board and adopted by the clergy members in full connection.[21] Those probationary members under appointment January, 1981 shall not be subject to the provisions of this paragraph unless the Annual Conference otherwise provides; (2) been previously elected as probationary members and ordained deacons; (3) met the following educational requirements: *(a)* graduation with a Bachelor of Arts or equivalent degree from a college or university listed by the University Senate or demonstrated competency equivalence through a process designed in consultation with the Division of Ordained Ministry; *(b)* graduation with a Master of Divinity degree from a school of theology listed by the University Senate or its equivalent as determined by the Division of Ordained Ministry; *(c)* educational requirements in every case shall include a minimum of two semester or three quarter hours in each of the fields of United Methodist history, doctrine, and polity; *provided* that a candidate may meet the requirements by undertaking an independent study program provided and administered by the Division of Ordained Ministry *(see* ¶ 1529.2); *(d)* under conditions regarded as exceptional, candidates who completed the first two years of the advanced course of study for ordained ministry and were admitted to probationary membership by a three-fourths vote (¶ 416.2), upon recommendation by the Board of Ordained Ministry when they have completed two additional years of advanced studies specified by and under the direction of the Division of Ordained Ministry and have met all the other requirements, may be received into full membership by a three-fourths vote of the clergy members in full connection,

---

[21]*See* Judicial Council Decisions 440, 555.

present and voting; (4) satisfied the board regarding physical, mental, and emotional health; (5) prepared and preached at least one written sermon on a biblical passage specified by the Board of Ordained Ministry; (6) presented a plan and outline for teaching a book or books of the Bible; (7) responded to a written or oral doctrinal examination administered by the Board of Ordained Ministry. The candidate should demonstrate the ability to communicate clearly in both oral and written form. The candidate's reflections and the board's response should be informed by the insights and guidelines of Part II of the Discipline. The following questions are guidelines for the preparation of the examination:

a) Theology.

(1) How has the practice of ministry affected your experience and understanding of God?

(2) What effect has the practice of ministry had on your understanding of humanity and the need for divine grace?

(3) What changes has the practice of ministry had on your understanding of *(a)* the "Lordship of Jesus Christ" and *(b)* the work of the Holy Spirit?

(4) The United Methodist Church holds that Scripture, tradition, experience, and reason are sources and norms for belief and practice but that the Bible is primary among them. What is your understanding of this theological position of the Church?

(5) How do you understand the following traditional evangelical doctrines: *(a)* repentance; *(b)* justification; *(c)* regeneration; *(d)* sanctification? What are the marks of the Christian life?

(6) For the sake of the mission of Jesus Christ in the world and the most effective witness to the Christian gospel, and in consideration of your influence as an ordained minister, are you willing to make a complete dedication of yourself to the highest ideals of the Christian life; and to this end will you agree to exercise responsible self-control by personal habits conducive to physical health, intentional intellectual development, fidelity in marriage and celibacy in singleness, social responsibility, and growth in grace and the knowledge and love of God?[22]

---

[22]*See* Judicial Council Decision 542.

(7) What is the meaning and significance of the Sacraments?

(8) Describe the nature and mission of the Church. What are its primary tasks today?

(9) What is your understanding of *(a)* the Kingdom of God; *(b)* the Resurrection; *(c)* eternal life?

b) Vocation.

(1) How do you conceive your vocation as an ordained minister?

c) The Practice of Ministry.

(1) How has the practice of ordained ministry affected your understanding of the expectations and obligations of the itinerant system?

(2) Do you offer yourself without reserve to be appointed and to serve as the appointive authority may determine?

(3) Describe and evaluate your personal gifts for ministry. What would be your areas of strength and areas in which you need to be strengthened?

(4) Are you willing to relate yourself to all persons without regard to race, color, national origin, or social status?

(5) Will you regard all pastoral conversations of a confessional nature as a trust between the person concerned and God?

(6) Provide evidence of experience in peace and justice ministries.

¶ **425.** *Historic Examination for Admission into Full Connection and Associate Membership.*—The bishop as chief pastor shall engage those seeking to be admitted in serious self-searching and prayer to prepare them for their examination before the conference. At the time of the examination the bishop shall also explain to the conference the historic nature of the following questions and seek to interpret their spirit and intent. The questions are these and any others which may be thought necessary:

1. Have you faith in Christ?

2. Are you going on to perfection?

3. Do you expect to be made perfect in love in this life?

4. Are you earnestly striving after it?

5. Are you resolved to devote yourself wholly to God and his work?

6. Do you know the General Rules of our Church?

7. Will you keep them?

8. Have you studied the doctrines of The United Methodist Church?

9. After full examination do you believe that our doctrines are in harmony with the Holy Scriptures?

10. Will you preach and maintain them?

11. Have you studied our form of Church discipline and polity?

12. Do you approve our Church government and polity?

13. Will you support and maintain them?

14. Will you diligently instruct the children in every place?

15. Will you visit from house to house?

16. Will you recommend fasting or abstinence, both by precept and example?

17. Are you determined to employ all your time in the work of God?

18. Are you in debt so as to embarrass you in your work?

19. Will you observe the following directions?

a) Be diligent. Never be unemployed. Never be triflingly employed. Never trifle away time; neither spend any more time at any one place than is strictly necessary.

b) Be punctual. Do everything exactly at the time. And do not mend our rules, but keep them; not for wrath, but for conscience' sake.[23]

ORDAINED MINISTERS FROM OTHER ANNUAL CONFERENCES, OTHER METHODIST AND CHRISTIAN DENOMINATIONS

¶ **426.** *Appointments.*—Ordained ministers from other Annual Conferences and Christian denominations may receive an appointment in the Annual Conference in the following manner:

1. *Ordained Ministers from Other Annual Conferences and Other Methodist Denominations.*—With approval and consent of the bishops or other judicatory authorities involved, ordained

---

[23]These are the questions which every Methodist preacher from the beginning has been required to answer upon becoming a full member of an Annual Conference. These questions were formulated by John Wesley and have been little changed throughout the years. *See* Judicial Council Decision 555.

ministers of other Annual Conferences or other Methodist churches may receive appointments in the Annual Conference while retaining their home conference membership or denominational affiliation. Appointments are to be made by the resident bishop of the conference in which the ordained minister is to serve. Upon the recommendation of the Board of Ordained Ministry, clergy in such appointments may be granted voice but not vote in the Annual Conference to which they are appointed. Their membership on conference boards and agencies is restricted to the conference of which they are a member. They shall be compensated no less than the equitable salary provisions of the Annual Conference in which they serve and participate in the pension and insurance programs of that Annual Conference. Such appointments are renewable annually up to a period of five years. Furthermore, it shall be the responsibility of the Board of Pensions of the Annual Conference in which the appointment is received to enroll such ordained ministers in the Ministerial Pension Plan and the Comprehensive Protection Plan (*see* ¶ 1606.20).[24]

2. *Ministers from Other Denominations.*—On recommendation of the Board of Ordained Ministry, the clergy members in full connection may approve annually clergy in good standing in other Christian denominations to serve appointments or ecumenical ministries within the bounds of the Annual Conference while retaining their denominational affiliation; *provided* they present suitable credentials, give assurance of their Christian faith and experience, and other qualifications. They shall give evidence of their agreement with and willingness to support and maintain United Methodist doctrine, discipline, and polity. Their ordination credentials shall be examined by the bishop and the Board of Ordained Ministry, and upon its recommendation may be recognized as valid in The United Methodist Church while they are under appointment. When the Board of Ordained Ministry certifies that their credentials are at least equal to those of associate members, although they are not associate members, they may be accorded all the rights and privileges of associate

---

[24]*See* Judicial Council Decisions 16, 361, 554.

membership in the Annual Conference (¶ 419.2, .3). They shall not have security of appointment.

3. Between conference sessions, the Board of Ordained Ministry may approve them for appointment pending the recognition of their orders. The bishop may make ad interim recognition of valid ordination after consultation with the Cabinet and executive committee of the Board of Ordained Ministry pending recognition by the vote of the clergy members in full connection. In every case prior examination shall be made of the ordained minister's understanding, acceptance, and willingness to support and maintain United Methodist doctrine, discipline, and polity.[25]

¶ **427.** *Transfers.*—1. *From Other Annual Conferences.*— Ordained ministers from other Annual Conferences of The United Methodist Church may be received by transfer into probationary, associate, or full membership with the consent of the bishops involved. Where possible, consultation with the chairperson or executive committee of the Board of Ordained Ministry shall be held prior to the transfer. This consultation is to be at the bishop's initiative.

2. *From Other Methodist Denominations.*—*a)* Ordained ministers from other Methodist churches may be received by transfer into probationary, associate, or full conference membership with the consent of the bishops or other authorities involved without going through the process required for ministers from other denominations. Where feasible, prior consultation with the chairperson or executive committee of the Board of Ordained Ministry shall be held.

b) Ordained ministers being transferred from Autonomous Methodist Churches, Affiliated Autonomous Methodist Churches, or other Methodist denominations shall meet the educational requirements of The United Methodist Church, or the equivalent approved by the General Board of Higher Education and Ministry.

c) In cases of transfer, the Division of Ordained Ministry shall certify the completion of the education requirements for conference membership based on guidelines developed by the

---

[25]*See* Judicial Council Decision 444.

Division of Ordained Ministry. In cases where additional education is required, the Board of Ordained Ministry shall develop an educational program in consultation with the Division of Ordained Ministry.

3. *From Other Denominations.—a)* On recommendation of the Board of Ordained Ministry, the clergy members in full connection may recognize the orders of ministers from other denominations and receive them into probationary or associate membership in the Annual Conference. They shall present their credentials for examination by the bishop and Board of Ordained Ministry and give assurance of their Christian faith and experience. They shall give evidence of their agreement with and willingness to support and maintain United Methodist doctrine, discipline, and polity, and present a satisfactory certificate of good health on the prescribed form from a physician approved by the Board of Ordained Ministry. They shall make themselves available for any psychological or aptitude tests the board may require. The Board of Ordained Ministry in consultation with the Division of Ordained Ministry shall determine whether they meet the educational requirements for conference membership.

b) Ordained ministers from other Christian denominations must serve as probationary members for at least two years and complete all the requirements of ¶ 424, including courses in United Methodist history, doctrine, and polity, before being admitted into full conference membership.

4. The Board of Ordained Ministry of an Annual Conference is required to ascertain from an ordained minister seeking admission into its membership on credentials from another denomination whether or not membership in the effective relation was previously held in an Annual Conference of The United Methodist Church or one of its legal predecessors, and if so when and under what circumstances the ordained minister's connection with such Annual Conference was severed.

5. Ordained ministers seeking admission into an Annual Conference on credentials from another denomination who have previously withdrawn from membership in the effective relation in an Annual Conference of The United Methodist Church or one of its legal predecessors shall not be admitted or readmitted without the consent of the Annual Conference from which they

withdrew or its legal successor, or the Annual Conference of which the major portion of their former conference is a part, such consent to be granted upon recommendation of its Board of Ordained Ministry.

¶ **428.** *Recognition of Orders.*—1. Clergy from other denominations may have their orders recognized by the clergy members in full connection of the Annual Conference after examination of their credentials by the bishop and Board of Ordained Ministry. Prior to admission to membership in the Annual Conference such recognition of orders may be given upon recommendation of the bishop and Board of Ordained Ministry.

2. When the orders of an ordained minister of another church shall have been duly recognized, the certificates of ordination by said church shall be returned to the minister with the following inscription written plainly on the back:

These orders are recognized by the _____ Annual Conference of The United Methodist Church, this _____ day of _____ , 19_____ .

_____, President

_____, Secretary

The ordained minister also will be furnished with a certificate of recognition of orders signed by the bishop.

Section IV.   Ordination.

¶ **429.** *Ordination and the Apostolic Ministry.*—1. The whole Church receives and accepts the call of God to embody and carry forth Christ's ministry in the world. Ordination originates in God's will and purpose for the Church. There are persons within the Church community whose gifts, evidence of God's grace, and promise of future usefulness are observable to the community, who respond to God's call and offer themselves in leadership as ordained ministers.

2. The pattern for this response to the call is provided in the development of the early Church. The apostles led in prayer and preaching, organized the Christian community to extend Christ's ministry of love and reconciliation, and provided for guardian-

ship and transmission of the gospel, as entrusted to the early Church, to later generations. Their ministry, though distinct, was never separate from the ministry of the whole people of God.

¶ **430.** *The Purpose of Ordination.*—1. Ordination for such ministry is a gift from God to the Church. In ordination, the Church affirms and continues the apostolic ministry which it authorizes and authenticates through persons empowered by the Holy Spirit. As such, those who are ordained are committed to becoming conscious representatives of the whole gospel and are responsible for the transmission of that gospel to the end that all the world may be saved. Their ordination is fulfilled in the ministry of Word, Sacrament, and Order.

2. Ordained persons are authorized to preach and teach the Word of God, administer the Sacraments of Baptism and the Lord's Supper, equip the laity for ministry, exercise pastoral oversight, and administer the Discipline of the Church.

3. The efficacy of the mission of the Church is dependent on the viable interaction of the general ministry and the ordained ministry of the Church. Without creative use of the diverse gifts of the entire Body of Christ, the ministry of the Church is not effective. Without responsible leadership, there is no focus and definition of such ministry.

¶ **431.** *Qualifications for Ordination.*—Acceptance of the call to ordained ministry, together with the acknowledgment and authentication of such call by the Church, grants to the person ordained authority to serve the Church through sacramental and functional leadership. In this, the ordained person becomes representative of the entire ministry of Christ in the Church and of the ministry required of the entire Church to the world. Though no singular manifestation of God's call can be structured or required by the Church, the consciousness of such a call is crucial, and it must be submitted to the Church for authentication. It is expected that persons to be ordained shall:

1. Have personal faith in Christ and be committed to him as Savior and Lord.

2. Nurture and cultivate spiritual disciplines and patterns of holiness.

3. Be aware of a call by God to give themselves completely to their ministry, accepting God's call to be his servant.

4. Be committed to and engage in leading the ministry of the whole Church in loving service to humankind.

5. Be able to give evidence of the possession of gifts, evidence of God's grace, and promise of future usefulness.

6. For the sake of the mission of Jesus Christ in the world and the most effective witness to the Christian gospel, and in consideration of his/her influence as an ordained minister, be willing to make a complete dedication of himself/herself to the highest ideals of the Christian life; and to this end agree to exercise responsible self-control by personal habits conducive to bodily health, mental and emotional maturity, fidelity in marriage and celibacy in singleness, social responsibility, and growth in grace and the knowledge and love of God.

7. Be persons in whom the community can place trust and confidence.

8. Be persons who accept the authority of Scripture and are competent in the disciplines of Scripture, theology, church history, and church polity, and in the understanding and practice of the art of communication and human relations.

9. Be accountable to The United Methodist Church, accept its Discipline and authority, abide by the demands of the special relationship of its ordained ministers, and be faithful to their vows as ordained ministers of the Church of God.

¶ **432.** *The Act of Ordination.*—Ordination is a public act of the Church which indicates acceptance by an individual of God's call to the upbuilding of the Church through the ministry of Word, Sacrament, and Order and acknowledgment and authentication of this call by the Christian community through prayers and the laying on of hands.

It is a rite of the Church following New Testament usage as appears in the words of Paul to Timothy: "I remind you to rekindle the gift of God that is within you through the laying on of my hands" (II Timothy 1:6).

United Methodist tradition has entrusted persons in the ordained ministry with the responsibility for maintaining standards: for education and training and for examination and granting credentials to those who seek ordination. By the authorization of the clergy members of the Annual Conference, candidates are elected into the Annual Conference and are ordained by the bishop, who will use the historic language of the Holy Trinity: Father, Son, and Holy Spirit.

Ordination, thus, is that act by which the Church symbolizes a shared relationship between those ordained for sacramental and functional leadership and the Church community from which the person being ordained has come. The community is initiated by God, is given meaning and direction by Christ, and is sustained by the Holy Spirit. This relationship is a gift which comes through the grace of God in assurance of the ministry of Christ throughout the world.

¶ **433.** *Classification of Ordination.*—The ordained ministry of The United Methodist Church consists of elders and deacons. No designations are to be applied so as to deprive any person of any right or privilege permanently granted by either The Methodist Church or The Evangelical United Brethren Church.[26]

1. Elders are ordained ministers who have completed their formal preparation for the ministry of Word, Sacrament, and Order; have been elected itinerant members in full connection with an Annual Conference; and have been ordained elders in accordance with the Order and Discipline of The United Methodist Church.

2. Deacons are ordained ministers who have progressed sufficiently in their preparation for the ministry to be received by an Annual Conference as either probationary members or associate members and who have been ordained deacons in accordance with the Order and Discipline of The United Methodist Church.

¶ **434.** *The Order of Deacon.*—A deacon is an ordained minister who has been received by an Annual Conference either as a probationary member or as an associate member and has been ordained deacon. Deacons have authority to conduct divine worship, to preach the Word, to perform the marriage ceremony where the laws of the state or province permit, and to bury the

---

[26]*See* Judicial Council Decision 337.

dead. When invited to do so by an elder, they may assist in the administration of the Sacraments. When serving as regularly appointed pastors of charges, they shall be granted authority to administer the Sacraments on the charges to which they are appointed. Persons of the following classes are eligible for the order of deacon:

1. Local pastors who have been received into associate membership after having met the requirements of ¶ 420.

2. Theological students who have been received into probationary membership after having met the requirements of ¶ 414.

3. A deacon shall be ordained by a bishop, employing the Order of Service for the Ordination of Deacons.

¶ **435.** *The Order of Elder.*—An elder is an ordained minister who has met the requirements of ¶ 424 and therefore has full authority for the ministry of Word, Sacrament, and Order; who has been received as a minister in full connection with an Annual Conference; and who has been ordained elder.

Ordained ministers of the following classes are eligible for the order of elder:

1. Deacons who have been probationary members of an Annual Conference, are graduates of theological schools listed by the University Senate, and have been elected to membership in full connection with an Annual Conference after having met the requirements of ¶¶ 424-425.

2. Deacons who have been probationary members of an Annual Conference for at least two years since being received from associate membership and who have been elected to membership in full connection with an Annual Conference after having met the requirements of ¶ 424.

3. An elder shall be ordained by a bishop, employing the Order of Service for the Ordination of Elders. The bishops shall be assisted by other elders and may include laity designated by the bishop representing the Church community in the laying on of hands.

4. The bishop and the secretary of the Annual Conference shall provide credentials to all members in full connection, certifying their ministerial standing and their ordination as elders.

Section V.   Appointments to Various Ministries.

¶ **436.** *General Provisions.*—All clergy members who are in good standing in an Annual Conference shall receive annually appointment by the bishop unless they are granted a sabbatical leave, a disability leave, or are on leave of absence or retired.[27]

In addition to the ordained ministers, persons who have been granted a license as local pastors and who have been approved by vote of the clergy members in full connection may be appointed as pastors in charge under certain conditions which are specified in ¶¶ 406-408. All clergy members and licensed local pastors to be appointed shall assume a lifestyle consistent with Christian teaching as set forth in the Social Principles.

¶ **437.** *The Itinerant System.*—The itinerant system is the accepted method of The United Methodist Church by which ordained ministers are appointed by the bishop to fields of labor. All ordained ministers shall accept and abide by these appointments. Persons appointed to multiple-staff ministries, either in a single parish or in a cluster or larger parish, must have personal and professional access to the bishop and Cabinet, the Committee on Pastor-Parish Relations, as well as to the pastor in charge. The nature of the appointment process is specified in ¶¶ 529-533.

1. Full-time service shall be the norm for ordained ministry in the Annual Conference. Full-time service shall mean that the person's entire vocational time is devoted to the work of ministry in the field of labor to which one is appointed by the bishop.

2. Less than full-time service may be rendered by a clergy member under the conditions stipulated in this paragraph. Less than full-time service shall mean that a specified amount of time less than full time agreed upon by the bishop and the Cabinet, the ordained minister, and the Annual Conference Board of Ordained Ministry is devoted to the work of ministry in the field of labor to which the person is appointed by the bishop. At his/her own initiative, a clergy member may request and may be appointed by the bishop to less than full-time service without loss of essential rights or membership in the Annual Conference.

---

[27]*See* Judicial Council Decisions 380, 462, 492, 524.

Division of Chaplains and Related Ministries–endorsed appointments beyond the local church may be for less than full-time service. Appointment to less than full-time service is not a guarantee but may be made by the bishop provided that the following conditions are met:

a) The ordained minister seeking less than full-time service should present a written request to the bishop and the chairperson of the Board of Ordained Ministry at least three months prior to the Annual Conference session at which the appointment is made. Exceptions to the three-month deadline must be approved by the Cabinet and the executive committee of the Board of Ordained Ministry.

b) Following appropriate consultation, as established in ¶¶ 444 and 529-533, and upon joint recommendation of the Cabinet and the Board of Ordained Ministry, the less than full-time category shall be confirmed by a two-thirds vote of the clergy members of the Annual Conference.

c) Reappointment to less than full-time service shall be requested by the ordained minister and approved annually by the bishop and Cabinet and shall not be granted for more than a total of eight years except by a three-fourths vote of the clergy members in full connection of the Annual Conference.

d) Ordained ministers who receive appointment at less than full-time service remain within the itineracy and as such remain available, upon consultation with the bishop and Cabinet, for appointment to full-time service. A written request to return to full-time appointment shall be made to the bishop and Cabinet at least six months prior to the Annual Conference session at which the appointment is to be made.

e) The bishop may make ad interim appointments at less than full-time service upon request of the ordained minister following consultation as specified in ¶¶ 529-533 and upon recommendation of the Cabinet and executive committee of the Board of Ordained Ministry, the same to be acted upon by the next regular session of the Annual Conference.[28]

3. Interim appointments may be made: to charges that have

---

[28]*See* Judicial Council Decision 579.

special transitional needs or to charges whose pastor is on sabbatical leave.

¶ **438.** A pastor is an ordained or licensed person approved by vote of the clergy members in full connection, appointed by the bishop to be in charge of a station, circuit, cooperative parish, extension ministry, or on the staff of one such appointment.[29]

¶ **439.** *Responsibilities and Duties of a Pastor.*—The pastor(s) shall oversee the total ministry of the local church in its nurturing ministries and in fulfilling its mission of witness and service in the world by: (1) giving pastoral support, guidance, and training to the lay leadership in the church, equipping them to fulfill the ministry to which they are sent as servants under the Lordship of Christ; (2) providing ministry within the congregation and to the world; (3) administering the temporal affairs of the congregation. In the context of these basic responsibilities, the pastor shall give attention to the following specific duties:

1. *Ministering Within the Congregation and to the World.*—*a)* To preach the Word, read and teach the Scriptures, and engage the people in study and witness.

b) To administer the Sacraments of Baptism and the Lord's Supper and all the other means of grace. It shall be the duty of ordained ministers before baptizing infants or children to prepare the parents and sponsors by instructing them concerning the significance of Holy Baptism, the responsibilities of parents and sponsors for the Christian training of the baptized child, and how these obligations may be properly discharged.

c) To give oversight to the total educational program of the church and encourage the distribution and use of United Methodist literature in each local church.

d) To be involved and to lead the congregation in evangelistic outreach in order to win persons on profession of faith.

e) To instruct candidates for membership and receive them into the Church.

f) To perform the marriage ceremony after due counsel with the parties involved. The decision to perform the ceremony shall be the right and responsibility of the pastor. Qualifications

---

[29]*See* Judicial Council Decision 555.

for performing marriage shall be in accordance with the laws of the state and The United Methodist Church.

g) To counsel those who are under threat of marriage breakdown and explore every possibility for reconciliation.

h) To counsel bereaved families and conduct appropriate funeral and memorial services.

i) To counsel with members of the church and community concerning military service and its alternatives.

j) To counsel persons struggling with personal, ethical, or spiritual issues.

k) To visit in the homes of the church and community, especially among the sick, aged, and others in need.

l) To participate in community and ecumenical concerns and to lead the congregation to become so involved.

m) To search out from among the membership and constituency men and women for pastoral ministry and other church-related occupations: to help them interpret the meaning of the call of God, to advise and assist when they commit themselves thereto, to counsel with them concerning the course of their preparation, and to keep a careful record of such decisions.

n) To give diligent pastoral leadership in ordering the life of the congregation for discipleship in the world.

2. *Equipping and Supervising.—a)* To give diligent pastoral leadership ordering the life of the congregation for nurture and care.

b) To offer counsel and theological reflection in the following:

(1) The development of goals for fulfilling the missions of the congregation, the Annual Conference, and the general Church.

(2) The development of plans for implementing the goals of the congregation and a process for evaluating their effectiveness.

(3) The selection, training, and deployment of lay leadership within the congregation and the development of a process for evaluating lay leadership.

c) To lead the congregation in experiencing the racial and ethnic inclusiveness of The United Methodist Church and to help prepare it for participation in the itineracy of all ordained men and women.

d) To participate in denominational and conference programs and training opportunities, and to seek out opportunities for cooperative ministries with other United Methodist pastors and churches.

3. *Administration.—a)* To be the administrative officer of the local church and to assure that the organizational concerns of the congregation are adequately provided for.

b) To administer the provisions of the Discipline and supervise the working program of the local church.

c) To give an account of their pastoral ministries to the Charge and Annual Conference according to the prescribed forms. The care of all church records and local church financial obligations shall be included.

¶ **440.** *Special Provisions.*—1. Pastors shall first obtain the written consent of the district superintendent before engaging for an evangelist any person who is not a conference-approved evangelist, a regular member of an Annual Conference, a local pastor, or a certified lay speaker in good standing in The United Methodist Church.

2. No pastor shall discontinue services in a local church between sessions of the Annual Conference without the consent of the Charge Conference and the district superintendent.

3. No pastor shall arbitrarily organize a pastoral charge. (*See* ¶ 268 for the method of organizing a local church.)

4. Ordained ministers of The United Methodist Church are charged to maintain all confidences inviolate, including confessional confidences.

¶ **441.** *Support for Ordained Ministers Appointed to a Pastoral Charge.*—Assumption of the obligations of the itinerant ministry required upon admission to the traveling connection places upon the Church a counterobligation to provide adequate support for the entire ministry of the Church (¶ 717). The Church shall provide and the ordained minister is entitled to receive not less than the equitable salary established by the Annual Conference for clergy members according to provisions of ¶ 722.3.

1. *Support for Ordained Ministers Appointed to Pastoral Charges Who Render Full-Time Service.*—Each pastor of an Annual

Conference who is in good standing and who is appointed to full-time service under the provision of ¶ 437.1 shall have a claim upon the conference Equitable Salary Fund and a right to receive not less than minimum salary established by the Annual Conference for persons in full-time service.[30]

2. *Support for Ordained Ministers Appointed to Pastoral Charges Who Render Less than Full-Time Service.*—Each pastor who is in good standing and who is appointed by the bishop to less than full-time service under the provisions of ¶ 437.2 shall have a claim upon the conference Equitable Salary Fund in one-quarter increments according to the guidelines established by the Annual Conference Commission on Equitable Salaries.

¶ **442.** *Appointments Beyond the Local United Methodist Church.*—Clergy members in effective relationship may be appointed to serve in ministry settings beyond the local church which extend the witness and service of Christ's love and justice. Persons in these appointments remain within the itineracy and shall be accountable to the Annual Conference. They shall be given the same moral and spiritual support by it as are persons in appointments to pastoral charges.[31] Their effectiveness shall be evaluated in the context of the specific setting in which their ministry is performed.

The institution or agency desiring to employ a conference member shall, when feasible, through its appropriate official, consult the member's bishop and secure approval before completing any agreement to employ the member. If the institution or agency is located in another area, the bishop of that area shall also be consulted.

¶ **443.** Clergy in appointment beyond the local church are full participants in the itinerant system. Therefore, a conference member in an appointment beyond the local church must be willing upon consultation to receive an appointment in a pastoral charge. When either the conference member or the Annual Conference requests appointment to a pastoral charge, the request shall be made in writing to or from the bishop and the Cabinet. Such a request should be made at least six months prior

---

[30]*See* Judicial Council Decisions 579, 587.
[31]*See* Judicial Council Decisions 321, 325, 466, 579.

to Annual Conference. In both instances, consultation shall give due regard to the individual's special training, experience, skills, and leadership potential.

1. *Categories of Appointment.*—In order to establish a clear distinction between the work to which all Christians are called and the tasks for which ordained ministers are appropriately prepared and authorized, the following categories are established for appointments within the itineracy of The United Methodist Church.

a) Appointments within the connectional structures of United Methodism: district superintendents, staff members of conference councils, boards, and agencies, treasurers, bishops' assistants, superintendents or directors of parish development, staff of general agencies, missionaries, faculty and administrators of United Methodist schools of theology and other educational institutions, approved by The University Senate, campus ministers, and staff members of ecumenical agencies.[32]

b) Appointments to extension ministries of persons under endorsement by the Division of Chaplains and Related Ministries of the General Board of Higher Education and Ministry, such as: chaplaincy in the armed forces, Veterans Administration, industry, correctional institutions, health care fields, community service organizations, and other related ministries which the bishop and conference Board of Ordained Ministry may designate.[33] The division shall annually verify the appropriate employment of persons under its endorsement and request their reappointment.

c) Conference members in service under the World Division of the General Board of Global Ministries may be appointed to the ministries listed in *(a)* and *(b)* above. They may be assigned to service either in Annual Conferences or Central Conferences, or with affiliated autonomous churches, independent churches, churches resulting from the union of Methodist Churches and other communions, or in other denominational or ecumenical bodies. They may accept such rights and privileges, including affiliate membership, as may be offered them by overseas Annual

---

[32]*See* Judicial Council Decisions 166, 167.
[33]*See* Judicial Council Decisions 321, 325, 329.

Conferences or by other churches to which they are assigned, without impairing their relationship to their home Annual Conference.

d) Conference members may receive appointments beyond the ministry usually extended through the local church and other institutions listed above in *(a)* and *(b)*[34] when considered by the bishop and the Annual Conference Board of Ordained Ministry to be a true extension of the Christian ministry of the Church. These ministries shall be initiated in missional response to the needs of persons in special circumstances and unique situations and shall reflect the commitment of the clergy to intentional fulfillment of their ordination vows to Word, Sacrament, and Order. These appointments may involve clergy with expertise from other vocations. Conference members in such appointments retain conference membership, and the Annual Conference may choose to extend financial support and benefits for its clergy by vote of the Annual Conference. (*See* ¶ 722.4.)

The Division of Chaplains and Related Ministries of the Board of Higher Education and Ministry will provide standards to assist in determining the appropriateness of special ministry settings. In addition, it will provide advocacy for persons serving in settings approved under this paragraph.

Those seeking such an appointment shall submit to the Cabinet, the Board of Ordained Ministry, and the Division of Chaplains and Related Ministries a written statement describing in detail the proposed setting for their ministry, sharing a sense of calling to that ministry and their gifts and evidence of God's grace for it, and expressing the intentional fulfillment of their ordination vows. This material will be submitted not later than 120 days before desired appointment to the proposed setting. On recommendation of the Cabinet and the Board of Ordained Ministry, such positions are to be confirmed by a two-thirds vote of the clergy members of the Annual Conference.

The bishop may make ad interim appointments in this category after consultation with the Cabinet and executive committee of the Board of Ordained Ministry, the position to be formally acted upon by the next session of the Annual Conference.

---

[34]*See* Judicial Council Decision 380.

2. *Relation to the Annual Conference.—a) Accountability to the Annual Conference.*—Conference members under appointment beyond the local church are amenable to the Annual Conference of which they are members and insofar as possible should maintain close working relationship with and effective participation in the work of their Annual Conference, assuming whatever responsibilities they are qualified and requested to assume.

Persons under appointment beyond the local church shall submit annually to the bishop, the district superintendent, and the Board of Ordained Ministry a written report, on the official form developed for the Church by the General Council on Finance and Administration for use by the Annual Conference. This report shall serve as the basis for the evaluation of these clergy in light of the missional needs of the Church and the fulfillment of their ordination to be minister of Word, Sacrament, and Order. Persons formally evaluated by the institutions in which they serve will provide, instead of an evaluation, a narrative report reflecting their ministry. Clergy serving in appointments outside the conference in which they hold membership shall furnish a copy of their report also to the bishop of the area in which they reside and work. Annual Conferences shall review the qualifications of persons in extension ministry status and integrate them into the ongoing work of the Annual Conference.

b) Responsibility of the Annual Conference.—The bishop, representatives of the Cabinet, and the Committee on Chaplains and Related Ministries of the Board of Ordained Ministry shall provide an opportunity to meet annually with ordained ministers appointed beyond the local church who carry on their ministry within the bounds of Annual Conference, both of that Annual Conference and those who hold membership elsewhere. The bishop shall convene the meeting which is to be planned by the Cabinet and the Board of Ordained Ministry. The purpose of this meeting is to gain understanding of one another's role and function in ministry, to report to other ordained ministers appointed beyond the local church and to discuss with them matters concerning the overall approach to ministry in the episcopal area, to interpret the role and function of extension ministries to the larger church through the offices of the bishop and his/her representatives, to nurture the development of various ministries as significant in assisting the mission of the Church, and to discuss specific programs and services which the bishop and his/her representatives may initiate in which the various ordained ministers serving in appointments beyond the local church may be qualified as consultants and supervisors. Using the appropriate resources and personnel of the Annual Conference, the bishop shall provide for an annual visit to the ministry setting of all persons under appointment beyond the local church assigned within the geographical bounds of the Annual Conference, and shall provide a report of the visit to the bishop of persons from other Annual Conferences.

3. *Relation to the Local Church.*—*a)* Conference members appointed beyond the local church shall establish membership in a Charge Conference in their home Annual Conference in consultation with the pastor in charge and with approval of the district superintendent and the bishop. They shall submit to their home Charge Conference an annual report of pastoral duties and the fulfillment of their ordination through their special appointment, including ministerial activities in the charge where they have an affiliate membership relation and in other units of the Church at large, as well as continuing education work completed and anticipated. This report may be the one submitted to the bishop, district superintendent, and Board of Ordained Ministry (¶ 443.2*a*). District superintendents, because of the nature of their work, and the relationship defined in ¶¶ 529.3, 453.1*a*, 752, shall not be required to have a Charge Conference affiliation.

All conference members, including those in extension ministries, shall be available and on call to administer the Sacraments of Baptism and the Lord's Supper as required by the Discipline (¶ 439.1*b*) and requested by the district superintendent of the district in which the appointment is held.

b) Affiliate Relation to a Local Church.—Ordained ministers under appointment beyond the local church and serving outside of the geographical bounds of their home Annual Conference shall promptly notify the bishop of the area in which they reside of their names, addresses, and the Annual Conferences in which their credentials are held. They shall be affiliate members without vote of a Charge Conference either within the district where they carry out the primary work of their appointment or within the district where they reside. Persons serving outside the geographic bounds of any Annual Conference are exempt from this requirement. The selection of the Charge Conference shall be made after consultation between the minister and the pastor of the local United Methodist church.

These ordained ministers under appointment beyond the local church and serving outside the geographical boundaries of their home Annual Conference shall submit to the Charge Conference of which they are affiliate members a copy of the report submitted to their home Charge Conference and/or an oral report concerning their ministry and the fulfillment of their ordination. The district superintendent shall be responsible for the notification to these ministers concerning the time and place of the Charge Conference.

4. *Affiliate Relation to Annual Conference.*—Ordained clergy appointed beyond the local church outside the boundary of their Annual Conference may, at their own initiative, apply to the Board of Ordained Ministry for affiliate membership in the Annual Conference in which their appointment is located or in which they reside. By a two-thirds vote of the executive session,[35] such clergy may be received with rights and privileges, including service on conference boards, agencies, task forces, and committees, with voice but without vote. Voting membership shall be retained in the appointee's home Annual Conference for the duration of affiliate member relationship. Nomination to general church boards and agencies and election as delegates to General and Jurisdictional Conferences shall originate in the appointee's home Annual Conference. Such persons may serve on the board, agency, task force, or committee of only one Annual Conference at any one time.[36]

5. *General Provisions.*—*a*) These appointments shall be made only to positions related to adequate accountability structures according to guidelines established by the Board of Ordained

---

[35]*See* Judicial Council Decision 555.
[36]*See* Judicial Council Decision 554.

Ministry and Cabinet in the Annual Conferences in which membership is held.

b) For information regarding pensions, the conference will continue to list the source of annuity claim for each of its clergy.

c) All conference secretaries shall submit to the editors of the General Minutes a list of such appointments beyond the local church made in their Annual Conferences, and there shall be published in the General Minutes a list of ordained ministers in the Church serving in the major categories under these appointments.

d) Conference members appointed beyond the local church shall attend the Annual Conference in which membership is held.

e) Individual participation in Armed Forces Reserve or National Guard units and part-time employment with the Veteran's Administration shall be reflected in Annual Conference journals.

Section VI.   Evaluation and Continuing Education for Full and Associate Members.

¶ **444.** *Evaluation.*—Evaluation is a continuous process which must take place in a spirit of understanding and acceptance.

1. The pastors in local churches shall receive evaluation annually from the Committee on Pastor-Parish Relations for use in an ongoing effective ministry and for identifying continuing education needs and plans (¶ 269.2*f*[2]), using criteria, processes, and training developed by the Board of Ordained Ministry and the Cabinet. The district superintendent will evaluate annually the pastors' effectiveness for ministry (¶¶ 423.1*b*, 520, 733.2*n, o*), using criteria, processes, and training developed by the Cabinet and the Board of Ordained Ministry.

2. Clergy serving in appointments beyond the local church will undergo annual evaluation by their immediate supervisors, engage in annual self-evaluation, and include copies of these evaluations in the annual report submitted to the bishop, district superintendent, and the Board of Ordained Ministry (¶ 443.2*a*).

¶ **445.** *Continuing Education.*—1. Clergy shall be expected to continue their education throughout their careers, including carefully developed personal programs of study augmented periodically by involvement in organized educational activities.

2. In most cases the ordained ministers' continuing education program should allow for study leaves at least one week each year and at least one month during one year of each quadrennium. Such study leaves shall not be considered as part of the ministers' vacations and shall be planned in consultation with their charges or other agencies to which they are appointed as well as the bishop, district superintendent, and Annual Conference Continuing Education Committee.

3. An ordained minister may request an educational leave of up to six months while continuing to hold a pastoral appointment. An Annual Conference may make such educational leaves available to its ordained ministers who have held full-time appointments for at least five years. Such a leave must be with the approval of the Committee on Pastor-Parish Relations, the Administrative Board/Council, and the district superintendent.

4. Financial arrangements for continuing education shall be negotiated in the following manner: *(a)* for pastors it shall be done in consultation with the district superintendent and the Committee on Pastor-Parish Relations; *(b)* for district superintendents, with the district Committee on Superintendency; *(c)* for conference staff, with the appropriate committee of the Council on Ministries; *(d)* for others in appointments beyond the local church, with the appropriate persons in their agency.

5. Pastors shall be asked by the district superintendent in the Charge Conference to report on their programs of continuing education for the past year and plans for the year to come. The district superintendent shall also ask the local church to describe its provision for time and financial support for the pastor's program of continuing education.

6. Clergy in appointment beyond the local church shall give evidence of their continuing education program and future plans in their annual reports (¶ 443.2a).

¶ **446.** *Sabbatical Leave.*—A sabbatical leave should be allowed for a program of study or travel, approved by the conference Board of Ordained Ministry. Ordained ministers who have been serving in a full-time appointment for six consecutive years from the time of their reception into full membership or for eight consecutive years from the time of their reception into associate membership may be granted a sabbatical leave for up to one year. Whenever possible, the salary level of the last appointment served before the leave should be maintained in the appointment made at the termination of the leave. The appointment to sabbatical leave is to be made by the bishop holding the conference upon the vote of the Annual Conference after recommendation by the Board of Ordained Ministry. Ordained ministers shall submit a written request for a sabbatical leave, including plans for study or travel, to the Board of Ordained Ministry, with copies to the bishop and district superintendent, ordinarily six months before the opening session of the Annual Conference. To be eligible for an additional sabbatical leave, ordained ministers shall have served six consecutive years under full-time appointment following the previous sabbatical leave.[37]

Section VII. Changes of Conference Relationship for Full, Probationary, and Associate Members.

¶ **447.** Ordained ministers seeking a change in conference relationship shall make written request to their Board of Ordained Ministry stating the reasons for the requested change of relationship. In addition, the Board of Ordained Ministry may request personal interviews with the minister requesting the change in relationship, except where personal appearance results in undue hardship.[38]

¶ **448.** *Leave of Absence.*—1. This relationship is granted to ordained ministers who are probationary, associate, and full members who because of impaired health, emotional and/or physical exhaustion, ineffectiveness or incompetence, or other equally sufficient reason, are temporarily unwilling or unable to perform the duties of full-time itinerant ministry. This relationship may be initiated by the minister or the Cabinet, with or without the consent of the clergy member, through the Board of Ordained Ministry, and granted or renewed by the vote of the clergy members in full connection upon the board's recommendation. The person in question has the right to a hearing before

---

[37]*See* Judicial Council Decision 473.
[38]*See* Judicial Council Decisions 524, 530.

the bishop, Cabinet, and executive committee of the Board of Ordained Ministry prior to the granting of a leave of absence without the minister's consent. Between sessions of the Annual Conference this relation may be granted or terminated with the approval of the bishop, district superintendents, and executive committee of the Annual Conference Board of Ordained Ministry. This interim action shall be subject to the approval of the Annual Conference at its next session. This relation shall be approved annually upon written request of the clergy member or the Cabinet with or without the consent of the clergy member and shall not be granted for more than five years in succession except by a two-thirds vote of the clergy members in full connection. The written request for this relationship should be made at least ninety (90) days prior to Annual Conference. This leave shall be counted as a part of the eight-year limit for probationary members unless the Board of Ordained Ministry recommends otherwise.

After consultation with the pastor, ordained ministers on leave of absence shall designate a Charge Conference within the bounds of the Annual Conference in which they shall hold membership and to which they shall submit an annual report. The exercise of their ministry shall be limited to the Charge Conference in which their membership is held and under the supervision of the pastor in charge, to whom they shall report all marriages performed, Baptisms administered, and funerals conducted, and shall be held amenable for their conduct and the continuation of their ordination rights to the Annual Conference. In case of failure to report to the Charge Conference, the Annual Conference may locate them without their consent. They shall have no claim on the conference funds except by vote of the clergy members in full connection. They shall not be eligible for membership on conference committees, commissions, or boards.[39]

2. Persons on voluntary leave of absence may, with the permission of the Charge Conference in which membership is held and with the approval of the Division of Chaplains and Related Ministries, continue to hold an existing reserve commis-

---

[39]*See* Judicial Council Decision 581.

sion as an armed forces chaplain but may not voluntarily serve on extended active duty.

3. When a member requests an end to the leave of absence, it shall be by written request at least six months prior to the session of Annual Conference. The Board of Ordained Ministry shall review the circumstances surrounding the granting of the relationship for the purpose of determining whether those circumstances have been alleviated.

4. When clergy members do not request an extension of the leave of absence annually during the five-year period, or do not indicate willingness to return to the itinerant ministry at the end of the five-year period, the provisions of ¶ 453 shall be invoked.[40]

¶ **449.** *Maternity/Paternity Leave.*—Maternity/paternity leave not to exceed one-fourth of a year will be available and shall be granted by the bishop and the Cabinet and the executive committee of the Board of Ordained Ministry to any probationary member, associate member, or ordained minister in full connection who so requests it at the birth or arrival of a child into the home for purposes of adoption.

1. Persons desiring maternity/paternity leave should file their request with the Committee on Pastor-Parish Relations after consulting with the district superintendent at least ninety (90) days prior to its beginning to allow adequate pastoral care for the churches involved to be developed.

2. During the leave, the ordained minister's Annual Conference relations will remain unchanged, and the insurance plans will remain in force.

3. A maternity/paternity leave of up to one quarter of a year will be considered as an uninterrupted appointment for pension credit purposes.

4. The ordained minister's salary will be maintained for no less than the first six weeks of the leave.

5. During the leave time pastoral responsibility for the church or churches involved will be handled through consultation with the Committee on Pastor-Parish Relations of the local church(es) and the district superintendent.

---

[40]*See* Judicial Council Decisions 450, 459, 473, 508, 524, 530.

6. Special arrangements shall be made for district superintendents, bishops, and those under special appointment.

¶ **450.** *Disability Leave.*—1. When ordained ministers who are local pastors under full-time appointment, associate members, probationary members, or members in full connection in an Annual Conference are forced to give up their ministerial work because of their physical or emotional disability, upon recommendations of the conference Board of Ordained Ministry and the conference Board of Pensions and by a majority vote of the clergy members of the Annual Conference in full connection who are present and voting, they may be granted annual disability leave without losing their relationship to the Annual Conference; *provided*, however that such leave may be granted or renewed only after a thorough investigation of the case by the Joint Committee on Disability of the Annual Conference, which will report its findings to the conference Board of Ordained Ministry and the conference Board of Pensions. When an ordained minister is granted disability leave by the Annual Conference, if the medical evidence has not yet met the standards for the receipt of disability benefits as set forth in the Comprehensive Protection Plan, subsection 5.4, the conference Board of Pensions may authorize payment of the disability benefits in the amount that would otherwise be payable from the Comprehensive Protection Plan. The payments shall be made by the General Board of Pensions as a charge to the Annual Conference granting the disability leave. If payments from the Comprehensive Protection Plan are subsequently approved, the Annual Conference will be reimbursed for benefits already paid, not to exceed the amount otherwise payable from the Comprehensive Protection Plan. Each disability leave granted by the Annual Conference shall be recorded in the conference minutes.

2. When ordained ministers who are full-time local pastors, associate members, probationary members, or members in full connection in an Annual Conference are forced to give up their ministerial work between sessions of the Annual Conference on account of physical or emotional disability, with the approval of a majority of the district superintendents, after consultation with the executive committee of the conference Board of Ordained Ministry and the executive committee of the conference Board of

Pensions, a disability leave may be granted by the bishop for the remainder of the conference year; *provided,* however, that such leave may be granted only after a thorough investigation of the case by the Joint Committee on Disability of the Annual Conference; which will report its findings to the conference Board of Ordained Ministry and the conference Board of Pensions. When an ordained minister is granted disability leave by the bishop, if the medical evidence has not yet met the standards for receipt of disability benefits as set forth in the Comprehensive Protection Plan, subsection 5.4, the conference Board of Pensions may authorize payment of the disability benefits in the amount that would otherwise be payable from the Comprehensive Protection Plan. The payments shall be made by the General Board of Pensions as a charge to the Annual Conference granting the disability leave. If payments from the Comprehensive Protection Plan are subsequently approved, the Annual Conference will be reimbursed for benefits already paid, not to exceed the amount otherwise payable from the Comprehensive Protection Plan.

3. When ordained ministers or local pastors on disability leave recover sufficiently to resume ministerial work, they may receive an appointment from a bishop between sessions of the Annual Conference, thereby terminating the disability leave. Such appointment shall be reported immediately by the Cabinet to the Annual Conference Board of Pensions and to the General Board of Pensions. Such termination of leave, together with the effective date, shall also be recorded in the minutes of the Annual Conference at its next regular session.[41]

¶ **451.** *Retirement.*—Retired ordained ministers are those who have been placed in the retired relation either at their own request or by action of the clergy members in full connection upon recommendation of the Board of Ordained Ministry.[42] (*See* ¶¶ 1606-1609 for pension information.) Requests for retirement shall be stated in writing to the bishop, Cabinet, and Board of Ordained Ministry at least ninety days prior to the conference session at which retirement is to be effective. The Board of

---

[41]*See* Judicial Council Decision 473.
[42]*See* Judicial Council Decisions 87, 88, 531.

Ordained Ministry shall provide guidance and counsel to the retiring member and family as they begin a new relationship in the local church.

1. *Mandatory Retirement.*—Every clergy member of an Annual Conference who will have attained age seventy on or before July 1 in the year which the conference is held shall automatically be retired.[43]

2. *Voluntary Retirement.*—*a) With Twenty Years of Service.*— Any members of the Annual Conference who have completed twenty years or more of service under appointment as ordained ministers or as local pastors with pension credit for service before 1982 or with full participation in the Comprehensive Protection Plan since 1981 prior to the opening date of the session of the conference may request the Annual Conference to place them in the retired relation with the privilege of receiving their pensions for the number of approved years served in the Annual Conference or conferences and such other benefits as the final Annual Conference may provide, payment to begin the first of any month after the session of the Annual Conference which occurs in the year in which the ordained minister attains age sixty-two on or before July 1. If pension begins prior to the age at which retirement under ¶ 452.2c could have occurred, then the provisions of ¶ 1606.4i shall apply.

b) With Thirty-five Years of Service or at Age Sixty-two.—At their own request and by vote of the clergy members in full connection, any clergy members who will have attained age sixty-two on or before July 1 or will have completed thirty-five years of service under appointment as ordained ministers, or as local pastors with pension credit for service before 1982 or with full participation in the Comprehensive Protection Plan since 1981, in the year in which the session of the Annual Conference is held may be placed in the retired relation with an annuity claim for an actuarially reduced pension, payment to begin the first of the month after the session of the Annual Conference (*see* ¶ 1606.4i).[44]

c) With Forty Years of Service or at Age Sixty-five.—At their own request and by vote of the clergy members in full connection, any

---

[43]*See* Judicial Council Decisions 7, 165, 413, 578.
[44]*See* Judicial Council Decision 428.

clergy members who will have attained age sixty-five on or before July 1 in the year in which the session of the conference is held or will have completed forty years of service under appointment as an ordained minister, or as a local pastor with pension credit for service before 1982 or with full participation in the Comprehensive Protection Plan since 1981, as of the conference session may be placed in the retired relation with the privilege of making an annuity claim.[45]

d) The Annual Conference, at its discretion, upon joint recommendation of the Board of Ordained Ministry and the conference Board of Pensions, may designate any time within the ensuing conference year as the effective date of retirement of an ordained minister who is placed in the retired relation under the provisions of §2*b* or §2*c* above.

3. *Involuntary Retirement.*—By a two-thirds vote of those present and voting, the clergy members of the Annual Conference in full connection may place any clergy members in the retired relation with or without their consent and irrespective of their age if such relation is recommended by the Board of Ordained Ministry and the Cabinet.[46] Written notice of the intended action shall be given to such member by the Board of Ordained Ministry at least ninety (90) days prior to Annual Conference. This process shall not preclude the rights to appeal and trial by any person so guaranteed by our Constitution.

4. *Pre-retirement Counseling.*—The Board of Ordained Ministry in cooperation with the conference Board of Pensions shall offer to all clergy members anticipating retirement, pre-consultation at least five years prior to the date of anticipated retirement (¶ 733.2*n*). The purpose of the consultation will be to assist the clergy and spouses to plan and to prepare for the psychological and financial adjustments of retirement, as well as providing guidance and counsel for their return to a new relationship in the local church. In pre-retirement counseling the Board of Ordained Ministry and the conference Board of Pensions may relate to the Annual Conference Association of Retired Ministers or similar organization where it exists. The boards shall take

[45]*See* Judicial Council Decision 379.
[46]*See* Judicial Council Decision 522.

initiative in assisting retirees to establish such organizations.

5. *Charge Conference Membership.—a)* All retired ordained ministers who are not appointed as pastors of a charge, after consultation with the pastor, shall have a seat in the Charge Conference and all the privileges of membership in the church where they elect to hold such membership except as set forth in the Discipline. They shall report to the Charge Conference and to the pastor all marriages performed, Baptisms administered, and other pastoral functions. If they reside outside the bounds of the conference, they shall forward annually to the conference a report of their Christian and ministerial conduct, together with an account of the circumstances of their families, signed by the district superintendent or the pastor of the charge within the bounds of which they reside. Without this report the conference, after having given thirty days' notice, may locate them without their consent.

6. *Appointment of Retired Ordained Ministers.—*A retired ordained minister shall be eligible to receive an appointment when requested by the bishop and Cabinet but not the same appointment from which he/she has been retired. A retired ordained minister appointed to a pastoral charge shall have neither a claim upon minimum salary nor further pension credit. Retired ordained ministers may serve on conference agencies.[47]

7. *Return to Effective Relationship.—*A clergy member who has retired under the provisions of ¶ 451.2 may at his/her own request be made an effective member upon recommendation of the Board of Ordained Ministry, the bishop, and Cabinet, and by majority vote of the clergy members of the Annual Conference and thereby eligible for appointment so long as he/she remains in the effective relation or until ¶ 451.1 applies. Each ordained minister requesting return to effective relationship after voluntary retirement must meet the following conditions: (1) Presentation of their certificate of retirement. (2) A satisfactory certificate of good health on the prescribed form from a physician approved by the Board of Ordained Ministry. However, any pension being received through the General Board of Pensions shall be discontinued upon their return to the effective relationship. The pension shall be reinstated upon subsequent retirement.

---

[47]*See* Judicial Council Decisions 87, 88, 531, 558.

Section VIII. Review of Full and Associate Conference Membership.

¶ **452.** 1. *Honorable Location.—a)* An Annual Conference may grant associate members or members in full connection certificates of honorable location at their own request; *provided* that it shall first have examined their character at the conference session when the request is made and found them in good standing; and *provided* further, that this relation shall be granted only to one who intends to discontinue service in the itinerant ministry. The Board of Ordained Ministry shall provide guidance and counsel to the locating member and family as they return to a new relationship in the local church.[48] Upon recommendation of the Board of Ordained Ministry, an Annual Conference may offer financial assistance in this transition from the Equitable Salary Fund or other conference resources.

b) Location shall be certified by the presiding bishop. Ordained ministers located according to the provisions of this paragraph shall not continue to hold membership in the Annual Conference. After consultation with the pastor, located ordained ministers shall designate the local church in which they shall hold membership. As clergy members of the Charge Conference, they shall be permitted to exercise ministerial functions under supervision of the pastor in charge. They shall have all the privileges of membership in the church where they elect to hold membership except as set forth in the Book of Discipline. When approved by the executive committee of the Board of Ordained Ministry, a person on honorable location may be appointed ad interim by the bishop as a local pastor. Otherwise the exercise of their ministry shall be limited to the Charge Conference in which their membership is held. A copy of the Annual Report to the Charge Conference must be forwarded to the registrar of the Board of Ordained Ministry in order for location to be continued. Failure to submit the report for two consecutive years shall result in location being discontinued. If location is discontinued, the provisions of ¶ 455 shall be invoked. They shall report to the Charge Conference and the pastor all marriages

---

[48]*See* Judicial Council Decision 366.

performed, Baptisms administered, and funerals conducted; and shall be held amenable for their conduct and the continuation of their ordination rights to the Annual Conference within which the Charge Conference membership is held. The provisions of this paragraph shall not apply to persons granted involuntary location prior to the General Conference of 1976. The names of located members after the annual passage of their character shall be printed in the journal.

2. *Withdrawal to Unite with Another Denomination.*—When ordained ministers in good standing withdraw to unite with another denomination or to terminate their membership in the denomination, their credentials should be surrendered to the conference, and if they shall desire it and the conference authorize it, the credentials may be returned with the following inscription written plainly across their face:

A. B. has this day been honorably dismissed by the _____ Annual Conference from the ministry of The United Methodist Church.

Dated: _____

_____, *President*

_____, *Secretary*

3. *Surrender of the Ordained Ministerial Office.*—Associate members or members in full connection of an Annual Conference in good standing who desire to surrender their ministerial office and withdraw from the conference may be allowed to do so by the Annual Conference at its session. The ordained minister's credentials shall be surrendered to the district superintendent for deposit with the secretary of the conference, and his/her membership may be transferred to a church which he/she designates, after consultation with the pastor, as the local church in which he/she will hold membership.[49]

4. *Withdrawal under Complaints or Charges.*—When clergy members are accused of an offense under ¶ 2621 and desire to withdraw from the membership of the Annual Conference, it

---

[49]*See* Judicial Council Decision 552.

may permit them to withdraw under the provisions of ¶ 2626.2. The ordained ministers' credentials shall be surrendered to the district superintendent for deposit with the secretary of the conference, and their membership may be transferred to a local church which they designate, after consultation with the pastor.[50]

7. *Withdrawal between Conferences.*—In the event that withdrawal by surrender of the ministerial office, to unite with another denomination, or under complaints or charges, should occur in the interval between sessions of an Annual Conference, the member's credentials shall be surrendered to the bishop or district superintendent along with a letter of withdrawal from the ordained ministry. Both the credentials and the letter of withdrawal shall be deposited with the secretary of the conference. This action shall be reported by the Board of Ordained Ministry for confirmation by the Annual Conference at its next session.[51]

¶ **453.** *Grievance Procedures.*—1. *General Provisions.*—Ordination and membership in an Annual Conference in The United Methodist Church is a sacred trust. The qualifications and duties of associate members, probationary members, and full members are set forth in the Book of Discipline of The United Methodist Church, and we believe they flow from the gospel as taught by Jesus the Christ and proclaimed by his Apostles. Whenever an ordained minister in any of the above categories violates this trust, the membership of his/her ministerial office shall be subject to review.

This review shall have as its purpose the reconciliation and restoration of the ordained minister and the strengthening of the Church. If the remedial process is unfruitful, discontinuance or termination may follow.

a) Supervision.—In the course of the ordinary fulfillment of the superintending role, the bishop or district superintendent may receive or initiate grievances about the performance or character of an ordained minister. A grievance is a written and signed statement claiming misconduct or unsatisfactory performance of ministerial duties. The person filing the grievance shall be informed of the process for filing the grievance and the

---

[50]*See* Judicial Council Decision 552.
[51]*See* Judicial Council Decision 552.

ordained minister shall be informed of the process and its purpose. The supervisory response shall be directed toward a reconciliation between all parties and the ordained minister and may include consultation with the Committee on Pastor-Parish Relations for pastors, the district Committee on Superintendency for district superintendents, or appropriate personnel committee. If supervisory activity does not achieve the desired results, the district superintendent or the bishop may refer the matter as a complaint to the chairperson of the Board of Ordained Ministry who shall forward it on to the Joint Review Committee.

b) Complaints.—A complaint must be based on incompetence, ineffectiveness, or any one or more of the offenses listed in ¶ 2621 and shall be submitted in written form and signed by the district superintendent or the bishop. No complaint shall be considered for any misconduct or unsatisfactory performance which shall not have been committed within two years immediately preceding the filing of the grievance (¶ 455.1*a*). Complaints may be initiated by the bishop, a district superintendent, or the Cabinet. Complaints shall be lodged with the chairperson of the Annual Conference Board of Ordained Ministry, who shall forward the complaint to the Joint Review Committee and the ordained minister against when the complaint is lodged within ten days of receipt.

c) Joint Review Committee.—In each Annual Conference there shall be a Joint Review Committee composed of two district superintendents appointed annually by the bishop, two Board of Ordained Ministry members nominated by the chairperson and elected annually by the board and two non-Cabinet, non-board members in full connection, one nominated by the bishop and Cabinet, one by the board, and elected annually by the members in full connection in ministerial executive session. An alternate shall be provided in each of the three categories. The alternate who is not a member of the Cabinet or Board of Ordained Ministry shall be nominated by the bishop and Cabinet. When a person serving on the Joint Review Committee is involved in or related to the complaint, the alternate shall serve. The committee shall elect its own officers.

This committee shall receive from the chairperson of the Board of Ordained Ministry all complaints and seek resolution of them. The work of this committee shall be informal and confidential and shall guarantee that the person or persons lodging the complaint and the person against whom the complaint is lodged shall have the right to be heard. No counsel shall be present. However, should the ordained minister under complaint desire it, a clergyperson chosen by the ordained minister may accompany him/her at meetings of the committee. If resolution of the matter is not achieved, the Joint Review Committee shall refer the complaint with any recommendations to the Board of Ordained Ministry.

d) Disposition of Complaints.—When a complaint has been received from the Joint Review Committee, the Board of Ordained Ministry shall develop a response based on the report of the Joint Review Committee and the needs of the church and the ordained minister. The Board of Ordained Ministry may recommend remedial action, discontinuance, leave of absence, administrative location, termination, or it may dismiss the complaint. In rare instances, following the Joint Review process, the board may refer the complaint as charges to the Committee on Investigation for possible trial. The board's recommendation will be shared with the minister, the bishop, the Cabinet, and the complainant.

e) Remedial Action.—In cooperation with the Cabinet and in consultation with the ordained minister, the Board of Ordained Ministry may choose or recommend one or more of the following options for a program of remedial action, subject to regular oversight by the board and annual review:

(1) Program of continuing education (¶ 445)

(2) Leave of absence (¶ 448)

(3) Early retirement (¶ 451.1)

(4) Sabbatical leave (¶ 446)

(5) Honorable location (¶ 452.2)

(6) Surrender of ordained ministerial office (¶ 452.3)

(7) Personal counseling or therapy

(8) Program of career evaluation

(9) Peer support and supervision

(10) Private reprimand: A letter signed by the chairperson of the Board of Ordained Ministry and the ordained minister's district superintendent, addressed to the minister with a file copy

in the permanent file of the Board of Ordained Ministry (¶ 705.6) stating the appropriateness of the complaint, the specific remedial action required, and the conditions under which the letter shall be withdrawn from the file and destroyed.

f) Recommendation to Terminate Membership.—The Board of Ordained Ministry shall recommend the discontinuance of a probationary member in keeping with the provisions of ¶ 418. The board's recommendation to terminate the membership of an associate member or member in full connection must be preceded by the Joint Review process and must be based on any one or more of the offenses listed in ¶ 2621. The board shall notify the ordained minister, the bishop, and district superintendent of the recommendation and shall forward the recommendation to the clergy executive session of the Annual Conference. The notice to the ordained minister shall also inform the minister of his/her right to elect trial (¶ 453.2) or withdraw under complaints (¶ 452.4). The recommendation of the Board of Ordained Ministry shall be acted upon by the clergy executive session unless the ordained minister shall choose withdrawal or trial. Such choice by the ordained minister must be made and notification of the choice sent to the bishop and the chairperson of the Board of Ordained Ministry within ten days following receipt of notice of the board's recommendation. If a full member or associate member is terminated, he/she shall no longer be permitted to exercise ordained ministerial functions and shall surrender his/her credentials to the district superintendent for deposit with the secretary of the conference, and the minister's membership transferred by the district superintendent to the local church which he/she designates after consultation with the pastor.

If upon notice of a recommendation from the Board of Ordained Ministry to terminate membership, a full member or associate member chooses trial, the Board of Ordained Ministry shall submit the formal complaint as charges and other appropriate material to the Committee on Investigation.

2. *By Trial.*—If a bishop or clergy member of an Annual Conference chooses trial, the procedures are provided for in ¶ 2623.[52]

---

[52]*See* Judicial Council Decision 485.

268

3. *Recommendation to Administrative Location.—a)* Upon recommendation of the Board of Ordained Ministry, the Annual Conference may grant members certificates of administrative location when, in the judgment of the Annual Conference, members have demonstrated an inability effectively and competently to perform the duties of itinerant ministry; *provided* that the Annual Conference shall have first examined their character and found them in good standing.

b) The Board of Ordained Ministry shall notify the ordained minister, bishop, and district superintendent of the recommendation to administrative location at least sixty (60) days before the opening of the next Annual Conference.

The notice to the ordained minister shall also inform the minister of his/her right to a hearing before the bishop, Cabinet, and executive committee of the Board of Ordained Ministry prior to the recommendation being forwarded to the executive session of the Annual Conference for consideration and action. Such choice by the ordained minister must be made and notification of the choice sent to the bishop and the chairperson of the Board of Ordained Ministry within ten (10) days following receipt of notice from the board.[53] The recommendation of the Board of Ordained Ministry shall be acted upon by the clergy executive session.

c) The provisions of ¶ 453.3*b* above apply to administrative location, except that a person on administrative location may not be given ad interim appointments by the bishop. Upon recommendation of the Board of Ordained Ministry, an Annual Conference may offer financial assistance from conference resources in this transition.

Section IX. Readmission to Conference Relationship.

¶ **454.** *Readmission to Probationary Membership.*—Ordained ministers who have been discontinued as probationary members under the provisions of ¶ 418 from an Annual Conference of The United Methodist Church or one of its legal predecessors may be readmitted by the Annual Conference in which they held previously such membership and from which they requested

---

[53]*See* Judicial Council Decisions 384, 485.

discontinuance or were discontinued or its legal successor or the Annual Conference of which the major portion of their former conference is a part upon their request and recommendation by the district Committee on Ordained Ministry, the Board of Ordained Ministry, and the Cabinet after review of their qualifications as required in ¶ 414 and the circumstances relating to their discontinuance. When reinstated by vote of the clergy members in full connection, their probationary membership in the conference and their credentials shall be restored, and they shall be authorized to perform those ministerial functions for which they are qualified. They shall resume ministerial studies as required by ¶¶ 415, 416.

¶ **455.** *Readmission after Honorable or Administrative Location.*—Ordained ministers requesting readmission after honorable or administrative location must meet the following conditions:

1. Presentation of their certificate of location.

2. A satisfactory report and recommendation by the Charge Conference and pastor of the local church in which their membership is held.

3. A satisfactory certificate of good health on the prescribed form from a physician approved by the Board of Ordained Ministry. The Board of Ordained Ministry should require psychological evaluation.

4. Recommendation by the district Committee on Ordained Ministry, the Board of Ordained Ministry, and the Cabinet, after review of their qualifications and the circumstances relating to their location. When reinstated by vote of the clergy members in full connection of the Annual Conference that granted the location, their membership in the conference shall be restored, and they shall be authorized to perform all ministerial functions. The conference Board of Ordained Ministry may require at least one year of service as a local pastor prior to readmission to conference membership.

¶ **456.** *Readmission after Surrender of the Ministerial Office.*—Ordained ministers who have surrendered the ministerial office under the provisions of ¶ 452.2, .3, .4, .5 to an Annual Conference of The United Methodist Church or one of its legal predecessors may be readmitted by the Annual Conference in which they held previously such membership and to which they surrendered the ministerial office or its legal successor or the Annual Conference of which the major portion of the former conference is a part upon their request and recommendation by the district Committee on Ordained Ministry, the Board of Ordained Ministry, and the Cabinet after review of their qualifications and the circumstances relating to the surrender of their ministerial office. A period of at least one year service as a local pastor shall be required prior to readmission to conference membership. When reinstated by vote of the clergy members in full connection, their membership in the conference and their credentials shall be restored, and they shall be authorized to perform all ministerial functions.[54]

¶ **457.** *Readmission after Termination by Action of the Annual Conference.*—Persons who have been terminated by an Annual Conference of The United Methodist Church or one of its legal predecessors may seek full membership in the Annual Conference in which they previously held membership and from which they were terminated or its legal successor or the Annual Conference of which the major portion of their former conference is a part upon recommendation of the Cabinet and completion of all requirements for full membership, including all requirements for election to candidacy and probationary membership. The provisions of this paragraph shall apply to all persons terminated or involuntarily located prior to General Conference of 1976.

[54]*See* Judicial Council Decisions 515, 552.

Chapter Four
THE SUPERINTENDENCY

Section I. Nature of Superintendency.

¶ **501.** *Task.*—The task of superintending in The United Methodist Church resides in the office of bishop and extends to the district superintendent, with each possessing distinct responsibilities. From apostolic times, certain ordained persons have been entrusted with the particular tasks of superintending. Those who superintend carry primary responsibility for ordering the life of the Church. It is their task to enable the gathered Church to worship and to evangelize faithfully.

It is also their task to facilitate the initiation of structures and strategies for the equipping of Christian people for service in the Church and in the world in the name of Jesus Christ and to help extend the service in mission. It is their task, as well, to see that all matters, temporal and spiritual, are administered in a manner which acknowledges the ways and the insights of the world critically and with understanding while remaining cognizant of and faithful to the mandate of the Church. The formal leadership in The United Methodist Church, located in these superintending offices, is an integral part of the system of an itinerant ministry.[1]

¶ **502.** *Guidelines for Superintending in this Age.*—The demands of this age on the leadership of bishops and district superintendents in The United Methodist Church can be seen in mode, pace, and skill:

1. *Mode.*—Leaders need to be able to read consensus and integrate it into a living tradition, to be open to the prophetic word, to be skilled in team-building, and to be effective in negotiation. The style of leadership should rise out of nurtured and cultivated spiritual disciplines and patterns of holiness, for the Spirit is given to the community and its members to the extent that they participate.

2. *Pace.*—Beyond formal systems of accountability, leaders need to open themselves to forms of accountability that they

---

[1]*See* Judicial Council Decision 524.

cultivate for themselves through a support group. Such a group can listen, can help, and can clarify, as well as participate with the leader, as he/she thinks through time demands and constraints in the process of sorting out of priorities. Appropriate time must be taken for reflection, study, developing friendships, and self-renewal.

3. *Skill.*—Among the skills needed by leaders are spiritual discipline, theological reflection, building the unique inclusive community of the Church and of the larger community as well. Reading the signs of the times, analyzing, designing strategy, assessing needs, organizing a wide range of resources, and evaluating programs and personnel are yet other skills crucial for leaders.

Section II.   Offices of Bishop and District Superintendent.

¶ **503.** The offices of **bishop** and **district superintendent** exist in The United Methodist Church as particular ministries for which persons are elected or selected from the group of elders who are ordained to be ministers of Word, Sacrament, and Order and thereby participate in the ministry of Christ, in sharing a royal priesthood which has apostolic roots (I Peter 2:9; John 21:15-17; Acts 20:28; I Peter 5:2-3; I Timothy 3:1-7).

¶ **504.** Bishops and superintendents share in the full ministry as ordained elders. The Body of Christ is one; yet many members with differing functions are all joined together in the one body (I Corinthians 12:28).

Section III.   Election, Assignment, and Termination of Bishops.

¶ **505.** *Bishops in Jurisdictions.*—1. Each jurisdiction having 500,000 church members or less shall be entitled to six bishops, and each jurisdiction having more than 500,000 church members shall be entitled to one additional bishop for each additional 500,000 church members or major fraction thereof; *provided,* however, that in those jurisdictions where this requirement would result in there being an average of more than 55,000 square miles per episcopal area, such jurisdiction shall be entitled to six bishops for the first 400,000 church members or less, and for each additional 400,000 church members or two-thirds thereof shall be entitled to one additional bishop; and *provided* further, that any episcopal area having two or more Annual Conferences with more than 125,000 members each may be divided into two episcopal areas by the Jurisdictional Conference with the addition of the needed bishop(s) made necessary by the division.[2] This legislation shall take effect upon adjournment of the 1988 General Conference.

¶ **506.** *Election.*—1. *Nomination.*—An Annual Conference, in the session immediately prior to the next regular session of the Jurisdictional Conference, may name one or more nominees for episcopal election. Balloting at Jurisdictional Conferences shall not be limited to nominees of Annual Conferences nor shall any Jurisdictional Conference delegate be bound to vote for any specific nominee. Each Jurisdictional Conference shall develop appropriate procedures for furnishing information about nominees from Annual Conferences. This shall be done at least two weeks prior to the first day of the Jurisdictional Conference. Similar procedures shall be developed for persons nominated by ballot who receive ten votes, or 5 percent of the valid votes cast, and the information shall be made available to the delegates at the site of the conference.

2. *Process.*—*a)* Jurisdictional Conference delegates, in electing bishops, shall give due consideration to the inclusiveness of The United Methodist Church with respect to sex, race, and national origin. In addition, consideration shall be given to the nature of superintendency as described in ¶¶ 501-502.

b) The Jurisdictional and Central Conferences are authorized to fix the percentage votes necessary to elect a bishop. It is recommended that at least 60 percent of those present and voting be necessary to elect.

c) Consecration of bishops may take place at the session of the conference at which election occurs or at a place and time designated by the conference. The consecration service may include bishops from other Jurisdictional and Central Conferences. It is strongly urged that the consecration service also include representatives from other Christian communions (*see* ¶ 512.1).

---

[2]*See* Judicial Council Decisions 84, 598.

¶ **507.** *Assignment Process.*—1. *Jurisdictional Committee on Episcopacy.*—The Jurisdictional Committee on Episcopacy, after consultation with the College of Bishops, shall recommend the assignment of the bishops to their respective residences for final action by the Jurisdictional Conference; it shall not reach any conclusion concerning residential assignments until all elections of bishops for that session are completed and all bishops have been consulted. A bishop may be recommended for assignment to the same residence for a third quadrennium only if the Jurisdictional Committee on Episcopacy, on a two-thirds vote, determines such assignment to be in the best interest of the jurisdiction.

The effective date of assignment for all bishops is September 1, following the Jurisdictional Conference.

A newly elected bishop shall be assigned to administer an area other than that within which his/her membership was most recently held, unless by a two-thirds vote the jurisdictional committee shall recommend that this restriction be ignored and by majority vote the Jurisdictional Conference shall concur.[3]

2. *Central Conferences.*—In the case of death, expiration of a term of service, or any disability of a bishop of a Central Conference, the Council of Bishops may assign one of its members to provide the episcopal supervision for the conference.[4]

3. *Special Assignments.*—The Council of Bishops may, with consent of the bishop and the concurrence of the Jurisdictional or Central Conference Committee on Episcopacy, assign one of its members for one year to some specific churchwide responsibility deemed of sufficient importance to the welfare of the total Church. In this event a bishop shall be released from the presidential responsibilities within the episcopal area for that term. Another bishop or bishops, active or retired, and not necessarily from the same Jurisdictional or Central Conference, shall be named by the Council of Bishops on recommendation of the College of Bishops of the jurisdiction involved to assume presidential responsibilities during the interim. This assignment

---

[3]*See* Judicial Council Decisions 48, 57, 416, 517, 538.
[4]*See* Judicial Council Decision 248.

may be renewed for a second year by a two-thirds vote of the Council of Bishops and majority vote of the Jurisdictional or Central Committee on Episcopacy and the consent of the bishop and the College of Bishops involved. The bishop so assigned shall continue to receive regular salary and support.

¶ **508.** *Vacancy in the Office of Bishop.*—A vacancy in the office of bishop may occur due to death, retirement (¶ 509.1, .2, .3), resignation (¶ 509.4), judicial procedure (¶ 2624.2), or disability (¶ 511.3). In case assignment of a bishop to presidential supervision of an episcopal area is terminated by any of the above causes, the vacancy shall be filled by the Council of Bishops on nomination of the College of Bishops of the jurisdiction concerned; or, if the vacancy should occur within twenty-four months of the episcopal assumption of presidential supervision of that area, the College of Bishops of the jurisdiction concerned may call a special session of the Jurisdictional Conference as provided in ¶ 619.2.

¶ **509.** *Termination of Office.*—An elder who is serving as a bishop up to the time of retirement shall have the status of a retired bishop; this provision includes all bishops of Central Conferences.[5]

1. *Mandatory Retirement.*—*a*) A bishop shall be retired on August 31 next following the regular session of the Jurisdictional Conference if the bishop's sixty-sixth birthday has been reached on or before July 1 of the year in which the Jurisdictional Conference is held.[6]

b) Pension as approved by the General Conference shall be payable on September 1 following the close of the Jurisdictional Conference.

c) If, however, the retired bishop accepts any one of the following assignments of churchwide responsibility, the General Council on Finance and Administration, after consultation with the Council of Bishops, shall set a level of compensation not to exceed a maximum determined by the General Conference on recommendation of the General Council on Finance and Administration: (1) assignment of a special nature with direct

---

[5]*See* Judicial Council Decisions 361, 407.
[6]*See* Judicial Council Decisions 413, 578.

relationship and accountability to the Council of Bishops, or (2) assignment to a general agency or United Methodist Church–related institution of higher education. Only the difference between the compensation as established and the continuing pension shall be paid from the Episcopal Fund. Assignment of retired bishops to United Methodist Church–related institutions of higher education must be at the initiative of the institutions, with service not to exceed the mandatory retirement ages of the institutions.

If a bishop is assigned to a general agency or United Methodist Church–related institution of higher education, that agency or United Methodist Church–related institution of higher education shall participate by payment of 50 percent of the difference between the compensation herein established and the pension of the bishop. The general agency or United Methodist Church–related institution of higher education shall further assume all responsibility for the bishop's operational and travel expenses related to the assignment.

Compensation for any special assignment shall cease after the bishop has reached the mandatory age of retirement for all ordained ministers (¶ 451.1) or completes the assignment, whichever comes first. No assignment to a jurisdiction, Central Conference, Annual Conference, or non–United Methodist agency shall qualify for additional compensation from the Episcopal Fund under the provisions of this paragraph. The status of a retired bishop on special assignment shall, for purposes of housing and other benefits, be that of a retired bishop.

2. *Voluntary Retirement.—a)* Bishops who have completed twenty years or more of service under full-time appointment as ordained ministers, or as local pastors with pension credit, prior to the opening date of the session of the Jurisdictional Conference, including at least one quadrennium as bishop, may request the Jurisdictional Conference or Central Conference to retire them with the privilege of receiving their pension as determined by the General Council on Finance and Administration, payment of which may begin the first of any month when such payments would be permissible under the provisions of the Ministerial Pension Plan. If the bishop has not reached age

sixty-five or completed forty years of service at the time of retirement, the pension benefit for years of service prior to January 1, 1982, may be actuarially reduced as provided under guidelines adopted by the General Conference.

b) Bishops who have attained age sixty-two or have completed thirty-five years of service under full-time appointment as an elder or bishop may request the Jurisdictional or Central Conference to place them in the retired relation with the privilege of receiving their pension as determined by the General Council on Finance and Administration.

c) Any bishop who seeks a voluntary retired status shall notify the president of the Council of Bishops at least six months prior to the General Conference.

d) A bishop may seek voluntary retirement for health reasons and shall be so retired by the Jurisdictional or Central Conference Committee on Episcopacy upon recommendation by the involved College of Bishops and upon presentation of satisfactory medical evidence. Such bishops shall receive their pensions as provided by the General Council on Finance and Administration in consultation with the Jurisdictional or Central Conference Committee on Episcopacy.

e) Pension as approved by the General Conference shall be payable on September 1 following the close of the Jurisdictional Conference.

3. *Involuntary Retirement.—a)* A bishop may be placed in the retired relation regardless of age by a two-thirds vote of the Jurisdictional or Central Conference Committee on Episcopacy if, after not less than a thirty-day notice in writing is given to the affected bishop and hearing held, such relationship is found by said committee to be in the best interests of the bishop and/or the Church. Appeal from this action may be made to the Judicial Council with the notice provisions being applicable as set forth in ¶ 2625.2.

b) A bishop, for health reasons, may be retired between sessions of the Jurisdictional or Central Conference by a two-thirds vote of the Jurisdictional or Central Conference Committee on Episcopacy upon the recommendation of one third of the membership of the involved College of Bishops. The affected bishop, upon request, shall be entitled to a review of his/her health condition by a professional diagnostic team prior to action by the involved College of Bishops. Notification of action to retire shall be given by the chairperson and secretary of the Jurisdictional or Central Conference Committee on Episcopacy to the secretary of the Council of Bishops and the treasurer of the Episcopal Fund. Appeal from this action may be made to the Judicial Council with the notice provisions being applicable as set forth in ¶ 2625.2. Upon such retirement, the bishop shall receive a pension as determined by the General Council on Finance and Administration. *See also* §2d above.

4. *Resignation.*—A bishop may voluntarily resign from the episcopacy at any time. A bishop may resign from the office by submitting his/her resignation to the Council of Bishops. The Council of Bishops shall have authority to take appropriate actions concerning matters relating to the resignation, including the appointment of an acting bishop to act until a successor is elected and assigned. The consecration papers of a bishop in good standing so resigning shall be properly inscribed by the secretary of the Council of Bishops and returned. He/she shall be furnished with a certificate of resignation which shall entitle him/her to membership as a traveling elder in the Annual Conference (or its successor) in which membership was last held. Notification of this action shall be given by the secretary of the Council of Bishops to the chairperson and secretary of the Jurisdictional or Central Conference Committee on Episcopacy. When the resigned bishop or surviving spouse and dependent children become conference claimants, the Episcopal Fund shall pay a pension as determined by the General Council on Finance and Administration.

¶ **510.** *Status of Retired Bishops.*—A retired bishop is a bishop of the Church in every respect and continues to function as a member of the Council of Bishops in accordance with the Constitution and other provisions of the Discipline.

1. Retired bishops may participate in the Council of Bishops and its committees but without vote. They may preside over sessions of an Annual Conference, Provisional Annual Conference, or Mission if requested to do so by the bishop assigned to that conference, or in the event of that bishop's incapacity, by the president of the College of Bishops to which the conference is

related. In emergency situations, where the resident bishop is unable to preside, the College of Bishops shall assign an effective or retired bishop to preside over the sessions of the Annual Conference (¶ 51). They may not make appointments or preside at the Jurisdiction or Central Conference. However, when a retired bishop is appointed by the Council of Bishops to a vacant episcopal area or parts of an area under the provisions of ¶ 510.3 or ¶ 511.2, that bishop may function as a bishop in the effective relationship.[7]

2. A retired bishop may be considered a member of an Annual Conference, without vote, for purposes of appointment to a local charge within the said conference.

3. A bishop retired under ¶ 509.1, .2 above may be appointed by the Council of Bishops upon recommendation of the involved College of Bishops to presidential responsibility for temporary service in an area in the case of death, resignation, disability, or procedure involving a resident bishop (¶ 2624.2). This appointment shall not continue beyond the next Jurisdictional or Central Conference.

4. Each Central Conference shall determine the rules for retirement of its bishops, *provided* that the age of retirement shall not exceed that fixed for bishops in the jurisdictions. In the event that retirement allowances are paid from the Episcopal Fund, these rules shall be subject to the approval of the General Conference.[8]

5. A bishop of a Central Conference who served as bishop up to the time of mandatory age retirement prior to the time of Union in 1968 shall be entitled to the following status and emoluments, prospectively and from the time of adoption of this provision: (1) has the right to use the title "bishop"; (2) has the right to attend sessions of the Council of Bishops; (3) has the right to have expenses paid for attendance at sessions of the Council of Bishops; (4) has the right to be seated among the bishops and retired bishops on the platform of the General Conference; (5) has the right to have expenses paid for attendance at sessions of the General Conference.

---

[7]*See* Judicial Council Decision 248.
[8]*See* Judicial Council Decisions 199, 407.

The foregoing provisions are separable and if the Judicial Council should hold one or more to be ineffective or invalid that shall not affect the others.

¶ **511.** *Leaves.*—1. *Renewal Leave.*—Every bishop in the active relationship shall take up to three consecutive months' leave from his/her normal episcopal responsibilities, for purposes of reflection, study, and self-renewal, once during each quadrennium. The College of Bishops, in consultation with the appropriate Jurisdictional or Central Conference Committee on Episcopacy, shall coordinate details pertaining to such leaves.

2. *Sabbatical Leave.*—A bishop who has served for at least two quadrenniums may be granted a sabbatical leave of not more than one year for a justifiable reason other than health if the request is made and if the involved College of Bishops, the Committee on Episcopacy of that jurisdiction or Central Conference, and the Council of Bishops or its executive committee approve. In this event the bishop shall, for the period for which the leave is granted, be released from the presidential responsibilities within the episcopal area; and another bishop or bishops, active or retired and not necessarily from the same jurisdiction or Central Conference, shall be designated by the Council of Bishops, on recommendation of the College of Bishops of the jurisdiction or Central Conference involved, to assume the presidential duties during the interim. The bishop shall receive one-half salary and, where applicable, housing allowance for the period of the leave.

3. *Disability Leave.*—Bishops who by reason of impaired health are temporarily unable to perform full work may be released by the Jurisdictional or Central Conference Committee on Episcopacy from the obligation to travel through the connection at large. They may choose a place of residence, and the Council of Bishops shall be at liberty to assign them to such work as they may be able to perform. They shall receive support as provided by the Episcopal Fund.

¶ **512.** *Bishops in Central Conferences.*—The Central Conferences shall elect bishops, in the number determined by the General Conference, whose episcopal supervision shall be within the territory included in the Central Conference by which they have been elected, subject to such other conditions as the General

Conference shall prescribe; *provided,* however, that a bishop elected by a Central Conference may exercise episcopal supervision in another Central Conference or a Jurisdictional Conference when so requested by such other Central Conference or Jurisdictional Conference.

1. Bishops elected by a Central Conference shall be constituted by election in a Central Conference and consecrated by the laying on of hands of three bishops or at least one bishop and two elders.

2. Bishops elected by a Central Conference shall have the same authority as that exercised by bishops elected by or administering in a Jurisdictional Conference.

3. Bishops elected by a Central Conference shall have the same status, rights, and duties as a bishop elected by or functioning in a Jurisdictional Conference. A bishop elected by a Central Conference shall have membership in the Council of Bishops and shall have the privilege of full participation with vote. Attendance at the annual meetings of the Council of Bishops by bishops elected by Central Conferences shall be left to the option of the bishops in each Central Conference.

4. In a Central Conference where term episcopacy prevails, bishops whose term of office expires prior to the time of compulsory retirement because of age and who are not reelected by the Central Conference shall be returned to membership as traveling elders in the Annual Conference (or its successor) of which they ceased to be a member when elected bishop. Their term of office shall expire at the close of the Central Conference at which their successor is elected, and they shall therefore be entitled to participate as a bishop in the consecration of the successor. The credentials of office as bishop shall be submitted to the secretary of the Central Conference, who shall make thereon the notation that the bishop has honorably completed the term of service for which elected and has ceased to be a bishop of The United Methodist Church.[9]

¶ **513.** *Involuntary Termination of Office.*—1. Episcopal leadership in The United Methodist Church shares with all other ordained persons in the sacred trust of their ordination. The

------

[9]*See* Judicial Council Decisions 61, 236, 370.

ministry of bishops as set forth in the Book of Discipline of The United Methodist Church also flows from the gospel as taught by Jesus the Christ and proclaimed by his apostles. Whenever a bishop violates this trust or is unable to fulfill appropriate responsibilities, continuation in the episcopal office shall be subject to review. This review shall have as its purpose the reconciliation and restoration of the bishop and the strengthening of the Church. If a remedial process is unfruitful, it shall be the responsibility of the Jurisdictional Committee on Episcopacy to make appropriate response.

2. Any grievance concerning the effectiveness, competence, or one or more of the offenses listed in ¶ 2621 shall be submitted to the president of the College of Bishops in that jurisdiction. If the grievance concerns the president, it may be submitted to any other office of the College of Bishops. A grievance is a written statement claiming misconduct, unsatisfactory performance of ministerial duties, or one or more of the offenses listed in ¶ 2621.

3. *Review Committee, Jurisdictional Committee on Episcopacy.*— In each jurisdiction there shall be a **Review Committee** composed of four clergy members from the Annual Conferences of that jurisdiction and two bishops other than the current officers of the College of Bishops. The Review Committee shall be appointed by the Jurisdictional Committee on Episcopacy and shall serve for the quadrennium.

This Review Committee shall receive from the College of Bishops all grievances concerning bishops in that jurisdiction and seek resolution of them. The work of this committee shall be informal and confidential and shall guarantee that the person or persons lodging the grievance and the bishop against whom the grievance is lodged shall have the right to be heard. No witnesses will be called and no counsel shall be present. Should the bishop desire it, another bishop or a clergyperson chosen by the bishop may accompany him/her at the meeting of the committee.

If resolution of the matter is not achieved, the Review Committee may prepare a complaint and forward it to the Jurisdictional Committee on Episcopacy with any recommendations.

4. *Complaints.*—A complaint prepared by the Review Committee, to the Jurisdictional Committee on Episcopacy, must be

based on incompetence, ineffectiveness, or one or more of the offenses listed in ¶ 2621 and shall be submitted in written form and signed by the chairperson of the Review Committee. No complaint shall be considered for any misconduct or unsatisfactory performance which shall not have been committed within two years immediately preceding the receipt of the grievance. The bishop named in the complaint shall be informed of the process and its purpose. Complaints shall be lodged with the chairperson of the jurisdictional committee.

5. *Disposition of Complaint.*—When a complaint with any attached recommendations has been received by the Jurisdictional Committee on Episcopacy, that committee shall develop a response based on the report of the Review Committee and the needs of the Church and the bishop. The jurisdictional committee may recommend involuntary retirement (¶ 509.3), sabbatical leave (¶ 511.2), disability leave (¶ 511.3), remedial action (as listed in ¶ 453.1e), or it may dismiss the complaint. In rare instances when the jurisdictional committee deems the matter serious enough and when one or more offenses listed in ¶ 2621 are involved, the Jurisdictional Committee on Episcopacy may refer the complaint to the Jurisdictional Committee on Investigation for possible trial (¶ 2623.2).

6. Any actions of the jurisdictional committee taken on a complaint shall be reported to the next session of the Jurisdictional Conference.

Section IV. Specific Responsibilities of Bishops.

¶ **514.** *Leadership.—Spiritual and Temporal.*—1. To lead and oversee the spiritual and temporal affairs of The United Methodist Church, which confesses Jesus Christ as Lord and Savior, and particularly to lead the Church in its mission of witness and service in the world.

2. To travel through the connection at large as the Council of Bishops (¶ 526) to implement strategy for the concerns of the Church.

3. To provide liaison and leadership in the quest for Christian unity in ministry, mission, and structure and in the search for strengthened relationships with other living faith communities.

4. To organize such Missions as shall have been authorized by the General Conference.

5. To promote and support the evangelistic witness of the whole Church.

6. To discharge such other duties as the Discipline may direct.

¶ **515.** *Presidential Duties.*—1. To preside in the General, Jurisdictional, Central, and Annual Conferences.[10]

2. To provide general oversight for the fiscal and program operations of the Annual Conference(s). This may include special inquiry into the work of agencies to assure that the Annual Conference and general church policies and procedures are followed.

3. To form the districts after consultation with the district superintendents and after the number of the same has been determined by vote of the Annual Conference.[11]

4. To appoint the district superintendents annually (¶¶ 517-518).

5. To consecrate bishops, to ordain elders and deacons, to consecrate diaconal ministers, to commission deaconesses and missionaries, and to see that the names of the persons commissioned and consecrated are entered on the journals of the conference and that proper credentials are furnished to these persons.

6. To fix the appointments of deaconesses and missionaries and to see that the names and appointments are printed in the journals of the conference.

¶ **516.** *Working with Ordained Ministers.*—1. To make and fix the appointments in the Annual Conferences, Provisional Annual Conferences, and Missions as the Discipline may direct (¶¶ 530-534).

2. To divide or to unite a circuit(s), station(s), or mission(s) as judged necessary for missional strategy and then to make appropriate appointments.

3. To read the appointments of deaconesses, diaconal ministers, lay persons in service under the World Division of the General Board of Global Ministries, and home missionaries.

---

[10]*See* Judicial Council Decision 395.
[11]*See* Judicial Council Decision 422.

4. To fix the Charge Conference membership of all ordained ministers appointed to ministries other than the local church in keeping with ¶ 443.

5. To transfer, upon the request of the receiving bishop, clergy member(s) of one Annual Conference to another; *provided* said member(s) agrees to said transfer; and to send immediately to the secretaries of both conferences involved, to the conference Boards of Ordained Ministry, and to the clearing house of the General Board of Pensions written notices of the transfer of members and of their standing in the course of study if they are undergraduates.[12]

6. To appoint associate members, probationary members, or full members to attend any school, college, or theological seminary listed by the University Senate, or to participate in a program of Clinical Pastoral Education in a setting certified by the Association of Clinical Pastoral Educators. Such persons are not to be considered as appointments beyond the local church.

Section V. Selection, Assignment, and Term of District Superintendents.

¶ **517.** *Selection and Assignment.*—Inasmuch as the district superintendency is an extension of the general superintendency, the bishop shall appoint elders to serve as district superintendents. Prior to each appointment, the bishop shall consult with the Cabinet and the Committee on District Superintendency of the district to which the new superintendent will be assigned (¶ 531), for the purpose of determining leadership needs of the Annual Conference and the district (¶¶ 501-502). In the selection of superintendents, bishops shall give due consideration to the inclusiveness of The United Methodist Church with respect to sex, race, national origin, and age except for the provisions of mandatory retirement.

¶ **518.** *Limitations on Years of Service.*—An elder may not be appointed a district superintendent for more than six years in any consecutive nine years. No elder shall serve as district superintendent more than twelve years. In addition, consideration shall

---

[12]*See* Judicial Council Decisions 114, 254, 554.

be given to the nature of superintendency as described in
¶¶ 501-502.[13]

Section VI. Specific Responsibilities of District Superintendents.

¶ **519.** The district superintendent shall oversee the total
ministry of the pastors and the churches in the communities of
the district in its mission of witness and service in the world: (1) by
giving pastoral support and supervision to the clergy of the
district; (2) by encouraging their personal, spiritual, and
professional growth; (3) by encouraging their personal commitment to the mandate of inclusiveness in the life of the Church; (4)
by participating with the bishops in the appointment-making
process; (5) by enabling programs throughout the district that
may assist local churches to build and extend their ministry and
mission with their people and to the community; (6) by working
in cooperation with appropriate district and Annual Conference
agencies to explore long-range, experimental, ecumenical,
multi-cultural, multi-racial, and cooperative ministries; (7) by
encouraging local congregations to work with ecumenical
agencies and coalitions in the sharing of resources, and to
develop an understanding of and relationship to other living
faith communities; (8) by assisting the bishop in the administration of the Annual Conference; (9) by participating in the
conference Council on Ministries and the district Council on
Ministries where it exists. In the fulfillment of this ministry, the
superintendent shall consult at least annually (¶ 751.3) with the
Committee on District Superintendency. In the context of these
basic responsibilities, the district superintendent shall give
attention to the following specific tasks.[14]

¶ **520.** *Supervision.*—1. To work with pastors, diaconal
ministers, and Charge Conferences in formulating statements of
purpose for congregations in fulfilling their mission, and
Committees on Pastor-Parish Relations to clarify the pastors' and
diaconal ministers' priorities for ministry.

---

[13]*See* Judicial Council Decisions 368, 512.
[14]*See* Judicial Council Decision 398.

2. To establish a clearly understood process of supervision for clergy of the district, including observation of all aspects of ministry, direct evaluation, and feedback to the clergy involved.

3. To consult with Committees on Pastor-Parish Relations to update their profiles for appointment in accordance with ¶ 532.1 and with pastors to update their profiles for appointment in accordance with ¶ 532.2.

4. To make specific provision for the supervision of probationary members and local pastors appointed within the district and for building clusters for supervision with the assistance of counseling or supervising elders in the district.

5. To receive annually from each clergy person a report of his/her program of continuing education, to give counsel concerning future plans, and to encourage congregations to give time and financial support for such programs.

¶ **521.** *Personnel.*—1. To work with pastors and diaconal ministers, Committees on Pastor-Parish Relations, and congregations in interpreting the meaning of ministry and in identifying and enlisting candidates of the highest quality for ordained and diaconal ministry, with special concern for the inclusiveness of the Church with respect to sex, race, and national origin.

2. To work with the district Committee on Ordained Ministry in enabling a meaningful and appropriate examination of candidates into ordained ministry; to issue and renew licenses to preach when authorized (¶ 407); to keep careful records of all such candidates; to maintain regular communication with all candidates in order to advise and encourage them in spiritual and academic preparation for their ministry. The district superintendent shall not serve as chairperson of the district Committee on Ordained Ministry.

3. To work with the bishop and Cabinet in the process of appointment and assignment for ordained ministers.

4. To cooperate with the Board of Ordained Ministry in its efforts to provide or arrange support services and liaison for pastors at times of changing conference relationships or termination (¶¶ 410, 447-453, 454-455).

5. To work with the bishop, conference Board of Diaconal Ministry, and diaconal ministers in matters of mutual concern for the personal and professional support of diaconal ministers.

¶ **522.** *Pastoral.*—1. To give pastoral support and care to the clergy and diaconal ministers and their families by traveling through the district, preaching, visiting, and maintaining the connectional order of the Discipline.

2. To counsel with clergy concerning their pastoral responsibilities and diaconal ministers concerning their ministerial duties as well as other matters affecting their ministry and personal life.

3. To encourage the building of peer groups among the clergy and diaconal ministers for mutual support and discipline; to build systems of mutual support for clergy and diaconal families.

¶ **523.** *Administration.*—1. To schedule and preside, or authorize an elder to preside, in each annual Charge Conference or Church Conference within the district (¶¶ 246, 248).

2. To administer the district office including supervision of support staff (¶¶ 710.1*a*; 751.4*a*).

3. To develop adequate salary support for all clergy, including provision for housing, utilities, travel, and continuing education.

4. To cooperate with the district Board of Church Location and Building and local church Boards of Trustees or building committees in arranging acquisitions, sales, transfers, and mortgages of property; and to ensure that all charters, deeds, and other legal documents conform to the Discipline and to the laws, usages, and forms of the county, state, territory, or country within which such property is situated, and to keep copies thereof.

5. Prior to consenting to the proposed action to sell or transfer any United Methodist Church property to ensure that an investigation be made and a plan of action be developed for the future missional needs of the community by The United Methodist Church.

6. To keep accurate and complete records for one's successor including:

a) All abandoned church properties and cemeteries within the bounds of the district;

b) All church properties being permissively used by other religious organizations, with the names of the local trustees thereof;

c) All known endowments, annuities, trust funds, investments, and unpaid legacies belonging to any pastoral charge or organization connected therewith in the district and an accounting of their management;

d) Membership of persons from churches which have been closed.

7. To promote current and deferred financial support in local churches for district, conference, and denominational causes.

8. To transfer members of a discontinued church to another United Methodist church of their choice or to such other churches as members may elect.

9. To recommend to the bishop for approval, after consultation with the churches involved, any realignment of pastoral charge lines and report them to the Annual Conference.

10. To serve within the district as acting administrator of any pastoral charge in which a pastoral vacancy may develop or where no pastor has been appointed.[15]

11. To see that the provisions of the Discipline are observed and to interpret and decide all questions of church law and discipline raised by the churches in the district, subject to an appeal to the president of the Annual Conference.

12. Secure an annual audit report of any and all district funds and send a copy to the District Conference or Annual Conference Council on Finance and Administration.

¶ **524.** *Program.*—1. To oversee the programs of the Church within the bounds of the district in cooperation with pastors and congregations, working with and through the district Council on Ministries where it exists.

2. To serve as a member of the Annual Conference Council on Ministries and to work cooperatively with the conference council and its staff in all program concerns of the Church.

3. To establish long-range planning which is responsive to ecumenical and racially inclusive perspectives and to initiate new and vital forms of ministry.

4. To participate with the Cabinet in submitting to the Annual Conference a report reflecting the state of the conference, with recommendations for greater effectiveness.

---

[15]*See* Judicial Council Decision 581.

¶ **525.** A district superintendent may take up to three consecutive months' leave from his/her normal superintendent responsibilities for purposes of reflection, study, and self-renewal once during his/her term as superintendent. The bishop and Cabinet, in consultation with the Committee on District Superintendency, shall coordinate details pertaining to such leaves.

Section VII.   Expressions of Superintendency.

¶ **526.** The offices of bishop and district superintendent are linked with each other in ways described elsewhere (¶ 503). The interdependence of the offices calls for a collegial style of leadership. However, both the office of bishop and that of district superintendent are embedded in their own contexts.

¶ **527.** *Council of Bishops.*—1. Bishops, although elected by Jurisdictional or Central Conferences, are elected general superintendents of the whole Church. As all ordained ministers are first elected into membership of an Annual Conference and subsequently appointed to pastoral charges, so bishops become through their election members first of the Council of Bishops before they are subsequently assigned to areas of service.

2. The Council of Bishops is thus the collegial expression of episcopal leadership in the Church and through the Church into the world. The Church expects the Council of Bishops to speak to the Church and from the Church to the world, and to give leadership in the quest for Christian unity and interreligious relationships.

3. In order to exercise meaningful leadership, the Council of Bishops is to meet at stated intervals. The Council of Bishops is charged with the oversight of the spiritual and temporal affairs of the whole Church, to be executed in regularized consultation and cooperation with other councils and service agencies of the Church.

¶ **528.** *Conference of Methodist Bishops.*—There may be a Conference of Methodist Bishops, composed of all the bishops elected by the Jurisdictional and Central Conferences and one bishop or chief executive officer from each Affiliated Autonomous Methodist or United Church, which shall meet on call of the Council of Bishops after consultation with other members of the Conference of Methodist Bishops. The travel and other necessary expense of bishops of Affiliated Autonomous Methodist or United Churches related to the meeting of the Conference of Methodist Bishops shall be paid on the same basis as that of bishops of The United Methodist Church.

¶ **529.** *Cabinet.*—1. District superintendents, although appointed to districts, are also to be given conference-wide responsibilities. As all ordained ministers are first elected into membership of an Annual Conference and subsequently appointed to pastoral charges, so district superintendents become through their selection members first of a Cabinet before they are subsequently appointed to service in districts.

2. The Cabinet under the leadership of the bishop is the expression of superintending leadership in and through the Annual Conference. It is expected to speak to the conference and for the conference to the spiritual and temporal issues that exist within the region encompassed by the conference.

3. The Cabinet is thus also the body in which the individual district superintendents are held accountable for their work, both for conference and district responsibilities.

4. In order to exercise meaningful leadership, the Cabinet is to meet at stated intervals. The Cabinet is charged with the oversight of the spiritual and temporal affairs of a conference, to be executed in regularized consultation and cooperation with other councils and service agencies of the conference.

5. To consult and plan with the district committee and conference Board of Ordained Ministry in order to make a thorough analysis of the needs of the district for clergy, implementing this planning with a positive and conscious effort to fill these needs (¶ 733.2*a*).

6. When the Cabinet considers matters relating to coordination, implementation, or administration of the conference program, and other matters as the Cabinet and director may determine, the conference council director shall be present. The director shall not be present during the Cabinet discussions on matters related to the making of appointments.

Section VIII.   Appointment-Making.

¶ **530.** *Responsibility.*—1. Pastors and clergy in appointments beyond the local church shall be appointed by a bishop, who is empowered to make and fix all appointments in the episcopal area within which the Annual Conference is a part. Appointments are to be made with consideration of the gifts and evidence of God's grace of those appointed, to the needs, characteristics, and opportunities of congregations and institutions, and with faithfulness to the commitment to an open itineracy. Open itineracy means appointments are made without regard to race, ethnic origin, sex, color, or age, except for the provisions of mandatory retirement. Through appointment-making, the connectional nature of the United Methodist system is made visible.

2. To make visible the connectional nature of the United Methodist system and to relate appointment-making to the missional needs of the whole church, itineracy across conference lines shall be encouraged. The Jurisdictional Conference may authorize a Jurisdictional Committee on Ordained Ministry to support this policy in cooperation with bishops, Cabinets, and Boards of Ordained Ministry. Part of the jurisdictional committee responsibility should be to make a study of anticipated clergy supply and demand in the conferences of the jurisdiction during the last quarter of each calendar year and provide this information to bishops, Cabinets, and Boards of Ordained Ministry by January 15. A part of this responsibility should be an annual study of the supply, demand, and mobility of ethnic clergy, clergy couples, and clergywomen within and across jurisdictions.

¶ **531.** *Consultation and Appointment-Making.*—Consultation is the process whereby the bishop and/or district superintendent confer with the pastor and Committee on Pastor-Parish Relations, taking into consideration the criteria of ¶ 532, a performance evaluation, needs of the appointment under consideration, and mission of the Church. Consultation is not merely notification. Consultation is not committee selection or call of a pastor. The role of the Committee on Pastor-Parish Relations is advisory. Consultation is both a continuing process and a more intense involvement during the period of change in appointment.[16]

---

[16]*See* Judicial Council Decisions 101, 501.

1. The process of consultation shall be mandatory in every Annual Conference.

2. The Council of Bishops shall inquire annually of their colleagues about the implementation of the process of consultation in appointment-making in their respective areas.

¶ **532.** *Criteria.*—Appointments shall take into account the unique needs of a charge in a particular setting and also the gifts and evidence of God's grace of a particular pastor. To assist bishops, Cabinets, pastors, and congregations to achieve an effective match of charges and pastors, criteria must be developed and analyzed in each instance and then shared with pastors and congregations.

1. *Congregations.*—The district superintendent shall develop with the pastor and the Committees on Pastor-Parish Relations of all churches profiles which include reflecting the needs, characteristics, and opportunities for mission of the charge consistent with the church's statement of purpose (¶ 520.1). These profiles shall be reviewed annually and updated when appropriate to include:

a) The general situation in which a congregation finds itself in a particular setting: size, financial condition, quality of lay leadership, history.

b) The convictional stance of the congregation: theology; prejudices, if any; spiritual life.

c) The ministry of the congregation among its people for the sake of the community: service programs, basis for adding new members, reasons for losing members, mission to community and world, forms of witness.

d) The qualities and functions of pastoral ministry needed to fulfill the mission and goals of the congregation.

2. *Pastors.*—The district superintendent annually shall develop with the pastor profiles reflecting the pastor's gifts, evidence of God's grace, and professional experience and expectations, and also the needs and concerns of the pastor's spouse and family. These profiles shall be reviewed annually and updated when appropriate to include:

a) Spiritual and personal sensibility: personal faith, call and commitment to ordained ministry, work through the institutional

Church, integration of vocation with personal and family well-being, life-style.

b) Academic and career background: nature of theological stance, experience in continuing education, professional experience, record of performance.

c) Skills and abilities: in church administration, leadership development, worship and liturgy, preaching and evangelism, teaching and nurturing, counseling and group work, ability to work in cooperation, and ability in self-evaluation, and other relational skills.

d) Family situation: health and educational needs of the family, and the spouse's career.

¶ **533.** *Process of Appointment-Making.*—The process used in appointment-making shall include:

1. A change in appointment may be initiated by a pastor, a Committee on Pastor-Parish Relations, a district superintendent, or a bishop.

2. The bishop and the Cabinet shall consider all requests for change of appointment in light of the profile developed for each charge and the gifts and evidence of God's grace, professional experience, and family needs of the pastor.

3. When a change in appointment has been determined, the district superintendent should meet together or separately with the pastor and the Committee on Pastor-Parish Relations where the pastor is serving, for the purpose of sharing the basis for the change and the process used in making the new appointment.

4. All appointments shall receive consideration by the bishop and the district superintendent(s) and the Cabinet as a whole until a tentative decision is made.

5. The process used in making the new appointment shall include:

a) The district superintendent shall confer with the pastor about a specific possible appointment (charge) and its congruence with gifts, evidence of God's grace, professional experience and expectations, and the family needs of the pastor identified in consultation with the pastor (¶ 532.2).

b) If the appointment is to a Cooperative Parish Ministry or to a charge which is part of a Cooperative Parish Ministry, the following shall be included in the consultation process.

(1) The prospective appointee shall be informed prior to the appointment that the charge under consideration is part of a Cooperative Parish Ministry.[17]

(2) The coordinator or director of the cooperative ministry, or, if there is no coordinator or director, a representative of the staff of the cooperative ministry, shall be conferred with concerning the prospective appointment and shall have the opportunity to meet with the prospective appointee prior to the appointment being made.[18]

6. The district superintendent shall confer with the receiving Committee on Pastor-Parish Relations about pastoral leadership (¶ 532.1).

7. When appointments are being made to less than full-time ministry, the district superintendent shall consult with the ordained minister to be appointed and the Committee on Pastor-Parish Relations regarding proportional time, salary, and pension credit.

8. If during this consultative process it is determined by the bishop and Cabinet that this decision should not be carried out, the process is to be repeated until the bishop, basing his/her decision on the information and advice derived from consultation, makes and fixes the appointment.

9. A similar process of consultation shall be available to persons in appointments beyond the local church.

10. When the steps in the process have been followed and completed, the announcement of that decision shall be made to all parties directly involved in the consultative process; that is, the appointment Cabinet, the pastor, and the Committee on Pastor-Parish Relations, before a public announcement is made.

¶ **534.** *Frequency.*—While the bishop shall report all pastoral appointments to each regular session of an Annual Conference, appointments to charges may be made at any time deemed advisable by the bishop and Cabinet.

---

[17]*See* Judicial Council Decision 556.
[18]*See* Judicial Council Decision 556.

Chapter Five
THE CONFERENCES

The United Methodist Church is a connectional structure maintained through its chain of conferences.

Section I. The General Conference.

¶ **601.** *Definition of Powers.*—The General Conference has full legislative power over all matters distinctively connectional (*see* ¶ 15, Division Two, Section II, Article IV, The Constitution). It has no executive or administrative power.

¶ **602.** *Composition.*—1. The voting membership of the **General Conference** shall consist of:

a) An equal number of clergy and lay delegates elected by the Annual Conferences as provided in the Discipline. The Missionary Conferences and Provisional Annual Conferences shall be considered as Annual Conferences for the purposes of this paragraph.

b) Delegates from The Methodist Church in Great Britain and other Autonomous Methodist Churches with which concordat agreements have been established providing for mutual election and seating of delegates in each other's highest legislative conferences (¶¶ 12.2, 12.3; 653).

2. The number of delegates to which an Annual Conference is entitled shall be computed on a two-factor basis: the number of clergy members of the Annual Conference and the number of members of local churches in the Annual Conference.[1]

The term "clergy members" as used in this paragraph shall refer to both active and retired members of the Annual Conference (¶ 701.1).

3. The secretary of the General Conference shall calculate the number of delegates to be elected by each Annual Conference, based on the factors specified above, as follows:

a) One clergy delegate for the first 140 clergy members of the Annual Conference and one clergy delegate for each additional 140 clergy members or major fraction thereof,[2] and

---

[1]*See* Judicial Council Decisions 109, 333, 592.
[2]*See* Judicial Council Decisions 327, 558.

b) One clergy delegate for the first 44,000 members of local churches of the Annual Conference and one clergy delegate for each additional 44,000 local church members or major fraction thereof, and

c) A number of lay delegates equal to the total number of clergy delegates authorized as above.

d) Every Annual Conference shall be entitled to at least one clergy and one lay delegate.

e) This formula is designated to comply with the Constitution, Division Two, Section II, Article I (¶ 12), which defines the minimum and maximum number of delegates to a General Conference. Should the computations provided in the paragraph result in a figure below the prescribed minimum or above the prescribed maximum for delegates, the secretary of the General Conference shall be authorized to remedy the situation by adjusting up or down the numbers of clergy members and members of local churches of the Annual Conference necessary to entitle an Annual Conference to elect delegates, any such adjustment to be proportionally the same for the two factors.

4. Delegates to the General Conference shall be elected at the session of the Annual Conference held in the calendar year preceding the session of the General Conference. At least thirty days prior to the beginning of that calendar year, the secretary of the General Conference shall notify the bishop and the secretary of each Annual Conference of the number of delegates to be elected by that Annual Conference.

5. The secretary of each Annual Conference, using the certificate of election form supplied by the secretary of the General Conference, shall report to the secretary of the General Conference the names, addresses, and such other information as may be required for delegates and reserves elected by the Annual Conference.

6. The secretary of the General Conference shall prepare and send to each Annual Conference secretary credentials to be signed and distributed to the delegates and reserves elected by the Annual Conference.

¶ **603.** *Presiding Officers.*—The bishops shall be the presiding officers at the General Conference.

¶ **604.** *Election of Secretary-Designate.*—The Council of Bishops shall present a nomination from the ordained ministry or lay membership of The United Methodist Church for secretary-designate. Other nominations shall be permitted from the floor. The election, if there be two or more nominees, shall be by ballot.

¶ **605.** The secretary-designate shall assume the responsibilities of the office of secretary as soon after the adjournment of the General Conference as all work in connection with the session, including the preparation, printing, and mailing of the journal, has been completed. The exact date of the transfer of responsibility to the secretary-designate shall be determined by the Commission on the General Conference, but shall not be later than twelve months after the adjournment of the General Conference. The secretary shall, at the request of the Commission on the General Conference, assist in initiating procedures to inform delegates from outside the United States concerning both the operation of the General Conference and materials it will consider. After consultation with the Council of Bishops and the General Commission on Christian Unity and Interreligious Concerns the secretary shall issue invitations to ecumenical representatives.

¶ **606.** *Rules of Order.*—The Plan of Organization and Rules of Order of the General Conference shall be the Plan of Organization and Rules of Order as published in the journal of the preceding General Conference until they have been altered or modified by the action of the General Conference.

¶ **607.** *Quorum.*—When the General Conference is in session, it shall require the presence of a majority of the whole number of delegates to the General Conference to constitute a quorum for the transaction of business; but a smaller number may take a recess or adjourn from day to day in order to secure a quorum, and at the final session may approve the journal, order the record of the roll call, and adjourn sine die.

¶ **608.** *Petitions to General Conference.*—Any organization, ordained minister, or lay member of The United Methodist Church may petition the General Conference in the following manner:

1. Three copies of the petition must be sent to the secretary of the General Conference or a designated petitions secretary.

2. Each petition must address only one paragraph of the Discipline or, if the Discipline is not affected, one issue.

3. Each petition must be signed by the person submitting it, accompanied by appropriate identification, such as address, local church, or United Methodist board or agency relationship.

4. All petitions submitted to the General Conference, except those submitted by individual members of The United Methodist Church and local church groups, which call for the establishment of new programs or the expansion of existing programs will be invalid unless accompanied by supporting data which addresses the issue of anticipated financial requirements of the program.

5. Petitions must be postmarked by a national postal service no later than sixty days prior to the opening session of the General Conference.

6. If petitions are transmitted by a means other than a national postal service, they must be in the hands of the petitions secretary no later than forty-five days prior to the opening session of the General Conference.

Exceptions to the time limitations shall be granted for petitions originating from an Annual Conference session held within forty-five days prior to the opening session of the General Conference, and for other petitions at the discretion of the Committee on Reference.

7. Petitions adopted and properly submitted by Annual Conferences, Jurisdictional and Central Conferences, the National Youth Ministry Organization, or general agencies or councils of the Church shall be printed in the Advance Edition of the Daily Christian Advocate.

8. Petitions and/or resolutions not printed in the Advance Edition of the Daily Christian Advocate shall be printed or copied and provided to the appropriate legislative committee in sufficient quantity for every committee member to have a copy. Where the content of petitions is essentially the same, the petition will be printed once, with multiple authors listed.

¶ **609.** All legislation of the General Conference of The United Methodist Church shall become effective January 1 following the session of the General Conference at which it is enacted unless otherwise specified (¶ 637.22).

¶ **610.** *Speaking for the Church.*—1. No person, no paper, no organization, has the authority to speak officially for The United Methodist Church, this right having been reserved exclusively to the General Conference under the Constitution. Any written public policy statement issued by a general church agency shall clearly identify either at the beginning or at the end that the statement represents the position of that general agency and not necessarily the position of The United Methodist Church (¶ 817).[3]

2. Any individual member called to testify before a legislative body to represent The United Methodist Church shall be allowed to do so only by reading, without elaboration, the resolutions and positions adopted by the General Conference of The United Methodist Church.

¶ **611.** The secretary of the General Conference shall be responsible for the permanent record of the General Conference which shall include:

1. A journal to be edited by the secretary and published and distributed at cost by The United Methodist Publishing House. Memoirs of members of the Council of Bishops who have died during the quadrennium shall be included.

2. A Book of Resolutions to be edited by The United Methodist Publishing House. The book shall contain all valid resolutions of the General Conference.

a) Resolutions and positions adopted by the General Conference of The United Methodist Church are valid until they are specifically rescinded, amended, or superseded by action of subsequent sessions of the General Conference. All valid resolutions and positions of the General Conference of The United Methodist Church beginning with those adopted by the 1968 Uniting Conference shall be listed in each edition of the Book of Resolutions. There shall be a complete subject index to all valid resolutions of the General Conference of The United Methodist Church in each edition of the Book of Resolutions.

b) The General Council on Ministries and the program boards and agencies shall review all valid resolutions and recommend to the General Conference the removal of time-dated material.

---

[3]*See* Judicial Council Decision 458.

3. The Advance Edition of the Daily Christian Advocate and the Daily Christian Advocate.

4. All original documents of a General Conference shall be filed with the General Commission on Archives and History.

Section II. The Jurisdictional Conference.

¶ **612.** 1. There shall be an **Interjurisdictional Committee on Episcopacy** elected by the General Conference consisting of the persons nominated by their Annual Conference delegations to serve on the several Jurisdictional Committees on Episcopacy.[4] The committee shall meet not later than the fifth day of the conference session and at the time and place set for their convening by the president of the Council of Bishops and shall elect from their number a chairperson, vice-chairperson, and secretary. The function of this joint committee shall be to discuss the possibility of transfers of bishops across jurisdictional lines at the forthcoming Jurisdictional Conferences for residential and presidential responsibilities in the ensuing quadrennium. It shall elect an executive committee consisting of the officers named above and two clergy and two lay persons from the nominees to each jurisdictional committee, elected by that committee to conduct consultations with bishops and others interested in possible episcopal transfers. The executive committee shall be responsible to the interjurisdictional committee.

2. No bishop shall be transferred across jurisdictional lines unless that bishop has consented to such transfer and has served at least one quadrennium in or under assignment by the jurisdiction in which the bishop was elected and unless a concurrent transfer is effected into the jurisdiction from which the bishop is transferring or unless the Jurisdictional Conference which is receiving that bishop has voted to waive this right. Such a transfer shall not be concluded until the Committee on Episcopacy of each jurisdiction involved has approved the plan insofar as it affects its own jurisdiction, by majority vote of those present and voting, and the Jurisdictional Conferences, meeting concurrently, have also approved.

¶ **613.** All Jurisdictional Conferences shall have the same

---

[4]*See* Judicial Council Decision 472.

status and the same privileges of action within the limits fixed by the Constitution.

¶ **614.** The membership of each Jurisdictional Conference shall consist of an equal number of clergy and lay delegates elected by the Annual Conferences as provided in the Discipline. The number of delegates to which an Annual Conference is entitled shall be computed on a two-factor basis: the number of clergy members of the Annual Conference and the number of church members in the Annual Conference, as follows:

1. One clergy delegate for every seventy clergy members of the Annual Conference and one additional clergy delegate for each major fraction thereof, and

2. One clergy delegate for the first 22,000 church members of the Annual Conference and one clergy delegate for each additional 22,000 church members and an additional clergy delegate for each major fraction of 22,000 church members, and

3. A number of lay delegates equal to the total number of clergy delegates authorized as above; *provided* that no Annual Conference shall be denied the privilege of four delegates, two lay and two clergy.

¶ **615.** The clergy and lay delegates and reserves to the Jurisdictional Conferences shall be elected by ballot in accordance with the provisions of the Constitution.

¶ **616.** The clergy and lay delegates shall deliberate in one body.

¶ **617.** Each Jurisdictional Conference shall meet within the period prescribed by the Constitution at such time and place as shall have been determined by the preceding Jurisdictional Conference or by its properly constituted committee.

¶ **618.** The Jurisdictional Conference shall adopt its own procedure, rules, and plan of organization. It shall take a majority of the whole number of delegates elected to make a quorum for the transaction of business; however, a smaller number may take a recess or adjourn from day to day, and at the final session may approve the journal, order the record of the roll call, and adjourn sine die.

¶ **619.** The Jurisdictional Conference shall provide for the expenses of its sessions.

¶ 620. 1. The Jurisdictional Conference may order a special session in such manner as it shall determine.

2. The College of Bishops of a jurisdiction by a two-thirds vote shall have authority to call a special session of the Jurisdictional Conference when necessary; *provided,* however, that if an episcopal area is left vacant by reason of death, retirement, or other cause within twenty-four months of the close of the preceding Jurisdictional Conference, the College of Bishops may by majority vote convene within three months, after giving not less than thirty days' notice, a special session of the Jurisdictional Conference for the purpose of electing and consecrating a bishop and of considering any other matters specified in the call; and *provided* further, that in such case the standing Committee on Episcopacy may recommend to the conference reassignment of one or more of the previously elected bishops.

3. The delegates to a special session of the Jurisdictional Conference shall be the delegates last elected by each Annual Conference.

4. A called session of the Jurisdictional Conference cannot transact any other business than that indicated in the call.

¶ 621. The Jurisdictional Conference shall be presided over by the bishops of the jurisdiction or a bishop of another jurisdiction or of a Central Conference. In case no bishop of the jurisdiction is present, the conference may elect a president from the clergy delegates.

¶ 622. Bishops elected by or administering in a Jurisdictional Conference shall be amenable for their conduct to their Jurisdictional Conference. Any bishop shall have the right of appeal to the Judicial Council.

¶ 623. *Jurisdictional Committee on Episcopacy.*—1. There shall be a **Jurisdictional Committee on Episcopacy** consisting of one clergy and one lay delegate to the Jurisdictional Conference from each Annual Conference elected by the Jurisdictional Conference upon nomination of their respective Annual Conference delegations.[5]

The committee shall be convened by the president of the College of Bishops at the close of the Jurisdictional Conference to

---

[5]*See* Judicial Council Decision 472.

which the delegates have been elected. It shall serve through the succeeding Jurisdictional Conference.

The committee shall elect from its members a chairperson, a vice-chairperson, and a secretary. It shall meet at least biennially.

Should there be a vacancy in an Annual Conference's elected representation on the Jurisdictional Committee on Episcopacy by death, resignation, election to the episcopacy, cessation of membership in the Annual Conference from which one is elected, or in the event that a member on the Jurisdictional Committee on Episcopacy is not reelected by the Annual Conference as a delegate to the Jurisdictional Conference, or for other reasons that the Annual Conference delegation may determine, the Annual Conference delegation shall nominate another person to fill the vacancy. That person may begin to serve on the committee as a nominee until the Jurisdictional Conference can elect.

2. The Jurisdictional Conference shall provide funding for the expenses of the Jurisdictional Committee on Episcopacy.

3. The Jurisdictional Committee on Episcopacy shall:

a) Review the work of the bishops, pass on their character and official administration, and report to the Jurisdictional Conference its findings for such action as the conference may deem appropriate within its constitutional warrant of power.

b) Recommend boundaries of the episcopal areas and the assignments of the bishops.[6]

c) Be available to the Council/College of Bishops for consultation on matters of mutual concern.

d) Determine the number of effective bishops eligible for assignment.

e) Receive and act upon requests for possible voluntary and involuntary retirement of bishops.

f) Consult with the conference Committees on Episcopacy with respect to the needs for episcopal leadership and how best they can be fulfilled.

g) Establish a consultation process with each bishop regarding his/her episcopal assignment.

h) Prepare a report of its decisions, activities, and recom-

---

[6]*See* Judicial Council Decision 517.

mendations to be transmitted to its successor through the office of the secretary of the Jurisdictional Conference. The report shall be made available to delegates of the Jurisdictional Conference prior to the Jurisdictional Conference.

¶ **624.** The **Jurisdictional Conference** shall have powers and duties as described in the Constitution. It shall also have such other powers and duties as may be conferred by the General Conference, and in exercise thereof it shall act in all respects in harmony with the policy of The United Methodist Church with respect to elimination of discrimination based upon race.

¶ **625.** In all elections in a Jurisdictional Conference which are based on the number of church members within that jurisdiction, the number counted shall include lay members, clergy members, and bishops assigned to that jurisdiction.

¶ **626.** The Jurisdictional Conference shall have authority to examine and acknowledge the journals of the Annual Conferences within its bounds and shall make such rules for the drawing up of the journals as may seem necessary.

¶ **627.** The Jurisdictional Conference shall keep an official journal of its proceedings, duly signed by the secretary and president or secretary of the College of Bishops, which shall be deposited in accordance with ¶ 1741 and with the secretary of the General Conference. The printing shall be done at the expense of the jurisdiction by The United Methodist Publishing House.

The provisions of this paragraph are to become effective upon adjournment of the 1988 General Conference.

JURISDICTIONAL AGENCIES

¶ **628.** The Jurisdictional Conference shall have the authority to appoint or elect such agencies as the General Conference may direct or as it deems necessary for its work. Insofar as possible the membership on councils, boards, and agencies of the Jurisdictional Conference shall include one-third clergy, one-third laywomen, and one-third laymen in keeping with the policies for general church agencies, except for the Board of Ordained Ministry and the Jurisdictional Committee on Episcopacy. Special attention shall be given to the inclusion of clergywomen, youth, young adults, older adults, single adults, persons with a handicapping condition, and racial and ethnic persons. (*See* ¶ 810.8*a-c.*)

¶ **629.** In each jurisdiction of The United Methodist Church there may be a **Jurisdictional Council on Ministries** or **Jurisdictional Administrative Council** organized as the jurisdiction shall determine and with the authority to coordinate the programs of the general agencies within the jurisdiction. This legislation is to become effective upon adjournment of the General Conference.

¶ **630.** In each jurisdiction there may be jurisdictional program agencies related to the general program agencies and the appropriate Annual Conference program agencies organized as the Jurisdictional Conference shall determine.

¶ **631.** 1. There may be a **Jurisdictional Commission on Archives and History,** auxiliary to the general commission, to be composed of the chairperson of each Annual Conference Commission on Archives and History or the historian of each Annual Conference, the president of the Jurisdictional Historical Society, and at least five members at large to be elected by the jurisdictional commission, or composed in a way the Jurisdictional Conference determines.

2. The jurisdictional commission may organize and promote a Jurisdictional Historical Society.

¶ **632.** *Jurisdictional Youth Ministry Organization Convocation.*—There shall be a **Jurisdictional Youth Ministry Organization Convocation** to be held every other year in each jurisdiction (alternating years with the National Youth Ministry Organization Convocation ¶ 1305). Among the membership of the convocation for the purpose of the election of steering committee members, there shall be four voting representatives from each conference: the conference coordinator of youth ministries or designate; the conference Council on Youth Ministry chairperson or designate; two youth at large, to be elected as shall be determined by the conference Council on Youth Ministry. It is recommended that at least two members from each Annual Conference be racial/ethnic persons. Each youth shall be a member (full or preparatory) of The United Methodist Church. Other persons may be added by jurisdictions according to their respective operational guidelines provided that the above categories are cared for and the recommended 50/50 racial/ethnic representation is observed. The expenses of the Jurisdictional Youth Ministry Organization

Convocation shall be borne by the participating Annual Conferences or the jurisdiction.

There shall be a **Jurisdictional Youth Coordinator** who shall be accountable to the jurisdictional Council on Ministries and the Jurisdictional Youth Ministry Organization. This coordinator may or may not be the same person as the adult representative to the National Youth Ministry Organization Steering Committee (¶ 1307). This decision is to be determined by the representatives of the Jurisdictional Youth Ministry Organization Convocation, or the Jurisdictional Youth Ministry Organization.

A responsibility of the Jurisdictional Youth Ministry Organization shall be to elect youth members to the National Youth Ministry Organization Steering Committee (*see* ¶ 1307). It is strongly recommended that two youth shall be elected from each jurisdiction, insofar as possible at least one of whom shall be a racial/ethnic person. Youth shall be sixteen years of age entering into the eleventh grade or younger; if not in school their age shall be sixteen or under at the time of their selection. Nominations shall come from Annual Conference Councils on Youth Ministry. The nominating process followed by the conference Councils on Youth Ministry shall include the solicitation of nominations from local churches, subdistricts, and districts. As far as possible members of the National Youth Ministry Organization Steering Committee from each jurisdiction shall be from five different Annual Conferences in that jurisdiction.

In addition to enabling the election of its two steering committee youth members, the following are suggested responsibilities for the Jurisdictional Youth Ministry Organization:

1. To initiate and support jurisdictional events (camps, conferences, workshops, etc.).

2. To recommend priorities, concerns, and/or policies to the National Youth Ministry Organization Steering Committee.

3. To promote the establishment and awareness of racial/ethnic needs, concerns, issues, etc., through caucuses, camps, consultations, etc.

4. To promote the spiritual growth of participants in the Jurisdictional Youth Ministry Organization Convocation.

5. To promote an evangelistic outreach to and through youth.

6. To provide training and supportive experiences for conference youth personnel.

7. To enable communication between general and conference levels of youth ministry.

8. To nominate the jurisdictional youth member to the General Council on Ministries (¶ 1007.1[3]) in the years that Jurisdictional Conference meets.

9. An additional responsibility of the Jurisdictional Youth Ministry Organization Convocation will be to elect a Steering Committee or executive body to carry out the functions and suggested responsibilities of the convocation during the interval between convocations. The convocation shall determine the representation of such body, the manner of election, any funding thereof and the relationship of the body to the Annual Conferences and to the jurisdictional Council on Ministries or equivalent.

¶ **633.** There may be **Jurisdictional Committees on both Ordained and Diaconal Ministries** or a joint jurisdictional committee related to the respective Divisions of Ordained and Diaconal Ministry. These committees shall include representation from each conference Board of Diaconal and Ordained Ministry. When a Jurisdictional Board of Higher Education and Ministry exists, this board may be a part of that structure.

¶ **634. Constitution of United Methodist Women in the Jurisdiction.**—*Article 1. Name.*—In each jurisdiction there shall be a jurisdictional organization named United Methodist Women, auxiliary to the Women's Division of the General Board of Global Ministries.

Article 2. Authority.—Each jurisdictional organization of United Methodist Women shall have authority to promote its work in accordance with the program and policies of the Women's Division of the General Board of Global Ministries.

Article 3. Membership.—The jurisdictional organization of United Methodist Women shall be composed of the members of the Core Planning Group; six delegates from each conference organization, all of whom shall be conference officers; members of the Women's Division living within the jurisdiction; a representative of the jurisdictional Association of Deaconesses/Home Missionaries; and all the bishops of the jurisdiction.

Article 4. Meetings and Elections.—*a)* There shall be a meeting of the jurisdictional organization of United Methodist Women during the last year of the quadrennium. At that time the women nominees to the General Board of Global Ministries shall be elected according to the Discipline (¶¶ 742.6*d*, 1429), and the president and any other officers shall also be elected.

b) There may be other meetings as needed.

Article 5. Amendments.—Proposed amendments to the constitution shall be sent to the recording secretary of the Women's Division prior to the last annual meeting of the division in the quadrennium.

¶ **635.** *Committee on United Methodist Men.*—In each jurisdiction there may be a **Jurisdictional Committee on United Methodist Men,** auxiliary to the General Board of Discipleship.

Each jurisdictional Committee on United Methodist Men shall have authority to promote its work in accordance with the policies and programs of the board.

The conference presidents within the jurisdiction (or their representatives) shall elect the jurisdictional president during the last year of the quadrennium. The jurisdictional president or, because of the inability of the president to serve, another elected by and from the Jurisdictional Committee of United Methodist Men shall be a member of the General Board of Discipleship (*see* ¶ 1204.1).

There may be meetings, retreats, and cooperative training events held by the jurisdiction United Methodist Men.

Section III. Central Conferences.

¶ **636.** *Authorization.*—1. In territory outside the United States, Annual Conferences, Provisional Annual Conferences, Missionary Conferences, Mission Conferences, and Missions in such numbers as the General Conference by a two-thirds vote shall determine may be organized by the General Conference into Central Conferences or Provisional Central Conferences, with such duties, privileges, and powers as are hereinafter set forth and as the General Conference by a two-thirds vote shall prescribe.[7]

2. There shall be such **Central Conferences** as have been authorized or shall be hereafter authorized by the General

---

[7]*See* Judicial Council Decisions 470, 549.

Conference; *provided* that a Central Conference shall have a total of at least thirty clergy and thirty lay delegates on the basis of representation as set forth in this section, except as the General Conference may fix a different number. A Central Conference in existence at the time of union may be continued with a lesser number of delegates for reasons deemed sufficient by the Uniting Conference.

3. The United Methodist Church shall have Central Conferences made up as follows:

a) Africa Central Conference: Angola, Burundi, Central Zaire, Mozambique (Southeast Africa), North Shaba, Southern Zaire, Zimbabwe.

b) Central and Southern Europe Central Conference: Austria Provisional, Bulgaria Provisional, Czechoslovakia, Hungary Provisional, Poland, Switzerland/France, Yugoslavia Provisional.

c) Central Conference in the Federal Republic of Germany and West Berlin: German Northwest, German South, German Southwest.

d) Central Conference in the German Democratic Republic: Annual Conference in the German Democratic Republic.

e) Northern Europe Central Conference: Denmark, Estonia Provisional, Finland-Finnish Provisional, Finland-Swedish Provisional, Norway, Sweden.

f) Philippines Central Conference: Middle Philippines, Mindanao, Northern Philippines, Northwest Philippines, Philippines, Southwest Philippines Provisional.

g) West Africa Central Conference: Liberia, Muri Provisional (Nigeria), Sierra Leone.

¶ **637.** *Organization.*—1. The **Central Conference** shall be composed of clergy and lay members in equal numbers, the clergy members elected by the clergy members of the Annual Conference and the lay members by the lay members thereof. Their qualifications and the manner of election shall be determined by the Central Conference itself, subject only to constitutional requirements. Each Annual Conference and Provisional Annual Conference shall be entitled to at least two clergy and two lay delegates, and no other selection of delegates shall be authorized which would provide for more than one clergy delegate for every six clergy members of an Annual Conference, except that a majority of the number fixed by a Central Conference as the ratio of representation shall entitle an

Annual Conference to an additional clergy delegate and to an additional lay delegate. Each Missionary Conference and Mission is authorized to elect and send one of its members to the Central Conference concerned as its representative, said representative to be accorded the privilege of sitting with the committees of the Central Conference with the right to speak in the committees and in the regular sessions of the Central Conference but without the right to vote. Representatives of Missionary Conferences or Missions shall have the same claim for payment of expenses as is allowed to members of the Central Conference.[8]

2. The first meeting of a Central Conference shall be called by the bishop or bishops in charge at such time and place as they may elect, to which members of the Annual Conferences, Provisional Annual Conferences, Missionary Conferences, and Missions concerned shall be elected on the basis of representation as provided herein. The time and place of future meetings shall be determined by the Central Conference or its executive committee.

3. Each Central Conference shall meet within the year succeeding the session of the General Conference at such time and place as the Central Conference itself or its bishops may determine, with the right to hold such adjourned sessions as it may determine. The sessions of said conference shall be presided over by the bishops. In case no bishop is present, the conference shall elect a temporary president from among its own members. The bishops resident in a Central Conference or a majority of them, with the concurrence of the executive committee or other authorized committee, shall have the authority to call an extra session of the Central Conference to be held at the time and place designated by them.[9]

4. The Council of Bishops may assign one or more of its number to visit any Central Conference or Provisional Central Conference. When so assigned, the bishop shall be an accredited representative of the general Church, and when requested by a majority of the bishops resident in that conference may exercise therein the functions of the episcopacy.

5. The presiding officer of the Central Conference shall

---

[8]*See* Judicial Council Decision 371.
[9]*See* Judicial Council Decision 371.

decide questions of order, subject to an appeal to the Central Conference, and shall decide questions of law, subject to an appeal to the Judicial Council, but questions relating to the interpretation of the rules and regulations made by the Central Conference for the governing of its own session shall be decided by the Central Conference.[10]

6. Each Central Conference within the bounds of which the General Board of Global Ministries has work shall maintain a cooperative and consultative relationship with the said board through a duly constituted executive committee, executive board, or council of cooperation; but the legal distinction between the General Board of Global Ministries and the organized Church on the field shall always be kept clear.

7. The journal of the proceedings of a Central Conference, duly signed by the president and secretary, shall be sent for examination to the General Conference through its secretary.

8. A Provisional Central Conference may become a Central Conference upon the fulfillment of the necessary requirements and upon the authorization of the General Conference.

9. In the case of a Central Conference the rule of proportionate representation shall be applied by each Annual Conference, and in the case of the delegates to the Central Conference of Central and Southern Europe the rule shall be applied to delegates coming from the Annual Conference of Switzerland/France.

¶ **638.** *Powers.*—1. To a Central Conference shall be committed for supervision and promotion, in harmony with the Discipline and interdenominational contractual agreements, the missionary, educational, evangelistic, industrial, publishing, medical, and other connectional interests of the Annual Conferences, Provisional Annual Conferences, Missionary Conferences, and Missions within its territory and such other matters as may be referred to it by said bodies or by order of the General Conference; and it shall provide suitable organizations for such work and elect the necessary officers for the same.

2. A Central Conference, when authorized by a specific enabling act of the General Conference, may elect one or more

---

[10]*See* Judicial Council Decisions 375, 376, 381.

bishops from among the traveling elders of The United Methodist Church. The number of bishops to be elected by each Central Conference shall be determined from time to time by the General Conference.

3. When a Central Conference shall have been authorized to elect bishops, such elections shall be conducted under the same general procedure as prevails in the Jurisdictional Conferences for the election of bishops. A Central Conference shall have power to fix the tenure of bishops elected by the said Central Conference.[11]

4. A Central Conference shall participate in the General Episcopal Fund on payment of its apportionment on the same percentage basis as that fixed for Annual Conferences in Jurisdictional Conferences. When the total estimated support, including salaries and all allowances for the bishops elected by it, and the estimated receipts on apportionment have been determined by a Central Conference, a statement of these amounts in itemized form shall be submitted to the General Council on Finance and Administration. This council, after consideration of the relative cost of living in various Central Conferences, shall determine the amount to be paid from the General Episcopal Fund in meeting the budget, after which the treasurer of the General Episcopal Fund shall pay the amount established to the bishop concerned, or as the Central Conference may determine.

5. An ordained minister who has served a term or part of a term as a bishop in a Central Conference where term episcopacy has prevailed shall upon retirement from the effective relation in the ministry be paid an allowance from the General Episcopal Fund in such sum as the General Council on Finance and Administration shall determine for the years during which the ordained minister served as a bishop.[12]

6. A Central Conference, in consultation with the bishops of that Central Conference, shall fix the episcopal areas and residences and make assignments to them of the bishops who are to reside in that Central Conference. The bishops of a Central Conference shall arrange the plan of episcopal visitation within its bounds.

---

[11]*See* Judicial Council Decisions 311, 430.
[12]*See* Judicial Council Decision 394.

7. The secretary of a Central Conference in which one or more bishops have been chosen shall report to the secretary of the General Conference the names of the bishop or bishops and the residences to which they have been assigned by the Central Conference.

8. A Central Conference shall have authority to elect and support general officers in all departments of the work of the Church within the boundaries of the Central Conference but may not determine the number of bishops.

9. A Central Conference shall have power to make such changes and adaptations as the peculiar conditions on the fields concerned require regarding the local church, ministry, special advices, worship, and temporal economy within its territory, including the authorizing of associate members to participate in the offices of the local church under such rules as it may see fit; *provided* that no action shall be taken which is contrary to the Constitution and the General Rules of The United Methodist Church. Subject to this restriction, a Central Conference may delegate to an Annual Conference within its boundaries the power to make one or the other of the changes and adaptations referred to in this paragraph, upon the request of such Annual Conference.[13]

10. A Central Conference shall have the authority to change the provisions for the ordination of ministers in such way that the ordination of an elder may follow immediately upon ordination as a deacon; *provided* that other conditions are fully met.

11. A Central Conference shall fix the boundaries of the Annual Conferences, Provisional Annual Conferences, Missionary Conferences, and Missions within its bounds, proposals for changes first having been submitted to the Annual Conferences concerned as prescribed in the Discipline of The United Methodist Church; *provided,* however, that the number of Annual Conferences which may be organized within the bounds of a Central Conference shall first have been determined by the General Conference. No Annual Conference shall be organized with fewer than thirty-five clergy members except as provided by an enabling act for the quadrennium, which shall not reduce the number below twenty-five. Nor shall an Annual Conference be

---

[13]*See* Judicial Council Decision 313.

continued with fewer than twenty-five clergy members except as provided by an enabling act for the quadrennium.[14]

12. A Central Conference may advise its Annual Conferences and Provisional Annual Conferences to set standards of character and other qualifications for admission of lay members.

13. A Central Conference shall have power to make changes and adaptations in procedure pertaining to the Annual, District, and Charge Conferences within its territory and to add to the business of the Annual Conference supplementary questions considered desirable or necessary to meet its own needs.

14. A Central Conference shall have authority to examine and acknowledge the journals of the Annual Conferences, Provisional Annual Conferences, Missionary Conferences, and Missions located within its bounds and to make rules for the drawing up of the journals as may seem necessary.

15. A Central Conference may have a standing **Committee on Women's Work.** This committee should preferably be composed of the women delegates and such other persons as the Central Conference may elect. The duty of this committee shall be to study the relation of women to the Church and to devise ways and means of developing this portion of the church membership to the end that it may assume its rightful responsibilities in the extension of the kingdom. The committee shall make recommendations to the Central Conference regarding women's organizations within its areas. A Central Conference organization may become a member of the World Federation of Methodist Women and may elect a representative to the World Federation of Methodist Women within the provisions of the Federation.

16. A Central Conference may organize a women's unit, after consultation with the Committee on Women's Work, in connection with any Annual Conference or Provisional Annual Conference within its bounds and provide a constitution and bylaws for it.

17. A Central Conference shall have authority to adopt rules of procedure governing the investigation and trial of its clergy, including bishops, and lay members of the Church and to provide the necessary means and methods of implementing the said

---

[14]*See* Judicial Council Decisions 525, 541, 549.

rules; *provided,* however, that the ordained ministers shall not be deprived of the right of trial by a clergy committee, and lay members of the Church of the right of trial by a duly constituted committee of lay members; and *provided* also, that the rights of appeal shall be adequately safeguarded.[15]

18. A Central Conference is authorized to prepare and translate simplified or adapted forms of such parts of the Ritual as it may deem necessary, such changes to require the approval of the resident bishop or bishops of the Central Conference.

19. A Central Conference shall have the power to conform the detailed rules, rites, and ceremonies for the solemnization of marriage to the statute laws of the country or countries within its jurisdiction.

20. Subject to the approval of the bishops resident therein, a Central Conference shall have the power to prescribe courses of study, including those in the vernaculars, for its ministry, both foreign and indigenous, including local preachers, lay speakers, Bible women, deaconesses, teachers both male and female, and all other workers whatsoever, ordained or lay. It shall also make rules and regulations for examination in these courses.

21. A Central Conference shall have authority to edit and publish a Central Conference Discipline which shall contain, in addition to the Constitution of the Church, such sections from the general Discipline of The United Methodist Church as may be pertinent to the entire Church and also such revised, adapted, or new sections as shall have been enacted by the Central Conference concerned under the powers given by the General Conference.

22. In a Central Conference or Provisional Central Conference using a language other than English, legislation passed by a General Conference shall not take effect until twelve months after the close of that General Conference in order to afford the necessary time to make adaptations and to publish a translation of the legislation which has been enacted, the translation to be approved by the resident bishop or bishops of the Central Conference. This provision, however, shall not exclude the election of delegates to the General Conference by Annual

---

[15]*See* Judicial Council Decisions 310, 595.

Conferences within the territory of Central Conferences or Provisional Central Conferences.

23. A Central Conference is authorized to interpret Article XXIII of the Articles of Religion *(page 67)* so as to recognize the governments of the country or countries within its territory.

24. A Central Conference shall have power to authorize the congregations in a certain state or country to form special organizations in order to receive the acknowledgment of the state or country according to the laws of that state or country. These organizations shall be empowered to represent the interests of the Church to the authorities of the state or country according to the rules and principles of The United Methodist Church, and they shall be required to give regular reports of their activities to their respective Annual Conferences.

25. A Central Conference may, with the consent of the bishops resident in that conference, enter into agreements with churches or missions of other denominations for the division of territory or of responsibility for Christian work within the territory of the Central Conference.

26. A Central Conference shall have the right to negotiate with other Protestant bodies looking toward the possibility of church union; *provided* that any proposals for church union shall be submitted to the General Conference for approval before consummation.[16]

27. A Central Conference, where the laws of the land permit, shall have the power to organize and incorporate one or more executive committees, executive boards, or councils of cooperation, with such membership and such powers as may have been granted by the Central Conference for the purpose of representing it in its property and legal interests and for transacting any necessary business that may arise in the interval between the sessions of the Central Conference or that may be committed to said boards or committees by the Central Conference.

28. A Central Conference, through a duly incorporated property-holding body or bodies, shall have authority to purchase, own, hold, or transfer property for and on behalf of all the unincorporated organizations of The United Methodist

---

[16]*See* Judicial Council Decision 350.

Church within the territory of that Central Conference or on behalf of other organizations of The United Methodist Church which have entrusted their property to that Central Conference.

29. A Central Conference shall have authority to make the necessary rules and regulations for the holding and management of such properties; *provided,* however, that *(a)* all procedure shall be subject to the laws of the country or countries concerned, *(b)* no transfer of property shall be made from one Annual Conference to another without the consent of the conference holding title to such property, and *(c)* the status of properties held by local trustees or other holding bodies shall be recognized.

30. A Central Conference shall not, directly or indirectly through its incorporated property-holding body or bodies, alienate property or proceeds of property without due consideration of its trusteeship for local churches, Annual Conferences, the General Board of Global Ministries and other organizations, local or general, of the Church.

31. A Central Conference or any of its incorporated organizations shall not involve the General Board of Global Ministries or any organization of the Church in any financial obligation without the official approval of said board or organization. All invested funds, fiduciary trusts, or property belonging to an Annual Conference, a Provisional Annual Conference, a Missionary Conference, or a Mission, or any of its institutions, acquired by bequest, donation, or otherwise and designated for a specific use, shall be applied to the purpose for which they were designated. They shall not be diverted to any other purpose except by the consent of the conference or mission involved, and with the approval of the Central Conference concerned, and civil court action when necessary. The same rule shall apply to similar funds or properties acquired by a Central Conference for specific objects. In cases involving the diversion of trust funds and properties within the territory of a Central Conference, the Central Conference concerned shall determine the disposition of the interests involved, subject to an appeal to the Judicial Court of the Central Conference.

32. When former Central Conferences of The United Methodist Church become or have become autonomous churches, or entered into church unions, retired bishops therein

shall continue to have membership in the Council of Bishops if the retired bishops involved so desire.

33. A Central Conference which adapts and edits the Discipline as provided in ¶ 638.21 shall establish a **Judicial Court** which, in addition to other duties which the Central Conference may assign to it, shall hear and determine the legality of any action of the Central Conference taken under the adapted portions of the Discipline or of a decision of law by the presiding bishop of the Central Conference pertaining to the adapted portions of the Discipline upon appeal by the presiding bishop or by one fifth of the members of the Central Conference. Further, the Judicial Court shall hear and determine the legality of any action of an Annual Conference taken under the adapted portions of the Discipline or of a decision of law by the presiding bishop of the Annual Conference pertaining to the adapted portion of the Discipline upon appeal of the presiding bishop or of such percentage of the members of the Annual Conference as may be determined by the Central Conference concerned.

Section IV. Provisional Central Conferences.

¶ **639.** Annual Conferences, Provisional Annual Conferences, Missionary Conferences, and Missions outside the United States which are not included in Central Conferences or in the territory of Affiliated Autonomous Churches, and which because of geographical, language, political, or other considerations have common interests that can best be served thereby, may be organized into **Provisional Central Conferences** as provided in ¶ 636.1.[17]

¶ **640.** The organization of Provisional Central Conferences shall conform to the regulations prescribed for Central Conferences insofar as they are considered applicable by the bishop in charge.

¶ **641.** The General Conference may grant to a Provisional Central Conference any of the powers of a Central Conference except that of electing bishops.[18]

¶ **642.** In the interval between General Conferences, the General Board of Global Ministries, upon the recommendation

---

[17]*See* Judicial Council Decision 525.
[18]*See* Judicial Council Decision 403.

of the bishops in charge and after consultation with the Annual Conferences, Provisional Annual Conferences, Missionary Conferences, and Missions concerned, may make changes in the boundaries of a Provisional Central Conference and may grant to a Provisional Central Conference or to any of its component parts any of the powers of a Central Conference except that of electing bishops. All changes in boundaries and all grants of powers authorized by the General Board of Global Ministries shall be reported to the ensuing session of the General Conference and shall expire at the close of that session unless renewed by the General Conference.

¶ **643.** An Annual Conference or a Provisional Annual Conference in the field of a Provisional Central Conference shall have the power to set standards of character and other qualifications for admission of its lay members.

¶ **644.** To Annual Conferences, Provisional Annual Conferences, Missionary Conferences, and Missions which are outside the United States and are not included in Central Conferences or Provisional Central Conferences, the General Conference may grant any of the powers of Central Conferences except that of electing bishops; and in the interval between General Conferences, the General Board of Global Ministries may grant such powers when requested to do so by the bishop in charge and by the Annual Conference, Provisional Annual Conference, Missionary Conference, or Mission concerned.

¶ **645.** The General Conference shall make provision for the episcopal supervision of work in the territory outside the United States which is not now included in Central Conferences.

¶ **646.** The Council of Bishops may provide, if and when necessary, for episcopal visitation of mission fields not included in Central or Provisional Central Conferences.

Section V. Autonomous Methodist Churches, Affiliated Autonomous Methodist Churches, Affiliated United Churches, Covenanting Churches, Concordat Churches.

¶ **647.** *Autonomous Methodist Churches.*—1. A self-governing Methodist church in whose establishment The United Methodist Church or one of its constituent members (The Evangelical

United Brethren Church and The Methodist Church) has assisted, but which has not entered into the Act of Covenanting with The United Methodist Church shall be known as an **Autonomous Methodist Church.**

2. When the requirements of such a Methodist church for its ministry are comparable to those of The United Methodist Church, clergy may be transferred between its properly constituted ministerial bodies and the Annual and Provisional Annual Conferences of The United Methodist Church, with the approval and consent of the appointive authorities involved.

3. A program of visitation may be mutually arranged by the Council of Bishops in cooperation with the equivalent leadership of the Autonomous Methodist Church, and/or United Church.

4. If desired by the Autonomous Methodist Church, the Council of Bishops, in consultation with the General Board of Global Ministries, shall work out plans of cooperation with that church. The General Board of Global Ministries shall serve as the agent of The United Methodist Church for a continuing dialogue looking to the establishment of mission priorities with special reference to matters of personnel and finance.

5. An Autonomous Methodist Church may enter into a concordat agreement with The United Methodist Church under the provisions of ¶ 653.

6. An Autonomous Methodist Church or other church of the Wesleyan tradition may enter into the Act of Covenanting with The United Methodist Church under the provisions of ¶ 650.

¶ **648.** *Affiliated Autonomous Methodist Churches.*—A self-governing church in whose establishment The United Methodist Church or one of its constituent members (The Evangelical United Brethren Church and The Methodist Church) has assisted, and which, by mutual agreement has entered into a covenant of relationship or in an Act of Covenanting (*see* ¶ 650) with The United Methodist Church, shall be known as an **Affiliated Autonomous Methodist Church.**

Such a covenant shall include the following provisions:

1. Certificates of church membership given by clergy in one church shall be accepted by clergy in the other church.

2. Clergy may be transferred between Annual and Provisional Annual Conferences of The United Methodist Church

and of Affiliated Autonomous Methodist Churches, and their ordination(s) recognized as valid, with the approval and consent of the bishops or other appointive authorities involved.

3. Each Affiliated Autonomous Methodist Church shall be entitled to two delegates, one clergy and one lay person, to the General Conference of The United Methodist Church in accordance with ¶ 2401.2. They shall be entitled to all the rights and privileges of delegates, including membership on committees, except the right to vote. Such a church having more than seventy thousand full members shall be entitled to one additional delegate. At least one of the three delegates shall be a woman. The bishop or president of the Affiliated Autonomous Methodist Churches may be invited by the Council of Bishops to the General Conference.

4. A program of mutual visitation may be arranged by the Council of Bishops in cooperation with the equivalent leadership of the affiliated autonomous church. The Council of Bishops may assign one or more of its members for visitation to such churches.

5. Other provisions shall be as mutually agreed upon by the two churches.

6. The Council of Bishops, in consultation with the General Board of Global Ministries, shall work out plans of cooperation with that church. The General Board of Global Ministries shall serve as the agent of The United Methodist Church for a continuing dialogue looking to the establishment of mutual mission priorities including, but not limited to, the exchange of personnel and financial resources.

BECOMING AN AFFILIATED AUTONOMOUS METHODIST OR UNITED CHURCH

¶ **649.** When conferences outside the United States which are parts of The United Methodist Church desire to become an **Affiliated Autonomous Methodist** or **Affiliated United Church,** approval shall first be secured from the Central Conference involved and this decision be ratified by the Annual Conferences within the Central Conference by two-thirds majority of the aggregate votes cast by the Annual Conferences.[19]

1. The conference shall prepare an historical record with reasons why autonomy is requested and shall consult with the

---

[19]*See* Judicial Council Decision 548.

Commission on Central Conference Affairs (¶ 2301) on proceedings for autonomy.

2. The Commission on Central Conference Affairs and the conferences involved shall mutually agree on the confession of faith and the constitution of the new church. These shall be prepared with care and shall be approved by the conferences.

3. Preparation of its Discipline is the responsibility of the conference(s) desiring autonomy.

4. Upon recommendation of the Commission on Central Conference Affairs, when all Disciplinary requirements for affiliated autonomous relationship have been met, the General Conference through an enabling act shall approve of and grant permission for the conference(s) involved to become an Affiliated Autonomous Methodist or United Church.

5. Then the Central Conference involved shall meet, declare the present relationship between The United Methodist Church and the conference(s) involved dissolved, and reorganize as an Affiliated Autonomous Methodist or Affiliated United Church in accordance with the enabling act granted by the General Conference. The Commission on Central Conference Affairs shall assist in this process, and when the plans are consummated, report to the Council of Bishops. The proclamation of affiliated autonomous status shall then be signed by the president of the Council of Bishops and the secretary of the General Conference.

6. A plan of cooperation shall be developed in accordance with ¶ 648.6 above.

BECOMING A COVENANTING CHURCH

¶ **650.** *A Covenanting Church.*—1. There may be established with other Christian churches and The United Methodist Church a covenanting relationship whose elements are described in the 1988 Book of Resolutions or otherwise developed.

a) The purpose of an **Act of Covenanting** with another Christian church is to encourage a new sense of global common cause, mutual support, mutual spiritual growth, common study of Scripture and culture, creative interaction as ministers in the mission of God's Church, cross fertilization of ideas about ways to be in that mission, sharing of resources, and exploration of new forms of service directed at old and emerging needs.

b) An Act of Covenanting will include recognition of our respective Baptisms as different facets of the one Baptism, recognition of each other as authentic expressions of the one, holy, catholic, and apostolic Church of Jesus Christ; recognition of the ordained ministries of the two churches; commitment to systematic participation in full eucharistic fellowship; commitment to function in new ways of partnership, visitations, and programs.

c) For The United Methodist Church, oversight of the covenantal relationships is the responsibility of the Council of Bishops with the assistance of the General Commission on Christian Unity and Interreligious Concerns, while participation in specific projects is the responsibility of the appropriate general agency or agencies.

2. The Council of Bishops shall represent The United Methodist Church in developing an Act of Covenanting with a prospective partner church. The Council of Bishops shall make recommendations to General Conference as to the specific covenanting agreements. When approved by General Conference and by the chief legislative body of the partner church, the Act of Covenanting becomes effective when signed by the president of the Council of Bishops and the secretary of the General Conference of The United Methodist Church and by the authorized persons in the covenanting church. The text of each Act of Covenanting as adopted shall be printed in the appropriate General Conference journal.

¶ **651.** *Affiliated United Churches.*—An Affiliated United Church shall have the same relationship and privileges as Affiliated Autonomous Methodist Churches in accordance with ¶¶ 648-649 above.

Becoming an Autonomous Methodist or United Church

¶ **652.** When conferences in nations other than the United States which are parts of The United Methodist Church desire to become an **Autonomous Methodist** or **United Church,** approval shall first be secured from the Central Conference involved and this decision be ratified by the Annual Conferences within the Central Conference by two-thirds majority of the aggregate votes cast by the Annual Conferences.

1. The conference shall prepare an historical record with reasons why autonomy is requested, and shall consult with the Commission on Central Conference Affairs (¶ 2301) on proceedings for autonomy.

2. The Commission on Central Conference Affairs and the conferences involved shall mutually agree on the confession of faith and the constitution of the new church. These shall be prepared with care and shall be approved by the conferences.

3. Preparation of its Discipline is the responsibility of the conference(s) desiring autonomy.

4. Upon recommendation of the Commission on Central Conference Affairs, when all Disciplinary requirements for autonomous relationship have been met, the General Conference through an enabling act shall approve of and grant permission for the conference(s) involved to become an Autonomous Methodist or United Church.

5. Then the Central Conference involved shall meet, declare the present relationship between The United Methodist Church and the conference(s) involved dissolved, and reorganize as an Autonomous Methodist or United Church in accordance with the enabling act granted by the General Conference. The Commission on Central Conference Affairs shall assist in this process, and, when the plans are consummated, report to the Council of Bishops. The proclamation of autonomous status shall then be signed by the president of the Council of Bishops and the secretary of the General Conference.

6. A plan of cooperation shall be developed in accordance with ¶ 647.6 above.

¶ 653. *Concordat Agreements.*—1. There may be **concordats** with other Methodist churches in accordance with ¶ 12.2 and for The Methodist Church of Great Britain, in accordance with ¶ 12.3.

2. The purposes of such concordats are:

a) to manifest the common Methodist heritage,

b) to affirm the equal status of the two churches and express mutual acceptance and respect,

c) to create opportunities for closer fellowship between the two churches especially on the leadership level.

3. With the exception of The Methodist Church of Great

Britain, such concordats may be established by the following procedure:

a) The Methodist church shall, through its major decision-making body, request a concordat relationship with The United Methodist Church through the Council of Bishops. Concordats may also be initiated by The United Methodist Church acting through the Council of Bishops who shall, in cooperation with the Methodist church in question, ascertain that all Disciplinary conditions are met and then prepare the necessary enabling legislation for adoption by the General Conference.

b) When such concordat agreement has been approved by the General Conference, the Council of Bishops shall prepare a statement of the concordat agreement, to be signed by the president of the Council of Bishops and the secretary of the General Conference and two representatives of the Methodist church with whom the concordat agreement is made. Such concordats shall be printed in the journal of that General Conference.

4. Such concordat agreement shall entitle the two churches to the following rights and privileges:

a) The two churches shall each elect two delegates, one clergy and one lay, to be seated in each other's General Conference or equivalent bodies, with all rights and privileges except the right to vote. Agreements in existing concordats shall be honored.

b) The host church shall make provisions for full hospitality, including room and board, for the delegates of the other concordat church. Travel and other expenses shall be the responsibility of the visiting church.

c) A program of mutual visitation may be arranged by the Council of Bishops in cooperation with the equivalent leadership of the other concordat church. The Council of Bishops may assign one or more of its members for episcopal visitation to concordat churches.

d) Clergy may be transferred between the two churches in accordance with ¶¶ 427.2*b* and 648.2.

BECOMING PART OF THE UNITED METHODIST CHURCH

¶ **654.** 1. An Autonomous Methodist Church or Affiliated Autonomous Methodist Church outside the United States may become a part of The United Methodist Church, when all of the following requirements are fulfilled:

a) Said church shall accept and approve the Constitution, Articles of Faith, Discipline, and polity of The United Methodist Church.

b) Said church, if it is within the boundaries of a Central or Provisional Central Conference, shall apply for membership in that conference. Such application shall be approved by the Central or Provisional Central Conference and by the General Conference. In the event that said church is not within the boundaries of an existing Central or Provisional Conference, then its membership application shall be reviewed by the Council of Bishops and shall be approved by the General Conference.

c) Said church shall declare its own constitution and church order null and void.

d) The Commission on Central Conference Affairs shall advise and assist said church in this process, and prepare the necessary enabling act for approval by the General Conference.

e) The General Conference shall approve legislation authorizing the necessary adjustments in the organization of the Central or Provisional Central Conference involved. In the event that said church is not within the boundaries of an existing Central or Provisional Central Conference, then legislation shall be approved to either change boundaries of a contiguous conference or to establish a new Central or Provisional Central Conference.

f) The Commission on Central Conference Affairs shall assist said church in the process of becoming a part of The United Methodist Church, determine when all requirements are met, and report to the General Conference.

2. Other churches outside the United States may become a part of The United Methodist Church by following the same procedure.

Section VI. Provisional Annual Conferences.

¶ **655.** A **Provisional Annual Conference** is a conference which, because of its limited membership, does not qualify for Annual Conference status.

¶ **656.** Any Missionary Conference or Mission established under the provisions of the Discipline may be constituted as a Provisional Annual Conference by the General Conference in consultation with the Central Conference, Provisional Central Conference, or Jurisdictional Conference within which the Missionary Conference or Mission is located; *provided* that

1. no Provisional Annual Conference shall be organized with fewer than ten clergy members, or be continued with fewer than six clergy members;

2. the total financial support from the General Board of Global Ministries, including the Advance, shall not exceed an appropriate percentage as determined in consultation with the division to which the conference relates;

3. the membership and contributions of the conference have shown a reasonable increase during the previous quadrennium and give evidence of an aggressive program for continued progress in both areas.

¶ **657.** *Organization.*—A Provisional Annual Conference shall be organized in the same manner and have the same powers and functions as an Annual Conference, subject to the approval of the presiding bishop; and its members shall share pro rata in the proceeds of The United Methodist Publishing House with members of the Annual Conferences, with the following exceptions:

1. The bishop having episcopal supervision of a Provisional Annual Conference in a foreign or a home mission field may appoint a representative as **superintendent,** to whom may be committed specific responsibility for the representation of the General Board of Global Ministries in its relation to the indigenous church and also in cooperation with other recognized evangelical missions. Such duties shall be exercised so as not to interfere with the work of the district superintendent. This superintendent may also be a district superintendent; *provided* the superintendent is a member of the said conference. The superintendent shall be responsible directly to the bishop appointed to administer the work in that episcopal area, and shall make adequate reports of the work and needs of the field to the bishop and to the secretaries of the General Board of Global Ministries immediately concerned.

2. A Provisional Annual Conference shall meet annually at the time appointed by the bishop. If there is no bishop present, the superintendent shall preside. In the absence of both, the presidency shall be determined as in an Annual Conference (¶ 702.5). The conference or a committee thereof shall select the place for holding the conference.

3. In a Provisional Annual Conference receiving major funding from the General Board of Global Ministries, the assigned staff of the appropriate division shall provide consultation and guidance in setting up the annual budget and Advance projects within the conference and in the promotion of new mission projects. The conference, in making requests for appropriations for support, including grants and loans for building projects, shall submit to the General Board of Global Ministries a statement of the proposed annual budget and proposed financial plan for new mission and building plans. Items involving increased appropriations from the General Board of Global Ministries, or increased askings from the Advance, shall be subject to modifications by the General Board of Global Ministries.

4. A Provisional Annual Conference shall elect one ordained minister and one lay person as delegates with full voting and other rights to the General Conference and to the Jurisdictional Conference. Delegates to Central Conferences shall be elected in accordance with ¶ 636.1.

¶ **658.** In a Provisional Annual Conference in the United States, Puerto Rico, or the Virgin Islands, there shall be a conference Board of Global Ministries constituted as in an Annual Conference and having the same duties and powers.

Section VII. The Missionary Conference.

¶ **659.** *Definition.*—A conference is a **Missionary Conference** because of its particular mission opportunities, its limited membership and resources, its unique leadership requirements, its strategic regional or language considerations, and ministerial needs. The General Board of Global Ministries shall provide administrative guidance and major financial assistance including attention to the distinctive property matters.

¶ **660.** *Organization.*—A Missionary Conference shall be organized in the same manner and with the same rights and powers as an Annual Conference (¶¶ 701-703), but with the following exceptions:

1. The College of Bishops shall provide episcopal supervision for any Missionary Conference(s) within its jurisdictional boundaries as are organized. The bishop thus placed in charge and having episcopal supervision within the respective episcopal area in cooperation with the General Board of Global Ministries shall appoint a conference superintendent and/or district superintendents. Such conference and/or district superintendent(s) shall be an elder(s), and may not be appointed for more than eight years. Years of service may be either consecutive or nonconsecutive. Years of service as a conference and/or district superintendent in a Missionary Conference shall be counted toward the total of twelve years permitted in a regular Annual Conference.[20]

2. The General Board of Global Ministries shall give close supervision and guidance in setting up the administrative and promotional budgets and Advance projects within the conference and in the promotion of new mission projects. The conference, in making requests for appropriations for support and grants and loans for building projects, shall submit to the General Board of Global Ministries a statement of the proposed annual promotional and administrative budget and the proposed financial plan for new mission and building projects. New work and building projects involving increased appropriations from the General Board of Global Ministries shall first have the approval of the General Board of Global Ministries. (*See also* ¶ 1414.)

3. Missionary Conferences shall elect clergy and lay delegates to General and Jurisdictional Conference on the same basis as Annual Conferences as provided in ¶¶ 602 and 613.

4. *a) Membership.*—A Missionary Conference shall determine by majority vote whether it will establish the right of full ministerial membership.

b) An ordained minister in full connection with an Annual Conference who is appointed to a Missionary Conference which has previously voted to include full membership under §4*a* may

---

[20]*See* Judicial Council Decisions 448, 512.

choose either to request the bishop of the Missionary Conference to seek the transfer of his/her membership into full membership with the Missionary Conference or retain his/her membership in a home conference and be considered in an affiliated relationship to the Missionary Conference. Affiliated relationship shall entitle the ordained minister to the fellowship of the conference, to full participation in its activities, including holding office and representing the Missionary Conference in General and Jurisdictional Conferences. An affiliate member of a Missionary Conference shall not vote in his or her Annual Conference while retaining the affiliate relationship to a Missionary Conference. Such affiliate relationship to a Missionary Conference shall be only for the duration of the ordained minister's appointment to the conference.

An affiliate member elected to a General or Jurisdictional Conference from a Missionary Conference shall not be eligible to be elected to such position from the conference where his or her membership is held.

c) A Missionary Conference may elect into full ministerial membership those persons desiring full membership in accordance with ¶ 662.

d) A pastor under full-time appointment in a Missionary Conference upon consultation with and the approval of the bishop and conference or district superintendent/Cabinet, may waive his or her claim upon the conference minimum salary. This waiver is to be reviewed annually and is to be effective until the time of subsequent appointment.

5. A Missionary Conference may include in its membership representation of such mission agencies within its boundaries as it deems advisable; *provided,* however, such representation shall not exceed a number equal to one third of the total membership of the Missionary Conference and that such representatives shall be members of The United Methodist Church in accordance with constitutional requirements.[21]

6. In order to provide traditional and experimental ministries, the bishop of the Missionary Conference may appoint an effective elder to other than full-time pastoral appointment

---

[21]*See* Judicial Council Decision 511.

combined with secular employment. This will in no way affect the conference relationship. Pension and other benefits shall be provided in consultation with the parties involved and with the approval of the Missionary Conference.

¶ **661.** Only the General Conference can create a Missionary Conference or change a Missionary Conference to a Provisional Annual Conference or an Annual Conference. A petition to the General Conference for change in status from a Missionary Conference shall set forth details of the history and status of the conference and shall be accompanied by a report and recommendation of the General Board of Global Ministries.

¶ **662.** Missionary Conferences shall have the same rights as those given to the Central Conferences in ¶ 638.9, .10 to make such changes and adaptations regarding the ministry and ordination of ordained ministers and the consecration of diaconal ministers as the effective use of indigenous leadership in the Missionary Conference may require; *provided* that no action shall be taken which is contrary to the Constitution and the General Rules of The United Methodist Church.

Section VIII. Mission.

¶ **663.** *Definition.*—A **Mission** is an administrative body for a field of work inside or outside the structures of any Annual Conference, Provisional Annual Conference, or Missionary Conference, which is under the care of the General Board of Global Ministries and exercises in a general way the functions of a District Conference.

The purpose of a Mission is to provide ministry with a particular group or region whose needs cannot be fully met with the existing structures and resources of the Annual Conference(s). It may also be the initial stage in moving toward the formation of a Provisional or Missionary Conference.

The establishment of a Mission may involve special considerations in areas of leadership, language resources, and/or property.

¶ **664.** *Establishment and Administration of a Mission.*—1. The General Board of Global Ministries, in consultation with the presiding bishop or bishops (¶ 514.4) of an Annual Conference(s), shall determine the need and set the boundaries for the

Mission established within an Annual Conference, across conference lines, or for another extended region or constituency.

2. A Mission shall be made up of all regularly appointed missionaries, both lay and clergy (¶ 1418.3), mission traveling preachers, and other lay members. The Mission shall determine the number of lay members and the method of their selection. In so doing it shall assure that all aspects of the Mission's work are represented.[22]

3. When the Mission lies within the bounds of one episcopal area, the resident bishop shall preside over the Mission. When the Mission crosses the boundaries of one or more episcopal areas or jurisdictions, the College(s) of Bishops shall assign a bishop to the Mission.

The bishop assigned to a Mission, in consultation with the deputy general secretary of the appropriate division of the General Board of Global Ministries, may appoint one or more superintendents of the Mission as may be determined and for whom support has been provided. The bishop shall decide which groups or charges the respective superintendents shall supervise.

4. A Mission shall meet annually at the time and place designated by the bishop in charge, who shall preside. In the absence of the bishop a superintendent of the Mission shall preside. The presiding officer shall bring forward the regular business of the meeting and arrange the work.

5. The annual meeting shall have the power to certify candidates for the ordained ministry, to pass on the character of preachers who are not members of an Annual Conference, to receive mission traveling preachers, and to recommend to an Annual Conference proper persons for probationary membership and deacon's orders. The examination of local pastors shall be held by the Mission and certified to an Annual Conference.

Mission traveling preachers are members of the Mission without being members of an Annual Conference. The Mission shall determine the requirements for a mission traveling preacher in order to most effectively utilize the indigenous leadership. They are limited in their itineration to the bounds of the Mission.

---

[22]*See* Judicial Council Decision 341.

6. The Bishop shall, at the annual meeting, assign the missionaries and mission traveling preachers to the several charges for the ensuing year provided that transfer of National Division–related missionaries shall be completed only after consultation with the National Division of the General Board of Global Ministries.

7. Administration, initiation, and coordination of a Mission in the United States, Puerto Rico, the Virgin Islands, and U.S. Trust Territories shall be in the National Division. Administration of a Mission in other areas shall be in the World Division.

Section IX. The Annual Conference.

¶ **701.** *Composition and Character.*—1. The clergy membership of an Annual Conference (¶ 412) shall consist of members in full connection (¶ 421), probationary members (¶ 413), associate members (¶ 418), affiliate members (¶ 1431.5a), and local pastors under full-time appointment to a pastoral charge (¶ 408.1).[23] (*See also* ¶ 35.)

a) Clergy members in full connection shall have the right to vote on all matters in the Annual Conference except in the election of lay delegates to the General and Jurisdictional or Central Conferences and shall have sole responsibility for all matters of ordination, character, and conference relations of clergy.

b) Probationary clergy members shall have the right to vote in the Annual Conference on all matters except constitutional amendments, election of clergy delegates to the General and Jurisdictional or Central Conferences, and matters of ordination, character, and conference relations of clergy.

c) Associate and affiliate clergy members shall have the right to vote in the Annual Conference on all matters except constitutional amendments, election of clergy delegates to the General and Jurisdictional or Central Conferences, and matters of ordination, character, and conference relations of clergy.

d) Local pastors under full-time appointment to a pastoral charge shall have the right to vote in the Annual Conference on all matters except constitutional amendments, election of

---

[23]*See* Judicial Council Decisions 341, 371, 477, 552, 584.

delegates to the General and Jurisdictional or Central Conferences, and matters of ordination, character, and conference relations of clergy.

e) Under special conditions, and for missional reasons, an Annual Conference may, by a two-thirds majority vote of its members present, allow local and student part-time pastors under appointment to a pastoral charge the right to vote at Annual Conference on all matters except constitutional amendments, election of clergy delegates to General and Jurisdictional or Central Conferences and matters of ordination, character and conference relations of clergy.

2. The following shall be seated in the Annual Conference and shall be given the privilege of the floor without vote: part-time and student local pastors; official representatives from other denominations, especially from member churches of the Consultation on Church Union, invited by the Annual Conference; lay missionaries regularly appointed by the General Board of Global Ministries in nations other than the United States and certified lay missionaries from nations other than the United States serving within the bounds of the Annual Conference.

3. Diaconal ministers are lay members of the Annual Conference. Also, by authorization of a Central Conference national diaconal ministers may be given the same privileges.[24]

4. The lay member or alternate, whoever was last seated in the Annual Conference, shall be seated in a special session of the Annual Conference when convened; *provided* that no local charge shall be deprived of its lay member due to death, serious illness, or cessation of membership. Under such circumstances another lay member may be elected by the Charge Conference.[25] (*See* ¶ 35.)

5. The lay members of the Annual Conference shall participate in all deliberations and vote upon all measures except on the granting or validation of license, ordination, reception

[24]*See* Judicial Council Decision 505.
[25]*See* Judicial Council Decision 319.

into full conference membership, or any question concerning the character and official conduct of ordained ministers. Lay members shall serve on all committees except those on ministerial relations and for the trial of clergy.[26]

6. When at any time a lay member is excused by the Annual Conference from further attendance during the session, the alternate lay member may be seated instead. The lay member, or the alternate, shall be the lay member of the Annual Conference, and it shall be the duty of the lay member to report on actions of the Annual Conference.

7. It is the duty of every member and all probationers and local pastors of the Annual Conference to attend its sessions and furnish such reports in such form as the Discipline may require. Any such person unable to attend shall report by letter to the conference secretary, setting forth the reason for the absence. Should any minister in active service be absent from the session of the Annual Conference without a satisfactory reason for the absence, the matter shall be referred by the conference secretary to the Board of Ordained Ministry.

¶ **702.** *Organization.*—1. Annual Conferences may become severally bodies corporate, whenever practicable, under the law of the countries, states, and territories within whose bounds they are located.[27]

2. The bishops shall appoint the times for holding the Annual Conferences.

3. The Annual Conference or a committee thereof shall select the place for holding the conference, but should it become necessary for any reason to change the place of meeting, a majority of the district superintendents, with the consent of the bishop in charge, may change the place.

4. A special session of the Annual Conference may be held at such time and in such place as shall have been determined by the Annual Conference after consultation with the bishop, or by the bishop, with the concurrence of three-fourths of the district superintendents. A special session of the Annual Conference shall have only such powers as are stated in the call.[28]

---

[26]*See* Judicial Council Decisions 109, 505, 592.
[27]*See* Judicial Council Decision 108.
[28]*See* Judicial Council Decision 397.

5. The bishop assigned shall preside over the Annual Conference or, in case of inability, arrange for another bishop to preside. In the absence of a bishop the conference shall by ballot, without nomination or debate, elect a president pro tempore from among the traveling elders. The president thus elected shall discharge all the duties of a bishop except ordination.[29]

6. The Annual Conference at the first session following the General Conference or Jurisdictional or Central Conferences (or, if it may desire, at the last session preceding the General, Jurisdictional, or Central Conferences) shall elect a secretary and statistician to serve for the succeeding quadrennium. In the case of a vacancy in either office in the interim of the sessions, the bishop, after consultation with the district superintendents, shall appoint a person to act until the next session of the Annual Conference. (*See* ¶ 715 for election of the treasurer.)

7. The Annual Conference may designate a person who is a member in good standing of one of the local churches and who is a member of the bar of the state as chancellor. The chancellor, who shall be nominated by the bishop and elected by the Annual Conference, shall serve as legal advisor to the bishop and to the Annual Conference.[30]

8. *a)* The **conference lay leader** is the elected leader of conference laity. The lay leader will have responsibility for fostering awareness of the role of the laity both within the congregation and through their ministries in the home, work place, community, and world in achieving the mission of the Church, and enabling and supporting lay participation in the planning and decision-making processes of the Annual Conference, district, and local church in cooperation with the bishop, district superintendents, and pastors. The lay leader is a member of the Annual Conference, the conference Council on Ministries, the conference Committee on Nominations, the conference Committee on Episcopacy, and the executive committee, if any, of the conference Council on Ministries, and may serve on the committee planning Annual Conference sessions and may be designated by virtue of office to membership on any conference agency by the Annual Conference.

---

[29]*See* Judicial Council Decisions 367, 373.
[30]*See* Judicial Council Decision 570.

b) Where there is no Board of Laity or equivalent organization, the lay leader with the approval of the Council on Ministries may organize a coordinating committee on lay work. The membership may include representatives of groups such as United Methodist Men, United Methodist Women, United Methodist Youth, age level councils, and district lay leaders, and such other members as may be desired to support lay work and help coordinate lay activities. In forming such a committee, special attention shall be given to the inclusion of women, men, young adults, older adults, persons with a handicapping condition, and racial and ethnic persons.

c) The conference lay leader shall act as chairperson of the conference Board of Laity, or its equivalent, and shall relate to the organized lay groups in the conference such as United Methodist Men, United Methodist Women, and United Methodist Youth, and support their work and help them coordinate their activities. The conference lay leader shall also have the general responsibility in (1) developing the advocacy role for laity in the life of the Church, (2) increasing the participation of laity in the sessions and structure of the Annual Conference, and (3) encouraging lay persons in the general ministry of the Church.

d) The conference lay leader shall be elected by the Annual Conference as the Annual Conference may determine. The method of nomination and term of office shall be determined by the Annual Conference. Associate lay leader(s), to work with the conference lay leader, may be elected by the Annual Conference as it may determine.

¶ **703.** *Powers and Duties.*—1. The Annual Conference for its own government may adopt rules and regulations not in conflict with the Discipline of The United Methodist Church; *provided* that in exercise of its powers each Annual Conference shall act in all respects in harmony with the policy of The United Methodist Church with respect to elimination of discrimination on the basis of race.[31]

2. An Annual Conference cannot financially obligate any

---

[31]*See* Judicial Council Decisions 43, 74, 109, 141, 318, 323, 367, 373, 418, 432, 435, 476, 536, 584, 590, 592.

organizational unit of The United Methodist Church except the Annual Conference itself.

3. The Annual Conference may admit into clergy membership only those who have met all the Disciplinary requirements for membership and only in the manner prescribed in the Discipline.[32]

4. The Annual Conference shall have power to make inquiry into the moral and official conduct of its clergy members. Subject only to the provisions of ¶¶ 2620-2626, the Annual Conference shall have power to hear complaints against its clergy members and may try, reprove, suspend, deprive of clergy office and credentials, expel, or acquit any against whom charges may have been preferred. The Annual Conference shall have power to locate a clergy member for unacceptability or inefficiency.[33]

5. The status of a clergy member and of a probationer and the manner and conditions of a transfer of a clergy member from one Annual Conference to another are governed by the section on the ordained ministry (Chapter Three).

6. Transfers of traveling preachers are conditioned on the passing of their character by the conference to which they are amenable. The official announcement that a preacher is transferred changes the preacher's membership so that all rights and responsibilities in the conference to which that preacher goes begin from the date of transfer. Such member of an Annual Conference shall not vote twice on the same constitutional question, nor be counted twice in the same year in the basis for election of delegates, nor vote twice in the same year for delegates to the General, Jurisdictional, or Central Conferences.

7. Whenever clergy members, whether on trial or in full connection, are transferred to another Annual Conference, either in connection with a transfer of the pastoral charge to which they are appointed or by reason of the dissolution or merger of the Annual Conference, they shall have the same rights and obligations as the other members of the conference to which they are transferred.

---

[32]*See* Judicial Council Decision 440.
[33]*See* Judicial Council Decision 534.

8. The Annual Conference shall have power to make inquiry into the financial status of the local churches, and where there is a deficit in finances, it may require the pastor and the lay member to appear before the appropriate committee and make explanation. Based upon its findings it shall provide counsel to help the church overcome such a deficit position.

9. The Annual Conference shall have the power to make inquiry into the membership status of the local churches, and where no members have been received on confession of faith during the year, it may require the pastor and the lay member to appear before the appropriate agency and make explanation.

10. The Annual Conference shall give recognition to any new churches that have been organized during the year and shall, through the presiding bishop and the secretary, send to each new church a certificate of organization, which the district superintendent shall, on behalf of the conference, present to the new church in an appropriate ceremony.

11. The Annual Conference shall secure, during the course of its annual session, the answers to the questions for conducting Annual Conference sessions, and the secretary to the Annual Conference shall include the answers to these questions in the conference journal and in the report to the Council on Finance and Administration.

12. If any Annual Conference initiates, joins, monitors, or terminates a boycott, the guidelines in the 1988 Book of Resolutions should be followed. The General Conference is the only body that can initiate, empower, or join a boycott in the name of The United Methodist Church.

¶ **704.** *Business of the Conference.*—1. The session shall open with a period of devotion, followed by a call of the roll, including the roll of the local pastors and diaconal ministers.

2. The Annual Conference, to expedite the transaction of its business, may adopt an agenda as a basis of its procedure. Such agenda shall be prepared by the bishop, the district superintendents, the conference lay leader and such others as the conference may name, and shall be submitted to the conference for adoption.

3. Members for all standing committees, boards, and commissions of the Annual Conference shall be selected in such

manner as the Annual Conference may determine or as the Discipline may specifically require.[34]

For the purpose of adjusting tenure a certain number of members may be elected or appointed for particular terms. Members shall hold office until their successors are elected. For the Annual Conference agencies provided for by the Discipline see ¶ 706.1 and for the agencies established by the Annual Conference itself see ¶ 706.2.

4. The business of the Annual Conference shall include the receiving and acting upon reports from the district superintendents, the officers, the standing and special committees, the boards, commissions, and societies and also the making of such inquiries as the Council of Bishops shall recommend by the provision of a supplemental guide.[35]

5. The agenda of the Annual Conference may provide time for a "State of the Laity" address which shall be the responsibility of the conference lay leader.

6. The Annual Conference shall make inquiry into the moral and official conduct of its ordained ministers. In response to the inquiry whether all clergy members of the conference are blameless in their life and official administration, the district superintendent may answer for all the preachers in the district in one answer, or the Board of Ordained Ministry may make inquiry of each district superintendent about each ordained minister in the district and make one report to the bishop and the conference in open session; *provided* that the conference or the bishop may order an executive session of the clergy members to consider questions relating to matters of ordination, character, and conference relationships.[36]

An executive session shall consist of the ordained ministers in full connection unless others are admitted by express action and invitation of the executive session. No one so invited shall have vote, nor, unless specifically granted by the executive session, shall have voice (¶ 422).

7. At the conclusion of the examination of the standing of the ordained ministers in the conference or at such later times as

---

[34]*See* Judicial Council Decision 559.
[35]*See* Judicial Council Decision 367.
[36]*See* Judicial Council Decisions 42, 406, 534, 555.

the bishop may designate, the presiding bishop may call to the bar of the conference the class to be admitted into full connection and receive them into conference membership after asking the questions to be found in ¶ 425. This examination of the ordained ministers and the passing of their characters may be the business of one session.

¶ **705.** *Records and Archives.*—1. The Annual Conference shall keep an exact record of its proceedings according to the forms provided by the General, Jurisdictional, and Central Conferences. If there are no archives of the Annual Conference, the secretary shall keep the bound copy or copies to be handed on to the succeeding secretary. The conference shall send to its Jurisdictional Conference or Central Conference copies of the minutes of the quadrennium for examination.

2. Each Annual Conference shall send to the General Council on Finance and Administration two printed copies of its annual journal and one printed copy to the General Council on Ministries.[37]

3. The Annual Conference journal shall include the following divisions, preferably in the following order:

- *a)* Officers of Annual Conference
- *b)* Boards, commissions, committees; rolls of conference members
- *c)* Daily proceedings
- *d)* Disciplinary questions
- *e)* Appointments
- *f)* Reports as ordered by the Annual Conference
- *g)* Memoirs as ordered by the Annual Conference
- *h)* Roll of dead—deceased clergy members
- *i)* Historical
- *j)* Miscellaneous
- *k)* Pastoral record (including the records of accepted local pastors in such manner as the conference may determine)
- *l)* Statistics
- *m)* Index

---

[37]*See* Judicial Council Decision 481.

4. An Annual Conference in the United States and Puerto Rico shall include in its journal a list of the deaconesses and missionaries, clergy and lay, active and retired, who have gone from the conference into mission service.

5. The Annual Conference journal shall include a listing of the consecrated diaconal ministers and their service records.

6. The secretary, treasurer, or other administrative officer named by the Annual Conference shall keep a complete service record of ordained and diaconal ministry personnel in the Annual Conference. Service records shall include but not be limited to biographical information supplied by the individual, a list of appointments, and a record of Annual Conference actions with regard to conference relationships. In addition to service records, the secretary, treasurer, or other administrative officer named by the Annual Conference shall keep descriptions of circumstances related to changes in conference relationships, credentials surrendered to the bishop or district superintendent, and confidential trial records.

7. All records of secretaries, statisticians, and treasurers shall be kept according to the forms prepared by the General Council on Finance and Administration so that all statistical and financial items shall be handled alike in all conferences and that uniformity of reporting shall be established as a churchwide policy.

8. All records of candidates and ordained and diaconal ministry personnel maintained by the conference secretary, treasurer, or other administrative officer named by the Annual Conference, Board of Ordained Ministry, Board of Diaconal Ministry, Board of Pensions, and the district Committee on Ordained Ministry are to be kept on behalf of the Annual Conference in conformity with guidelines provided by the General Council on Finance and Administration, in consultation with the General Board of Higher Education and Ministry and the General Board of Pensions, and the following principles:

a) the Annual Conference is the owner of its personnel records and files;

b) individuals in whose name a record is kept shall have access to the information contained in a record or file, with the exception of surrendered credentials and information for which a right-of-access waiver has been signed;

c) access to unpublished records by persons other than the bishop, district superintendent, conference secretary, treasurer, or other administrative officer or the Board of Ordained Ministry, Board of Diaconal Ministry, Board of Pensions, and the district Committee on Ordained Ministry shall require written consent of the person in whose name a record is kept; access to trial records shall be governed by the provisions of ¶ 2624.2*e*, .3*e*).

CONFERENCE AGENCIES

¶ 706. The Annual Conference shall provide for the connectional relationship between the general boards and commissions and the conference, district, and local church.

1. The Annual Conference shall structure itself for effective mission in any mode deemed appropriate. In each Annual Conference, there may be conference program boards related to the general program boards organized as the Annual Conference shall determine. The Annual Conference shall provide for the connectional relationship between the general program boards and the conference, districts, and local churches, and shall specifically assign the program responsibilities related to the objectives and scope of the general program boards to agencies of the Annual Conference.[38]

2. The Annual Conference may appoint additional committees for the purpose of promoting the work of The United Methodist Church within the bounds of the said Annual Conference and may prescribe their membership and their powers and duties.

3. Each Annual Conference may make its agencies of such size as its work may require; *provided* that consideration shall be given to the inclusion of lay and clergy persons from small membership churches. Full-time local pastors serving charges are eligible for election or appointment to such agencies, except those dealing with qualifications, orders, and status of clergy and local pastors.

4. Insofar as possible, the membership on councils, boards,

---

[38]*See* Judicial Council Decisions 411, 417, 418.

and agencies of the Annual Conference shall include one-third clergy, one-third laywomen, and one-third laymen, except for the Board of Ordained Ministry.[39] Special attention shall be given to the inclusion of clergywomen, youth, young adults, older adults, persons with a handicapping condition, and racial and ethnic persons in keeping with policies for general church agencies.

5. Members of general agencies (¶ 801) shall serve as ex officio members of the corresponding Annual Conference agency or its equivalent structure (*see* ¶ 810.4, .5). If this results in a person being a member of more than one Annual Conference agency in violation of either Annual Conference policy or another provision of the Book of Discipline, the person shall choose the Annual Conference agency on which to serve.

THE CONFERENCE COUNCIL ON FINANCE AND ADMINISTRATION

¶ **707.** In each Annual Conference there shall be a **conference Council on Finance and Administration,** hereinafter called the council.

¶ **708.** The council's purpose, membership, organization, and relationships shall be as follows:

1. *Purpose.*—The purpose of the council shall be to develop, maintain, and administer a comprehensive and coordinated plan of fiscal and administrative policies, procedures, and management services for the Annual Conference.

2. *Membership.*—*a)* Each Annual Conference shall elect, at its session next succeeding the General Conference or Jurisdictional Conference, a conference Council on Finance and Administration, composed of not less than five nor more than twenty-one members; in every case there shall be at least one lay person more than clergy included on the council.[40] Persons shall be nominated for membership in a manner determined by the conference, in accordance with ¶ 706.4. Churches of less than two hundred members may be represented on the conference Council on Finance and Administration at least as high as the proportion of their total membership to the conference membership. The term

---

[39]*See* Judicial Council Decisions 446, 558.
[40]*See* Judicial Council Decision 441.

of office shall begin with the adjournment of the Annual Conference session at which they are elected and shall be for a period of four years and until their successors are elected. No member or employee of any conference agency and no employee, trustee, or director of any agency or institution participating in the funds of any conference budget shall be eligible for voting membership on the council.[41] Any vacancy shall be filled by action of the council until the next conference session, at which time the Annual Conference shall fill the vacancy.

b) The following shall be ex officio members of the council in addition to the number set by the Annual Conference under ¶ 708.2*a*: (1) the conference treasurer/director of administrative services, without vote; (2) any members of the General Council on Finance and Administration who reside within the bounds of the conference, with vote, unless voting membership is in conflict with another provision of the Book of Discipline, in which case their membership shall be without vote; in either case, they shall not be eligible to serve on an agency receiving funding; (3) the presiding bishop, without vote; (4) a district superintendent chosen by the Cabinet, without vote; and (5) the conference council director or another representative of the conference Council on Ministries, without vote.

3. *Officers.*—The council shall elect from its voting membership a president, a vice-president, a secretary, and such other officers as it may deem necessary. The conference treasurer (¶ 715) shall be the treasurer of the council. The treasurer shall not be eligible for voting membership on the council and shall not be eligible for election to any of those offices which are to be filled by voting members of the council.

4. *Organization.*—*a)* The council may establish committees and task forces and define their duties and authority as it deems necessary for fulfilling its purpose and responsibilities.

b) The Annual Conference may enact bylaws governing meetings, quorum, and other matters of procedure for the council, or it may authorize the council to enact such bylaws; in any event such by-laws shall not be in conflict with the Book of Discipline.

c) If deemed necessary for the fulfillment of its functions,

---

[41]*See* Judicial Council Decisions 10, 493.

and if so authorized by the Annual Conference, the council may be incorporated.

5. *Amenability.*—The council shall be amenable and report directly to the Annual Conference.[42]

6. *Relationships.*—*a)* The council and the Annual Conference Council on Ministries shall cooperate in the development of the conference benevolences budget (¶ 710.3).

b) In the interest of developing and implementing coordinated Annual Conference policies in the areas of fiscal management and administrative services, it shall serve in a liaison role among conference agencies with responsibilities in these areas. The council shall be authorized to convene representatives of Annual Conference administrative and clergy support agencies for the purpose of consulting on matters of mutual concern, such as the coordination of fiscal management, fund-raising activities, and administrative services in the Annual Conference.

¶ **709.** *Responsibilities.*—The council shall have authority and responsibility to perform the following functions:

1. To recommend to the Annual Conference for its action and determination budgets of anticipated income and proposed expenditures for all funds which provide for Annual Conference clergy support, Annual Conference administrative expenses, and Annual Conference benevolence and program causes (¶ 710).[43]

2. To receive, consider, report, and make recommendations to the Annual Conference regarding the following, prior to final decision by the Annual Conference: *(a)* any proposal to raise capital funds for any purpose; *(b)* funding considerations related to any proposal which may come before the conference; *(c)* any requests to conduct a special conference-wide financial appeal, whether by special collections, campaigns, or otherwise, in the local churches of the conference.

3. To recommend to the Annual Conference for its action and decision, the methods or formulas by which apportionments to churches, charges, or districts for duly authorized general, jurisdictional, conference, and district funds shall be determined (¶ 711).

---

[42]*See* Judicial Council Decisions 551, 560.
[43]*See* Judicial Council Decision 521.

4. To cooperate with the Committee on Communication in providing district superintendents, pastors, and appropriate officers of the local churches and charge conferences with interpretive aids which will assist in gaining understanding and support of the conference budget and other approved conference causes.

5. To develop policies governing the investment of conference funds (except for pension funds as provided in ¶ 1608), whether in debt or equity, short-term or long-term instruments, with the aim of maximizing funds available for mission in a manner consistent with the preservation of capital and with the Social Principles of the Church. A statement of such policies shall be printed in the conference journal at least once in each quadrennium.

6. To recommend to the Annual Conference for its action and decision procedures for dealing responsibly with situations in which budgeted funds, as approved by the Annual Conference, are inadequate to meet emerging missional needs or unforeseen circumstances.[44]

7. To review at least quarterly and to account to the Annual Conference for the disbursement of funds in accordance with budgets approved by the conference.

8. To recommend to the Annual Conference for its action and determination the conditions under which it may borrow funds for current expense purposes and the maximum amount of such borrowing.

9. To have authority and supervision over the treasurer/director of administrative services subject to ¶¶ 715-716; to establish policies governing the treasurer/director's work.

10. To work in cooperation with other Annual Conference agencies for the design and implementation of a plan by which the Annual Conference may designate the conference treasury as a central treasury for funds designated for any or all conference agencies participating in conference funds.

11. To establish uniform and equitable policies and practices in the employment and compensation of personnel, in consultation and cooperation with other conference agencies

---

[44]*See* Judicial Council Decision 551.

which employ staff, unless the Annual Conference has designated another agency to carry this responsibility. These policies and practices shall be in accordance with the Social Principles (¶ 72A, E, F, and G).

12. To cooperate with the General Council on Finance and Administration and with the General Board of Discipleship in promoting and standardizing the financial recording and reporting system in the local churches of the conference.

13. In cooperation with the General Council on Finance and Administration, related Annual Conference agencies and institutions, and local churches, to make recommendations to the Annual Conference regarding the development, promotion, and review of a broad general program of insurance protection and risk management, except for employee benefit programs.

14. To make recommendations to the Annual Conference for its action and determination regarding plans to initiate or cause to be organized a foundation or similar organization for the purpose of securing, conserving, or expending funds for the direct or indirect benefit or support of the Annual Conference, or of any conference agency or any of its programs or work. The council shall have opportunity to make its recommendations regarding such plans if the foundation or similar organization is: (1) proposed to be organized by the Annual Conference itself, whether acting alone or in concert with other Annual Conferences; (2) proposed to be organized by any conference council, board, commission, committee, or other agency; (3) to make use of the name "United Methodist" in its title or solicitation; or (4) proposed for the purpose of soliciting gifts primarily from the United Methodist constituency.

15. To perform such other administrative and fiscal functions and services as the Annual Conference may assign.

¶ **710.** *Budgets.*—The council shall recommend to the Annual Conference for its action and determination budgets of anticipated income and proposed expenditures for all funds to be apportioned to the churches, charges, or districts.[45] Prior to each regular session of the Annual Conference the council shall make a diligent and detailed study of the needs of all the conference

---

[45]*See* Judicial Council Decisions 551, 560.

agencies and causes asking to be included in the budget of any conference fund. The chairperson of each conference agency, or other duly authorized representative, shall have opportunity to represent the claims of that agency before the council.

1. *Clergy Support Budgets.—a)* It shall be the duty of the council, unless otherwise provided, to estimate the total amount necessary to furnish a sufficient and equitable support for the district superintendents of the conference, including salary, travel, staff, office, and housing. The council shall report specific recommendations to the Annual Conference for conference action (¶¶ 523.2; 754.4*a*).[46]

b) The council shall report to the Annual Conference at each session the percentage approved by the General Conference as the basis for the Episcopal Fund apportionment to the Annual Conference and shall include in its recommended clergy support budget the amount determined by the treasurer of the General Council on Finance and Administration as necessary to meet this apportionment.

c) Based on recommendations from the Episcopal Residence Committee (¶ 736.4*d*), the council shall recommend the amount to be raised as the Annual Conference share of the cost of the bishop's housing.

d) After consultation with the conference Board of Pensions, the council shall report to the Annual Conference the amounts computed by that agency as necessary to meet the needs for pensions and benefit programs of the conference. Such amounts need not be derived solely from apportionments.

e) It shall recommend to the Annual Conference an amount determined in consultation with the Commission on Equitable Salaries to be used for compliance with the approved schedule of equitable salaries for pastors (¶ 722.3).

f) It shall recommend to the Annual Conference estimates of the amounts needed for any other programs of clergy support the conference may adopt, such as a Sustentation Fund (¶ 723) or provision for the moving expenses of pastors.

2. *Administration Budget.—a)* The council shall recommend to the Annual Conference estimates of the amounts needed for

---

[46]*See* Judicial Council Decisions 44, 584, 590, 591.

administrative expenses of the conference, including its own expenses and those of the conference treasurer's office. It shall consult with the conference agencies and officers to be included in the administrative budget regarding the estimated budgets of their expenses and base its conference administration budget recommendations on information thus received.

b) It shall include in its estimates recommendations regarding the conference's share of an area expense fund, if any, and apportionments for administration properly made by the Jurisdictional Conference and the General Conference (¶ 911.5).

3. *World Service and Conference Benevolences Budget.—a)* In preparing the conference benevolences budget the council, working together with the conference Council on Ministries as provided in ¶ 710.3*b*, shall make diligent effort to secure full information regarding all conference benevolence and service causes that none may be neglected, jeopardized, or excluded. Basing its judgment of needs upon the information secured, the council shall recommend to the Annual Conference for its action and determination the total amount to be apportioned for the conference benevolences budget. After receiving the recommendations of the conference Council on Ministries, the council shall also recommend the amount or the percentage of the total of the conference benevolences budget which shall be allocated to each cause included in the said budget. Such recommendations should reflect agreement with the conference Council on Ministries on program agency allocations as specified below.[47]

b) The Council on Finance and Administration and the Annual Conference Council on Ministries shall work together to establish and follow a procedure which shall preserve the following principles:

(1) It is the responsibility of the conference Council on Finance and Administration to establish the total amount to be recommended to the Annual Conference as the conference benevolences budget and, within that amount, the total sum to be recommended for distribution among the conference program agencies. It is likewise the responsibility of the council to study the budget requests for any agencies or causes to be included in the

---

[47]*See* Judicial Council Decisions 400, 521, 551, 582.

conference benevolences budget other than the conference program agencies, including the requests of the conference Council on Ministries, and to give the chairpersons or other authorized representatives of such agencies and causes opportunity to represent their claims before the council.[48]

(2) It is the responsibility of the conference Council on Ministries to study the budget requests of the conference program agencies and to recommend to the conference Council on Finance and Administration amounts to be allocated from the conference benevolences budget to each such agency, within the total established by the conference Council on Finance and Administration.[49]

(3) It is the responsibility of the conference Council on Finance and Administration to present the conference benevolences budget recommendations to the Annual Conference. The recommended allocations to conference program agencies should reflect agreement between the council and the conference Council on Ministries.[50]

c) The term **conference benevolences** shall include those conference allocations and expenditures directly associated with the program, mission, and benevolent causes of Annual Conference program agencies and institutions. Annual Conference program agencies and institutions shall be defined as those agencies with responsibilities parallel to those of the program-related general agencies (¶ 803) and institutions whose work is within the field of responsibility of one or more of those agencies. Administrative expenses which are directly related to the program, mission, and benevolent causes of conference program agencies, including the expenses of the conference Council on Ministries, may also be included in the conference benevolences budget. The term "conference benevolences" shall not include allocations and expenditures for other conference agencies and officers whose work is primarily administrative. It shall likewise not include Annual Conference clergy support funds as set forth in ¶¶ 717-724, allocations and expenditures of conference agencies responsible for administering clergy support funds, or

[48]*See* Judicial Council Decisions 521, 551.
[49]*See* Judicial Council Decisions 521, 551.
[50]*See* Judicial Council Decision 551.

apportionments made to the Annual Conference by the General or Jurisdictional Conferences.

d) The council, on receiving from the treasurer of the General Council on Finance and Administration a statement of the amount apportioned that Annual Conference for World Service, shall combine the total World Service apportionment, without reduction for the quadrennium, and the approved conference benevolences budget (¶ 710.3*a*). The sum of these two amounts shall be known as **World Service and Conference Benevolences.** The World Service and Conference Benevolences budget thus established shall include a statement of the percentage for World Service and the percentage for conference benevolences.[51] (*See also* ¶ 711.)

4. *Other Apportioned Causes.*—The council shall include in its budget recommendations specific amounts recommended for all other funds properly apportioned to the Annual Conference for the support of duly authorized general or other connectional funds. The budget recommendations shall likewise include any other amounts to be apportioned to the districts, charges, or churches by the Annual Conference for conference or district causes of any kind.

5. *Special Appeals.*—*a)* No Annual Conference agency or interest, including any related agency or institution such as a school, college, university, hospital, home, housing project, or other service institution, shall make a special conference-wide appeal to the local churches for funds without the approval of the Annual Conference upon recommendation of the council except in case of an extreme emergency when such approval may be the council, acting jointly. Neither shall special conference-wide appeals to local churches for funds be made by such boards, interests, agencies, or institutions which are not related to the Annual Conference in which the appeal is to be made, unless approval for such an appeal is granted by the Annual Conference upon recommendation of the council. The Annual Conference approvals specified in this paragraph shall not be required for special churchwide financial appeals which have been approved under the provisions of ¶ 911.4, for solicitations which have been

---

[51]*See* Judicial Council Decision 348.

approved under the provisions of ¶ 912.3, or for any other general fund promotion or appeal authorized by the General Conference or approved and conducted under other provisions of the Book of Discipline.

b) When application is made to the council for the privilege of a special conference-wide financial appeal, whether by special collections, campaigns, or otherwise, the council shall investigate the application and its possible relation to other obligations of the conference, and in the light of the facts make recommendations to the conference for its action and determination. If application for privilege of a special appeal is made directly to the conference, the application shall be referred to the council before final action is taken.

c) The council may include in its budget recommendations to the Annual Conference amounts to be considered as goals for special appeals or other nonapportioned causes.

6. The council shall make its budget recommendations to the Annual Conference in a format based on guidelines suggested by the General Council on Finance and Administration.

¶ **711.** *Apportionments.*—The council shall recommend to the Annual Conference for its action and determination the methods or formulas by which the approved budgeted amounts for clergy support, administration, World Service and Conference Benevolences, and other apportioned causes (¶¶ 711.1-.4) shall be apportioned to the districts, churches, or charges of the conference.

1. The council, on receiving from the General Council on Finance and Administration a statement of the amount apportioned to the Annual Conference for the several general funds authorized by the General Conference, shall apportion the same to the several districts, charges, or churches by whatever method the conference may direct, but without reduction.

2. The council shall recommend to the Annual Conference for its action and determination whether the apportionments referred to in this paragraph shall be made by the council to the districts only or to the churches or charges of the conference. If the apportionments are made to the districts only, then the distribution to the churches or charges of each district shall be made as provided in ¶ 711.3. The conference may order that

the entire distribution to all the churches or charges of the conference be made by the district superintendents.

3. Should the Annual Conference make the apportionments to the districts only, the distribution to the churches or charges of each district shall be made by its district Board of Stewards, composed of the district superintendent as chairperson and the district stewards elected by the several Charge Conferences (¶ 250.1). In that case the board, meeting on call of the district superintendent as soon as practicable after the adjournment of the Annual Conference, shall make the distribution to the churches or charges of the district, using such methods as it may determine, unless the Annual Conference shall have determined the method of distribution to the churches or charges.

4. The World Service and Conference Benevolences apportionment to the churches or charges of the conference, whether made by the conference directly, by the district Board of Stewards as provided in ¶ 711.3, or by the district superintendents, shall not be combined with any other General, Jurisdictional, or Annual Conference apportionment made to the churches or charges of the conference.[52]

¶ **712.** The council shall be responsible for designating a depository of depositories for conference funds.

¶ **713.** The council shall have the following authority and responsibility with respect to the auditing of the financial records of the conference and its agencies:

1. To have the accounts of the conference treasurer for the preceding fiscal year audited by a certified public accountant within 120 days after the close of the conference fiscal year, and to receive, review, and report such audit to the Annual Conference.[53]

As a part of the audit, the accountant shall confer with the presiding bishop of the Annual Conference and the president of the council.

2. To require and review at least annually audited reports, in such detail as it may direct, from all conference agencies and from all agencies, institutions, and organizations receiving any

---

[52]*See* Judicial Council Decision 591.
[53]*See* Judicial Council Decision 334.

financial support from conference funds or from any authorized conference-wide appeal.

3. The council may establish an Audit Review Committee to review all of the reports and audits required by ¶ 713.1, .2. If the council chooses to establish such a committee, at least half of its members should be persons who are not members of the council and who are chosen for their expertise in areas related to the work of the committee.

¶ **714.** The council shall have the following authority and responsibility with respect to the bonding of conference and conference agency officers and staff whose responsibilities include the custody or handling of conference funds or other negotiable assets:

1. The council shall provide for the fidelity bonding of the conference treasurer and other staff under its authority and supervision in amounts it judges to be adequate.

2. In the case of those agencies, institutions, and organizations for which the conference treasurer does not serve as treasurer, the council shall have authority to require fidelity bonding of their treasurers in such amounts as it deems adequate and to withhold payment of the allocation of any such agency, institution, or organization until evidence of the required bonding has been submitted.

3. The council may provide, or require any conference agency to provide, directors' and officers' liability insurance in amounts it judges to be adequate.

4. The council shall require compliance with the policies established as provided by this paragraph and shall report annually to the Annual Conference on such compliance.

¶ **715.** *Conference Treasurer.*—1. Each Annual Conference, on nomination of its Council on Finance and Administration, shall at the first session of the conference after the quadrennial session of the General Conference or Jurisdictional Conference, or at such other times as a vacancy exists, elect a **conference treasurer.**[54] The treasurer shall serve for the quadrennium or until a successor shall be elected and qualify. If a vacancy should occur during the quadrennium, the council shall fill the vacancy

---

[54]*See* Judicial Council Decision 185.

until the next session of the Annual Conference. After consultation with the bishop in charge, the council may remove the treasurer from office for cause and fill the vacancy until the next session of the conference. The treasurer shall be directly amenable to the council. The treasurer may sit with the council and its committees at all sessions and have the privilege of voice but not vote.

2. The conference treasurer shall receive and disburse, in accordance with the actions of the Annual Conference and the provisions of the Book of Discipline, remittances from local church treasurers for all duly authorized general, jurisdictional, Annual Conference, and district causes.[55]

a) Local church treasurers shall remit monthly to the conference treasurer all amounts contributed in each local church for (1) the World Service and Conference Benevolences fund; (2) all other funds authorized by the General Conference and apportioned to the Annual Conferences by the General Council on Finance and Administration; (3) all other jurisdictional, Annual Conference, and district funds or causes apportioned in accordance with ¶ 711, unless otherwise directed by the Annual Conference; (4) special Sunday offerings (¶ 274); (5) special appeals (¶¶ 710.5, 911.4); (6) Advance special gifts (¶ 914); (7) World Service special gifts (¶ 913); (8) Youth Service Fund (¶ 1310); and (9) all other general, jurisdictional, Annual Conference, and district funds not otherwise directed.

b) The treasurer shall each month divide the total amount received from local churches for World Service and Conference Benevolences, setting aside the proper amount for World Service and the proper amount for conference benevolences, according to the ratio of each established by the Annual Conference in the total World Service and Conference Benevolences budget (¶ 710.3c). The treasurer shall, from the share received for conference benevolences, credit monthly the accounts of the several agencies or causes included in the conference benevolences budget or make monthly remittances to the treasurers of such agencies or causes according to the rightful share and proportion of each (¶ 710.3a) or according to a payment schedule

---

[55]*See* Judicial Council Decisions 456, 591.

approved by the conference Council on Finance and Administration which shall provide that the total allocated to each agency or cause during the year shall be equal to the rightful share and proportion of each. The treasurer shall remit each month to the treasurer of the General Council on Finance and Administration the total share received during the month for World Service. When the share so designated for World Service during a year exceeds the amount apportioned to the Annual Conference, the entire share contributed for World Service shall be remitted in regular order to the treasurer of the General Council on Finance and Administration before the end of the fiscal year.[56]

c) The treasurer shall, as far as practicable, remit monthly to the several district superintendents the amount due each of them (¶ 710.1*a*).

d) The treasurer shall likewise credit or remit each month all funds received and payable for other jurisdictional, Annual Conference, and district causes in accordance with budgets adopted by the Annual Conference.

e) The conference treasurer shall remit each month to the treasurer of the General Council on Finance and Administration the amounts received during the month for the General Administration Fund, the Episcopal Fund, the Interdenominational Cooperation Fund, the Black College Fund, the Temporary General Aid Fund, the Ministerial Education Fund, the Missional Priority Fund, World Service special gifts, Advance special gifts, general church special Sunday offerings (¶ 274), special churchwide appeals (¶ 911.4), and all other general causes not otherwise directed.

3. The conference treasurer may serve as treasurer for any or all agencies served by a conference central treasury (¶ 709.10). The treasurer shall enter the proper credits to each at the end of each month's business. Disbursements from funds allocated to any conference agency shall be made only on proper order from the agency.[57]

4. The treasurer shall prepare at regular intervals such financial statements and reports as may be required for the

---

[56]See Judicial Council Decisions 306, 332, 400, 521, 539.
[57]*See* Judicial Council Decisions 400, 521, 539.

bishop in charge, the district superintendents, the Annual Conference, the council, the agencies served by the conference central treasury and its officers, and the treasurer of the General Council on Finance and Administration.

a) The treasurer shall make each month a full report of all general funds handled to the treasurer of the General Council on Finance and Administration and to the presiding bishop of the conference.

b) The treasurer shall prepare annually a report of all receipts, disbursements, and balances of all funds under his/her direction, which report shall be printed in the conference journal. The reports shall be made on forms authorized by the General Council on Finance and Administration so that all financial items going outside the local church shall be handled alike in all districts and conferences, and uniformity of financial reporting shall be established as a churchwide policy.

5. The treasurer may be authorized by the council to invest funds in accordance with policies and procedures established by the council (¶ 709.5). A listing of securities held shall be printed annually in the conference journal.

6. The treasurer shall provide counsel and guidance to local church business administrators, treasurers, financial secretaries, and Committees on Finance in the development of standardized financial recording and reporting systems (¶ 709.12).

7. The treasurer shall perform such other staff services as the council may require in the fulfillment of its functions and responsibilities.

¶ **716.** An Annual Conference may authorize its Council on Finance and Administration to assign to its conference treasurer the additional title and responsibilities of a **director of administrative services,** to have responsibility in one or more of the following areas: office management; payroll and personnel services; the provision of administrative services for Annual Conference officers and agencies; property management with respect to property owned by the Annual Conference or any of its agencies; and such other responsibilities of an administrative nature as the council, by mutual agreement with other Annual Conference officers and agencies, may assign. The council shall have authority and supervision over the director and shall, after consultation with those Annual Conference officers and agencies for whom the director might be expected to perform services, define his/her specific responsibilities.

CLERGY SUPPORT

¶ **717.** Assumption of the obligations of the itineracy, required to be made at the time of admission into the traveling connection, puts upon the Church the counterobligation of providing support for the entire ordained ministry of the Church. In view of this the claim for clergy support in each pastoral charge shall include provisions for the support of pastors, district superintendents, bishops, and conference claimants.[58]

¶ **718.** Each Annual Conference shall determine what plan and method shall be used in distributing the apportionments to its several districts and charges for the Episcopal Fund (¶ 923), for the support of district superintendents and conference claimants, and for the Equitable Salary Fund (¶ 722), whether by percentages based on the current cash salary paid to the ordained ministers serving pastoral charges under episcopal appointment and to local pastors or by some other method.[59]

¶ **719.** When the apportionments for bishops, district superintendents, conference claimants, and the Equitable Salary Fund for the several districts and charges have been determined, payments made to the same in each pastoral charge shall be exactly proportional to the amount paid on the clergy salary or salaries (¶ 925). The treasurer or treasurers of each pastoral charge shall accordingly make proportional distribution of the funds raised in that charge for the support of the ordained ministry and shall remit, monthly if practicable and quarterly at the latest, the items for bishops, district superintendents, conference claimants, and the Equitable Salary Fund to the proper treasurer or treasurers.[60]

[58]*See* Judicial Council Decisions 306, 455, 551, 579.
[59]*See* Judicial Council Decisions 208, 455.
[60]*See* Judicial Council Decisions 320, 401.

¶ **720.** The several Charge Conferences shall determine the pastors' salaries according to the provisions of ¶ 247.13.

¶ **721.** No pastor shall be entitled to any claim for unpaid salary against any church or charge served after pastoral connection with the church or charge has ceased.

¶ **722.** *Equitable Salaries.*—1. There shall be in each Annual Conference a **Commission on Equitable Salaries** composed of an equal number of lay and clergy persons—including at least one layperson and one clergyperson from churches of fewer than two hundred members—who are nominated by the conference Nominating Committee and elected by and amenable to the Annual Conference. Selection of commission members shall ensure, insofar as possible, adequate representation of racial and ethnic persons. In addition, one district superintendent named by the Cabinet shall be a member.

2. It is the purpose of the Commission on Equitable Salaries to support ordained ministry in the charges of the Annual Conference by (1) recommending conference standards for clergy support; (2) administering funds to be used in salary supplementation; and (3) providing counsel and advisory material on clergy support to district superintendents and Committees on Pastor-Parish Relations.

3. The commission shall carefully study the needs for additional support within the conference and the sources of income, and shall recommend annually to the conference for its action a schedule of minimum salaries for all full-time pastors or those clergy members of the Annual Conference appointed less than full time to a local church, subject to such rules and regulations as the conference may adopt (¶ 437.1, .2).[61]

4. Consistent with the provisions of this paragraph, the primary responsibility for the payment of pastoral salaries remains with individual pastoral charges.[62]

5. On recommendation of the Commission on Equitable Salaries, the Annual Conference may authorize the utilization of the Equitable Salary Fund to provide for supplementing salaries beyond the minimum salary schedule. Special attention shall be

---

[61]*See* Judicial Council Decisions 383, 579.
[62]*See* Judicial Council Decision 461.

given to ethnic pastors serving ethnic ministries, with particular attention given to Native American pastors serving Native American ministries.

6. In consultation with the Commission on Equitable Salaries, the Council on Finance and Administration shall recommend to the conference its estimate of the amount required to support the schedule of minimum salaries and salary supplements for the pastors, as adopted by the conference. The conference Council on Finance and Administration shall apportion the amount approved by the conference as an item of clergy support to the districts or the charges as the conference may direct (¶ 710.1*e*).[63]

7. The **Equitable Salary Fund,** secured as described above in ¶ 722.6, shall be disbursed under the direction of the Commission on Equitable Salaries.

8. The Equitable Salary Fund, secured as described in §6, shall be used to provide each pastor who receives less than the minimum salary with an additional amount sufficient to make the salary approved by the pastoral charge plus the supplemental aid or income from other sources equal to the minimum salary approved by the conference; *provided* that nothing in this paragraph shall be construed as limiting the right of an Annual Conference to set a maximum amount to be used in attaining such minimum salary in any given case.[64]

9. The commission shall assemble and distribute to the charges and the district superintendents advisory material for use in the process of negotiating the total of each pastoral support package, the schedule of minimum salaries, and other information relevant to the establishment of more equitable salaries by all the charges of the conference.

10. The guidelines of the Annual Conference program of equitable clergy support shall insofar as possible be observed by the bishops and district superintendents in arranging charges and making appointments. Each full-time pastor or those clergy members of the Annual Conference appointed less than full time under episcopal appointment to a local church are eligible for

---

[63]*See* Judicial Council Decisions 90, 179.
[64]*See* Judicial Council Decisions 456, 492, 579, 587.

participation in the Annual Conference program of equitable salaries (¶ 441.1, .2).

11. The commission may suggest to the Annual Conference for its consideration equitable salary ranges for the pastors and/or charges, and the Annual Conference may suggest such equitable salary ranges to the charges for their consideration.

Nothing in this paragraph shall be construed as limiting the rights of an Annual Conference to set its own policy regarding the number of years for which a pastor is eligible to receive equitable salary funds.

¶ **723.** *Sustentation Fund.*—An Annual Conference may establish a **Sustentation Fund** for the purpose of providing emergency aid to the clergy of the conference who may be in special need. On recommendation of the conference Council on Finance and Administration, the amount needed for this purpose may be apportioned to the pastoral charges as the conference may determine. The fund, if established, shall be administered jointly by the bishop, the appropriate district superintendent, and the chairperson of the Commission on Equitable Salaries or the chairperson of such other agency as the Annual Conference may determine.

¶ **724.** The total of all travel, automobile, and other expenses allowed and paid to a pastor in addition to salary shall be reported for insertion in the journal of the Annual Conference, in a separate column from that of pastor's salary and adjacent thereto. These expenses shall be distinguished from the moving expenses of a new appointee to a pastoral charge.

¶ **725.** Every clergy member of an Annual Conference appointed beyond the local church shall furnish annually to the conference secretary, at such time as the secretary shall direct, a statement of his/her total compensation (including salary, travel, automobile, housing, and other expenses allowed and paid) for the year then ending, and said compensation of all clergy appointed beyond the local church shall be published in the journal of the Annual Conference.[65] When this information is not furnished, the appointment of the clergyperson shall be subject to review by the resident bishop and the Cabinet.

---

[65]*See* Judicial Council Decisions 345, 465.

ANNUAL CONFERENCE COUNCIL ON MINISTRIES

¶ 726. In each Annual Conference of The United Methodist Church there shall be a **conference Council on Ministries;** *provided* that such council or any component thereof may be organized on an area basis.

1. *Purpose.*—The purpose of the Annual Conference Council on Ministries, as part of the total mission of the Church, is to facilitate the Church's program life in the Annual Conference. The council's task is to be responsible for the development, administration, and evaluation of the program of the Annual Conference and to encourage, coordinate, and support the conference agencies, districts, and local churches in their ministry and various programs in accordance with the mission of The United Methodist Church.

2. *Membership.*—The membership of the Annual Conference Council on Ministries shall consist of the presiding bishop; the district superintendents; representatives of conference agencies and commissions described in ¶¶ 739-741; representatives of other conference agencies as determined by the Annual Conference; the conference secretary; the area or conference superintendent or director of parish development; two representatives of the conference youth organization; two representatives of the conference United Methodist Women, one of whom shall be the president; two representatives of the conference United Methodist Men, one of whom shall be the president; two young adults; the conference lay leader; one lay person from each district; chairpersons of age-level and family departments; and such additional members as the Annual Conference may determine.

The person or persons serving as members of the General Council on Ministries shall be member(s) of the Annual Conference Council on Ministries as full voting member(s).

The following shall be members of the council without vote: salaried and volunteer Annual Conference staff, the conference treasurer, and one or more members of the Council on Finance and Administration.

3. *Officers.*—The officers of the council shall be a chairperson, a vice-chairperson, a secretary, and such other officers as the council shall determine. They shall be elected by the council.

4. *Executive Committee.*—There may be an executive committee consisting of the officers, the bishop, at least one district superintendent chosen by the Cabinet, the conference lay leader, the conference council director, the elected representative of the General Council on Ministries, and other members as the council may determine. Approximately one-half of the members of the executive committee shall be lay persons.

The executive committee may also serve as the **Personnel Committee** of the conference Council on Ministries.

5. *Committees, Task Forces, and Consultations.*—The council may appoint a **Committee on Ethnic Local Church Concerns,** a **Committee on Communication,** a **Committee on Planning and Research,** a **Committee on Leadership Development,** and a **Committee on Evaluation**. It may appoint such other committees, task forces, and consultations as may be deemed essential to effective discharging of its responsibilities.

a) Committee for the Coordination of Ethnic Local Church Concerns.—There shall be a committee organized in each Annual Conference on **Ethnic Local Church Concerns** which shall relate to all conference agencies for the implementation of the conference's Comprehensive Plan. The committee shall comprise one-third laywomen, one-third laymen, and one-third clergy. At least one-half of this committee shall be racial/ethnic persons, where feasible. It shall also include a Cabinet representative. The committee shall develop a comprehensive plan for implementation by the Council on Ministries, and also shall develop criteria for use in evaluating racial/ethnic projects and programs within the conference and in reporting on its work to the Council on Ministries.

b) Committee on Communication.—In each Annual Conference Council on Ministries, chosen by it and amenable to it, there may be a **Committee on Communication.** It may assist the council in the performance of the responsibilities listed in ¶ 726.10*g-i*, and may perform such other functions as are assigned to it by the council. A full-time conference or area staff person may be employed as director of communications to assist the committee in carrying out its functions. In the absence of a full-time staff person, responsibilities in communication shall be assigned as a part of the work of a member of the conference staff.

c) Committee on Planning and Research.—It should not be deemed necessary for all members of the **Committee on Planning and Research** to be members of the conference council. Due consideration should be given to the inclusion in the membership of the committee persons with expertise in planning and research. Its function shall be:

(1) To engage in planning and research on behalf of the council in the continuing ministry of The United Methodist Church within the conference.

(2) To serve as an advisory group in planning and research for the Annual Conference and its agencies.

(3) To serve as the clearinghouse for all planning and research projects under the sponsorship of the Annual Conference and its agencies.

(4) To relate to and cooperate with the planning and research projects of the General Council on Ministries.

d) Committee on Evaluation.—It should not be deemed necessary for all members of the **Committee on Evaluation** to be members of the conference council. Due consideration should be given to the inclusion in the membership of committee persons with expertise in program review and evaluation. Its function shall be:

(1) To review program criteria and goals for every conference program board and agency;

(2) To evaluate recommendations for the continued funding of these programs.

e) Committee on Publishing House Liaison.—There may be organized in each Annual Conference a **Committee on Publishing House Liaison.** The committee shall consist of three members nominated and elected by the Annual Conference. The committee shall have lay and clergy members. Members of the General Board of Publication shall be members ex officio. The committee chairperson shall be a member of the conference Council on Ministries. The committee shall provide liaison contact with The United Methodist Publishing House to relate the work of the house to the work of the conference.

6. *Age-Level and Family Councils.*—The council may establish children, young adult, adult, older adult, single adults, and family ministry councils as it deems necessary to the performance

of its duties. (*See* ¶ 743 concerning the establishment of a Council on Youth Ministry.)

7. *a) Director.*—The council shall elect, upon nomination by the Cabinet, in consultation with the Personnel Committee of the council or its equivalent, an executive officer to be known as the **conference council director.** The director shall be present when the Cabinet considers matters relating to coordination, implementation, and administration of the conference program, and other matters as the Cabinet and director may determine. The director shall not be present during the Cabinet discussions on matters related to the making of appointments. A limit to the term of service for the director may be set by the Annual Conference.

b) Responsibilities.—The responsibilities of the conference council director shall be but are not limited to the following:

(1) To serve as the executive officer of the Annual Conference Council on Ministries.

(2) To be a communication link between the Annual Conference program agencies and the Jurisdictional (where they exist) and General Conference program agencies.

(3) To facilitate communication among the Annual Conference program agencies and the local churches.

(4) To serve as a resource person for district programs and the Annual Conference Council on Ministries agencies in their planning, implementation, and evaluation process.

(5) To supervise the Annual Conference Council on Ministries staff members.

(6) To serve on other Annual Conference agencies as determined by the Annual Conference, and/or by the conference Council on Ministries.

(7) To serve as a consultant to the conference Committee on Nominations.

8. *Staff.*—All Annual Conference council staff may be employed by, directed by, and amenable to the Annual Conference Council on Ministries. Insofar as possible, employees of the conference shall include women, racial and ethnic persons, lay and clergy, at every level. Ordained ministers on the staff are subject to being appointed by the presiding bishop in consultation with the Personnel Committee of the council or its

equivalent. A limit to the term of service for the council staff may be set by the Annual Conference.

9. *Relationships.*—The council shall have the following relationships, including the amenabilities indicated:

a) Between sessions of the Annual Conference, all Annual Conference program agencies shall cooperate with and be amenable to the Council on Ministries of the Annual Conference in matters relating to the development, implementation, and administration of the program.[66]

b) All Annual Conference agencies shall submit the elements of program which are to be promoted in, supported by, or implemented by the local churches of the conference to the council for consideration, coordinating, and calendaring prior to presentation to the local churches. The council may request district or Annual Conference agencies to implement a program for the entire conference.

c) The council staff shall be responsible, in cooperation with the district superintendents, for the implementation of the conference program.

d) The council may develop and carry out a program of conference Advance special giving (*see* ¶¶ 727.1, 1007.5).

10. *Responsibilities.*—The responsibilities of the Annual Conference Council on Ministries are:

a) To describe, coordinate, and organize opportunities to respond to the missional priority, should any be adopted by the General Conference.

b) To assist the Annual Conference and local churches in discovering their mission and to determine program emphases which will enable them to fulfill their mission.

c) To receive program recommendations from the local churches, the district and Annual Conference agencies, and the Jurisdictional and General Council on Ministries; to evaluate these recommendations; and to formulate a coordinated conference program to be presented to the Annual Conference for consideration.

d) To provide staff personnel and necessary resources for

---

[66]*See* Judicial Council Decision 400.

the implementation and administration of the program adopted by the conference.

e) To receive and coordinate the budget askings of all conference program agencies and to determine priorities to make budget recommendations to the Conference Council on Finance and Administration.

f) To cooperate in ecumenical projects and events which have been approved by the Annual Conference.

g) To interpret the programs of the general Church, the Jurisdictional or Central Conference, and the Annual Conference to the local churches; and to promote all General and Annual Conference benevolences.

h) To provide two-way channels of communication among Annual Conference agencies, district Councils on Ministries, and local churches.

i) To provide for relationships with all news media within the conference; to lead the conference in making creative use of television and telecommunication ministries; to provide training in communication; and to perform public relations functions for the conference.

j) To give leadership in research and planning for the Annual Conference.

k) To provide guidance and training for district and/or local-church leaders.

l) To provide linkage with general program agencies and provide names of Annual Conference agencies and persons who carry program responsibilities related to each general program agency.

¶ **727.** 1. There may be a **conference Advance program,** established and carried out in the same spirit of partnership as the general Advance program.

2. A conference Advance special gift is one made to a conference Advance special project within bounds of the Annual Conference or episcopal area authorized by an Annual Conference upon recommendation by the conference Board of Global Ministries or its equivalent structure and consistent with the goals of the Advance. The funds as received shall be administered by the conference Board of Global Ministries or such structure as designated by the conference.

3. An Annual Conference may undertake a conference-wide campaign for a lump sum to be applied to its missionary and church extension. The funds so received shall be designated as conference Advance specials and shall be administered by the conference Board of Global Ministries or equivalent structure. Local churches shall report their contributions as conference Advance specials.

4. With the approval of the Annual Conference, a district within the conference may authorize and promote Advance specials for church extension and missionary needs within the district, such funds to be administered by a district missionary society organized for that purpose or by a similar body set up by the district. Such special funds secured and administered on a district level shall be reported by each local church to the Annual Conference as conference Advance specials.

5. Local churches shall report their contributions to general Advance specials and conference Advance specials to the charge conference and in the manner indicated on the Annual Conference report form.

OTHER CONFERENCE AGENCIES

¶ **728.** 1. The Annual Conference shall organize a **Board of Church and Society** or an equivalent structure that shall provide for Church and society responsibilities related to the purpose, objectives, and responsibilities of the General Board of Church and Society, as set forth in ¶¶ 1102-1104.

2. The conference Board of Church and Society or equivalent structure shall be composed of those persons as determined by the Annual Conference including as an ex officio member the mission coordinator for Christian social involvement of the conference United Methodist Women. Guidelines for inclusiveness in the membership shall be followed (¶ 706.4).

3. The conference board, in cooperation with the General Board of Church and Society and the Annual Conference Council on Ministries, shall develop and promote programs on Church and society within the bounds of the conference. To this end it may divide its membership into committees of approximately equal size, patterned after the issue departments of the

General Board of Church and Society, inclusive of the areas of political and human rights, human welfare, environmental justice and survival, peace and world order, and social and economic justice. Committees of the board shall have responsibility to cooperate with one another to advance the respective and mutual concerns of their respective divisions in social education, service, witness, and action.

4. The conference Board of Church and Society shall serve to connect the General Board of Church and Society and the district and local churches in relating the gospel of Jesus Christ to the members of the Church and to the persons and structures of the communities, nation, and world in which they live. Program shall be developed which provides education and action on issues confronting the Church consistent with the Social Principles and the policies adopted by the General Conference.

5. The board shall estimate annually the amount necessary for support of its work and shall report this amount according to the procedure of the Annual Conference. The work of the board may be considered a benevolence interest of the Church within the conference.

6. The Annual Conference may employ a person or persons to further its purposes. Two or more Annual Conferences may cooperate in developing their programs and in employing one or more persons.

¶ **729.** *Conference Board of Discipleship.*—The Annual Conference shall organize a **Board of Discipleship** or equivalent structure that shall provide for the connectional relationship between the General Board of Discipleship and the conference, district, and local church, and provide for discipleship functions related to the objectives and scope of work of the General Board of Discipleship, as set forth in ¶¶ 1201, 1202. The person or persons serving as member(s) of the General Board of Discipleship shall be member(s) of the conference Board of Discipleship and may be granted voting privileges.

1. *General Responsibilities.*—*a)* To lead and assist the congregations and districts in the conference in their efforts to win persons as disciples of Jesus Christ, to build up the Christian community, and to celebrate and communicate the redeeming

and reconciling love of God as revealed in Jesus Christ to persons of every age, ethnic background, and social condition.

b) To foster and promote such ministries as Christian education, camping and outdoor activities, evangelism, stewardship, worship, lay development, devotional life, age-level and family life ministries, leadership education, United Methodist Men, and such other areas of work as the Annual Conference may determine.

c) To foster and promote camping experiences for persons with handicapping conditions including camps specifically designed for persons with handicapping conditions, and the participation of persons with handicapping conditions, when feasible, in camps sponsored by the district and conference.

d) To provide training for clergy and laity in ministries with a population with handicapping conditions, including the areas of the Sunday School, camps and retreats, and faith development.

e) To provide guidance and training for related district leaders and agencies and for local church administrative boards, officers, and committees, Councils on Ministries, age-level and family councils, work area chairpersons of evangelism, stewardship, worship, and education, and work area commissions and task groups.

f) To develop a unified and comprehensive program for leadership training to serve all age groups in the home, Church, and community.

g) To provide continued training for pastors in effective ministry with children, child and faith development of children, and interpretation of curriculum resources.

h) To enable and strengthen the ministry with and to youth at all levels of the Church.

i) To determine the necessary directors, coordinators, or designated leaders for discipleship responsibilities at the Annual Conference level, including the maintenance of linkage with the General Board of Discipleship and related district committees within the Annual Conference.

2. *Responsibilities in the Area of Education.—a)* To develop and promote a conference program of Christian education that gives children, youth, young adults, and adults a knowledge of and

experience in the Christian faith as motivation for Christian service in the Church, the community, and the world. This may include guidance and training for district leaders responsible for Christian education and for local church chairpersons of the work area and commissions on education, superintendents of the church school, church school division superintendents, church school teachers, and other leaders in the educational ministry of local churches.

b) To develop and maintain an organized system for communicating and working with persons responsible for Christian education programs in local churches, districts, jurisdictions, and the General Board of Discipleship.

c) To encourage the observance of the first Sunday of Christian Education Week, or some other day designated by the Annual Conference, in each local church as Christian Education Sunday for the purpose of emphasizing the importance of Christian education and for receiving an offering for the work of Christian education. (*See* ¶ 276.1.)

d) To develop and recommend to the Annual Conference plans for the acquisition of or disposition of conference camps and/or retreat properties in accordance with standards of camping developed by the General Board of Discipleship (¶ 1209.5).

e) To promote church school extension by (1) encouraging the development of new United Methodist church schools; (2) starting new classes; (3) expanding teaching/learning opportunities in the congregation and community.

f) To assist local congregations in initiating programs of teacher recruitment, development, training, and retraining in biblical, theological, and ethical thinking, as well as in the procedures and methods of Christian education.

g) To cooperate in the promotion of knowledge about the support for all schools, colleges, universities, and seminaries related to the conference, the campus Christian movement, and the campus ministry of the conference, region, or area through the establishment and support of such programs as may be approved by the Annual Conference in harmony with the policies and procedures of the General Board of Higher Education and Ministry.

3. *Responsibilities in the Area of Evangelism.—a)* To plan and promote an effective program of comprehensive evangelism throughout the conference.

b) To create an understanding of, interest in, and commitment to evangelism throughout the conference.

c) To provide for the training of clergy and lay persons in evangelism, the distribution of promotional literature, and the encouragement and enlistment of local church participation in a year-round program of evangelism.

d) To give guidance to the groups responsible for the work of evangelism in the districts and to the work area chairperson of evangelism in the local church.

e) To give particular emphasis to the promotion of programs of evangelism in order that all persons living in a community where there is a local United Methodist church, and who are without a church affiliation or who make no profession of faith, will be included within the nurturing and caring responsibility of that local church.

f) To recommend annually, in consultation with the Board of Ordained Ministry, to the conference and to the bishop in charge the appointment of certain effective members of the conference as conference-approved evangelists, provided that such persons shall meet the standards set for approved evangelists by the General Board of Discipleship, the conference Board of Discipleship, or its equivalent, and the conference Board of Ordained Ministry.

4. *Responsibilities in the Area of Worship.—a)* To be responsible for the concerns of worship within the Annual Conference.

b) To foster the use of the best resources for worship at conference meetings and in all the churches of the conference, promote the use of the Book of Worship and the hymnal in all the churches of the conference, foster creative and regular individual and family worship throughout the conference, plan and promote seminars and demonstrations on forms of worship and the use of music and other arts.

c) To provide exhibits at the conference sessions, cooperate with the Fellowship of United Methodists in Worship, Music, and Other Arts, the General Board of Discipleship, and the conference Council on Ministries in promoting seminars and training events in the area of worship, including music and other arts.

5. *Responsibilities in the Area of Stewardship.*—*a)* To plan and promote a comprehensive program of stewardship throughout the conference in such areas as stewardship education, proportionate giving and tithing, funding the Church's ministries, planned giving, time and abilities, economics and money management, and life-style.

b) To interpret the biblical and theological basis for stewardship.

c) To promote giving consistent with a Christian life-style.

d) To develop funding concepts within Annual Conference, district, and local church consistent with sound stewardship principles and the doctrine of The United Methodist Church.

e) To inform the local church that tithing is the minimum standard of giving in The United Methodist Church.

f) To design and schedule training events, to distribute promotional material, and to enlist local church participation in a year-round program of stewardship.

g) To give guidance to the work area of stewardship in the districts and to the work area chairperson of stewardship and the Committee on Finance in the local church.

h) To develop a program that will create concern on the part of every local church for the ecological and environmental problems that confront the world and to motivate them to accept responsibility for aiding in the solution of such problems.

i) To participate in the work of national and jurisdictional organizations related to stewardship, such as the National Association of Stewardship Leaders and the National Association of United Methodist Foundations.

6. *Responsibilities in the Area of Devotional Life.*—*a)* To promote the development of the devotional life throughout the conference.

b) To conduct seminars and training events in the areas of private and corporate prayer.

c) To encourage and assist with the distribution and use of devotional resources as provided by The Upper Room and the General Board of Discipleship.

7. *Responsibilities in the Area of Lay Life and Work.*—*a)* To

develop and promote programs to cultivate an adequate understanding of the theological and biblical basis for lay life and work among the members of the churches of the Annual Conference; to give special emphasis to programs and services which will enable laity of all ages to serve more effectively as leaders in both Church and community.

b) To provide support and direction for such lay programs as United Methodist Men, lay speaking, the observance of Laity Day, and the work of lay leaders on the local and district levels.

c) To provide support, training, and guidance for district coordinators, leaders, and groups for age-level and family ministries and for local church coordinators of age-level and family ministries.

d) To give support and direction to the conference and district program for local church officer development, coordinating and developing training experiences that will enable persons of all ages to serve more effectively as members of local church Councils on Ministries, Administrative Boards, and of the committees, commissions, and task forces related to these groups.

e) To encourage and support the involvement of older persons in ministries of service and mission, recognizing that as persons of insight and wisdom they represent a creative resource bank for the Church at all levels.

¶ **730.** 1. *Conference Board of Laity.*—There shall be in every Annual Conference a **conference Board of the Laity** or equivalent structure which shall provide for the ministry of the laity related to the objectives of the General Board of Discipleship as set forth in ¶¶ 1201-1300.

2. The purpose of the conference Board of Laity shall be:

a) To foster an awareness of the role of the laity both within the local congregation and through their ministries in the home, work place, community, and world in achieving the mission of the Church.

b) To develop and promote stewardship of time, talent, and possessions within the Annual Conference in cooperation with the conference Council on Ministries.

3. The following membership of the board is recommended: the conference lay leader, associate conference lay leaders, the presidents and two representatives elected by each of the

conference organizations of United Methodist Men, United Methodist Women, United Methodist Young Adults, and the conference Council on Youth Ministries, and in addition, the district lay leaders, two laymen, two laywomen, and two youth elected by the Annual Conference upon nomination of the conference Nominating Committee, a district superintendent designated by the Cabinet, the director of the conference Council on Ministries, and the presiding bishop. Special attention shall be given to the inclusion of persons with handicapping conditions and racial and ethnic persons.

4. The conference lay leader shall chair the board. Other officers shall be elected as the board shall deem necessary.

5. The board shall relate to the lay speaking program and to the organized lay groups in the conference, such as United Methodist Men, United Methodist Women, United Methodist Young Mdults, and United Methodist Youth, and shall support their work and help them coordinate the activities of the organized laity of the conference.

¶ **731.** 1. The Annual Conference shall organize a Board of Global Ministries or an equivalent structure which shall provide for global ministries responsibilities related to the objectives and scope of work of the General Board of Global Ministries as set forth in ¶¶ 1402-1403.

2. The **conference Board of Global Ministries** or equivalent structure shall be composed of those persons as determined by the Annual Conference and shall fulfill those responsibilities as assigned.

3. There shall be elected annually a conference **coordinator of Christian global concerns** of the conference United Methodist Women who shall be a member of the Annual Conference board and may be a member of the Annual Conference Council on Ministries. This person shall work with the Annual Conference Board of Global Ministries and the Annual Conference Council on Ministries to provide the necessary liaison between the Annual Conference and the General Board of Global Ministries.

4. The Annual Conference and the General Board of Global Ministries shall cooperate in carrying out the policies and promoting all phases of the work as related to the scope of the board as set forth in ¶ 1402.

Responsibilities.—(1) To designate the necessary committees, sections, or commissions and individual secretaries, coordinators, or other leaders for global ministries responsibilities at the Annual Conference level.

(2) To interpret to the Annual Conference the programs, plans, and policies of the General Board of Global Ministries and to plan and promote emphases on global ministries. To undergird with education, constructive evaluation, communication, and cultivation the total program of the General Board of Global Ministries.

(3) To interpret to the General Board of Global Ministries the mission program, priorities, and concerns of the Annual Conference and the local churches to enable the board to fulfill its responsibilities as an extension of the local church.

(4) To plan and promote various kinds of meetings and experiences throughout the conference for the purpose of developing a spirit of mission and participation in global ministries for training, education, and leadership development of mission leaders and persons in the field of human services, and health and welfare ministries.

(5) To cooperate with the General Board of Global Ministries in its program outside the United States.

(6) To identify with all who are alienated and dispossessed and to assist them in achieving their full human development—body, mind, and spirit, including encouraging and implementing affirmative action programs.

(7) To engage in direct ministries to human need, both emergency and continuing institutional and noninstitutional, however caused.

(8) To cooperate with the conference organization of United Methodist Women and help equip all women for full participation in the mission of the Church.

(9) To cultivate, through the channels of the Church other than United Methodist Women, the Advance special gifts for national and overseas ministries administered by the National and World Divisions, and the United Methodist Committee on Relief Department.

(10) To encourage, maintain, and strengthen the relationships between the Annual Conference and agencies related to the appropriate divisions and departments of the General Board of

Global Ministries and provide a channel through which these agencies shall report to the Annual Conference.

(11) To develop and implement church financial support of conference mission projects and programs, health and welfare ministries, with particular emphasis on benevolent care and Golden Cross, education and social service ministries, and Crusade Scholarships.

(12) To enable, encourage, and support the development of congregations, cooperative parishes, community centers, education and human services, and health and welfare ministries so that they may be units of mission in urban and rural areas, and partners with others in the worldwide mission of the Christian church.

(13) To encourage and support specialized urban and town and country ministries enabling comprehensive mission related to broad metropolitan and rural issues, services ministering to the needs of persons, and supportive programs strengthening the local church.

(14) To assist districts and local churches in exploring and developing new methods and direct service ministries as changing conditions and societal forms demand.

(15) To cooperate with Church and secular leaders at all levels in strategic planning, developing programs, and advocating legislation which impacts community and national issues.

(16) To envision and engage in imaginative new forms of mission appropriate to changing needs and to share the results of experimentation.

(17) To develop strategies in response to critical community issues, with special attention to the needs of ethnic and language groups, persons with handicapping conditions, people in transitional relationships, and those living under repressive systems.

(18) To support United Methodist Committee on Relief's refugee resettlement ministry by encouraging an Annual Conference Refugee Resettlement Committee capable of encouraging, advising, and assisting churches sponsoring the resettlement of refugees.

(19) To assist Annual Conference Disaster Response Coordinators and the United Methodist Committee on Relief by

encouraging the formation of an Annual Conference Disaster Response Committee which includes, when possible, members of the General Board of Global Ministries from the Annual Conference.

(20) To assist the program of Church and Community Ministry in setting goals, developing programs, providing funding, and evaluating the ministries.

(21) To cooperate with the General Board of Global Ministries in the recruitment of missionary personnel, and to cooperate with the appropriate conference units in the promotion and recruitment of persons for health and welfare service careers and other church-related occupations.

(22) To review and certify applications to the General Board of Global Ministries for loans, donations, and grants; to administer such funds for their designated purposes in accordance with the established guidelines, and to participate with the General Board of Global Ministries in planning and evaluation processes related to these funds.

(23) To cultivate gifts for those special Sunday offerings which are administered through the General Board of Global Ministries.

(24) To work with health and welfare institutions and programs related to the Annual Conference to develop a mutual agreement between the Annual Conference and each institution concerning their relationships. The term "related to" shall mean any relationship defined by the Annual Conference.

The Annual Conference and each health and welfare institution shall have a clearly stated document which describes their legal and financial relationships; *provided* that no such document shall impose as a party to it The United Methodist Church and/or the General Board of Global Ministries.

The Annual Conference may consult with a health and welfare institution when that institution plans to establish a new facility, alter its major purpose or function, or make a plan for expansion of an existing facility. The purpose of such a consultation would be to review the mission of the Annual Conference in health and welfare ministries and to ensure that the new institution, the new facility, the new purpose, or the expansion be in harmony with the mission of the Annual

Conference, and that there not be unnecessary duplication of existing services. The consultation may include a discussion of proposed plans of development, financing, and types of services to be rendered.

(25) To strive to ensure mutual representation between the Annual Conference unit responsible for health and welfare ministries and each health and welfare institution related to the Annual Conference where such representation is called for by mutual agreement of the institution and the Annual Conference.

(26) To encourage the health and welfare institutions and programs within the Annual Conference related to a connectional unit of The United Methodist Church to utilize the programmatic standards, self-study, and peer review available through the Health and Welfare Ministries Department.

(27) To assist the Annual Conference in assessing needs in health and welfare ministries. To assist the Annual Conference in development of health and welfare services in local communities and within the Annual Conference.

(28) To work with the General Board of Global Ministries in leadership development programs and the promotion of health and welfare ministries, and to work with the United Methodist Association of Health and Welfare Ministries in leadership development programs and the promotion of health and welfare ministries.

(29) To promote Christian, financial, and professional standards in health and welfare ministries within the Annual Conference.

(30) To aid in planning and developing a religious ministry in Annual Conference–related institutions and programs and, wherever practical, in state and other institutions and programs not related to the conference where there is a need.

(31) To serve in an advisory capacity to the conference nominating processes where the Annual Conference participates in the selection of trustees for health and welfare institutions and programs related to the Annual Conference.

(32) To provide a channel through which health and welfare programs and institutions report to the Annual Conference.

(33) To promote an annual Golden Cross offering or other

means of giving to be received in every local church on a day or days designated by the Annual Conference in support of the health and welfare ministries within the Annual Conference, and to provide financial support to care for sick persons, older persons, children and youth, and persons with handicapping conditions; with special emphasis given to aiding those ministries which provide direct financial assistance to persons in need. Promotion also should include World Division, National Division, and UMCOR Advance Specials related to health and welfare ministries.

(34) To make available program and other resources to local churches to help assure physical accessibility of church buildings.

5. The Annual Conference shall either establish a **Committee on Parish and Community Development** or assign this responsibility to an existing agency in the Annual Conference that will fulfill these responsibilities as related to the objectives and scope of the National Division, General Board of Global Ministries (¶ 1414). The committee shall initiate and develop programs with institutional and voluntary ministries related to the National Division, Church and Community Ministries, Congregational Development, Town and Country Ministries, Urban Ministries, and other concerns as desired. The committee may form subcommittees for these areas. The committee shall be accountable to the conference Board of Global Ministries, or to such other agency as the conference may determine. The chairperson of the committee and the chairpersons of the subcommittees shall be members of the conference Board of Global Ministries or such body to which the committee shall be amenable.

a) The committee shall include persons involved in significant types of parish and community ministries, the area or conference superintendent or director of parish development, representatives of related church agencies and groups, and at-large community representatives.

b) The general responsibilities of the committee shall include research, evaluation, planning and strategy development, policy formulation, program implementation, local and national liaison related to parish and community development, and such other functions as the conference or agency to which the committee is accountable may determine.

c) Responsibilities of the subcommittee on Institutional and Voluntary ministries related to the National Division may include developing a relationship to all such institutional and voluntary ministries within the Annual Conference; consulting with them in cooperative planning and strategy for the implementation of national mission concerns relative to needs in the area of social welfare as implemented through the ministries of community centers, residences, health care agencies, schools, and other educational agencies; and working with funding sources to provide the support needed for effective service in such agencies.

d) In Annual Conferences where church and community workers are assigned through the National Division of the General Board of Global Ministries, responsibilities of the subcommittee on Church and Community Ministry shall include reviewing and evaluating projects; serving as liaison between projects and the National Division; and securing consultative and financial support for workers.

e) Responsibilities of the subcommittee on Congregational Development shall include encouraging and supporting the development of new and established congregations; conducting research studies and community surveys that plan for and assist with developing innovative strategies for mission; and reviewing, evaluating, and making recommendations for loans, donations, and grants from the National Division.

f) Responsibilities of the subcommittee on Town and Country Ministries shall include mission development and ministry in rural and town areas with under 50,000 population. These shall include small cities of 10,000 to 50,000 and rural areas under 2,500, fulfilling the functions outlined in ¶ 731.5*h.*

g) Responsibilities of the subcommittee on Urban Ministries shall include long-range mission strategy development and ministry for metropolitan communities with over 50,000 population, fulfilling the functions outlined in ¶ 731.5*h.*

h) Responsibilities of the subcommittees on Town and Country Ministries and Urban Ministries shall include the following: consulting with the bishop, Cabinet, area or conference superintendent/director of parish development, district representatives of Town and Country Ministries and Urban Ministries, and the conference agencies in the development of policies for Cooperative Parish Ministries, securing of funding for staff, and in initiating and strengthening these ministries; developing of a comprehensive related missional strategy for the mission of the Annual Conference, the districts, and the local churches, and, reporting this plan to the Annual Conference for consideration, with the understanding that the plan may relate to a regional mission organization for purposes of larger geographical coordination; initiating and/or assisting with programs to deal with needs such as: local church/community outreach organization and development; ministries with specialized constituencies and sectors of community life, agricultural and industrial production and other issue-oriented ministries; the development and strengthening of regional and/or national networks and/or association; ethnic and language groups; churches in transitional communities; small membership churches; the impact of oppressive systems on town and country and urban people and their communities; and to fulfill other functions as related to the objectives and scope of work of the National Division, General Board of Global Ministries as set forth in ¶ 1414.

i) In metropolitan areas over 50,000 population consideration shall be given to the establishment of a **Metropolitan Commission** whose purpose shall be to promote long-range planning and to provide a coordinating framework for United Methodism's mission strategy for that metropolitan area. The membership may include the bishop or bishop's representative; the district superintendents involved; a selected group of clergy and laypersons representing the Annual Conference Board of Global Ministries and the Annual Conference Committee on Urban Ministry; the conference Commission on Religion and Race; the Annual Conference United Methodist Women and United Methodist Men; representatives from community-based ministries; representatives from district Council(s) on Ministries; representatives from other boards and agencies deemed appropriate; and groups and individuals who have skills and experience enabling them to fulfill creative planning and strategy functions for United Methodism in the metropolitan area.

When the metropolitan area includes more than one Annual Conference, representatives shall be elected from each conference's constituent boards and agencies to the Metropolitan Commission.

6. There may be a short-term **Volunteer-in-Mission coordinator** who will coordinate the short-term Volunteer-in-Mission ministries of the Annual Conference, in cooperation with the General Board of Global Ministries short-term Volunteer-in-Mission office and the Jurisdictional short-term Volunteer-in-Mission Agency (where one exists).

a) The coordinator shall be elected annually and shall be a member of the Annual Conference Board of Global Ministries.

b) The coordinator will be responsible to:

(1) match volunteers with mission opportunities;

(2) be responsive to volunteers' desire to serve;

(3) train and mobilize volunteers for short-term Volunteer-in-Mission;

(4) disseminate information on what is happening in the area of short-term Volunteer-in-Mission programs.

¶ **732.** 1. There shall be in each Annual Conference a Board of Higher Education and Campus Ministry. The number of members shall be determined by the Annual Conference, including representation from appropriate constituencies.

2. The **Annual Conference Board of Higher Education and Campus Ministry** shall provide for the connectional relationship between the Division of Higher Education of the General Board of Higher Education and Ministry and the conference, district, and local church and shall provide for a ministry in higher education related to the objectives and scope of work of the General Board of Higher Education and Ministry and the Division of Higher Education.

3. The Annual Conference chairperson of higher education and campus ministry shall be a member of the Annual Conference Council on Ministries.

4. The specific responsibilities of an Annual Conference Board of Higher Education and Campus Ministry include:

a) General Responsibilities.—(1) To interpret and promote the United Methodist ministries in higher education which are supported by the general Church and those specifically related to the Annual Conference.

(2) To provide the connectional relationship between the

Division of Higher Education of the General Board of Higher Education and Ministry and the conference, districts, and local churches.

(3) To recommend the policies guiding the Annual Conference in its program of ministry in higher education.

(4) To provide counsel, guidance, and assistance to United Methodist schools, colleges, universities, and campus ministries within the Annual Conference regarding their relationships to the state, and to interact with public higher education as it reflects on the wholeness of persons and the meaning of life.

(5) To represent the Annual Conference in its relationship to United Methodist schools, colleges, and universities, especially those related to the Annual Conference.

(6) To oversee the management of the Annual Conference program of campus ministry in Wesley Foundations, local churches, and ecumenical campus ministries.

(7) To train and provide resources for district committees and local church work areas of higher education and campus ministry.

(8) To identify and work with the Annual Conference, church-related colleges, and campus ministries on issues of public policy that bear on higher education, especially issues bearing on access, equity, academic freedom, peace, and justice.

(9) To apprise United Methodists of their historic commitment to and present mission in higher education.

(10) To present to the Council on Ministries and then to the Council on Finance and Administration of the Annual Conference the financial needs for adequate support of the schools, colleges, universities, theological schools, campus Christian movements, Wesley Foundations,[67] and other campus ministries related to the Annual Conference for allocations of apportionments to the churches within the conference.

(11) To determine the distribution of the funds received from undesignated gifts, returns from special days, and Annual Conference and district Advance Specials for higher education.

---

[67]*See* Judicial Council Decision 191.

(12) To establish, where appropriate, foundations or other means to ensure the ongoing support of the Annual Conference program of ministry in higher education.

(13) To work with the Annual Conference Council on Ministries and with districts and local churches to interpret and promote higher education ministries supported by special days and funds: Black College Fund; Hispanic, Asian, and Native Americans (HANA) Educational Ministries; United Methodist Student Day; World Communion Sunday; and other funds and special days related to higher education ordered by the General Conference or Annual Conference.

(14) To promote use of the United Methodist Loan Fund and to designate appropriate persons to represent the United Methodist Loan Fund on campuses, such persons normally being Wesley Foundation Directors or ecumenical campus ministers supported by the Annual Conference; to provide the Office of Loans and Scholarships with the names and addresses of those persons; and to apprise students of alternative ways to apply for loans in the event there is no campus minister.

(15) To administer the scholarship funds rebated to the Annual Conference by the Office of Loans and Scholarships in accordance with the guidelines of that office.

(16) To encourage the establishment of loan and scholarship funds in the Annual Conference and local churches, and to administer the loan and scholarship funds of the Annual Conference.

(17) To counsel United Methodist schools, colleges, universities, and campus ministries related to the Annual Conference with regard to their charters and constitutions, reversionary clauses, and liability.

(18) To counsel United Methodist institutions about property and endowments entrusted to the institutions and to maintain and enforce trust and reversionary clauses in accordance with the provisions of the Division of Higher Education under ¶ 1516.3c.

(19) To monitor fiduciary and legal relationships with United Methodist schools, colleges, universities, and campus ministries and to assist Annual Conferences in their responsibilities in these matters.

(20) To evaluate schools, colleges, universities and campus ministries related to the Annual Conference with concern for the quality of their performance, the integrity of their mission, and their response to the missional goals of the general Church and the Annual Conference.

(21) To confer at once with representatives of the General Board of Higher Education and Ministry to determine what resources and aid the board may be able to provide and to enable the Division of Higher Education to carry out its responsibilities in the event that any educational institution, Wesley Foundation, or other campus ministry moves to sever or modify its connection with the Church or violate the rules adopted by the division in accordance with ¶ 1516.3.

(22) Members of the Wesley Foundation Board of Directors shall be elected at the direction of the Annual Conferences according to the method selected by the Annual Conference Boards of Higher Education and Campus Ministry to be the most functional for each Wesley Foundation.

(23) To provide that two or more Annual Conferences may, on recommendation of their Boards of Higher Education and Campus Ministry, join in constituting an area or regional Committee or Commission on Higher Education and Campus Ministry, the membership, scope, and functions of which shall be determined by the cooperating conferences, in consultation with their bishop or bishops. The area committee or commission shall include a majority of its members from the participating Annual Conference Boards of Higher Education and Campus Ministry, with appropriate representation of college presidents, campus ministers, students, and ethnic persons.

(24) To provide resources for local churches and districts with programs of ministry with students or to campuses, and, where those programs receive financial support from or are designated as ministries on behalf of the Annual Conference, to ensure that the policies, standards, and goals of the Annual Conference Board of Higher Education and Campus Ministry are observed.

b) Responsibilities with Schools, Colleges, and Universities.—In addition to its general responsibilities, the Annual Conference Board of Higher Education and Campus Ministry shall carry out the following duties with regard to United Methodist schools, colleges, and universities.

(1) To make known to the district, subdistricts, and all local churches the names and location of all United Methodist educational institutions and, wherever possible, provide resources interpreting their work and special missions.

(2) To assist institutions related specifically to the Annual Conference in their efforts to raise funds, scholarships, recruit students, and extend services to the Annual Conference.

(3) To assume responsibility, after consultation with the Annual Conference Committee on Nominations and the nominating committee of the institution's Board of Trustees, for the nomination of those trustees who are to be nominated and elected by the Annual Conference to the Boards of Trustees of United Methodist schools, colleges, and universities. In the event that the Annual Conference confirms or elects trustees nominated by trustee-nominating committees, to consult with those committees, having special concern for the selection of persons who will appropriately address the financial, missional, and educational progress of the institution.

(4) To provide for interpretation of the programs of United Methodist schools, colleges, and universities throughout the educational program of the Annual Conference, and especially in cooperation with those committees and persons responsible for youth and young adult ministries.

(5) To interpret systematically to the districts, subdistricts, and local churches the conference program with United Methodist schools, colleges, and universities, encouraging their support and participation.

c) Responsibilities with Campus Ministries.—In addition to the general responsibilities listed above, the Annual Conference Board of Higher Education and Campus Ministry shall have the following responsibilities with regard to campus ministry:

(1) To have available the names and addresses of all campus ministries supported by The United Methodist Church, and to supply the names and addresses of campus ministries supported by the Annual Conference to all districts and local churches.

(2) To ensure representation of the Annual Conference board on the boards of all campus ministries supported by the Annual Conference.

(3) To interpret systematically to the districts, subdistricts, and local churches the conference program of campus ministry as a ministry to the whole campus (students, faculty, staff, and administration), encouraging their support, and urging United Methodist students of all ages to participate.

¶ **733.** 1. Each Annual Conference at the first session following the General Conference shall elect for a term of four years a **Board of Ordained Ministry** consisting of not fewer than six ordained ministers in full connection.[68] Lay observers shall be elected to participate in the work of the board but without vote. An ordained minister in retired relationship may be included as a member of the board. At least one member of the board will be engaged in an appointment beyond the local church and will represent to the board all other clergy so assigned. The board membership shall include women and ethnic persons.

a) This board shall be directly amenable to the Annual Conference, notwithstanding its organizational relationship within any other program or administrative unit of the Annual Conference. At least two-thirds of the members shall be graduates of seminaries listed by the University Senate. Members shall be nominated by the presiding bishop, after consultation with the chairperson of the board, the executive committee, or a committee elected by the board of the previous quadrennium, and with the Cabinet. To ensure adequate board membership, consultation shall include an evaluation of the workload of the board in meeting disciplinary and Annual Conference responsibilities. The Annual Conference Council on Finance and Administration shall recommend adequate administrative funds for the board in light of its workload.

b) It is recommended that each district be represented by a member of the board. The board may invite at least one member of the Cabinet to serve as a member of the board, if the Cabinet is not already represented in its membership. Vacancies shall be filled by the bishop after consultation with the chairperson or a committee of the board.

c) The board shall organize by electing from its membership a chairperson, registrars, and such other officers as it may deem

---

[68]*See* Judicial Council Decision 415.

necessary. The board shall designate its executive committee.

d) To ensure maximum contact with and support of persons in appointments beyond the local church, the board shall maintain relationships with all general agencies which have responsibility for persons in such appointments.

e) The board shall meet at least once prior to its meeting at the time of the Annual Conference session and may set a deadline prior to Annual Conference for transacting its business.

f) The board shall select from its own membership an official representative to serve on each district Committee on Ordained Ministry, preferably from within said district.

2. The duties of the Annual Conference Board of Ordained Ministry shall be:

a) To assume the primary responsibility for the enlistment and recruitment of ordained clergy, by working in consultation with the Cabinet and the Division of Ordained Ministry, to study and interpret the clergy needs and resources of the Annual Conference, with due regard to the inclusive nature of the Church. It shall, with the assistance of the local church Committee on Pastor-Parish Relations, conference agencies, and every ordained minister of the conference, enlist women and men of all races and ethnic origins for the ordained ministry and guide those persons in the process of education, training, and ordination, recommending colleges and schools of theology listed by the University Senate. Persons recruited should have an understanding of and appreciation for persons of different racial/ethnic heritages.

b) To seek from a school of theology information about the personal and professional qualities of an applicant for probationary membership or of a probationary member; *provided,* however, that the applicant or member consent to the provision of such information.

c) To receive annual reports on the progress made by each ministerial student enrolled in a theological school and to record credit for work satisfactorily completed.

d) It shall require a transcript of credits from each applicant before recognizing any of the applicant's educational claims. In case of doubt, the board may submit a transcript to the Division of Ordained Ministry for evaluation.

e) The board shall annually appoint and train a sufficient number of supervising pastors, in each district, in consultation with the district superintendent.

f) To guide the candidate for ordained ministry who is not enrolled in a theological school and who is pursuing the course of study as adopted by the Division of Ordained Ministry.

g) To examine all applicants as to their fitness for the ordained ministry and make full inquiry as to the fitness of the candidate for: (1) annual election as local pastor; (2) election to associate membership; (3) election to probationary membership; (4) election to full conference membership.

h) To provide all candidates for ordained ministry a written statement on the Disciplinary and Annual Conference requirements for the local pastor, associate, probationary, and full membership.

i) To interview and report recommendation concerning: (1) students, not yet elders in full connection, to be appointed to attend school and assigned to a Charge Conference; (2) candidates for ordination as deacons; (3) candidates for ordination as elders.[69]

j) To assign a board member to serve as liaison to retired clergy in the conference.

k) To interview applicants and make recommendation concerning: (1) changes from the effective relation to a leave of absence or retirement; (2) return to the effective relation from other relations; (3) honorable location; (4) readmission of located persons and persons discontinued from probationary membership; (5) sabbatical leave; (6) disability leave; (7) appointment as a student; (8) termination; (9) changes to or from less than full-time ministry.

The board shall keep a record of these changes and the reason behind them and place a copy in the permanent records of the Annual Conference maintained by the secretary of the conference.

l) To ensure confidentiality in relation to the interview and reporting process. The personal data and private information provided through the examinations of and by the Board of

----

[69]*See* Judicial Council Decision 405.

Ordained Ministry will not be available for distribution and publication. There are occasions when the Board of Ordained Ministry would not report privileged information, which in the judgment of the board, if revealed in the executive session would be an undue invasion of privacy without adding measurably to the conference's information about the person's qualifications for ordained ministry.[70]

m) To be in consultation with the bishop through the chairperson or the executive committee regarding transfers. This consultation is to be at the bishop's initiative and, where possible, to take place prior to transfers into the Annual Conference.

n) To provide support services for the ordained minister's career development, including personal and career counseling, continuing education, assistance in preparation for retirement, and all matters pertaining to clergy morale. In providing such support, the board in cooperation with the Cabinet shall give training and guidance to each local Committee on Pastor-Parish Relations regarding its work and role.

o) To provide a means of evaluating the effectiveness of ordained ministers in the Annual Conference (¶¶ 704.6; 269.2*f*[3]; 444).

p) To interpret the high ethical standards of ordained ministry set forth in the Discipline and to study matters pertaining to character (¶ 704.6).

q) To recommend to the full members of the Annual Conference for validation special ministries for which members seek appointment. The appointment to such ministries is the prerogative of the bishop and the Cabinet.

r) To administer the portion of the Ministerial Education Fund for use by the Annual Conference in its programs of enlistment, basic professional educational aid, continuing education, ethnic ministry and language training, and professional growth of ordained ministers; and to confer with the conference Board of Diaconal Ministry concerning the same uses for diaconal ministers.

s) To cooperate with the Division of Ordained Ministry and assist in: (1) the interpretation of current legislation

---

[70]*See* Judicial Council Decision 406.

concerning ordained ministry; (2) the interpretation and promotion of the Ministerial Education Fund; (3) the promotion and observance of Ministry Sunday; (4) the supplying of a record of all information, recommendations, and action on each candidate for ordained ministry after each session of the Annual Conference.

t) To promote in the Annual Conference and/or Jurisdictional Conference a system of financial aid to ministerial students. A conference transferring a person with less than three years of active service into another conference may require reimbursement either from the person or from the receiving conference for outstanding obligations for theological education financed through conference funds.

u) To work in cooperation with the Board of Diaconal Ministry, meeting together at least annually, to enhance the total ministry of the Church, recognizing that both diaconal ministry and ordained ministry are components of the professional ministry of the Church.

v) To approve, train, and assign counseling elders recommended by the Cabinet (¶ 411).

3. The board shall elect a **registrar** and such associate registrars as it may determine; one such associate registrar to be given responsibility for candidacy, including giving leadership to the training and guidance of supervising pastor(s) in each district. A staff executive may be named by the board to fulfill the functions of registrar.

a) The registrar shall keep full personnel records for all candidates for ordained ministry, under the care of the board, including essential biographical data, transcripts of academic credit, instruments of evaluation, and, where it applies, psychological and medical test records, sermons, theological statements, and other pertinent data.

b) Pertinent information and recommendations concerning each candidate shall be certified to the Annual Conference in duplicate; one copy of this record shall be kept by the registrar and one copy shall be mailed after each conference session to the Division of Ordained Ministry. The registrar shall forward an acknowledgment of transfer to the pastor of the local church where each newly elected probationary and associate member held membership.

c) The registrar shall keep a record of the standing of the students in the course of study and report to the conference when required. This record shall include the credits allowed students for work done in accredited schools of theology, in approved course of study schools, or the course of study correspondence.

d) The registrar shall file in the bishop's office for permanent record a copy of circumstances involving the discontinuance of probationary membership or termination of the local pastor status.

e) The records and files of the Board of Ordained Ministry are kept on behalf of the Annual Conference and shall be maintained under guidelines provided by the General Council on Finance and Administration in consultation with the General Board of Higher Education and Ministry and the General Board of Pensions.

4. Administrative costs of the Board of Ordained Ministry shall be a claim on the conference operating budget. The Board of Ordained Ministry shall have direct access to the conference Council on Finance and Administration in support of its program.

¶ **734.** 1. Each Annual Conference at the first session following General Conference shall elect for a term of four years a **Board of Diaconal Ministry,** consisting of not fewer than nine persons, of whom at least one-third shall be clergy, two-thirds lay members, and at least one-half of the lay members shall be in diaconal ministry careers, preferably diaconal ministers. (*See* ¶¶ 303-317.)

a) The board shall be directly responsible to the Annual Conference, notwithstanding its organizational relationship with any other program or administrative unit of the Annual Conference. Administrative costs of the board shall be a direct claim on the conference operating budget.

b) The board shall be nominated by the presiding bishop after consultation with the executive committee of the board of the previous quadrennium. The bishop shall designate a member of the Cabinet and may designate a staff person from the conference Council on Ministries to be ex officio members of the board.

c) The board shall organize by electing from its membership a chairperson, a secretary, a registrar, other officers as may be necessary, and may name committees as needed.

d) Where there is a Board of Higher Education and Ministry the Board of Diaconal Ministry may function as the Division of Diaconal Ministry.

2. The board shall work in cooperation with the conference Board of Ordained Ministry, or, if necessary, the executive committees, meeting together, at least annually to enhance the total ministry of the Church, recognizing that both diaconal ministry and ordained ministry are components of the representative ministry of the Church.

3. The duties of the conference Board of Diaconal Ministry for the office of diaconal minister shall be:

a) To study diaconal ministry needs and resources of the Annual Conference with due regard to the inclusive Church.

b) To interpret diaconal ministry in the Annual Conference and to cooperate in the promotion of the observance of Ministry Sunday (¶ 733.2*s*).

c) To enlist women and men of all races and ethnic origins for diaconal ministry, in cooperation with conference agencies, district superintendents, and all ordained ministers of the conference.

d) To guide persons in the process of education, training, and consecration for diaconal ministry, recommending colleges, universities, and schools of theology listed by the University Senate.

e) To provide counsel and resources to the local church for its examination and recommendation of persons for candidacy as diaconal ministers (¶ 303).

f) To examine all applicants as to their fitness for diaconal ministry, and to make recommendations concerning their candidacy for diaconal ministry (¶¶ 304-305).

g) To guide and counsel candidates for diaconal ministry throughout their candidacy.

h) To maintain accurate records of work satisfactorily completed by candidates engaged in academic preparation for diaconal ministry, based on reports received from the appropriate bodies.

i) To transfer records of candidates who move to another Annual Conference.

j) To ensure confidentiality in the interview and reporting process. Personal data and private information will not be available for distribution and publication without proper authorization.

k) To work with the presiding bishop to provide for an appropriate service of consecration during the session of Annual Conference, following the guidelines of the Division of Diaconal Ministry, General Board of Higher Education and Ministry. The services for consecration and ordination may be incorporated into one service.

l) To be responsible for the evaluation of the character and effectiveness of diaconal ministers in the Annual Conference and to make one report to the bishop and the conference in open session annually.

m) To examine candidates who have completed their candidacy for diaconal ministry and to make recommendations to the Annual Conference concerning their consecration as diaconal ministers and their relationship to the Annual Conference (¶ 306).

n) To interview a diaconal minister requesting a change in his/her Annual Conference relationship and make recommendations for Annual Conference action concerning disability leave, maternity/paternity leave, study/sabbatical leave, personal leave, retirement, termination, and reinstatement. The board shall keep a record of these changes and the reasons for them and place a copy in the permanent ministerial records of the Annual Conference.

o) To consult with receiving bishop and to transfer the credentials and records of a diaconal minister from another Annual Conference. Following the consent of the receiving bishop, the receiving Annual Conference shall initiate the action for transfer.

p) To recommend annually for review by the Cabinet and approval by the bishop of the Annual Conference the names of all persons consecrated to the office of diaconal minister and their places of service.

q) To report annually to the Annual Conference for reading by the bishop and for publication in the conference journal the names of all persons consecrated to the office of diaconal minister and their places of service.

r) To ensure that the significance of consecration into and retirement from diaconal ministry is appropriately recognized by the Annual Conference.

s) To work with the Annual Conference and the employing agency to assure responsible conditions of employment for the diaconal minister, to provide a supportive atmosphere that will empower his/her ministry, and to see that entrance into employment and departure from employment are open and fair to all persons involved.

t) To work with the Annual Conference and the employing agency to assure for the diaconal minister a pension plan, an insurance program, an adequate salary base, and other employee benefits commensurate with the diaconal minister's training, ability, and experience.

u) To provide support services for the diaconal minister's career development, including personal and career counseling, continuing education, assistance in preparation for retirement, and all matters pertaining to morale.

v) To work with the bishop and district superintendents in matters of mutual concern for the personal and professional support for diaconal ministers.

w) To confer with the conference Board of Ordained Ministry concerning the use of Ministerial Education Funds for enlistment, basic professional educational aid, continuing education, and professional growth of diaconal ministers.

x) To maintain the records and files of the conference Board of Diaconal Ministry on behalf of the Annual Conference, and they shall be maintained under guidelines provided by the General Council on Finance and Administration in consultation with the General Board of Higher Education and Ministry and the General Board of Pensions.

4. The duties of the conference Board of Diaconal Ministry for certification shall be:

a) To determine in consultation with the Division of Diaconal Ministry of the General Board of Higher Education and Ministry whether applicants meet the standards of the General

Board of Higher Education and Ministry for professional certification in education, evangelism, music, and other areas that may be assigned.

b) To recommend to the Annual Conference persons who have met the standards and have been mutually approved by the conference Board of Diaconal Ministry and the Division of Diaconal Ministry of the General Board of Higher Education and Ministry for professional certification in education, evangelism, music, and other areas that may be assigned; and to report the action of the Annual Conference to the General Board of Higher Education and Ministry.[71]

c) To keep a current record of all persons in the Annual Conference who have been certified in professional church careers, including places of service address.

d) To renew or discontinue professional certification based on an annual review and evaluation of all persons who have been certified in education, evangelism, music, or other areas that may be assigned.

e) To report annually to the Annual Conference for publication in the conference journal a roster of all persons certified in professional careers and the careers in which they are certified.

f) To work with the Annual Conference and the employing agency to assure responsible conditions of employment for the certified person, to provide a supportive atmosphere that will empower his/her service, and to see that entrance into employment and departure from employment are open and fair to all persons involved.

5. The duties of the conference Board of Diaconal Ministry for deaconesses and home missionaries shall be:

a) To keep a record of all persons in the Annual Conference who have been commissioned to the office of deaconess or the office of home missionary.

b) To report annually to the Annual Conference for publication in the conference journal a roster of all persons commissioned as deaconess and home missionary.

6. The board shall cooperate with the Division of Diaconal Ministry and assist in the study, interpretation, promotion, and

---

[71]*See* Judicial Council Decision 507.

support of diaconal ministry; the maintenance of standards and processes for consecration and certification; and the interpretation and promotion of the Ministerial Education Fund.

¶ **735.** *Conference Committee on Episcopacy.*—1. There shall be a **conference Committee on Episcopacy** elected quadrennially by the Annual Conference at the session following the General Conference. The committee's membership shall number at least seven but no more than seventeen. In addition to the lay and clergy members of the jurisdictional Committee on Episcopacy, who shall be ex officio members with vote, the committee shall consist of the following representatives: one-fifth laywomen, one-fifth laymen, one-fifth clergypersons, one-fifth persons to make possible the representation of racial and ethnic groups, youth, young adults, and older adults and one-fifth persons appointed by the bishop; *provided* that one lay person shall be the conference lay leader.

Two or more conferences under the presidency of a single bishop may decide to have one Committee on Episcopacy, in which case each Annual Conference shall be represented as stated in the preceding paragraph and shall each elect its own representatives.

2. The committee shall meet at least annually. It shall be convened by the bishop and shall elect a chairperson, a vice-chairperson, and a secretary. The bishop and/or chairperson are authorized to call additional meetings when desired.

3. The functions of the conference Committee on Episcopacy shall be:

a) To support the bishop of the area in the oversight of the spiritual and temporal affairs of the Church, with special reference to the area where the bishop has presidential responsibility.

b) To be available to the bishop for counsel.

c) To assist in the determination of the episcopal needs of the area and to make recommendations to appropriate bodies.

d) To keep the bishop advised concerning conditions within the area as they affect relationships between the bishop and the people of the conference agencies.

e) To interpret to the people of the area and to conference agencies the nature and function of the episcopal office.

f) To engage in annual consultation and appraisal of the work of the bishop in the episcopal area including concern for the inclusiveness of the Church and its ministry with respect to sex, race, and national origin, and understanding and implementation of the consultation process in appointment-making.

g) To report needs for episcopal leadership to the jurisdictional Committee on Episcopacy through the duly elected conference members of that committee.

4. The conference Council on Finance and Administration shall make provision in its budget for the expenses of this committee.

¶ **736.** *Episcopal Residence Committee.*—1. The provision of housing for effective bishops in the Jurisdictional Conferences shall be the responsibility of the Annual Conference or conferences comprising the episcopal area to which the bishop is assigned.

2. In each episcopal area in the Jurisdictional Conferences there shall be an **Episcopal Residence Committee**. It is recommended that the committee be composed of the following persons:

a) The president, or his/her designate, of the conference Committee on Episcopacy from each conference.

b) The president, or his/her designate, of the conference Council on Finance and Administration from each Annual Conference.

c) The chairperson, or his/her designate, of the conference Board of Trustees from each Annual Conference.

3. The chairperson of the Episcopal Residence Committee shall be the representative of the Committee on Episcopacy of the Annual Conference in which the episcopal residence is currently located.

4. It shall be the responsibility of the Episcopal Residence Committee:

a) To make recommendations to the Annual Conference(s) regarding the purchase, sale, or rental of an episcopal residence.

b) To prepare an annual budget covering the cost of providing the episcopal residence which may also include utilities, insurance, and normal costs of upkeep in maintaining the residence.

c) To forward the proposed budget annually to the General Council on Finance and Administration for its action as to that portion of the episcopal residence expense which shall be paid from the Episcopal Fund (*see* ¶ 927).

d) To forward the proposed budget annually and recommend to each conference Council on Finance and Administration the proportionate share of the proposed budget to be borne by that Annual Conference, such proportionate share to be approved by each Annual Conference as it acts on budget recommendations (¶ 710).

e) To supervise the expenditure of funds allocated from all sources for expenses related to the provision of the episcopal residence, and to account for such expenditures annually to each Annual Conference in the episcopal area and to the General Council on Finance and Administration.

f) To give oversight in all matters related to upkeep, maintenance, improvements, and appropriate insurance coverages for the episcopal residence.

5. Titles to properties held as episcopal residences shall be held in accordance with ¶ 2514.

¶ **737.** *Conference Board of Pensions.*—1. *Authorization.*—There shall be organized in each Annual Conference a conference board, auxiliary to the General Board of Pensions, to be known as the **conference Board of Pensions,** hereinafter called the board, which shall have charge of the interests and work of providing for and contributing to the support, relief, assistance, and pensioning of clergy and their families, other church workers, and lay employees of The United Methodist Church, its institutions, organizations, and agencies within the Annual Conference, except as otherwise provided for by the general board.

2. *Membership.*—*a)* The board shall be composed of not less than twelve members not indebted to pension and benefit funds, plans, and programs; one-third laywomen, one-third laymen, and one-third clergy, and in accordance with ¶ 704.3, elected for a term of eight years and arranged in classes as determined by the Annual Conference; in addition thereto, any clergy member of the conference or lay member of a church within the conference

who is a member of the General Board of Pensions. A vacancy in the membership of the board may be filled by the board for the remainder of the conference year in which the vacancy occurs, subject to the same qualifications before provided, and at its next session the conference shall fill the vacancy for the remainder of the unexpired term.

b) The members shall assume their duties at the adjournment of the conference session at which they were elected.

3. *Organization.*—The board shall organize by electing a chairperson, vice-chairperson, secretary, and treasurer, who shall serve during the ensuing quadrennium or until their successors shall have been elected and qualified. These officers shall constitute an executive committee; *provided,* however, that three members may be added thereto by the board. The duty of the executive committee shall be to administer the work of the board during the conference year in the interim between regular or special meetings of the board. The office of secretary may be combined with that of treasurer. The treasurer may be a person who is not a member of the board, in which case the person shall be an ex officio member of the executive committee, without vote. Calls for special meetings of the board shall be issued by the secretary on request of the chairperson, or the vice-chairperson when the chairperson is unable to act.

4. *Proportional Payment.*—The board shall compare the records of the amounts paid by each pastoral charge for the support of pastors and for pension and benefit programs, computing the proportional distribution thereof and keeping a permanent record of defaults of the clergy of the conference who have failed to observe the following provisions pertaining to proportional payment, and shall render annually to each clergy who is in default a statement of the amounts in default for that and preceding years.[72]

a) When the apportionment to the pastoral charges for the pension and benefit program of the Annual Conference has been determined; payments made thereon by each pastoral charge shall be exactly proportionate to payments made on the salary or salaries of the ordained minister or clergy serving it.

---

[72]*See* Judicial Council Decisions 50, 390, 401, 471.

b) The treasurer of the pastoral charge shall be primarily responsible for the application of proportional payment; but in the event of the treasurer's failure to apply it, the pastor shall adjust cash salary and payment according to the proper ratio, as provided above, before the pastor enters the respective amounts in the statistical report to the Annual Conference.

c) The conference statistical tables shall provide separate columns for reporting the amount apportioned to each pastoral charge for pension and benefit purposes and the amount paid thereon.

d) On retirement, the amount that a pastor is in default shall be subject to deduction from the pastor's pension, in accordance with rules and regulations of the specific program or programs under which the pension is provided.

e) If a retired ordained minister, while serving as a supply pastor, fails to observe the provisions of this paragraph pertaining to proportional payment in any conference year, the amount of such default shall be deducted from the pastor's pension the ensuing conference year.

f) It shall not be permissible for a pastor to receive a bonus or other supplementary compensation tending to defeat proportional payment. The board may recommend to the conference that a lien be placed on the pension of the pastor in the amount of the bonus or supplementary compensation received.

5. *Reports to the Annual Conference and the General Board.—* *a)* The board shall report to the Annual Conference and to the General Board of Pensions the names, addresses, and years of service approved for pension credit of the annuitants of the conference, the names of those who have died during the year, and the names of dependent children of deceased clergy members of the conference, and shall show separately the amount paid to each beneficiary by the conference from the annuity and necessitous funds.

b) The board shall report to the General Board of Pensions immediately following the session of the conference, on forms provided for that purpose by the general board, and shall report also the names and addresses of clergy who are members of funds, plans, or programs administered by the general board.

¶ **738.** 1. In each Annual Conference there shall be a **conference Commission on Archives and History.** The commission shall be elected by the Annual Conference upon the nomination of its nominating committee. The number of members of the commission and their terms of office shall be as the conference may determine and may include an ex officio representative of each United Methodist shrine or landmark in its bounds. It shall be the duty of the commission to cooperate with and report, when requested, to the General and Jurisdictional Commissions on Archives and History; to preserve the records of the Annual Conference and of closed churches; to collect and preserve data relating to the organization and history of the conference; to maintain a firesafe historical and archival depository and to see that all current items which obviously will have value for future history are preserved therein; to provide for the ownership of real property and to receive gifts and bequests; to provide liaison with shrines, landmarks, and conference historical sites in their bounds; to assist the bishop or the conference program committee in planning for the historical hour and other appropriate historical observances at Annual Conference sessions; to establish retention and disposition schedules for local church records under standards or guidelines established by the General Commission on Archives and History; to encourage and assist the local churches in preserving their records and compiling their histories; and to engage with other Wesleyan, Methodist, or Evangelical United Brethren–related denominations in lifting up our joint heritage.

2. The commission may organize a **conference Historical Society** and encourage individuals to become members of it for the purpose of promoting interest in the study and preservation of the history of the conference and its antecedents. The officers of the conference Commission on Archives and History may be the officers of the conference Historical Society. Individuals may become members of the Historical Society by paying dues as the society may direct, and in return they shall receive official publications and publicity materials issued by the commission and the society.

3. Each Annual Conference may have a historian to undertake specific duties as may be designated by the commis-

sion. The **Annual Conference historian** may be a member of the Annual Conference Commission on Archives and History.

4. The Annual Conference Commission on Archives and History shall work with the ethnic congregations of the conference to develop and preserve the historical records of those congregations and antecedent conferences.

¶ **739.** 1. Each Annual Conference shall create a **conference Commission or Committee on Christian Unity and Interreligious Concerns** to work with the General Commission on Christian Unity and Interreligious Concerns. The commission or committee will report each year to the conference in such manner as the conference may direct.[73]

2. It is recommended that this commission or committee be composed of two United Methodists from each district (complying with ¶ 706.4), one of whom shall be district coordinator for Christian unity and interreligious concerns and shall serve as liaison with local church work areas on Christian unity and interreligious concerns. Additional members may include persons from The United Methodist Church or other member churches of the Consultation on Church Union as directed by the conference to assure ecumenical expertise and interchange with other agencies.

Ex officio members of the Annual Conference Commission on Christian Unity and Interreligious Concerns shall include any United Methodists residing within the conference bounds who are members of the following: the General Commission on Christian Unity and Interreligious Concerns, the Governing Board of the National Council of the Churches of Christ in the U.S.A., the World Methodist Council, the United Methodist delegation to the most recent World Council of Churches Assembly, and the United Methodist delegation to the most recent plenary meeting of the Consultation on Church Union.

3. There shall be a representative of the commission who serves as one of the conference representatives to state councils or conferences of churches.

4. The duties of the commission or committee shall be to act in cooperation with the Annual Conference Council on

---

[73]*See* Judicial Council Decision 576.

Ministries, in coordination with the duties of the General Commission on Christian Unity and Interreligious Concerns, as outlined in ¶¶ 2002-2003, and as it may recommend, and to take initiative in ecumenical and interreligious concerns as follows:

a) To interpret, advocate, and work for the unity of the Christian Church in every aspect of the life of the conference and its churches, and to encourage dialogue and cooperation with persons of other living faiths.

b) To recommend to the conference the goals, objectives, and strategies and to assist the conference, in cooperation with the bishop and the Cabinet, in the development of ecumenical relationships and planning for mission with other judicatories, particularly in the establishment of new churches, yoked congregations, and in the process of local church union efforts.

c) To stimulate participation in and evaluation of mission programs ecumenically planned and implemented, such as experimental parishes, ecumenical parish clusters, ecumenical task forces, and united ministries in higher education, and in other issue-oriented tasks.

d) To stimulate conference, district, and congregational participation in councils, conferences, or associations of churches, in coalition task forces, and in interreligious groups through ecumenical educational or shared time programs, jointly approved curriculum resources, interreligious study programs, or ecumenical community action projects such as institutional ministries and media communications and various other modes of interchurch cooperation.

e) To participate in the selection of conference delegates to state councils or conferences of churches, which participation may include nomination, in cooperation with the conference nominating committee, for conference election the delegates to these bodies; the selecting of representatives to district, area, and regional ecumenical and interreligious task groups and workshops; and acting as the body to which such delegates are accountable through the receiving of and action on their reports and recommendations.

f) To promote and interpret the work of national and world ecumenical bodies such as the National Council of the Churches of Christ in the U.S.A., the World Council of Churches, the Consultation on Church Union, and the World Methodist Council, and to cooperate in and provide leadership for specific ecumenical experiences of worship and celebration, such as the Week of Prayer for Christian Unity, Pentecost Sunday, World Communion Sunday, Reformation Sunday, and other appropriate occasions.

g) To stimulate understanding and conversations with all Christian bodies, to encourage continuing dialogue with Jewish and other living faith communities, and to encourage an openness of mind toward an understanding of other major world religions.

h) To fulfill other functions assigned by the Annual Conference and to respond to such requests as may be made by its leadership.

¶ **740.** 1. There shall be in each Annual Conference a **conference Commission on Religion and Race,** following the general guidelines and structure of the General Commission on Religion and Race as outlined in ¶¶ 2102, 2108 where applicable.

2. The basic membership of the Annual Conference commission shall be nominated and elected by established procedure of the respective Annual Conferences. Each Annual Conference shall determine the number and composition of the total membership which shall consist of a minimum of twelve. The commission membership shall include representation from each district. Care shall be taken to ensure that the total membership shall maintain the one-third laywomen, one-third laymen, and one-third clergy balance. It is strongly urged that the Annual Conference commissions be constituted so that the majority of the membership be represented by racial and ethnic persons (Asian Americans, Black Americans, Hispanic Americans, and Native Americans) reflecting the racial and ethnic constituency of the Annual Conference. Selection of commission members shall ensure adequate representation of women, youth, young adults, older adults, and persons with handicapping conditions. Members of the General Commission on Religion and Race residing in the Annual Conference shall be ex officio members of the Annual Conference Commission on Religion and Race with vote.

3. The Annual Conference commission will assume responsibility for such matters as:

a) Providing resources and training to enable the work of local church work area chairpersons of religion and race as specified in ¶ 261.7.

b) Examining ethnic representation on all of the conference boards, agencies, commissions, and committees, as well as the governing boards of related institutions. After such an examination, appropriate recommendations for total inclusiveness should be made to the Annual Conference.

c) Working with Annual Conference boards and agencies as they seek to develop programs and policies of racial inclusiveness.

d) Providing a channel of assistance to racial and ethnic groups as they seek to develop programs of empowerment and ministry to their communities.

e) Consulting with the Board of Ordained Ministry and the Cabinet to determine what provisions are made for the recruitment and itineracy of racial and ethnic ordained ministers.

f) Serving as a resource and support group to promote understanding between pastors appointed to local congregations across racial and ethnic lines, and such congregations.

g) Consulting with local churches which are seeking to establish multiracial fellowships and encouraging and supporting local churches in maintaining a Christian ministry in racially changing neighborhoods.

h) Coordinating the conference support and cooperation with various movements for racial and social justice in consultation with the conference Board of Church and Society, as appropriate.

i) Providing opportunities for multiracial and interethnic dialogue and meetings throughout the conference.

j) Providing programs of sensitization and education at every level of the conference, on the nature and meaning of racism—attitudinal, behavioral, and institutional.

k) Coordinating in consultation with the General Commission on Christian Unity and Interreligious Concerns the conference programs of cooperation with black and other racial and ethnic denominations, especially those of the Methodist family.

l) Evaluating the priorities of the Annual Conference in light of the needs in the area of race relations. The commission shall develop recommendations to present to the appropriate agencies and report directly to the Annual Conference session. These recommendations shall lift up the need to deal with the pressing issue of racism, racial and ethnic group empowerment, and reconciliation among the races.

m) Evaluating the effects of merger and making appropriate recommendations to the Annual Conference session.

n) Reviewing the Annual Conference practices of employment, of Annual Conference program, business and administration, and office personnel, and reporting and recommending to the Annual Conference steps to be taken to actualize racial and ethnic inclusiveness; reviewing the Annual Conference–related institutions such as colleges, hospitals, homes for the aged, child-care agencies, etc., concerning their practices of racial and ethnic inclusiveness in clientele and employment and reporting to Annual Conference session.

o) Serving in consultation with the bishop and other appropriate conference leadership to investigate and assist in resolution of complaints of racial discrimination made by clergy or laity.

p) Maintaining a close relationship with the General Commission on Religion and Race, seeking its guidance, utilizing its training and resources, and interpreting to Annual Conference the programs, plans, and policies of the General Commission on Religion and Race.

4. The Annual Conference Commission on Religion and Race shall develop an adequate budget for its operation as a commission for inclusion in the Annual Conference budget.

¶ **741.** There shall be in each Annual Conference, including the Central Conferences, a **conference Commission on the Status and Role of Women.**

1. The responsibility of this commission shall be in harmony with the responsibility of the general commission (*see* ¶ 2203) with the following objectives established as guidelines for adaptation to the needs of the respective Annual Conferences:

a) To be informed about the status and role of all women in the total life of the conference. Data shall be gathered which relate to all structural levels of the conference, including the local church. Such information will be regularly updated and disseminated.

b) To initiate cooperation with United Methodist Women at the Annual Conference level, and other levels as appropriate, in order to achieve full participation of women in the decision-making structures.

c) To develop ways to inform and sensitize the leadership within the conference at all levels on issues that affect women, which shall be projected into and through all districts within the conference by the commission.

d) To focus on major priorities of issues related to women and to enlist the support of the bishop, Cabinet, and conference staff in policies, plans, and practices related to those priorities.

e) To advise the general commission about the progress and effectiveness of efforts to achieve full participation of women in the life of the Church.

f) To participate in connectional programs and plans initiated or recommended by the general commission; and to utilize the resources available from the general commission as needed.

2. The basic membership of the conference commission shall be nominated and elected by established procedures of the respective Annual Conferences. Each Annual Conference shall determine the number and composition of the total membership which shall consist of not fewer than twelve nor more than thirty-six. All must be members of The United Methodist Church. Special consultants without vote may be used as resource persons. Among the basic members of the commission shall be representatives from each district. There shall be at least six members at large. The addition of the at-large membership shall ensure that the total membership shall maintain the one-third laywomen, one-third laymen, one-third clergy balance. The majority of the commission shall be women, including both clergy and lay. In an Annual Conference where there is not a sufficient number of clergywomen to meet the required balance, additional laywomen shall be elected beyond the one-third proportion to bring the total membership to a majority of women.

Selection of commission members shall ensure adequate

representation of racial and ethnic groups, youth, young adults, older adults, and persons of varying life-styles.

At least one member shall be named by the conference United Methodist Women.

3. The chairperson of the commission shall be a woman.

4. The commission shall propose a budget and submit it for inclusion in the budget of the Annual Conference, according to procedures for funding of all boards, commissions, and agencies of the Annual Conference.

¶ 742. United Methodist Women.—*Constitution of United Methodist Women in the Conference.*—*Article 1. Name.*—In each Annual Conference there shall be a conference organization named United Methodist Women, auxiliary to the jurisdictional organization of United Methodist Women and to the Women's Division of the General Board of Global Ministries.

Article 2. Function.—The function of the conference organization of United Methodist Women shall be to work with the district organizations and the local units of United Methodist Women in developing programs to meet the needs and interests of women and the concerns and responsibilities of the global Church; to encourage and support spiritual growth, missionary outreach, and Christian social action; and to promote the plans and responsibilities of the Women's Division.

Article 3. Authority.—Each conference organization of United Methodist Women shall have authority to promote its work in accordance with the plans, responsibilities, and policies of the Women's Division of the General Board of Global Ministries.

Article 4. Membership.—The conference organization of United Methodist Women shall be composed of all members of local units within the bounds of the conference. The resident bishop shall be a member of the conference organization of United Methodist Women and of its executive committee.

Article 5. Officers and Committees.—The conference organization shall elect a president, a vice-president, a secretary, a treasurer, and a Committee on Nominations. Additional officers and committees shall be elected or appointed in accordance with the plans of the Women's Division as set forth in the bylaws of the conference organizations of United Methodist Women.

Article 6. Meetings and Elections.—*a)* There shall be an annual meeting of the conference organization of United Methodist Women, at which time there shall be presented a program designed to meet the needs of the women of the conference in harmony with the Purpose and the plans and responsibilities of the Women's Division of the General Board of Global Ministries. Officers and the Committee on Nominations shall be elected, the necessary business transacted, and pledges made for the ensuing year.

b) The voting body of the annual meeting of the conference organization shall be composed of representatives from units in local churches as determined by the conference organization; such district officers as the conference organization may determine; the conference officers and chairpersons of committees; members of the Women's Division and officers of the jurisdictional organization residing within the bounds of the conference.

c) At the annual meeting of the conference organization prior to the quadrennial meeting of the jurisdictional organization, six conference officers shall be elected according to provisions in ¶ 634.3 for membership in the jurisdictional organization.

d) At the annual meeting of the conference organization prior to the quadrennial meeting of the jurisdictional organization, the conference organization shall nominate three women for membership on the General Board of Global Ministries, the names to be sent to the jurisdiction organization according to ¶ 634.4.

Article 7. Relationships.—a) The president of the conference organization of United Methodist Women is a member of the Annual Conference, as set forth in ¶ 35.

b) Designated officers shall represent the conference organization on the various agencies, councils, commissions, and committees of the conference as the constitutions and bylaws of such agencies provide.

c) The conference organization shall encourage women to participate in the total life and work of the Church, and shall support them in assuming positions of responsibility and leadership.

*Article 8. Amendments.—*Proposed amendments to this constitution may be sent to the recording secretary of the Women's Division prior to the last annual meeting of the division in the quadrennium.

¶ **743.** 1. In each Annual Conference there shall be a **conference Council on Youth Ministry** composed of both youth and adults. Its purpose shall be to strengthen the youth ministry in the local churches and districts of the Annual Conference. For administrative purposes the council shall be related to the Annual Conference Council on Ministries. (*See* ¶ 1311 for the National Youth Ministry Organization Convocation and the National Youth Ministry Organization Steering Committee.)

2. *Membership.*—No more than one-third of the membership of the council shall be adults, one of whom may be the conference lay leader or his/her representative. It is recommended that the council be composed of 50 percent racial and ethnic group members. (It is suggested that members at large may be added toward achieving 50/50 ethnic/white membership in a manner to be determined by the conference Council on Youth Ministry.) Where ethnic or language conferences overlap nonethnic conferences, provision shall be made for the inclusion of members of the ethnic or language conferences and vice-versa. Those serving on the conference Council on Youth Ministry shall be members (full or preparatory) of The United Methodist Church.

3. *Responsibilities.*—*a*) To initiate and support plans and activities and projects that are of particular interest to youth.

b) To be an advocate for the free expression of the convictions of youth on issues vital to them.

c) To support and facilitate, where deemed needed, the formation of youth caucuses.

d) To cooperate with the boards and agencies of the Annual Conference, receiving recommendations from and making recommendations to the same.

e) To recommend to the Annual Conference Committee on Nominations qualified youth for membership on boards and agencies.

f) To elect and certify Annual Conference representatives to the Jurisdictional Youth Ministry Organization Convocation and the National Youth Ministry Organization Convocation in keeping with the provisions of ¶¶ 632 and 1301.2*a*.

g) To receive and set the policy and criteria for its portion of the Youth Service Fund (¶ 1310). No more than one-third shall be used for administrative purposes; at least one-third shall be used for projects within the geographic bounds of the Annual Conference; and at least one-third shall be used for projects outside the geographic bounds of the Annual Conference.

h) To establish the policy for Youth Service Fund education and be responsible for its promotion throughout the Annual Conference, in cooperation with the National Youth Ministry Organization Steering Committee.

i) To establish a Project Review Committee as an advisory committee with regard to the use of the Youth Service Fund receipts for projects. It is recommended that the committee be composed of at least 50 percent racial and ethnic group persons.

j) To participate with the appropriate conference agencies in the nomination of the conference coordinator of youth ministry, who shall serve as its advisor.

¶ **744.** There shall be a **Joint Committee on Disability** in each Annual Conference. It shall be composed of a minimum of two representatives each from the Board of Ordained Ministry and the conference Board of Pensions, who may be elected by those boards at the beginning of each quadrennium and at other times when vacancies occur, and a district superintendent appointed from time to time by the bishop to represent the Cabinet. Unless and until other members are elected, the chairperson and registrar of the Board of Ordained Ministry and the chairperson and secretary of the conference Board of Pensions, or others designated by them, shall be authorized to represent their respective boards. The committee shall organize at the beginning of each quadrennium by the election of a chairperson and a secretary. The duties of the Joint Committee on Disability shall be:

a) To study the problems of disability in the Annual Conference.

b) To provide for a continuing personal ministry to any disabled clergy of the conference and to aid them in maintaining fellowship with the members of the conference.

c) To determine what medical doctor or doctors it will approve for medical examinations and reports regarding disabled clergy and what medical doctor or doctors it will recommend to the General Board of Pensions for that purpose.

d) To make recommendations to the Board of Ordained Ministry, the conference Board of Pensions, and the Cabinet on matters related to disability, including steps for its prevention, disability leave, benefits, and programs of rehabilitation.

e) To cooperate with and give assistance to the General Board of Pensions in its administration of disability benefits through the Ministers Reserve Pension Fund or the Comprehensive Protection Plan.

¶ **745.** There may be a **Committee on Ministry to Persons with Handicapping Conditions** in each Annual Conference with such members and responsibilities as the Annual Conference may determine.

Section X. The District Conference.

¶ **746. A District Conference** shall be held if directed by the Annual Conference of which it is a part and may be held upon the call of the district superintendent, which call shall specify the time and place.

¶ **747.** 1. A District Conference shall be composed of members as determined and specified by the Annual Conference.

2. The District Conference may choose its own order of business. The secretary duly elected shall keep an accurate record of the proceedings and submit it to the Annual Conference for examination.

3. The District Conference shall issue certificates of candidacy for the ordained ministry on recommendation of the district Committee on Ordained Ministry and shall consider for approval the reports of this committee.

4. The District Conference may incorporate a **District Union,** under the laws of the state in which it is located, to hold and administer district real and personal property, receive and administer church extension and mission funds for use within the district, and exercise such other powers and duties as may be set forth in its charter or articles of incorporation as authorized by

the Annual Conference having jurisdiction over said district. All such District Unions chartered or incorporated by districts of the churches which joined and united in adopting the Constitution of The United Methodist Church are declared to be disciplinary agencies of The United Methodist Church as though originally created and authorized by that Constitution, and may act for or as a District Conference when convened for that purpose by the district superintendent, who shall be its executive secretary, or by its president or other executive officer.

5. If any district or conference initiates, joins, monitors, or terminates a boycott, the guidelines in the 1988 Book of Resolutions should be followed. The General Conference is the only body that can initiate, empower, or join a boycott in the name of The United Methodist Church.

¶ **748.** 1. The **district lay leader** is the elected leader of the district laity. The district lay leader shall provide for the training of local church lay leaders for their ministries in the local churches in relation to ¶ 251.1. The district lay leader shall have responsibility for fostering awareness of the role of the laity in achieving the mission of the Church, and supporting and enabling lay participation in the planning and decision-making processes of the district and the local churches in cooperation with the district superintendent and pastors. The district lay leader is a member of the District Conference and shall be a member of the district Council on Ministries and its executive committee. The district lay leader shall also be a member of the Committee on District Superintendency of his/her district.

2. There may be an associate district lay leader within a district. The associate district lay leader shall be elected as determined by the Annual Conference. The method of nomination and term of office shall be determined by the Annual Conference.

3. The district lay leader shall relate to the organized lay groups in the district such as United Methodist Women, United Methodist Men, and United Methodist Youth and support their work and help them coordinate their activities.

4. With the approval of the district Council on Ministries, the district lay leader may, where there is no district Board of Laity or equivalent organization, organize a coordinating committee on lay

work which may include the district lay leader, district president of United Methodist Women, district president of United Methodist Men, district president of United Methodist Youth, district president of United Methodist Young Adults, and, where organized, the district president of the Older Adult Council, and others as deemed necessary. The district lay leader shall be chairperson of this coordinating committee. In forming such a committee, special attention shall be given to the inclusion of women, men, youth, young adults, and older adults; persons with a handicapping condition; and racial and ethnic group persons.

5. The district lay leader may designate persons to serve as proxy in any of the above groups except the District Conference, district Council on Ministries, and the Council on Ministries executive committee.

6. The district lay leader shall be elected as determined by the Annual Conference. The method of nomination and term of office shall be determined by the Annual Conference.

7. The district lay leader shall serve on the district and the Annual Conference Committee on Lay Speaking.

¶ **749.** Each district of an Annual Conference may organize a **district Council on Ministries.**

1. *Purpose.*—The purpose of the district Council on Ministries shall be to assist local churches to minister more effectively; to serve as a channel of communication between the local churches, the Annual Conference Council on Ministries, and the general agencies of the Church; to initiate programs for the district; and to help the Annual Conference Council on Ministries in the performance of its functions.

2. *Membership.*—Each Annual Conference may determine the membership and the method of election of its district Councils on Ministries. The membership structure need not be identical in each district. It may include the following: district coordinators of age-level and family ministries; the district director/president of United Methodist Men; representatives of town and country ministry and urban ministry, except in those districts where one of these population categories is not present; representatives of program agencies (i.e., district directors of evangelism, education, religion and race, status and role of

women, district missionary secretaries, district directors for Church and society, work area chairpersons on stewardship) and representatives of clusters of local churches. It is recommended that a member of the Annual Conference Council on Ministries staff be included as a resource person in each district Council on Ministries. Membership shall be chosen, insofar as possible, to include one-third clergy, one-third laywomen, and one-third laymen (with special attention to the inclusion of clergywomen, youth, young adults, older adults, persons with handicapping conditions, and racial and ethnic persons) in keeping with policies for general church agencies. The Annual Conference may ask the District Conferences (¶ 746) to elect the membership of the district Council on Ministries.

3. *Officers.*—The officers of the district Council on Ministries shall be the chairperson, who shall be elected from the membership of the council, and such other officers as the Annual Conference or the district deems necessary. The district superintendent shall have executive oversight responsibility for the work of the district Council on Ministries.

4. *Responsibilities.*—The responsibilities of the district Council on Ministries may be determined by the Annual Conference or the district Council on Ministries. The following functions may be incorporated into its work:

a) To study the needs of the local churches in the district and help them establish and provide more effective ministry in and through the churches.

b) To keep local churches informed on the work of the whole Church and challenge each church to full participation.

c) To encourage local churches to engage in creative, innovative approaches to ministry.

d) To serve as a two-way channel of communication between the local churches and the Annual Conference and to assist local churches in communication with each other.

e) To study the needs of the district and establish priorities for district action.

f) To study the needs of the district and establish priorities and guidelines for the development of cooperative ministries in town and country and urban situations.

g) To develop experimental types of ministry within the

district and especially in urban districts to facilitate structures as provided in ¶¶ 731.5*f*, *g*; 1414.5.

h) To provide leadership training events for local church leaders.

i) To relate the Annual Conference Council on Ministries and its staff to local church needs.

j) To make program and other recommendations to the Annual Conference Council on Ministries.

k) To assist in the implementation of the program of the Annual Conference.

l) To cooperate in ecumenical programs and events on the district level.

m) To plan and conduct inspirational events.

n) To elect the lay representative(s) from the district to membership on the Annual Conference Council on Ministries when requested by the Annual Conference Council on Ministries.

o) The district superintendent, after consultation with the chairperson of the conference Board of Global Ministries and the conference secretary of global ministries, may appoint a district secretary of global ministries who shall serve on the district Council on Ministries and chair the district Committee of Global Ministries, where these exist, in cases where the Annual Conference has not directed otherwise.

p) To help congregations attain a higher level of financial giving through The United Methodist Church.

q) To help local churches discover the resources they have for a viable ministry and to find ways to employ these resources in fulfilling our ministry in the local and worldwide community.

The district Councils on Ministries in an Annual Conference shall cooperate with the Annual Conference Council on Ministries so that a harmonious and holistic approach to the total ministry of the conference may be achieved. In order to coordinate the calendar and program plans of each district with the Annual Conference, the Annual Conference Council on Ministries may require the district councils to submit their program plans for approval.

The district Council on Ministries may appoint a **district**

coordinator of communications to work in cooperation with the district and conference Councils on Ministries and with the conference Committee on Communication, if organized. The district Council on Ministries may create a district Committee on Communication to assist the council in carrying out district communication functions.

5. *Finances.*—Each Annual Conference shall determine the method by which its district Councils on Ministries shall be financed. It is recommended that an amount for the general operating expense of the district Councils on Ministries be included in the Annual Conference budget. As a general rule, major program expenditures for any district should be made through the budget of the Annual Conference Council on Ministries or the appropriate Annual Conference program board.

¶ **750.** The district superintendent, after consultation with the conference board, may appoint a **district director of Church and Society.** Also, if desirable, a district may create a Committee on Church and Society of laypersons and clergy, to work with the district superintendent to further the purposes of the conference board. The coordinator of the area of Christian social involvement of the district United Methodist Women shall be an ex officio member.

¶ **751.** The district superintendent, after consultation with the Annual Conference Commission on Religion and Race, shall appoint a **district director of Religion and Race**. A district may establish a Committee on Religion and Race of lay persons and clergy, to work with the district superintendent to further the purposes of the Annual Conference commission.

¶ **752.** There shall be a **district Committee on Ordained Ministry.**

1. The **district Committee on Ordained Ministry** shall be amenable to the Annual Conference through the Board of Ordained Ministry. It shall be composed of a representative from the Board of Ordained Ministry, named by the board after consultation with the district superintendent, and who may be named chairperson; the district superintendent, who may serve as the executive secretary; and at least five other ordained ministers in full connection in the district, including women and ethnic clergy wherever possible, nominated annually by the

district superintendent in consultation with the chairperson or executive committee of the Board of Ordained Ministry and approved by the Annual Conference. Interim vacancies may be filled by the district superintendent.

At least one layman observer and one laywoman observer may be members of the committee, nominated annually by the district superintendent and approved by the Annual Conference.

2. The district Committee on Ordained Ministry shall elect its officers at the first meeting following the Annual Conference session when the members are elected.

3. The committee shall maintain a list of all persons who have declared their candidacy for the ordained ministry and are pursuing candidacy studies under a supervising pastor. A duplicate list shall be forwarded to the Annual Conference registrar for candidacy; such list being made current at least prior to each session of the Annual Conference.

4. The committee shall offer counsel to candidates regarding pretheological studies.

5. The committee shall supervise all matters dealing with candidacy for the ordained ministry and with the license for local pastor.

6. The vote of the committee on all matters of candidacy shall be by individual written ballot, with a three-fourths majority vote of the committee present required for certification or approval or recommendation.

7. The committee shall maintain a service record and file on every local pastor and candidate for the ordained ministry until the individual becomes an associate or probationary member of the Annual Conference, at which time a copy of the files shall be forwarded to the registrar of the Board of Ordained Ministry. The records and files of the committee are kept on behalf of the Annual Conference and shall be maintained under guidelines provided by the General Council on Finance and Administration in consultation with the General Board of Higher Education and Ministry and the General Board of Pensions.

8. The committee shall recommend to the Board of Ordained Ministry those persons who qualify for associate and probationary membership, for continuance as local pastors, and for restoration of credentials. All persons shall have been current

members of The United Methodist Church for at least one year immediately preceding certification, shall have been recommended by their Charge Conference, and shall, in the judgment of the committee, show evidence that their gifts, evidence of God's grace, and usefulness warrant such recommendation.[74]

9. The committee shall examine all persons who apply in writing for certification or renewal of certificate. Where there is evidence that their gifts, evidence of God's grace, and usefulness warrant and that they are qualified under ¶¶ 406-409, and on recommendation of their Charge Conference, or the conference Board of Ordained Ministry, the committee shall issue or renew their certificate.

10. The committee shall assist the conference Board of Ordained Ministry in providing support services for all clergy under appointment within the district.

¶ **753.** *District Committee on Lay Speaking.*—There may be a **district Committee on Lay Speaking.**

1. The purpose of the district Committee on Lay Speaking shall be to plan and supervise the lay speaker program within the district.

2. Membership shall be the district lay leader, district superintendent, director of lay speaking (if elected), an instructor of lay speaking courses, other resource persons as desired.

3. The responsibilities of the district Committee on Lay Speaking shall be to plan and supervise the lay speaking program within the district that will provide basic training for local church lay speakers as recommended by the General Board of Discipleship and advanced courses for the certified lay speaker.

4. The district committee shall plan advanced courses for lay speaking that will enable the recertification of the certified lay speakers.

5. The district committee will report to the pastor and Charge Conference of each certified lay speaker the courses that have been satisfactorily completed by the certified lay speaker.

¶ **754.** *Committee on District Superintendency.*—There shall be a **Committee on District Superintendency.**

1. *Membership.*—This committee shall be composed of the

---

[74]*See* Judicial Council Decision 586.

district lay leader, two laywomen, two laymen, two clergy, and two at-large members selected to make possible the representation of racial and ethnic persons, youth, young adults, and older adults, and two additional persons appointed by the district superintendent; *provided* that at least three of the eleven persons are clergy and seven are lay persons.

2. *Selection.*—The members shall be selected in such manner as may be determined by the District Conference or, where there is no District Conference, by the Annual Conference. The district committee shall be authorized to co-opt members as advisory members who have expertise in areas of special need. The bishop of the area, or his/her authorized representative, shall be an ex officio member of said committee.

3. *Meeting.*—The district committee shall meet at least annually and upon call of the district superintendent and/or the chairperson of the committee. The committee shall elect a chairperson, vice-chairperson, and secretary.

4. *Purpose.*—The purpose of the Committee on District Superintendency shall be to support the district superintendent of the district in the oversight of the spiritual and temporal affairs of the Church with special reference to the district where the superintendent has responsibilities. In fulfilling this purpose, the committee shall give attention to the following responsibilities:

a) To advocate for adequate budget support services for the district superintendent; such as, adequate secretarial support, travel, continuing education, and parsonage needs (¶¶ 523.2; 710.1*a*).

b) To be available for counsel.

c) To keep the district superintendent advised concerning conditions within the district as they affect relations among the district superintendent, the laity, the clergy, and the district agencies.

d) To establish a clearly understood process for observing the district superintendent's ministry with direct evaluation and feedback; with special concern for the inclusiveness of the Church and its ministry with respect to sex, race, and national origin, and implementation of the consultative process in appointment making.

e) To consult with the district superintendent concerning

continuing education and to arrange with the Cabinet and bishop for the necessary time and financial assistance for the attendance of the district superintendent at such continuing education events as may serve his/her professional and spiritual growth.

f) To interpret to the people of the district and to the district boards and agencies the nature and function of the district superintendency.

5. *Consultation.*—The district committee and the district superintendent shall engage in an annual consultation and appraisal of the work of the district superintendent in the district and shall serve in an advisory relationship with the bishop of the area.

¶ **755. United Methodist Women.**—*Constitution of United Methodist Women in the District.*—*Article 1. Name.*—In each district there shall be a district organization named United Methodist Women, auxiliary to the conference organization of United Methodist Women and the Women's Division of the General Board of Global Ministries.

Article 2. Responsibilities.—The responsibilities of the district organization of United Methodist Women shall be to work with local units in developing programs to meet the needs and interests of women and the concerns and responsibilities of the global Church; to encourage and support spiritual growth, missionary outreach, and Christian social action; and to promote the plans and responsibilities of the Women's Division and the conference organization of United Methodist Women.

Article 3. Authority.—Each district organization of United Methodist Women shall have authority to promote its work in accordance with the plans, responsibilities, and policies of the conference organization and the Women's Division of the General Board of Global Ministries.

Article 4. Membership.—All members of organized units of United Methodist Women in the local churches of the district shall be considered members of the district organization. The district superintendent shall be a member of the district organization of United Methodist Women and of its executive committee.

Article 5. Officers and Committees.—The district organization shall elect a president, a vice-president, a secretary, a treasurer, and a Committee on Nominations. Additional officers and committees shall be elected or appointed in accordance with the plans of the Women's Division as set forth in the bylaws for the district organization of United Methodist Women.

Article 6. Meetings and Elections.—There shall be an annual meeting of the district organization of United Methodist Women, at which time there shall be presented a program designed to meet the needs of the women of the district in harmony with the Purpose and the plans and the responsibilities of the conference organization and the Women's Division of the General Board of Global Ministries. Officers and the Committee on Nominations shall be elected, the necessary business transacted, and pledges made for the ensuing year.

Article 7. Relationships.—*a)* Designated officers shall represent the district organization of United Methodist Women on the various boards, councils, commissions, and committees of the district as the constitution and bylaws of such agencies provide.

b) The district president shall be the only district representative with vote on the conference executive committee.

c) The district organization shall encourage women to participate in the total life and work of the Church, and shall support them in assuming positions of responsibility and leadership.

Article 8. Amendments.—Proposed amendments to this constitution may be sent to the recording secretary of the Women's Division of the General Board of Global Ministries prior to the last annual meeting of the division in the quadrennium.

¶ **756.** Each district of an Annual Conference may organize a **district Council on Youth Ministry.**

1. *Purpose.*—The purpose of the district Council on Youth Ministry is defined as follows: to assist local churches in ministry for, with, and by junior-high and senior-high youth more effectively; to serve as a channel of communication and involvement among the youth ministry in the local churches, the conference Council on Youth Ministry, and the general agencies of the Church; to initiate youth programs for the district to influence the total programming of the district and conference as it relates to the concerns and needs of youth, and to take primary

responsibility for promoting and raising money for the Youth Service Fund.

2. *Membership.*—Each district may determine the membership and the method of election of its district Council on Youth Ministry in consultation with the conference Council on Youth Ministry. It is recommended that the membership include the following; *(a)* no more than one-third of the membership shall be adults; *(b)* at least 50 percent ratio of nonwhite persons, if possible; *(c)* the district Youth Coordinator to be a member by virtue of his/her office; *(d)* representatives on the conference Council on Youth Ministry.

3. *Functions.*—The functions of the district Council on Youth Ministry may be determined by the Annual Conference Council on Youth Ministry and/or the district Council on Youth Ministry. The following functions may be incorporated in its work;

a) To study the needs of the junior-high and senior-high youth ministry of the local churches in the district and help them establish and provide more effective ministry in and through the district.

b) To keep local churches informed of the work of the whole Church in youth ministry and to challenge each church to full participation.

c) To serve as a two-way channel of communications between the local church youth and the Annual Conference, and to assist local church youth in communication with one another.

d) To cooperate with the programming and ministry of the district Council on Ministries as it serves to provide leadership training to persons in the district.

e) To assist in the implementation of the program of the Annual Conference, and particularly of the Annual Conference Council on Youth Ministry.

f) To serve as an advocate for the free expression of youth in the district and local churches of the district.

g) To provide leadership training.

h) To promote, educate, and be a resource to local churches on Youth Service Fund.

i) To participate with the district superintendent and the conference Coordinator of Youth Ministry, who shall serve as its advisor. The district Council on Youth Ministry's responsibilities shall include organizing, programming, consulting with local churches, and nurturing adult workers with youth in the district.

4. *Finances.*—Each district Council on Youth Ministries, in consultation with the conference Council on Ministries and the district Council on Ministries, shall determine the method by which it will be financed.

Chapter Six

ADMINISTRATIVE ORDER

Section I. General Provisions.

¶ **801.** *Agencies and General Agencies.*—1. The term "agency," wherever it appears in the Book of Discipline, is a term used to describe the various councils, boards, commissions, committees, divisions, or other units constituted within the various levels of church organization (General, Jurisdictional, Central, Annual, District, and Charge Conferences) under authority granted by the Book of Discipline; the term does not and is not meant to imply a master-servant or principal-agent relationship between these bodies and the conference or other body which creates them, except where the authority is specifically granted.

2. The general agencies of The United Methodist Church are the regularly established councils, boards, commissions, committees, or other units with ongoing responsibilities which have been constituted by the General Conference. Not included are such commissions and committees as are created by the General Conference to fulfill a special function within the ensuing quadrennium, ecumenical groups on which The United Methodist Church is represented, or committees related to the quadrennial sessions of the General Conference.[1] The term "general agency" or "agency" wherever it appears in the Book of Discipline in reference to a general agency does not and is not meant to imply a master-servant or principal-agent relationship between such a body and the General Conference or any other unit of the denomination, or the denomination as a whole.

¶ **802.** *Amenability and Program Accountability.*—1. All the general agencies of The United Methodist Church that have been constituted by the General Conference are amenable to the General Conference, except as otherwise provided.

2. Between sessions of the General Conference, the following general agencies are accountable to the General Council on Ministries: the General Board of Church and Society, the General Board of Discipleship, the General Board of Global

---

[1]*See* Judicial Council Decision 139.

Ministries, the General Board of Higher Education and Ministry, the General Commission on Christian Unity and Interreligious Concerns, the General Commission on Religion and Race, the General Commission on the Status and Role of Women, the General Commission on Archives and History and the General Commission on Communications in matters pertaining to their program responsibilities.[2]

3. Evaluation of general agencies by the General Council on Ministries shall be part of the accountability relationship (¶ 1006.13). The evaluation process and its results shall be reported to each General Conference. The purpose for agency evaluation is to assist the agency in the process of fulfilling and supporting its ministry. Local church groups, district, and Annual Conference organizations may receive an explanation of the evaluation process by requesting it from the General Council on Ministries.

4. Questions and concerns about programs, projects, or decisions of a particular agency may be addressed to that agency, with copies to the General Council on Ministries. Agencies shall acknowledge receipt of requests for information within thirty days and provide information as soon thereafter as it is available.

5. If any district, Annual Conference, or general agency initiates, joins, monitors, or terminates a boycott, the guidelines in the 1988 Book of Resolutions should be followed. The General Conference is the only body that can initiate, empower, or join a boycott in the name of The United Methodist Church.

6. In all matters of accountability episcopal oversight as provided in ¶ 526 is assumed.

¶ **803.** *Definitions, Structures, and Titles.*—1. *General Council.*— An organization created by the General Conference to perform defined responsibilities of review and oversight on behalf of the General Conference in relation to the other general agencies and to perform other assigned functions shall be designated as a general council. General councils are amenable and accountable to the General Conference and report to it. These councils are the General Council on Finance and Administration and the General Council on Ministries.[3]

---

[2]*See* Judicial Council Decisions 429, 496.
[3]*See* Judicial Council Decision 496.

(Note: The Council of Bishops and Judicial Council are authorized by the Constitution and not created by the General Conference.)

2. *General Board.*—A continuing body of the Church created by the General Conference to carry out assigned functions of program, administration, and/or service shall be designated as a general board. Each general board, so far as possible, shall adopt the following levels in agency organization:

a) Division.—An organizational unit within a general board along functional lines for the purpose of accomplishing a part of the total work of the general board.[4]

b) Department.—A specialized unit within a general board to give organizational identity for the purpose of accomplishing specific program responsibilities and assignments.

c) Section.—A functional subunit of a division or department.

d) Office.—A support service unit within a general board.

3. *General Commission.*—An organization created by the General Conference for the fulfillment of a specific function for an indefinite period of time.

4. *Study Committee.*—An organization created by the General Conference for a limited period of time for the purpose of making a study ordered by the General Conference. The General Council on Ministries shall provide for coordination with and among the study committees except where General Conference otherwise designates.

5. *Program-Related General Agencies.*—The general boards and commissions which have program and/or advocacy functions shall be designated as program-related general agencies. These agencies are amenable to the General Conference and between sessions of the General Conference are accountable to the General Council on Ministries: the General Board of Church and Society, the General Board of Discipleship, the General Board of Global Ministries, the General Board of Higher Education and Ministry, the General Commission on Christian Unity and Interreligious Concerns, the General Commission on Religion and Race, and the General Commission on the Status and Role of

---

[4]*See* Judicial Council Decision 535.

Women.[5] In all matters of accountability episcopal oversight as provided in ¶ 526 is assumed.

6. *Administrative General Agencies.*—The general boards and commissions which have primarily administrative and service functions shall be designated as administrative general agencies. These agencies are the General Board of Pensions, the General Board of Publication, and the General Commission on Archives and History and General Commission on Communication, both of which also carry program-related responsibilities for which they are accountable to the General Council on Ministries.

7. Each general agency, unless otherwise provided, shall adopt the following executive staff titles:

a) General Secretary—the chief staff officer of a general agency. Each general agency is entitled to only one general secretary, who is its chief administrative officer.

b) Deputy General Secretary—the chief staff officer of a division of the General Board of Global Ministries.

c) Associate General Secretary—the associate staff officer of a general agency or the chief staff officer of a division or a department of a general agency.

d) Assistant General Secretary—the assistant staff officer of a general agency or the chief staff officer of a section or office of a general agency.

e) Treasurer—the staff financial officer of a general agency, entrusted with the receipt, care, and disbursement of agency funds. In some general agencies there may be associate and/or assistant treasurers. There are general agencies in which "treasurer" is not a staff title but is an officer elected from the voting membership of the agency.

8. *Theme.*—A theme is a theological focus, missional emphasis, prophetic statement, or program catalyst for ministry. A theme enhances programs or ministries basic to the life of the Church and serves as a rallying point for constituents involved in those programs.

9. *Missional Priority.*—A missional priority is a response to a critical need in God's world which calls for The United Methodist Church's massive and sustained effort through primary attention

---

[5]*See* Judicial Council Decision 496.

and ordering or reordering of program and budget at every level of the Church, as adopted by the General Conference or in accord with ¶ 1006.1. This need is evidenced by research or other supporting data, and the required response is beyond the capacity of any single general agency or Annual Conference. However, the ongoing priority of The United Methodist Church both in program and budget is to proclaim the good news that salvation comes through Jesus Christ.

10. *Special Program.*—A special program is a quadrennial emphasis approved by the General Conference and assigned to a general agency, designed in response to a distinct opportunity or need in God's world which is evidenced by research or other supporting data, and proposes achievable goals within the quadrennium.

11. *Program.*—A program is an ongoing or special activity designed and implemented to fulfill a basic Disciplinary responsibility of a general agency accountable to the General Council on Ministries.

12. *Association or Fellowship.*—Organizations not created by nor officially related to the General Conference, and intended to provide professional relationships conducive to sharing professional techniques and information for groups within the denomination, shall be designated as associations or fellowships.

¶ **804.** All the general agencies of the Church, including councils, boards, commissions, and committees constituted by the General Conference, shall account for receipts and expenditures of funds in a format designed by the General Council on Finance and Administration. A quadrennial report of such accounting shall be included in the report of General Council on Finance and Administration made to the General Conference.

Annual reports shall be made available by the respective agencies upon the request of Annual Conferences and local church Administrative Councils or Boards. The annual reports prepared by the agencies shall include a listing of organizations, individuals, associations, fellowships, coalitions, consultants, programs, and entities not formally part of the Church, and the amount (expended annually) of monetary and in-kind contributions. The listing shall include but not be limited to office space, printing, staff assistance, purchases, travel expense, and other forms of financial assistance that have been granted to such entities.

¶ **805.** *General Agency Membership.*—All provisions pertaining to the nomination and election of general agency members shall take effect immediately upon the adjournment of the General Conference which enacts them. The secretary of the General Conference shall coordinate the processes pertaining to nominations and elections of general agency members. The following provisions shall govern the nomination and election of the voting membership of those general agencies to which the Jurisdictional Conferences elect members:[6]

1. *Nominations by Conferences.*—*a)* Each Annual and Missionary Conference in the United States and Puerto Rico, upon recommendation from a committee composed of the bishop and the General and Jurisdictional Conference delegation, and having allowed opportunity for nominations from the floor, shall elect persons to be submitted to a jurisdictional pool from which the Jurisdictional Nominating Committee shall select persons for election to the following general agencies: General Council on Ministries; General Board of Church and Society; General Board of Discipleship; General Board of Global Ministries; General Board of Higher Education and Ministry; General Board of Pensions; General Board of Publication; General Commission on Christian Unity and Interreligious Concerns; General Commission on Communication; General Commission on Religion and Race; and General Commission on the Status and Role of Women. Jurisdictional Conferences may decide that persons elected by the Annual and Missionary Conferences in the United States and Puerto Rico for inclusion in the jurisdictional pool shall not serve as members of the Jurisdictional Nominating Committee.

b) Each Annual and Missionary Conference in the United States and Puerto Rico shall nominate the persons most recently elected as delegates to the General Conference to the jurisdictional pool. In addition, it shall nominate at least fifteen persons to the jurisdictional pool, including, where available, at least one and not more than five persons in each of the following eight

---

[6]*See* Judicial Council Decision 467.

categories: (1) clergy (including at least one woman), (2) laywomen, (3) laymen, (4) racial and ethnic persons (at least one from each ethnic group—Asian American, Black American, Hispanic American, Native American), (5) youth (¶ 263.2), (6) young adults (¶ 263.3), (7) older adults (¶ 262.5), and (8) persons with a handicapping condition. No nominee shall be listed in more than one of these eight categories.[7]

c) Each Central Conference, or a body authorized by it, shall nominate to each general board at least one person from each of the following three categories: (1) clergy, (2) laymen, and (3) laywomen, to form a pool from which each board is to elect the additional members that are to come from the Central Conferences pursuant to ¶ 805.2*c*(1).

d) All nominees shall list one to three preferences for agency membership. In addition all nominees shall prepare an up-to-100-word biographical statement listing experience, gifts, and training which qualify him/her for general agency membership. Biographical statements for all persons in the jurisdictional pool shall be given to each member of the nominating committee. Names and biographical data of all persons nominated by the Annual and Missionary Conferences in the United States and Puerto Rico but not elected by the jurisdiction shall be forwarded by the Jurisdictional Conference secretary to the general agencies to be in a pool from which additional members may be elected (¶¶ 805.2*c*, 3*b*).[8]

2. *General Program Board Membership.—a) Basic Membership.*—Each jurisdiction shall elect one person from each of its Annual and Missionary Conferences to each program board. The jurisdiction membership on each program board shall incorporate one-third clergy (at least one of whom shall be a woman), one-third laymen (with the exception of ¶ 1204.1), and one-third laywomen (with the exception of ¶ 1412.2),[9] and shall ensure adequate representation of youth (¶ 263.2), young adults (¶ 263.3), and older adults (¶ 263.5). (*See also* ¶¶ 1412.6, 1507.) The episcopal members shall not be counted in the computation of the clergy membership. In order to ensure adequate

---

[7]*See* Judicial Council Decision 600.
[8]*See* Judicial Council Decisions 520, 538.
[9]*See* Judicial Council Decisions 446, 558.

representation of racial and ethnic persons (Asian Americans, Black Americans, Hispanic Americans, Native Americans), it is recommended that at least 30 percent of a jurisdiction's membership on each general program board be racial and ethnic persons. Special attention shall be given to the inclusion of persons with a handicapping condition.[10] *Provided,* however, that effective immediately, when a new Annual Conference or conferences are created by a Jurisdictional Conference and come into being following the Jurisdictional Conference, each such new Annual Conference or conferences shall be authorized to elect one person directly to General Council on Ministries and each general program board on which no person from the new Annual Conference already has been elected by the Jurisdictional Conference under the provisions of this paragraph.[11]

b) Episcopal Membership.—The episcopal membership of not less than five nor more than ten members shall be nominated by the Council of Bishops and elected by the General Conference (*see* exception, ¶ 1412.6). At least one of the episcopal members of each general program board shall be a Central Conference bishop.

c) Additional Membership.—(1) *United Methodist.*—Additional members shall be elected by each general program board in order to bring into the board persons with special knowledge or background which will aid in the work of the agency, to consider differing theological perspectives, and to perfect the representation of racial and ethnic persons, youth (¶ 263.2), young adults (¶ 263.3), older adults (¶ 263.5), women and men, persons with a handicapping condition, and persons from small-membership churches, and distribution by geographic area. There shall be not less than five nor more than twelve additional members of each general program board. Such additional membership shall maintain the one-third laymen, one-third laywomen, and one-third clergy balance.[12] In addition, each board shall elect three persons from the Central Conferences, one clergy, one layman, one laywoman, and one alternate for each who may attend if the elected member cannot attend.

---

[10]*See* Judicial Council Decisions 451, 467.
[11]*See* Judicial Council Decision 538.
[12]*See* Judicial Council Decisions 377, 446, 520.

(2) *Other.*—It is recommended that each general agency elect at least one member without vote from among the member churches of the Consultation on Church Union other than The United Methodist Church.

3. *Other General Agencies.*—*a)* Each Jurisdictional Conference shall elect members from the jurisdictional pool nominated by the Annual and Missionary Conferences in the United States and Puerto Rico (¶ 805.1) in accordance with the specific membership provisions of those agencies as set forth in the Book of Discipline: General Council on Ministries (¶ 1007), General Board of Pensions, (¶ 1602.1*a*), General Board of Publication (¶ 1702), General Commission on Christian Unity and Interreligious Concerns (¶ 2006), General Commission on Communication (¶ 1907), General Commission on the Status and Role of Women (¶ 2204), and the General Commission on Religion and Race (¶ 2103).

b) Episcopal and additional members, if any, of the general agencies listed in ¶ 805.3*a* shall be nominated and elected by the procedures specified in the paragraphs listed in ¶ 805.3*a*. The agencies shall consider names forwarded to them by the jurisdictions as having been nominated by the Annual and Missionary Conferences in the United States and Puerto Rico but not elected by the Jurisdictional Conferences to general agency membership. Additional names may be considered in order to perfect the representation as provided in ¶ 805.2*c*.

4. The membership of all agencies of The United Methodist Church, at the level of General and Jurisdictional Conferences and insofar as possible at the level of Annual and Missionary Conferences and local church, shall ensure adequate representation of racial and ethnic groups—Asian American, Black American, Hispanic American, and Native American; all such boards, committees, and agencies whose membership is set forth in the Discipline shall be authorized to elect as many additional members as necessary to meet this requirement.

¶ **806.** *Committee to Nominate Additional Members.*—1. Each jurisdiction shall designate one clergy, one laywoman, and one layman whom it has elected to a general program agency or to the General Council on Ministries to nominate the additional members of that program agency or council (¶ 805.4). The fifteen members thus designated by the five jurisdictions in each general program agency and in the General Council on Ministries shall constitute a committee to nominate additional members for that agency and shall be convened as provided in ¶ 806.2.

2. An active bishop designated by the president of the Council of Bishops shall convene the committee as soon as practical after jurisdictional elections have been completed. The committee shall consider, but not be limited to, names forwarded to it by the jurisdictions as having been nominated by the Annual and Missionary Conferences in the United States and Puerto Rico to their jurisdictional pool as well as names from caucuses and other appropriate groups. To aid the committee, biographical data submitted by the Annual Conferences (¶ 805.1*d*) shall be made available from the Jurisdictional Conference secretaries. In addition, general agencies shall submit to the committee names and biographical data of persons eligible for reelection and who are willing to serve.

3. The committee shall complete its work prior to the organizational meeting (¶ 807) of any of the agencies listed in ¶ 803.5 and report by mail to the previously elected members of each of those agencies the names of persons nominated as additional members of that agency. All members shall be elected and seated before an agency proceeds to the election of officers or any other business.

¶ **807.** *Organizational Meetings.*—1. In those years in which the General Conference holds its regular session, all general program agencies shall meet, organize, and conduct such business as may properly come before the agency not later than ninety (90) days after the close of the Jurisdictional Conferences. Each organizational meeting shall be convened by an active bishop designated by the president of the Council of Bishops.

2. All councils, boards, commissions, and committees established by a General, Jurisdictional, Central, Annual, or other Conference shall meet and organize as promptly as feasible following the selection of their members.

3. Unless otherwise specified in the Discipline or by the establishing conference, every council, board, commission, and

committee shall continue in responsibility until its successor council, board, commission, or committee is organized.

¶ **808.** *Board Organization.*—1. Each program board shall elect a president and one or more vice-presidents from the voting membership of the board, and a secretary, treasurer, and such other officers as it deems appropriate; *provided* that all officers shall be members of The United Methodist Church.

2. Each program board shall elect chairpersons for its divisions and departments from the voting membership of the board. The divisions and departments shall elect a vice-chairperson, a secretary, and such other officers as it deems appropriate.

3. Terms of officers of boards, divisions, and departments, shall be for the quadrennium or until their successors are elected.

4. No person shall serve as president or chairperson of more than one general agency or division or department thereof.

¶ **809.** *Membership.*—The membership of each program board shall be divided among the divisions or other subunits of the board in such number as the board determines.

¶ **810.** *Provisions Pertaining to General Agency Membership.*—1. Members of all general agencies shall be members of The United Methodist Church except as provided in ¶ 805.2c(2).

2. Members of all general agencies shall be persons of genuine Christian character who love the Church, are morally disciplined and loyal to the ethical standards of The United Methodist Church as set forth in the Social Principles, and are otherwise competent to serve as members of general agencies.

3. A voting member of a general agency shall be eligible for membership on that agency for no more than two consecutive four-year terms. The four-year term shall begin at the first organizational meeting of that agency following General Conference. Service of more than one year in fulfilling an unexpired or vacated position shall be considered as a full four-year term. To provide a continuing membership on these agencies, it is recommended that each nominating and electing body give special attention to continuing and effective membership on these agencies. If a general agency is merged with another agency, the years served by members prior to the

merger shall be counted as part of the maximum specified above.[13]

A person who has been a voting member of general agencies for four consecutive quadrenniums shall be ineligible for election to a general agency in the succeeding quadrennium. The foregoing shall not apply to episcopal members.

4. No person shall serve at the same time on more than one general agency or any part thereof, except where the Discipline specifically provides for such interagency representation; *provided*, however, that if this limitation would deprive a jurisdiction of its full episcopal representation on an agency, it may be suspended to the extent necessary to permit such representation.[14] (*See* ¶ 1007.1*b*.)

5. A voting member of a general agency, by virtue of such membership, shall become a voting member of the corresponding agency or its equivalent structure of the Annual Conference, unless such membership would conflict with ¶ 708.2*b*(2) or ¶ 733.1. This provision shall not apply to episcopal members of general agencies nor to salaried Annual Conference staff who are members of a general agency, unless such voting membership is specifically provided by another provision of the Discipline or by action of the Annual Conference.[15] If this results in a person being a member of more than one Annual Conference agency in violation of either Annual Conference policy or another provision of the Book of Discipline, the person shall serve on the conference agency which corresponds to the primary general agency to which they were elected. (*See* ¶ 706.5.)

6. No person who receives compensation for services rendered or commissions of any kind from an agency shall be eligible for voting membership on that agency.[16]

7. No elected member, officer, or other employee shall vote on or take part in deliberations on significant matters directly or indirectly affecting his or her business, income, or employment, or the business, income, or employment of a member of his/her immediate family.

---

[13]*See* Judicial Council Decision 495.
[14]*See* Judicial Council Decision 224.
[15]*See* Judicial Council Decision 495.
[16]*See* Judicial Council Decision 139.

8.*a)* If any clergy member of a general or jurisdictional agency who was elected to represent a certain Annual Conference ceases to be a member of that Annual Conference, or if any lay member so elected changes permanent residence to a place outside the bounds of that Annual Conference, that member's place shall automatically become vacant.

b) If any clergy member of a general agency who was chosen to represent a certain jurisdiction ceases to be a member of an Annual Conference in that jurisdiction, or if any lay member so elected changes permanent residence to a place outside the bounds of that jurisdiction, that member's place shall automatically become vacant.

c) If any clergy member of a jurisdictional agency ceases to be a member of an Annual Conference in that jurisdiction, or if any lay member so elected changes permanent residence to a place outside the bounds of the jurisdiction, that member's place shall automatically become vacant.

9. If a member of a general agency is absent from two consecutive meetings of the agency without a reason acceptable to the agency, that person shall cease to be a member thereof. In that case the person shall be so notified, and that place shall be filled in accordance with the appropriate provisions of the Discipline.

10. When a bishop is unable to attend a meeting of an agency of which that bishop is a member, that bishop may name another bishop to attend that meeting with the privilege of vote. When an alternate to a Central Conference bishop must be named, that alternate shall be another Central Conference bishop.

¶ **811.** The councils, boards, committees, or commissions elected, authorized, or provided for by the General Conference shall have full power and authority to remove and dismiss at their discretion any member, officer, or employee thereof:

1. Who has become incapacitated so as to be unable to perform official duties.

2. Who is guilty of immoral conduct or breach of trust.

3. Who for any reason is unable to, or who fails to, perform the duties of the office, or for other misconduct which any council, board, committee, or commission may deem sufficient to warrant such dismissal and removal.

In the event that any member, officer, or employee of such council, board, committee, or commission, elected, authorized, or provided for by the General Conference, is found guilty of any crime involving moral turpitude by any federal, state, or county court or pleads guilty thereto, then and in that event, the council, board, committee, or commission of which that person is a member, officer, or employee shall be and is hereby authorized to remove such member, officer, or employee so convicted; and the place so vacated shall be filled as provided in the Discipline.

¶ **812.** *Vacancies.*—Unless otherwise specified, vacancies on general agencies occurring during the quadrennium shall be filled as follows: an episcopal vacancy shall be filled by the Council of Bishops; a vacancy in the basic membership shall be filled by the College of Bishops of that jurisdiction with notice of the vacancy sent by the agency to the secretary of the Council of Bishops; a vacancy in the additional membership shall be filled by the agency itself.

¶ **813.** The general secretary of each general program agency that is accountable to the General Council on Ministries shall be elected annually by ballot of the General Council on Ministries upon the nomination of the agency involved. Any general secretary of a general program agency who has not been elected by the General Council on Ministries shall not serve in such capacity beyond the end of that calendar year. Each general program agency shall elect annually by ballot its deputy and associate general secretary(ies) and may elect or appoint such other staff as may be necessary.[17]

¶ **814.** *Provisions Pertaining to Staff.*—1. No elected general program agency staff shall hold the same position more than twelve years. Years of service prior to January 1, 1989, are not counted. The agency responsible for the election of such staff may annually suspend this provision by a two-thirds ballot vote.[18]

2. Official travel of the staffs of agencies shall be interpreted to include all travel which is necessary in the performance of official duties directly related to the agency functions. No staff person shall accept honoraria for such official duties. A staff

---

[17]*See* Judicial Council Decisions 499, 567.
[18]*See* Judicial Council Decision 567.

member may accept an engagement not related to the functions of the employing agency when such an engagement does not interfere with official duties; the staff member may accept an honorarium for services rendered in connection with such engagements.

3. Normal retirement for all general agency staff personnel shall be at age sixty-five or the completion of forty years of service to The United Methodist Church in an elective, appointive, or employed capacity. Mandatory retirement shall be at age seventy. An employee may elect to retire at any time after attaining age sixty-two or completing thirty-seven years of service.

4. Provisions of the Staff Pension Plan shall be reviewed, with recommendations, by the Committee on Personnel Policies and Practices (¶ 907.7*b*).

5. The general secretary of the General Council on Ministries and/or the general secretary of the General Council on Finance and Administration may convene the general secretaries of the general agencies as necessary for the purpose of obtaining opinion and recommendations to assist the councils in discharging their functions.

6. All general secretaries, deputy general secretaries, associate general secretaries, and assistant general secretaries of all general agencies shall be members of The United Methodist Church. This provision shall not apply to persons employed prior to the 1976 General Conference.[19]

7. No member of the staff of a general agency shall be eligible for voting membership on any general or jurisdictional agency of The United Methodist Church except where the Discipline specifically provides for such interagency representation.

8. Elected staff shall be allowed voice but not vote in the agency and its subunits.

9. All management staff persons of general agencies shall be persons of genuine Christian character who love the Church and are committed to the oneness of the body of Christ, are morally disciplined and loyal to the ethical standards of The United Methodist Church as set forth in the Social Principles, and are competent to administer the affairs of a general agency.

---

[19]*See* Judicial Council Decision 426.

¶ **815.** *Policies Relative to Nondiscrimination.*—It shall be the policy of The United Methodist Church that all administrative agencies and institutions, including hospitals, homes, and educational institutions, shall: *(a)* recruit, employ, utilize, recompense, and promote their professional staff and other personnel in a manner consistent with the commitment of The United Methodist Church to ethnic, racial, and sexual inclusiveness; *(b)* fulfill their duties and responsibilities in a manner which does not involve segregation or discrimination on the basis of race, color, age, sex, or handicapping condition; and *(c)* provide for adequate representation by laity.

¶ **816.** *Policies Relative to Socially Responsible Investments.*—It shall be the policy of The United Methodist Church that all general boards and agencies, including the General Board of Pensions, and all administrative agencies and institutions, including hospitals, homes, and educational institutions, shall, in the investment of money, make a conscious effort to invest in institutions, companies, corporations, or funds which make a positive contribution toward the realization of the goals outlined in the Social Principles; and shall endeavor to avoid investments that appear likely, directly or indirectly, to support racial discrimination or the production of nuclear armaments, alcoholic beverages or tobacco, or companies dealing in pornography. The boards and agencies are to give careful consideration to shareholder advocacy, including advocacy of corporate disinvestment.

¶ **817.** Each general agency shall keep a continuous record of its advocacy roles, coalitions, and other organizations supported by membership or funds, and endorsement or opposition of federal or state legislation. Information concerning these activities shall be available to United Methodist churches upon written request. Organizations not officially related to the General Conference may take positions only in their own names and may not speak for a general agency or the denomination as a whole (¶ 610.1).

¶ **818.** All general funds administered by any general agency of The United Methodist Church which are proposed to be used for funding a program within an Annual Conference shall be disbursed after consultation with the presiding bishop, the conference council director, and the Council on Ministries of that Annual Conference. Consultation in matters of funding and relationships among various agencies, conferences, and other bodies of the Church requires communication, including written documentation, in which each party reveals plans and intents in such a way as to assure dialogue and mutual awareness, even if not agreement.[20]

¶ **819.** The General Board of Global Ministries, through its World Division, shall facilitate and coordinate the program relationships of other program agencies of The United Methodist Church with colleague churches and agencies in nations other than the United States. The resources of the General Board of Global Ministries shall also be available to the Council of Bishops in the implementation of its responsibilities as defined in ¶ 516.2, .3. Central Conferences of The United Methodist Church may request program and other assistance through direct relationships with the program agencies of The United Methodist Church.

¶ **820.** *Church Year and Quadrennium.*—1. The program and fiscal year for The United Methodist Church shall be the calendar year.

2. Unless otherwise specified in the Discipline for a specific purpose, the term "quadrennium" shall be deemed to be the four-year period beginning January 1 following the adjournment of the regular session of the General Conference.[21]

¶ **821.** In the spirit of openness and accountability, all meetings of councils, boards, agencies, commissions, and committees of the Church, including subunit meetings and teleconferences, shall be open to news media, both church and public. Portions of a particular meeting may be closed for consideration of certain specific subjects, if such a session is authorized by at least a three-fourths majority vote of duly selected members present when the vote is taken in public session and entered in the minutes. Documents distributed in open meetings shall be considered public.

Subjects which may be considered in closed session are limited to considerations of sale or purchase of real property,

---

[20]*See* Judicial Council Decision 518.
[21]*See* Judicial Council Decision 559.

personnel matters, issues related to the accreditation or approval of institutions, discussions relating to civil litigation or collective bargaining, deployment of security personnel or devices, negotiations involving confidential third-party information, and deliberations of the Judicial Council.

A report on the results of a closed session is to be made immediately upon its conclusion, or as soon thereafter as is practicable.

¶ **822.** *Evangelical United Brethren Council of Administration.*—The General Council on Finance and Administration shall preserve the corporate existence of the Evangelical United Brethren Council of Administration until such time as attorneys shall advise its dissolution. The General Council on Finance and Administration shall nominate for election the Board of Trustees of the Evangelical United Brethren Council of Administration.

¶ **823.** *Church Name Outside the United States of America.*—The name of The United Methodist Church may be translated by any Central Conference into languages other than English. The United Methodist Church in the Central and Southern Europe Central Conference and the Central Conference in the German Democratic Republic and the Central Conference in the Federal Republic of Germany and West Berlin may use the name *Evangelisch-methodistische Kirche.*

¶ **824.** *Church Founding Date.*—The United Methodist Church (¶ 112) has become the successor to all rights, powers, and privileges of The Evangelical United Brethren Church and The Methodist Church; the two churches, from their beginnings, have had a close relationship.

The Methodist Church, the first of the two churches to organize, dates from the Christmas Conference of 1784. Therefore, The United Methodist Church recognizes as its founding date the year 1784.

All General Conferences shall be designated not in numerical sequence from any particular date, but merely by the calendar years in which they are respectively held. An Annual Conference, local church, or other body within The United Methodist Church which is composed of uniting units with differing dates of origin shall use as the date of its founding the date of founding of the older or oldest of the uniting units, or it may use such other founding-date formula as it may determine.

Section II. General Council on Finance and Administration.

¶ **901.** *General Statement on Church Finance.*—The work of the Church requires the support of our people, and participation therein through service and gifts is a Christian duty and a means of grace. In order that all members of The United Methodist Church may share in its manifold ministries at home and abroad and that the work committed to us may prosper, the following financial plan has been duly approved and adopted.

¶ **902.** *Name.*—There shall be a **General Council on Finance and Administration** of The United Methodist Church, hereinafter called the council.

¶ **903.** *Incorporation.*—The council shall be incorporated in such state or states as the council shall determine. This corporation shall be the successor corporation and organization to the Council on World Service and Finance (including the Council on World Service and Finance of The United Methodist Church, an Illinois corporation; the World Service Commission of the Methodist Episcopal Church, an Illinois corporation; the General Council of Administration of The Evangelical United Brethren Church, an Ohio corporation; the Board of Administration, Church of the United Brethren in Christ, an Ohio corporation) and the Board of Trustees.

This corporation shall receive and administer new trusts and funds, and so far as may be legal be the successor in trust of: The Board of Trustees of The United Methodist Church; The Board of Trustees of The Evangelical United Brethren Church, incorporated under the laws of Ohio; The Board of Trustees of the Church of the United Brethren in Christ, incorporated under the laws of Ohio; The Board of Trustees of the Evangelical Church, an unincorporated body; The Board of Trustees of The Methodist Church, incorporated under the laws of Ohio; The Trustees of the Methodist Episcopal Church, incorporated under the laws of Ohio; The Board of Trustees of the Methodist Episcopal Church, South, incorporated under the laws of Tennessee; and The Board of Trustees of the Methodist Protestant Church, incorporated under the laws of Maryland;

and so far as may be legal, as such successor in trust, it is authorized to receive from any of its said predecessor corporations all trust funds and assets of every kind and character, real, personal, or mixed, held by them or any one of them, or to merge into itself any one or more of its said predecessor corporations. Any such trusts and funds coming to it as successor corporation, either by transfer or by merger, shall be administered in accordance with the conditions under which they have been previously received and administered by said predecessor corporations or unincorporated body.

¶ **904.** *Amenability.*—The council shall report to and be amenable to the General Conference, and it shall cooperate with the General Council on Ministries in the compilation of budgets for program agencies participating in World Service Funds, as defined in ¶ 906.1.

¶ **905.** *Organization.*—1. *Membership.*—The members of the council shall be elected quadrennially by the General Conference as follows: three bishops, nominated by the Council of Bishops; two clergy in full connection, two laymen, and two laywomen from each jurisdiction, nominated by the bishops of that jurisdiction; nine members at large, one-third laymen, one-third laywomen, and one-third clergy, at least one of whom shall not be over thirty years of age at the time of election, and at least two of whom shall be racial and ethnic persons, and most of whom shall be elected for special skills; and one youth under the age of eighteen at the time of election. The at-large members and the youth member shall be nominated by the Council of Bishops without reference to jurisdictions. The general secretaries who serve as the chief executive officers of the general agencies and the publisher of The United Methodist Church shall be members of the council but without vote. The voting members, including bishops, shall not be eligible for membership on, or employment by, any other agency receiving funds administered by the council except where the Discipline specifically provides for such interagency representation. They shall serve until their successors are elected and qualified. Vacancies occurring between sessions of the General Conference shall be filled by the council on nomination of the College of Bishops of the jurisdiction concerned (*see* ¶ 812) or, in the event of a vacancy among the youth, episcopal, or at-large members, on nomination of the Council of Bishops.

2. *Meetings.*—The council shall meet annually and at such other times as are necessary on call of the president or on written request of one fifth of the members. Twenty-two voting members shall constitute a quorum.

3. *Officers.*—The officers of the council shall be a president, a vice-president, a recording secretary, and a general secretary, who shall also be the treasurer of the council, all of whom shall be elected by the council (*see* §5). They shall serve until the adjournment of the next succeeding quadrennial session of the General Conference after their election and until their successors are duly elected and qualified. The president, vice-president, and recording secretary shall be elected from the membership of the council. The general secretary shall sit with the council and its executive committee at all sessions and shall have right to the floor without the privilege of voting.

4. *Committees.*—*a) Executive Committee.*—There shall be an executive committee of the council consisting of the episcopal members, the officers of the council, chairpersons of the committees on services, as defined in the council bylaws, the chairperson of the Committee on Council Operations, and up to three members at large to assure that, in addition to the episcopal members, there is at least one member from each jurisdiction and there is racial and ethnic participation. The executive committee shall meet on call of the president or of a majority of the membership and shall act for the council and exercise its powers in the interim between the meetings of the council, but it shall not take any action contrary to or in conflict with any action or policy of the council. A copy of the minutes of each meeting of the executive committee shall be sent from the central office to each member of the council as soon after the meeting as practicable.

b) Committee on Audit and Review.—The executive committee of the council shall appoint a **Committee on Audit and Review,** no members of which shall be officers or members of the executive committee of the council, and at least half of whom shall not be members of the council, whose duty it shall be to review financial reports and audits of all treasuries receiving general church funds, including the funds of the council. The committee shall report its findings to the annual meeting of the council.

c) Committee on Official Forms and Records.—The council shall maintain and supervise under the direction of its general secretary a **Committee on Official Forms and Records,** which shall have the duty of preparing and editing all official statistical forms, record forms, and record books for use in the Church. The committee shall consist of one bishop elected by the Council of Bishops and nine persons elected by the General Council on Finance and Administration, as follows: one member of the council from each jurisdiction and one conference secretary, one conference treasurer, one conference statistician, and one district superintendent. The following persons shall be consultants to this committee ex officio without vote: a staff representative of the council, the director of the Department of Statistics, a staff representative of the General Council on Ministries, a representative of The United Methodist Publishing House, and representatives of other general agencies when their programs are directly involved. All official statistical forms, record forms, and record books required for use in The United Methodist Church shall be printed and published by The United Methodist Publishing House.

d) Committee on Personnel Policies and Practices.—The council shall organize a committee consisting of three representatives from the General Council on Finance and Administration, one of whom shall serve as chairperson, two representatives from the General Council on Ministries, and one representative of each of the following agencies: the General Board of Church and Society, the General Board of Discipleship, the General Board of Global Ministries, the General Board of Higher Education and Ministry, the General Commission on Archives and History, the General Commission on Christian Unity and Interreligious Concerns, the General Commission on Communication, the General Commission on Religion and Race, and the General Commission on the Status and Role of Women. Each of the aforementioned representatives shall be selected by the council, board, or commission represented from its membership. The committee shall have duties and responsibilities as defined in ¶ 907.7*b*.

e) Committee on Legal Responsibilities.—The council shall

organize a committee composed of six persons, three of whom shall be members of the council. The committee shall be amenable to the council and shall make recommendations to the council regarding the fulfillment of the responsibilities defined in ¶ 907.4.

f) Other Committees.—The council shall elect or appoint such other committees and task forces as needed for the performance of its duties.

5. *Staff.*—The council shall elect a general secretary as provided in § 3 above. On nomination of the general secretary, the council may elect associate general secretaries, who shall work under the direction of the general secretary. All employed personnel of the council shall be selected by and shall be amenable to the general secretary. The provisions of this paragraph shall become effective upon adjournment of the General Conference.

¶ **906.** *Fiscal Responsibilities.*—All moneys contributed by a local church to the World Service Fund, including World Service special gifts and Advance special gifts, the General Administration Fund, the Episcopal Fund, the Interdenominational Cooperation Fund, the Ministerial Education Fund, the Black College Fund, the Missional Priority Fund, the Temporary General Aid Fund, the World Communion Fund, the Human Relations Day Fund, the United Methodist Student Day Fund, the One Great Hour of Sharing Fund, the Youth Service Fund, the World Order Sunday Fund, Peace with Justice Sunday Fund, Native American Awareness Sunday Fund, and such other funds as may have been authorized by the General Conference shall be held in trust by the council and distributed only in support of the ministries of the respective funds. The council shall be accountable to The United Methodist Church through the General Conference in all matters relating to the receiving, disbursing, and reporting of such funds, and agencies receiving such funds shall be fiscally accountable to the council. In the exercise of its fiscal accountability role the council shall have the authority and responsibility to perform the following functions:

1. It shall submit to each quadrennial session of the General Conference, for its action and determination, budgets of expense for its own operation, the World Service Fund, the General

Administration Fund, the Episcopal Fund, the Interdenominational Cooperation Fund, the Ministerial Education Fund, the World Communion Offering, the One Great Hour of Sharing Fund, the Temporary General Aid Fund, the Black College Fund, the Human Relations Day Fund, the United Methodist Student Day Fund, the World Order Sunday Fund, Peace with Justice Sunday Fund, Native American Awareness Sunday Fund, and such other general funds as the General Conference may establish. It shall also make recommendations regarding all other funding considerations to come before General Conference.

a) The council shall make recommendations to the General Conference as to the amount and distribution of all funds provided for in §1 above.

b) In the case of the World Service Fund, the General Council on Finance and Administration and the General Council on Ministries shall proceed in the following manner in developing budget recommendations as they relate to allocations to the general program agencies of the Church:

(1) The General Council on Ministries shall, in consultation with the General Council on Finance and Administration and the general program agencies, develop recommendations to the General Council on Finance and Administration on needs of the general program agencies for the programs, missional priorities, and special programs.

(2) The General Council on Finance and Administration shall then establish and communicate to the General Council on Ministries the total sum proposed for distribution from the World Service Fund among the general program agencies.

(3) The General Council on Ministries, after reviewing both the program priorities and the total funds available to the general program agencies, shall recommend to the General Council on Finance and Administration the amount of the annual World Service allocation to each of those agencies, within the total sum proposed by the General Council on Finance and Administration for distribution among such agencies.

(4) Only when the General Council on Finance and Administration and the General Council on Ministries agree on the allocations to the several general program agencies shall these allocations be included in the World Service budget to be

recommended to the General Conference by the General Council on Finance and Administration.

(5) The General Council on Finance and Administration shall establish the total sum to be recommended to the General Conference for the annual budget of the World Service Fund.

(6) Before the beginning of each year the General Council on Finance and Administration shall determine and communicate to the General Council on Ministries the sum available at that time from World Service contingency funds to meet requests for additional funding from the general program agencies. The General Council on Ministries shall be authorized to approve allocations to the general program agencies for additional program funding up to the limit so established. No money shall be allocated by the General Council on Ministries from this source for general administrative costs, fixed charges, or capital outlay without approval by the General Council on Finance and Administration.

(7) The General Council on Ministries shall receive from the General Council on Finance and Administration copies of the proposed annual budgets of the general program agencies, in order that it may review such budgets in relation to the program proposals made by those agencies in their quadrennial budget requests.

c) It shall recommend the formulas by which all apportionments to the Annual Conferences shall be determined, subject to the approval of the General Conference.

d) The expenses of the council, including the cost of all its operations, shall be a first claim against all general funds received and disbursed by the council. The charges against the several funds or beneficiary agencies, except for the charge against the General Administration Fund, shall be in proportion to the funds' receipts. On recommendation of the council, the General Conference shall determine the amount of the council's expenses to be charged to the General Administration Fund.

2. It shall receive and disburse in accordance with budgets approved by the General Conference all funds raised throughout the Church for:

a) The World Service Fund, including World Service special gifts and Advance special gifts, *b)* The General Administration Fund,

c) The Episcopal Fund,

d) The Interdenominational Cooperation Fund,

e) The Ministerial Education Fund,

f) The Black College Fund,

g) The Missional Priority Fund,

h) The Temporary General Aid Fund,

i) The World Communion Fund,

j) The Human Relations Day Fund,

k) The United Methodist Student Day Fund,

l) The One Great Hour of Sharing Fund,

m) The World Order Sunday Fund,

n) The Peace with Justice Sunday Fund,

o) The Native American Awareness Sunday Fund,

p) The Youth Service Fund, and

q) any other fund or funds as directed by the proper authority.

3. To perform the accounting and reporting functions for the General Council on Ministries, the agencies accountable to it (¶ 803.5), and any administrative general agencies (¶ 803.6) which request the service and with which a plan of operation mutually agreeable to the agency and the council is established. In the interest of sound fiscal management, the council will ensure that expenditures of agencies receiving general church funds do not exceed receipts and available reserves, and this within an approved budget. If necessary for the efficient performance of the accounting and reporting function, the council may establish branch offices.

4. It shall require all agencies receiving general church funds to follow uniform accounting classifications and procedures for reporting. It shall require an annual audit of all treasuries receiving general church funds, following such auditing procedures as it may specify. It shall have authority to pass on the acceptability of any auditing firm proposed by an agency. It shall also require annually one month in advance of its annual meeting, or as is deemed necessary, and in such form as the council may require, statements of proposed budgets of all treasuries or agencies receiving general church funds. It shall review the budget of each agency receiving general church funds

in accordance with guidelines which it shall establish and communicate to the agencies, including the relationship between administration, service, and promotion. It shall include in its quadrennial report to the General Conference a fiscal report for each of the general agencies, including councils, boards, commissions, and committees of The United Methodist Church that have been constituted by the General Conference. Such report shall be available upon request.

5. To establish policy governing the functions of banking, payroll, accounting, and budget control for all agencies receiving general church funds. The council may upon mutual consent of the agencies involved, perform the functions of banking, check preparation, and payroll on behalf of an agency in order to maximize efficiency of operation.

6. To develop investment policies for, suggest investment counselors for, and review, at the council's discretion but on at least an annual basis, the performance of all invested funds of all agencies receiving general church funds. The council shall have complete authority to manage any portfolio of less than $1,500,000. The council is encouraged to invest in institutions, companies, corporations, or funds which make a positive contribution toward the realization of the goals outlined in the Social Principles of The United Methodist Church (¶¶ 70-76).

7. To receive, collect, and hold in trust for the benefit of The United Methodist Church, its general funds, or its general agencies, any and all donations, bequests, and devises of any kind, real or personal, that may be given, devised, bequeathed, or conveyed to The United Methodist Church as such or to any general fund or agency of The United Methodist Church for any benevolent, charitable, or religious purposes, and to administer the same and the income therefrom in accordance with the directions of the donor, trustor, or testator; and, in cooperation with the Board of Discipleship, to take such action as is necessary to encourage United Methodists to provide for their continued participation in World Service, in one or more of the World Service agencies, or in other general church benevolence funds or interests, through wills and special gifts (*see* ¶ 1215.6).

8. In consultation with the National Association of United

Methodist Foundations, to establish standardized gift annuity rates for the writing of annuities by United Methodist foundations and institutions and agencies operating under the auspices of the denomination.

9. Where Annual Conferences, individually or in groups, have established United Methodist foundations, the council may provide staff leadership on request to advise in matters of financial management, to the end that foundation assets shall be wisely managed on behalf of the Church.

10. To approve plans for financing all national conferences and convocations to be held under the auspices or sponsorship of any general agency of the Church.

11. To make recommendations to the General Conference, in consultation with the General Council on Ministries and the Council of Bishops, regarding any offerings to be received in connection with special days observed on a churchwide basis. These recommendations shall include the number and timing of such special days with offerings, the amount, if any, to be established as a goal for each such offering, the causes to be benefited by each, the method by which the receipts on each such offering shall be distributed among the causes benefiting from it, and the method by which such receipts shall be remitted and reported by local churches. All such recommendations are subject to the approval of the General Conference.

12. The council shall be responsible for ensuring that no board, agency, committee, commission, or council shall give United Methodist funds to any "gay" caucus or group, or otherwise use such funds to promote the acceptance of homosexuality. The council shall have the right to stop such expenditures.[22]

¶ **907.** *Other Administrative Responsibilities.*—The council shall have the authority and responsibility to perform the following functions:

1. To establish general policy governing the ownership, sale, rental, renovation, or purchase of property by a general agency in the United States or Puerto Rico. The council shall consider the plans of any general agency proposing to acquire or sell real

_____
[22]*See* Judicial Council Decisions 491, 597.

estate or erect a building or enter into a lease in the continental United States and determine whether the proposed action is in the best interest of The United Methodist Church. On the basis of that determination it shall approve or disapprove all such proposed actions. In the case of such proposed action by a general program agency, it shall solicit and consider the recommendation of the Council on Ministries. If either council disapproves, the agency shall delay the project until it can be considered by the next General Conference. Nothing in the foregoing shall include the operational requirements of the General Board of Publication or the General Board of Pensions.

2. To act in concert with the General Council on Ministries to establish a procedure for making a quadrennial review, initiating proposals and/or responding to proposals by the general agencies regarding the location of headquarters and staff and report the same to the General Conference. (*See* ¶ 1006.25.)

3. To exercise on behalf of General Conference a property reporting function by receiving reports annually from general agencies of the Church concerning property titles, values, debts, general maintenance, lease or rental costs, space usage, and such other information as the council may deem relevant. The council may consult and advise with the general agencies concerning any property problems that may arise. A summary of the property data shall be reported to each quadrennial General Conference. This provision shall apply to headquarters buildings but not to properties which are part of the program responsibilities of the General Board of Global Ministries or to any of the properties of the General Board of Publication. Titles to historical shrines, landmarks, and such historical properties as may be acquired in the future shall be held by the General Council on Finance and Administration.

4. To take all necessary legal steps to safeguard and protect the interests and rights of the denomination; to maintain a file of legal briefs related to cases involving the denominational interests of The United Methodist Church, and to make provisions for legal counsel where necessary to protect the interests and rights of the denomination. The council shall recommend to each general agency and unit thereof and to each Annual Conference Council on Finance and Administration a

uniform procedure to be followed by the aforesaid agencies and, where applicable, local churches, relative to the certification and payment of ordained ministers' housing allowances in accordance with provisions of the Internal Revenue Code of the United States. The council shall have the authority to pursue policies and procedures necessary to preserve the tax-exempt status of the denomination and its affiliated organizations.[23]

5. To provide direction and coordination in the design and implementation of operating systems in order to maximize the efficiency of operating personnel, equipment, and resources between and within agencies. During the quadrennium these agencies shall study their respective responsibilities, programs, and internal operations and institute such improvements and economies in their work as they find to be feasible and practicable. They shall cooperate with the council in working out, in advance of these studies, the general areas to be included and methods of carrying out this objective. They shall report their accomplishments in improvements and economies to the council before the close of the third fiscal year of each quadrennium, at a time determined by the council, which shall prepare from this information a combined report for the General Conference.

6.*a)* To advise and consult with general agencies receiving general church funds about the ownership, lease, and use of electronic data processing or electronic word processing.

b) When a general agency receiving general church funds proposes to purchase or lease any electronic computer that will be used for data processing, word processing, or management information functions, the council shall:

(1) Consult with the agency regarding the hardware and software configurations for the purpose of overall coordination of computing devices in the agencies and,

(2) Review the proposed computer purchase for cost effectiveness and fiscal appropriateness. This review shall be for advisory and consultative purposes.

c) Electronic data or word processing shall include information gathering, manipulation, storage, retrieval, and dissemination as achieved by an electronic computer or similar device.

---

[23]*See* Judicial Council Decision 458.

7. *a)* The council shall: (1) require each general agency as listed in (¶ 905.4*d*), including itself, to follow uniform policies and practices in the employment and remuneration of personnel, recognizing differences in local employment conditions, and (2) be authorized to gather from all general agencies, at such intervals as it may determine, information regarding the number of agency employees and staff and the salary paid each such employee or staff member; salary information shall be collected by job classification or title only.

b) The Committee on Personnel Policies and Practices (¶ 905.4*d*) shall: (1) prepare quadrennially, review annually, and recommend to the council an appropriate salary schedule, based upon responsibilities, for executive staff personnel of the councils, boards, and commissions represented on the committee; (2) develop and recommend to the council a schedule of benefits for an employee benefit program for general agency personnel and any changes required thereto from time to time; and (3) receive from agencies and institutions receiving general church funds statements regarding their compliance with the policy stated in ¶ 911.1. Based on these statements, and in consultation with and upon the advice of the General Commission on Religion and Race and the General Commission on the Status and Role of Women, the committee shall prepare for the General Council on Finance and Administration reports and recommendations deemed appropriate by the committee.

In the event it is determined by the council that an agency or institution receiving general church funds is not in compliance with the equal employment opportunity policies and the salary and employee benefit schedules established by the committee, the council shall notify in writing the agency so named and suspend, after a three-month period of grace, an appropriate amount of future funding until the agency or institution complies.

8. To maintain a consultative service to assist general agencies in planning and making arrangements for national meetings, conferences, and convocations.

9. To maintain an accurate record of the mail addresses of all bishops; ordained ministers in effective relation; local pastors, including retired ordained ministers serving charges; and such

lists of general, jurisdictional, conference, and district boards, commissions, and committees, and officers of same, and of local church commission chairpersons, as may be deemed necessary. No one other than authorized bodies or officers of the Church shall be permitted to use these records.

10. To prepare the important statistics relating to The United Methodist Church for the General Minutes, or such other publications and releases as may be approved by the council. It shall provide for the distribution of statistical information to Annual Conferences, the general planning and research agencies of the Church, and other interested parties. The council may establish an appropriate schedule of fees and charges to defray the cost of such information distribution services.

11. To assist and advise the jurisdictions, Annual Conferences, districts, and local churches in all matters relating to the work of the council. These matters shall include, but shall not be limited to, business administration, investment and property management, data processing, and auditing. Matters related to resourcing the development and implementation of financial programs within the local church Committee on Finance shall be the responsibility of the General Board of Discipleship. The council may perform certain functions for the jurisdictions, Annual Conferences, districts, or local churches if the particular organization so elects and a suitable plan of operation can be determined.

12. To provide guidance and consultation in the area of local church business administration, including establishment of professional standards, a training program, certification of church business administrators and associate church business administrators, and sponsorship of an association of United Methodist church business administrators.

13. To provide guidance and consultation in the work of church secretaries, including establishment of professional standards, training and certification programs, and sponsorship of a professional association of United Methodist church secretaries.

14. To sponsor a **National Association of Commissions on Equitable Salaries of The United Methodist Church.** Under the sponsorship of the council, the association shall provide guidance

and counsel to Annual Conference Commissions on Equitable Salaries in their areas of responsibility (¶ 722) by means of consultations, workshops, development of educational materials and informational resources, and other appropriate means. The council, in its sponsorship role, may provide such staff and in-kind services to the association as it deems appropriate.

15. To institute, manage, and maintain an insurance program available, where approved by regulatory agencies, to all United Methodist local churches in the United States and Puerto Rico and, where acceptable on an underwriting basis, to all United Methodist Annual Conferences, agencies, and institutions in the United States and Puerto Rico.

16. To designate the **business manager of the General Conference** who shall be related operationally to the Commission on the General Conference.

¶ **908.** The treasurer of the General Council on Finance and Administration shall, not less than ninety days prior to the session of each Annual Conference or as soon thereafter as practical, transmit to the presiding bishop thereof, to the president of the conference Council on Finance and Administration, and to the conference treasurer a statement of the apportionments to the conference for the World Service Fund, the General Administration Fund, the Episcopal Fund, the Interdenominational Cooperation Fund, the Ministerial Education Fund, the Temporary General Aid Fund, the Black College Fund, the Missional Priority Fund, and such other funds as may have been apportioned by the General Conference. The treasurer shall keep an account of all amounts remitted by the conference treasurers and from other sources intended for the funds listed in ¶ 906.2. and any other fund so directed by the proper authority, and shall disburse the same as authorized by the General Conference and directed by the council. A separate account shall be kept of each such fund, and none of them shall be drawn on for the benefit of another fund.

¶ **909.** The treasurer shall report annually to the council and to the respective conference councils as to all amounts received and disbursed during the year. The treasurer shall also make to each quadrennial session of the General Conference a full report of the financial transactions of the council for the previous four fiscal years. The treasurer shall be bonded for such an amount as may be determined by the council. The books of the treasurer shall be audited annually by a certified public accountant approved by the Committee on Audit and Review (¶ 905.4*b*).

<small>GENERAL FUNDS</small>

¶ **910.** *Definition of "General Funds."*—The terms "general fund(s)" and "general church fund(s)," wherever they appear in the Book of Discipline, refer to: the World Service Fund, including World Service special gifts and Advance special gifts; the General Administration Fund; the Episcopal Fund; the Interdenominational Cooperation Fund; the Ministerial Education Fund; the Black College Fund; the Missional Priority Fund; the Temporary General Aid Fund; the World Communion Fund; the Human Relations Day Fund; the United Methodist Student Day Fund; the One Great Hour of Sharing Fund; the World Order Sunday Fund; Peace with Justice Sunday Fund; Native Awareness Sunday Fund; the Youth Service Fund; and such other funds as may have been established by the General Conference and have been specifically authorized by the General Conference to be raised on a churchwide basis. They are restricted assets and are not funds of local churches, Annual or Jurisdictional Conferences, or other units of the denomination. Such general funds are to be disbursed for the purpose or purposes set forth in ¶¶ 912-932 and budgets or similar directives adopted for the respective funds by the General Conference. The General Council on Finance and Administration, in the fulfillment of its fiscal responsibilities pursuant to ¶ 906, shall only have authority to disburse moneys contributed to any of these funds in a manner specifically authorized by the Book of Discipline or for a purpose set forth in the budget or directives adopted by the preceding General Conference for that particular fund.

¶ **911.** *General Policies.*—1. The General Council on Finance and Administration is authorized to withhold approval of a portion or all of the budget of any agency or any church-related institution receiving general church funds until such agency or church-related institution certifies to the council in writing that it has established and has complied with a policy of (*a*) recruiting, employing, utilizing, recompensing, and promoting professional staff and other personnel without regard to race, color, age, or sex, (*b*) fulfilling its duties and responsibilities in a manner which does not involve segregation or discrimination on the basis of race, age, or sex, and (*c*) insofar as possible, purchasing goods and services from vendors who are in compliance with such policies as are described in sections (*a*) and (*b*) of this paragraph. In the fulfillment of this directive the council shall take the following steps to ensure that concerns of the General Commission on Religion and Race and the General Commission on the Status and Role of Women are represented: (1) consult with the two commissions in the development of a certification form to be submitted to the council by agencies and institutions receiving general church funds; (2) share copies of such certifications with the two commissions; (3) receive and consider recommendations from either of the two commissions regarding possible noncompliance with these policies by agencies and institutions receiving general church funds.

2. It may withhold approval of any item or items in the budget or budgets receiving general church funds which in its judgment represent unnecessary duplication of administrative function; in cooperation with and on recommendation of the General Council on Ministries, it may withhold approval of any such item which represents unnecessary duplication of program within an agency or between two or more agencies. If the council finds that there is such duplication in existing activities, it shall promptly direct the attention of the agencies involved to the situation and shall cooperate with them in correcting the same, and may decline to supply from general fund receipts money to continue activities which have been held to duplicate each other unnecessarily or plainly violate the principle of correlation as applied to the total benevolence program of the Church.

3. An agency of The United Methodist Church proposing to borrow funds for a period in excess of twelve months or in an amount in excess of 25 percent of its annual budget or one hundred thousand dollars, whichever amount is smaller, whether for building or current expense purposes, shall submit such proposal, accompanied by a plan for amortization, to the council

for approval. If the council disapproves, the agency shall delay such borrowing until it can be considered by the next General Conference.

4. Any general board, cause, agency, or institution or any organization, group, officer, or individual of The United Methodist Church or to which The United Methodist Church contributes financial support desiring or proposing to make a special churchwide financial appeal during the quadrennium shall present a request for authorization to make such appeal to the General Council on Finance and Administration at the time budgets for the ensuing quadrennium are being considered. All such appeals shall be reviewed by the General Council on Ministries and its actions shall be reported to the General Council on Finance and Administration. The council shall then report such request to the General Conference with a recommendation for its action thereon. "Special appeal" shall be understood to mean any appeal other than the general appeal for support of the World Service program as represented in the World Service budget. "Churchwide appeal" shall be understood to mean any appeal to the Church at large except appeals to such special groups as alumni of an educational institution. In the interim between the quadrennial sessions of the General Conference such proposed churchwide financial appeal shall require the approval of the General Council on Finance and Administration and the Council of Bishops. In case of emergency the executive committee of either of these bodies may act in such matter for the body itself, but only by a three-fourths vote. Any individual or agency authorized to make a churchwide appeal for funds shall channel all gifts through the General Council on Finance and Administration. The General Council on Finance and Administration may withhold payment of the allocation from any general fund to any agency or institution which it finds to be in violation of the provisions of this paragraph.

5. The apportionments for all apportioned general church funds, as approved by the General Conference, shall not be subject to reduction either by the Annual Conference or by the charge or local church (¶ 710.2*b*).

6. Individual donors or local churches may make contributions to the support of any cause or project which is a part of the

work of any general church agency. Such miscellaneous gifts shall be sent to the General Council on Finance and Administration, which shall then forward the gift to the agency for which it is intended. Agencies receiving miscellaneous gifts shall acknowledge receipt of the gift to the donor. No agency shall solicit or cultivate gifts for any cause or project which has not been approved for support through World Service Special gifts (¶ 913), general Advance special gifts (¶ 914), or a special appeal (¶ 911.4).

7. No general council, board, commission, or committee shall initiate or cause to be organized without approval of the General Council on Finance and Administration a foundation or similar organization for the purpose of securing, conserving, or expending funds for the direct or indirect benefit or support of any general agency or any of its programs or work. Foundations related directly or indirectly to any general church agency shall report annually to the council in a manner determined by the council.

¶ **912.** *The World Service Fund.*—**The World Service Fund** is basic in the financial program of The United Methodist Church. World Service on apportionment represents the minimum needs of the general agencies of the Church. Payment in full of these apportionments by local churches and Annual Conferences is the first benevolent responsibility of the Church.

1. The council shall recommend to each quadrennial session of the General Conference the amount of the annual World Service budget for the ensuing quadrennium and the method by which it shall be apportioned to the Annual Conferences. In cooperation with the General Council on Ministries it shall prepare and recommend a plan of distribution of World Service receipts among the World Service agencies, in accordance with the procedures described in ¶ 906.1*b*. In the planning of the World Service budget it shall be the role of the General Council on Finance and Administration to facilitate sound fiscal and administrative policies and practices within and among the general agencies of the Church. It shall be the role of the General Council on Ministries to relate the budget askings of the program agencies to one another in such a way as to implement the program and missional priorities of the Church.

2. The general secretary or other duly authorized representative of each agency of The United Methodist Church requesting support from the World Service Fund and the authorized representative of any other agency for which askings are authorized by the General Conference shall have the right to appear before the council at a designated time and place to represent the cause for which each is responsible, provided that such representation has been previously made to the Council on Ministries.

3. The World Service agencies shall not solicit additional or special gifts from individual donors or special groups, other than foundations, unless approval for such solicitation is first secured from the council.

¶ **913.** *World Service Special Gifts.*—A World Service Special gift is a designated financial contribution made by an individual, local church, organization, district, or Annual Conference to a project authorized as a World Service Special project by the General Council on Ministries. General agencies which qualify under the provisions of ¶ 1007.6*b*(1) shall be eligible to recommend projects for approval by the General Council on Ministries as World Service Special projects.

2. General guidelines governing the types of projects which may be recommended for approval as World Service Special projects shall be approved by the General Conference on recommendation of the General Council on Ministries and the General Council on Finance and Administration.

3. The World Service Special gifts program shall be under the supervision of the General Council on Ministries, which shall be responsible for *(a)* establishing project approval criteria consistent with the guidelines adopted by the General Conference; *(b)* establishing the process by which projects may be recommended and approved; *(c)* approving projects to receive World Service Special gift support; and *(d)* providing adequate staff administration and program accountability.

4. Churches and individuals shall give priority to the support of World Service and Conference Benevolences and other apportioned funds. World Service Special gift giving shall be voluntary and in addition to the support of apportioned

funds. World Service Special gifts shall not be raised as a part of a fund apportioned by an Annual Conference.

5. World Service Special gifts shall be remitted in full by local church treasurers to Annual Conference treasurers, who shall remit each month to the General Council on Finance and Administration the total amounts received during the month as World Service Special gifts. The council shall remit such gifts in full to the administering agencies, which shall acknowledge the receipt of every gift to the donor or the local church.

6. The promotion of this program may include general promotion, for purposes of name identification and visibility, which shall be the responsibility of United Methodist Communications.

7. Specific cultivation of approved projects shall be done by the administering agencies to specific audiences that have demonstrated previously their interest and concern for the ministry contained in the approved project. Expenses for specific cultivation shall be borne by the administering agencies. No promotional or cultivation expenses shall be paid from World Service Special Gifts receipts. Such expenses shall not exceed amounts approved by the General Council on Finance and Administration and the General Council on Ministries under guidelines approved by the General Conference.

¶ **914.** *The Advance.*—1. The Advance for Christ and His Church (hereafter referred to as the Advance) is an official program within The United Methodist Church through which support may be designated for projects approved by the Advance Committee of the General Council on Ministries. (*See* ¶ 1411.2*b*.)

2. A general Advance special gift is a designated financial contribution made by an individual, local church, organization, district, or conference to a project authorized for this purpose by the Advance Committee.

a) Gifts as Advance specials may be made for specific projects or purposes authorized by the Advance Committee.

b) Gifts as Advance specials may be made for broadly designated causes (such as a type of work, a country, or a region), or for use as block grants to a certain country or administrative unit, provided such causes are authorized by the Advance Committee. In such case the administering agency shall provide the donor with information about the area to which the funds have been given and, where practicable, establish communication with a person or group representative of that type of work.

c) An Advance special gift may be given to an authorized agency (¶ 1007.5*d*) rather than to a specific project, in which case the agency shall determine the Advance special project or projects to which such a gift shall be allocated, shall inform the donor where the gift has been invested, and as far as practicable shall establish communication between donor and recipient.

3. Funds given and received as a part of the general Advance shall be subject to the following conditions:

a) Churches and individuals shall give priority to the support of the World Service and Conference Benevolences and other apportioned funds. Advance giving shall be voluntary and in addition to the support of apportioned funds.

b) Funds shall be solicited or received only for authorized projects. Programs and institutions having general Advance special projects shall promote only for the projects approved and shall ask that gifts be remitted in the manner described in ¶ 914.4 below.

c) Funds received through the Advance shall be used solely for project support and are not to be used for administration or promotional costs.

d) Advance special gifts shall not be raised as a part of a fund apportioned by an Annual Conference. (For conference Advance special gifts *see* ¶ 727.)

e) Upon receipt of funds for a general Advance special each administering agency shall communicate promptly with the donor, acknowledging receipt of the gift and suggesting avenues for communication, if communication has not already been established.

4. Receipts for general Advance specials shall be remitted by the local church treasurer to the conference treasurer, who shall make remittance each month to the participating agencies in a manner determined by the treasurer of the General Council on Finance and Administration. Individuals may remit directly to respective agencies in a manner determined by the treasurer of the General Council on Finance and Administration, with these remittances reported to the Annual Conference treasurer by the respective agencies.

¶ **915.** The following general directives shall be observed in the promotion and administration of the Advance and One Great Hour of Sharing:

1. In the appeal and promotion of Advance specials and One Great Hour of Sharing offerings there shall be no goals or quotas except as they may be set by the Annual Conferences for themselves.

2. The treasurer of the General Council on Finance and Administration shall be treasurer of the Advance and One Great Hour of Sharing.

3. The expense of promotion for Advance specials shall be borne by the respective participating agencies in proportion to the amount received by each in Advance specials. The causes of the Advance shall be coordinated with other financial appeals and shall be promoted by the Division of Program and Benevolence Interpretation of the General Commission on Communication.

4. The appeal for Advance specials shall be channeled through bishops, district superintendents, and pastors, the details of the procedure to be determined by the Division of Program and Benevolence Interpretation of the General Commission on Communication in consultation with the Mission Education and Cultivation Department of the General Board of Global Ministries and the Advance Committee.

5. In each Annual Conference the conference Board of Global Ministries (if any; *see* ¶ 730), in cooperation with the General Board of Global Ministries, shall promote Advance specials and One Great Hour of Sharing offerings through district missionary secretaries, conference and district missionary institutes, and other effective means as it may determine.

6. Should a clear emergency arise, any feature of the structure and administration of the Advance may be altered on the approval of a majority of the Council of Bishops and of the General Council on Finance and Administration.

¶ **916.** *General Church Special-Day Offerings.*—The following are the special days with offerings to be used in support of general church causes:

1. *Human Relations Day.*—A **Human Relations Day** shall be observed during the season of Epiphany on the Sunday before

the observance of Martin Luther King, Jr.'s birthday with an offering goal recommended by the General Council on Finance and Administration and adopted by the General Conference. The purpose of the goal is to further the development of better human relations through funding programs determined by the General Conference upon recommendation of the General Council on Finance and Administration after consultation with the General Council on Ministries. Net receipts from this observance shall be allocated as predetermined on ratio (*see* ¶ 274.1), with the funds being administered by the general boards under which approved programs are lodged.

2. *One Great Hour of Sharing.*—There shall be an annual observance of the **One Great Hour of Sharing** as a special offering for relief (¶ 274.2). The observance shall be under the general supervision of the General Commission on Communication (¶ 1906.12) in accordance with the following directives:

a) The One Great Hour of Sharing shall be observed annually on the fourth Sunday in Lent. All local churches shall be fully informed and encouraged to receive a freewill offering in behalf of the relief program.

b) Insofar as possible, the planning and promotion of the One Great Hour of Sharing shall be done cooperatively with other denominations through the National Council of the Churches of Christ in the U.S.A., it being understood, however, that receipts of the offerings shall be administered by The United Methodist Church.

c) Receipts from the offering, after payment of the expenses of promotion, shall be remitted by the treasurer of the General Council on Finance and Administration to the United Methodist Committee on Relief (¶ 1459.7) to be administered by that committee.

3. *United Methodist Student Day.*—The **United Methodist Student Day** offering, taken annually, the Sunday after Thanksgiving, shall be received for the support of the United Methodist Scholarships and the United Methodist Student Loan Fund (¶ 274.4). Receipts from the offering, after payment of the expenses of promotion, shall be remitted by the treasurer of the General Council on Finance and Administration to the General

Board of Higher Education and Ministry to be administered by that board.

4. *World Communion Offering.*—In connection with **World Communion Sunday** there shall be a churchwide appeal conducted by the General Commission on Communication in accord with the following directives:

a) Each local church shall be requested to remit as provided in ¶ 916.8 all the Communion offering received on World Communion Sunday (on the first Sunday in October) and such portion of the Communion offering received at other observances of the Sacrament of the Lord's Supper as the local church may designate.

b) The net receipts, after payment of promotional costs, shall be divided as follows: 50 percent to the Crusade Scholarship Committee, 35 percent to the Ethnic Scholarship Program, and 15 percent to the Ethnic In-Service Training Program, the last two administered by the General Board of Higher Education and Ministry in consultation with the various ethnic groups (¶ 274.3).

5. *Peace with Justice Sunday.*—**Peace with Justice Sunday** shall be observed on the Second Sunday after Pentecost. The observance shall be under the general supervision of the General Board of Church and Society (*see* ¶ 274.5). There shall be a churchwide appeal and offering. The net receipts from the offering will be distributed as follows:

a) The Annual Conference treasurer shall retain 50 percent of the moneys for Peace with Justice Ministries in the Annual Conference to be administered by the Annual Conference Board of Church and Society or equivalent structure.

b) The Annual Conference treasurer shall remit the remaining 50 percent of the moneys to the General Council on Finance and Administration.

c) Net receipts from the offering, after payment of the expenses of promotion, shall be remitted by the treasurer of the General Council on Finance and Administration to the General Board of Church and Society for Peace with Justice Ministries.

6. *Native American Sunday.*—**Native American Sunday** shall be observed annually on a day to be set by the General Council

on Ministries. The purpose of the churchwide appeal is to develop and strengthen Native American ministries in the Annual Conferences, in target cities of the Native American Urban Initiative of the General Board of Global Ministries, and for scholarships for Native Americans attending United Methodist schools of theology (¶ 274.6).

7. Promotion of all authorized general church special Sunday offerings shall be by the General Commission on Communication in consultation with the participating agencies. Expenses of promotion for each offering shall be a prior claim against the receipts of the offering promoted. In each case such expenses shall be within a budget approved by the General Council on Finance and Administration upon recommendation of the General Commission on Communication after consultation with the participating agencies. In the promotion of these offerings there shall be an emphasis on the spiritual implications of Christian stewardship.

8. Receipts from all authorized general church special Sunday offerings shall be remitted promptly by the local church treasurer to the Annual Conference treasurer, who shall remit monthly to the treasurer of the General Council on Finance and Administration. A special-gift voucher for contributions to the offerings will be issued when appropriate. Local churches shall report the amount of the offerings in the manner indicated on the Annual Conference report form.

¶ **917.** *The General Administration Fund.*—1. **The General Administration Fund** shall provide for the expenses of the sessions of the General Conference, the Judicial Council, such special commissions and committees as may be constituted by the General Conference, and such other administrative agencies and activities as may be recommended for inclusion in the general administration budget by the General Council on Finance and Administration and approved by the General Conference. Any agency or institution requiring or desiring support from the General Administration Fund shall present its case for the same to the council at a time and place which shall be indicated by the officers of the council. The council, having heard such requests, shall report the same to the General Conference with recommendations for its action and determination.

2. The treasurer of the council shall disburse the funds received for the General Administration Fund as authorized by the General Conference and as directed by the council. Where the General Conference has not allocated definite sums to agencies receiving money from the General Administration Fund, the council or its executive committee shall have authority to determine the amount to be allocated to each.

3. The expenses of the Judicial Council shall be paid from the General Administration Fund and within a budget submitted annually by the Judicial Council to the General Council on Finance and Administration for its approval.

¶ **918.** *The Interdenominational Cooperation Fund.*—1. The General Commission on Christian Unity and Interreligious Concerns, in consultation with the Council of Bishops, shall recommend to the General Council on Finance and Administration the amount of the annual **Interdenominational Cooperation Fund** allocation to each of the recipients of the fund. The council shall recommend to the General Conference the amounts to be included in the annual Interdenominational Cooperation Fund budget.

2. This fund shall provide the United Methodist share of the basic budgets of those organizations which relate to the ecumenical responsibilities of the Council of Bishops and of the General Commission on Christian Unity and Interreligious Concerns. Such organizations shall include the Consultation on Church Union, National Council of the Churches of Christ in the U.S.A., and the World Council of Churches. The fund shall also provide for the expenses of representatives chosen by the Council of Bishops or by the General Commission on Christian Unity and Interreligious Concerns to meetings and committees of such ecumenical agencies. The General Council on Finance and Administration shall reimburse such expenses from vouchers approved by persons designated by the general secretary of the General Commission on Christian Unity and Interreligious Concerns or by the general secretary of the General Council on Finance and Administration.

3. Before the beginning of each calendar year the General Council on Finance and Administration shall determine and communicate to the General Commission on Christian Unity and

Interreligious Concerns the sum available from the Interdenominational Cooperation Fund Contingency Reserve to be allocated by the commission to meet emerging needs of ecumenical agencies.

¶ **919.** *Black College Fund.*—The General Council on Finance and Administration shall recommend to the General Conference the sum which the Church shall undertake for the black colleges and the method by which it shall be apportioned to the Annual Conferences. The purpose of the fund is to provide financial support for current operating budgets and capital improvements of the black colleges related administratively to the Church.

1. The current funds received annually shall be distributed to those black colleges whose eligibility under adopted guidelines of management, educational quality, and measurement by announced objectives shall be the precondition of participation. These guidelines shall be revised and administered by the Division of Higher Education of the General Board of Higher Education and Ministry, in consultation with the Council of Presidents of the Black Colleges. The Division of Higher Education of the General Board of Higher Education and Ministry shall administer the fund according to the guidelines for support and a formula approved by the General Conference.

2. In the interim between sessions of the General Conference, the guidelines for support and formula for distribution may be changed as necessary upon recommendation of the Council of Presidents of the Black Colleges and the General Board of Higher Education and Ministry and with the consent of the General Council on Finance and Administration.

3. Promotion of the **Black College Fund** shall be by the Division of Higher Education and in consultation with the Council of Presidents of the Black Colleges, in cooperation with and with the assistance of the Division of Program and Benevolence Interpretation of the General Commission on Communication, the cost being a prior claim against the Black College Fund receipts and within a budget approved by the Division of Higher Education and the General Council on Finance and Administration.

¶ **920.** *The Temporary General Aid Fund.*—The council shall recommend to the General Conference, either as a separate apportioned general fund or as a part of another apportioned general fund, the sum which the Church shall undertake for the purpose of providing grants-in-aid for pensions and minimum salaries to those Annual and Missionary Conferences that qualify under a formula adopted by the General Conference. The purpose of this fund is to assist in raising the level of pensions and minimum salaries in conferences which have merged with conferences of the former Central Jurisdiction. In consultation with the General Commission on Religion and Race, the pension portion of this fund is to be administered by the General Board of Pensions, and the minimum salary portion by the council (*see* ¶ 2108.16). The distribution of fund receipts is to be made by the council in accordance with formulas approved by the General Conference. The provisions of this paragraph shall become effective immediately upon adjournment of the General Conference.

¶ **921.** *The Ministerial Education Fund.*—The council shall recommend to the General Conference the sum which the Church shall undertake for the **Ministerial Education Fund** and the method by which it shall be apportioned to the Annual Conferences, in accordance with the provisions adopted by the 1968 General Conference in establishing the Ministerial Education Fund. The purpose of the fund is to enable the Church to unify and expand its program of financial support for the recruitment and education of ordained and diaconal ministers and to equip the Annual Conferences to meet increased demands in this area.[24] The maximum amount possible from this fund shall go directly for programs and services in theological education, the enlistment and continuing education of ordained and diaconal ministers, and the courses of study.

1. Of the total money raised in each Annual Conference for the Ministerial Education Fund, 25 percent shall be retained by the Annual Conference which raised it, to be used in its program of ministerial education as approved by the Annual Conference and administered through its Board of Ordained Ministry. The Boards of Ordained Ministry and Diaconal Ministry will confer concerning use of the Ministerial Education Fund. Administra-

---

[24]*See* Judicial Council Decision 545.

tive costs of the Boards of Ordained and Diaconal Ministry shall be a claim on the conference operating budget. No Annual Conference which had been participating in a 1 percent plan or other conference program of ministerial student scholarships and loan grants prior to the establishment of this fund shall receive less for this purpose than it received in the last year of the quadrennium preceding the establishment of the fund, provided the giving from that conference for ministerial education does not fall below the level achieved in the quadrennium preceding the establishment of the fund.

2. Of the total money raised in each Annual Conference for the Ministerial Education Fund, 75 percent shall be remitted by the conference treasurer to the treasurer of the council for distribution to the Division of Ordained Ministry and the Division of Diaconal Ministry for support of ministerial education and administered by the Division of Ordained Ministry. It shall be distributed as follows:

a) At least 75 percent of the amount received by the divisions shall be distributed to the theological schools of The United Methodist Church on a formula established by the Division of Ordained Ministry and Division of Diaconal Ministry after consultation with the theological schools. All the money allocated to the theological schools shall be used for current operations, not for physical expansion.

b) The remaining portion of the amount received shall be used for supplemental distributions to the theological schools and for board use in its program of ministerial enlistment and development. The Division of Ordained Ministry and the Division of Diaconal Ministry will consult and recommend to the general secretary of the General Board of Higher Education and Ministry appropriate funding for divisional programs of ministerial enlistment and development.

3. This fund shall be regarded by Annual Conferences as a priority to be met before any additional benevolences, grants, or funds are allocated to a theological school or school of religion.

¶ **922.** *Missional Priority Fund.*—There may be a **Missional Priority Fund,** established by the General Conference as a part of its action in the adoption of a missional priority (¶ 803.9). The council, following consultation with the General Council on

Ministries and the Council of Bishops, shall recommend to the General Conference the sum which the Church shall undertake for this purpose and the method by which it shall be apportioned to the Annual Conferences. Receipts shall be administered by an agency or agencies designated by the General Conference upon recommendation of the General Council on Ministries and the General Council on Finance and Administration.

The Episcopal Fund

¶ **923.** The **Episcopal Fund,** raised in accordance with ¶ 925, shall provide for the salary and expenses of effective bishops and for the support of retired bishops and surviving spouses and minor children of deceased bishops. Subject to the approval of the General Council on Finance and Administration, the treasurer shall have authority to borrow for the benefit of the Episcopal Fund such amounts as may be necessary for the proper execution of the orders of the General Conference.[25]

¶ **924.** The council shall recommend to each quadrennial session of the General Conference for its action and determination: (1) the amounts to be fixed as salaries of the effective bishops or a formula by which the council shall fix the salaries; (2) a schedule of such amounts as may be judged adequate to provide for their office expense; (3) provision for an annual operating budget for the Council of Bishops, including the office of the secretary of the Council of Bishops; (4) guidelines governing the payment of bishops' travel expenses, including all travel authorized by the Council of Bishops; (5) the minimum amounts to be fixed as annual pensions for the support of retired bishops and/or the method by which their annual pensions shall be determined; and (6) provisions for allowance for the surviving spouses and for the support of minor children of deceased bishops. From the facts in hand the council shall estimate the approximate total amount required annually during the ensuing quadrennium to provide for the items of episcopal support above mentioned and shall report the same to the General Conference. This amount as finally determined shall be the estimated

---

[25]*See* Judicial Council Decision 365.

episcopal budget. The administration of the Episcopal Fund budget as determined by the General Conference shall be under the direction and authority of the General Council on Finance and Administration, including annual fiscal statements and audits. Nothing in this paragraph shall preclude the Annual Conference or conferences of an episcopal area from including in their budgets amounts for an area expense fund.[26] This legislation shall become effective immediately upon adoption by the Annual Conference.

¶ **925.** The council shall estimate what percentage of the total salaries paid pastors and associate pastors by the entire Church will yield an amount equal to the estimated episcopal budget and shall make recommendations to the General Conference concerning the same for its action and determination. When such percentage has been approved by the General Conference, it shall be the basis of the annual apportionment to each Annual Conference for the Episcopal Fund. The apportionment to each Annual Conference shall be an amount equal to the approved percentage of the total cash salaries paid to the pastors and associate pastors serving charges under episcopal appointment or as local pastors in the most recent complete year as reported to the Annual Conference. This apportionment shall be distributed to the pastoral charges as the conference may determine. In every case the amount apportioned to a charge for the Episcopal Fund shall be paid in the same proportion as the charge pays its pastor.

¶ **926.** The treasurer of the General Council on Finance and Administration shall remit monthly to each effective bishop one-twelfth of the annual salary as determined by the General Conference, and office expenses as approved by the council, less such deductions or reductions from the salary or office expense allowance as each bishop may authorize. Allowances for retired bishops and for the surviving spouses and minor children of deceased bishops shall be paid in equal monthly installments.

¶ **927.** Upon receipt of a budget from the Episcopal Residence Committee, the General Council on Finance and Administration shall provide funds from the Episcopal Fund to

---

[26]*See* Judicial Council Decision 365.

share in the costs of providing an episcopal residence, the amount of such funds to be set by the council in accordance with a policy approved by the General Conference on recommendation of the council. The treasurer of the General Council on Finance and Administration shall remit monthly one-twelfth of the share approved for payment from the Episcopal Fund to the person or office designated by the Episcopal Residence Committee to receive such housing payments. (*See also* ¶ 736.)

¶ **928.** The treasurer of the council shall pay monthly the claim for the official travel of each bishop upon presentation of an itemized voucher with such supporting data as may be required by the General Council on Finance and Administration. "Official travel" of an effective bishop shall be interpreted to include: (1) all visitations to local churches and to institutions or enterprises of The United Methodist Church within the area, (2) such travel outside the area, but within the jurisdiction, as is approved by the College of Bishops, and (3) such other travel as may be consistent with guidelines approved by the General Conference as being within the meaning of "official travel." No part of the expense and no honoraria for any such visitations shall be accepted from local churches or enterprises or institutions of The United Methodist Church, such expense being a proper claim against the Episcopal Fund. Nothing in this interpretation is intended to preclude special or nonofficial engagements of a bishop, other than the oversight of the temporal and spiritual affairs of the Church, such as series of lectures in educational institutions, baccalaureate addresses, and preaching missions for several days' duration when such engagements do not interfere with official duties, nor does it preclude the acceptance of honoraria for such services.

¶ **929.** Fiscal reporting and audit procedures of each area office shall be determined according to a schedule as set forth by the council upon recommendation of the Committee on Episcopal Services.

¶ **930.** *Pensions.*—1. The pensions for the support of retired bishops elected by General, Jurisdictional, or Central Conferences and the surviving spouses and minor dependent children of such deceased bishops shall be administered by the General Council on Finance and Administration in consultation with the

General Board of Pensions and in accordance with such program and procedures as may from time to time be determined by the General Council on Finance and Administration with the approval of the General Conference. For service years beginning January 1, 1982, and thereafter, the pensions for the support of bishops elected by Jurisdictional Conferences and those of their surviving spouses and dependent children shall include the benefits provided by the Ministerial Pension Plan and the Comprehensive Protection Plan of the General Board of Pensions.

2. A bishop in active service may contribute to individual tax-sheltered annuity plans or other savings plans approved by the Council. The treasurer of the Episcopal Fund shall be authorized to withhold from such bishop's salary the amount so designated by the bishop for this purpose and make payments to the selected plan(s).

¶ **931.** Should any effective bishop in the interim of the quadrennial sessions of the Jurisdictional Conference be relieved by the College of Bishops of the jurisdiction from the performance of regular episcopal duties on account of ill health or for any other reason, the president of the said College of Bishops shall so notify the treasurer of the Episcopal Fund. Beginning ninety days after such notification, the said bishop shall receive at least the minimum regular pension allowance of a retired bishop; the amount of such benefit for which the Episcopal Fund is responsible shall be reduced by the amount of any disability benefit payable from the Comprehensive Protection Plan of the General Board of Pensions. Such pension allowance shall continue until the regular duties of an effective bishop are resumed or until the bishop's status shall have been determined by the Jurisdictional Conference. Assignment of another bishop or bishops to perform the regular episcopal duties of a bishop so disabled or otherwise incapacitated, for a period of sixty days or more, shall be interpreted as a release of the said bishop from the performance of regular episcopal duties. This legislation is to be effective at the close of the 1988 General Conference.

¶ **932.** Should any retired bishop, in the interim of the quadrennial sessions of the Jurisdictional Conference, be called into active service and assigned to active episcopal duty (¶ 507.3), that bishop shall be entitled to remuneration for such service. The Episcopal Fund shall be responsible for the difference between the pension of the retired bishop and the remuneration of an active bishop as set by General Conference. In the event of such assignment of a retired bishop to active episcopal duty, the president or secretary of the Council of Bishops shall notify the treasurer of the Episcopal Fund. The treasurer of the Episcopal Fund shall make remittance accordingly.

Section III. The General Council on Ministries.

¶ **1001.** *Name.*—There shall be a **General Council on Ministries** of The United Methodist Church, hereinafter called the council.

¶ **1002.** *Incorporation.*—The council shall be incorporated in such state or states as the General Council on Ministries shall determine. This corporation shall be the successor corporation and organization to the Program Council of The United Methodist Church.

¶ **1003.** *Amenability.*—The council shall report to and be amenable to the General Conference.

¶ **1004.** *Purpose.*—The purpose of the council, as a part of the total mission of the Church, is to facilitate the Church's program life as determined by the General Conference. The council's task is to encourage, coordinate, and support the general agencies as they serve on behalf of the denomination.

¶ **1005.** *Objectives.*—The objectives of the General Council on Ministries are:

1. To study missional needs and propose priorities of the general church; and, when necessary, adjust emphases between sessions of the General Conference.

2. To establish the processes and relationships pertaining to the coordination and funding of the ministries and program emphases of the denomination through its general agencies and to minimize unnecessary overlapping or conflicting approaches to the local church and the Annual Conferences.

3. To enhance the effectiveness of our total ministries by reviewing and evaluating the performance of the general

program agencies and their responsiveness to the needs of the local churches and Annual Conferences.

4. To facilitate informed decision making at all levels of the church by engaging in research and planning in cooperation with the general agencies and the Annual Conferences.

¶ **1006.** *Responsibilities.*—The responsibilities of the council shall include, but not be limited to, the following:

1. Upon a two-thirds vote of the members of the General Council on Ministries present and voting, and upon a two-thirds vote of the Council of Bishops present and voting, to make changes in missional priorities or special programs necessitated by emergencies or by other significant developments between General Conferences which substantially affect the life of the Church, and to make adjustments in program budget allocations accordingly; *provided* that such adjustments are made within the total budget set by the previous General Conference; and *provided,* further, that such adjustments are made after consultation with the affected boards and agencies and approval by a two-thirds vote of the General Council on Finance and Administration.

2. To take the following actions, in sequence, with respect to recommendations to the General Council on Finance and Administration for the allocation of World Service funds to general program agencies:

a) The General Council on Ministries shall, in consultation with the General Council on Finance and Administration and the general program agencies, develop recommendations to the General Council on Finance and Administration on needs of the general program agencies for the programs, missional priorities, and special programs.

b) The General Council on Ministries shall receive the recommendation the General Council on Finance and Administration proposes to make to the General Conference as to that portion of the total World Service budget to be available for distribution among the general program agencies.

c) The General Council on Ministries, after reviewing both the program priorities and the total funds available to the general program agencies, shall recommend to the General Council on Finance and Administration the amount of the annual World

Service allocation to each of those agencies, within the total sum proposed by the General Council on Finance and Administration for distribution among such agencies.

d) Only when the General Council on Ministries and the General Council on Finance and Administration agree on the allocations to several general agencies shall these allocations be included in the World Service budget to be recommended to the General Conference by the General Council on Finance and Administration.

e) Before the beginning of each year the General Council on Finance and Administration shall determine and communicate to the General Council on Ministries the sum available at that time from World Service contingency funds to meet requests for additional funding from the general program agencies. The General Council on Ministries shall be authorized to approve allocations to the general program agencies for such additional program funding up to the limit so established. No money shall be allocated by the General Council on Ministries from this source for general administrative costs, fixed charges, or capital outlay without approval by the General Council on Finance and Administration.

f) The General Council on Ministries shall receive from the General Council on Finance and Administration copies of the proposed annual budgets of the general program agencies, in order that it may review such budgets in relation to the program proposals made by those agencies in their quadrennial budget requests.

3. To designate, in cooperation with the General Council on Finance and Administration, the general agency to undertake a special study ordered by the General Conference when the conference fails to make such a designation.

4. To assign responsibilities for implementation of themes, missional priorities, and/or special programs initiated between sessions of the General Conference to the general program agencies or to special task forces created by the General Council on Ministries.

5. To assure the development of a unified and coordinated program for promoting of the connectional ministries of the Church by:

a) Approving the scheduling and timing of all national conferences, convocations, and/or major consultations, subject to the approval of the General Council on Finance and Administration of plans for financing such meetings;

b) Maintaining a calendar of meetings on behalf of all agencies of The United Methodist Church as an aid to the agencies in regulating the number and the timing of such meetings;

c) Reviewing all plans of the general program agencies for the production, distribution, and timing of the release of free literature and promotional resource materials (except church school literature), avoiding duplication of both materials and activities.

6. To recommend to the General Conference, after consultation with the Council of Bishops, the number and timing of special days which are to be observed on a churchwide basis; *provided* that the General Council on Finance and Administration shall make recommendations to the General Conference as set forth in ¶ 906.11 regarding the special days to be observed with offering; and *provided* further, that the Council of Bishops and the General Council on Finance and Administration may authorize a special financial appeal in an emergency.

7. To relate to Annual Conferences, their Councils on Ministries, or other corresponding structures:

a) To provide resources for them related to their basic tasks;

b) To enhance two-way communication with them;

c) To assist the conference councils in developing comprehensive approaches to planning, research, evaluation, and coordination; and

d) To inform conference councils of significant issues identified through the monitoring of trends in society and the Church.

8. To consider the plans of any general program agency to publish a new periodical (except church school literature). Any general program agency proposing to publish such a new periodical shall submit its request to the council. If the council disapproves, the agency shall delay such publication until the proposal can be submitted to the General Conference for determination.

9. To consult with the general program agencies, the General Commission on Communication, and the president and publisher of The United Methodist Publishing House with regard to their publishing and communication policies in order to avoid unnecessary overlapping and duplication.

10. To resolve any overlapping in structure or functions or lack of cooperation among the general program agencies by:

a) coordinating interagency programs where two or more general program agencies are involved, unless otherwise specified by the General Conference;

b) approving the creation of any ongoing interagency committee or task force;

c) receiving reports and recommendations from such committees or task forces; and

d) appointing, when appropriate, observers to attend the meetings of any interagency group, including those that are part of the structure of program agencies.

11. To study the connectional structures of The United Methodist Church and, after consultation with the general agencies, recommend to the General Conference such legislative changes as may be appropriate to effect desirable modifications of existing connectional structures. Any such proposed legislative changes that would affect general fund budget allocations shall be studied in connection with the General Council on Finance and Administration and shall be recommended to the General Conference by these two councils acting in concert.

12. To provide for the training of the Annual Conference Council on Ministries directors and to provide jointly with the Division of Ordained Ministry of the General Board of Higher Education and Ministry and the Council of Bishops the training of district superintendents.

13. To review and evaluate the effectiveness of the general program agencies in fulfilling the ministries assigned to them (*see* ¶ 802.3).

14. To keep under review the concurrence of general program agencies with the Social Principles (¶¶ 70-76) of The United Methodist Church.

15. The general secretary of each general program agency that is accountable to the General Council on Ministries shall be

elected annually by ballot of the General Council on Ministries upon the nomination of the agency involved. Any general secretary of a general program agency who has not been elected by the General Council on Ministries shall not serve in such capacity beyond the end of that calendar year. Each program agency shall elect annually by ballot its deputy and associate general secretary(ies) and may elect or appoint such other staff as may be necessary.[27]

16. To give leadership to and participate in planning and research for The United Methodist Church, thereby helping all levels of the Church to evaluate needs, set goals, and plan strategy; to coordinate planning and research for the denomination in cooperation with the general program agencies of The United Methodist Church; and maintain a list of research and planning documents received from the general program agencies and the Annual Conferences.

17. To determine the need for and to develop and implement plans for themes, missional priorities, and/or special programs for the ministry of the Church for any particular quadrennium and, after consultation with the Council of Bishops, to recommend them to the General Conference for consideration.

18. To devise and implement measures to assure full, effective representation and participation of Central Conference members in the work of The United Methodist Church.

19. To report to the General Conference for its approval a summary of all decisions and recommendations made dealing with program changes and structure overlap.

20. To review, with the program agencies, all valid resolutions and positions adopted by the General Conference, and recommend to the General Conference the removal of time-dated materials.

21. To receive reports from and refer matters to the General Commission on Christian Unity and Interreligious Concerns on the participation of The United Methodist Church in the various aspects of ecumenism.

---

[27]*See* Judicial Council Decisions 499, 567.

22. To organize the Advance Committee which shall have general oversight of the Advance program.

23. To organize the World Service Special Gifts Committee which shall have general oversight of the World Service Special gifts program.

24. To relate to and cooperate with the National Association of Conference Council Directors.

25. To act in concert with the General Council on Finance and Administration to establish a procedure for making a quadrennial review, initiating proposals, and/or responding to proposals by the general agencies regarding the location of headquarters and staff and report the same to the General Conference. (*See* ¶ 907.2.)

¶ **1007.** *Organization.*—1. *Membership.*—*a)* The membership of the council shall consist of:

(1) One member from each Annual Conference and Missionary Conference within the United States and Puerto Rico elected by the Jurisdictional Conference from a list of nominees submitted by each Annual Conference and each Missionary Conference which shall include at least one laywoman, one layman, and one from the clergy, with special attention to the inclusion of clergywomen. The nominations from the Annual Conference shall be made from the General Conference delegates. If there is not an adequate number of persons from the nominees, additional nominees may be selected from the jurisdictional delegates, and if additional nominees are further required, they may be selected from the membership of the Annual Conference. The above members shall consist, so far as possible, of one-third laywomen, one-third laymen, and one-third clergy.

(2) A bishop from each jurisdiction and one bishop from the Central Conferences selected by the Council of Bishops (*see* ¶ 810.10);

(3) One youth from each jurisdiction under the age of eighteen at the time of their election nominated by the Jurisdictional Youth Ministry Organization and elected by the Jurisdictional Conference;

(4) One young adult under age thirty at the time of their election from each jurisdiction elected by the Jurisdictional Conference;

(5) One nonstaff representative or alternate selected by each of the general program agencies;

(6) Fifteen additional members to be elected by the council;

(7) Three persons from Central Conferences, one clergy, one laywoman, one layman, and one alternate for each (who may attend if the elected member for whom he/she is the alternate cannot attend) nominated by the Council of Bishops and elected by the General Council on Ministries;

(8) The general secretaries who serve as the chief executive officers of the general program agencies; the publisher and a representative of the General Board of Publication; the general secretary and a representative of the General Commission on Archives and History; the general secretary and a representative of the General Commission on Communication; and the director of the Advance shall be members with voice but without vote.[28]

b) Members of the council representing Annual Conferences, members at large, and bishops, except the bishop from the Western Jurisdiction, shall not serve on any boards or commissions or the divisions thereof having representation on the General Council on Ministries.

c) Of the additional members elected by the council, in order to ensure that one-fourth of the council's membership may represent racial and ethnic groups, it is recommended that there shall be not less than two representatives from each of the following groups: Asian Americans, Black Americans, Hispanic Americans, and Native Americans. (The council shall receive nominations from the racial and ethnic caucuses and ethnic Annual Conferences of these respective groups prior to the report of their nominating committee.) Insofar as possible, these additional members should be one-third laywomen, one-third laymen, and one-third clergy, with special attention to the inclusion of at least one clergywoman from each jurisdiction.

d) In order to ensure representation of older adults, it is recommended that at least one clergy member, one layman member, and one laywoman member be over sixty-five years of age.

e) It is recommended that each Jurisdictional Conference

---

[28]*See* Judicial Council Decision 423.

give consideration to electing to membership on the council at least one-third of the same persons elected to the council by the preceding Jurisdictional Conference.

f) When the committee selected to nominate the additional members of the General Council on Ministries meets prior to the organizational meeting, it shall determine the number of persons nominated by the Annual Conference and elected by the Jurisdictional Conference who were members of the council the previous quadrennium. If the number is less than twenty, the Nominating Committee shall nominate enough persons from the eligible membership of the council in the previous quadrennium to bring this number to twenty. These persons shall be in addition to the fifteen additional members.

g) The members of the council shall serve for four years or until the convening of the organizational meeting. No voting member shall be eligible to serve for more than two consecutive four-year terms.

h) If a bishop is unable to attend a meeting of the council, that bishop may designate an alternate bishop from the same jurisdiction.

2. *Meetings.*—Before the end of the calendar year in which regular sessions of the Jurisdictional Conferences are held, all persons who have been elected to membership on the council, including additional members nominated, shall be convened by an active bishop designated by the president of the Council of Bishops for the purpose of organizing.

The council shall meet at least once during each calendar year. It may meet in special session or at other times upon the call of the president or upon the written request of one-fifth of its members.

3. *Officers.*—The council shall have a president, one or more vice-presidents, a recording secretary, and a treasurer elected from the membership of the council. The president of the council shall be its presiding officer. Officers shall be elected for terms of four years and shall continue until their successors are duly elected.

4. *Internal Structure.*—The council shall determine its internal structure as it deems necessary for the performance of its duties.

5. *Advance Committee.*—There shall be an **Advance Committee,** which shall have general oversight of the Advance for Christ and His Church. It shall be organized under the authority and direction of the General Council on Ministries. It shall consist of twenty members of the General Council on Ministries.

a) Director of Advance.—(1) There shall be a **Director of the Advance,** nominated by the Advance Committee from the staff of one of the participating agencies and elected by the General Council on Ministries. The participating agencies are National and World Divisions and United Methodist Committee on Relief and Mission Education and Cultivation Departments of the General Board of Global Ministries; Division of Program and Benevolence Interpretation of the General Commission on Communication; General Council on Ministries; and the General Council on Finance and Administration.

(2) The salary and related benefits of the director shall be paid by the participating agency. Other administrative costs of the Advance shall be borne by the General Council on Ministries.

(3) While continuing as a staff member of the participating agency, the director shall be a staff member of the General Council on Ministries related to the Advance Committee.

b) Responsibilities of Director.—The responsibilities of the Director of the Advance shall be:

(1) To coordinate the total program of the Advance, including its promotion, cultivation, and administration.

(2) To coordinate the staff work required of the participating agencies within the Advance.

(3) To report directly to the Advance Committee concerning the program and progress of the Advance.

(4) To keep a record of all general Advance special projects.

c) General Advance Special Projects.—It shall be the responsibility of the Advance Committee to determine which projects are approved to receive general Advance special gifts (¶ 914.2). The Advance fosters partnership between those who give and those who receive and affirms the right of persons to determine the priority of their own needs. Projects shall therefore be proposed by authorized persons closely related to the project and shall be recommended to the Advance Committee by the administering agency. The Advance Committee may consider and approve proposals for either specific projects or broadly designated causes, such as a type of work, a country, a region, or an administrative unit.

d) Administering Agencies.—Agencies authorized to recommend projects and receive and administer funds for general Advance special projects shall be the World and National Divisions and United Methodist Committee on Relief Department of the General Board of Global Ministries, and such other agencies as are designated by the General Council on Ministries. The administering agencies shall report annually to the Advance Committee on the financial progress of projects and assist in providing programmatic information as requested.

No project within the boundaries of an Annual Conference shall be approved by the Advance Committee for promotion, cultivation, and administration as a mission Advance Special without consultation with the Annual Conference Council on Ministries and the board or agency delegated responsibility for missions by the Annual Conference.

6. *World Service Special Gifts Committee.*—*a)* There shall be a **World Service Special Gifts Committee** within the council to give administrative oversight to the World Service Special gifts program, including establishing the procedure and criteria for approving specific projects, providing for staff administration of the program, and assuring program accountability to the council by the administering agencies. The council shall make provisions for the General Council on Finance and Administration and administering agencies to have representation with voice but not vote. Any costs related to such representation shall be borne by the respective agencies.

b) In the World Service Special gifts program, it shall be the responsibility of the General Council on Ministries to determine which projects are approved to receive World Service Special gifts (¶ 913) under guidelines approved by the General Conference.

(1) All general boards and commissions except those units of general agencies authorized to receive general Advance special gifts are authorized to recommend World Service Special gift projects for approval by the council, provided the project is specifically related to one or more of the Disciplinary functions of the recommending agency.

(2) The participating agencies shall report annually to the council on the financial progress of World Service Special gift projects and assist in providing programmatic information as requested.

(3) No World Service Special gift project within the boundaries of an Annual Conference shall be approved by the council without consultation with the director of Annual Conference Council on Ministries.

7. *Staff.*—The council shall elect annually a general secretary and associate general secretaries as needed. The elected staff shall sit with the council with voice but without vote.

Section IV. General Board of Church and Society.

¶ **1101.** *Name.*—There shall be a **General Board of Church and Society** in The United Methodist Church, as an expression of the mission of the Church.

¶ **1102.** *Purpose.*—The purpose of the board shall be to relate the gospel of Jesus Christ to the members of the Church and to the persons and structures of the communities and world in which they live. It shall seek to bring the whole of human life, including all activities, possessions, and community and world relationships, into conformity with the will of God. It shall show the members of the Church and the society that the reconciliation which God effected through Christ involves personal, social and civic righteousness.[29]

¶ **1103.** *Objectives.*—To achieve its purpose, the board shall project plans and programs that challenge the members of The United Methodist Church to work through their own local church, through ecumenical channels, and through society toward personal, social, and civic righteousness; to assist the District and Annual Conferences with needed resources in areas of such concerns; to analyze the issues which confront the person, the local community, the nation, and the world, and to encourage Christian lines of action which assist humankind to move toward a world where peace and justice are achieved.

¶ **1104.** *Responsibilities.*—Prime responsibility of the board is to seek the implementation of the Social Principles and other

---

[29]*See* Judicial Council Decision 387.

policy statements of the General Conference on Christian social concerns. Furthermore, the board and its executives shall provide forthright witness and action on those social issues that call Christians to respond as forgiven people for whom Christ died. In particular, the board shall conduct a program of research, education, and action on the wide range of issues confronting the Church consistent with the Social Principles and the policies adopted by the General Conference.

The board shall analyze long-range social trends underlying ethical values, systemic alternatives, and strategies for social change and explore alternate futures.

The board shall develop, promote, and distribute resources and conduct programs to inform, motivate, train, organize, and build networks for action toward social justice throughout society, particularly on the specific social issues prioritized by the board. Special attention shall be given to nurturing the active constituency of the board by encouraging an exchange of ideas on strategy and methodology for social change and enabling church members through conferences, districts, coalitions, and networks to identify and respond to critical social issues at the community, state and regional level.

The board will maintain a close relationship with the General Commission on Religion and Race as they both seek to coordinate the denominational support and cooperation with various movements for racial and social justice.

The board shall speak to the Church, and to the world, its convictions, interpretations, and concerns, recognizing the freedom and responsibility of all Christians to study, interpret, and act on any or all recommendations in keeping with their own Christian calling.[30]

¶ **1105.** *Incorporation.*—The General Board of Church and Society shall be a corporation existing under the laws of the District of Columbia, and shall be the legal successor and successor in trust of the corporations, boards, departments or entities, known as the General Board of Christian Social Concerns of The United Methodist Church; the Department of Christian Social Action of The Evangelical United Brethren

---

[30]*See* Judicial Council Decision 387.

Church; the Board of Christian Social Concerns of The Methodist Church; the Division of General Welfare of the General Board of Church and Society of The United Methodist Church; the Division of General Welfare of the General Board of Christian Social Concerns of The United Methodist Church; the Division of Alcohol Problems and General Welfare of the Board of Christian Social Concerns of The Methodist Church; the Division of Temperance and General Welfare of the Board of Christian Social Concerns of The Methodist Church; the Board of Temperance of The Methodist Church; the Board of Temperance, Prohibition and Public Morals of The Methodist Episcopal Church; the Board of World Peace of The Methodist Church; the Commission on World Peace of The Methodist Church; the Commission on World Peace of The Methodist Episcopal Church; the Division of World Peace of the General Board of Church and Society of The United Methodist Church; the Board of Social and Economic Relations of The Methodist Church; the Division of Human Relations of the General Board of Church and Society of The United Methodist Church.

¶ **1106.** *Organization.*—The General Board of Church and Society shall be composed according to the instructions defined for all program boards in ¶¶ 802-810 of the General Provisions.

The board, however, may decide to designate its program units as departments, and the chief staff officer of each department, a director.

¶ **1107.** *Vacancies.*—Vacancies in the board membership shall be filled by the procedure defined in ¶ 812 of the General Provisions.

¶ **1108.** *Officers.*—The board shall elect such officers as it may determine in accordance with the General Provisions (¶ 808).

¶ **1109.** *Executive Committee.*—The executive committee shall be composed of the officers of the board and such other members as the board may designate. The committee shall include representatives of racial and ethnic groups, women, age groups, and of each jurisdiction. The committee shall have the power ad interim to fill any vacancies occurring in the elected staff and to transact such business and adopt such resolutions and statements as are authorized between the meetings of the board.

It shall report all of its actions to the board promptly after each of its meetings and again for confirmation at the next meeting of the board. It shall have special responsibility for long-range planning, for reviewing and recommending program priorities to the board, and for recommending allocations of staff, budget, and program resources in accordance with such priorities. This would include long-range planning that anticipates the future needs of the board, the Church, and the society.

¶ **1110.** *Nominating Committee.*—A nominating committee of six members shall be constituted. It shall be composed of one member, clergy or lay, from each jurisdiction, chosen by board members from that jurisdiction, and one bishop chosen by the bishops who are board members. The bishop shall serve as convenor. This committee shall nominate the officers of the board.

¶ **1111.** *Meetings.*—The board shall hold an annual meeting, at a time and place to be determined by its executive committee, and such other meetings as its work may require, and shall enact suitable bylaws governing the activities of the board and its employees. A majority of the membership shall constitute a quorum.

¶ **1112.** *Financial Support.*—1. The work of the board shall be supported from the general benevolences of the Church, the amount to be determined by the General Conference following the budgeting procedures established in ¶ 906.

2. Either on behalf of its total work or on behalf of one of its programs, the board may solicit and create special funds, receive gifts and bequests, hold properties and securities in trust, and administer all its financial affairs in accordance with its own rules and provisions of the Discipline. Funds vested in any of the predecessor boards shall be conserved for the specific purposes for which such funds have been given.

¶ **1113.** *Internal Organization.*—The internal organization and the operation of the board shall be developed and conducted by the board in the manner it determines insofar as this does not conflict with other provisions of the Discipline.

¶ **1114.** *Staff.*—1. The **general secretary** shall be the chief administrative officer of the board, responsible for the coordination of the total program of the board, the supervision of staff, and for the administration of the headquarters office. The general secretary shall be an ex officio member of the executive committee, without vote, and shall sit with the board when it is in session with voice, but without vote.

2. All other staff are to be elected or appointed in a manner prescribed by the board and in keeping with the affirmative action policies of the general Church and the board.

¶ **1115.** *Headquarters.*—The headquarters location shall be determined in accordance with ¶ 907.2. A United Nations Office shall be conducted in cooperation with the Women's Division of the General Board of Global Ministries.

¶ **1116.** *Bylaws.*—The General Board of Church and Society shall provide its own bylaws, which shall not violate any provisions of the Constitution or the Discipline, and which may be amended by a two-thirds vote of the members present and voting thereon at a regular or special meeting; *provided* that notice of such amendment has previously been given to the members.

Section V. General Board of Discipleship

¶ **1201.** *Purpose.*—There shall be a **General Board of Discipleship,** the purpose of which is found within the expression of the total mission of the Church outlined in the objectives of mission. Its primary purpose shall be to assist Annual Conferences, districts, and local churches in their efforts to win persons to Jesus Christ as his disciples and to help these persons to grow in their understanding of God that they may respond in faith and love, to the end that they may know who they are and what their human situation means, increasingly identifying themselves as children of God and members of the Christian community, to live in the Spirit of God in every relationship, to fulfill their common discipleship in the world, and to abide in the Christian hope.

The board shall use its resources to enhance the meaning of membership as defined in ¶¶ 211-215 which emphasizes the importance of the identification of church membership with discipleship to Jesus Christ. The board shall work with persons and through structures, such as districts and Annual Conferences, to lead and assist local churches in becoming communities of growing Christians, celebrating and communicating the redeeming and reconciling love of God as revealed in Jesus Christ to persons of every age, racial and ethnic background, and social condition, and to advocate and encourage the development of new congregations.

The board members and staff shall seek to fulfill this purpose in theory and practice.

¶ **1202.** *Responsibilities.*—All the responsibilities assigned to the units within the board shall be considered to be the responsibilities of the board. In addition to these, the board shall have authority:

1. To coordinate and harmonize the work of its units so as to provide its services to the Church in a unified manner.

2. To review and act upon reports of the units, the committees, and their officers and staffs.

3. To assign to one or several of its units any programs adopted by the General Conference or the General Council on Ministries and assigned to the board.

4. To provide for special publications directed toward the local church age-level and family ministry coordinators, the work area chairpersons, the pastor, and the other local church officers for whom the board has primary responsibility.

5. To manage and publish *The Upper Room, alive now!,* and other devotional life publications.

6. To provide resources, guidance, and training to related district and Annual Conference agencies and their committees; to local church administrative officers; Councils on Ministries; age-level and family ministry councils; work area chairpersons for evangelism, stewardship, worship, and local church education; and work area commissions and task groups.

7. To cooperate with the various agencies of the Church in the training and nurturing of pastors and lay persons for leadership in the areas of evangelism, stewardship, worship, and local church education; in creating new congregations; and in initiating new forms of ministry.

8. To provide programs for the training of pastors, parents, teachers, officials, and others in the work of the local church and to promote these programs through various types of training events, correspondence work, and such other agencies as it may see fit to establish. It shall have authority also to promote and

conduct conferences, consultations, assemblies, and other meetings to further the work assigned to the board.

9. To develop and provide organizational, written, and consultative resources for cooperative parish ministries (*see* ¶ 206) in consultation with appropriate units of other boards and to interpret how local church programming can be enriched by participating in a cooperative ministry.

10. To develop a unified and comprehensive program and resources for leadership training to serve all age groups in the home, Church, and community.

11. To plan and administer a comprehensive youth ministry; to enable and strengthen the ministry with and to youth at all levels of the Church, including the calling together of youth and adults.

12. To provide representation in ecumenical and interdenominational agencies as they relate to the work of the board.

13. To cooperate with the General Board of Global Ministries in jointly developing and recommending architectural standards for facilities needed to house the Church's program of worship, education, and fellowship; and to cooperate in recommending training ventures to interpret these recommended standards.

14. To respond to requests and needs for ministries in other lands in consultation with the General Board of Global Ministries and other agencies.

15. To engage in research, experimentation, innovation, and the testing and evaluation of programs, resources, and methods to discover more effective ways to help persons achieve the purpose set forth in ¶ 1201. This responsibility will include authority for experimentation and research in all areas of ministry assigned to the General Board of Discipleship and will encourage cooperation with other agencies in the conduct of such research and experimentation. This research and experimentation may be assigned to appropriate units within the board.

¶ **1203.** *Incorporation.*—The General Board of Discipleship shall be a corporation existing under the laws of Tennessee, and shall be the legal successor and successor in trust of the corporations known as the General Board of Evangelism of The United Methodist Church and the General Board of Laity of

The United Methodist Church, and shall further be responsible for the performance of the functions previously conducted by the Commission on Worship of The United Methodist Church, the Division of the Local Church, and the Division of Curriculum Resources of the General Board of Education of The United Methodist Church.

The General Board of Discipleship is authorized to take such action as is appropriate under the corporation laws of Tennessee so as to accomplish the end result stated above, and under which the General Board of Discipleship shall be one legal entity.

The divisions of the General Board of Education were not incorporated separately; it is the intent, however, that responsibility for the functions delegated to the divisions by prior legislative action be transferred consistent with the separation of the divisions between the General Board of Discipleship and the General Board of Higher Education and Ministry. In the division of the assets of the General Board of Education, it is the intent that all assets be used in keeping with the original intent and purpose for which they were established or acquired, and so be assigned as appropriate to the General Boards of Discipleship and Higher Education and Ministry respectively. It is further intended that the annuities, bequests, trusts, and estates formerly held by the General Board of Education be used for the benefit and use of the General Boards of Discipleship and Higher Education and Ministry (in accord with their purposes as defined in the Discipline) respectively as their interests may appear, and that real estate titles be authorized to be conveyed as appropriate and apportioned where indicated.

In the event that the intent of the original donor of existing annuities, bequests, trusts, and estates cannot clearly be determined in relation to the interests of the two boards, such assets shall be divided equally between the two boards.

It is further intended that should additional assets accrue to the former General Board of Education by reason of annuities, bequests, trusts, and estates not now known and where the intent of the donor can be clearly ascertained, the assets shall be used in keeping with the original intent and purpose for which they were established or acquired and so be assigned as appropriate to the

General Boards of Discipleship and Higher Education and Ministry respectively.

It is further intended that should additional assets accrue to the former General Board of Education by reason of annuities, bequests, trusts, and estates not now known and where the intent of the original donor cannot be clearly determined in relation to the interests of the two boards, such assets shall be divided equally between the two boards.

The president of the board, the general secretary, and the treasurer shall have the power to execute on behalf of the board legal paper such as conveyances of real estate, releases on mortgages, transfer of securities, contracts, and all other legal documents.

¶ **1204.** *Organization.*—1. The board shall consist of the number of members as defined in ¶ 805 of the general provisions with the addition of these Central Conference persons (one of whom shall be a woman): one bishop or an alternate bishop (¶ 810.10), one clergy, and one layperson, to be elected by the Council of Bishops. In addition there shall be one layman from each jurisdiction who shall be the president of the Jurisdictional Committee of United Methodist Men or, because of the inability of the president to serve, another elected by and from the Jurisdictional Committee on United Methodist Men (¶ 635). It shall be organized to accomplish its work through elected officers as prescribed in ¶ 808.

2. The board may elect an executive committee and establish such rules as necessary for the carrying out of its duties.

3. The board shall determine and establish the appropriate organization of the board and its staff, and may create or discontinue as deemed necessary, divisions, sections, committees, task forces, and consultations to carry out the regular or special duties of the board.

4. The board shall provide such bylaws as necessary to facilitate the work of the board, which shall not violate any provisions of the Discipline and which may be amended by a two-thirds vote of the members present and voting thereon at a regular or special meeting; provided that written notice to such amendment has been given to the members and the vote thereon shall be delayed at least one day.

5. Adequate provisions shall be made in its organizational structure for all responsibilities assigned to the board. These organizational units shall be amenable to and report regularly to the board and its executive committee.

¶ **1205.** *Organizational Units.*—The organizational units shall be organized by the board so as to fulfill the objectives and the responsibilities assigned to them within the mandate of the board (*see* ¶ 1204.3). The basic organization of these units shall be as follows:

1. *Membership.*—The units shall be composed of board members as provided in ¶ 805. In order to provide for unit members with special knowledge and experience, the board shall have authority to elect members at large to the units on nomination of the units and in accord with ¶ 805.

2. *Meetings.*—The units shall meet in conjunction with the meetings of the board. Special meetings may be called in a manner prescribed by the board. Presence of one-third of the members of a unit shall constitute a quorum.

3. *Officers.*—Each unit shall have a chairperson, elected by the board; such vice-chairpersons as necessary; and a recording secretary, elected by the unit.

4. *Executive Committee.*—Each unit may elect an executive committee and establish such rules as necessary for the carrying out of its duties.

5. *Unit Staff.*—The administrative officer of each unit shall be elected by the board and shall sit with the unit and all its regular committees. In all of these relationships he/she shall have the right of the floor without the power to vote. All other staff persons are to be elected or appointed in a manner prescribed by the board (¶ 814).

¶ **1206.** *Financial Support.*—1. The financial support of the board shall be determined as follows: the General Conference shall determine and provide the budget for the board in accord with procedures defined in ¶ 906.

2. The board shall have authority to receive and administer funds, gifts, or bequests that may be committed to it for any portion of its work and to solicit, establish, and administer any special funds that may be found necessary for the carrying out of its plans and policies in accordance with ¶ 911.3. In the

investment of any funds, the board shall adhere to the specific investment guidelines adopted by the General Conference.

3. No funds, property, and other investments either now in hand or hereafter accumulated by *The Upper Room* or other devotional and related literature hereafter produced by The Upper Room shall be used for the support of other features of the board's work, but all funds from the sale of such publications shall be conserved by the board for the purpose of preparing and circulating such literature and cultivating the devotional life; *provided,* however, that this shall not prevent the setting up of a reserve fund out of such income as a protection against unforeseen emergencies.

4. When special missions are conducted or special projects are undertaken by the board, offerings and contributions may be received toward defraying expenses.

5. In the discharge of its responsibility for Christian education in The United Methodist Church, the board may establish, and provide for participation by church school groups in a fund (or funds) for missions and Christian education in the United States and overseas. Plans for the allocation of, administration of, and education for this fund(s) shall be developed cooperatively by such means as the board shall determine in consultation with the General Board of Global Ministries.

EDUCATION

¶ **1207.** 1. The board shall have general oversight of the educational interests of the Church as directed by the General Conference. The board shall be responsible for the development of a clear statement of the biblical and theological foundations of Christian education, consistent with the doctrines of The United Methodist Church and the purpose of the board. The board shall devote itself to studying, supervising, strengthening, researching, evaluating, and extending the educational ministry of the Church. The board shall be responsible for the educational program which is carried on through the structure adopted for the local church.

2. The total Christian educational program of The United Methodist Church for use in local churches shall be developed by

the board. The educational program shall seek to encourage persons to commit themselves to Christ and membership in his Church; to learn about and participate in the Christian faith and life, including study of the Bible, and to develop skills which enable them to become effectively involved in the ministry of God's people in the world. It shall include the educational emphases and activities of all the general departments and interests of the denomination, such as evangelism, stewardship, missions, Christian social action, and Bible instruction. It shall be developed as a comprehensive, unified, and coordinated Christian education program for children, youth, adults, and families in local churches. It shall be promoted and administered by the board in cooperation with those agencies responsible for Christian education in jurisdictions, Annual Conferences, districts, and local churches. It shall give careful consideration to the needs of all churches, such as small and larger churches, rural and urban settings, ethnic populations.

3. The educational ministry in local churches shall provide for study, worship, fellowship, and service, including social action, recreational, evangelistic, stewardship, and missionary activities as education in the Christian way of life.

¶ **1208.** *Education Responsibilities.*—The board shall organize as may be necessary for carrying on the educational ministry throughout the whole life-span of persons. The board shall be responsible for the following:

1. Formulating and interpreting the educational philosophy and approach which shall undergird and give coherence to all the educational work of the Church; the church school and related activities; individual or group study; fellowship and action groups for children, youth, and adults (including the United Methodist Youth Fellowship); related educational programs provided by civic youth-serving agencies; week-day nurseries and kindergartens; day care centers; choirs, drama groups, mission studies; preparation for confirmation; education for leisure; outdoor education; camping; education of the mentally retarded and others of special need; special Bible study groups; human relations workshops; training in church membership responsibilities; continuing education for adults and educational ministries with older adults.

2. Developing, resourcing, and supporting flexible systems of organization and administration to provide for the Church's educational ministries with children, youth, adults, and families at the local, district, and conference levels with the cooperation of other agencies.

Developing educational approaches in a variety of settings which appeal to persons with different life-styles and theological perspectives and which will enable persons of different racial, ethnic, and cultural groups to appropriate the gospel for their own life situations.

Providing guidance for local churches to promote participation through membership and attendance among children, youth, and adults in a wide variety of settings.

Providing guidance for local churches in organizing church schools for the study of the Bible and Christian tradition, beliefs, and values (*see* ¶ 263.1).

Developing the education ministries of the Church in keeping with the levels of faith development, learning capacities, and needs of persons and providing field and support services for leaders, teachers, and others responsible for the education of persons across the life-span.

3. Initiating programs of teacher recruitment, development, training, and retraining in biblical, theological, and ethical thinking, as well as in procedures and methods.

Providing guidance and training for volunteer workers recruited for Christian service.

Offering training courses and other aids needed for vocational guidance.

Providing programs for the training of pastors, parents, teachers, education work area chairpersons, superintendents of the church school, division superintendents, officials, and others in educational ministries of the local church and promoting these programs through various types of training schools, correspondence work, and such other agencies as it may see fit to establish.

Designing, guiding, resourcing, and conducting leadership development enterprises specifically for teachers and educational leaders at all levels including district and conference, and such other leaders as may be assigned.

Working with the colleges and seminaries of the Church

wherever possible to forward the common interest in the training of professional Christian educators and the training of ministerial students in local church Christian education.

Providing programs of Christian education outdoors and camping through the training of Annual Conference camp directors, district camp directors, camp committee persons, director/managers and managers of sites. Provide national camp training events and assist jurisdictions and Annual Conferences in designing, guiding, and resourcing camp training programs.

4. Providing guidance resources and services related to the training and work of local church directors, ordained and diaconal ministers, and associates of Christian education and educational assistants.

Providing resources, models, and training to support Annual Conferences and local churches as they help people make decisions related to their general Christian vocation as well as their specific occupations or careers. Providing resources developed by the General Board of Global Ministries and the General Board of Higher Education and Ministry to persons interested in considering professional church-related ministries.

5. Planning for and providing education in the processes and procedures by which teaching, learning, and educational communication occur; in the selection, development, and use of learning resources, media, and technology; and in the application of experimentation, innovation, and new approaches in education.

6. The board shall review and recommend for approval the curriculum plans developed in cooperation with the other boards and agencies in the Curriculum Resources Committee and shall interpret and support the curriculum developed by the committee.

7. The board shall be responsible for promoting the observance of Christian Education Sunday (¶¶ 276.1, 1906.12).

8. Only those special funds which are approved by the General Board of Discipleship may be promoted nationally in the church schools (¶ 1206.5).

¶ **1209.** *Educational Standards.*—The board shall establish and maintain standards and shall give direction to the program of Christian education in local churches, in districts, in conferences, and elsewhere as will nurture growth toward these standards.

1. The board shall set standards and provide guidance concerning programming, leadership, grouping, and grading procedures for the various educational settings of the Church.

2. The board shall establish standards for the church school, for programs of Christian education, for the functioning of educational leaders, for church school membership, for the organization and administration of the church school and for recording and reporting membership and attendance of the church school.

3. The board in cooperation with the General Board of Higher Education and Ministry, shall develop performance standards that encourage the continuing growth of local church directors, clergy, diaconal ministers, and associates of Christian education; educational assistants; and director/managers of church camping.

4. The board shall cooperate with the General Board of Higher Education and Ministry in developing standards for certifying professional ministry careers as provided in ¶ 1526.2.

5. The board shall develop standards governing all types of camping in regard to physical facilities, program, and leadership. To the extent possible, all camps shall be accessible to persons with handicapping conditions.

6. The board shall develop educational standards and provide guidance for local churches in equipment, arrangement, and design for church school buildings and rooms.

¶ **1210.** The board shall cooperate with other boards and agencies as follows:

1. The board shall cooperate with other general boards and agencies in the promotion of stewardship, evangelism, worship, mission education, and social action, and in the evaluation of these ministries from the perspective of sound educational procedure.

2. The board shall, in cooperation with the General Board of Higher Education and Ministry, give guidance to training which encourages the continued growth of local church directors, ordained and diaconal ministers, and associates of Christian education; educational assistants; director/managers of camping; and directors and ministers of music. Particular

emphasis will be given to ministry to persons with handicapping conditions.

3. The board shall be responsible for developing a unified program of mission education for all age groups in the local church and for developing aids for use in colleges, universities, and schools of theology. The board shall cooperate with the General Board of Global Ministries in the interest of effective mission education. The mission education program shall include provisions for the following:

a) Linking emerging philosophies of mission and of education through information flow and cooperative work of the respective staffs and boards;

b) Developing and interpreting varied styles of mission education appropriate to different groups, including age groupings and the various racial and ethnic cultures;

c) Curriculum planning for education in mission, providing mission information about projects supported by The United Methodist Church (including ecumenical projects) through the church school resources, and preparing curricular and other materials for mission education;

d) Participating with various agencies in the design, development, and promotion of ecumenical mission education resources;

e) Developing and interpreting educational approaches and channels for mission giving of children, youth, and adults, such as the Children's Fund for Christian Mission;

f) Developing and interpreting models for new approaches to mission study and educational participation in mission, including travel and study seminars;

g) Certifying leaders for schools of mission through developing educational criteria;

h) Disseminating a comprehensive listing of mission resources for leaders.

4. The board shall have authority to cooperate with the jurisdictional, Annual Conference, district, and local church agencies responsible for education, with other agencies of the Church, and with ecumenical agencies in cooperative enterprises to further the cause of Christian education.

5. The board is authorized to cooperate with the Christian Educators Fellowship of The United Methodist Church in such

ways as will develop and strengthen the educational ministries of the Church.

6. The board is authorized to cooperate with the General Board of Global Ministries in the planning and execution of programs for the strengthening and development of the town and country, urban, and ethnic local church ministries of The United Methodist Church and of interdenominational cooperation in these fields.

¶ **1211.** *Church School Extension.*—1. The board shall be authorized to project and promote plans for church school extension throughout the Church and to cooperate in the strengthening of the Church through Christian education inclusive of the three following ways: *a)* sponsoring new United Methodist church schools; *b)* starting new church school classes; *c)* expanding teacher/learning opportunities in the congregation and community.

2. The board shall have the responsibility to develop, in cooperation with jurisdictional agencies responsible for education, a general program and plan to further within the Annual Conferences all the interests of the Christian education within the purview of the board.

EVANGELISM

¶ **1212.** 1. The board shall have general oversight of the evangelism ministries of the Church as directed by the General Conference. The Christian evangelism program of The United Methodist Church shall be developed by the board.

2. The board shall share the blessing of the gospel of the Lord Jesus Christ with all persons by the development, promotion, and support of all phases of evangelism throughout The United Methodist Church worldwide.

3. The local congregation in its ministry of evangelism seeks to reach out to persons with the good news of Jesus Christ, to invite and receive them into the fellowship of the Church, to help them be related to God, to grow in faith, and to send persons out to witness and live as Christian disciples.

¶ **1213.** *Evangelism Responsibilities.*—1. To set forth an adequate biblical and theological basis and understanding for the personal, corporate, and social aspects of evangelism, consistent with the doctrine and tradition of The United Methodist Church, and to communicate and interpret the same to the membership of the Church.

2. To give particular emphasis to the promotion and interpretation of comprehensive and practical ministries and programs of evangelism at the conference, district, and local church levels, so that persons who are not active Christian disciples through any local church will be cared for and invited by a United Methodist church.

3. To give guidance to the Church in using leisure time and the appropriate days and seasons of the Christian calendar for special evangelistic emphasis as a part of the ongoing ministries of evangelism.

4. To provide training and resources for strategies, ministries, and programs in evangelism, including resources for the local church work areas on evangelism (¶ 261.4) and related committees and task forces.

5. To cooperate with other program agencies of the Church in supporting and equipping both clergy and laity at all levels in involvement in evangelism, church growth, and new congregational development.

6. To provide and encourage research in what creative congregations are doing in effective evangelism that can serve as models for other churches, and to foster experimentation and demonstration of additional evangelistic approaches, consistent with the nature of the Christian gospel and the Church, at all levels of the Church's life including new congregations and all racial and cultural groups.

7. To provide resources and services for those serving as pastors and directors of evangelism in local churches, and associate and assistant pastors and directors of evangelism.

8. To cooperate with the General Board of Higher Education and Ministry (¶ 1526.2) to set minimal standards for elders desiring to serve as conference-approved evangelists. The board shall send copies of these standards quadrennially to the bishops, district superintendents, conference Boards of Discipleship and conference evangelists. An elder who feels called of God to be a conference-approved evangelist should prepare definitely

for such service under the guidance of the Annual Conference to which the person belongs.

9. To maintain and service the General Military Roll for The United Methodist Church and to work in cooperation with the General Board of Higher Education and Ministry so that United Methodist chaplains may be aware of and informed concerning all forms and phases of evangelism.

10. To relate and provide liaison services to denominational and ecumenical associations and fellowships of evangelism.

11. To seek mutual cooperation among and with the seminaries of the Church and the General Board of Higher Education and Ministry in the training and nurturing of persons for ministry and in continuing education where the responsibilities intersect.

12. To communicate with other agencies in whose programs the subject matter of evangelism would be included, and to provide counsel, guidance, and resources for the implementation of such programs.

13. To participate in and cooperate with the work of the Curriculum Resources Committee of the board for the inclusion of evangelism concepts and resources in local church study curriculum.

14. To provide, as needed, consultation with conference, district leaders, local congregations, and other agencies to develop strategies in evangelism for church growth and new congregational development.

15. To work with the General Board of Global Ministries for the extension of the Church. To this end there shall be a **Joint Committee on Congregational Development** with equal representation of members from the General Board of Discipleship and the General Board of Global Ministries which shall meet at least annually to expedite cooperation between these two boards in the field of congregational development of both new congregations as well as the revitalization of existing congregations.

WORSHIP

¶ **1214.** *Worship Responsibilities.*—1. To cultivate the fullest possible meaning in the corporate worship celebrations of the

Church, including liturgy, preaching, the Sacraments, music, and related arts. The Section on Worship shall encourage observance of the seasons of the Christian year.

2. To develop standards and resources for the conduct of public worship in the churches, including liturgy, preaching, the Sacraments, music, and related arts.

3. To make recommendations to the General Conference regarding future editions of the book of worship and the hymnal and, as ordered, to provide editorial supervision of the contents of these publications, which shall be published by The United Methodist Publishing House. The hymnal of The United Methodist Church is The United Methodist Hymnal. The Ritual of the Church is that contained in the Book of Ritual of The Evangelical United Brethren Church, 1959, "The General Services of the Church" in The Book of Worship for Church and Home of The Methodist Church, The Ordinal 1981, and "The General Services of the Church 1984" (English and Spanish versions).

4. To prepare revisions of the Ritual of the Church and approved orders of worship for recommendation to the General Conference for adoption.

5. To work with other North American Christian denominations through the Consultation on Common Texts in the continuing development of a Common Calendar and Lectionary and to encourage the voluntary use of the Common Lectionary and of resources based upon it.

6. To prepare and sponsor the publication of supplemental orders and texts of worship.[31]

7. To maintain a cooperative but not exclusive relationship with The United Methodist Publishing House in the preparation and publication of worship resources.

8. To advise the general agencies of the Church in the preparation, publication, and circulation of orders of service and other liturgical materials bearing the imprint of The United Methodist Church, including racial and ethnic worship resources and other language publications, incorporating sensitivities to

---

[31]*See* Judicial Council Decision 445.

language which embodies paragraph 4 (Article IV) of the Constitution of The United Methodist Church and serves the needs of the several constituencies of the Church.

9. To counsel with the editors of the periodicals and publications of The United Methodist Church concerning material offered in the fields of worship, including preaching, music, and the other liturgical arts.

10. To participate in and cooperate with the Curriculum Resources Committee of the board for the inclusion of worship concepts and resources in local church study curriculum.

11. To encourage in the schools of theology and pastors' schools and other settings, the offering of instruction in the meaning and conduct of worship. This should include the worship practices and expressions of the various racial cultures.

12. To counsel with those responsible for planning and conducting the worship services of the General Conference and other general assemblies of the Church.

13. To develop, in cooperation with the General Board of Higher Education and Ministry, performance standards that encourage the continuing growth of local church directors, ordained ministers, and associates of music; music assistants; and others in the local church related to music and the other arts. (*See* ¶¶ 1209.4, 1505.7, 1526.2.)

14. To cooperate with the Fellowship of United Methodists in Worship, Music, and Other Arts and The Order of St. Luke in affirming the sacramental life embracing liturgy, preaching, music, and other arts appropriate for the inclusive worship life of the Church.

15. To give guidance to, and develop performance standards for, directors and ministers of music, in cooperation with the General Board of Higher Education and Ministry, and to cooperate with the General Board of Higher Education and Ministry in their certification of directors and ministers of music as provided in ¶ 1526.2.

STEWARDSHIP

¶ **1215.** *Stewardship Responsibilities.*—1. To interpret the biblical and theological basis for stewardship consistent with the doctrines of The United Methodist Church and inform the Church of the same through educational channels and study materials.

2. To develop and promote programs, resources, and training materials in such basic subject areas of stewardship as stewardship education, proportionate giving and tithing, funding, planned giving, financial planning, time and ability, economics and management, and life-style.

3. To participate in and cooperate with the work of the Curriculum Resources Committee of the board for inclusion of stewardship concepts and resources in local church school curriculum.

4. To provide education, counsel, resourcing, and training for the local church stewardship work area chairperson, Commission on Stewardship, Board of Trustees, Committee on Finance, Committee on Finance chairperson, financial secretaries, and treasurers and to develop program resources and training materials for use with and by the above-named persons and/or groups (*see* ¶ 907.11). Matters relating to procedures involving official records, forms, and reporting of finances shall be the responsibility of the General Council on Finance and Administration.

5. To develop strategies, provide resources, and implement actions that lead to a continuing improvement in the level of giving of United Methodists in providing adequate support for the mission of the Church.

6. To encourage United Methodists to provide for their continued participation in World Service, or in one or more of the World Service agencies, in Annual Conference, district, and local church programs, and in other humanitarian causes, through current and planned giving, special gifts, estate planning, wills, and United Methodist foundations.

7. To counsel in the area of stewardship and finance with jurisdictional and Annual Conference program agencies relative to their organizational structure and program responsibilities and assist them in their interpretation of program and resources.

8. To develop and promote sound methods to aid local churches, districts, Annual Conferences, areas, and their related

institutions to raise funds for benevolent causes, current expenses, and capital needs. When projects of this nature are extended a fee may be negotiated.

9. To develop programs and materials to assist in securing adequate financial support for all United Methodist ordained ministers and church-related employees.

10. To create within The United Methodist Church a renewal of personal and corporate Christian stewardship which includes the use and sharing of wealth, resources, and the practice of a Christian life-style.

11. To furnish counsel and guidance to associations such as the National Association of United Methodist Foundations and the National Association of Stewardship Leaders.

12. To furnish counsel and resources to conference and area foundations as they fulfill their stewardship functions.

13. To communicate and work cooperatively with the general agencies whose programs include the subject matter of stewardship, and any interagency groups.

14. To cooperate with the National Division of the General Board of Global Ministries in the development, planning, and utilization of stewardship principles, guidelines, strategies, and resources for fundraising programs to assist local churches, Annual Conferences, and denominational institutions to obtain funds necessary for their continuing viability in mission. (*See* ¶ 1414.14.)

¶ **1216.** *Devotional Life Responsibilities.*—1. To interpret and communicate the biblical and theological basis for the devotional life which takes seriously both personal and corporate worship and Christian involvement in the world.

2. To develop literature and programs for the cultivation of the devotional life.

3. To maintain and extend the worldwide ministry of *Upper Room* and other publications, including other language editions, with continuing focus upon our ecumenical stance.

4. To cooperate with all other units within the board and other groups within United Methodism, as well as other denominations whose programs are related to the devotional life.

MINISTRY OF THE LAITY

¶ 1217. The board shall interpret and spread through the Church all the rich meanings of the universal priesthood of believers, of Christian vocation, and of the ministry of the laity.

The United Methodist Church has the responsibility of training and enabling the *laos*—the whole body of its membership—to enter into mission and to minister and witness in the name of Jesus Christ, the Head of the Church. Although all units of the Church have some responsibility for this imperative, the General Board of Discipleship has a preeminent responsibility in that it is charged with developing discipleship.

¶ 1218. *Leadership and Ministry Development.*—1. To help develop an adequate understanding of the theological and biblical basis for lay life and work.

2. To develop and interpret ministry of the laity both within and without the institutional Church.

3. To provide resources, support services, and designs for the development and improvement of leaders in the local church, except as specifically delegated to other agencies, and especially those who serve as members of Charge Conferences, Administrative Councils, Administrative Boards, Councils on Ministries, Committees on Pastor-Parish Relations, Personnel Committees, Committees on Nominations and Personnel, and those who serve as lay leaders and lay members of Annual Conferences.

4. To provide consultative services in organizational development and management skills for leadership development committees and other organizations in jurisdictions, conferences, and districts.

5. To provide resources and suggested plans for the observance of Laity Day in the local church.

6. To provide resources and support services for the lay speaker program, including standards for the local church lay speaker and certified lay speaker and designs and resources for use by Annual Conferences and districts in the training of local church lay speakers and certified lay speakers.

7. To provide support services to conference and district lay leaders and conference and district Boards of Laity or equivalent structures, the National Association of Annual Conference Lay

Leaders, and to other appropriate conference and district officers and agencies.

8. To initiate a process of coordination and collaboration in developing a comprehensive approach to leadership development and training within all program areas for which the General Board of Discipleship has responsibility.

¶ **1219.** *Age-Level and Family Ministries.*—1. To provide a coordinated and integrated approach for developing resources and support for children, youth, adults of all ages, family and singles programs.

2. To provide interpretation, resources, consultative and support services to age-level and family ministry coordinators and other leaders as they carry out their responsibilities:

a) To encourage and resource programs in local churches addressed to the differing needs and aspirations of persons in each age group and of families as centers for the formation of spiritual growth, values, and vocation consistent with Christian teaching and practice.

b) To provide in collaboration with other appropriate agencies resources, training, consultative and administrative services, and support for specialized programs in age-level and family ministries. This includes, but is not limited to, marital growth programs, parenting programs, human sexuality training programs with children, youth, adults of all ages, families and singles in settings of service and leisure; intergenerational ministries and preparation for life-long process of aging also may be included.

3. To provide liaison relationships and joint programming services with specialized interdenominational and cooperative programs in age-level and family ministries. This includes, but is not limited to, the International Christian Youth Exchange and Scouting.

¶ **1220.** *Committee on Family Life.*—1. There shall be a **Committee on Family Life** which shall be administratively related to the General Board of Discipleship.

The committee shall provide the arena for information sharing, cooperative planning, and joint program endeavors as determined in accordance with the responsibilities and objectives of the participating boards and agencies. The committee shall serve as an advocate for family life concerns with all general agencies of The United Methodist Church and in the larger society.

The responsibilities of the committee shall include the following:

a) To identify the needs and concerns of families in our complex society.

b) To survey the Church's ministry with families and to collect and disseminate information on models and programs which inform the work of all boards and agencies to strengthen, enrich, and enable family living consistent with Christian teaching and practice.

c) To encourage exploration of the biblical, theological, and experiential understandings of family living and the Church's role in ministry to and with families.

d) To advocate the development and implementation of programs, policies, and services by agencies of The United Methodist Church which are designed to impact those systems and concepts which adversely affect family life.

e) To relate and provide liaison services to interdenominational and ecumenical agencies in the area of family life, including The World Methodist Council Committee on Family Life and the Commission on Family Ministries and Human Sexuality of the National Council of the Churches of Christ in the U.S.A.

2. The committee shall consist of staff and/or member representatives from the General Board of Discipleship, General Board of Global Ministries, General Board of Church and Society, General Board of Higher Education and Ministry, the General Commission on the Status and Role of Women, and two bishops selected by the Council of Bishops. Each general agency may name at least one additional member in order to provide additional expertise and consultation. It is strongly urged that the committee be inclusive.

¶ **1221.** *Comprehensive Youth Ministry.*—1. There shall be four component parts to a comprehensive approach to development and implementation of youth ministry programming at all levels of the Church:

a) Curriculum.—Through the Curriculum Resources Committee (¶ 1223) the General Board of Discipleship shall ensure the availability of curriculum and leaders' guides for use in a variety of settings suitable for the specific needs of all persons in the 12 to 18-year-old age group.

b) Program Resources. Additional and supplemental guidebooks and other program aids shall be developed and promoted for effective youth ministry programs in the local church and at the district, conference, jurisdictional, and general church levels.

c) Leadership Training and Networking. Leadership training shall be provided to encourage and support adult workers with youth and youth leaders in their roles as teachers, counselors, advisors, and enablers at all levels of the Church. Networking shall be developed to maintain ongoing communication through workshops, special mailings, and publications between leaders in youth ministries across the denomination for the enhancement of skills and the sharing of effective models and resources.

d) Structures. Active and effective structures for youth ministry programming shall be promoted and maintained at the local church, district, conference, jurisdictional, and general church levels for the full involvement of youth in leadership and membership, and for the advocacy of youth concerns in all areas of Church life, planning, and administration.

United Methodist Men's Division

¶ **1222.** *Men's Work Responsibilities.*—1. To provide resources and support services to foster the development of units of United Methodist Men.

a) Provide specific and optional models for these organizations.

b) Receive recommendations from the National Association of Conference Presidents of United Methodist Men.

c) Promote the chartering and annual recertification of local church men's units with the General Board of Discipleship.

d) Establish models for jurisdictional, Annual Conference, and district level organizations for the purpose of carrying out the objectives as set out in ¶ 264.

e) Recognize officers of the National Association of Conference Presidents as the national officers of United Methodist Men.

2. To seek methods for involving men in a growing relationship to the Lord Jesus Christ and his Church.

a) Provide resources and support for programs of evangelism in cooperation with the area of evangelism which are geared to men's needs.

b) Provide resources and support for programs of stewardship in cooperation with the area of stewardship which will lead men to an understanding of their responsibility for stewardship, including time, talent, money, and prayer.

c) Seek resources and support for men as husbands and fathers in a rapidly changing society.

d) Continue in a constant search for new and better ways for The United Methodist Church to minister to and through men.

CURRICULUM RESOURCES COMMITTEE

¶ **1223.** There shall be a **Curriculum Resources Committee,** organized and administered by the General Board of Discipleship, which shall be responsible for constructing plans for curriculum and curriculum resources to be used in the church school. (*See* ¶ 263.1.) The plans for curriculum and curriculum resources shall be designed to help local churches carry out the Church's educational ministry with children, youth, young adults, adults, and families, and to meet the needs of various racial, ethnic, age, cultural, and language constituencies, as well as the needs of persons of various learning capacities, backgrounds, levels of psychological development, sight and hearing impairments, and Christian maturity. Plans for curriculum shall give particular attention to the characteristics and needs of small membership congregations. They shall be for use in a variety of settings, both formal and informal, including Sunday schools, fellowship groups, outdoor experiences, family life, leadership education, campus ministries, and confirmation preparation classes. The plans for curriculum and curriculum resources shall be consistent with the educational philosophy and approach formulated for the educational ministry of the Church by the General Board of Discipleship and shall reflect a unity of purpose and a planned comprehensiveness of scope. They shall be designed to support the total life and work of the Church and shall reflect the official positions of The United Methodist Church as authorized by the General Conference.

¶ **1224.** When the plans for curriculum and curriculum resources have been approved by the General Board of Discipleship, the editorial staff of Church School Publications shall be responsible for the development of curriculum resources based on the approved plans. The curriculum resources shall be based on the Bible, shall reflect the universal gospel of the living Christ, and shall be designed for use in the various settings which are defined by the board.

¶ **1225.** The Curriculum Resources Committee shall review and may approve and recommend existing or projected resources from other agencies. All curriculum resources that are approved by the General Board of Discipleship shall be authorized for use in the church school.

¶ **1226.** *Relationships.*—1. The Curriculum Resources Committee shall be related to the General Board of Discipleship as follows:

a) The committee shall be responsible to the board with respect to educational philosophy and approaches and shall seek to maintain the standards set by the board.

b) The committee shall work with the General Board of Discipleship in setting policies for interpreting and promoting the use of approved curriculum resources.

c) The chairperson of the Curriculum Resources Committee shall serve as a member of the executive committee of the General Board of Discipleship.

d) In preparation of the budget for presentation to the General Board of Publication (¶ 1736), the editor of Church School Publications shall consult with the general secretary of the General Board of Discipleship.

2. The Curriculum Resources Committee shall be related to The United Methodist Publishing House and the General Board of Publication as follows:

a) The publisher or chairperson of the General Board of Publication may sit with the General Board of Discipleship for consideration of matters pertaining to joint interests of the Curriculum Resources Committee and the General Board of Publication and shall have the privilege of the floor without vote.

b) The General Board of Publication shall publish, manufacture, and distribute, through the facilities of The United Methodist Publishing House, the curriculum resources prepared by the editorial staff of Church School Publications. The United Methodist Publishing House and the General Board of Discipleship shall be responsible jointly for interpretation and support of these resources.

c) The United Methodist Publishing House shall cooperate with the editor of Church School Publications in developing formats and types of curriculum resources, such as periodicals, books, booklets, graphics, recordings, and other audiovisual materials. The publishing house shall have final responsibility in relation to publishing and financial matters, and in these matters the editor of Church School Publications shall recommend changes in formats of publications to be produced and shall work cooperatively with the publisher in the design and layout and in handling of proofs and equivalent steps in the case of nonprinted resources.

d) The work of the Curriculum Resources Committee shall be financed by the General Board of Publication.

3. The committee shall exercise these additional relationships:

a) The committee shall cooperate with other agencies of The United Methodist Church so that their assigned concerns are reflected in and supported by the church school resources.

b) The committee may explore and implement opportunities at home and overseas for cooperative planning and publishing wherever such cooperation seems best for all concerned and when it is found to be practicable and in harmony with editorial and publishing policies.

c) The committee may cooperate with The United Methodist Publishing House and the General Board of Discipleship in educational research, in the development of experimental resources, and in the evaluation of resources that are provided for the church school.

¶ **1227.** *The Editor of Church School Publications.*—1. The **editor of Church School Publications** shall be responsible for the administration of the work of the Curriculum Resources Committee and the editorial staff of Church School Publications, the general editorial policy, and shall be responsible for final determination of editorial content of the church school publications.

2. The editor shall be elected by the General Board of Discipleship upon nomination by a joint committee composed of the president of the General Board of Discipleship, the chairperson of the Curriculum Resources Committee, one other member of the General Board of Discipleship representing educational concerns, the chairperson and two other members of the General Board of Publication. The election of the editor shall be subject to confirmation by the General Board of Publication.

3. The editor shall be responsible to the General Board of Discipleship for seeing that the content of church school publications is consistent with the educational philosophy formulated by the board.

¶ **1228.** *Membership.*—1. The Curriculum Resources Committee shall consist of twenty-one voting members elected quadrennially by the General Board of Discipleship as follows:

a) A bishop who is a voting member of the General Board of Discipleship, to be nominated by the executive committee of the board.

b) Twenty members, nominated by the executive committee of the board, of whom at least seven shall be pastors, at least three of whom shall be voting members of the board, at least one of whom shall be at the time of election serving a church of two hundred members or less; at least seven shall be laypersons actively participating as member/leader/teacher in the educational ministry in the local church; at least three of whom shall be voting members of the board; at least one of whom shall be at the time of election serving a church of two hundred members or less; six additional members shall be nominated, three of whom shall be members of the board, with due consideration to the diversity in theological perspectives, educational attainments, sex, age, racial and ethnic differences, and sizes of local churches, and in consultation with the directors of Councils on Ministries or Boards of Discipleship in each of the Annual Conferences.

c) Twenty persons from the program boards shall participate in Curriculum Resources Committee meetings with the privilege of the floor without vote. These persons shall be: the general secretaries of the General Board of Discipleship, the General Board of Global Ministries, the General Board of Church and Society, and the General Board of Higher Education and Ministry, or someone designated by them; the editor of Church School Publications; the president and publisher, and the vice-president in charge of publishing of The United Methodist Publishing House; and with due consideration to providing for diversity in sex, age, racial, and ethnic differences, five staff members of Church School Publications, and eight other staff members representing the broad concerns of the General Board of Discipleship.

d) The chairperson of the committee shall be a member of the General Board of Discipleship.

2. The Curriculum Resources Committee may select other persons to assist in its work, including persons nominated by the boards, agencies, and general commissions of the Church.

The committee may prepare such bylaws and operating guidelines as are necessary to facilitate the work of the committee.

Section VI. United Methodist National Youth Ministry Organization.

¶ 1301. There shall be a **National Youth Ministry Organization** of The United Methodist Church.

¶ 1302. *Purpose.*—The purpose of the National Youth Ministry Organization shall be:

1. To advocate for youth and the concerns of youth within The United Methodist Church.

2. To empower youth as full participants with the life and mission of The United Methodist Church.

3. To be a forum for the expression of youth needs and concerns.

4. To provide a means of outreach through the Youth Service Fund.

¶ 1303. *Accountability.*—National Youth Ministry Organization shall be accountable to the General Board of Discipleship. The accountability will involve evaluation by the General Board of Discipleship of National Youth Ministry Organization's Disciplinary mandates.

¶ **1304.** *Structure.*—National Youth Ministry Organization shall be composed of three basic units:

(1) National Youth Ministry Organization Convocation;

(2) National Youth Ministry Organization Legislative Assembly; and

(3) National Youth Ministry Organization Steering Committee.

¶ **1305.** *National Youth Ministry Organization Convocation.*— There shall be a **National Youth Ministry Organization Convocation.**

1. *Objectives and responsibilities of the National Youth Ministry Organization Convocation.*—

a) The objectives of the National Youth Ministry Organization Convocation shall be:

(1) To provide leadership training for youth.

(2) To provide for spiritual growth of the participants.

(3) To promote evangelistic outreach by and for youth.

(4) To support and facilitate renewal in the life of the Church.

(5) To strengthen the connectional ties of youth ministry in The United Methodist Church.

b) The responsibilities of the National Youth Ministry Organization Convocation shall be: providing opportunities for worship and the renewal of Christian commitment; offering workshops for youth and adult workers with youth in areas of vital concern to youth; training for designated conference youth leaders; and providing the context and setting for the National Youth Ministry Organization Legislative Assembly.

2. *Participants.*—Participation in the National Youth Ministry Organization Convocation shall be open to:

a) all United Methodist youth as defined in ¶ 263.2;

b) adult workers in youth ministry;

c) youth members of general agencies; and

d) National Youth Ministry Organization Steering Committee members.

Each participant of the National Youth Ministry Organization Convocation with the exception of the National Youth Ministry Organization Legislative Assembly voting members, shall be an observer to the National Youth Ministry Organization Legislative Assembly without voice or vote.

3. *Meetings.*—The National Youth Ministry Organization Convocation shall be held biennially, preferably during the summer months, at a location designated by the National Youth Ministry Organization Steering Committee. The National Youth Ministry Organization Convocation site shall rotate among the jurisdictions in the following order: Southeastern, North Central, South Central, Northeastern, and Western. Every third National Youth Ministry Organization Convocation shall be held at an historically ethnic institution, insofar as possible.

4. *Expenses.*—The expenses of participants, other than those participants listed in ¶ 1306.3 shall be arranged by the individual.

It is strongly recommended that Annual Conference Councils on Youth Ministry secure scholarships for National Youth Ministry Organization Convocation participants, giving special attention to economic factors, inclusiveness, and expressed interest in National Youth Ministry Organization and attending the convocation.

¶ **1306.** *National Youth Ministry Organization Legislative Assembly.*—The **National Youth Ministry Organization Legislative Assembly** shall serve as a national delegated assembly of United Methodist youth and adult workers with youth. The National Youth Ministry Organization Legislative Assembly shall be convened by the National Youth Ministry Organization Steering Committee (¶¶ 1307.2*a* and 1306.1*b*[3]).

1. *a)* Central to the objectives of the National Youth Ministry Organization Legislative Assembly shall be:

(1) To be a forum for the expression of issues vital to youth and to direct the National Youth Ministry Organization Steering Committee in the advocacy of these issues.

(2) To empower youth by supporting and communicating with youth ministry structures at both Annual Conference and jurisdictional levels.

(3) To support and facilitate renewal in the Church.

b) The responsibilities of the National Youth Ministry Organization Legislative Assembly shall be:

(1) To set national Youth Service Fund monetary goals.

(2) To set the policy and criteria for the selection of projects and the distribution of the national portion of the Youth Service Fund.

(3) To elect the National Youth Ministry Organization Steering Committee in accordance with ¶ 1307.2a.

(4) To initiate and support special projects which are of particular interest to youth.

(5) To make recommendations to appropriate boards and agencies of The United Methodist Church on ways to strengthen youth ministry in areas of vital concern.

(6) To support and facilitate formation of racial/ethnic youth caucuses on the Annual Conference, jurisdictional, and general levels of the Church.

(7) To select the National Youth Ministry Organization priority for the next four years.

2. The membership of the National Youth Ministry Organization Legislative Assembly shall be:

a) Voting Members.—Three representatives from each Annual Conference selected by the Annual Conference Council on Youth Ministry. Of those selected, two are to be youth (¶ 263.2), one of whom is the conference Council on Youth president or designate; and one adult, who shall be the conference youth coordinator or designate. It is strongly recommended that at least one of the conference representatives, preferably a youth, shall be a person from one of these four racial/ethnic groups: Pacific and Asian Americans, Black Americans, Hispanic Americans, and Native Americans. If the Annual Conference is not represented by a voting member that represents one of the four racial/ethnic groups, the adult member will sit on the floor with voice but no vote. An Annual Conference must have a youth present in order to exercise voting privileges. Voting members shall be members (full or preparatory) of The United Methodist Church. The youth chairpersons from each jurisdiction shall be in addition to the two youth and one adult from their Annual Conference.

b) Nonvoting Members.—(1) Youth members of the general agencies and (2) members of the National Youth Ministry Organization Steering Committee shall have the right to participate in the National Youth Ministry Organization Legislative Assembly with voice but without vote.

3. *Expenses.*—*a)* The expenses of the members of the National Youth Ministry Organization Steering Committee, with

the exception of the general board and agency representatives, shall be paid from National Youth Ministry Organization funds.

b) The expenses of conference representatives shall be paid by the Annual Conference they represent. It is also recommended that the expense of alternates be paid by the Annual Conference they represent. A travel fund shall be established in order to equalize the expense of each conference.

c) The jurisdictional Council on Ministries or equivalent body shall provide funding for expenses for the jurisdictional youth chairperson.

d) The general agencies shall be responsible for the expenses of their youth members as well as representatives.

¶ **1307.** *National Youth Ministry Organization Steering Committee.*—There shall be a **National Youth Ministry Organization Steering Committee.**

1. *Membership.*—The National Youth Ministry Organization Steering Committee shall consist of youth who are members (full or preparatory) of The United Methodist Church. It is strongly recommended that at least one-half of these youth shall be from these racial/ethnic groups: Pacific and Asian Americans, Black Americans, Hispanic Americans, and Native Americans, so elected that each racial/ethnic group is represented. In addition, there shall be on the National Youth Ministry Organization Steering Committee one adult involved in youth ministry on the Annual Conference level from each jurisdiction; a bishop chosen by the Council of Bishops, an elected member, and a staff member related to youth ministry of the General Board of Discipleship, and one board or staff member, with voice but not vote, from each of the following agencies (to be selected at a regular meeting of the agency): the General Board of Church and Society, the General Board of Global Ministries, the General Board of Higher Education and Ministry, the General Board of Discipleship, the Curriculum Resources Committee, the General Council on Ministries, the General Commission on Religion and Race, the General Commission on the Status and Role of Women, and the General Commission on Christian Unity and Interreligious Concerns. Additional board or staff representatives may be added at the discretion of the steering committee. All youth elected to the steering committee shall be at the time of their

election entering into the eleventh grade or under or their age shall be sixteen or younger.

2. *Election.*—*a)* Each jurisdiction shall elect two youth and one adult worker with youth to the National Youth Ministry Organization Steering Committee at the National Youth Ministry Organization Legislative Assembly. It is strongly recommended that the legislative assembly shall elect members at large so that all four racial and ethnic groups are represented on the National Youth Ministry Organization Steering Committee. It is strongly recommended that if no racial/ethnic group adult is elected to the National Youth Ministry Organization Steering Committee, the National Youth Ministry Organization Legislative Assembly shall elect a racial/ethnic adult at large to be a National Youth Ministry Organization Steering Committee member. Ten youth (two from each jurisdiction; it is strongly recommended that at least one of whom must be a racial/ethnic group member) shall be elected in the alternate years at the Jurisdictional Youth Ministry Convocation (¶ 632). It is strongly recommended that if all four racial/ethnic groups are not represented, the National Youth Ministry Organization Steering Committee shall elect additional members at large so that all four groups are represented on the National Youth Ministry Organization Steering Committee.

b) Any vacancy that occurs due to an unfulfilled term shall be filled as follows: (1) The jurisdictional convocation shall determine the definition of vacancy and the process for filling jurisdictional vacancies. (2) The National Youth Ministry Organization Steering Committee shall fill vacancies to maintain racial/ethnic representation as required by §2*a* above (3) Youth shall be elected to fill youth vacancies and adults shall be elected to fill vacancies in adult positions.

3. *Term.*—The term for National Youth Ministry Organization Steering Committee members (with the exception of general board and agency representatives) shall be two years.

a) Members cannot serve two consecutive terms.

b) Members shall begin their term immediately upon adjournment of the jurisdictional convocation or National Youth Ministry Organization Legislative Assembly at which they were elected and shall conclude upon the adjournment of the next respective jurisdictional convocation or National Youth Ministry Organization Legislative Assembly.

c) The term for board and agency representatives begins immediately following the organizational meeting of their respective board or agency and concludes at the end of the National Youth Ministry Organization Steering Committee meeting following the next General Conference.

4. *Responsibilities.*—The National Youth Ministry Organization Steering Committee shall be responsible:

a) To administer the national portion of the Youth Service Fund, including the selection of the national projects. It shall fulfill this responsibility according to the criteria set by the National Youth Ministry Organization Legislative Assembly.

b) To promote Youth Service Fund education throughout The United Methodist Church in cooperation with the Annual Conference Councils on Youth Ministry (¶ 742.3*h*).

c) To develop comprehensive agenda concerns for each National Youth Ministry Organization Legislative Assembly via a thorough and intentional survey of each conference Council on Youth Ministry, providing an outlet for local churches to voice specific concerns for the National Youth Ministry Organization and The United Methodist Church.

d) To plan the National Youth Ministry Organization Convocation and make arrangements for the National Youth Ministry Organization Legislative Assembly.

e) To convene the National Youth Ministry Organization Legislative Assembly and to implement its decisions.

f) To recommend action goals and issues to the National Youth Ministry Organization Legislative Assembly.

g) To advocate youth concerns and participation in the Church at all levels: general, jurisdictional, conference, district, and local.

h) To call together, when necessary, groups of concerned youth to study and recommend action on vital issues.

i) To encourage participation of youth in appropriate denominational and interreligious enterprises and deliberations.

j) To recommend youth to nominating committees of general boards and agencies, considering suggestions from

Annual Conference Councils on Youth Ministry (¶ 742) and other appropriate youth organizations.

k) To communicate the work of National Youth Ministry Organization to the General Board of Discipleship for its information and response.

¶ **1308.** *Staff.*—The National Youth Ministry Organization shall have an executive director.

1. The responsibilities of the executive director shall be:

a) To provide managerial oversight of National Youth Ministry Organization and staff.

b) To communicate the decisions of National Youth Ministry Organization.

c) To communicate the concerns of youth to the general boards and agencies.

d) To interpret the actions of National Youth Ministry Organizations to The United Methodist Church.

2. Administrative staff persons shall be nominated by the National Youth Ministry Organization Steering Committee and elected by the General Board of Discipleship.

3. The National Youth Ministry Organization Steering Committee shall also determine the need for additional staff. The National Youth Ministry Organization Steering Committee shall also determine the responsibilities of the additional staff member(s).

4. In all meetings of the National Youth Ministries Organization Steering Committee, National Youth Ministry Organization Convocation, and National Youth Ministry Organization Legislative Assembly the staff shall have the right of voice without vote.

5. The General Board of Discipleship in consultation with the National Youth Ministry Organization Steering Committee, shall provide access to office space and support service to the staff of National Youth Ministry Organization. The staff shall be governed by the personnel policies and guidelines of the Committee on Personnel Policies and Practices (¶ 905.4*d*) and the National Youth Ministry Organization Steering Committee.

¶ **1309.** *National Youth Ministry Organization Funding.*—The National Youth Ministry Organization shall be responsible for administering its own budget. The operating funds shall be derived from two main sources: general church funds and the national portion of the Youth Service Fund. A minimum of 80 percent of the national portion of the Youth Service Fund shall be used for projects.

¶ **1310.** *Youth Service Fund.*—There shall be a **Youth Service Fund** which shall be a means of stewardship education and mission support of youth within The United Methodist Church. As a part of its cultivation the youth shall have been challenged to assume their financial responsibilities in connection with the total program and budget of the church of which they are members. Local church treasurers shall send the full amount of Youth Service Fund offerings to the treasurer of the Annual Conference, who shall retain 70 percent of the amount for the Annual Conference Council on Youth Ministry. The Annual Conference Treasurer shall send monthly the remaining 30 percent to the treasurer of the General Council on Finance and Administration to be forwarded to the National Youth Ministry Organization. All other Youth Service Fund money raised in the Annual Conference shall be divided in the same manner and distributed in the same way.

¶ **1311.** *Project Selection.*—The National Youth Ministry Organization Steering Committee shall constitute a **Project Review Committee** to advise the National Youth Ministry Organization Steering Committee in the selection of projects. The Project Review Committee shall be composed of five youth from the National Youth Ministry Organization Steering Committee and two adults who are members of The United Methodist Church but not members of the National Youth Ministry Organization Steering Committee or related to any general agency. The projects shall be chosen according to the policies and criteria established by the National Youth Ministry Organization Legislative Assembly.

Section VII. General Board of Global Ministries.

¶ **1401.** There shall be a **General Board of Global Ministries,** hereinafter referred to as "the board," the purpose of which is found within the expression of the total mission of the Church. It is a missional instrument of The United Methodist

Church, its Annual Conferences, Missionary Conferences, and local congregations in the context of a global setting.

The Church in mission is a sign of God's presence in the world. By the authority of God and the power of the Holy Spirit, the Church:

1. Joins God's mission to reclaim, restore, and redeem the life of all creation to its divine intention;

2. Confesses by word and deed the redeeming activity of God in Christ among the whole human family;

3. Seeks to embody and realize the potential of new life in Christ among all human beings;

4. Looks forward in faith and hope for the fulfillment of God's reign and the completion of God's mission.

¶ **1402.** *Responsibilities.*—1. To discern those places where the gospel has not been heard or heeded and to witness to its meaning throughout the world, inviting all persons to newness of life in Jesus Christ through a program of global ministries.

2. To encourage and support the development of leadership in mission for both the Church and society.

3. To challenge all United Methodists with the New Testament imperative to proclaim the gospel to the ends of the earth, expressing the mission of the Church, to recruit, send, and receive missionaries; enabling them to dedicate all or a portion of their lives in service across racial, cultural, national, and political boundaries.

4. To plan with others and to establish and strengthen Christian congregations where opportunities and needs are found, so that these congregations may be units of mission in their places and partners with others in the worldwide mission of the Christian church.

5. To advocate the work for the unity of Christ's Church through witness and service with other Christian churches and through ecumenical councils.

6. To engage in dialogue with all persons, including those of other faiths and to join with them where possible in action on common concerns.

7. To assist local congregations and Annual Conferences in mission both in their own communities and across the globe by

raising awareness of the claims of global mission and by providing channels for participation.

8. To express the concerns of women organized for mission and to help equip women for full participation both locally and globally in Church and world.

9. To engage in direct ministries to human need, both emergency and continuing, institutional and noninstitutional, however caused.

10. To work within societies and systems so that full human potential is liberated and to work toward the transformation of demonic forces which distort life.

11. To identify with all who are alienated and dispossessed and to assist them in achieving their full human development—body, mind, and spirit.

12. To envision and engage in imaginative new forms of mission appropriate to changing human needs and to share the results of experimentation with the entire Church.

13. To facilitate the development of cooperative patterns of ministry so that the unified strength of local congregations and other units of the Church in designated areas can respond with more effective ministries of justice, advocacy, compassion, and nurture.

14. To affirm the concept of volunteers-in-mission (short-term) as an authentic form of personal missionary involvement and devise appropriate structure to interpret and implement such opportunities for short-term volunteers in the global community.

15. To facilitate the receiving and assignment of missionaries from churches in nations other than the United States in cooperation with the World Division, the National Division, the Mission Personnel Resources Department, with other general agencies, and with Annual Conferences.

¶ **1403.** *Objectives.*—1. The objectives of the board shall be:

a) To plan for the implementation of the responsibilities of the board in the missional outreach of The United Methodist Church.

b) To establish the appropriate organization of the board and staff to accomplish its program and fulfill the responsibilities of the board.

c) To determine, in cooperation with the divisions, departments, and mission constituencies, the areas to be served and the nature of the work to be undertaken.

d) To determine policy and program, to establish goals and priorities, to project long-range plans, to evaluate the program and services of the board and its divisions and departments as to the progress made in fulfilling its purpose in accordance with ¶ 1401 and ¶ 1402, and to seek to achieve its objectives through the programs of the divisions and departments of the board.

e) To coordinate and harmonize the work of the board.

f) To elect or appoint, according to the bylaws, the staff of the board.

g) To assign responsibility and delegate authority to staff and to provide oversight of the staff.

h) To receive and properly administer all properties, trust funds, permanent funds, annuity funds, and other special funds.

i) To receive, secure, appropriate, and expend funds, to underwrite its program and fulfill its responsibilities.

j) To receive and act upon the reports of its divisions, departments, committees, and their staff.

k) To make a report of its activities during the quadrennium to the General Conference.

l) To develop and maintain cooperative relations with other general agencies and with Jurisdictional, Central, Annual, and Missionary Conferences.

m) To be responsible for implementing a policy stating that The United Methodist Church is not a party to any international agreement that limits the ability of any Annual Conference in any jurisdiction to develop and resource programs of ministry of any kind among Native Americans, including the organization of local churches where necessary.

2. The board shall develop and maintain cooperative working relationships with churches and ecumenical agencies on matters of mutual concern in the implementation of Disciplinary responsibilities.

3. The board through its World Division shall facilitate and coordinate the program relationships of other program agencies of The United Methodist Church with churches and agencies in nations other than the United States.

¶ **1404.** *Authority of the Board.*—The board shall have authority to make bylaws and regulate its proceedings in harmony with the Discipline of The United Methodist Church. Bylaws may be amended by a two-thirds vote of the members present and voting thereon at a regular or special meeting, *provided* that required notice of such amendment has previously been given to the members. The board shall have the power and right to do any and all things which shall be authorized by its charter. It shall have authority to develop and carry out its responsibilities as described in ¶ 1402; to buy, acquire, or receive by gift, devise, or bequest property, real, personal, and mixed; to hold, mortgage, sell, and dispose of property; to sue and be sued; to borrow money in case of necessity in a manner harmonious with ¶¶ 906-907; to develop and maintain ecumenical relations to carry out its responsibilities; and to administer its affairs through the board and its respective divisions, departments, and committees.

¶ **1405.** *Authority of the Divisions and Departments.*—The divisions and departments shall have authority to make bylaws and to regulate their proceedings in harmony with the charter of the board and, with its approval, to develop and carry out the functions of the divisions and departments; to buy and sell property; to solicit and accept contributions subject to annuity under the board's regulations and ¶¶ 906-907; and to recommend the appropriation of their funds for the work of the board.

¶ **1406.** *Incorporation.*—1. The General Board of Global Ministries shall be incorporated and shall function through the board, its divisions and departments. Within the board there shall be three divisions—namely: the National Division, the Women's Division, and the World Division; and four departments—namely: the Health and Welfare Ministries Department, the Mission Education and Cultivation Department, the Mission Personnel Resources Department, and the United Methodist Committee on Relief Department. The divisions and departments may each also be incorporated upon approval of the board. These divisions and departments shall be the corporate successors, respectively, of the Health and Welfare Ministries Division, the Education and Cultivation Division, the United Methodist Committee on Relief Division, the Joint Commission on Education and Cultivation, the

National Division, the United Methodist Committee on Relief, the Women's Division, the World Division of the Board of Missions of The Methodist Church, and the corporate successor of the Board of Missions of The Evangelical United Brethren Church, the Board of Missions of The United Methodist Church, and the General Board of Health and Welfare Ministries of The United Methodist Church. The board, its divisions, and departments shall be incorporated in such a state or states as the board may elect.

2. The General Board of Global Ministries of The United Methodist Church shall be the successor to the following corporations: the Board of Missions of The Evangelical United Brethren Church, the Home Missions and Church Erection Society of the Church of the United Brethren in Christ, the Foreign Missionary Society of the United Brethren in Christ, the Women's Missionary Association of the Church of the United Brethren in Christ, the Missionary Society of the Evangelical Church, and the Board of Church Extension of the Evangelical Church, and as such successor it shall be and is authorized and empowered to receive from its said predecessor corporations all trust funds and assets of every kind and character, real, personal, or mixed, held by them, and it shall and hereby is authorized to administer such trusts and funds in accordance with the conditions under which they have been previously received and administered by the said predecessor corporations.

3. It shall have control of all the work formerly controlled and administered by the following: the Board of Health and Welfare Ministries; the Board of Missions of The United Methodist Church; the Board of Missions and Church Extension of The Methodist Church; the Missionary Society, the Board of Foreign Missions, the Board of Home Missions and Church Extension, the Woman's Foreign Missionary Society, the Woman's Home Missionary Society, the Wesleyan Service Guild, and the Ladies' Aid Societies of the Methodist Episcopal Church; the Board of Missions, including the Woman's Missionary Society, the Woman's Board of Foreign Missions, the Woman's Board of Home Missions, the Woman's Missionary Council, and the Board of Church Extension of the Methodist Episcopal Church, South; the Board of Missions of the Methodist

Protestant Church; and such other corporations or agencies of the General Conference as do similar work; but this list shall not be construed as exclusive.

4. Subject to the limitations hereinafter specified, each of the incorporated divisions shall be subject to the supervision and control of the General Conference of The United Methodist Church in all things not inconsistent with the Constitution and laws of the United States and of the states of incorporation.

5. The board, its divisions, and departments shall have the power to create those subsidiary units or sections needed in the fulfillment of designated functions, upon approval of the board.

¶ **1407.** *Administrative Committee.*—There shall be an administrative committee whose membership and powers shall be determined by the board.

¶ **1408.** *Corporate Officers.*—1. *Board Officers.*—The board shall elect as its corporate officers a president, three vice-presidents who shall be the presidents of the divisions, a treasurer, a recording secretary, and such other officers as it shall deem necessary.

The Women's Division shall elect its president, who shall be one of the three vice-presidents of the board. The board shall determine the powers and duties of its officers.

2. *Division and Department Officers.*—The board shall elect the chairpersons of the four departments. Each division shall elect at least one vice-president. Each department shall elect a vice-chairperson. Each division and department shall also elect a treasurer, a recording secretary, and such other officers as it shall deem necessary. Vacancies shall be filled by the divisions and departments or their executive committees. The divisions and departments shall determine the power and duties of their officers.

¶ **1409.** *Elected Staff.*—1. *Board Staff.*—*a)* The board, through a personnel and nominations committee, shall make nominations to the General Council on Ministries for the office of general secretary. As chief staff officer of the board, the general secretary shall have direct involvement in staff selections.

b) The board shall elect an associate general secretary for administration, a board treasurer, a board planner, and an ombudsperson.

c) The board shall elect additional staff as needed.

2. *Division and Department Staff.—a)* The board personnel and nominations committee, in consultation with the general secretary of the board, the divisions, and departments, shall recommend candidates for the positions of deputy and associate general secretaries for election by the board. The Women's Division shall nominate its deputy general secretary for election by the division and the board after consultation with the president and general secretary of the board.

The deputy general secretaries shall have administrative responsibility for the divisions and shall be responsible to the divisions and to the general secretary. The associate general secretaries shall have administrative responsibility for the departments and shall be responsible to the departments and to the general secretary.

b) The divisions and departments shall nominate for election by the board such other staff persons as are deemed necessary to carry out the work assigned.

3. The president, general secretary, and treasurer of the board are ex officio members of the divisions and departments and their executive committees, without vote.

The board shall elect, on nomination of each division and department and in consultation with the general secretary, an associate treasurer of the General Board of Global Ministries, who shall have fiscal responsibility for the division or department. He or she will be responsible to the treasurer of the General Board of Global Ministries for board fiscal procedures and to the deputy or associate general secretary for all division or department administrative and fiscal procedures (¶ 803.7*e*).

¶ **1410.** *Personnel.—*1. *Selection.—*The board and its divisions and departments shall elect and appoint staff on the basis of competency and with representation of ethnic and racial groups, young adults, and women, in accordance with policies in ¶ 814.

2. *Staff Participation of Women.—a)* Of the following staff positions within the board—namely, the general secretary, the treasurer of the board, the deputy general secretaries, the associate general secretaries, the planner, and the ombudsperson—a minimum of 40 percent shall be occupied by women.

b) In each division and in each department a minimum of 40 percent of the staff elected to the positions of deputy general secretary, associate general secretaries, treasurer, and assistant treasurers, as well as 40 percent of the appointed staff, shall be women.

¶ 1411. 1. All properties, trust funds, annuity funds, permanent funds, and endowments now held and administered by the Board of Missions, the Board of Health and Welfare Ministries, and the United Methodist Committee on Relief of The United Methodist Church; the Board of Missions of The Methodist Church; the Board of Missions of The Evangelical United Brethren Church; and their respective divisions shall be carefully safeguarded. The General Board of Global Ministries of The United Methodist Church and its divisions and departments shall endeavor to invest in institutions, companies, corporations, or funds which make a positive contribution toward the realization of the goals outlined in the Social Principles of The United Methodist Church and to administer such investments in the interest of those persons and causes for which said funds were established. Such properties, trust funds, annuity funds, permanent funds, and endowments shall be transferred to the General Board of Global Ministries of The United Methodist Church or its respective divisions and departments from merged boards and societies only when such transfers can be made in accordance with the laws of the states where the several boards and societies are chartered and on the recommendation of the respective divisions and departments and the approval of such boards and societies. Funds of the administrative divisions and departments and their preceding corporations and societies which are subject to appropriation shall be appropriated only on recommendation of the respective divisions and departments. (*See* ¶¶ 906.6, .8.)

2. The financial affairs of the board shall be as follows:

a) The income of the divisions and departments of the board, exclusive of the Women's Division, shall be derived from apportionments, assessments, or askings distributed to jurisdictions, Annual Conferences, and pastoral charges by the budget-making process of the General Conference in such manner as the General Conference may prescribe, and from church schools, gifts, donations, freewill offerings, annuities, bequests, specials, and other sources from which missionary and benevolence funds are usually derived, in harmony with the Discipline of The United Methodist Church and actions of the General Conference. Funds for the fulfillment of the responsibilities of the Women's Division shall be derived from annual voluntary pledges, offerings, gifts, devises, bequests, annuities, or money received through special emphases and from meetings held in the interest of the division.

b) Cultivation for the Advance shall be through channels of the Church other than United Methodist Women.

c) All contributions to and income on all funds of the board or its respective divisions and departments should be used for current expenses and annual appropriations unless otherwise designated by the donor.

3. Askings shall be received from the fields, and budgets shall be prepared by the divisions and departments in such manner as the board may prescribe, consistent with its constitution and charter, and this combined budget shall be presented to the General Council on Ministries in accordance with ¶ 906.

¶ **1412.** *Membership.*—The policies, plans of work, management, business, and all affairs of the General Board of Global and administered by the board, which shall be composed according to the conditions defined in ¶¶ 805, 809 of the General Provisions, with the following conditions:

1. The basic members (clergy, laymen, and laywomen) are elected by the jurisdiction upon the nomination of the Annual Conferences in accord with ¶ 805.1. The additional members of the board are nominated by a committee composed of three persons from each jurisdiction—a clergy member, a layman, and a laywoman—elected within each jurisdiction. The committee is to be convened by the president of the board, or if there be none, the secretary of the Council of Bishops.

2. The Women's Division membership procedures are an exception to those described in ¶¶ 805, 809 of the general provisions. This formula is defined in ¶ 1429. The basic members of the Women's Division shall also serve on the

membership of other divisions, departments, and committees of the board.

3. The composition of the board and its divisions and departments should reflect the major recognized categories of church members. (*See* ¶ 805.1*b*, 2*a.*) One-half of the membership should be women.

4. Members of the board shall be distributed across the component divisions, departments, and standing committees of the board in accord with board bylaws.

5. The term of office of all members whose election is provided for in this paragraph shall begin and the board shall organize at a meeting to be held within ninety days after the adjournment of the last meeting of the several Jurisdictional Conferences held after the adjournment of the General Conference.

6. In addition to the episcopal members provided for by ¶ 805, on nomination of the Council of Bishops, the General Conference shall elect to the board three Central Conference bishops, and each Central Conference, or a body authorized by it, shall elect to the board one clergy, one laywoman, and one layman.

7. The general secretary and treasurer of the board, the deputy general secretaries, and the associate general secretaries shall be members without vote.

8. Salaried members of staff of any agency receiving appropriation funds from any division or department of the board shall not be eligible to serve as voting members of said board, except in order to fulfill the provisions of ¶ 805.

National Division

¶ 1413. *Purpose.*—Within the expression of the total mission of the Church outlined in the objectives of mission and the purposes of the General Board of Global Ministries, the **National Division** exists to proclaim and witness to the saving grace of Jesus Christ through mission and ministries in the United States, Puerto Rico, the Virgin Islands, and U.S. Trust Territories.

The National Division is committed to an expression of faith which understands that God, through Jesus Christ, is active in all of life and works in church and secular society for dignity and justice among persons and communities. This faith directs the development of national mission strategies and program to include developing and strengthening congregations as centers of Christian mission, creating ministries of compassion with persons and groups who suffer in body and spirit, assigning personnel, responding to the efforts of people for self-determination, and changing social patterns which cause and continue suffering.

¶ **1414.** *Responsibilities.*—The National Division shall:

1. Develop, administer, and supervise the national mission strategy of The United Methodist Church within the objectives and responsibilities of the General Board of Global Ministries, providing overall coordination for programs within the United States, Puerto Rico and the Virgin Islands.

2. Identify and analyze national mission concerns through research and planning.

3. Advocate justice and human dignity related to the mission concerns and objectives of the National Division and the board.

4. Assist congregations, cooperative parishes, transitional community parishes, church-related institutional ministries, districts, Annual Conferences, and other units of the Church in planning and research processes, experimental and creative ministries, long-term financing and grants, architectural services, fund-raising efforts, and disaster response.

5. Enable, encourage, and support the missional outreach of the Church in local communities through the development of new or existing ethnic and language ministries, congregations, community centers, health, education, and social welfare ministries in urban, suburban and rural settings—and programs for enlisting and training leadership committed to global consciousness and mission.

6. Develop strategies for church and community development including grants, loans, and technical assistance that address particular needs of women, children, and older adults including self-determination efforts pertaining to social needs

arising from concerns for ethnic and cultural pluralism, economic and sexual exploitation, and political/racial oppression.

7. Facilitate and coordinate the program relationships of other program agencies of The United Methodist Church with institutions related to the National Division, including community centers, residences, health-care agencies, child care agencies, schools, and other educational agencies.

8. Develop, administer, supervise, and evaluate other units of the General Board of Global Ministries and the Annual Conferences.

9. Provide counsel and assistance in the coordination of local and national mission strategy to institutions related to the National Division, including community centers, residences, health-care agencies, child-care agencies, schools, and other educational agencies.

10. Maintain the United Methodist Development Fund for the purpose of making first mortgage loans to United Methodist churches, districts, city societies, district unions, or Annual Conference church extension agencies for the purchase, construction, expansion, or major improvement of churches, parsonages, or mission buildings. The United Methodist Development Fund shall operate under policies set by the National Division, and the National Division shall be responsible for the supervision and administration of the United Methodist Development Fund.

11. Maintain relationships and fulfill responsibilities with Missions, Missionary Conferences, and Provisional Annual Conferences in accordance with Disciplinary provisions; establish missional structures that assist Annual Conferences, districts, and local churches working together cooperatively and strategically; and work with special regional or national agencies or organizations, including the Appalachian Development Committee and Southwest Border Committee, to further the national mission strategy of the Church.

12. Work cooperatively with agencies of the Church, other denominations, and both ecumenical and secular coalitions.

13. Work with the Parish and Community Development Committee or its equivalent in an Annual Conference by providing resources on the initiation and development of

programs with agencies related to the National Division, church and community ministry, congregational development, ministries in town and country and urban areas, and other missionally oriented ministries.

14. Work with the General Board of Discipleship for the extension of the Church. To this end there shall be a **Joint Committee on Congregational Development** with equal representation of members from the National Division and the General Board of Discipleship, which shall meet at least annually to expedite cooperation between these two boards in the field of congregational development including new missional congregations and the renewal and revitalization of existing congregations.

¶ **1415.** *Authority and Organization.*—The National Division shall have the authority and power to:

1. Receive and properly administer funds assigned to the National Division, including:

a) World Service and other funds designated for the program of the National Division;

b) the Advance special gifts for work related to the National Division which are cultivated through the Mission Education and Cultivation Department;

c) donation aid, loan funds, and endowments contributed and established for the work of church extension;

d) funds allocated by the Women's Division, keeping in mind the special concerns of women;

e) bequests, earnings on investments, and other income in accordance with the provisions by which they are given and available for work related to the National Division;

f) funds appropriated by the United Methodist Committee on Relief Department for coordination of disaster response ministries and church property damage caused by disasters.

2. Receive and properly administer all properties and funds, including:

a) all properties and trust funds, permanent funds, annuity funds, and other special funds coming into the possession of the National Division as part of a board for missionary and other purposes, in accordance with ¶ 1405;

b) all trust funds and assets of every kind and character, real, personal, or mixed, held by predecessor corporations, in accordance with the conditions under which such trusts and funds have been previously received and administered by the said predecessor corporations (¶ 1406.2).

3. Represent within The United Methodist Church and provide financial support and consultative services for new and historically related mission institutions of the National Division of the General Board of Global Ministries, including community centers, residences, multi-service mission complexes, child-care institutions, schools, and other educational institutions.

4. Assign staff to develop programs, administer such appropriations as are committed to them, and cooperate with other divisions within the board, other boards, and agencies, as their work may affect the group itself.

5. Receive from Health and Welfare Ministries Department counsel and field consultation related to health care and services to the aging and children and youth.

6. Conduct research and distribute information which will assist congregational development, cooperative parishes, districts, conferences and other units of The United Methodist Church in identifying mission opportunities and appropriate responses.

7. Encourage rural, town, city, metropolitan, or district mission structures according to the following:

a) Such structures may be organized, under such names as may be determined, wherever, in the judgment of the bishop or bishops and district superintendents concerned, it is deemed advisable. When two or more districts, conferences, episcopal areas, or jurisdictions have churches in the same area, it is recommended that the structure be organized to include all United Methodist churches. "Metropolitan" or "rural" shall be defined with sufficient flexibility to include separate communities which are economically or socially related.

b) It is recommended that a majority of the governing body be from the laity, men and women, young adults and youth. All bishops, district superintendents, and superintendents of ethnic ministries having jurisdiction within the geographic territory served by the structure may be ex officio members of the organization. Membership may also include representation from conference Boards of Global Ministries, conference or district United Methodist Women, community-based young adult ministries (¶ 263.3), rural, city and suburban parish churches, community centers, and other nonparish rural and urban ministries, poverty communities, youth, and racial and ethnic groups.

c) The purpose of such a structure shall be to promote and coordinate the work of the Church (¶¶ 201-204) in town and country or metropolitan areas. It may:

(1) Develop special ministries and new forms of mission appropriate to new metropolitan or town and country needs, including recruitment, training, involvement of clergy and laity, and cooperative models of ministry.

(2) Promote long-term regional planning and provide coordinating framework for town and country and metropolitan mission strategy for United Methodism, especially with small congregations and ethnic and language groups.

(3) Enable and support rural, central city, and suburban church extension, including research, organization (but not the constituting) of churches, acquisition of real estate, and the erection and maintenance of buildings (having first secured the approval of the district Board of Church Location and Building). Wherever possible, consideration should be given to new concepts of church extension, such as leased space, shared facilities, revitalized small congregations, and other experimental styles.

(4) Help to initiate and participate in rural and urban coalitions and other associations with leaders in business, finance, industry, agriculture, labor, education, welfare, etc., to work cooperatively for mutually desired social change.

(5) Encourage and support the development of effective community organizations in rural, inner-city, and suburban communities, to the end that people may share in the decision-making processes, and open more effective channels of communication between all peoples.

(6) Participate with federal, state, and local governments in programs of rural and urban renewal and development, with special reference to protection and enhancement of human values, families, and family farms and businesses.

(7) Cooperate with representatives of other churches and faiths in developing, implementing, and funding new patterns of joint mission.

(8) Raise funds for the support of its work in cooperation with the Annual Conference Council on Finance and Administration, including the securing and holding of endowments for general purposes and for designated churches, institutions, or types of mission. Consideration shall be given to the use of an area or conference United Methodist foundation for the investment management of bequests, endowments, trusts, and special gifts.

d) In order to receive financial assistance from the division the structure shall meet the following conditions:

(1) It shall be organized according to the Discipline.

(2) It shall have a governing board or executive committee meeting at least once each quarter.

(3) It shall be actively at work.

(4) It shall have made a report to the division in the prescribed form provided for that purpose.

e) Each Annual Conference shall promote the work of such mission structures within its boundaries and receive annual reports through the Annual Conference Board of Global Ministries. All moneys received shall be reported in the conference journal.

f) If a full-time executive officer is employed, it is recommended that he or she be invited into consultation with the bishop and district superintendents in the consideration of the appointments that affect missions or churches administered or aided by the organization which he or she represents.

g) Each such mission organization shall, in cooperation with the Annual Conference Board of Global Ministries, annually present its financial needs to the Annual Conference Council on Finance and Administration of the conference to which it is related, to determine how the needs shall be met, including possible apportionments to the churches in its geographic area.

h) All pastors whose charges lie within the territory of the mission organization shall each year present the interests of the organization to their congregations, taking an offering or otherwise promoting support of its work.

i) Any local church expecting to receive aid from the mission organization for building or improvement shall be required, as a condition of receiving such aid, to secure its approval with respect to location, plans, and methods of financing.

j) In a metropolitan area the National Division may cooperate, with the approval of the bishops and the conferences, in the organization of a Metropolitan Commission, which may be composed of bishops and district superintendents involved and a selected group of ordained ministers, laymen, and laywomen, representing Annual Conference Boards of Global Ministries, Committees on Urban Ministries, Annual Conference United Methodist Women, community-based young adult ministries (¶ 263.3), city missionary societies, local churches, representatives of other boards and agencies, and others who have skills and experience enabling them to fulfill creative planning and strategy functions for United Methodism in the metropolitan area.

The purpose of such a commission is to promote long-term planning and to provide a coordinating framework for United Methodism's metropolitan mission strategy. These functions may be fulfilled by other city, metropolitan, or district mission structures as deemed appropriate.

¶ **1416.** There shall be an executive committee of the division whose powers shall be determined by the division, subject to the approval of the board. It shall be composed of fifteen persons including the chairperson of the division, one clergy in full connection, two laymen, two from ethnic groups, and one from youth or young adult. One-half of the nonepiscopal members shall be women, elected by the Women's Division in accordance with ¶ 1425.

¶ **1417.** *Membership.*—The basic membership of the National Division shall be constituted in accord with the bylaws of the board and consistent with the provisions of ¶ 1412.3.

OFFICE OF DEACONESS

¶ **1418.** *Office of Deaconess.*—1. There shall be in The United Methodist Church the **office of deaconess**. Persons who have been commissioned to the office of home missionary and who are continuing in that office shall be so recognized. The purpose of the office of deaconess shall be to express representatively the love and concern of the believing community for the needs in the world, and enable, through education and involvement, the full ministry and mission of the people of God. Deaconesses function through diverse forms of service directed toward the world to make Jesus Christ known in the fullness of his ministry and mission which mandate that his followers:

a) Alleviate suffering.

b) Eradicate causes of injustice and all that robs life of dignity and worth.

c) Facilitate the development of full human potential.

d) Share in building global community through the Church Universal.

2. Deaconesses are persons who have been led by the Holy Spirit to devote their lives to Christlike service under the authority of the Church. They are approved by the General Board of Global Ministries upon recommendation of the Mission Personnel Resources Department and the National Division. They are commissioned by a bishop at a session of the General Board of Global Ministries. They shall have a continuing relationship to The United Methodist Church through the General Board of Global Ministries.

Deaconesses are available for service with any agency or program of The United Methodist Church. Both deaconesses and home missionaries may also serve in other than United Methodist Church agencies or programs provided that approval be given by the National Division in consultation with the bishop of the receiving area.

3. Full-time service is the norm for the ministry of a deaconess, meaning that the person's entire vocational time is devoted to work of ministry in the field of labor to which one is appointed by the bishop.

a) The program office shall process appointments for deaconesses in consultation with the bishop of the area, in accordance with the policies and procedures of the National Division.

b) The appointment shall be fixed by the bishop (¶ 515.5) at the session of Annual Conference and printed in the list of appointments in the Annual Conference journal.

c) The Annual Conference secretary shall:

(1) Keep a record of all persons in the Annual Conference who have been commissioned to the Office of Deaconess or the Office of Home Missionary.

(2) Publish annually in the Annual Conference journal the list of appointments of deaconesses and home missionaries.

4. A deaconess shall hold church membership in a local church within the conference where her appointment is located and shall be a voting member of the Charge Conference of that church.

5. Deaconesses shall be seated at the sessions of the Annual Conference with voice.

6. A deaconess may become a member of the Annual Conference when elected in accordance with ¶¶ 35 and 251.2.

7. Deaconesses shall be subject to the administrative authority of the program or agency to which they are appointed. In matters of their assignment they are subject to the authority of the General Board of Global Ministries through the National Division and may not contract for service which would nullify this authority.

8. Each deaconess shall enroll in a pension plan. The rights of any deaconess or home missionary in any prior or existing agreement or pension plan shall be fully protected.

9. A deaconess shall relinquish the commissioned relationship:

a) when no longer available for appointment as a deaconess of The United Methodist Church, or

b) when not eligible for appointment as determined by the National Division.

10. Persons who have relinquished the commissioned relationship may be reinstated on the joint recommendation of the National Division and the Mission Personnel Resources Department with approval of the General Board of Global Ministries.

¶ **1419.** *Committee on Deaconess Service.*—1. There shall be a **Committee on Deaconess Service,** which shall be advisory to the General Board of Global Ministries through the National Division.

2. The Committee on Deaconess Service shall be composed

of one bishop who is a member of the General Board of Global Ministries; four active deaconesses and two active home missionaries selected by national vote of the active deaconesses and home missionaries; two directors of the National Division and two directors of the Women's Division chosen by the respective divisions, at least one of whom shall also be a director of the Mission Personnel Resources Department.

3. There shall be an executive committee and other committees as necessary for carrying out the duties of the Committee on Deaconess Service.

4. The work of the committee shall be carried out in accordance with the bylaws as approved by the National Division of the General Board of Global Ministries.

¶ **1420.** *The Deaconess Program Office.*—There shall be a program office for deaconesses to represent the deaconess relationship on a national level and to maintain the corps of professionally competent persons who are committed to service under authority of the Church.

1. For purposes of administration, all provisions for the office of deaconess shall apply to persons continuing in the office of home missionary.

2. The General Board of Global Ministries shall assign the administration of the program office to the National Division or such other division or department as it may determine (¶ 1403.1*b*). The executive secretary of the program office shall be a deaconess.

3. There may be a national organization of deaconesses which shall operate according to policies approved by the National Division.

WOMEN'S DIVISION

¶ **1421.** *Purpose.*—The **Women's Division** shall be actively engaged in fulfilling the mission of Christ and the Church and shall interpret the purpose of United Methodist Women. With continuing awareness of the concerns and responsibilities of the Church in today's world, the Women's Division shall be an advocate for the oppressed and dispossessed with special attention to the needs of women and children; shall work to build a supportive community among women; and shall engage in activities which foster growth in the Christian faith, mission education, and Christian social involvement throughout the organization.

¶ **1422.** *Responsibilities.*—The responsibilities of the Women's Division shall be:

1. To recommend program and policies to United Methodist Women.

2. To interpret the role and responsibility of the division in fulfilling the mission of Christ and the Church.

3. To provide resources and opportunities for women that enrich their spiritual life and increase their knowledge and understanding of the needs of the world and their responsibility in meeting those needs.

4. To secure funds through the channels of United Methodist Women for the support of the program of the Church through the General Board of Global Ministries, with special concern for the needs and responsibilities of women.

5. To project plans specially directed toward leadership development of women through appropriate planning with the other divisions and agencies of the board.

6. To strengthen the Church's challenge to women to enlist in the diaconate as missionaries and deaconesses.

7. To enlist women in activities that have a moral and religious significance for the public welfare and that contribute to the establishment of a just global society.

8. To work with the other agencies of the Church and community in areas of common concern and responsibility. A United Nations Office shall be conducted in cooperation with the General Board of Church and Society.

9. To give visible evidence of oneness in Christ by uniting in fellowship and service with other Christians, including the World Federation of Methodist Women, Church Women United, and other similar groups, thereby strengthening the ecumenical witness and program of the Church.

10. To formulate concepts of contemporary mission.

¶ **1423.** *Authority.*—1. The Women's Division shall have the authority to make its bylaws and to regulate its proceedings in harmony with the charter of the board, and with its approval, to develop and carry out the functions of the board as described in ¶ 1402; to buy and sell property; to solicit and accept contributions, subject to annuity under the board's regulations; and to appropriate its funds.

2. The division shall meet annually at the time of the meeting of the board, and at such other times as it shall deem necessary.

3. The Women's Division shall include in its responsibilities:

a) Those formerly carried by the Woman's Society of Christian Service of The Methodist Church and the Women's Society of World Service of the Evangelical United Brethren Church, the Women's Society of Christian Service of The United Methodist Church, and those other organizations of women of similar purposes which have operated in the churches forming the United Methodist tradition; including the Women's Missionary Association of the Church of the United Brethren in Christ; the Woman's Missionary Society of the Evangelical Church; the Woman's Foreign Missionary Society, the Woman's Home Missionary Society, the Wesleyan Service Guild, and the Ladies' Aid Societies of the Methodist Episcopal Church; the Woman's Missionary Society, the Woman's Board of Foreign Missions, the Woman's Board of Home Missions, the Woman's Missionary Council of the Methodist Episcopal Church, South; and the Woman's Convention of the Board of Missions of the Methodist Protestant Church. This list shall not be construed as exclusive.

b) All policy matters pertaining to the homes for retired workers owned by the Women's Division.

4. The Women's Division shall have the authority:

a) To organize jurisdictional, conference, district, and local church organizations of United Methodist Women, which shall be auxiliary to the General Board of Global Ministries, through the Women's Division, of The United Methodist Church.

b) To recommend constitutions and make bylaws for United Methodist Women.

c) To appropriate funds received through United Methodist Women.

d) To serve as the national official policy-making body of United Methodist Women, with the officers of the Women's Division designated as the national officers.

¶ **1424.** *Organization.*—The Women's Division shall elect an executive committee which shall exercise the powers of the division ad interim. It shall be composed of nineteen members, of whom the division shall elect six to serve on the executive committee of the World Division, six to serve on the executive committee of the National Division, two to serve on the executive committee of the Mission Education and Cultivation Department. Members of the executive committee may also be named by the division to serve on other department executive committees. The deputy general secretary and the treasurer of the division and the officers of the board as defined in ¶ 1409.3 shall be members ex officio.

¶ **1425.** The Women's Division shall be organized into such sections as the division shall determine.

¶ **1426.** *Assembly.*—There may be an assembly of United Methodist Women, including a delegated body termed the Assembly. The division shall determine the time and place of meeting and the purpose, composition, functions, and powers of the Assembly.

¶ **1427.** *Finances.*—The funds for the fulfillment of the responsibilities of the Women's Division shall be derived from annual voluntary pledges, offerings, gifts, devises, bequests, annuities, or money received through special emphases and meetings held in the interest of the division. All funds, except those designated for local purposes, shall be forwarded through the channels of finance of United Methodist Women to the treasurer of the division. Undesignated funds received by the Women's Division shall be allocated by the division, on recommendation of the appropriate section or committee, for the work of the several sections of the Women's Division and to such other divisions and agencies of the General Board of Global Ministries as the division shall determine for the fulfillment of the responsibilities of the division. Funds appropriated for the work of the other divisions and agencies of the board may be given with specific designations and time limits, after which unspent funds are to be returned to the division.

¶ **1428.** *Membership.*—The Women's Division shall be composed of board members as follows: one of the episcopal members of the board, with residence in the United States; six basic members of the board: two clergy in full connection, two laymen and two laywomen; and fifty-eight women, forty of whom shall be nominated by the jurisdictional organizations of United Methodist Women and elected by the Jurisdictional Conferences (¶ 634.4); five shall be the jurisdiction presidents of United Methodist Women; and thirteen shall be elected by the division to board membership. Officers of the board (¶ 1409.3), the deputy general secretary, and the treasurer of the division shall be members ex officio.

¶ **1429.** *Constitution of United Methodist Women.*—For the Constitution of United Methodist Women in the jurisdiction, *see* ¶ 634; for the Constitution of United Methodist Women in the conference, *see* ¶ 742; for the Constitution of United Methodist Women in the district, *see* ¶ 755; for the Constitution of United Methodist Women in the local church, *see* ¶ 263.6.

WORLD DIVISION

¶ **1430.** *Purpose.*—The **World Division** exists to confess Jesus Christ as divine Lord and Savior to all people in every place, testifying to his redemptive and liberating power in every sphere of human existence and activity, and calling all people to Christian obedience and discipleship.

The World Division, through responsibilities delegated to it by the General Board of Global Ministries and on behalf of The United Methodist Church, seeks to fulfill the purpose by:

1. Coordination of relationships and administration of program of The United Methodist Church as it relates to areas outside the United States.

2. Engaging mutually in mission with colleague churches and other bodies outside the United States, and facilitating their interaction with the Church and society in the United States so that all become more effective in Christian mission.

¶ **1431.** *Responsibilities.*—The responsibilities of the World Division, in order to fulfill its purpose, shall be:

1. To develop and administer the missional relationships of The United Methodist Church with Central Conferences, Autonomous Methodist and United Churches, and ecumenical bodies in nations other than the United States.

2. To formulate the objectives and strategies for the world mission of The United Methodist Church, within the context of the cultural and historical understandings out of which relationships have developed with the Christian communities in nations other than the United States.

3. To foster the interaction of churches and ecumenical groups in nations other than the United States with the Church and society in the United States with the purpose of mutuality in the definition and implementation of Christian mission and of international concerns.

4. To administer programs of support for churches and ecumenical bodies in nations other than the United States through the provision of financial resources and the training and support of persons in mission, including missionaries assigned by the division and national persons in service in their own or in other countries.

5. To facilitate the receiving and assignment of missionaries from nations other than the United States, in cooperation with the National Division, the Mission Personnel Resources Department, with other boards and agencies, and with Annual Conferences.

a) Ordained clergy from Methodist or United Churches in nations other than the United States serving within the boundaries of an Annual Conference as missionaries certified by the General Board of Global Ministries may be affiliate members of the Annual Conference.They may serve local churches, conference or district positions, under the supervision of the bishop. They may also serve in ecumenical, institutional, or United Methodist general agency ministries.

b) Missionaries from churches in nations other than the United States with affiliate relationship to the Annual Conference shall have come in response to the initiative of the agency calling them, under a letter of agreement in which the specific task, the length of term of service, and the responsibilities of each party have been defined to the satisfaction of the affiliated member, the sending church, the receiving body, and the General Board of Global Ministries.

c) Missionaries from churches in nations other than the United States as affiliated members are responsible to the bishop and to the conference Board of Global Ministries in the conference where they are serving. They shall submit annually to the bishop, the district superintendent, the conference Board of Global Ministries, and the Charge Conference of the local church to which they are related a written report outlining the progress in the work to which they have been assigned. They shall also send copies of this report to the bishop or chief appointive officer of the conference or governing church body from which they have come.

d) They shall be governed by the privileges and limitations of affiliate members as defined in ¶ 443.4.

6. To provide services and information which facilitate the advocacy of public policies which support justice according to the Social Principles of The United Methodist Church and are relevant to the mission concerns and objectives of the World Division and of the General Board of Global Ministries.

¶ 1432. *Authority.*—The General Board of Global Ministries through its World Division shall facilitate and coordinate the program relationships of other program agencies of The United Methodist Church in nations other than the United States (*see* ¶¶ 1430.1 and 1431.1).

¶ 1433. The World Division shall prohibit the use of its personnel as paid or unpaid informer to any official or unofficial intelligence agency of any government.

¶ 1434. The division shall meet annually at the time of the meeting of the board and at such other times as it shall deem necessary.

¶ 1435. *Executive Committee.*—There shall be an executive committee, whose membership and powers shall be determined by the division.

¶ 1436. *Liaison Committee.*—1. The General Board of Global Ministries, through its World Division, shall request each Central Conference and its conferences, both Annual and Provisional, each Affiliated Autonomous Methodist Church or United Church, where applicable, to make provision for liaison functions with the board through a committee which is representative of all phases of the world mission, particularly of the needs and responsibilities of women.

2. There may be a subcommittee on women's work of the

committee, which shall deal with all the concerns of women in the Church appropriate to the committee. This subcommittee may be composed of all women members of the committee and additional co-opted members as desired.

¶ **1437.** *Administration of New Commitments.*—Where the World Division, with the approval of the General Board of Global Ministries, plans to develop mission relationships in countries where it presently has no commitments, the division shall do so by pursuing a working agreement with the church or churches already in the area or with a united mission organization or with ecumenical bodies related to the area. Where these approaches are not available, the World Division may participate in the formation of a new United Methodist denominational structure, in which case it may request the Council of Bishops to provide any necessary episcopal oversight.

¶ **1438.** *Membership.*—The basic membership of the World Division shall be constituted in accord with the bylaws of the board and consistent with provisions of ¶ 1412.3. The deputy general secretary and treasurer of the division and the officers of the board as defined in ¶ 1409.3 shall be members ex officio.

HEALTH AND WELFARE MINISTRIES DEPARTMENT

¶ **1439.** *Purpose.*—The purpose of the **Health and Welfare Ministries Department** shall be to assist United Methodists to become involved globally in health and welfare ministries, especially in areas of child care, aging, health care, and persons with handicapping conditions; and to assist organizations, institutions, and programs related to Annual Conferences and other units of The United Methodist Church in their involvement in direct service to persons in need through both residential and nonresidential ministries.

¶ **1440.** *Responsibilities.*—1. To provide upon request consultation services to existing and emerging health and welfare institutions and programs, and to jurisdictional, conference, district, and local church units.

a) Consultation services include assistance in: organization and administration, financial management and support, securing management-level personnel, evaluation of current services, planning for new services and methods, and the development of affirmative action programs (*see* ¶ 815).

b) Upon request of the Annual Conference unit responsible for health and welfare ministries, or other appropriate unit, the department shall assist in evaluating plans for new or expanded residential or nonresidential ministries seeking approval from the Annual Conference or other unit (*see* ¶ 730.4[24]).

2. To recommend programmatic standards, self-study, and peer review that will assist health and welfare institutions and programs to improve their services, and to encourage them to attain these standards.

3. To provide leadership development opportunities for programs, institutions, Annual Conferences, districts, and local churches to improve the quality of professional and volunteer leadership in health and welfare ministries, including attention to fund development work by the Annual Conferences, and to help Annual Conferences and health and welfare institutions clarify their relationship with one another, including matters of legal and financial responsibility.

4. To identify health and welfare needs and to advocate and educate on behalf of the health and welfare rights and needs of all persons.

5. To develop printed, audiovisual, and other resources to interpret and support health and welfare ministries in cooperation with the Mission Education and Cultivation Department.

6. To provide a program to encourage awareness of the gifts and needs of persons with handicapping conditions for Annual Conferences, districts, and local churches.

7. To assist Annual Conferences in assessing emerging needs in health and welfare ministries within Annual Conferences.

¶ **1441.** The department shall, in cooperation with the Mission Education and Cultivation Department, and the General Commission on Communication, encourage Golden Cross and similar offerings within each Annual Conference to collect moneys and provide other material assistance for care of sick persons, children, youth, older persons, and persons with handicapping conditions, especially emphasizing support for those ministries which provide assistance to persons in need.

¶ **1442.** *Relationship with the United Methodist Association of Health and Welfare Ministries.*—The department shall work with the United Methodist Association of Health and Welfare Ministries in leadership development and may make services available to the association.

¶ **1443.** *Meetings.*—The department shall meet annually at the time of the meeting of the board and at such other times as it shall deem necessary. Written notice stating the place and purpose of all meetings must be given to all members at least ten days prior to the meeting. A majority of the members of the department shall constitute a quorum.

¶ **1444.** *Executive Committee.*—There shall be an executive committee of the department whose powers shall be determined by the department subject to approval of the board. It shall be composed of nine persons: the chairperson, vice-chairperson, recording secretary, and six other persons elected by the department, one of whom shall be a member of the Women's Division Executive Committee serving on the Health and Welfare Ministries Department.

The executive committee shall include at least two persons from racial and ethnic groups. The associate general secretary and treasurer of the department shall be members of the executive committee, ex officio and without vote.

¶ **1445.** *Financial Support.*—The department shall derive its financial support from World Service and other funds designated for the program of the Health and Welfare Ministries Department of the General Board of Global Ministries, including such proportion of undesignated gifts as may be determined by the board, and from gifts, wills, and trust funds given especially to the Health and Welfare Ministries Department. The department shall properly administer special gifts for approved work related to the Health and Welfare Ministries Department cultivated by the Mission Education and Cultivation Department. The department is authorized to receive financial grants and trusts from private foundations and funds from public agencies and is empowered to act as trustee for the administration of bequests.

¶ **1446.** *Membership.*—The basic membership of the Health and Welfare Ministries Department shall be in accordance with the bylaws of the board and consistent with the provisions of ¶ 1412.3.

¶ 1447. *Limitation of Responsibility.*—The department shall not be responsible, legally or morally, for the debts, contracts, or obligations or for any other financial commitments of any character or description created, undertaken, or assumed by any institution or interest related to a unit of The United Methodist Church, whether or not such institution or interest shall be approved, accepted, or recognized by the department, or shall be affiliated with the department, or whether or not the promotion or establishment of the same shall be approved by the constitution of the department. No such institution or interest related to a unit of The United Methodist Church and no officer or member of this department shall have any authority whatsoever to take any action directly or by implication at variance with, or deviating from, the limitation contained in the preceding sentence hereof, except as the department may directly own and manage an institution in its own name.

MISSION EDUCATION AND CULTIVATION DEPARTMENT

¶ 1448. *Purpose.*—The **Mission Education and Cultivation Department** exists:

a) To undergird the total program of the General Board of Global Ministries affirming that relating persons to mission through communication, education, and cultivation is itself mission.

b) To initiate and develop programs and resources through which individuals and groups may understand the biblical background and theological basis of the Christian world mission, the involvement of The United Methodist Church in global ministries, the special concerns of women in mission, and the possibilities for personal and corporate witness involvement in and support of those ministries.

c) To initiate and develop programs and resources through which children and youth may understand the mission of the Church. This should be done by the Mission Education and Cultivation Department in cooperation with the General Board of Discipleship.

¶ **1449.** *Responsibilities.*—The program responsibilities of the Mission Education and Cultivation Department are:

1. To interpret to the Church the programs, plans, and policies of the board and to plan and promote emphases on global ministries.

2. To initiate and develop, in consultation with appropriate divisions/departments, programs and resources through which individuals and groups may understand and participate in the global ministries of the Church and to make known channels through which these ministries may be supported.

3. To prepare, sell, and distribute printed, audiovisual, and video and other electronic resources and periodicals for the General Board of Global Ministries.

4. To cultivate, through channels of the Church other than United Methodist Women, the Advance special gifts for national and overseas ministries administered by the National and World Divisions, and the United Methodist Committee on Relief Department, in accordance with the General Council on Finance and Administration, assuming responsibility for providing information to the donors (¶ 914).

5. To work with ecumenical agencies in fulfilling department responsibilities.

6. To develop and coordinate the plans for cultivating mission giving in consultation with the divisions and departments of the General Board of Global Ministries, the General Board of Discipleship, the General Council on Finance and Administration, and the General Commission on Communication, subject to and in harmony with the general financial system of The United Methodist Church as adopted by the General Conference.

7. To cooperate with the Curriculum Resources Committee of the General Board of Discipleship in providing opportunities for missional involvement and understanding at all age levels (¶ 1223).

8. To cooperate with the General Commission on Communication in all ways as mutually agreed upon, including communications, training, audiovisual, and video and other electronic production, benevolence interpretation, and other areas of common concern.

9. To cooperate with the General Board of Higher

Education and Ministry in providing an emphasis on mission education in the schools of theology.

10. To cooperate with divisions, departments, Jurisdictional and Annual Conferences, district superintendents, pastors, local churches, United Methodist Women, men's groups, and other groups within the Church in fulfilling these responsibilities.

11. To coordinate the itineration of missionaries on furlough, retired or on home assignment, providing to them a specific period of training and assistance in effective communication, to include audiovisual techniques, public speaking, briefing on current issues, an overview of the board's work, and an expert's critique of their planned presentation and slides.

¶ **1450.** *Authority.*—The Mission Education and Cultivation Department shall have the authority to make bylaws, to regulate its proceedings in harmony with the charter of the board, and with the approval of the board to develop and carry out its responsibilities (¶ 1402); to recommend a budget for the department to the general secretary, to the Women's Division, and United Methodist Committee on Relief Department; to receive and administer funds allocated to it and to solicit Advance special funds for the work of the World Division, National Division, and United Methodist Committee on Relief Department, in cooperation with the General Council on Finance and Administration.

¶ **1451.** *Executive Committee.*—There shall be an executive committee whose composition, duties, and powers shall be determined by the department. One-half of the members shall be women elected in accordance with ¶¶ 1412.3 and 1424.

¶ **1452.** *Membership.*—The basic membership of the Mission Education and Cultivation Department shall be in accordance with the bylaws of the board and consistent with the provisions of ¶ 1412.3.

MISSION PERSONNEL RESOURCES DEPARTMENT

¶ **1453.** *Purpose.*—The purpose of the **Mission Personnel Resources Department** is to serve the Church in the identification, recruitment, selection, preparation, training, and support of persons in mission service, as well as assisting in the identification of opportunities for Christian service and in representing mission personnel concerns before the board.

¶ **1454.** *Responsibilities.*—1. To administer the Crusade Scholarship Program which enables persons from churches in nations other than the U.S. and from ethnic and racial groups in the U.S. to prepare for leadership in mission in Church and society.

2. To administer the Crusade Scholarship resources in harmony with the mission leadership strategies of the program divisions with fiscal accountability to the General Council on Finance and Administration.

3. To promote the opportunities for mission service related to the General Board of Global Ministries throughout the constituencies of the Church.

4. To recruit and select persons for missionary and deaconess service, and to cooperate with personnel-assigning divisions in orientation, training, and evaluation of personnel and in the staffing of mission agencies.

5. To recommend persons as candidates for commissioning as deaconesses and missionaries, to supervise and confirm the completion of all requirements for commissioning, and assist in arranging for the act of commissioning.

6. To engage in referral, transfer procedures, and career counseling to assist persons in mission in fulfillment of their missional vocation.

7. To establish criteria and procedures and to develop in cooperation with jurisdictional and conference officers opportunities for persons to participate as short-term volunteers in mission.

8. To work with ecumenical agencies in fulfilling departmental responsibilities.

9. To cooperate with the General Board of Higher Education and Ministry in matters related to Crusade Scholarships and the preparation of persons to participate in the representative and commissioned ministries of the Church.

¶ **1455.** *Authority.*—1. To write bylaws as may be needed for the operation of the department.

2. To set broad policies and establish criteria for the awarding of grants for leadership development provided

through the World Communion Sunday Offering and other sources.

3. To plan for the promotion and interpretation of Crusade Scholarship objectives through the Mission Education and Cultivation Department, the Advance Committee, and the General Commission on Communication.

4. To set standards and qualifications for the selection and training of mission personnel and otherwise facilitate their participation in mission through the divisions/departments.

5. To constitute the relationships of deaconesses and missionaries through the act of commissioning.

¶ **1456.** *Executive Committee.*—There shall be an executive committee whose composition, duties, and powers shall be determined by the department. One-half of the members shall be women.

¶ **1457.** *Membership.*—The basic membership of the Mission Personnel Resources Department shall be in accordance with the bylaws of the board and consistent with the provisions of ¶ 1412.3.

UNITED METHODIST COMMITTEE ON RELIEF DEPARTMENT

¶ **1458.** *Purpose.*—The **United Methodist Committee on Relief Department** shall have as its purpose assisting churches in direct ministry to persons in need through programs of relief, rehabilitation, and service: to refugees, to those suffering from root causes of hunger and their consequences, and to those caught in other distress situations. These ministries shall be administered in the spirit of Jesus Christ, shall advance the dignity of persons without regard to religion, race, nationality, or sex, and shall seek to enhance the quality of life in the human community.

¶ **1459.** *Objectives and Responsibilities.*—The objectives and responsibilities of the United Methodist Committee on Relief shall be:

1. To provide immediate relief of acute human need.

2. To respond to the suffering of persons in the United States caused by natural and civil disaster.

3. To work for the rehabilitation of persons outside the

United States caught in distress situations caused by natural disaster, political turmoil, persecution from any cause, or endemic factors.

4. To assist in rehabilitation ministries with refugees, including resettlement, and to work cooperatively with each Annual Conference's Refugee Resettlement Committee, if organized.

5. To attack root causes of hunger and their consequences through programs of economic and social development.

6. To work with ecumenical agencies in fulfilling department responsibility.

7. To participate in the promotion of the One Great Hour of Sharing and to administer its receipts.

8. To communicate with Annual Conferences and churches concerning appeals for help.

¶ **1460.** *Finances.*—Sources of funds for the department shall include: voluntary gifts, One Great Hour of Sharing offering, Advance special gifts, supplementary gifts of United Methodist Women, churchwide appeals made by authority of the Council of Bishops and the General Council on Finance and Administration, and designated benevolence funds. Sources of funds for administrative functions of the General Board of Global Ministries shall be other than designated funds for the United Methodist Committee on Relief. Financial promotion shall be by the Mission Education and Cultivation Department and the General Commission on Communications, in consultation with the associate general secretary of the department.

¶ **1461.** The United Methodist Committee on Relief is authorized to provide for its necessary expense of administration and promotion out of undesignated receipts.

¶ **1462.** The United Methodist Committee on Relief shall receive and allocate funds contributed by churches, groups, or individuals for the purposes designated.

¶ **1463.** Churchwide appeals for funds shall be made only with the approval of the Council of Bishops and the General Council on Finance and Administration.

¶ **1464.** The response of the United Methodist Committee on Relief in the United States shall include only the meeting of human needs growing out of natural or civil disaster. This response shall be made at the request of the appropriate body of The United Methodist Church. Repair and reconstruction of local church property and other church-related property shall be included in the funding response of the United Methodist Committee on Relief only when such response has been included in the appeal made for funds or the Advance special gifts made for this purpose. When this condition has been met, the United Methodist Committee on Relief shall respond in cooperation with the National Division as follows:

1. UMCOR, in consultation with conference disaster response coordinators, bishops, and district superintendents, shall identify specific locations where local church property and church-related properties have suffered damage.

2. This information shall be relayed to the National Division, which shall contact the conference disaster response coordinator to arrange an onsite visit to evaluate damages and initiate an ongoing consultative process.

¶ **1465.** *Organization.*—In fulfilling its purpose the United Methodist Committee on Relief shall:

1. Relate to other divisions and departments of the General Board of Global Ministries in carrying out assigned functions and responsibilities by:

a) Consulting/cooperating with the National Division in domestic natural or civil disaster response.

b) Consulting/cooperating with the World Division in relationship to colleague churches in meeting emergency needs, development programs, rehabilitation and refugee concerns.

c) Consulting/cooperating with the Mission Personnel Resources Department in regard to short-term volunteers.

2. Work in partnership with colleague churches, ecumenical bodies and with interdenominational agencies.

3. Cooperate with colleague churches, ecumenical bodies, and interdenominational agencies in responding to their requests for short-term volunteers.

¶ **1466.** The United Methodist Committee on Relief shall elect an executive committee which shall have the powers granted to it by the department. It shall be composed of five members, including the president, vice-president, and secretary of the department. The associate general secretary and the treasurer of the department and the officers of the board as defined in ¶ 1409.3 shall be members ex officio. At least one-half of the members shall be women. The executive committee shall meet as determined by the department or on call of the president.

¶ **1467.** *Membership.*—The basic membership of the United Methodist Committee on Relief Department shall be constituted in accordance with the bylaws of the board and consistent with provisions of ¶ 1412.3. The associate general secretary and treasurer of the department and the officers of the board as defined in ¶ 1409.3 shall be members ex officio.

Section VIII. General Board of Higher Education and Ministry.

¶ **1501.** *Name.* There shall be a **General Board of Higher Education and Ministry,** hereinafter referred to as the board.

¶ **1502.** *Incorporation.*—The General Board of Higher Education and Ministry shall be a corporation under the laws of Tennessee and shall be responsible for the functions previously conducted by the Division of Higher Education of the General Board of Education and the Commission on Chaplains and Related Ministries of The United Methodist Church.

The General Board of Higher Education and Ministry is authorized to take such action as is appropriate under the corporation laws of Tennessee so as to accomplish the end result stated above, and under which the General Board of Higher Education and Ministry shall be one legal entity.

The divisions of the General Board of Education were not incorporated separately; it is the intent, however, that responsibility for the functions delegated to the divisions by prior legislative action be transferred consistent with the separation of the divisions between the General Board of Discipleship and the General Board of Higher Education and Ministry. In the division of the assets of the General Board of Education, it is the intent that all assets be used in keeping with the original intent and purpose for which they were established or acquired, and so be assigned as appropriate to the General Boards of Discipleship and Higher Education and Ministry respectively. It is further intended that the annuities, bequests, trusts and estates formerly held by the General Board of Education be used for the benefit and use of the General Boards of Discipleship and Higher Education and Ministry (in accord with their purposes as defined in the Discipline) respectively as their interests may appear, and that real estate titles be authorized to be conveyed as appropriate and apportioned where indicated.

In the event that the intent of the original donor of existing annuities, bequests, trusts, and estates cannot be clearly determined in relation to the interests of the two boards, such assets shall be divided equally between the two boards.

It is further intended that should additional assets accrue to the former General Board of Education by reason of annuities, bequests, trusts, and estates not now known and where the intent of the donor can be clearly ascertained, the assets shall be used in keeping with the original intent and purpose for which they were established or acquired and so be assigned as appropriate to the General Boards of Discipleship and Higher Education and Ministry respectively.

It is further intended that should additional assets accrue to the former General Board of Education by reason of annuities, bequests, trusts, and estates not now known and where the intent of the original donor cannot be clearly determined in relation to the interests of the two boards, such assets shall be divided equally between the two boards.

¶ **1503.** *Amenability and Accountability.*—The board shall be amenable to the General Conference and between sessions of the General Conference it shall be accountable to the General Council on Ministries.

¶ **1504.** *Purpose.*—The board exists, within the expression of the total mission of the Church, for the specific purpose of preparing and assisting persons to fulfill their ministry in Christ in the several special ministries, ordained and diaconal; and to provide general oversight and care for campus ministries and institutions of higher education, including schools, colleges, universities, and theological schools.

¶ **1505.** *Objectives.*—All the objectives assigned to the divisions shall be considered to be the objectives of the board. In summary, the board shall have authority:

    1. To maintain the historic mission of The United Methodist

Church in higher education and to serve as advocate for the intellectual life of the Church.

2. To seek to understand and communicate the significance of the Christian mission in higher education and ministry throughout the world as the context in which values and Christian life-style are shaped.

3. To ensure that the board's programs and policies address the needs and concerns for ministry with racial and ethnic persons.

4. To provide counsel, guidance, and assistance to Annual Conferences through their Boards of Ordained Ministry, Diaconal Ministry, and Higher Education and Campus Ministry, and other such program units as may be organized in the Annual Conferences.

5. To study needs and resources for representative ministries, ordained and diaconal, including identification of new types of ministry.

6. To develop and maintain standards and procedures for certification in ministry careers, for consecration into the diaconal ministry and for ordination into the ordained ministry.[32]

7. To promote and give direction to work among racial and ethnic groups for enlistment, training, and placement of persons in the professional church-related ministries.

8. To coordinate and make visible information about career assessment opportunities and continuing education that will assist persons in professional church-related ministries with their professional growth and development.

9. To recruit, endorse, and provide general oversight of United Methodist ordained ministers, including persons who speak languages in addition to English, who desire to serve as chaplains in specialized institutional ministry settings in both private and governmental sectors.

10. To represent The United Methodist Church in, and provide liaison with United Methodist ordained ministers certified by professional certifying and accrediting organizations related to ministry in specialized settings.

11. To plan and implement a continuing ministry to United

---

[32]*See* Judicial Council Decision 507.

Methodist laity in institutions and armed forces who are separated from their local churches.

12. To develop and provide services directed to enlistment for specialized church-related ministries, professional growth and development, and counseling.

13. To offer personnel and placement assistance for persons involved in professional church-related ministries.

14. To conduct research on human needs to be met by the Church through its resources in higher education.

15. To provide for the allocation of funds to institutions and to programs related to the board.

16. To maintain adequate fiduciary/legal relationships with institutions and ministries and to assist Annual Conferences and other judicatories in their responsibilities in these matters.

17. To provide counsel, guidance, and assistance to institutions of higher education in their relationships with governmental agencies.

18. To guard property and endowments entrusted to the institutions and to maintain and enforce adequate trust and reversionary clauses.

19. To monitor and interact with public higher education in terms of its reflection on the wholeness of persons and the meaning of life, and to study and inform constituencies of public policy issues related to higher education, both independent and public.

20. To promote, in cooperation with the General Commission on Communication, special days and funds: Black College Fund, Ministerial Education Fund, United Methodist Student Day, World Communion Sunday, and other funds and special days ordered by the General Conference.

21. To evaluate United Methodist higher education and professional church-related ministries with concern for the quality of their performance and the integrity of their mission.

22. To provide standards and support for and interpretation of the work of United Methodist theological schools.

23. To analyze needs of those in church-related ministries for continuing education, including assessment of effectiveness, professional growth and development, and funding.

24. To provide professional ministerial courses of study for

orderly entrance into ordained and diaconal ministry. In providing these courses of study, consideration shall be given to languages other than English.

25. To provide for a continuing discussion of the theological bases for professional church-related ministries and higher education.

26. To provide such services as will create a climate of acceptance and empowerment for women and racial and ethnic persons in higher education and professional church-related ministries, and to be alert to the necessity of advocacy in behalf of these professional ministries in questions of equity and justice.

27. To provide counsel, guidance, and assistance to professional associations and fellowships related to diaconal and other church-related special ministries.

28. To interpret, promote, and administer the loan and scholarship programs of the board, and to cooperate with the General Board of Global Ministries in matters related to the Crusade Scholarship program (¶ 1454.9).

29. To engage in research related to personnel needs and interpretation of occupational opportunities in the Church.

30. To provide such support agencies as are deemed necessary to carry out the functions of the board.

31. To give priority to the planning and policy development functions of the board on behalf of the Church.

¶ **1506.** *Responsibilities.*—The responsibilities of the General Board of Higher Education and Ministry shall be:

1. To establish and review the objectives of the General Board of Higher Education and Ministry within the wider mission of The United Methodist Church.

2. To establish appropriate organizational structures within the board and staff to achieve established objectives, including writing bylaws, electing officers, establishing committees, electing staff, and filling vacancies in accord with ¶ 812.

3. To determine policy and program, establish goals and priorities, project long-range plans, and to evaluate program and services of the board.

4. To give direction to the staff and to delegate authority to board executives through general oversight of the administration.

5. To report the activities of the board to The United Methodist Church through appropriate agencies of the General and Jurisdictional Conferences.

6. To develop and maintain cooperative relationships with ecumenical agencies and other denominations for the full discharge of the objectives of the board.

7. To cooperate with other agencies in The United Methodist Church in the fulfillment of the programs of the General Conference.

8. To develop and maintain cooperative relationships with higher educational institutions, campus ministries, chaplains and related ministries, and diaconal ministries throughout the world in collaboration with the General Board of Global Ministries.

9. Upon request, to provide resources and technical assistance in higher education throughout the world in collaboration with churches of the Wesleyan tradition.

10. In cooperation with the General Council on Finance and Administration, develop long-range investments and fund-raising projects within the Church which shall guarantee, insofar as possible, the continuous flow of resources for United Methodist higher education for the decades and the centuries to come. In developing such long-range investments, the division shall adhere to the specific investment guidelines adopted by the General Conference.

¶ **1507.** *Organization.*—The membership of this board shall be constituted in accordance with ¶ 805 of the General Provisions and with the addition of these Central Conference members (one of whom shall be a woman): one bishop or an alternate bishop (¶ 810.10), one clergy, and one layperson, to be elected by the Council of Bishops. If a vacancy occurs in the board, it shall be filled in accordance with ¶ 812.

¶ **1508.** 1. *Divisions.*—The board shall be organized into four divisions: the Division of Chaplains and Related Ministries, the Division of Higher Education, the Division of Diaconal Ministry, and the Division of Ordained Ministry.

2. *Offices.*—The board, in implementing the objectives (¶¶ 1503, 1505), shall have authority to establish and maintain the following offices: *(a)* Interpretation; and *(b)* Loans and Scholarships.

¶ **1509.** 1. The work and program of the Divisions of Ordained and Diaconal Ministry shall be supported from the general benevolences of the Church and the Ministerial Education Fund. Funds received by the board for the divisions from the Ministerial Education Fund shall be restricted to the support of theological schools and the Divisions of Ordained and Diaconal Ministry in the development of their programs of enlistment, basic professional degree programs, and continuing education (in accordance with ¶ 921.2*a* and *b*).

2. Administration and other programs of the divisions shall be supported solely from World Service moneys. The associate general secretaries shall recommend through the general secretary of the board to the General Council on Finance and Administration the amount of financial support which should be allocated for the divisions.

DIVISION OF CHAPLAINS AND RELATED MINISTRIES

¶ **1510.** There shall be a **Division of Chaplains and Related Ministries** of the Board of Higher Education and Ministry.

¶ **1511.** The division shall represent The United Methodist Church.

1. All persons have the right to receive the full ministry of the gospel of Jesus Christ. The Church is aware of its responsibility to provide adequate professional ministry to persons in special situations beyond the local church which calls for an ecumenical ministry to persons of different denominations and faith groups. In order to assure high standards of competency, the Division of Chaplains and Related Ministries shall have responsibility for clergy in appointments beyond the local church (¶ 443.1*b*), such as: chaplaincy in the armed forces, Veterans Administration, industry, health-care fields, pastoral counseling, correctional institutions, community service organizations, and those other related areas of service which conference Boards of Ordained Ministry and bishops may designate. Clergy to be appointed to any of the above appointments beyond the local church shall receive ecclesiastical endorsement through the Division of Chaplains and Related Ministries.

2. *Duties.—a) Recruitment.*—The division, in cooperation with other units of the General Board of Higher Education and

Ministry, other agencies of the Church, and the Annual Conferences, shall recruit persons for ordained ministry in the above categories through contacts in undergraduate and graduate schools, including theological schools, national professional societies, and also within the structures of the local church and boards and agencies of the Annual Conferences.

b) Interpretation.—The division is charged with the responsibility to interpret to the Church at large the need to have trained clergy to staff health care settings, homes, correctional settings, industry, the armed forces, and counseling centers. The division will also interpret to its constituents the ongoing concerns of the denomination.

c) Endorsement.—All United Methodist ordained ministers appointed in the above categories shall receive endorsement from the division prior to such appointment. Endorsement is affirmation that a person is performing a valid ministry of The United Methodist Church and has presented evidence of having the special training and skills necessary to perform that ministry. Specific requirements of various ministries, requiring professional certification, shall be met prior to endorsement and appointment. When dictated by unique circumstances, provisional endorsement may be granted by the endorsing committee for appointment purposes. Provisional endorsement is a temporary status that implies verifiable, ongoing movement towards full endorsement and must be authorized annually by the endorsing committee. The division, through the evaluation of readiness of the candidate for endorsement, shall facilitate entry of clergy into these specialized ministry settings. The Division of Chaplains and Related Ministries shall have the authority to adopt rules of procedure for removal of endorsement, after appropriate recommendations, providing that the rights of appeal shall be adequately safeguarded. An endorsing committee, made up of ordained members of the Division of Chaplains and Related Ministries, and chaired by a bishop, shall represent The United Methodist Church in all endorsing procedures.

d) General Oversight.—The division shall provide general oversight for all those under endorsement, particularly for those serving outside the bounds of their Annual Conferences. The division shall assure conference Boards of Ordained Ministry of the validity of ministry and quality of performance of clergy serving under its endorsement.

e) Annual Recommendation.—The division shall verify annually to bishops and conference Boards of Ordained Ministry those clergy under its endorsement and request their reappointment.

f) Advocacy.—The division shall serve as an advocate for persons serving in extension ministries under its endorsement. Such advocacy may include: representing their interests within the nonchurch institutional systems where they serve; representing their interests within the connectional system of The United Methodist Church in conferences and boards and agencies; being in dialogue with the various professional and certifying agencies; helping to facilitate, as an agent on their behalf, the transition into or out of extension ministries; and giving attention to the needs for continuing education and ongoing spiritual formation for those under endorsement.

3. *Laity Outside the United States.*—The division shall assist in providing a ministry to United Methodist laity in or associated with the armed forces stationed in locations outside the United States. The General Board of Higher Education and Ministry through the division shall cooperate with the General Board of Discipleship, General Board of Global Ministries, and other agencies of the Church in preparing materials, planning programs, and providing a continuing ministry that includes such activities as retreats, confirmation classes, and other pastoral functions. Basic to all such ministry will be involvement in the life of the local United Methodist community and existing ecumenical and interreligious programs. These shall take into account the language and cultural needs of the persons involved.

¶ **1512.** The division is authorized to receive such World Service funds as may be allocated for the support of its responsibilities. The division shall also receive and distribute other funds and special gifts as have been or shall be given specifically to the division.

DIVISION OF HIGHER EDUCATION

¶ **1513.** *General Responsibilities.*—1. Higher education is a significant part of our Wesleyan heritage, our present task, and our future responsibility. The Church continues its historic mission of uniting knowledge and vital piety by maintaining educational institutions and a campus ministry, and through them an intellectual, spiritual, and material ministry to all persons within the academic community without respect to sex, race, creed, or national origin.

2. There shall be a **Division of Higher Education** representing The United Methodist Church in its relationships with educational institutions and the campus ministry. The division shall have an advisory relationship to all United Methodist–affiliated institutions, including universities, colleges, secondary and special schools, Wesley Foundations, and similar organizations as well as ecumenical campus ministry groups. The division will, on request, serve in an advisory and consultative capacity to all agencies of the Church owning or administering educational institutions and campus ministry units.

3. The nominating committee of the board shall, insofar as possible, provide representation for nomination as members of the Division of Higher Education an equitable number of persons directly related to the areas of concern of the division.

4. Principal objectives of the division are:

a) To determine the nature of the United Methodist mission in and through its elementary, secondary, and higher educational institutions and campus ministries.

b) To develop policy that enables The United Methodist Church to engage effectively in higher education throughout the world.

c) To encourage the Church in programs designed to nurture and sustain educational institutions and campus ministry units as invaluable assets in the ongoing life of the Church.

d) To promote a campus Christian movement and a concerned Christian ministry of the educational community; to witness in the campus community to the mission, message, and life of Jesus Christ; to deepen, enrich, and mature the Christian faith of college and university students, faculty, and staff through commitment to Jesus Christ and the Church and to assist them in their service and leadership to the world, in and through the Church.

e) To interpret both the Church and its educational institutions and campus ministry to each other; to help the agencies of the Church and higher education participate in the greater realization of a fully humane society committed to freedom and truth, love, justice, peace, and personal integrity.

f) To foster within educational institutions the highest educational standards, effective programs of church relationships, the soundest business practices, the finest ethical and moral principles, and especially Christian ideals; to help people experience release from enslavement, fear, and violence; and to help people live in love.

g) To preserve and protect resources, property, and investments of The United Methodist Church or any conference, agency, or institution thereof, in any educational institution, Wesley Foundation, or other campus ministry unit founded, organized, developed, or assisted under the direction or with the cooperation of The United Methodist Church.

h) To relate to professional organizations of higher education and campus ministry on behalf of The United Methodist Church.

i) To enable the division's constituencies to develop an interest in and response to public policies bearing on higher education, both independent and public.

j) To provide resources and suggest guidelines for Annual Conference Boards of Higher Education and Campus Ministry.

5. The division shall appoint personnel, including an assistant general secretary for campus ministry and an assistant general secretary for schools, colleges, and universities, and shall establish such committees and commissions as may be necessary for effective fulfillment of its objectives. It may adopt such rules and regulations as may be required for the conduct of its business.

¶ **1514.** *Responsibilities to General and Annual Conferences.*— The Division of Higher Education will cooperate with and assist the General and Annual Conferences and their respective boards and area commissions organized in behalf of educational institutions and the campus ministry. (For Annual Conference boards *see* ¶ 732.2.)

1. The division shall:

a) Provide for the cooperative study of plans for maximum coordination of the work of United Methodist higher education with the Church's mission in Christian education.

b) Direct attention of church members to the contribution of United Methodist educational institutions and campus ministry units to the life and character of students, faculty, and staff, and to the place the institutions and campus ministry have in the preservation and propagation of the Christian faith for our time.

2. The division shall assess institutional and campus ministry relationships with and responsibilities to the Church, and shall aid in the determination of the degree of active accord between institutional and campus ministry policies and practices and the policies of the church as expressed in the Discipline and in General Conference enactments.

3. The division shall assist educational societies and foundations related to the Annual Conferences for the promotion of Christian higher education and the campus ministry and shall recognize such societies and foundations as auxiliaries of the division when their objectives and purposes, articles of incorporation, and administrative policies shall have been approved by the Annual Conference within whose boundaries they have been incorporated.

4. The division shall direct attention to the work and needs of those educational institutions which stand in special relationship to The United Methodist Church and shall request support for them. Due recognition shall be given to the needs of the black colleges historically related to The United Methodist Church. (*See* ¶¶ 919, 1523.)

5. The division shall develop policies and guidelines for Annual Conference Boards of Ordained Ministry that will recognize and empower Native American pastoral leadership which emerges from and is affirmed by a Native American community.

¶ **1515.** *Responsibilities to Institutions.*—The Division of Higher Education shall establish policy and practice providing for consultation with and support of United Methodist educational institutions, campus ministry units, and Annual Conference Boards of Higher Education and Campus Ministry in matters of institutional study and evaluation, promotion, interpretation, management, program, and finance.

1. The division shall, in cooperation with the University Senate:

a) Study trends in higher education, the needs of the Church, and public and private educational opportunities and requirements and make recommendations to the educational institutions, and to state commissions or other bodies or publics concerned with higher education.

b) Recommend and approve plans for institutional cooperation, consolidation, or merger between or among United Methodist–related colleges and/or between them and institutions of other denominations which ensure that the interests of The United Methodist Church are adequately protected.

c) Investigate, at its discretion, the objectives, academic programs, educational standards, personnel policies, plant and equipment, business and management practices, financial program, public relations, student personnel services, student development programs, religious life, and church relations of any educational institution claiming or adjudged to be related to The United Methodist Church.

d) Evaluate and classify institutions in order to authenticate relatedness to the Church; determine eligibility for church financial support in accord with the objectives of the Division of Higher Education.

e) Approve changes in institutional sponsorship, relationships to the General or Annual Conferences, including separation from United Methodist program boards, from the General or one or more Annual Conferences or from the University Senate as the certifying agency of The United Methodist Church.

2. The division shall, in regard to campus ministry, Wesley Foundations, and ecumenical campus ministry groups, provide a structure within the division in order to:

a) Assist in development of plans for the systematic evaluation of these units in cooperation with their regularly constituted boards of directors or trustees and with conference, area, or regional committees or commissions on Christian higher education and campus ministry or appropriate ecumenical agencies.

b) Study the trends in programming and funding in campus ministry; review reports from conference agencies and local units; and, interpret these findings to the constituency as appropriate.

c) Affirm its commitment to an ecumenical approach to campus ministry; encourage local, campus, state, and regional units of that ministry to work toward ecumenical programming and structures where appropriate to provide counsel and support to conference boards and agencies in reviewing, evaluating and strengthening existing and proposed local and regional ecumenical covenants for campus ministry; and to ensure that ecumenical covenants and procedures for these units are on file with the Annual Conference Boards of Higher Education and Campus Ministry.

d) Recognize and cooperate with agencies with whom relationships may serve to further the objectives of the division.

e) Provide for representation and participation, as deemed necessary, with other national ecumenical campus ministry agencies.

f) Provide services to meet specific denominational needs.

3. The division shall, as it seeks to interpret higher education:

a) Promote the Church's mission in higher education, including the special missions and educational ministries to ethnic groups, persons with handicapping conditions, and other peoples disadvantaged by world conditions.

b) Promote Christian instruction and provide opportunity for Christian service.

c) Encourage educational institutions and campus ministry units to inculcate human and humane values consistent with the gospel and the public good.

d) Foster the development of Christian community within the life of educational institutions and campus ministry units.

e) Make use of the existing church organization and publications for interpreting the mission of higher education.

f) Participate in the Crusade Scholarship program.

g) Design and organize the promotion of United Methodist Student Day to recognize United Methodist students in higher education.

¶ **1516.** *Financing Higher Education.*—1. In recognition of its heritage and the mandate to maintain its mission in higher education and in light of emergent fiscal concerns, The United Methodist Church affirms its commitment to higher education and to the means by which it can be continuously supported and renewed.

2. The Division of Higher Education shall be empowered to take such action as may be necessary to:

a) Promote the financial support of Christian higher education within the Church.

b) Create arrangements which shall provide for the flow of supporting funds from the whole Church to the institutions affiliated with the Church as affirmed by the University Senate (¶ 1519).

c) Develop corporations, or other fiscal or fiduciary agencies, for the purpose of financing, creating, recycling, managing, or otherwise caring for institutions and campus ministry units or their assets and liabilities.

3. The division, in regard to fiscal matters, shall:

a) Study the financial status of United Methodist educational institutions and campus ministry units, encourage the Church to give them continuous support, and provide consultative services in fiscal affairs and other aspects of institutional management. The division shall study all appropriate related data and may recommend to each conference or agency the support levels appropriate for each related institution or institutions.

b) Appropriate such funds as are available for the support of educational institutions, Wesley Foundations, or other campus ministry units related to The United Methodist Church under such rules as the board may adopt.

c) Take such action as is necessary to protect or recover resources, property, and investments of The United Methodist Church, or any conference, agency, or institution thereof, in capital or endowment funds of any educational institution, Wesley Foundation, or other campus ministry unit founded, organized, developed, or assisted under the direction or with the cooperation of The United Methodist Church should any such institution discontinue operation or move to sever or modify its connection with the Church or violate the terms of any rules adopted by the board or the terms of any such grant of new capital or endowment funds made by The United Methodist Church or any conference, agency, or institution thereof. In order to carry out its duties under this paragraph, the division shall at its discretion investigate, audit, and review all necessary records and documents of any educational institution claiming or adjudged by the division to be related to The United Methodist Church. In the event any such educational institution, Wesley Foundation, or other campus ministry unit shall endeavor to discontinue operation or move to sever or modify its connection with the Church or violate the rules adopted by the division in accordance with ¶ 1516.3*b*, it shall be the duty of the trustees and the administrators of such institutions, along with the conference agency on higher education and the resident bishop of the conference in which such institution is located, to confer at the earliest possible opportunity with appropriate representatives of the division to determine what resources and aid the division may be able to provide and to permit the division to carry out its responsibilities under this paragraph.

d) (1) Foster and aid through a special apportionment the United Methodist institutions historically related to education for black people. It shall have authority to institute plans by which colleges sponsored by the division may cooperate with or may unite with colleges of other denominations or under independent control; *provided* that the interests of The United Methodist Church are adequately protected. (2) Encourage such black colleges to secure adequate endowments for their support and maintenance. Whenever the division is assured that their support will be adequate and the property will be conserved and perpetuated for Christian education under the auspices and control of The United Methodist Church, it may transfer the colleges to boards of trustees under such conditions as the General Board of Higher Education and Ministry may prescribe, which shall include the right of reversion to the board under conditions prescribed by the board.

¶ **1517.** *Membership and Organization.*—1. The **University Senate** shall be the professional educational advisory agency for The United Methodist Church and all educational institutions related to it.[33]

2. The senate shall be composed of twenty-five voting members who, at the time of election, are actively engaged in the work of education through employment in an educational institution and are fitted by training and experience for the technical work of evaluating educational institutions. Election is for the quadrennium, except in cases where conflict of interest arises as a result of change in employment. Nine of these members shall be elected quadrennially by the National Association of Schools and Colleges of The United Methodist Church—seven of whom shall be chief executive officers of United Methodist–related educational institutions, the other two holding other positions relevant to academic or financial affairs or church relationships; four by the General Board of Higher Education and Ministry—two of whom shall be chief executive officers of United Methodist–related higher educational institutions, the other two holding other positions relevant to academic or financial affairs or church relationships; four by the General Conference—two of whom shall be chief executive officers of United Methodist–related educational institutions at the time of their election, the other two holding other positions relevant to academic or financial affairs or church relationships; four by the senate itself, without limitation other than the general provisions of this paragraph; and four shall be appointed by the Council of Bishops—two of whom shall be chief executive officers of United Methodist–related educational institutions, the other two holding other positions relevant to academic or financial affairs or church relationships. Each of the five electing bodies shall elect at least one woman.

Members elected by the General Conference shall be nominated and elected by the following procedure: Twelve persons shall be nominated by the Council of Bishops, six of

[33]*See* Judicial Council Decision 589.

whom shall be chief executive officers of United Methodist–related educational institutions, the other six holding other positions relevant to academic or financial affairs or church relationships. At the same daily session at which the above nominations are announced, additional nominations may be made from the floor but at no other time. From these nominations, the General Conference shall elect without discussion, by ballot and by plurality vote, the four persons to serve on the senate, two from each of the two categories of nominees. Should a vacancy occur in the members elected by General Conference in the interim prior to the next General Conference, the Council of Bishops shall appoint a replacement taken from the remaining nominees. The election process shall be repeated at each succeeding General Conference. Care should be taken that women, racial and ethnic persons, and representatives from the United Methodist–related black colleges and graduate theological seminaries shall be members of the senate. If a member (other than the four elected by the General Conference) retires from educational work, or for any other cause a vacancy occurs during the quadrennium, it shall be filled by the agency by which the retiring member was elected at its next meeting. The general secretary of the General Board of Higher Education and Ministry and the associate general secretaries of the Divisions of Higher Education, Ordained Ministry, and Diaconal Ministry of that board shall serve as ex officio members of the senate, with voice but without vote. There shall be one staff representative, with voice but without vote, from the General Board of Global Ministries on the senate named by the general secretary of the General Board of Global Ministries.

This legislation is to be effective upon the adjournment of the General Conference.

3. The associate general secretary of the Division of Higher Education shall be the executive secretary of the senate. The general secretary of the board shall convene it for organization at the beginning of each quadrennium. The senate shall elect its own officers, including a president, a vice-president, and a recording secretary, and may appoint such committees and commissions and delegate to them such powers as are incident to its work. Thereafter, it shall meet semiannually at such time and

place as it may determine. Special meetings may be called on the written request of five members or at the discretion of the president and the executive secretary.

4. After consultation with the officers of the senate, the Division of Higher Education shall provide in its annual budget for the expense of the senate as it may deem sufficient, except that expenses incurred by the senate on behalf of any other board of the Church shall be borne by that board.

¶ **1518.** *Purposes and Objectives.*—1. To be the professional educational agency representing the common interests of The United Methodist Church and its affiliated schools, colleges, universities, and graduate theological seminaries.

2. To support the development of institutions whose aims are to address and whose programs reflect significant educational, cultural, social, and human issues in a manner reflecting the values held in common by the institutions and the Church.

3. To provide an effective review process so that institutions that qualify for University Senate affiliation and church support will be recognized as having institutional integrity, well-structured programs, sound management, and clearly defined church relationships.[34]

4. To establish effective annual reporting procedures that will provide the senate with the data necessary to complete its review of the institutional viability and program integrity of member institutions.

¶ **1519.** *Institutional Affiliation.*[35]—1. Approval by the senate is prerequisite to institutional claim of affiliation with The United Methodist Church.

2. Every effort shall be made by both the Annual Conferences and institutions to sustain and support each other, but identification of an institution with The United Methodist Church shall depend upon its approval by the senate. The senate shall provide adequate guidelines and counsel to assist institutions seeking initial or renewed affiliation.

3. Only institutions affiliated with The United Methodist Church through approval by the senate shall be eligible for

---

[34]*See* Judicial Council Decision 589.
[35]*See* Judicial Council Decision 589.

funding by Annual Conferences, General Conference, general boards, or other agencies of The United Methodist Church.

4. To qualify for affiliation with The United Methodist Church, institutions must maintain appropriate academic accreditation.

5. Assessment of church relationships shall be a part of the process for those institutions seeking approval of the senate for affiliation with The United Methodist Church. Inasmuch as declarations of church relationships are expected to differ one from the other, and because of the diversity in heritage and other aspects of institutional life, declarations of church relationship will necessarily be of institutional design.

¶ **1520.** *Responsibilities.*—1. Each year the senate shall publish a list classifying United Methodist–affiliated institutions. These institutions shall include secondary schools, colleges, universities, graduate theological seminaries, and special schools.

2. The senate shall also prepare annually a list of approved schools, colleges, universities, and graduate theological seminaries for use by Annual Conference Boards of Ordained Ministry in determining candidate educational eligibility for admission into full connection.

3. An institution which chooses to disaffiliate with The United Methodist Church for any reason shall: *a)* inform the University Senate as soon as possible after discussions begin concerning disaffiliation; *b)* inform all appropriate United Methodist judicatories; *c)* seek technical and legal assistance from the Division of Higher Education regarding fiduciary issues.

4. The senate shall publish annually, with its list of United Methodist–affiliated institutions, the names of institutions of other historic Methodist churches which wish to participate in research projects, the insurance program, and technical services of the General Board of Higher Education and Ministry. Such institutions shall be designated as "associate" institutions.

¶ **1521.** *Consultative Relationship with Institutions.*—1. Support for approved institutions shall include, through the appropriate divisions of the General Board of Higher Education and Ministry, consulting teams with skills in comprehensive institutional design, management, governance, and program.

2. Support for approved institutions shall include an interpretation of and consultation on data in the annual institutional reports.

3. The Division of Higher Education shall report annually to the senate on the level and types of institutional support rendered by related conferences and agencies and shall evaluate such support, including specific responses of conferences and agencies to recommended levels.

NATIONAL METHODIST FOUNDATION FOR CHRISTIAN HIGHER EDUCATION

¶ **1522.** The **National Methodist Foundation for Christian Higher Education** is incorporated in the state of Tennessee as a nonprofit, charitable organization with permanent ties to the Division of Higher Education, which elects its Board of Trustees. The general purpose of the foundation is to foster the growth and development of institutions of higher education by encouraging persons and corporations to provide financial support and by acting as a foundation for such support. The foundation is also authorized to serve as a trustee and administrator of gifts and bequests designated by donors to specific institutions.

¶ **1523.** 1. There shall be an organization known as the **Council of Presidents of the Black Colleges.** It shall be composed of all the presidents of the United Methodist institutions historically related to the education of black people and with a current relationship to The United Methodist Church.

2. *Purposes and Objectives.*—The purpose of the council shall be to:

a) Help identify and clarify the roles of these colleges in higher education and The United Methodist Church.

b) Promote fund-raising efforts through the Church.

c) Study, review, and discuss programs of member institutions.

The council shall have a minimum of two regular meetings in each calendar year, and shall be amenable to the Division of Higher Education in the implementation of its responsibilities.

DIVISION OF DIACONAL MINISTRY

¶ **1524.** The Division of Diaconal Ministry shall be responsible for the work of the General Board of Higher Education and Ministry that relates to (1) persons preparing for the office of diaconal minister, (2) persons currently consecrated to the office of diaconal minister, (3) persons certified in various specialized ministries for which an agency of the church has set professional standards and (4) persons currently serving in professional ministry careers.

¶ **1525.** *Purpose.*—The purpose of the Division of Diaconal Ministry shall be:

1. To cooperate in the study of the needs of the United Methodist ministry, especially in regard to diaconal ministry, and to make recommendations accordingly.

2. To cooperate with other units of the board and other denominational agencies in interpreting the diaconal ministry as vocation and the educational preparation for such ministry.

3. To provide guidance and standards for the academic preparation for diaconal ministry.

4. To develop personal, church, and professional standards for persons in the diaconal ministry of The United Methodist Church and to provide guidance relating to the ethical and moral problems in specialized ministry.

5. To participate in the continuing study of the ministry so as to include matters of importance to the diaconal ministry in its reports to the General Board of Higher Education and Ministry and to the General Conference.

6. To study needs and develop standards and procedures for certification in professional ministry careers of The United Methodist Church.

7. To review the conference Boards of Diaconal Ministry recommendations of persons to be approved for professional certification by the Division of Diaconal Ministry of the General Board of Higher Education and Ministry.

8. To provide guidance and standards for the academic preparation for professional ministry careers.

9. To develop guidelines and resources for continuing education of persons subsequent to their consecration and/or

certification, and to develop means of in-service training and continuing education to strengthen their ministry.

10. To develop guidelines and resources for the work of the conference Board of Diaconal Ministry.

11. To provide resources and training to the conference Board of Diaconal Ministry concerning counseling and examination of candidates for consecration to the office of diaconal minister and for certification in professional ministry careers.

¶ **1526.** *Responsibilities.*—The Division of Diaconal Ministry shall:

1. Develop and recommend to the General Board of Higher Education and Ministry and to the General Conference the requirements and standards that shall be minimal for consecration to the office of diaconal minister in The United Methodist Church.

2. Develop and recommend to the General Board of Higher Education and Ministry and to the General Conference the requirements and standards that shall be minimal for certification in professional ministry careers of The United Methodist Church, after consultation with the agencies responsible for programs and areas of work related to the careers.

3. Work with the graduate theological seminaries, other graduate schools, colleges, and universities in development of curricula for the academic preparation of diaconal ministers and others in professional ministry careers, including the Foundational Studies for Diaconal Ministers and the Certification Studies in Ministry Careers.

4. Develop and recommend programs of continuing education for diaconal ministers and others in professional ministry careers.

5. Participate in the study and interpretation of career opportunities in the diaconal ministry.

6. Work with conference Boards of Diaconal Ministry in their responsibility to enlist women and men of all races and ethnic origins for diaconal ministry.

7. Work with conference Boards of Diaconal Ministry in their responsibility for administering the standards and requirements for the office of diaconal minister.

8. Work with conference Boards of Diaconal Ministry in their responsibility for administering the standards and requirements for certification in professional ministry careers.[36]

9. Work with the Annual Conference Boards of Diaconal Ministry to encourage the recognition of persons at the time of their entrance into a career in the diaconal ministry, and at the time of the completion of their service in that career.

10. Work with conference Boards of Diaconal Ministry to assure for the diaconal minister conditions of employment, support, and benefits commensurate with the diaconal minister's training, ability, and experience.

11. Work with conference Boards of Diaconal Ministry and other United Methodist agencies to foster cooperative relationships among persons in the diaconal ministry of The United Methodist Church, and with their colleagues in other denominations and faiths.

12. Cooperate with the Christian Educators Fellowship of The United Methodist Church; the Fellowship of United Methodists in Worship, Music, and Other Arts; and other professional associations and fellowships, in ways that will be supportive of their professional ministry careers.

13. Cooperate with other United Methodist agencies and general boards in their resourcing of members in the professional associations and fellowships.

14. Cooperate with the Division of Ordained Ministry and the Division of Chaplains and Related Ministries in the continuing study of the ordained ministry and in other areas of mutual concern.

Division of Ordained Ministry

¶ **1527.** 1. The **Division of Ordained Ministry** shall be responsible for the work of the General Board of Higher Education and Ministry that relates to persons preparing for the ordained ministry and those currently serving under the appointment of a bishop. This responsibility shall be discharged in active relation with schools of theology, jurisdic-

---

[36]*See* Judicial Council Decision 507.

tional Boards or Committees on Ordained Ministry, Annual Conference Boards of Ordained Ministry, and appropriate departments of interdenominational bodies. This division shall be responsible for the promotion of theological education and its support for the whole Church.

2. Areas of concern shall include enlistment, preparation, continuing education, and career development of women and men of all races and ethnic origins in and for the ordained ministry of the Church.

3. The Division of Ordained Ministry shall establish resources for the purpose of enlisting and supporting the effective ministry of women, particularly in Annual Conferences where 3 percent or less of full members are women.

¶ **1528.** The Nominating Committee of the General Board of Higher Education and Ministry, in carrying out its responsibilities, shall provide an equitable number of persons directly related to areas of concern for the division.

¶ **1529.** The specific responsibilities of the Division of Ordained Ministry shall be:

1. To study ministerial needs and resources in The United Methodist Church and to cooperate with appropriate groups in the interpretation of ministry as a vocation, in an effort to enlist suitable persons for ordained ministry.

2. To prescribe the course of study for ordained ministry, which shall include studies required for license as local pastor and the basic five-year course of study. It also shall provide advanced course of study for preachers who have finished the above courses and meet the requirements of ¶ 424.3. All work in the ministerial course of study for candidates for elder in full connection (¶¶ 422-425), renewal of licenses (¶ 405), associate member (¶ 420), probationary member (¶ 415), and local pastors qualifying for appointment (¶¶ 406-409), shall be taken under the direction of the Division of Ordained Ministry in an approved course of study school. The division shall cooperate with the Boards of Ordained Ministry and other conference boards in organizing, financing, and conducting course of study schools. (For exceptional provisions for taking the course of study for ordained ministry by correspondence, *see* ¶ 408.1.)

3. To cooperate with the Boards of Ordained Ministry in

Annual Conferences by (*a*) providing guidance in counseling and examination of ministerial students, and (*b*) assisting in interpretation of current legislation concerning ordained ministry.

4. To provide resources to the district Committee on Superintendency and to the Annual Conference Cabinet in the fulfillment of their work.

5. To provide jointly with the General Council on Ministries and the Council of Bishops the training of district superintendents.

6. To lead in the churchwide interpretation and promotion of the Ministerial Education Fund.

7. To recommend and help organize, finance, and conduct continuing education for all ordained ministers subsequent to ordination and to advise means of in-service training and evaluation, with special care being given that programs are available and relevant for all multiracial/multicultural groups within the denomination.

8. To maintain the educational standards of the ordained ministry of The United Methodist Church and to study problems relating to ministerial status, morale, and support, and to cooperate with the Boards of Ordained Ministry in (*a*) studying problems relating to clergy morale, clergy housing and itineracy and clergy families, and (*b*) developing resources and programs for clergy and clergy families.

9. To study and support coordination and mutual ministry including possibilities for merger of schools.

10. To certify the course offerings in non–United Methodist seminaries for meeting the requirements in United Methodist history, doctrine, and polity specified in ¶ 424.3 and provide Boards of Ordained Ministry with a list of the courses approved. The division will also monitor the implementation of ¶ 1531.

11. To provide for recruiting and preparation of persons for ordained ministry among ethnic groups, including Black Americans, Hispanic Americans, Native Americans, Asian Americans, and those of other national and ethnic origin. Provision for special resources in pretheological and theological education shall be undertaken as training for these distinctive ethnic ministries. Provision for evaluating the credentials and

training of such persons shall be undertaken in cooperation with bishops and Annual Conference Boards of Ordained Ministry.

12. To participate in the Crusade Scholarship program.

SCHOOLS OF THEOLOGY

¶ **1530.** 1. The schools of theology of The United Methodist Church are established and maintained for the education of ordained ministers and the clarification of the Church's faith through research and prophetic inquiry on behalf of the whole Church. They exist for the benefit of the whole Church, and support shall be provided by the Church. They shall receive financial support for the current operating expenses from the Ministerial Education Fund, administered by the Division of Ordained Ministry. (*See* ¶ 921.2.)

2. The Ministerial Education Fund shall be regarded by Annual Conferences as a priority to be met before any additional benevolences, grants, or funds are allocated to a theological school or schools of religion in the conference's region.[37]

3. No school of theology seeking affiliation and support from The United Methodist Church shall be established without first submitting its proposed organization to the Division of Ordained Ministry for prior approval.

¶ **1531.** United Methodist schools of theology, in addition to preparing their students for effective service for Christ and the Church, shall acquaint them with the current programs of The United Methodist Church, such as its educational, missional, social, other service programs; practical experience in administration, stewardship, and other such concerns of order; and with the polity, organization, and terminology of the Church. Each school of theology, in consultation with the General Board of Higher Education and Ministry, shall provide in its curriculum the courses in United Methodist history, doctrine, and polity specified in ¶¶ 424.3 and 306.3c. (*See also* ¶ 1529.10.)

¶ **1532.** The United Methodist schools of theology share with the Boards of Ordained Ministry the responsibility for the

---

[37]*See* Judicial Council Decision 545.

selection and education of candidates for admission to the Annual Conferences.

Section IX. General Board of Pensions.

¶ **1601.** *Name, Corporations, and Locations of Offices.*— 1. There shall be a **General Board of Pensions** of The United Methodist Church, hereinafter called the board, having the general supervision and administration of the support, relief, and assistance and pensioning of ordained ministers and their families, other church workers, and lay employees of The United Methodist Church, hereinafter referred to as beneficiaries, in succession to the Board of Pensions of The Evangelical United Brethren Church and in succession to the General Board of Pensions of The Methodist Church. The Board of Pensions of The Evangelical United Brethren Church, which is incorporated under the laws of the State of Ohio in that name, and the Board of Pensions of The Methodist Church, which is incorporated under the laws of the State of Illinois in that name, and the Board of Pensions of The Methodist Church, which is incorporated under the laws of the State of Maryland in that name, and the Board of Pensions of The Methodist Church, which is incorporated under the laws of the State of Missouri in that name, shall be continued, subject to the direction, supervision, and control of the General Board of Pensions of The United Methodist Church, but with their corporate names changed to and to be known as The Board of Pensions of The United Methodist Church, Incorporated in Ohio, and The Board of Pensions of The United Methodist Church, Incorporated in Illinois, and The Board of Pensions of The United Methodist Church, Incorporated in Maryland, and The Board of Pensions of The United Methodist Church, Incorporated in Missouri, respectively.

2. The general supervision and administration of the pension and benefit funds, plans, and programs of The United Methodist Church, subject to the direction, supervision, and control of the board, shall be conducted by and through the headquarters office.

3. The board shall have authority to establish, maintain, and discontinue from time to time such auxiliary offices as it shall deem proper and advisable.[38]

¶ **1602.** 1. *Membership.*—*a)* The board shall be composed of one bishop, elected by the Council of Bishops; one ordained minister, one layman, and one laywoman from each jurisdiction, elected by the respective Jurisdictional Conferences; two clergywomen in full connection, two laymen, and two laywomen, with not more than two from the same jurisdiction, elected by the General Conference on nomination of the Council of Bishops; and eight additional members for the purpose of bringing to the board special knowledge or background, with consideration given to representation by women and racial and ethnic groups, not more than two from the same jurisdiction, nominated and elected by the board in such manner as it shall provide in its bylaws.

b) The clergy membership of the board shall be limited to clergy members of an Annual Conference.[39]

c) The general secretary of the board shall be an ex officio member thereof, without vote.

d) The terms of all members so elected shall be four years, to take effect at the annual meeting of the board following the General Conference. Members shall serve during the terms for which they are elected and until their successors shall have been elected and qualified.

e) A vacancy in the membership shall be filled for the unexpired term by the board.

f) The members of the board shall constitute the membership of the respective Boards of Directors of the aforesaid four constituent corporations. The general secretary shall be an ex officio member of each, without vote.

2. *Meetings.*—The annual meetings of the board and of the Boards of Directors of the constituent corporations shall be held at the same date and place, at which time the board shall review and consider responsibilities committed to its care and take such action as it deems advisable in the furtherance of the best interest of the funds, plans, and programs administered by the board.

---

[38]*See* Judicial Council Decisions 577, 585.
[39]*See* Judicial Council Decision 558.

Special meetings of the board may be called by any two of the officers hereinafter named in ¶ 1603.

3. *Quorum.*—A majority of the members of the board shall constitute a quorum.

¶ **1603.** 1. *Officers.*—The board shall elect at its annual meeting next following the General Conference a president, a vice-president, and a recording secretary, all of whom shall be members of the board, and shall also elect a general secretary and a treasurer, all for four-year terms. The officers so elected shall serve during the terms for which they were elected and until their successors shall have been elected and qualified. The officers of the board shall also be elected by, and serve as the officers of, each of the four constituent corporations of the board. A vacancy in any of these offices may be filled by the board for the remainder of the unexpired term. Other offices that are deemed desirable and to the best interest of the board for carrying out its purposes may be created by the board, and persons may be elected or appointed to fill such offices.

2. *Executive Committee.*—An executive committee shall be elected by the board. The same committee shall also respectively be elected by, and serve as the executive committee of, each of the four constituent corporations unless otherwise required by applicable laws of the respective states of incorporations, in which case the board shall recognize such laws, and the board and the corporations shall have power to comply therewith.

3. *Committee on Rules and Regulations.*—The board shall elect quadrennially from its membership a Committee on Rules and Regulations, which shall consist of the bishop, one ordained minister, and one lay person from each jurisdiction and two ordained ministers and two lay persons from the membership of the board at large, whose responsibility it shall be to study the operation of the several pension and benefit funds, plans, and programs administered by the board, to present its recommendations for revision of the rules and regulations of the said pension and benefit funds, plans, and programs for consideration and action by the board, under authority granted to the board by the General Conference, and to present to the General Conference such proposed revisions of the Discipline as may be recommended by the board.

¶ **1604.** *General Authorizations.*—1. The General Board of Pensions, consistent with the Church's mandate for inclusiveness of the Church and for racial and social justice, is authorized to adopt and further any and all plans, to undertake any and all activities, and to create, obtain, accept, receive, manage, and administer any and all assets or property, absolute or in trust for specified purposes, for the purpose of increasing the revenues and of providing for, aiding in, and contributing to the support, relief, and assistance and pensioning of ordained ministers and their families and other church workers and lay employees in The United Methodist Church and its constituent boards, organizations, and institutions; to do any and all acts and things deemed by the board to be necessary and convenient in connection therewith or incident thereto; and to perform any and all other duties and functions from time to time imposed, authorized, or directed by the General Conference of The United Methodist Church. No proposal shall be made to the General Conference which changes a benefit presently in effect without first securing through the General Board of Pensions an actuarial opinion concerning the cost and other related aspects of the proposed change.

2. The board is authorized to manage and administer pension and benefit funds, plans, and programs in such manner as may be deemed by the board to be reasonably necessary to achieve an efficient, equitable, and adequate operation; and to receive, hold, manage, and disburse the moneys related thereto in accordance with the provisions of the respective funds, plans, and programs.

3. The board is authorized to receive, hold, manage, merge, consolidate, administer, and invest and reinvest, by and through its constituent corporations, all connectional pension and benefit funds. The board shall discharge its duties with respect to a plan solely in the interest of the participants and beneficiaries and for the exclusive purpose of providing benefits to participants and their beneficiaries and defraying reasonable expenses of administering the plan, with the care, skill, prudence, and diligence under the circumstances then prevailing that a prudent person acting in a like capacity and familiar with such matters would use in the conduct of an enterprise of a like character and with like

aims. The board is encouraged to invest in institutions, companies, corporations, or funds which make a positive contribution toward the realization of the goals outlined in the Social Principles of our Church, subject to other provisions of the Discipline, and with due regard to any and all special contracts, agreements, and laws applicable thereto.[40] Among the tools the board may use are shareholder advocacy, selective divestment, and advocacy of corporate disinvestment from certain countries or fields of business.

4. The board is authorized to receive, hold, manage, adminster, and invest and reinvest, by and through its constitutent corporations, endowment funds belonging to Annual Conferences or other funds for pension and benefit purposes to be administered for such Annual Conferences. The board is encouraged to invest in institutions, companies, corporations, or funds which make a positive contribution toward the realization of the goals outlined in the Social Principles of our Church; *provided,* however, that at no time shall any part of the principal of the endowment funds be appropriated by the board for any other purpose. The net income of such funds shall be accounted for annually by the board and paid over to the Annual Conferences concerned.

5. The board is authorized, on request of an Annual Conference or conference organization or agency of The United Methodist Church, to receive therefrom distributable and reserve pension funds and to make the periodic pension payments to the beneficiaries of such Annual Conference, conference organization, board, or agency, in accordance with a schedule of distribution which shall be provided for the guidance of the board in making such payments. The board shall report annually the details of transactions under this provision. The board shall be entitled to recover the cost of performing such services.

6. The board, by and through its constituent corporations, is authorized and empowered to receive any gift, devise, or bequest made or intended for beneficiaries of The United Methodist Church, being the legal successor to and vested with the legal title

---

[40]*See* Judicial Council Decisions 577, 585.

to any and all such gifts, devises, and bequests. If the language or terms of any gift, devise, or bequest are inexact or ambiguous, the board shall dispose of or administer the same in the manner deemed most equitable according to the apparent intent of the donor as determined by the board after careful inquiry into the circumstances in connection with the making of such gift, devise, or bequest, and after granting full opportunity to all interested parties to be heard, after due and timely written notice of the time and place of hearing. Such notice shall be mailed to each and all interested parties through their respectively known representatives, at their last known addresses.

7. The four constituent corporations shall, until otherwise determined by the board, continue to collect, receive, and administer such gifts, devises, and bequests, and other funds as may be specifically designated to them by donors, subject to the rules, regulations, and policies of the board with respect thereto. All undesignated gifts, devises, bequests, and donations shall be collected, received, and administered under the direction of the board.

8. The board shall not use for operational or administrative purposes funds raised for the World Service budget of The United Methodist Church.

9. The appropriations from the net earnings of the publishing interests which are contributed to the pension programs of The United Methodist Church, and of the several Annual Conferences, shall be distributed on the basis determined by the board.

10. The board shall compile and maintain complete service records of clergy members in full connection, associate members, and probationary members of the Annual Conferences of The United Methodist Church and of local pastors whose service may be related to potential annuity claims. Such service records shall be based on answers to the Business of the Annual Conference questions as published in the journals of the several Annual Conferences and in the General Minutes of The United Methodist Church, or in comparable publications of either or both of the uniting churches, and from information provided by Annual Conference Boards of Pensions. The conference Boards of Pensions

shall be responsible for providing census data when requested by the board on participants and their families including, but not limited to, such data as birthdates, marriage dates, and dates of death.[41]

11. The board shall administer a clearinghouse for the allocation of pension responsibility among the several Annual Conferences, in accordance with the principle of divided annuity responsibility, and for the collection and distribution of pension funds related to such responsibility.

a) For each beneficiary involved in the operation of the clearinghouse the board shall determine the division of responsibility on account of approved service rendered.

b) The board shall have authority to determine the pension responsibility of each Annual Conference, in accordance with the principle of divided annuity responsibility, and to collect from each Annual Conference, as determined on the basis of their respective pension programs, the amount required by the clearinghouse to provide the pension benefits related thereto. Each Annual Conference shall provide funds to meet its annuity responsibility to beneficiaries of other Annual Conferences on the same basis as it provides pension payments for beneficiaries related directly to itself.[42]

c) The board is authorized and empowered to make all the rules concerning details that may be necessary to the operation of the clearinghouse.

12. The board is authorized and empowered to continue the operation, management, and administration of the following pension and benefit funds, plans, and programs, these to include but not to be restricted to: The Ministerial Pension Plan; The Comprehensive Protection Plan; The Lay Pension Plan; The Basic Protection Plan; The Staff Pension Plan; The Senior Plan; Ministers Reserve Pension Fund; The Minister's Reserve Pension Plan; The Current Income Distribution Pension Plan; Joint Contributory Annuity Fund; Staff Pension Fund; The Pension Plan for Lay Employees; Lay Employees Pension Fund; Cumulative Pension and Benefit Fund; Tax-

---

[41]*See* Judicial Council Decision 165.
[42]*See* Judicial Council Decision 360.

Deferred Annuity Contributions Program; Hospitalization and Medical Expense Program; Death Benefit Program; Bishops Reserve Pension and Benefit Fund, in consultation with the General Council on Finance and Administration; The Printing Establishment of The United Brethren in Christ Fund; The Home Office Pension Fund of the General Board of Global Ministries, in consultation with the General Board of Global Ministries; Chaplains Pension Fund, in consultation with the Division of Chaplains and Related Ministries; Retirement Allowance for Bishops, General Church Officers, and Staff Personnel Plan of the former Evangelical United Brethren Church, with funds to be provided by the General Council on Finance and Administration; Temporary General Aid Fund, in consultation with the General Commission on Religion and Race, as determined by the General Conference, with funds to be provided by the General Council on Finance and Administration. The General Board of Pensions shall report to the General Conference, pension and benefit funds, plans, and programs to be proposed for the General Conference to receive, review, adopt, approve, or otherwise act upon this report.

13. The board is authorized to prepare and publish a pension manual related to the funds, plans, and programs administered by the General Board of Pensions, and such other materials not inconsistent with the Discipline as may be deemed reasonably necessary by the board to its efficient operation.

14. In all matters not specifically covered by General Conference legislation or by reasonable implication, the board small have authority to adopt rules, regulations, and policies for the administration of the support of beneficiaries of The United Methodist Church.

15. Pension for service approved for pension credit by an agency of The United Methodist Church receiving financial support from the World Service Fund, the General Administration Fund, the Episcopal Fund, or any authorized general benevolent or administrative fund shall be provided by the employing agency in uniformity with that provided by other agencies under one of the pension funds, plans, or programs administered by the General Board of Pensions of The United

Methodist Church; *provided,* however, that where service has been rendered in two or more agencies, the total pension benefit shall be calculated as if all such service had been with one agency and the final agency shall provide any additional pension benefits necessary to accomplish this; furthermore, such agency may not make any arrangement with a life insurance company or any other entity for the purchase of annuities for the benefit of individual effective or retired employees or take any steps to nullify, in whole or in part, the pension plans or program of The United Methodist Church by making contracts with outside parties.

¶ **1605.** *Permanent Funds.*—1. The **Chartered Fund** shall be administered by the General Board of Pensions for the benefit of all the Annual and Provisional Annual Conferences in The United Methodist Church, the boundaries of which are within the United States, its territorial and insular possessions, and Cuba, unless the General Conference shall order otherwise. Once a year the net earnings of the fund, after provision for depreciation, shall be divided equally among such Annual and Provisional Annual Conferences in accordance with the restrictive rule contained in ¶ 20.

2. The General Board of Pensions shall order and direct that the income from the **General Endowment Fund for Conference Claimants** (formerly known as the General Endowment Fund for Superannuates of The Methodist Episcopal Church, South) held by the General Board of Pensions of The United Methodist Church, Incorporated in Missouri, shall be distributed on account of service of conference claimants rendered in an Annual Conference of The United Methodist Church; *provided,* however, that such distribution shall be restricted to Annual Conferences which, directly or through their predecessor Annual Conferences, participated in raising this fund, in proportion to the number of approved years of annuity responsibility of each Annual Conference as shall be determined by the General Board of Pensions.

Annual Conference Administration

¶ **1606.** *Powers, Duties, and Responsibilities.*—1. The Annual Conference, on recommendation of the conference Board of

Pensions, shall determine the admissibility and validity of service approved, or compensation entering the contribution base, for pension credit and the payments, disallowances, and deductions thereunder, subject to the provisions of the Discipline and the rules and regulations of the pension funds, plans, and programs of The United Methodist Church.[43]

2. *a)* Service rendered prior to January 1, 1982, by an ordained minister or local pastor in The United Methodist Church, including service rendered in either or both of the uniting churches, prior to church union shall be approved for pension credit in accordance with provisions of the Discipline in effect and applicable thereto or as subsequently amended, at the time such service was rendered. Pension for such service shall be provided in accordance with the past service provisions of the Ministerial Pension Plan.

b) Pension for full-time service rendered by an ordained minister or local pastor in The United Methodist Church prior to January 1, 1982, shall be not less than an amount based upon pension credit for service prior to January 1, 1982, and the benefit levels in effect on December 31, 1981; *provided,* however, that the pension of a clergy member whose membership was terminated prior to January 1, 1982, shall be determined in accordance with the provisions of the Discipline, pension funds, plans, and programs in effect at the time of such termination.

c) Pensions earned by bishops (elected by a Jurisdictional Conference), ordained ministers, and local pastors, and protection benefits for such bishops, ordained ministers, and eligible local pastors in The United Methodist Church after December 31, 1981, shall be provided in accordance with the provisions of the Ministerial Pension Plan and the Comprehensive Protection Plan.[44]

3. For service rendered prior to January 1, 1982, the following years of approved service in an Annual Conference of The United Methodist Church shall be counted for pension credit subject to the conditions stated in this paragraph:

---

[43]*See* Judicial Council Decisions 81, 360, 379.
[44]*See* Judicial Council Decision 502.

a) By an ordained minister who is a probationary member or who is in the effective relation as an associate member or a member in full connection in the Annual Conference: (1) as pastor, associate or assistant pastor, or other ordained minister in a pastoral charge; (2) as district superintendent, presiding elder, conference president, conference superintendent, or other full-time salaried official of the conference; (3) under appointment beyond the local church to an institution, organization, or agency which in the judgment of the Annual Conference rendered to it some form of service, direct or indirect, sufficient to warrant pension credit, or to a community church, or as a conference-approved evangelist; *provided,* however, that such institution, organization, agency, community church, or evangelist accepts and pays such apportionments as the conference may require, with the recommendation that this apportionment shall be not less than twelve times the annuity rate of the conference; and *provided* further, that pension related to such service may be arranged through one of the pension funds or plans administered by the General Board of Pensions; (4) as a student appointed to attend school, but only if the ordained minister serves subsequently with pension credit in an Annual Conference or conferences for three or more years under appointment other than to attend school, such credit as a student not to exceed three years; *provided,* however, that all years for which pension credit was given under legislation in effect prior to the 1972 General Conference, on account of appointment to attend school, shall be counted in determining the pension claim thereon; and *provided* further, that, if a clergy member is again appointed to attend school after having served under appointment for six consecutive years as an ordained minister in full connection with pension credit in an Annual Conference or conferences other than under appointment to attend school, pension credit shall be given for up to but not more than three additional years under appointment to attend school if the ordained minister serves subsequently with pension credit in an Annual Conference or conferences for three or more additional years under appointment other than to attend school; (5) as an ordained minister on sabbatical leave, *provided* that not less than five of the ten years just preceding the granting of such leave were served with pension credit in the Annual

Conference which grants the sabbatical leave; and (6) as an ordained minister on disability leave subsequent to the 1968 Uniting Conference, not to exceed fifteen years.[45]

b) By a person classified by the Board of Ordained Ministry as eligible to be appointed as a full-time local pastor, and by an approved supply pastor prior to church union in 1968, as a pastor or assistant pastor of a pastoral charge in full-time service under appointment; *provided,* however, that such credit shall be conditional and subject to provisions hereinafter stated in this paragraph.[46]

c) By an ordained minister from another Christian denomination who has not attained the age of mandatory retirement for a conference clergy member, who has not retired from the denomination, and who is approved by the Annual Conference on recommendation of the Board of Ordained Ministry as provided in ¶ 426.2, who renders full-time service under appointment as a pastor or assistant pastor subject to provisions hereinafter stated in this paragraph.

d) In calculating fractions of years of service for pension credit earned prior to January 1, 1982, the following formula shall be used:

(1) Any period of up to and including forty-five days shall not be counted.

(2) Forty-six days up to and including one hundred thirty-six days shall be counted as one quarter of a year.

(3) One hundred thirty-seven days up to and including two hundred twenty-eight days shall be counted as one half of a year.

(4) Two hundred twenty-nine days up to and including three hundred nineteen days shall be counted as three quarters of a year.

(5) Three hundred twenty days up to and including three hundred sixty-five days shall be counted as one year.

4. Concerning the normal conditions for pension credit and pro rata pension credit, the following provisions shall apply for service rendered prior to January 1, 1982, in determining

---

[45]*See* Judicial Council Decisions 180, 219.
[46]*See* Judicial Council Decisions 73, 206.

approval for pension credit, eligibility for pension, and allocation of responsibility:

a) Normal Conditions.—The normal conditions required of a clergy member or a local pastor for full pension credit shall be:

(1) That full-time service is rendered by a person appointed to a field of labor under provisions of ¶ 437.1;

(2) That this person not be attending school as a regular student except as provided in ¶ 1606.3*a*(4);

(3) That this person not be substantially employed in work other than that to which he or she is appointed by the bishop;

(4) That this person receive not less cash support per annum from all church and/or conference-related sources than that provided in the schedule of equitable salaries adopted by the Annual Conference for those in this person's classification.

b) Proportional Pension Credit.—Effective as of the closing day of the 1980 Annual Conference session, pro rata pension credit may be granted to persons appointed to less than full-time service under the provisions of ¶ 437.2 by a three-fourths vote of those present and voting in the Annual Conference session on recommendation of the conference Board of Pensions. Such pension credit shall be in one-quarter year increments; *provided,* however, that no one individual receives in excess of one year of pension credit per annum.

c) Full Pension Credit.—Full pension credit may be granted for persons not meeting some or all of the above conditions by a three-fourths vote of those present and voting in the Annual Conference on recommendation of the conference Board of Pensions.[47]

d) Service as a chaplain on full-time duty prior to December 31, 1946, which previous legislation includes as eligible to be counted in determining the annuity claim on an Annual Conference, shall be so recognized.

e) Pension responsibility on account of the appointment of a clergy member of an Annual Conference to attend school prior to 1982 shall be allocated to the conference or conferences in which

---

[47]*See* Judicial Council Decision 386.

the ordained minister shall first thereafter render six years of service under appointment to a local church, to conference staff, as a district superintendent, or to an appointment beyond the local church normally considered to be eligible for pension by the Annual Conference. This allocation procedure shall continue through December 31, 1987, at which time any unallocated years shall be assigned on a pro rata basis to the conference or conferences in which service under appointment to a local church, to conference staff, as a district superintendent, or to an appointment beyond the local church normally considered to be eligible for pension coverage by the Annual Conference totalled less than six years; *provided,* however, that such allocation shall not apply in cases where pension payments were in effect prior to January 1, 1985, on the basis of the allocation of responsibility under previous legislation.

f) Service of a local pastor prior to 1982 may be approved for pension credit only by vote of the Annual Conference, on recommendation of the conference Board of Pensions, after consultation with the district superintendents. If such credit is granted, it should be included under the Discipline question, "What other personal notation should be made?"

g) Upon recommendation of the conference Board of Pensions and by a three-fourths vote of those present and voting in the Annual Conference, pension credit may be granted to a clergy member of the conference on account of full-time service previously rendered as an approved local pastor or approved supply pastor to an institution, organization, or agency, which in the judgment of the Annual Conference rendered to it some form of service sufficient to warrant pension credit; *provided,* however, that such institution, organization, or agency shall accept and pay such apportionment as the conference may require.

h) On recommendation of the conference Board of Pensions and approval by the Annual Conference, appointments beyond the local church shall be listed in the conference journal as follows: (1) with pension credit by the Annual Conference or (2) with pension responsibility on the institution or agency served. If at any session the conference fails to make such listing, it may be done subsequently, whenever desirable, under the Business of the Annual Conference question, "What other personal notation should be made?"[48]

i) In the event of retirement under ¶ 453.2*b*, the actuarially reduced pension or subsequent pension resulting from annuity rate increases for service rendered prior to January 1, 1982, shall be determined by multiplying the pension (years times rate) by a percentage factor; such percentage factor shall be the greater of 100 percent minus one-half percent per month or fraction of a month of age less than sixty-five years attained on the date the actuarially reduced pension is to commence (or the date of such annuity rate increase), or 100 percent minus one-half percent per month for each month of difference between the assumed date at which pension payments would have been permitted by retirement under ¶ 453.2*c* by completion of forty years of service under appointment and the actual date the actuarially reduced pension or annuity rate increase is to commence under ¶ 453.2*b*. Effective at the close of the 1988 General Conference, if retirement is granted in accordance with ¶ 453.2*d*, the actuarially reduced pension shall be calculated from the deferred retirement date. Such actuarially reduced pension shall be calculated by the General Board of Pensions and allocated pro rata to the Annual Conference or conferences which are charged with the pension responsibility.[49]

5. *a)* A pension shall be payable on account of pension credit for service prior to 1982 as a full-time local pastor or supply pastor if (1) the local pastor shall have been admitted as an associate or probationary member or member in full connection in an Annual Conference and has subsequently been placed in the retired relation by the conference, or (2) the local pastor shall have rendered no less than four consecutive years of full-time service with pension credit for service prior to 1982 or with full participation in the Comprehensive Protection Plan since 1981, or a combination thereof, in one Annual Conference and has been recognized by an Annual Conference as a retired local pastor.

b) On recommendation of the conference Board of Pensions,

---

[48]*See* Judicial Council Decision 95.
[49]*See* Judicial Council Decision 428.

a pension shall be payable on account of pension credit for service prior to 1982 for an ordained minister from another Christian denomination who shall have rendered not less than four consecutive years of full-time service with pension credit for service prior to 1982 or with full participation in the Comprehensive Protection Plan since 1981, or a combination thereof, in one Annual Conference while qualified under ¶ 426.2, who has attained the age of voluntary retirement for a conference clergy member and who has been retired by the denomination, providing the ordained minister is not receiving a pension for the same period of service from another denomination. (*See also* §3*c* above.)

6. The Annual Conference, on recommendation of the conference Board of Pensions, shall have the power to revise, correct, or adjust an ordained minister's record of pension credit as set forth in the minister's service record. Prior to the revision of such record, the General Board of Pensions may be requested to review relevant data and report its findings thereon. Such revisions, corrections, and adjustments shall be published in the journal of the Annual Conference in answer to Business of the Annual Conference questions and shall be reported to the General Board of Pensions by the conference Board of Pensions.[50]

7. The Annual Conference shall review annually the annuity rate for service rendered in the Annual Conference prior to January 1, 1982, for the purpose of adjusting the rate as appropriate, taking into account changes in economic conditions. Such annuity rate shall be determined each year without restriction, other than that contained in ¶ 1606.2*b*, but it is recommended that such rate be not less than 1 percent of the average compensation of the conference as computed by the General Board of Pensions. The annuity rate for approved service of local pastors shall also be determined by the conference each year and may be the same as the rate for service of conference members, but it shall be no less than 75 percent of that rate. A successor conference resulting from a merger involving a former Central Jurisdictional Conference shall establish for all

---

[50]*See* Judicial Council Decision 386.

for whom it has pension responsibility the same rate for past service of conference members in the Central Jurisdiction as for service in a geographic former Methodist jurisdiction and the same rate for past service of local pastors regardless of the jurisdiction in which the service was rendered.[51]

8. Persons who have served full-time appointments beyond the local church under endorsement by the Division of Chaplains and Related Ministries are eligible for pension support for those years of service so served for which no other pension is provided. Such pension support shall be in accordance with the Chaplains Pension Fund or the Ministerial Pension Plan under arrangements agreed to by the General Board of Higher Education and Ministry through its Division on Chaplains and Related Ministries and the General Board of Pensions.

9. The responsibility for pension for service approved for pension credit shall rest with the Annual Conference in which the service was rendered; *provided,* however, that in the event of mergers, unions, boundary changes, or transfers of churches, such responsibility shall rest with the successor Annual Conference within whose geographical boundaries the charge is located.[52]

10. Pension for service approved for pension credit by an Annual Conference shall be provided by the Annual Conference under one of the pension funds, plans, or programs administered by the General Board of Pensions of The United Methodist Church.

11. An Annual Conference may not make any arrangement with a life insurance company for the purchase of annuities for the benefit of individual effective or retired ministers or take any steps to nullify, in whole or in part, the pension plans and programs of The United Methodist Church by making contracts with outside parties.[53]

12. *Other Annual Conference Organizations.—a)* Annual Conferences, hereinafter called conferences, are authorized to establish, incorporate, and maintain investment funds, preachers aid societies, and organizations and funds of similar character,

---

[51]*See* Judicial Council Decisions 360, 389.
[52]*See* Judicial Council Decisions 203, 389, 523.
[53]*See* Judicial Council Decision 585.

under such names, plans, rules, and regulations as they may determine, the directors of which shall be elected or otherwise designated by the conference, where permissible under the laws of the state of incorporation, and the income from which shall be applied to the support of the pension program through the conference Board of Pensions.[54]

b) Distributable pension funds from all sources shall be disbursed by or under the direction of the conference Board of Pensions, excepting only such funds as are otherwise restricted by specific provisions or limitations in gifts, devises, bequests, trusts, pledges, deeds, or other similar instruments, which restrictions and limitations shall be observed.

c) It shall not be permissible for any conference or permanent fund organization thereof to deprive its beneficiaries who are beneficiaries in other conferences of the privilege of sharing in the distribution of the earned income of such funds through the clearinghouse administered by the General Board of Pensions.

d) (1) Prior to January 1, 1982, a conference subject to the laws of the state in which it is incorporated shall have power to require from its clergy members and local pastors who are serving with pension credit from the conference an annual contribution to either its permanent or reserve fund or for current distribution or to a preachers aid society for the benefit of its beneficiaries, subject to the following provisions:[55]

(a) The annual payment may be made in installments as provided by the conference.

(b) The making of such payment shall not be used as the ground of contractual obligations upon the part of the conference or as the ground of any special or additional annuity claim of a member against the conference; neither shall it prevent disallowance of a member's annuity claim by conference action.

(c) The conference may fix a financial penalty for failure of the member to pay.

(d) In case membership in the conference is terminated under the provisions of the Discipline, the conference may

---

[54]*See* Judicial Council Decision 218.
[55]*See* Judicial Council Decision 181.

refund the amount so paid, in whole or in part, after hearing has been given to the member, in case such hearing is requested.

(e) Ordained ministers entering a conference shall not be charged an initial entry fee by any organization mentioned in §*a* above; furthermore, the annual contribution required from a clergy member of the conference or a local pastor shall not exceed an amount equal to 3 percent of the ordained minister's or local pastor's support.

(2) If an ordained minister is participating in one of the pension funds, plans, or programs administered by the General Board of Pensions, the minister shall not be required by the conference or by an organization thereof related to the support of beneficiaries to make any other contribution for pension purposes.

e) Each conference, on recommendation of its conference Board of Pensions or one of the organizations mentioned in §*a* above, may select a Sunday in each year to be observed in the churches as Retired Ministers Day, in honor of the retired ordained ministers, their spouses, and the surviving spouses of ordained ministers in recognition of the Church's responsibility for their support. The bishop may request each conference in the area to insert a Retired Ministers Day in its calendar.

13. A conference Board of Pensions may make special grants to clergy members or former clergy members and to local pastors or former local pastors of an Annual Conference who have served under appointment in that conference; or to their spouses, former spouses, surviving former spouses, or surviving dependent children (including adult dependent children). A report of such special grants shall be made annually to the Annual Conference.

14. *a)* A former clergy member of an Annual Conference whose membership was terminated on or after January 1, 1973, and prior to January 1, 1982, after the completion of ten or more years of service with pension credit in an Annual Conference or conferences, shall retain the right to receive a pension, subsequent to the close of the Annual Conference session in which the former ordained minister last held membership which occurs in the year in which the former minister attains age

sixty-two on or before July 1, based on the years of service approved for pension credit. Such former ordained minister's pension shall be based on all years of service with pension credit if the former minister had twenty or more such years. If less than twenty such years but at least ten years, the years used in the calculation of the benefit shall be a percentage of the approved service years; such percentage shall be determined by multiplying the credited whole years by 5 percent, resulting in 50 percent of such years for ten years of credited service and 100 percent for twenty years of such service. If pension begins prior to the age at which retirement under ¶ 453.2*c* could have occurred, then the provisions of ¶ 1606.4*i* shall apply.

b) A former clergy member of an Annual Conference whose membership was terminated on or after January 1, 1982, after the completion of ten or more years of service under appointment in an Annual Conference or conferences, shall retain the right to receive a pension subsequent to the close of the Annual Conference session in which the former ordained minister last held membership which occurs in the year in which the former minister attains age sixty-two on or before July 1 based on the years of service prior to January 1, 1982, approved for pension credit. If pension begins prior to the age at which retirement under ¶ 453.2*c* could have occurred, then the provisions of ¶ 1606.4*i* shall apply.

c) Effective at the close of the 1976 General Conference, former clergy members of the Annual Conference whose membership was terminated on or after such date shall have any vested pension benefits calculated at the annuity rate in effect on the date such person's membership is terminated.

d) Clergy members in an Annual Conference who voluntarily withdraw from the ministry of The United Methodist Church to enter the ministry of another church or denomination, on the attainment of age sixty-two and on recommendation of the conference Board of Pensions and a three-fourths vote of those present and voting in any Annual Conference in which approved service was rendered prior to January 1, 1982, or the legal successor, may be recognized and granted pensions on account of approved service rendered in that conference. If pension begins prior to the age at which retirement under

¶ 453.2*c* could have occurred, then the provisions of ¶ 1606.4*i* shall apply.

15. The responsibility for providing pension on account of service rendered prior to January 1, 1982, in a Missionary Conference, Provisional Annual Conference, or former Mission within the United States or Puerto Rico, which has been approved for pension credit, shall rest jointly with *(a)* the Missionary Conference, Provisional Annual Conference, or former Mission concerned, *(b)* the General Board of Pensions with funds provided by the General Council on Finance and Administration, and *(c)* the National Division of the General Board of Global Ministries. The revenue for pension purposes covering such service shall be provided by the aforesaid parties in accordance with such plan or plans as may be mutually agreed to by them.

16. An ordained minister who has been granted the retired relation in a Central Conference or an Affiliated Autonomous Church, shall be entitled to a pension from a conference or conferences in the United States or Puerto Rico for the years of approved service rendered therein upon attainment of the required age or the completion of the required years of approved service. Such minister shall notify the General Board of Pensions upon his or her retirement. The General Board of Pensions shall certify the years of approved service to each Annual Conference concerned. Payments due thereunder shall be collected from the conference concerned and forwarded to the claimant by the General Board of Pensions in such manner as it may deem most expedient and economical.

17. Pension and benefit contributions are the responsibility of the salary-paying unit of a participant in the Ministerial Pension Plan and the Comprehensive Protection Plan. Unless otherwise determined by vote of the Annual, Missionary, or Provisional Conference, the treasurer of a local church or pastoral charge shall remit such contributions to the General Board of Pensions related to the participant's compensation which is provided from local church funds. If compensation from the local church or pastoral charge is supplemented from other church sources, pension and benefit contributions related to such supplements shall be paid from that same source. If the entire compensation for a participant is from a salary-paying unit other

than a local church or a pastoral charge, the unit responsible for compensation shall remit the pension and benefit contributions to the General Board of Pensions. Nothing in this paragraph shall be understood as preventing an Annual, Missionary, or Provisional Conference from raising part or all of the annual contributions for the pension program of its pastors by an apportionment to the churches of the conference, remitting payments to the General Board of Pensions on behalf of all the pastors covered; there is no time limit on this provision.

18. Actual compensation, limited by the denominational average compensation, is the basic contribution base of the Ministerial Pension Plan and Comprehensive Protection Plan. Other options setting the contribution base as actual compensation limited by 150 percent of the denominational average compensation, or actual compensation, may be elected by the Annual Conference or other participating groups as they may determine. The above limits do not apply to personal contributions or tax-deferred annuity contributions.

19. An Annual Conference may establish a Pension Support Fund to be administered by the conference Board of Pensions. Local churches may request pension assistance from this fund when special circumstances arise which result in nonpayment of pension contributions and/or apportionments for pension and benefit purposes. The board shall present its estimate of the amount required to the conference Council on Finance and Administration which shall include it in its recommendation to the conference. If the amount is approved by the conference, it shall be apportioned as an item of clergy support.

20. The Annual Conference Board of Pensions in consultation with the General Board of Pensions shall have the responsibility to enroll ordained ministers and local pastors of the Annual Conference in the Ministerial Pension Plan and the Comprehensive Protection Plan in accordance with the provisions of such plans (*see* ¶ 407.4).

21. Optional provisions contained in the Ministerial Pension Plan and Comprehensive Protection Plan may be adopted by vote of the Annual Conference subsequent to the receipt of a recommendation from the conference Board of Pensions.

The recommended contribution rate for service rendered after December 31, 1985, for the Ministerial Pension Plan is 12 percent of the contribution base. However, for service rendered after December 31, 1985, the percentage of the contribution base that may be paid to fund the Ministerial Pension Plan in any one year will be limited to:

a) 12 percent, if the then current annuity rate is at least nine-tenths of 1 percent of the conference average compensation, as computed by the General Board of Pensions.

b) For the period January 1, 1986 through December 31, 1989, not more than 11 percent, if the then current annuity rate is at least eight-tenths of 1 percent, but less than nine-tenths of 1 percent of the conference average compensation as computed by the General Board of Pensions.

c) For the period January 1, 1986, through December 31, 1989, not more than 10 percent, if the then current annuity rate is less than eight-tenths of 1 percent of the conference average compensation as computed by the General Board of Pensions.

d) Effective January, 1, 1990, 11 percent, if the then current annuity rate is less than nine-tenths of 1 percent of the conference average compensation, as computed by the General Board of Pensions.

¶ **1607.** *Financing Pension and Benefit Programs.*—The Annual Conference shall be responsible for annually providing moneys in the amount necessary to meet the requirements of the pension and benefit funds, plans, and programs of the conference.

1. The board shall compute the amount to be apportioned annually to meet the requirements of the pension and benefit programs of the conference.

2. After consultation with the board, the conference Council on Finance and Administration shall report to the Annual Conference the amounts computed by the board which are required to meet the needs of the pension, benefit, and relief programs of the conference.

3. Distributable pension funds from all sources, unless restricted by specific provisions or limitations, shall be disbursed by, or under the direction of, the conference Board of Pensions.

4. The board may accumulate a fund from the income for

pension purposes, in order to stabilize the pension program of the conference.[56]

¶ **1608.** *Financial Policy.*—The following rules shall apply to the financial administration of Annual Conference pension and pension-related funds:

1. A member of the board connected or interested in any way with the securities, real estate, or other forms of investment sold to or purchased from such funds, or with an insurance program or a contract under consideration by the board, shall be ineligible to participate in the deliberation of the investment committee or of the board or to vote in connection therewith.

2. No officer or member of a conference agency handling such funds shall receive a personal commission, bonus, or remuneration, direct or indirect, in connection with the purchase or sale of any property, the loan of any money, the letting of any annuity or insurance contract, the making or acceptance of any assignment, pledge, or mortgage to secure the payment of any loan, or for the purchase or sale of any securities or other properties from or to that agency, or be eligible to obtain a loan in any amount from funds committed to the care of that agency. No investment shall be purchased from or sold to any member of the board or any member of the family of a member of the board.

3. To prevent development of any conflict of interest or preferential treatment and to preserve good will and confidence throughout the Church, no local church, church-related institution, or organization thereof shall be eligible to obtain a loan in any amount from such funds.[57]

4. The principle of diversification of investments shall be observed, with the agency encouraged to invest in institutions, companies, corporations, or funds which make a positive contribution toward the realization of the goals outlined in the Social Principles of our Church, however with primary consideration given to the soundness and safety of such investments.

5. Real property may hereafter be accepted as consideration for gift annuity agreements only with the stipulation that the

---

[56]*See* Judicial Council Decision 50.
[57]*See* Judicial Council Decision 145.

annuity shall not exceed the net income from the property until such property shall have been liquidated. Upon liquidation, the annuity shall be paid upon the net proceeds at the established annuity rate.

6. An Annual Conference agency handling such funds shall not offer higher rates of annuity than those listed in the annuity schedule approved by the General Council on Finance and Administration.

7. *a)* There shall be printed in the Annual Conference journal a list of the investments held by each agency handling such funds directly or indirectly under the control of the Annual Conference, or such list may be distributed directly to the members of the Annual Conference at their request. A copy of all such lists of investments shall be filed annually with the General Board of Pensions.

b) The conference Board of Pensions shall require an annual audit of pension and pension-related funds setting forth the total asset value of such funds and the distribution of income from such funds from persons and organizations appointed or employed for the management of these funds.

8. The borrowing of money in any conference year by a conference corporation or organization to enable the conference Board of Pensions to meet the requirements of the pension and benefit programs shall be done only on authority of the conference granted by three-fourths vote of the members present and voting.

9. *Depositories and Bonding.—a)* The conference Board of Pensions shall designate a bank or banks or other depository or depositories for deposit of the funds held by the board and may require a depository bond from such depository or depositories.

b) The board, through the conference Council on Finance and Administration, shall provide a fidelity bond in suitable amount for all persons handling its funds.

¶ **1609.** *Joint Distributing Committees.—*1. *Authorizations.—* Whenever two or more Annual or Provisional Annual Conferences are to be merged, in whole or in part, there shall be elected by each conference affected a Distributing Committee of three members and three alternates, which shall act jointly with similar committees from the other conference or conferences. The Joint

Distributing Committee thus formed shall have power and authority: *(a)* to allocate the pension responsibility involved; *(b)* to distribute equitably the permanent funds and all other pension assets of the conference or conferences affected, taking into consideration the pension responsibility involved, such distribution to be made within twelve months of the date of the dissolution of the committee as provided in ¶ 1609.3*d*; *(c)* to the extent not otherwise previously provided for by the conference or conferences involved, to apportion or distribute equitably any other assets or property and any other liabilities or obligations. It shall be governed by the legal restrictions or limitations of any contract, trust agreement, pledge, deed, will, or other legal instrument.

2. *Organization.*—The committee shall be convened by the general secretary of the General Board of Pensions, or by some other officer of that board designated by the general secretary in writing, and shall elect from its membership a chairperson, a vice-chairperson, and a secretary.

3. *Powers, Duties, and Responsibilities.*—*a)* The committee shall determine the number of years of service approved for pension credit rendered in the conferences which will lose their identity in the merging of conference territories, and the findings of the committee shall be final unless substantial evidence to the contrary is presented, and the annuity payments by the continuing conference or conferences shall be made accordingly. The determination of pension benefits in The United Methodist Church shall recognize all pension rights to which clergy are entitled under the pension plans in existence at the time of church union and shall recognize all approved service which has been rendered in The Evangelical United Brethren Church and The Methodist Church prior to the date of church union.

b) The committee shall keep complete minutes of its transactions, and a copy thereof shall be filed with the secretary of each Annual Conference involved and with the General Board of Pensions.

c) Until the committee's work shall have been completed, the corporate organization of each conference in the process of merger shall be maintained. After the committee shall have completed its work, the officers of such corporation, subject to the completion of its business, shall dissolve or merge it, in after being authorized to do so by the conference involved.

d) The committee, having completed its work in connection with the merger or mergers for which it was organized and having filed copies of its findings and actions with the secretaries of the conferences involved for publication in the respective conference journals, and with the General Board of Pensions, shall be dissolved; subject, however, to recall by the general secretary of the General Board of Pensions in the event of the discovery and presentation to the general board of data substantially at variance with those previously submitted, for the purpose of reviewing such data and possible revision of its previous actions.

4. Whenever a single Annual Conference or Provisional Annual Conference is to be divided into two or more conferences, the provisions of ¶ 1609 shall be applied; *provided* the distributing committee members of each resulting conference shall be named subsequent to the effective date of the division and no later than the first regular annual session of such conferences.

Section X. General Board of Publication.

¶ **1701.** *Publishing Interests.*—The General Board of Publication comprises the publishing interests of The United Methodist Church and shall hereafter be designated as The United Methodist Publishing House. It shall have responsibility for and supervision of the publishing and printing for The United Methodist Church. The General Board of Publication shall through agencies or instrumentalities it deems necessary achieve the objectives set forth in ¶ 1713. The General Board of Publication shall provide publishing and printing services for other agencies of The United Methodist Church and shall share with other agencies of The United Methodist Church in the total program of The United Methodist Church, as well as share in the total ecumenical program in the area of printing and publishing for the advancement of the cause of Christ and his Kingdom as the General Board of Publication shall determine to be appropriate.

¶ **1702.** *Organization.*—The **General Board of Publication,** hereinafter called the board, shall consist of up to fifty members, including two bishops selected by the Council of Bishops. A maximum of ten of these members shall be elected by the board, with consideration given to representation of racial and ethnic groups not elected by the jurisdictions, and to special knowledge or background in publishing, marketing, graphic arts manufacturing, production of audiovisuals or electronic media, or other business fields. Thirty-eight members shall be elected by the Jurisdictional Conferences on a ratio providing for an equitable distribution among the various jurisdictions, based on the memberships thereof; *provided* that no jurisdiction shall be represented by fewer than two members. It is recommended that persons elected by each jurisdiction be inclusive of ethnic groups—Asian American, Black American, Hispanic American, and Native American. Membership on the board shall be equally divided, as far as practicable, between ordained ministers and lay persons. Other paragraphs of the Discipline notwithstanding, membership shall also be by classes based on term of office for one, two, or three quadrenniums, attention being given to the principle of rotation so that, as far as practicable, one-third of the membership shall be elected each quadrennium.[58] The principle of rotation is also applicable to the executive committee. At least two young adults, at the time of their election, shall be elected each quadrennium. It shall be the duty of the secretary of the General Conference to inform the various jurisdictional secretaries of the number of members to be elected from their jurisdictions, the ratio of such representation being computed on the basis of the latest official membership statistics available. In case a vacancy occurs between sessions of the Jurisdictional Conferences for any cause, the board shall fill the vacancy for the unexpired term from that jurisdiction in the representation of which the vacancy occurs, except in the case of members elected by the board where such vacancies would be filled by the board in the prescribed manner without regard to geographic or jurisdictional relationship. The publisher of The United Meth-

---

[58]*See* Judicial Council Decision 593.

odist Church (¶ 1714) shall be an ex officio member of the board without vote.

¶ **1703.** The board shall hold at least one meeting in each calendar year. The place and time of all meetings shall be designated by the board, but if it fails to do so, then the time and place shall be designated by the chairperson. It shall convene at such other times on call of the chairperson or by the board or by the executive committee. At all meetings of the board a majority of the members shall constitute a quorum.

¶ **1704.** The board shall keep a correct record of its proceedings and make written report thereof to the Church through the General Conference.

¶ **1705.** The members of the board and all officers of the board elected by it shall hold office until their successors are chosen and the new board is duly organized.

¶ **1706.** The board is authorized to perfect its organization from its membership, including the offices of chairperson, vice-chairperson, and secretary. The board shall elect from its membership an executive committee of sixteen members, including the chairperson, vice-chairperson, and secretary of the board, who shall serve respectively as chairperson, vice-chairperson, and secretary of the committee. Not more than four members of the executive committee shall be from any one jurisdiction. The bishops serving on the board shall be ex officio members, and the publisher of The United Methodist Church (¶ 1714) shall be an ex officio member without vote. Any vacancy occurring in the membership of the executive committee shall be filled by it, subject to confirmation by the board at its next meeting.

¶ **1707.** The executive committee shall have and may exercise all the powers of the board except those expressly reserved by the board and/or by the Discipline for board action. It shall meet quarterly to examine the affairs under its charge and shall keep and submit to the board correct records of its proceedings. Special meetings may be called by the chairperson on his or her own initiative and shall be called on the written request of five members of the executive committee. A majority of the members shall constitute a quorum.

¶ **1708.** The board shall be the successor in interest to and carry on the work of the Board of Publication of The Evangelical United Brethren Church and the Board of Publication of The Methodist Church.

¶ **1709.** *The United Methodist Publishing House.*—1. The board is empowered and authorized in its discretion to cause the general operations, if any, of the five existing corporations to be conducted under the name of **The United Methodist Publishing House.** The corporations are: The Methodist Book Concern, a corporation existing under the laws of the State of New York; The Methodist Book Concern, a corporation existing under the laws of the State of Ohio; The Board of Publication of the Methodist Protestant Church, a corporation existing under the laws of the State of Pennsylvania; Book Agents of the Methodist Episcopal Church, South, a corporation existing under the laws of the State of Tennessee; and the Board of Publication of The Methodist Church, a corporation existing under the laws of the State of Illinois.

2. The board is authorized and empowered at any time it may deem such action to be desirable or convenient to take corporate action in the name of said corporations to surrender the charter or charters of one or several or all of said corporations or to merge, consolidate, or affiliate such corporations, or any of them, in compliance with appropriate state corporation laws.

¶ **1710.** The members of the board shall serve and act as directors or trustees of the corporations named in ¶ 1709.

¶ **1711.** The corporations named in ¶ 1709 are agencies or instrumentalities through which The United Methodist Church conducts its publishing, printing, and distribution in the name of The United Methodist Publishing House in accordance with the objectives set forth in ¶ 1713. Each of these corporations shall comply with the policies set forth in ¶ 815.

¶ **1712.** The board shall examine carefully the affairs of The United Methodist Publishing House and make written report thereof to the Church through the General Conference.

¶ **1713.** *Objectives.*—The objectives of The United Methodist Publishing House shall be: the advancement of the cause of Christianity throughout the world by disseminating religious knowledge and useful literary, scientific, and educational information in the form of books, tracts, multimedia, and periodicals; the promotion of Christian education; the implementation of any and all activities properly connected with the publishing, manufacturing in a variety of media, and distribution of books, tracts, periodicals, materials, and supplies for churches and church schools, including the ecumenical outreach of Christianity, and such other activities as the General Conference may direct.

¶ **1714.** *Direction and Control.*—The United Methodist Publishing House shall be under the direction and control of the board, acting through an executive officer elected quadrennially by the board, who shall be the publisher of The United Methodist Church, and such other officers as the board may determine.

¶ **1715.** The net income from the operations of The United Methodist Publishing House, after providing adequate reserves for its efficient operation and allowing for reasonable growth and expansion, shall be appropriated by the board and distributed annually on the basis of an equitable plan provided by the General Board of Pensions to the several Annual Conferences for the persons who are and shall be conference claimants.

¶ **1716.** The net income from the operations of The United Methodist Publishing House shall be appropriated to no other purpose than its own operating requirements and for persons who are or shall be conference claimants as provided in ¶¶ 20 and 1715.[59]

¶ **1717.** The members of the board and their successors in office are declared to be the successors of the incorporators named in the charters of The Methodist Book Concern issued by the States of New York and Ohio and in the charter of The Board of Publication of the Methodist Protestant Church issued by the State of Pennsylvania. The executive officer of the board, elected from time to time under this or any subsequent Discipline, is declared to be the successor in office of the Book Agents of the Methodist Episcopal Church, South, named in the charter issued to the corporation of that name by the State of Tennessee.

¶ **1718.** Subject to the provisions of ¶ 1714 and to the

---

[59]*See* Judicial Council Decisions 322, 330.

continuing control and direction of the General Conference of The United Methodist Church as set forth from time to time in the Discipline, the board is authorized and empowered to cause the operations of The United Methodist Publishing House to be carried on and the objectives defined in ¶ 1713 to be achieved in such manner, through or by means of such agencies or instrumentalities, and by use of such procedures as the board may from time to time determine to be necessary, advisable, or appropriate, with full power and authority in the premises to take all such action and to do all such other acts and things as may be required or found to be advisable. In particular, and without limiting the generality of the foregoing, the board is authorized and empowered, for the purposes of this section:

1. To use, manage, operate, and otherwise utilize all property and assets of every kind, character, and description of four corporations—namely, The Methodist Book Concern, a corporation existing under the laws of the State of New York; The Methodist Book Concern, a corporation existing under the laws of the State of Ohio; The Board of Publication of the Methodist Protestant Church, a corporation existing under the laws of the State of Pennsylvania; and Book Agents of the Methodist Episcopal Church, South, a corporation existing under the laws of the State of Tennessee—as well as all income from such property and assets and the avails thereof, all with liability or obligation to account for such property and assets, the use thereof, the income therefrom, and avails thereof, only to the General Conference of The United Methodist Church or as it shall direct.

2. To cause each of the said corporations to take all such action and to do all such things as the board may deem necessary or advisable to carry out the intent and purposes of this paragraph. The governing body of each of the said corporations from time to time shall take all action which the board deems necessary or advisable to carry out the intent and purposes of this paragraph. The board shall cause all legal obligations of said four corporations, now existing or hereafter incurred, to be met, fulfilled, and performed.

3. To continue to exercise the powers and administer the duties and responsibilities conferred on it as an agency of The

United Methodist Church through the corporation named Board of Publication of The Methodist Church, incorporated under the laws of the State of Illinois in accord with authority delegated to it by the General Conference of 1952, or through such other means and agencies as it may from time to time determine to be expedient and necessary in order to give full effect to the purposes expressed in this section.[60]

¶ 1719. 1. The property, assets, and income of the Illinois corporation shall be held by it, under the direction of the board, as an agency of The United Methodist Church and shall at all times be subject to the control and direction of the General Conference of The United Methodist Church as set forth from time to time in the Discipline.

2. In carrying out and executing its operations and functions, the Illinois corporation shall be entitled to hold, use, manage, operate, and otherwise utilize all property and assets of every kind, character, and description of each of the four corporations identified in ¶ 1718.1 (other than its corporate powers and franchises) and all income therefrom and avails thereof for the purposes and objectives defined in this section.

3. The governing body of each of the five existing corporations under the direction of the board shall from time to time take all such action as the board deems necessary or advisable to carry out the intent and purposes of this paragraph and section.

4. The Illinois corporation shall be liable for and shall execute and satisfy all legal obligations of each of the four corporations named in ¶ 1718.1, but neither it nor the board shall have or be under any obligation to account for principal and income to any such other corporation or to otherwise report to any of them.

¶ 1720. Pursuant to the Declaration of Union of The Evangelical United Brethren Church and The Methodist Church and under the authority of ¶¶ 939, 950-954 of the Book of Discipline of The United Methodist Church, 1968, The Otterbein Press, an Ohio corporation, and The Evangelical Press, a Pennsylvania corporation, have been legally dissolved and their charters have been surrendered. The proceeds of their corporate

---

[60]*See* Judicial Council Decision 330.

assets have been and are being administered pursuant to said Disciplinary provisions.

¶ **1721.** *Officers of the Corporations.*—The officers of each corporation under the direction of the board shall be elected annually in accordance with its charter and bylaws.

¶ **1722.** The executive officer (publisher) elected pursuant to ¶ 1714 shall also be elected the president of each corporation under the direction of the board.

¶ **1723.** The board shall fix the salaries of the officers of the corporations and shall report the same quadrennially to the General Conference.

¶ **1724.** The board shall require the president to submit quarterly to the executive committee and annually to the board written reports of the financial condition and operating results of The United Methodist Publishing House.

¶ **1725.** The president (publisher) and the board shall have authority to extend the activities of The United Methodist Publishing House in such manner as they may judge to be for the best interests of the Church.

¶ **1726.** The board shall require the president and other corporate officers to give bond conditioned on the faithful discharge of their respective duties. It also shall authorize the execution of a blanket bond covering all staff personnel whose responsibilities justify such coverage. The amount of the bonds shall be fixed by the board, and the bonds shall be subject to the approval of the board. The premiums shall be paid by The United Methodist Publishing House, and the chairperson of the board shall be the custodian of the bonds.

¶ **1727.** The board shall have power to suspend, after hearing, and to remove, after hearing, the president or any of the officers for misconduct or failure to perform the duties of their offices.

¶ **1728.** *Book Editor.*—The board shall elect annually a book editor who shall be designated editorial director of general publishing. The book editor shall have joint responsibility with the publisher for approving manuscripts considered for publication. The book editor shall edit or supervise the editing of all books and materials of our publication. In the case of church school publications and official forms and records, the book editor shall collaborate with the editor of Church School Publications and the Committee on Official Forms and Records whenever such collaboration is mutually desirable and beneficial. The book editor shall perform such other editorial duties as may be required by the board.

¶ **1729.** The board, at its discretion, may continue the publication of the periodical *Quarterly Review,* with the book editor responsible for its editorial content.

¶ **1730.** The board shall fix the salary of the book editor.

¶ **1731.** The board shall have power to suspend or remove, after hearing, the book editor for misconduct or failure to perform the duties of the office.

¶ **1732.** *Church School Publications.*—There shall be an editor of Church School Publications, elected as set forth in ¶ 1227.

¶ **1733.** The editor of Church School Publications shall be responsible for the preparation of all curriculum materials as set forth in ¶ 1228.

¶ **1734.** The curriculum of the church school shall be determined by the Curriculum Resources Committee, which shall include in its membership the vice-president in charge of publishing and the publisher, as set forth in ¶ 1228.1*c.*

¶ **1735.** The board shall fix the salary of the editor of Church School Publications and shall have full financial responsibility for all expenses connected with this work.

¶ **1736.** The publications of the Curriculum Resources Committee shall be manufactured, published, and distributed through The United Methodist Publishing House. In matters involving financial responsibility the final determination in every case shall lie with the board. After consultation with the publisher, the editor of Church School Publications shall prepare a complete budget for this work, including salaries of assistants and office secretaries and travel, etc., to be effective when approved by the board, and shall direct its operation from year to year.

¶ **1737.** There shall be one complete, coordinated system of literature published by the board for the entire United Methodist Church. This literature is to be of such type and variety as to meet the needs of all groups of our people. The board president and publisher shall consult with the general program agencies, the

General Commission on Communication, and the General Council on Ministries with regard to their publishing needs in order to avoid unnecessary overlapping and duplication.

¶ **1738.** The board and the publisher shall have authority to decline to publish any item of literature when in their judgment the cost would be greater than should be borne by The United Methodist Publishing House.

¶ **1739.** The editor of Church School Publications (¶ 1227) and a member of the General Board of Discipleship designated by the president shall have the right to sit with the board and shall have the privilege of the floor without vote for the consideration of matters pertaining to their joint interests.

¶ **1740.** The United Methodist Publishing House shall explore and engage in cooperative publication of United Methodist church school curriculum resources wherever both The United Methodist Publishing House and the Curriculum Resources Committee of the General Board of Discipleship find this to be practicable and in harmony with related editorial and publishing policies.

¶ **1741.** *Printing for Church Agencies.*—It is recommended that the general agencies and institutions of The United Methodist Church have all their printing done by The United Methodist Publishing House (¶¶ 627, 905.4c).

¶ **1742.** *Distributing for Church Agencies.*—It is recommended that all general agencies of The United Methodist Church use the distribution system of The United Methodist Publishing House for distribution of resources, materials, and supplies needed for use in the local church.

¶ **1743.** *Real Estate and Buildings.*—The United Methodist Publishing House shall not buy any real estate costing in excess of $500,000 and shall not sell or exchange any real estate having a fair market value in excess of $500,000 except by the order of the General Conference or, between sessions of the General Conference, by a two-thirds vote of all the members of the board. In either case such vote shall be taken at a regular or called meeting of the board, and if at a called meeting, the purpose of this meeting shall have been stated in the call. The erection of a new building or improvement, alteration, or repair of an existing building or the purchase of real estate for retail purposes involving an expenditure of not more than $500,000, or the sale or exchange of real estate used by the publishing house for retail purposes which has a fair market value of not more than $500,000, may be authorized by the vote of a majority of the executive committee. These provisions shall not prevent the making of investments on mortgage security or the protection of the same or the collection of claims and adjustments.

Section XI. General Commission on Archives and History.

¶ **1801.** *Name.*—The name of the official historical agency of The United Methodist Church shall be the **General Commission on Archives and History.**

¶ **1802.** *Incorporation.*—The General Commission on Archives and History shall be incorporated under the laws of whatever state the commission may determine.

¶ **1803.** *Purpose.*—1. The purpose of the commission shall be to gather, preserve, hold title to, and disseminate materials on the history of The United Methodist Church and its antecedents. It shall cooperate with other bodies, especially the World Methodist Historical Society and the World Methodist Council. It shall do any and all things necessary to promote and care for the historical interest of The United Methodist Church. It shall maintain archives and libraries in which shall be preserved historical records and materials of every kind relating to The United Methodist Church. It shall provide guidance for the creation and preservation of archives and records at all levels of The United Methodist Church.

2. The commission shall be accountable to the General Council on Ministries for all programmatic assignments.

3. The commission shall have responsibility for and supervision of its archives and historical libraries and other depositories of similar character, if any, established by The United Methodist Church.

¶ **1804.** *Membership of the General Commission.*—1. The commission shall be constituted quadrennially, and its members and all officers elected by it shall hold office until their successors have been chosen. The commission may fill interim vacancies during a quadrennium where not otherwise provided by the Discipline.

2. The commission shall be composed of thirty members in the following manner: thirteen members shall be elected by the General Conference on nomination of the Council of Bishops, which number would include at least two women, one young adult, one youth, and two persons from racial and ethnic groups; two bishops; five presidents of the Jurisdictional Commissions on Archives and History, or where no commission exists or any Disciplinary conflict arises, a person designated by the jurisdictional College of Bishops and ten additional members elected by the general commission. Not less than ten of the total shall be women; not less than two shall be persons over sixty-five years of age; not less than four of the members should be from racial and ethnic groups, including one each of the following: Pacific and Asian American, Black American, Hispanic American, and Native American.

¶ **1805.** *Meetings.*—The commission shall meet annually at such time and place as it may determine, subject to the provisions of the act of incorporation. The commission may hold special meetings on the call of the president. A majority of the members of the commission shall constitute a quorum.

¶ **1806.** *Officers.*—The commission shall elect from its membership a president, vice-president, secretary, and such other officers as may be needed. The president shall be a bishop. The officers shall perform the duties usually incident to their positions.

¶ **1807.** *Staff.*—The commission shall elect a general secretary and such other staff officers as may be needed. The general secretary shall be the executive and administrative officer and shall carry on the work of the commission, keep the records and minutes, serve as editor of official publications of the commission, supervise the depositories, make an annual report to the commission, and furnish such reports as are required to the General Conference and General Conference agencies. The general secretary shall attend meetings of the commission and the executive committee and have the privilege of the floor without vote. Archivists, curators, and librarians employed by the commission shall be responsible to the general secretary. They shall attend meetings of the commission and the executive committee when it is deemed necessary by the general secretary.

When in attendance, they shall have the privilege of the floor without vote.

¶ **1808.** *Executive Committee.*—There shall be an executive committee, composed of the president, vice-president, secretary, and three other members of the commission elected by it. The executive committee shall perform the duties and exercise the authority of the commission between meetings. Its minutes shall be submitted to the commission for approval. The executive committee and the commission may vote on any matter by mail. Mail polls shall be directed by the general secretary, who shall state clearly the propositions to be voted on and announce the results to all the members.

¶ **1809.** *Finances.*—The commission shall be financed by appropriations of the General Conference, the sale of literature and historical materials, subscriptions to the commission's official publications, dues from associate members, and gifts, grants, and bequests of interested individuals and organizations.

¶ **1810.** *Historical Society.*—1. The general commission may organize a **Historical Society** of The United Methodist Church and encourage individuals to become members of it for the purpose of promoting interest in the study and preservation of the history of The United Methodist Church and its antecedents. They shall be encouraged to cooperate with the Annual Conference, Jurisdictional Conference, and General Commission on Archives and History in the promotion of the historical interests of the Church.

2. Individuals may become members of the Historical Society by paying such dues as the commission may direct, in return for which they shall receive such commission publications as are deemed suitable.

3. Once each quadrennium the commission may hold a Historical Convocation, to which may be invited members of the Historical Society, members of Jurisdictional and Annual Conference historical organizations, heads of departments of history in the universities, colleges, and seminaries of The United Methodist Church, and such other persons as may be interested.

¶ **1811.** 1. *Archival Definitions.*—*a) Archives,* as distinguished from libraries, house not primarily books, but documentary record material.

b) Documentary record material shall mean all documents, minutes, journals, diaries, reports, pamphlets, letters, papers, manuscripts, maps, photographs, books, audiovisuals, sound recordings, magnetic or other tapes, electronic data processing records, artifacts, or any other documentary material, regardless of physical form or characteristics, made or received pursuant to any provisions of the Discipline in connection with the transaction of church business by any general agency of The United Methodist Church or of any of its constituent predecessors.

c) General agency of The United Methodist Church or of its constituent predecessors shall, in turn, mean and include every church office, church officer or official (elected or appointed), including bishop, institution, board, commission, bureau, council, or conference at the national level.

2. *Custodianship of records.*—The church official in charge of an office having documentary record material shall be the custodian thereof, unless otherwise provided.

3. *Procedures.*—*a)* The general commission shall establish a central archives of The United Methodist Church and such regional archives and record centers as in its judgment may be needed.

b) The bishops, General Conference officers, general boards, commissions, committees, and agencies of The United Methodist Church shall deposit official minutes or journals, or copies of the same, in the archives quadrennially and shall transfer correspondence, records, papers, and other archival materials described above from their offices when they no longer have operational usefulness. No records shall be destroyed until a disposal schedule has been agreed upon by the General Commission on Archives and History and the agency. When the custodian of any official documentary record material of a general agency certifies to the General Commission on Archives and History that such records have no further use or value for official and administrative purposes and when the commission certifies that such records appear to have no further use or value for research or reference, then such records may be destroyed or otherwise disposed of by the agency or official having custody of them. A record of such certification and authorization shall be entered in the minutes or records of both the commission and the agency. The General Commission on Archives and History is hereby authorized and empowered to make such provisions as may be necessary and proper to carry this paragraph into effect.

c) The commission shall have the right to examine the condition of documentary record material and shall, subject to the availability of staff and funds, give advice and assistance to church officials and agencies in regard to preserving and disposing of documentary record material in their custody. Officials of general agencies shall assist the commission in the preparation of an inventory of records in their custody. To this inventory shall be attached a schedule, approved by the head of the agency having custody of the records and the commission, establishing a time period for the retention and disposal of each series of records. So long as such approved schedule remains in effect, destruction or disposal of documentary record material in accordance with its provisions shall be deemed to have met the requirements of ¶ 1811.3*b.*

d) The commission is authorized and directed to conduct a program of inventorying, repairing, and microfilming among all general agencies of The United Methodist Church for security purposes that documentary record material which the commission determines has permanent value and of providing safe storage for microfilm copies of such material. Subject to the availability of funds, such program may be extended to material of permanent value of all agencies of The United Methodist Church.

e) General documentary record material certified by the commission as being of permanent value shall be preserved in the custody of the agency in which the records are normally kept or in the custody of the commission. Any general church official or agency is hereby authorized and empowered to turn over to the commission any church records no longer in current use, and the commission is authorized in its discretion to accept such records, and having done so shall provide for their administration and preservation in the archives of the commission. When such records have thus been surrendered, photocopies, microfilms, typescripts, or other copies of them shall be made and certified under seal of the commission, upon application of the agency from which the records have been transferred. This certification shall have the same force and effect as if made by the official or agency by which the records were transferred to the commission.

f) The general boards, commissions, committees, and agencies of The United Methodist Church shall place two copies of all their publications, of whatever kind, as they are issued in the archives or in lieu thereof shall file a statement with the archivist affirming that they are preserving copies of all such items in their own libraries or depositories.

g) Official documents, or copies thereof, such as articles of incorporation, constitutions, bylaws, and other official papers of the boards and agencies of The United Methodist Church shall be deposited in the archives.

h) Whoever has the custody of any general agency records shall, at the expiration of the term of office, deliver to the successor, custodian, or, if there be none, to the commission all records, books, writings, letters, and documents kept or received in the transaction of official general agency business. This will also apply to the papers of temporary and special general church committees.

i) The bishops, General Conference officers, and the general boards, commissions, committees, and agencies of The United Methodist Church are urged to counsel with the central archivist concerning the preservation of all materials.

j) Jurisdictional and Annual Conference secretaries shall deposit two copies of their respective conference journals quadrennially or annually, as the case may be, in the central archives and in the appropriate regional archives.

k) Secretaries of Jurisdictional and Annual Conference boards, commissions, committees, and agencies shall deposit annually, or as often as they meet, copies of their minutes (as distinguished from reports which are printed separately or in the Jurisdictional and Annual Conference journals) in the central archives or in the appropriate regional archives.

l) Bishops, General Conference officers, general agency staff personnel, missionaries, and those ordained ministers and lay persons in positions of leadership and influence at any level of

637

the Church are urged to deposit or bequeath their personal papers to the archives of the general commission.

m) Organizations and individuals may negotiate appropriate restrictions on the use of materials which they deposit in the archives.

n) Upon recommendation of its executive committee, the commission may authorize the transfer of materials to an organization, agency, or family.

o) All materials in the archives shall be available for research and exhibition, subject to such restrictions as may be placed on them.

¶ **1812.** *Historic Shrines, Historic Landmarks, and Historic Sites.*—1. *a)* All nominations for the designation of buildings and locations as United Methodist historic shrines or historic landmarks shall be referred to the General Commission on Archives and History. Through its Committee on Historic Shrines and Historic Landmarks the commission shall consider the merits of each nomination and shall make such recommendations as it deems appropriate to the ensuing General Conference for its action and determination.

The commission shall recommend only a building or a location for designation as a historic shrine or historic landmark which has been registered as a historic site by an Annual or Jurisdictional Conference and has met the requirements established by the commission.

b) The commission shall be responsible for making a quadrennial review of the existing duly designated historic shrines and landmarks, according to the criteria which it shall prepare and which shall be compatible with the Discipline of The United Methodist Church. The commission shall further be responsible for recommending to the General Conference the redesignation or reclassification of the designated historic shrines and historic landmarks as such action may be appropriate in keeping with such criteria.

2. *a) Historic Shrines.*—To qualify for designation as a historic shrine of The United Methodist Church, a building must have been linked with significant events and outstanding personalities in the origin and development of The United Methodist Church or its antecedents so as to have distinctive historic interest and

value for the denomination as a whole, as contrasted with local or regional historic significance.

b) Present Historic Shrines.—The historic shrines of The United Methodist Church are: Acuff's Chapel, state highway 126 between Blountsville and Kingsport, TN; Albright Memorial Chapel, Kleinfeltersville, PA; Barratt's Chapel, near Frederica, DE; Edward Cox House near Bluff City, TN; Green Hill House, Louisburg, NC; John Street Church, New York City; Old McKendree Chapel, Jackson, MO; Old Otterbein Church, Baltimore, MD; Rehobeth Church, near Union, WV; St. George's Church, Philadelphia; St. Simon's Island, Brunswick, GA; Cemetery and Site of Old Stone Church, Leesburg, VA; Robert Strawbridge's Log House, near New Windsor, MD; Wyandot Indian Mission, Upper Sandusky, OH; Whitaker's Chapel, near Enfield, Halifax County, NC; the town of Oxford, GA; Peter Cartwright United Methodist Church, Pleasant Plains, IL; Bethune-Cookman College, Daytona Beach, FL; Boehm's Chapel, Willow Street, PA; Deadwood Cluster, Deadwood, SD; Zoar United Methodist Church, Philadelphia, PA; and Hanby House, Westerville, OH.

3. *a) Historic Landmarks.*—Locations which have little remaining in the way of structure or monuments but which otherwise qualify as historic shrines may be designated as historic landmarks.

b) Present Historic Landmarks.—The historic landmarks of The United Methodist Church are: the sites of the Lovely Lane Chapel, Baltimore, MD; Brooklyn Methodist Hospital, Brooklyn, NY; McMahan's Chapel, Bronson, TX; John Wesley's American Parish, Savannah, GA; Asbury Manual Labor School and Mission, Ft. Mitchell, AL; Cokesbury College, Abingdon, MD; the organization of the Methodist Episcopal Church, South, Louisville, KY; Keywood Marker, Glade Spring, VA; first church building and publishing house, Evangelical Association, New Berlin, PA; and Rutersville Cluster, Rutersville, TX.

4. *Sites.*—Jurisdictional and Annual Conferences may designate as historic sites buildings and locations within their regions which have been related to significant events and important personalities in the origin and development of The United Methodist Church or its antecedents. The president of the

Commission on Archives and History of the conference making such a designation shall advise the general commission, which shall in turn keep a register of all historic sites.

Section XII. General Commission on Communication.

¶ **1901.** *Preamble.*—As United Methodists, our theological understanding obligates us, as members of the Body of Christ, to communicate our faith by speaking and listening to persons both within and outside the Church throughout the world, and to utilize all appropriate means of communication.

The responsibility to communicate is laid upon every church member, every pastor, every congregation, every Annual Conference, every institution, and every agency of the Church. Within this total responsibility, there are certain functions that the General Conference has assigned to the General Commission on Communication, to be performed in behalf of all through the talents and resources at its command.

¶ **1902.** *Name.*—There shall be a General Commission on Communication of The United Methodist Church which for communication and public relations purposes may be designated as **United Methodist Communications (UMCom).**

¶ **1903.** *Incorporation.*—The **General Commission on Communication** is successor to the Joint Committee on Communications, incorporated in the State of Ohio, and shall be authorized to do business as United Methodist Communications (UMCom). It is authorized to create such other corporate substructures as the commission deems appropriate to carry out its functions.

¶ **1904.** *Amenability and Accountability.*—The General Commission on Communication shall be amenable to the General Conference. As an administrative general agency which carries significant program functions in addition to its many service and support responsibilities, the commission shall be accountable to, report to, and be evaluated by the General Council on Ministries in program matters and shall be accountable to and report to the General Council on Finance and Administration for matters of finance.

¶ **1905.** *Purpose.*—The General Commission on Communication shall give leadership to the Church in the field of communication in a holistic way. It shall serve in meeting the communication, public relations, and promotional needs of the entire Church, reflecting the cultural and racial diversity within The United Methodist Church. It shall be responsible for providing resources and services to local churches and Annual Conferences in the field of communication. It shall have a consultative relationship to all general agencies of the Church and to any structures for communication and public relations at the jurisdictional, episcopal area, Annual Conference, district, or local church level.

¶ **1906.** *Responsibilities.*—Specific responsibilities and functions of the General Commission on Communication and its staff are as follows:

1. It shall be the official news-gathering and distributing agency for The United Methodist Church and its general agencies. In discharging its responsibilities, in keeping with the historic freedom of the press, it shall operate with editorial freedom as an independent news bureau serving all segments of church life and society, making available to both religious and public news media information concerning the Church at large.

2. It shall have major responsibility on behalf of The United Methodist Church in the United States to relate to the public media in presenting the Christian faith and work of the Church to the general public through broadcast, the press, and audiovisual media. It may develop such structures for broadcast and audiovisual communication purposes as are deemed helpful to the Church in its witness through the media. It shall serve in unifying and coordinating public media messages and programs of United Methodist general agencies.

3. It shall give special attention to television, including broadcast television, cable, videotape, videodisc, and satellite. It shall provide counsel and resources to Annual Conferences—and through conferences to districts and local churches—to develop and strengthen their television ministries. Responsibilities of the commission shall include program production and placement, and relationships to commercial broadcasters at the national level in the U.S.A.

4. It shall represent The United Methodist Church in the Communication Commission of the National Council of the

Churches of Christ in the U.S.A., and in other national and international interdenominational agencies working in the area of mass communications. Budget allocations and other funds granted to these ecumenical agencies shall be administered in accordance with ¶ 918.

5. It shall have responsibility to work toward promotion and protection of the historic freedoms of religion and the press, and shall seek to increase the ethical, moral, and human values of media structures and programs.

6. It shall have general supervision over the conduct of public relations activities for The United Methodist Church in the United States, planning and carrying out public relations work at the denomination-wide level and giving counsel to the various units of the Church in regard to their public relations needs. It shall interpret to the constituency of the Church the significance of the denomination and its various programs.

7. It shall develop and oversee a unified and comprehensive program of audiovisual materials for the Church. It shall plan, create, produce or cause to be produced, and distribute or cause to be distributed, audiovisual materials that are informative and vital to the religious life of all United Methodists. It shall unify and coordinate the audiovisual programs of all United Methodist agencies dealing with projected pictures, recordings, videotape and other audiovisual or electronic materials.

8. It shall give oversight to a comprehensive communication system for the Church, providing a total view of communication structure and practices, including telecommunications. It shall create networks of communicators at all levels, including local church, district, conference, and general. These networks may include periodic consultations for such purposes as idea exchange, information sharing, joint planning, and monitoring and evaluating the total Church's communication enterprises. With respect to the use of computers for communication purposes, the agency shall cooperate with the General Council on Finance and Administration (*see* ¶ 907.6).

9. It shall provide guidance, resources, and training for the local church coordinator of communications (¶ 262.3), provided that training at the local level shall be through and in cooperation with Annual Conferences.

10. It shall be responsible for education and training in the principles and skills of communication, including the following: *(a)* national workshops and training experiences in communication skills related to the various media; *(b)* consultation with and assistance to Annual Conferences, districts, racial and ethnic groups, in the training of local church persons, especially the local church coordinator of communications; *(c)* training experiences for bishops, personnel of general church agencies, and other groups on request; *(d)* providing and facilitating apprenticeship, internship, and scholarship programs for church communicators; *(e)* counseling schools of theology and other institutions of higher education about the training of faculty, candidates for the ordained ministry, and lay persons in the principles and skills of communication, media resource development, and media evaluation.

11. It shall determine and implement, after consultation with the Council on Finance and Administration, policy for the interpretation, promotion, and cultivation of all financial causes demanding churchwide promotion or publicity. The General Commission on Communication shall assist episcopal areas, Annual Conferences, and districts by means of a field service program providing counsel and resources in communication, program interpretation, and the promotion of benevolence and administrative funds.

12. It shall be the central promotional agency for the purpose of promoting throughout the Church the following general church funds: World Service Fund (¶ 912.1), World Service Special Gifts (¶ 913), the Advance (¶ 914), One Great Hour of Sharing (¶ 916.2 and ¶ 274.2), World Communion Offering (¶ 916.4 and ¶ 274.3), Missional Priority Fund (¶ 922), General Administration Fund (¶ 917), Interdenominational Cooperation Fund (¶ 918), Temporary General Aid Fund (¶ 920), Ministerial Education Fund (¶ 921), Episcopal Fund (¶ 923), Human Relations Day (¶ 916.1 and ¶ 274.1), Black College Fund (¶ 919), United Methodist Student Day (¶ 916.3 and ¶ 274.4), Christian Education Sunday (¶ 276.1), Peace with Justice Sunday (¶ 916.5 and ¶ 274.5), Golden Cross Sunday (¶ 276.2), Youth Service Fund (¶ 1310), Native American Awareness Sunday (¶ 916.6 and ¶ 274.6) and all other general church funds approved by the

General Conference, as well as any emergency appeals that may be authorized by the Council of Bishops and the General Council on Finance and Administration (¶ 911.4). In the interpretation, promotion, and cultivation of these causes, this agency shall consult with and is encouraged to utilize content material provided by the program agency responsible for the area and with the agency responsible for the administration of the funds. Budgets for the above promoted funds shall be developed in cooperation with the General Council on Finance and Administration. In cases where the General Conference assigns a portion of the promotional responsibility to some other agency, such promotional work shall be subject to coordination by the General Commission on Communication. The cost of promotion of the funds shall be a prior claim against receipts, except that the cost of promotion for general Advance specials shall be billed to the recipient agencies in proportion to the amount of general Advance special funds received by each (¶ 915.3), and the promotion of World Service Special gifts shall be borne by administering agencies (¶ 913.6). The administration of the money thus set aside for promotion shall be the responsibility of the General Commission on Communication.

13. It shall undertake the promotion of any cause or undertaking, financial or otherwise, not herein mentioned, demanding churchwide promotion or publicity; *provided* that such action shall have been previously approved by the Council of Bishops and the General Council on Finance and Administration, or their respective executive committees. The General Council on Finance and Administration shall determine the source of the funding for any such authorized promotions.

14. Appeals for giving that are made to United Methodists shall be consistent with the aims of Christian stewardship. There shall be cooperation between this agency and the General Board of Discipleship in order that programs and resource materials of the two agencies may be in harmony in their presentation of Christian stewardship.

15. It shall publish a program journal for pastors and other church leaders that shall present the program and promotional materials of the general agencies in a coordinated manner and shall be in lieu of general agency promotional periodicals. This

agency shall determine the manner of selecting the principal editors, who shall be responsible for the content of the journal. This agency shall obtain from the churches or district superintendents the names of church officials entitled to receive the journal so as to compile a subscription list compatible with regulations of the U.S. Postal Service.

16. It shall supervise the use of the official insignia of The United Methodist Church and preserve the integrity of its design. It shall maintain appropriate registration to protect the insignia in behalf of The United Methodist Church. The insignia may be used by any official agency of the Church, including local churches, to identify the work, program, and materials of The United Methodist Church. Any commercial use of the design must be explicitly authorized by an appropriate officer of this agency.

17. It shall give leadership in study and research in the field of communication, applying research findings from the professional and academic communities to the work of the Church, and in evaluative research in the field of communication. It shall cooperate with other agencies and other levels of the Church in research and development work in the field of communication and share the findings of study and research.

18. It shall represent United Methodist interests in new technological developments in the field of communication, including research, the evaluation of new devices and methods, and the application of technological developments to the communication services of the Church.

19. It may develop information services and other innovative services which provide channels of communication to and from all levels of the Church.

20. It shall provide resources, counsel, and staff training for area, conference, and district communication programs and develop guidelines in consultation with persons working in areas, conferences, and districts.

21. It shall produce materials for program interpretation in cooperation with the General Council on Ministries and the general program boards.

¶ **1907.** *Organization.*—1. *Membership.*—The affairs of the General Commission on Communication shall be governed by a commission composed of: three bishops selected by the Council of Bishops, four persons (two men and two women including at least one clergy, one laywoman, and one layman) elected by each Jurisdictional Conference, fifteen additional members elected by the commission to ensure membership of persons with expertise in the field of communication, and two members of the General Council on Ministries, selected by the council. It is recommended that each of the following groups be represented in the commission: Asian Americans, Black Americans, Hispanic Americans, Native Americans, clergywomen, youth, young adults, and persons over sixty-five. The additional members shall be nominated by a committee composed of one commission member designated from each jurisdiction and one of the member bishops. Members from the General Council on Ministries shall be assigned to the Division of Program and Benevolence Interpretation.

2. *Meetings.*—The commission shall hold at least one meeting in each calendar year. Fifteen members shall constitute a quorum.

3. *Officers.*—The commission shall elect a president, at least one vice-president, a recording secretary, and such other officers as it determines.

There may be an executive committee comprised of not more than one-third of the total membership of the commission and elected by the commission. The membership of the executive committee shall be representative of the composition of the commission.

4. *Internal Organization.*—The General Commission on Communication is empowered to create internal structures as it deems appropriate for effective operation.

5. *Staff.*—The commission shall elect annually a general secretary upon nomination by the executive committee or a nominating committee and shall elect such associate general secretaries as needed and shall provide for election or appointment of other staff. The general secretary shall cooperate with the General Council on Ministries for program services and with the general secretary of the General Council on Finance and Administration for financial services.

¶ **1908.** *Finance.*—The General Conference shall provide for the financial needs of the General Commission on Communication upon recommendation by the General Council on Finance and Administration. The commission shall consult with the General Council on Ministries in the area of program matters in development of an annual budget which shall be reported to the General Council on Finance and Administration for approval.

¶ **1909.** *Religion in American Life, Incorporated* is recognized as an interdenominational and interfaith agency through which the denomination may work to direct attention to church attendance and religious values. United Methodist Communications shall nominate United Methodist representatives to be elected to its Board of Directors by Religion in American Life. In consultation with the General Council on Finance and Administration, United Methodist Communications shall determine the amount of the annual contribution to this program in behalf of The United Methodist Church, such funds being made available through the budget of United Methodist Communications.

Section XIII. General Commission on Christian Unity and Interreligious Concerns.

¶ **2001.** *Name.*—The name of this agency shall be the **General Commission on Christian Unity and Interreligious Concerns.**

¶ **2002.** *Purpose.*—The purpose of the General Commission on Christian Unity and Interreligious Concerns shall be to fulfill two major responsibilities.

1. To advocate and work toward the full reception of the gift of Christian unity in every aspect of the Church's life and to foster approaches to ministry and mission which more fully reflect the oneness of Christ's Church in the human community.

2. To advocate and work for the establishment and strengthening of relationships with other living faith communities, to further dialogue with persons of other faiths, cultures, and ideologies, and to work toward the unity of humankind.

¶ **2003.** *Responsibilities.*—The responsibilities of the General Commission on Christian Unity and Interreligious Concerns shall be:

1. To enable ecumenical and interreligious understanding and experience among all United Methodists, including assistance to all United Methodist agencies.

2. To provide resources and counsel to conference Commissions or Committees on Christian Unity and Interreligious Concerns and to local church leadership.

3. To develop or assist in the development of resources and other educational materials which will stimulate understanding and experience in ecumenical and interreligious relationships.

4. To develop and interpret the primary relationships of The United Methodist Church to ecumenical and interreligious organizations (such as the World Council of Churches, regional councils of churches, the National Council of the Churches of Christ in the U.S.A., the World Methodist Council, and Consultation on Church Union), to United Churches which include a church formerly related to The United Methodist Church or its predecessors, to churches with which a concordat of exchange of voting delegates has been established by General Conference and to churches which have entered into a formal covenanting act with The United Methodist Church.

5. To pursue or initiate relationships and conversations with other Christian churches on possible church unions and in general bilateral or multilateral dialogues.

6. To develop and engage in dialogue, cooperation, and unity discussions with the historic members of the Methodist denominational family in the United States; namely, the African Methodist Episcopal, the African Methodist Episcopal Zion, and the Christian Methodist Episcopal churches, and all those Wesleyan bodies in the United States related to the World Methodist Council.

7. To report to General Conference on developments in Christian unity and interreligious issues and to make recommendations on any specific proposals for church union.

8. To pursue or initiate relationships and conversations with the Jewish and other religious and ideological communities in dialogue and in cooperative efforts.

9. To consider resolutions, pronouncements, and actions of ecumenical and interreligious councils and agencies, to be responsible for appropriate United Methodist responses, and to initiate or to channel counsel to ecumenical and interreligious bodies.

10. To receive reports from the Consultation on Church Union, the National Council of the Churches of Christ in the U.S.A., the World Methodist Council, and the World Council of Churches on their work, such reports to include relevant financial information.

11. To receive copies of all requests for funds from ecumenical and interreligious bodies to all United Methodist agencies and to review for possible recommendations to both the ecumenical and United Methodist agencies.

12. To enable and review the ecumenical and interreligious involvements, programming, and funding of all United Methodist program agencies; to review funding of ecumenical agencies by United Methodist program agencies through examination of the disclosure records annually provided to the General Council on Finance and Administration; to report findings and make recommendations to those agencies and to the General Council on Ministries and to the General Council on Finance and Administration as requested.

13. To advocate for adequate funding for the core budgets of the major ecumenical and interreligious agencies.

14. To provide from its own budget where possible supplementary funding for cognate units in ecumenical agencies and ad hoc ecumenical and interreligious enterprises.

15. To recommend to the General Council on Ministries and the General Council on Finance and Administration the total goal and constituent allocations of the Interdenominational Cooperation Fund for submission to General Conference and to administer all aspects of the fund in accordance with guidelines established in consultation with the General Council on Finance and Administration and with the Council of Bishops. (*See* ¶ 918.)

16. To receive and administer funds allocated to it through the General Conference or the General Council on Finance and Administration and other sources.

17. To report annually to the Council of Bishops on aspects of Christian unity and interreligious developments, issues, and trends.

18. To channel and recommend to the Council of Bishops qualified United Methodists for service as representatives on ecumenical councils or agencies and to special meeting or

assemblies, and to name such representatives to councils, agencies, or assemblies not named by the Council of Bishops.

19. To work as partners with agencies of The United Methodist Church on matters of mutual concern.

20. To care for other matters as may be deemed necessary by the commission or requested by the General Conference, the Council of Bishops (*see* ¶ 2405), or the General Council on Ministries.

¶ **2004.** *Authority and Powers.*—The General Commission on Christian Unity and Interreligious Concerns shall have the authority and power to fulfill all the responsibilities noted in ¶ 2003 and to fulfill other functions that may be requested of it by the Council of Bishops, the General Council on Ministries, or the General Council on Finance and Administration and General Conference. (*See* ¶ 2405 on relationships with the Council of Bishops.)

¶ **2005.** *Organization.*—The General Commission on Christian Unity and Interreligious Concerns shall be organized quadrennially in conformity with ¶¶ 805-810. In addition:

1. The commission shall elect from its membership a chairperson and other officers as it may determine.

2. There shall be an executive committee of the commission with powers as determined by the commission. It shall be composed of the chairperson of the commission, other officers of the commission, and additional elected directors for a total voting membership of not less than eight or more than ten persons.

3. The general secretary shall be a member of the commission executive committee without vote.

4. The general secretary, in relationships with other churches, shall be referred to as the Ecumenical Staff Officer for The United Methodist Church, in conformity with common practice in other churches.

5. The commission shall meet annually and at such other times as it shall deem necessary. A majority of the members of the commission shall constitute a quorum.

6. The general commission shall nominate annually, according to approved process in ¶ 813, its general secretary and shall elect annually by ballot its associate general secretary(ies).

Other staff may be elected or appointed as the general commission shall determine.[61]

7. The responsibilities of the general secretary are to be defined by the commission.

¶ **2006.** 1. The General Commission on Christian Unity and Interreligious Concerns shall be composed of United Methodists as follows: four bishops appointed by the Council of Bishops, one of whom shall be the secretary of the Council of Bishops; four persons from each jurisdiction, elected by the Jurisdictional Conferences (see ¶ 805); fourteen other persons with vote selected by the elected commission at the organizational meeting. It is recommended that persons elected by each jurisdiction and by the General Commission on Christian Unity and Interreligious Concerns be inclusive of ethnic representation—Asian American, Black American, Hispanic American, and Native American. Two additional members with vote may include persons from the other churches in the Consultation on Church Union.

2. All members shall be selected with a view to balances envisioned in ¶ 805 and may well include persons from administration or faculty of United Methodist schools of theology and undergraduate colleges, campus ministers, seminarians, members of conference Commissions on Christian Unity and Interreligious Concerns, delegates to or members of Central or Executive Committees of the World Council of Churches and the National Council of the Churches of Christ in the U.S.A., the Consultation on Church Union, the World Methodist Council, and staff of regional and local cooperative agencies.

3. The general commission shall be authorized to fill vacancies in its membership during the quadrennium according to the three categories of membership: *(a)* by requesting appointment by the Council of Bishops; *(b)* by requesting replacement appointment by the appropriate Jurisdictional College of Bishops *(see ¶ 812)*; and *(c)* by its own nomination and election process for the other directors.

---

[61]*See* Judicial Council Decisions 496, 499.

Section XIV. General Commission on Religion and Race.

¶ 2101. *Name.*—There shall be a **General Commission on Religion and Race.**

1. *Amenability and Accountability.*—The general commission shall be amenable to the General Conference of the United Methodist Church. Between sessions of the General Conference, the commission shall be accountable to the General Council on Ministries by reporting and interpreting activities designed to fulfill the purpose of the commission and by cooperating with the Council in the fulfillment of its legislated responsibilities.

¶ 2102. *Purpose.*—The primary purpose of the General Commission on Religion and Race shall be to challenge the general agencies, institutions, and connectional structures of The United Methodist Church to a full and equal participation of the racial and ethnic constituency in the total life and mission of the Church through advocacy and by reviewing and monitoring the practices of the entire Church so as to further ensure racial inclusiveness.

¶ 2103. *Membership.*—The total membership of the commission shall be forty-eight, composed of two bishops appointed by the Council of Bishops, six persons elected by each jurisdiction from the Annual Conference nominations, and sixteen additional members to be elected by the commission. It is recommended that at least four of the six persons elected by each jurisdiction be from ethnic groups (Asian American, Black American, Hispanic American, and Native American). At least two of the six shall be women, and at least one under the age of thirty. Further, it is recommended that of the members at large, four members shall be elected from each of the four racial and ethnic groups (Asian American, Black American, Hispanic American, and Native American). Of the sixteen additional members there shall be two young adults between the ages of nineteen and thirty and two youth under nineteen.[62]

¶ 2104. *Vacancies.*—Vacancies in the commission membership shall be filled by the procedure defined in ¶ 812 of the General Provisions.

¶ 2105. *Officers.*—The General Commission on Religion

---

[62]See Decision 5, Interim Judicial Council.

and Race shall elect as its officers a president, vice-president, a secretary, and such other officers as it shall deem necessary.

¶ **2106.** *Staff.*—The General Commission on Religion and Race shall nominate its general secretary for election by the General Council on Ministries (¶ 813). The commission shall select by whatever process it chooses the additional staff needed to assist the general secretary in carrying out the commission's responsibilities.

¶ **2107.** *Finances.*—The General Council on Finance and Administration shall make provision for the support of the work of the commission, including provision for a general secretary and associated staff and an office for the commission.

¶ **2108.** *Responsibilities.*—The general commission will assume general church responsibility for such matters as:

1. Coordinating the denominational concern and providing a channel of assistance to ensure that ethnic and racial group members of The United Methodist Church will have equal opportunities for service, representation, and voice on every level of the Church's life and ministry.

2. Reviewing, evaluating, and assisting agencies and institutions of the Church as they seek to develop programs and policies to implement and mandate for racial inclusiveness.

3. Reviewing, evaluating, and assisting Annual Conferences and their appointive Cabinets as they seek to develop appointments, programs, and policies designed to achieve racial and ethnic inclusiveness.

4. Providing channels of assistance to racial and ethnic groups as they seek to develop programs of empowerment and ministry to their local churches and communities.

5. Relating to and coordinating the concerns of the racial and ethnic groups as they relate to minority group empowerment and ministry within the Church.

6. Reviewing, investigating, and conducting hearings where necessary in response to written allegations of violation of the Church's policy of racial and ethnic inclusiveness which have not been satisfactorily resolved in the Annual Conference, any general agency or other institution of the Church. All involved parties shall meet with the General Commission on Religion and Race, or its designated representatives, presenting their briefs,

653

arguments, and evidence related to said allegations. The commission will submit its findings and recommendations to the appropriate parties, conferences, general agencies, or institutions concerned, for the purpose of securing a satisfactory resolution to the case at hand.

7. Administering the Minority Group Self-Determination Fund.

8. Providing resources for the local church work area on religion and race.

9. Counseling local churches that are seeking to establish multiracial fellowships and encouraging and supporting local churches in maintaining a Christian ministry in racially changing neighborhoods.

10. Maintaining a close relationship with the General Board of Church and Society, as they both seek to coordinate the denominational support and cooperation with various movements for racial and social justice.

11. Being available to assist Central Conferences, Autonomous and Affiliated Autonomous Methodist and United Churches, and Methodist bodies in countries other than the United States as they address the issue of racism.

12. Providing opportunities for multiracial and interethnic dialogue and meetings throughout the Church.

13. Working directly with the Council of Bishops and the related Annual Conferences to plan workshops, seminars, and consultations on racism based on biblical and theological grounds.

14. Providing programs of sensitization and education at every level of the Church's life, on the nature and meaning of racism—attitudinal, behavioral, and institutional.

15. Relating to and assisting the Annual Conference Commission on Religion and Race.

16. Consulting with the General Board of Pensions in the administration of the Temporary General Aid Fund, recommending such adjustments from time to time as may be necessary under legislation to achieve the intended purpose. (*See* ¶ 920.)

17. Advising the General Council on Finance and Administration (¶ 911.1) with regard to the policies and practices of agencies and church-related institutions receiving general

church funds concerning their implementation of the denomination's policy of inclusiveness and nondiscrimination on the basis of race and ethnic heritage. This shall be done by (1) consulting with the council in development, review, and maintenance of the certification form to be submitted to the council by agencies and institutions receiving general church funds; (2) reviewing annually the submissions of certifications of compliance with ¶ 911.1*a, b,* and *c*; and (3) recommending to the council acceptance of the certifications, or other appropriate action, including withholding approval of the entire budget of an agency or institution because of noncompliance with ¶ 911.1*a, b,* or *c*.

18. Developing leadership among racial and ethnic groups for the total ministry in the life of the Church.

19. Facilitating the delivery of program services and information to racial and ethnic local churches.

20. Reporting to the General Conference on the role of racial and ethnic groups in The United Methodist Church and on the progress toward racial inclusiveness.

Section XV. General Commission on the Status and Role of Women.

¶ **2201.** *Name.*—There shall be a **General Commission on the Status and Role of Women** in The United Methodist Church.

¶ **2202.** *Purpose.*—The primary purpose of the General Commission on the Status and Role of Women shall be to challenge The United Methodist Church, including its general agencies, institutions, and connectional structures, to a continuing commitment to the full and equal responsibility and participation of women in the total life and mission of the Church, sharing fully in the power and in the policy making at all levels of the Church's life.

Such commitment will confirm anew recognition of the fact that The United Methodist Church is part of the Universal Church, rooted in the liberating message of Jesus Christ, that recognizes every person, woman or man, as a full and equal part of God's human family.

The general commission shall function as an advocate with and on behalf of women individually and collectively within

The United Methodist Church; as a catalyst for the initiation of creative methods to redress inequities of the past and to prevent further inequities against women within The United Methodist Church; and as a monitor to ensure inclusiveness in the programmatic and administrative functioning of The United Methodist Church.

¶ **2203.** *Responsibility.*—The general commission shall be charged with the responsibility of fostering an awareness of issues, problems, and concerns related to the status and role of women, with special reference to their full participation in the total life of the Church at least commensurate with the total membership of women in The United Methodist Church.

1. In the fulfillment of its mandate, this commission shall have the authority to initiate and utilize such channels, develop such plans and strategies, and assign staff as may be required in the implementation of the following primary needs across The United Methodist Church: leadership enablement, resources and communication, affirmative action and advocacy roles, and interagency coordination.

Such plans and strategies related to these needs shall be directed toward the elimination of sexism in all its manifestations from the total life of The United Methodist Church, including general agencies as well as the various connectional channels and structures that reach the local church. The commission shall work with the respective agencies as needs may determine in achieving and safeguarding representation and participation of women, including racial and ethnic groups.

2. The commission through its various research and monitoring processes shall continue to gather data, make recommendations, and suggest guidelines for action as appropriate to eradicate discriminatory policies and practices in any form or discriminatory language and images wherever found in documents, pronouncements, publications, and general resources.

3. The commission shall stimulate ongoing evaluation procedures and receive progress reports toward the end of effecting the guidelines in §2 above in all responsible bodies of the Church.

4. The commission shall establish and maintain a working relationship with Annual Conference commissions, taking into

account the objectives/guidelines for conferences in ¶ 741.1, and seeking to develop and strengthen the leadership of the conference for the realization of these objectives within the general context of the responsibilities of the general commission (¶ 2203.1).

5. The commission shall recommend plans and curricula for new understanding of theology and biblical history affecting the status of women.

6. The commission shall create needed policies and recommendations and program for immediate and long-range implementation related to the enhancement of the role of women in professional and voluntary leadership in the Church.

7. The commission shall serve in an advocacy role to ensure openness and receptivity in matters related to women's role in the Church's life, with particular attention to the contributions of clergy and lay professional women, racial and ethnic women, and those experiencing changing life-styles.

8. The commission shall generate active concern and give full support toward immediate efforts in the fulfillment of the following directive: councils, boards, commissions, committees, personnel recruitment agencies, schools of theology, and other related institutions are directed to establish guidelines and policies for specific recruitment, training, and full utilization of women in total employment, which includes but is not limited to pastoral and related ministries, health and welfare ministries, and faculties and staffs of seminaries and other educational institutions.

9. Advise the General Council on Finance and Administration (¶ 911.1) with regard to the policies and practices of agencies and church-related institutions receiving general church funds concerning their implementation of the denomination's policy of inclusiveness and nondiscrimination on the basis of gender. This shall be done by (1) consulting with the council in development, review, and maintenance of the certification form to be submitted to the council by agencies and institutions receiving general church funds; (2) reviewing annually the submissions of certifications of compliance with ¶ 911.1*a, b,* and *c;* and (3) recommending to the council acceptance of the certifications, or other appropriate action,

including withholding approval of the entire budget of an agency or institution because of noncompliance with ¶ 911.1*a*, *b*, or *c*.

¶ **2204.** *Membership.*—The policies, plans, and administration of the work of the general commission shall be determined by its membership which shall be composed in accord with the following guidelines:

1. The basic membership shall be nominated and elected by the Jurisdictional Conferences, assuring that the pluralism and diversity of the Church's membership is reflected in the representation of racial and ethnic minorities and various age categories. Each jurisdiction shall elect six persons for membership: two laywomen, two laymen, one clergywoman, and one clergyman. Of the persons elected by each Jurisdictional Conference, at least one should be from a racial and ethnic group and at least one shall be under thirty-one years of age at the time of election.

2. There shall be thirteen additional members elected by the general commission, in accord with the provisions of ¶ 805.3*b*. The election of the additional members shall take into account the need to provide adequate representation of racial and ethnic groups and of the various age categories, and to include persons of special competence. The additional membership shall assure that the total membership shall maintain the one-third laymen, one-third laywomen, one-third clergy balance as well as majority membership of women.

3. There shall be three women named by the Women's Division from its members or staff to serve as ex officio members with vote.

4. There shall be two bishops named by the Council of Bishops.

5. In the total membership:

a) Persons over sixty-five years of age shall be included.

b) There should be no less than four persons (two women and two men) from each of these four racial and ethnic groups: Pacific and Asian Americans, Black Americans, Hispanic Americans, and Native Americans.

c) There shall be at least one member who is a diaconal minister.

COMMISSION ON CENTRAL CONFERENCE ¶ 2301

6. The general commission shall be authorized to fill vacancies in its membership during the quadrennium.

¶ **2205.** *Officers.*—The president of the general commission shall be a woman elected by the total commission from its membership. Other officers shall be elected as the commission determines.

¶ **2206.** *Meetings.*—The general commission shall meet annually with such additional meetings as needs demand.

¶ **2207.** *Funding.*—The funds for carrying out the general commission's purpose shall be authorized by the General Conference.

¶ **2208.** *Staff.*—The general commission shall nominate for election by the General Council on Ministries its general secretariat or general secretary who shall provide executive, administrative, and program staff leadership (¶ 813). The commission shall elect such other staff members as needs require within the General Conference mandates and the authority vested in the commission to develop policies and programs directed toward the realization of its purpose.

¶ **2209.** *Relationships.*—In order to fulfill its responsibilities and the directives of the General Conference, the general commission shall work with the Council of Bishops, the general agencies, institutions, and other appropriate structures and channels at all levels of the Church.

Section XVI. Commission on Central Conference Affairs.

¶ **2301.** *Commission on Central Conference Affairs.*—1. Recognizing the differences in conditions that exist in various areas of the world and the changes taking place in those areas, there shall be a **Commission on Central Conference Affairs** to study the structure and supervision of The United Methodist Church in its work outside the United States and its territories and its relationships to other church bodies. The commission shall prepare such recommendations as it considers necessary for presentation directly to the General Conference. All resolutions and petitions related to Central Conferences presented to the General Conference shall be referred to the commission for consideration and the commission shall report its recommendations directly to the General Conference.

659

2. The commission shall be composed of one bishop, one ordained minister, and one lay person from each jurisdiction who are delegates to the General Conference and named by the Council of Bishops; one bishop, one ordained minister, and one lay person from each Central Conference who are delegates to the General Conference and named by the Council of Bishops; one bishop, one ordained minister, and one lay person who are elected members of the World Division of the General Board of Global Ministries and named by the Council of Bishops. Special attention shall be given to the inclusion of women, clergy and lay.

The chairperson of the commission shall be a bishop.

The commission shall meet at the seat of the General Conference.

3. The episcopal members of the commission shall act as the executive committee between sessions of the General Conference. The executive committee shall have authority to take necessary actions on behalf of the commission, including submitting petitions to General Conference under the provisions of ¶ 608.6.

4. The General Council on Finance and Administration shall recommend to the General Conference for its action and determination a provision in the budget of an appropriate general church fund for the expenses incurred by the commission and its executive committee in the interim between sessions of the General Conference.

Section XVII. Interdenominational Agencies.

¶ **2401.** *World Methodist Council.*—1. The United Methodist Church is a member of the World Methodist Council, its predecessor Methodist and Evangelical United Brethren Churches having been charter members of such body. The council is a significant channel for United Methodist relationships with other Methodist churches and with Autonomous Methodist Churches, Affiliated Autonomous Methodist Churches, and Affiliated United Churches formerly part of The United Methodist Church or its predecessor denominations, and with other churches with a Wesleyan heritage. The members of the section representing The United Methodist Church shall be nominated by the Council of Bishops, due regard being given to inclusiveness (in the spirit of ¶ 805) and geographical representation. United Methodist financial support of the World Methodist Council shall be remitted through the General Council on Finance and Administration and shall be in the manner directed by the latter council.

2. Each Affiliated Autonomous Methodist Church and each Affiliated United Church which is a member of the World Methodist Council may choose to send delegates either to the General Conference as proposed in ¶¶ 648.3 and 651, or to the World Methodist Council (receiving from the General Administration Fund the expense of travel and per diem allowances thereto). But no such church shall be entitled to send delegations at the expense of the General Administration Fund to both the World Methodist Council and the General Conference.

¶ **2402.** *Councils and Consultations of Churches.*—1. *The Consultation on Church Union.*

a) The United Methodist Church is a member of the Consultation on Church Union, its predecessor Methodist and Evangelical United Brethren Churches having been involved in its very beginnings and in all its committees and plenary consultations. It has borne its appropriate share of financial support, and through the Interdenominational Cooperation Fund is authorized and directed to continue its support (*see* ¶ 918).

b) United Methodist financial support of the Consultation on Church Union shall be remitted through the General Council on Finance and Administration in accordance with ¶ 918.

2. *The National Council of the Churches of Christ in the U.S.A.*

a) The United Methodist Church is a member of the National Council of the Churches of Christ in the United States of America, its predecessor Methodist and Evangelical United Brethren Churches having been charter members of such body. It has borne its proportionate share of financial support, and through the Interdenominational Cooperation Fund is authorized and directed to continue its support. United Methodist financial support of the National Council of the Churches of Christ in the U.S.A. shall be remitted through the General Council on Finance and Administration in accordance with ¶ 918.

b) The United Methodist representatives and proxies to the

National Council of the Churches of Christ in the U.S.A. Governing Board shall be selected by the Council of Bishops from nominations reviewed by the General Commission on Christian Unity and Interreligious Concerns. Recommendations of names for consideration may be sent by Annual Conferences to the Jurisdictional Conferences. Each Jurisdictional Conference shall provide to the General Commission on Christian Unity and Interreligious Concerns a panel of twelve names with biographical data recommending it include racial and ethnic persons, insofar as possible representing each ethnic group— Asian American, Black American, Hispanic American, and Native American, from which four persons will be chosen by the Council of Bishops as voting delegates. Persons named to the panel shall represent consideration of quotas and balances required both by The United Methodist Church and the National Council of Churches. To supplement the panel from the jurisdictions, if necessary in order to ensure inclusiveness in the delegation, the General Commission on Christian Unity and Interreligious Concerns may recommend additional names to the Council of Bishops. The Jurisdictional Conference may report order of selection or priority, if it desires.

In addition to the delegates representing the jurisdictions, the Council of Bishops shall name five of their number, one of whom is to be the secretary of the Council of Bishops, as part of the clergy quota. Also, the Council of Bishops shall, from the nominations by the General Commission on Christian Unity and Interreligious Concerns name as delegates the appropriate number of staff persons to complete the current complement of delegates allowed from The United Methodist Church.

The Council of Bishops shall approve a list of proxies for the jurisdictional representatives, drawing wherever possible on the original panel of names provided. The Council of Bishops shall provide proxies for any of their own representatives who are unable to attend a particular session of the Governing Board. The General Commission on Christian Unity and Interreligious Concerns shall choose proxies for a particular session for the designated staff delegates on recommendations from the chief executive of the agency from which the official delegate comes.

Representatives from The United Methodist Church to various unit committees and working groups of the National Council of Churches, normally nominated by the National Council of Churches' units, shall be cleared and affirmed or substitutions made by the general commission, in consultation with the Council of Bishops wherever necessary or desired by either the council or the commission.

c) United Methodist financial support of the National Council of the Churches of Christ in the U.S.A. shall include: that council's share of the Interdenominational Cooperation Fund, as determined by the General Conference; and such payments by the general agencies of the Church as each agency may deem its responsibility and proportionate share in the cooperative program of the council.

(1) United Methodist support of the basic budget of the National Council of the Churches of Christ in the U.S.A. shall be established by the General Conference in the budget of the Interdenominational Cooperation Fund. Such support shall be remitted in accordance with ¶ 918 through the General Council on Finance and Administration in the manner directed by the latter council.

(2) Payments by the general agencies of the Church to the National Council of the Churches of Christ in the U.S.A. shall be reported to the General Council on Finance and Administration.

(3) The General Council on Finance and Administration shall include a summary report for United Methodist gifts and contributions to the National Council of the Churches of Christ in the U.S.A. in its annual financial report to the Church.

3. *The World Council of Churches.*

a) The United Methodist Church is a member of the World Council of Churches, its predecessor Methodist and Evangelical United Brethren Churches having been charter members of such body. It should bear its proportionate share of financial support, and through the Interdenominational Cooperation Fund is authorized and directed to continue its support.

b) The representatives of The United Methodist Church to the Assembly and other agencies of the World Council of Churches shall be nominated by the General Commission on Christian Unity and Interreligious Concerns and named by the

Council of Bishops; due regard being given to geographical representation and inclusiveness in the spirit of ¶ 805.4.

c) United Methodist support of the World Council of Churches shall be remitted (in accordance with ¶ 918) through the General Council on Finance and Administration, which shall give due credit for United Methodist gifts and contributions received by the World Council of Churches and shall include them in its annual financial report to the Church.

¶ **2403.** *Commission on Pan-Methodist Cooperation.*—Given the historical relationship and shared traditions of the denominations of the Wesleyan tradition called Methodists in America, there shall be a Commission on Pan-Methodist Cooperation developed jointly with the African Methodist Episcopal Church, the African Methodist Episcopal Zion Church, and the Christian Methodist Episcopal Church. The representatives from The United Methodist Church shall be named by the Council of Bishops. Each delegation shall consist of six members: two bishops, a layman and a laywoman, a young adult and at least one other member of the clergy. The Commission on Pan-Methodist Cooperation shall work to define, determine, plan, and, in cooperation with established agencies of the several denominations, execute activities to foster meaningful cooperation among the four Methodist denominations in the collaboration. Such cooperation shall include, but not be limited to, evangelism, missions, publications, social concerns, and higher education. Each denomination will pay the expenses of its delegation to participate in commission affairs.

¶ **2404.** *The American Bible Society.*—To encourage the wider circulation and use of the Holy Scriptures throughout the world and to provide for the translation, printing, and distribution essential thereto, the American Bible Society shall be recognized as a means of mission outreach for The United Methodist Church, for which appropriate entities of The United Methodist Church shall offer means for seeking the financial support needed for this program.

¶ **2405.** *Liaison Role of the Council of Bishops.*—1. In formal relations with other churches and/or ecclesial bodies, the Council of Bishops shall be the primary liaison for The United Methodist Church. The secretary of the Council of Bishops shall be responsible for these relationships and shall work in cooperation with the General Commission on Christian Unity and Interreligious Concerns in the fulfillment of these functions.

2. The General Commission on Christian Unity and Interreligious Concerns shall consult with the Council of Bishops in establishing the guidelines for the administration of the Interdenominational Cooperation Fund (see ¶¶ 918 and 2003.15).

¶ **2406.** Notwithstanding the above provisions of this section, should structural changes be voted between sessions of the General Conference by any of the above ecumenical bodies, necessitating election of a new group of United Methodist delegates, the Council of Bishops is authorized to elect such delegates as may be required.

Chapter Seven
CHURCH PROPERTY

Section I. All Titles—in Trust.

¶ **2501.** *Titles to Properties.*—In consonance with the legal definition and self-understanding of The United Methodist Church (*see* ¶ 113), and with particular reference to its lack of capacity to hold title to property, The United Methodist Church is organized as a **connectional structure,** and titles to all properties held at General, Jurisdictional, Annual, or District Conference levels, or by a local church or charge, or by an agency or institution of the Church, shall be held in trust for The United Methodist Church and subject to the provisions of its Discipline. Titles are not held by "The United Methodist Church" (*see* ¶ 906.7) or by "The General Conference of The United Methodist Church," but instead by the incorporated conferences, agencies, or organizations of the denomination, or in the case of unincorporated bodies of the denomination, by boards of trustees established for the purpose of holding and administering property.

¶ **2502.** *Use of the Name "Methodist" or "United Methodist."*—The words "Methodist" or "United Methodist" are not to be used as, or as a part of, a trade name or trademark or as a part of the name of any business firm or organization, except by corporations or other business units created for the administration of work undertaken directly by The United Methodist Church.

¶ **2503.** *Trust Clauses in Deeds.*—1. Except in conveyances which require that the real property so conveyed shall revert to the grantor if and when its use as a place of divine worship has been terminated, all written instruments of conveyance by which premises are held or hereafter acquired for use as a place of divine worship for members of The United Methodist Church or for other church activities shall contain the following trust clause:

In trust, that said premises shall be used, kept, and maintained as a place of divine worship of the United Methodist ministry and members of The United Methodist Church; subject to the Discipline, usage, and ministerial appointments of said church as from time to time authorized and declared by the General Conference and by the Annual Conference within whose bounds the said premises are situated. This provision is solely for the benefit of the grantee, and the grantor reserves no right or interest in said premises.

2. All written instruments by which premises are held or hereafter acquired as a parsonage for the use and occupancy of the ministers of The United Methodist Church shall contain the following trust clause:

In trust, that such premises shall be held, kept, and maintained as a place of residence for the use and occupancy of the ordained ministers of The United Methodist Church who may from time to time be entitled to occupy the same by appointment; subject to the Discipline and usage of said church, as from time to time authorized and declared by the General Conference and by the Annual Conference within whose bounds the said premises are situated. This provision is solely for the benefit of the grantee, and the grantor reserves no right or interest in said premises.

3. In case the property so acquired is to be used for both a house of worship and a parsonage, the provisions of both trust clauses specified in §§1 and 2 above shall be inserted in the conveyance.

4. In case the property so acquired is not to be used exclusively for a place of worship, or a parsonage, or both, all written instruments by which such premises are held or hereafter acquired shall contain the following trust clause:

In trust, that said premises shall be kept, maintained, and disposed of for the benefit of The United Methodist Church and subject to the usages and the Discipline of The United Methodist Church. This provision is solely for the benefit of the grantee, and the grantor reserves no right or interest in said premises.

5. However, the absence of a trust clause stipulated in §§ 1, 2, 3, or 4 above in deeds and conveyances previously executed shall in no way exclude a local church or church agency from or relieve it of its connectional responsibilities to The United Methodist Church. Nor shall it absolve a local congregation or church agency or Board of Trustees of its responsibility and accountability to The United Methodist Church; *provided* that the

intent and desires of the founders and/or the later congregations or Boards of Trustees are shown by any or all of the following indications: (*a*) the conveyance of the property to the trustees of a local church or agency or any predecessor to The United Methodist Church; (*b*) the use of the name, customs, and polity of any predecessor to The United Methodist Church in such a way as to be thus known to the community as a part of such denomination; (*c*) the acceptance of the pastorate of ordained ministers appointed by a bishop or employed by the superintendent of the District or Annual Conference of any predecessor to The United Methodist Church.

¶ **2504.** *Effect of Union.*—Nothing in the Plan of Union at any time after the union is to be construed so as to require any existing local church of any predecessor denomination to The United Methodist Church to alienate or in any way to change the title to property contained in its deed or deeds at the time of union, and lapse of time or usage shall not affect said title or control. Title to all property of a local church, or charge, or agency of the Church shall be held subject to the provisions of the Discipline, whether title to the same is taken in the name of the local church trustees, or charge trustees, or in the name of a corporation organized for the purpose, or otherwise.

¶ **2505.** *Oil, Gas, and Mineral Leases.*—Subject to and in accordance with the laws of the state, province, or country, the governing body of any church unit or agency owning land in trust for The United Methodist Church as provided in this Discipline may lease said land for the production of oil, gas, coal, and other minerals, upon such terms as it may deem best; *provided*, however, that such production shall not interfere with the purpose for which said land is held. The moneys received from such leases as rentals, royalties, or otherwise, shall be used so far as practicable for the benefit of the church unit and for the promotion of the interests of The United Methodist Church. The lessee shall have no control over or responsibility for the payments made under such lease.

Section II. Compliance with Law.

¶ **2506.** *Conformity of Discipline with Local Law.*—All provisions of the Discipline relating to property, both real and personal, and relating to the formation and operation of any corporation, and relating to mergers, are conditioned upon their being in conformity with the local laws, and in the event of conflict therewith the local laws shall prevail; *provided,* however, that this requirement shall not be construed to give the consent of The United Methodist Church to deprivation of its property without due process of law or to the regulation of its affairs by state statute where such regulation violates the constitutional guarantee of freedom of religion and separation of Church and state or violates the right of the Church to maintain connectional structure; and *provided* further, that the services of worship of every local church of The United Methodist Church shall be open to all persons without regard to race, color, or national origin. "Local laws" shall be construed to mean the laws of the country, state, or other like political unit within the geographical bounds of which the church property is located.[1]

¶ **2507.** *Conformity of Deeds and Conveyances with Local Law.*—In order to secure the right of property, with the appurtenances thereof, of the churches and parsonages of The United Methodist Church, care shall be taken that all conveyances and deeds be drawn and executed in due conformity to the laws of the respective states, provinces, and countries in which the property is situated and also in due conformity to the laws of The United Methodist Church. Deeds shall be registered or recorded directly upon their execution.

¶ **2508.** *Instituting and Defending Civil Action.*—Because of the nature of The United Methodist Church (¶ 113) no individual or affiliated church body or unit, nor any official thereof, may commence or participate in any suit or proceeding in the name of or on behalf of The United Methodist Church, excepting, however, the following:

1. Any person or church unit served with legal process in the name of The United Methodist Church may appear for the purpose of presenting to the court the non-jural nature of The United Methodist Church and to raise issues of lack of jurisdiction of the court, lack of capacity of such individual or unit

---

[1]*See* Judicial Council Decisions 11, 315.

to be served with process, and related Constitutional issues in defense of denominational interests.

2. Any denominational unit authorized to hold title to property and enforce trusts for the benefit of the denomination may bring suit in its own name to protect denominational interests.

¶ **2509.** *Financial Obligations.*—No conference, council, board, agency, local church, or other unit can financially obligate the denomination or, without prior specific consent, any other organizational unit thereof.

Section III. Audits and Bonding of Church Officers.

¶ **2510.** All persons holding trust funds, securities, or moneys of any kind belonging to the General, Jurisdictional, Annual, or Provisional Annual Conferences or to organizations under the control of the General, Jurisdictional, Annual, or Provisional Annual Conferences shall be bonded by a reliable company in such good and sufficient sum as the conference may direct. The accounts of such persons shall be audited at least annually by a recognized public or certified public accountant. A report to an Annual Conference containing a financial statement which the Discipline requires to be audited shall not be approved until the audit is made and the financial statement is shown to be correct. Other parts of the report may be approved pending such audit.

Section IV. The Methodist Corporation.

¶ **2511.** 1. The General Council on Finance and Administration shall be the successor to all right, title, and interest in and to all assets of The Methodist Corporation for the following purposes: to hold, to manage and/or to liquidate such assets if and when it concludes that it is not in the best interest of The United Methodist Church to undertake a development of or further holding of the property.

2. The members of the General Council on Finance and Administration shall constitute the Board of Directors of The Methodist Corporation, which shall be continued as a legal entity until such time as said board shall deem it desirable and convenient to liquidate the corporation, at which time it is empowered and authorized to take the necessary corporate

action to effect the surrender of its charter or to merge, consolidate, or affiliate it into or with the General Council on Finance and Administration, a corporation.

3. Upon the liquidation of the assets of The Methodist Corporation, the resulting fund, after the payment and satisfaction of all debts, shall be conveyed, assigned, and transferred by the General Council on Finance and Administration to such religious, charitable, scientific, literary, or educational organization or organizations as the General Conference of The United Methodist Church shall direct. No funds or property shall be distributed among or inure to the benefit of any private shareholder or individual.

Section V. Annual Conference Property.[2]

¶ 2512. 1. *Annual Conference Board of Trustees.*—Each Annual Conference shall have a **Board of Trustees,** which shall be incorporated unless the conference is incorporated in its own name. In either case the board shall consist of twelve persons of which one-third shall be clergy, one-third laywomen, and one-third laymen, in accordance with the provisions of ¶ 706.4, said persons must be of legal age as determined by law, and lay members shall be members in good standing of local churches within the bounds of the conference. Such persons shall be the directors of the corporation. They shall be elected by the conference for terms of four years except for the first board, one-fourth of whom shall be elected for a term of one year, one-fourth for two years, one-fourth for a term of three years, and one-fourth for a term of four years and shall serve until their successors have been elected; *provided,* however, that existing incorporated trustees of any Annual Conference may continue unaffected while the charter or articles of incorporation are amended to bring them into conformity with this paragraph.

2. The Board of Trustees shall meet at least annually and organize by electing a president, vice-president, secretary, and treasurer, whose duties shall be those usually pertaining to such offices. They shall be amenable to the Annual Conference.

---

[2]For authority regarding property held by general agencies of the Church, *see* ¶¶ 907.1, .3.

Vacancies shall be filled by the Annual Conference for the unexpired term.

3. The said corporation shall receive, collect, and hold in trust for the benefit of the Annual Conference any and all donations, bequests, and devises of any kind or character, real or personal, that may be given, devised, bequeathed, or conveyed to the said board or to the Annual Conference as such for any benevolent, charitable, or religious purpose, and shall administer the same and the income therefrom in accordance with the directions of the donor, trustor, or testator, and in the interest of the church, society, institution, or agency contemplated by such donor, trustor, or testator, under the direction of the Annual Conference. The Annual Conference may include in any resolution authorizing proposed action regarding Annual Conference property a direction that any contract, deed, bill of sale, mortgage, or other necessary written instrument be executed by and on behalf of the Annual Conference Board of Trustees by any two of its officers, who thereupon shall be duly authorized to carry out the direction of the Annual Conference; and any written instrument so executed shall be binding and effective as the action of the Annual Conference. The board shall have the power to invest, reinvest, buy, sell, transfer, and convey any and all funds and properties which it may hold in trust, subject always to the terms of the legacy, devise, or donation; *provided*, however, that the foregoing shall not apply to churches, colleges, camps, conference grounds, orphanages, or incorporated boards. The conference Board of Trustees is encouraged to invest in institutions, companies, corporations, or funds that make a positive contribution toward the realization of the goals of the Social Principles of our Church. When the use to be made of any such donation, bequest, or devise is not otherwise designated, the same shall be used as directed by the Annual Conference. Funds committed to this board may be invested by it only in collateral that is amply secured and after such investments have been approved by the said board or its agency or committee charged with such investment, unless otherwise directed by the Annual Conference.[3]

---

[3]*See* Judicial Council Decisions 135, 160, 190.

4. The board may intervene and take all necessary legal steps to safeguard and protect the interests and rights of the Annual Conference anywhere and in all matters relating to property and rights to property whether arising by gift, devise, or otherwise, or where held in trust or established for the benefit of the Annual Conference or its membership.

5. It shall be the duty of the pastor within the bounds of whose charge any such gift, bequest, or devise is made to give prompt notice thereof to said board, which shall proceed to take such steps as are necessary and proper to conserve, protect, and administer the same; *provided,* however, that the board may decline to receive or administer any such gift, devise, or bequest for any reason satisfactory to the board. It shall also be the duty of the pastor to report annually to the Board of Trustees of the Annual Conference a list of all property, including real, personal, or mixed, within the charge belonging to or which should be under the control or jurisdiction of the said board.

6. The board shall make to each session of the Annual Conference a full, true, and faithful report of its doings, of all funds, moneys, securities, and property held in trust by it, and of its receipts and disbursements during the conference year. The beneficiary of a fund held in trust by the board shall also be entitled to a report at least annually on the condition of such fund and on the transactions affecting it.

¶ **2513.** *Foundations—Annual Conference or Conferences.*—An Annual Conference or conferences may establish a United Methodist Foundation. The purposes for establishing such a foundation may include:

1. Providing the services described in ¶ 2512.3 as designated by the donor or at the direction of the conference Board of Trustees;

2. The promotion of planned giving programs on behalf of local churches, conferences, and general church boards and agencies;

3. Furnishing counsel and guidance to local churches with regard to promotion and management of permanent funds;

4. Other responsibilities as determined by the Annual Conference. The United Methodist Foundation shall have a governing board as determined by the Annual Conference. The

governing board will establish policies upon which the foundation will operate.

¶ **2514.** *Episcopal Residence.*—When authorized by two-thirds of the Annual Conferences comprising an episcopal area, an episcopal residence for the resident bishop may be acquired, the title to which shall be held in trust by the trustees of the Annual Conference within which the residence is located. Any such property so acquired and held shall not be sold or disposed of except with the consent of a majority of the conferences that participate in the ownership. Whenever there is a plan to sell an episcopal residence or to transfer an Annual Conference from one episcopal area to another, that plan shall include provision for safeguarding each conference's equity, if any, in an episcopal residence; except that an Annual Conference, by its own decision, may relinquish its claims to an equity interest in an episcopal residence.[4]

¶ **2515.** *Sale, Transfer, Lease or Mortgage of Annual Conference Property.*—No Annual Conference property shall be sold, transferred, or leased for a term that exceeds twenty (20) years, or mortgaged without the consent of the Annual Conference or, ad interim, *(a)* the consent of the presiding bishop and of a majority of the district superintendents, and, in the case of discontinued or abandoned local church property, the consent of a majority of the district Board of Church Location and Building (*see* ¶ 2548); and *(b)* the bishop's determination that such transfer or encumbrance conforms to the Discipline. The bishop's written statement evidencing the satisfaction of this condition shall be affixed to or included in any instrument of transfer or encumbrance. Any required written instrument necessary to carry out the action so authorized shall be executed in the name of the conference corporation by any two of its officers or, where the conference is unincorporated, by any two officers of its Board of Trustees, and any written instrument so executed shall be binding and effective as the action of the conference.

¶ **2516.** *Camps, Conference Grounds, and Retreat Centers.*—Title to Annual Conference or district camps, conference grounds, and retreat centers held in trust by an incorporated

---

[4]*See* Judicial Council Decision 194.

board or agency of an Annual Conference or district, or by an unincorporated board, commission, society, or similar body of the conference or district, can be mortgaged or sold and conveyed by such corporation or unincorporated body only after authorization by the Annual or District Conference to which such body is related.

Section VI. District Property.

¶ **2517.** *District Parsonages and Boards of Trustees.*—1. A **district parsonage** for the district superintendent may be acquired, when authorized by the Charge Conferences of two-thirds of the charges in the district or when authorized by a two-thirds vote of the District Conference, subject to the advice and approval of the district Board of Church Location and Building as provided in ¶¶ 2518-2523.

2. The title of district property may be held in trust by a **district Board of Trustees.** Unless the District Union is incorporated in its own name, each district shall have a district Board of Trustees, which shall be incorporated. The board shall consist of not fewer than three nor more than nine members in accordance with ¶ 706.4, having the same qualifications provided for trustees of local churches (¶ 2524), who shall be nominated by the district superintendent in consultation with the district nominating committee, if one exists, and elected by the District Conference. Where there is no District Conference, they may be elected by the district Board of Stewards or by the Annual Conference on nomination of the district superintendent. They shall be elected for a term of one year and serve until their successors shall have been elected, and shall report annually to the District Conference or Annual Conference. Title to district property may be held in trust by the district Board of Trustees. If the title to the district parsonage is not held in trust by the district Board of Trustees, the same shall be held in trust by the trustees of the Annual Conference of which such district is a part, and such trustees shall the state, territory, or country prescribe otherwise, district property held in trust by a district Board of Trustees may be mortgaged or sold and conveyed by them only by authority of the District Conference or Annual Conference, or if such property is held in trust by the trustees of the Annual

Conference, it may be mortgaged or sold and conveyed by such trustees only by authority of the Annual Conference. The District Conference, or Annual Conference in the case of property held in trust by the trustees of the Annual Conference, may include in the resolution authorizing such proposed action a direction that any contract, deed, bill of sale, mortgage, or other necessary written instrument may be executed by and on behalf of the respective Board of Trustees by any two of its officers, who thereupon shall be duly authorized to carry out the direction of the District Conference or Annual Conference; and any written instrument so executed shall be binding and effective as the action of the District Conference or Annual Conference. The purchase price and maintenance cost of a district parsonage may be equitably distributed among the charges of the district by the district Board of Stewards. Where there is an incorporated District Union (¶ 745.4), the Board of Directors of the District Union shall have the same duties and reponsibilities with respect to district property as are described here for the district Board of Trustees.

3. When district boundaries are changed by division, rearrangement, or consolidation so that a district parsonage purchased, owned, and maintained by one district is included within the bounds of another district, each such district shall be entitled to receive its just share of the then reasonable value of the parsonage in which it has invested funds; and the amount of such value and just share shall be determined by a committee of three persons, appointed by the bishop of the area, who shall not be residents of any of the said districts. The committee shall hear claims of each district regarding its interest therein before making decision. From any such determination there is reserved unto each of the interested districts the right of appeal to the next succeeding Annual Conference. Any sum received as or from such share shall be used for no other purpose than purchase or building of a parsonage in the district. The same procedure shall be followed in determining equities of a district in any other property which may be included in another district by changes in district boundaries.

¶ **2518.** *Board of Church Location and Building.*—There shall be in each district of an Annual Conference a **district Board of**

Church Location and Building. The board shall consist of the district superintendent and a minimum of six and a maximum of nine additional persons (one-third clergy, one-third laymen, one-third laywomen), and where possible should be inclusive of sex, race, age, and persons with handicapping conditions, nominated by the district superintendent in consultation with the district nominating committee, if one exists, and elected annually by the Annual Conference; *provided* that in a district of great geographical extent an additional board may be so elected. The members of the board, excuding the district superintendent, shall be divided into three classes. One-third shall be elected annually for a three-year term. A chairperson and a secretary shall be elected annually at the first meeting following Annual Conference. The board shall file a report of any actions taken with the Charge Conference of each local church involved, and the report so filed shall become a part of the minutes of the said conference or conferences. The board shall also make a written report to the District Conference (or if there is no District Conference, to the district superintendent), and this report shall become a part of the records of that conference.

¶ **2519.** 1. *Local Church Building Sites and Plans.*—The Board of Church Location and Building shall investigate all proposed local church building sites, ascertaining that such sites are properly located for the community to be served and adequate in size to provide space for future expansion and parking facilities. (*See* ¶¶ 268.1, 2543.2.)

2. If there is a district Strategy Committee for Parish Development or a Metropolitan Commission (¶ 1415.5*j*) in the district, the board shall consider its recommendations in planning a strategy for continuing the service of The United Methodist Church in changing neighborhoods. If no parish development committee or commission is operative, the board shall study the duties assigned to each and seek ways to provide continuity of service in parishes where there is a change in the racial, ethnic, or cultural character of the residents to the end that the resolutions of the General Conference involving such neighborhoods be given careful consideration. One member of the board shall also have membership on the strategy committee or on the commission.

677

3. The Board of Church Location and Building shall investigate all proposed local church or parsonage buildings to determine the best method to make the structure energy efficient.

¶ **2520.** *Approval of Construction, Purchase, or Remodeling Plans for Local Churches.*—1. The board shall require any local church in its district, before beginning or contracting for construction or purchase of a new church or educational building or a parsonage, or remodeling of such a building if the cost will exceed 10 percent of its value, to submit for consideration and approval a statement of the need for the proposed facilities, preliminary architectural plans, an estimate of the cost, and a financial plan for defraying such costs, as provided in ¶¶ 2543.4-.5. Before finally approving the building project, the board shall ascertain whether the preliminary architectural design and financial programs have been reviewed, evaluated, and approved by proper authorities (¶ 2543.5).

2. When the local church has secured final architectural plans and specifications and a reliable and detailed estimate of the cost of the proposed undertaking as provided in ¶ 2543.8, the board shall require their submission for consideration and approval. The board shall study carefully the feasibility and financial soundness of the undertaking and ascertain whether the financial plan will provide funds necessary to assure prompt payment of all proposed contractual obligations, and it shall report its conclusions to the church in writing.

3. A final decision of the board approving purchase, building, or remodeling shall automatically terminate after a period of one year, where no action has been taken by the local church to carry out such decision.

¶ **2521.** A decision of the board disapproving such purchase, building, or remodeling shall be final unless overruled by the Annual Conference, to which there is reserved unto the local church the right of appeal.

¶ **2522.** The above provisions shall apply to the acquisition of a district parsonage.

¶ **2523.** *Sale, Transfer, Lease, or Mortgage of District Property.*—No district property shall be sold, transferred, or leased for a term which exceeds twenty years, or mortgaged without *(a)* the consent of the presiding district superintendent, and *(b)* the district superintendent's determination that such transfer or encumbrance conforms to the Discipline and to appropriate governmental requirements. The district superintendent's written statement evidencing the satisfaction of these conditions shall be affixed to any instrument or transfer or encumbrance. Any required written instrument necessary to carry out the action so authorized shall be executed in the name of the corporation by any two of its officers, or any two officers of its Board of Trustees, and any written instrument so executed shall be binding and effective as the action of the corporation.

Section VII. Local Church Property.

¶ **2524.** *Local Church Board of Trustees—Qualifications.*—In each pastoral charge consisting of one local church there shall be a **Board of Trustees,** consisting of not fewer than three nor more than nine persons, at least one-third of whom shall be laywomen, and at least one-third of whom shall be laymen, each of whom shall be of legal age as determined by law and at least two-thirds of whom shall be members of The United Methodist Church.[5]

¶ **2525.** *Local Church Board of Trustees—Election.*—The members of the Board of Trustees shall be divided into three classes, and each class shall as nearly as possible consist of an equal number of members. At the Charge Conference, on nomination by the Committee on Nominations or from the floor, it shall elect, to take office at the beginning of the ensuing calendar year or at such other times as the Charge or Church Conference may set to serve for a term of three years or until their successors have been duly elected and qualified, the required number of trustees to succeed those of the class whose terms then expire; *provided,* however, that nothing herein shall be construed to prevent the election of a trustee to self-succession.[6] The Charge Conference may assign the responsibility for electing trustees to a Church Conference.

¶ **2526.** *Church Local Conference—Duties, Authority and Membership.*—1. In a pastoral charge consisting of two or more local

---

[5]*See* Judicial Council Decision 500.
[6]*See* Judicial Council Decisions 130, 500.

churches, a **Church Local Conference,** constituted and organized under the Discipline of The United Methodist Church in each local church therein, shall be vested with authority and power in matters relating to the real and personal property of the local church concerned. Such Church Local Conference shall elect the Board of Trustees of such local church in number and manner described in ¶ 2525, and the duties of such trustees, duly elected, shall be the same as and identical with the duties described in ¶ 2528. The duties, authority, and power vested in the Church Local Conference, insofar as they relate to the property, real and personal, of the local church concerned, are the same as and identical with the authority and power vested in the Charge Conference of a pastoral charge of one local church (¶ 2528); and the authority, power, and limitations therein set forth shall be applicable to the Church Local Conference as fully and to the same extent as if incorporated herein. The effect of the provisions for a Church Local Conference is to give to each local church in a charge of two or more churches, rather than to the pastoral Charge Conference, supervision over and control of its own property, subject to the limitations prescribed in the Discipline with regard to local church property.

2. Whenever required under the Discipline of The United Methodist Church for matters relating to real or personal property of the local church or to mergers of churches, a local church in a pastoral charge consisting of two or more local churches shall organize a Church Local Conference. The membership of the Church Local Conference shall consist of the persons specified for membership of the Charge Conference (¶ 246.2) so far as the officers and relationships exist within the local church, except that the pastor shall be a member of each Church Local Conference. The provisions of ¶¶ 246.2-.10 relating to membership qualification and procedures of a Charge Conference shall be applicable to membership qualifications and procedures of a Church Local Conference.

¶ **2527.** *Charge or Cooperative Parish Board of Trustees.*—1. A pastoral charge composed of two or more churches, each having a local Board of Trustees, may have in addition a **Board of Trustees for the charge as a whole.** This board shall hold title to and manage the property belonging to the entire charge, such as parsonage, campground, burial ground, and such other property as may be committed to it. It shall receive and administer funds for the charge in conformity with the laws of the state, province, or country in which the property is located. This board shall consist of not less than three persons, at least two-thirds of whom shall be members of The United Methodist Church and of legal age as determined by law. These trustees shall be elected by the Charge Conference for three years or until their successors are elected.

2. A cooperative parish composed of two or more charges may have, in addition to its charge trustees and local church trustees, a Board of Trustees for the cooperative parish as a whole. This board shall hold title to and manage the property belonging to the cooperative parish in accordance with ¶¶ 2503, 2526, 2527. These trustees shall be elected by the Charge Conference and/or Church Local Conference related to the cooperative parish and shall be representative of each congregation which composes the cooperative parish.

3. The Board of Trustees of a charge shall provide for the security of its funds, keep an accurate record of its proceedings, and report to the Charge Conference to which it is amenable.

4. When two or more local churches compose a single pastoral charge having a parsonage and one or more thereof is separated from such charge and established as a pastoral charge or united with another pastoral charge, each such local church shall be entitled to receive its just share of the then reasonable value of the parsonage in which it has invested funds, and the amount of such value and just share shall be determined by a committee of three persons, appointed by the district superintendent, who shall be members of The United Methodist Church but not of any of the interested local churches. Such committee shall hear all interested parties and shall take into account the investment of any church in any such property before arriving at a final determination. From any such determination there is reserved to each of the interested churches the right of appeal to the next succeeding Annual Conference, the decision of which shall be final and binding. Any sum received as or from such share shall not be applied to current expense or current budget.

¶ 2528. In a pastoral charge consisting of one local church, the Charge Conference, constituted as set forth in ¶¶ 246-247, shall be vested with power and authority as hereinafter set forth in connection with the property, both real and personal, of the said local church, namely:

1. If it so elects, to direct the Board of Trustees to incorporate the local church, expressly subject, however, to the Discipline of The United Methodist Church and in accordance with the pertinent local laws and in such manner as will fully protect and exempt from any and all legal liability the individual officials and members, jointly and severally, of the local church, and the Charge, Annual, Jurisdictional, and General Conferences of The United Methodist Church, and each of them, for and on account of the debts and other obligations of every kind and description, of the local church.

2. To direct the Board of Trustees with respect to the purchase, sale, mortgage, encumbrance, construction, repairing, remodeling, and maintenance of any and all property of the local church.

3. To direct the Board of Trustees with respect to the acceptance or rejection of any and all conveyances, grants, gifts, donations, legacies, bequests, or devises, absolute or in trust, for the use and benefit of the local church, and to require the administration of any such trust in accordance with the terms and provisions thereof and of the local laws appertaining thereto. (*See* ¶ 2532.2.)

4. To do any and all things necessary to exercise such other powers and duties relating to the property, real and personal, of the local church concerned as may be committed to it by the Discipline.

¶ 2529. *Local Church Board of Trustees—Organization and Membership.*—The Board of Trustees shall organize as follows:

1. Within thirty days after the beginning of the ensuing calendar or conference year (whichever applies to the term of office) each Board of Trustees shall convene at a time and place designated by the chairperson, or by the vice-chairperson in the event that the chairperson is not reelected a trustee or because of absence or disability is unable to act, for the purpose of electing

officers of the said board for the ensuing year and transacting any other business properly brought before it.

2. The Board of Trustees shall elect from the membership thereof, to hold office for a term of one year or until their successors shall be elected, a chairperson, vice-chairperson, secretary, and if need requires, treasurer; *provided,* however, that the chairperson and vice-chairperson shall not be members of the same class; and *provided* further that the offices of secretary and treasurer may be held by the same person; and *provided* further that the chairperson shall be a member of the local church. The duties of each officer shall be the same as generally connected with the office held and which are usually and commonly discharged by the holder thereof. The Church Local Conference may, if it is necessary to conform to the local laws, substitute the designations "president" and "vice-president" for and in place of "chairperson" and "vice-chairperson."

3. Where necessity requires, as a result of the incorporation of a local church, the corporation directors, in addition to electing officers as provided in §2 above, shall ratify and confirm, by appropriate action, and if necessary elect, as officers of the corporation, the treasurer or treasurers, as the case may be, elected by the Charge Conference in accordance with the provisions of the Discipline, whose duties and responsibilities shall be as therein set forth. If more than one account is maintained in the name of the corporation in any financial institution or institutions, each such account and the treasurer thereof shall be appropriately designated.

4. "Trustee," "trustees," and "Board of Trustees," as used herein or elsewhere in the Discipline, may be construed to be synonymous with "director," "directors," and "Board of Directors" applied to corporations, when required to comply with law.

¶ **2530.** *Removal of Local Church Trustees.*—1. Should a trustee withdraw from the membership of The United Methodist Church or be excluded therefrom, trusteeship therein shall automatically cease from the date of such withdrawal or exclusion.

2. Should a trustee of a local church or a director of an incorporated local church refuse to execute properly a legal

instrument relating to any property of the church when directed so to do by the Charge Conference and when all legal requirements have been satisfied with reference to such execution, the said Charge Conference may by majority vote declare the trustee's or director's membership on the Board of Trustees or Board of Directors vacated.

3. Vacancies occurring in a Board of Trustees shall be filled by election for the unexpired term. Such election shall be held in the same manner as for trustees.

¶ **2531.** *Meetings of Local Church Boards of Trustees.*—The Board of Trustees shall meet at the call of the pastor or of its president at least annually at such times and places as shall be designated in a notice to each trustee and the pastor(s) at a reasonable time prior to the appointed time of the meeting. Waiver of notice may be used as a means to validate meetings legally where the usual notice is impracticable. A majority of the members of the Board of Trustees shall constitute a quorum.

¶ **2532.** *Board of Trustees—Powers and Limitations.*—1. Subject to the direction of the Charge Conference, the Board of Trustees shall have the supervision, oversight, and care of all real property owned by the local church and of all property and equipment acquired directly by the local church or by any society, board, class, commission, or similar organization connected therewith; *provided* that the Board of Trustees shall not violate the rights of any local church organization elsewhere granted in the Discipline; *provided* further, that the Board of Trustees shall not prevent or interfere with the pastor in the use of any of the said property for religious services or other proper meetings or purposes recognized by the law, usages, and customs of The United Methodist Church, or permit the use of said property for religious or other meetings without the consent of the pastor, or in the pastor's absence the consent of the district superintendent; and *provided* further, that pews in The United Methodist Church shall always be free; and *provided* further, that the Church Local Conference may assign certain of these duties to a building committee as set forth in ¶ 2543 or the chairperson of the parsonage committee, if one exists.

2. When a pastor and/or a Board of Trustees are asked to grant permission to an outside organization to use church

facilities, permission can be granted only when such use is consistent with the Social Principles (¶¶ 70-75) and ecumenical objectives.

3. The chairperson of the Board of Trustees or the chairperson of the parsonage committee if one exists, the chairperson of the Committee on Pastor-Parish Relations, and the pastor shall make an annual review of the church-owned parsonage to assure proper maintenance.

4. Subject to the direction of the Charge Conference as hereinbefore provided, the Board of Trustees shall receive and administer all bequests made to the local church; shall receive and administer all trusts; shall invest all trust funds of the local church in conformity with laws of the country, state, or like political unit in which the local church is located. The Board of Trustees is encouraged to invest in institutions, companies, corporations, or funds which make a positive contribution toward the realization of the goals outlined in the Social Principles of our Church.

¶ **2533.** *Permanent Endowment Fund Committee.*—A Charge Conference may establish a local church **Permanent Endowment Fund Committee**. The purposes for establishing such a committee may include the responsibilities to:

1. Provide the services described in ¶ 2532.2 as designated by the donor or at the direction of the Charge Conference. It is recommended that consideration be given to the placement of funds with the conference or area United Methodist Foundation for administration and investment.

2. Emphasize the need for adults of all ages to have a will and an estate plan and provide information on the preparation of these to the members of the congregation.

3. Stress the opportunities for church members and constituents to make provisions for giving through United Methodist churches, institutions, agencies, and causes by means of wills, annuities, trusts, life insurance, memorials, and various types of property.

4. Arrange for the dissemination of information that will be helpful in preretirement planning, including such considerations as establishing a living will and a living trust.

5. Other responsibilities as determined by the Charge Conference.

¶ **2534.** *Local Church Foundations.*—After securing the written consent of the pastor and of the district superintendent, local churches may, by Charge Conference action, establish local church foundations whose trustees, directors, or governing body shall be elected by the Charge Conference. Such foundations shall be incorporated, organized, and function in compliance with state law and subject to the provisions of the Discipline. Any such foundation shall not violate the rights of any other local church organization and shall be subject to the direction of the Charge Conference.

¶ **2535.** *Unincorporated Local Church Property—Title and Purchase.*—Unless otherwise required by local law (¶ 2506), title to all property now owned or hereafter acquired by an unincorporated local church, and any organization, board, commission, society, or similar body connected therewith, shall be held by and/or conveyed and transferred to its duly elected trustees, their successors and assigns in trust for the use and benefit of such local church and of The United Methodist Church. The trustees shall be named as the Board of Trustees of the local church in the written instrument conveying or transferring title. Every instrument of conveyance of real estate shall contain the appropriate trust clause as set forth in the Discipline (¶ 2503).

¶ **2536.** *Unincorporated Local Church Property—Notice and Authorization.*—Prior to the purchase by an unincorporated local church of any real estate, a resolution authorizing such action shall be passed at a meeting of the Charge Conference by a majority vote of its members present and voting at a regular meeting or a special meeting of the Charge Conference called for that purpose; *provided,* however, that not less than ten days' notice of such meeting and the proposed action shall have been given from the pulpit or in the weekly bulletin of the church; and *provided* further, that written consent to such action shall be given by the pastor and the district superintendent. (*See* ¶ 2543.)

¶ **2537.** *Incorporated Local Church Property—Title and Purchase.*—Unless otherwise required by local law (¶ 2506), the title to all property, now owned or hereafter acquired by an incorporated local church, and any organization, board, commission, society, or similar body connected therewith, shall be held by and/or conveyed to the corporate body in its corporate name, in trust for the use and benefit of such local church and of The United Methodist Church. Every instrument of conveyance of real estate shall contain the appropriate trust clause as set forth in the Discipline (¶ 2503).

¶ **2538.** *Incorporated Local Church Property—Notice and Authorization.*—Prior to the purchase by a local church corporation of any real estate, a resolution authorizing such action shall be passed by the Charge Conference in corporate session, or such other corporate body as the local laws may require, with the members thereof acting in their capacity as members of the corporate body, by a majority vote of those present and voting at any regular or special meeting called for that purpose; *provided* that not less than ten days' notice of such meeting and the proposed action shall have been given from the pulpit or in the weekly bulletin of the local church; and *provided* further, that written consent to such action shall be given by the pastor and the district superintendent; and *provided* further, that all such transactions shall have the approval of the Charge Conference.

¶ **2539.** Any real property owned by, or in which an unincorporated local church has any interest, may be sold, transferred, leased for a term which exceeds five years, or mortgaged subject to the following procedure and conditions:

1. Notice of the proposed action and the date and time of the regular or special meeting of the Charge Conference at which it is to be considered shall be given at least ten days prior thereto (except as local laws may otherwise provide) from the pulpit of the church or in its weekly bulletin.

2. A resolution authorizing the proposed action shall be passed by a majority vote of the Charge Conference members (in a pastoral charge consisting of two or more local churches, the Church Local Conference; *see* ¶ 2526) present and voting at a special meeting called to consider such action.

3. The written consent of the pastor of the local church and the district superintendent to the proposed action shall be necessary and shall be affixed to or included in the instrument of sale, transfer, lease, or mortgage. Prior to consenting to the proposed action to sell or transfer any United Methodist Church property, the pastor and district superintendent shall ensure that: *(a)* a full investigation shall be made and, if warranted, an

appropriate plan of action shall be developed for the future missional needs of the community; *(b)* the transfer or encumbrance shall conform to the Discipline; and *(c)* the congregation, if no longer to continue as an unincorporated local United Methodist church, does not sell its facilities to another United Methodist church. Certification by the district superintendent shall be conclusive evidence that the transfer or encumbrance conforms to the Discipline. The requirements of investigation and the development of a plan of action, however, shall not affect the merchantability of the title to the real estate or the legal effect of the instruments of sale or transfer.

4. The resolution authorizing such proposed action shall direct that any contract, deed, bill of sale, mortgage, or other necessary written instrument be executed by and on behalf of the local church by any two of the officers of its Board of Trustees, who thereupon shall be duly authorized to carry out the direction of the Charge Conference; and any written instrument so executed shall be binding and effective as the action of the local church.

¶ **2540.** *Incorporated Local Church Property—Sale, Transfer, Lease, or Mortgage.*—Any real property owned by, or in which an incorporated local church has any interest, may be sold, transferred, leased for a term which exceeds five years, or mortgaged subject to the following procedure and conditions:

1. Notice of the proposed action and the date and time of the regular or special meeting of the members of the corporate body, i.e., members of the Charge Conference at which it is to be considered, shall be given at least ten days prior thereto (except as local laws may otherwise provide) from the pulpit of the church or in its weekly bulletin.

2. A resolution authorizing the proposed action shall be passed by a majority vote of the members of the corporate body present and voting at any regular or special meeting thereof called to consider such action and by a majority vote of the members of said church present and voting at a special meeting called to consider such action; *provided* that for the sale of property which was conveyed to the church to be sold and its proceeds used for a specific purpose a vote of the members of said church shall not be required.

3. The written consent of the pastor of the local church and the district superintendent to the proposed action shall be necessary and shall be affixed to or included in the instrument of sale, conveyance, transfer, lease, or mortgage. Prior to consenting to the proposed action to sell or transfer any United Methodist church property the pastor and district superintendent shall ensure that: *(a)* a full investigation be made and, if warranted, an appropriate plan of action shall be developed for the future missional needs of the community; *(b)* the transfer or encumbrance shall conform to the Discipline; and *(c)* the congregation, if no longer to continue as an organized United Methodist church, does not sell its facilities to another United Methodist church. Certification by the district superintendent shall be conclusive evidence that the transfer or encumbrance conforms to the Discipline. The requirements of investigation and the development of a plan of action shall not affect the merchantability of the title to the real estate or the legal effect of the instruments of sale or transfer.

4. The resolution authorizing such proposed action shall direct and authorize the corporation's Board of Directors to take all necessary steps to carry out the action and to cause to be executed, as hereinafter provided, any necessary contract, deed, bill of sale, mortgage, or other written instrument.

5. The Board of Directors at any regular or special meeting shall take such action and adopt such resolutions as may be necessary or required by the local laws.

6. Any required contract, deed, bill of sale, mortgage, or other written instrument necessary to carry out the action so authorized shall be executed in the name of the corporation by any two of its officers, and any written instrument so executed shall be binding and effective as the action of the corporation.

¶ **2541.** *Disposition of Church Building or Parsonage.*—Real property acquired by a conveyance containing trust clauses may be sold in conformity with the provisions of the Discipline of The United Methodist Church when its use as a church building or parsonage, as the case may be, has been, or is intended to be, terminated; and when such real estate is sold or mortgaged in accordance with the provisions of the Discipline of The United

Methodist Church, the written acknowledged consent of the proper district superintendent representing The United Methodist Church to the action taken shall constitute a release and discharge of the real property so sold and conveyed from the trust clause or clauses; or in the event of the execution of a mortgage, such consent of the district superintendent shall constitute a formal recognition of the priority of such mortgage lien and the subordination of the foregoing trust provisions thereof; and no bona fide purchaser or mortgagee relying upon the foregoing record shall be charged with any responsibility with respect to the disposition by such local church of the proceeds of any such sale or mortgage; but the Board of Trustees receiving such proceeds shall manage, control, disburse, and expend the same in conformity to the order and direction of the Charge Conference or Church Local Conference, subject to the provisions of the Discipline of The United Methodist Church with respect thereto.

¶ **2542.** *Restriction on Proceeds of Mortgage or Sale.*—1. No real property on which a church building or parsonage is located shall be mortgaged to provide for the current (or budget) expense of a local church, nor shall the principal proceeds of a sale of any such property be so used. This provision shall apply alike to unincorporated and incorporated local churches.[7]

2. A local church, whether or not incorporated, on complying with the provisions of the Discipline, may mortgage its unencumbered real property as security for a loan to be made to a conference Board of Global Ministries or a city or district missionary society; *provided* that the proceeds of such loan shall be used only for aiding in the construction of a new church.

¶ **2543.** *Planning and Financing Requirements for Local Church Buildings.*—Any local church planning to build or purchase a new church or educational building or a parsonage, or to remodel such a building if the cost will exceed 10 percent of its value, shall first establish a study committee to analyze the needs of the church and community, project the potential membership with average attendance, and write up its program of ministry (¶¶ 201-204). This information will form the basis of a report to

---

[7]*See* Judicial Council Decision 399.

be presented to the Charge Conference and to be used by the building committee (¶¶ 2543.3-.4). The study committee's findings become a part of the report to the district Board of Church Location and Building (¶¶ 2543.5, 2520.1).

1. It shall secure the written consent of the pastor and the district superintendent.

2. It shall secure approval of the proposed site by the district Board of Church Location and Building as provided in the Discipline (¶ 2519.1).

3. Its Charge Conference shall authorize the project at a regular or called meeting, not less than ten days' notice (except as local laws may otherwise provide) of such meeting and the proposed action having been given from the pulpit or in the weekly bulletin, and shall elect a building committee of not fewer than three members of the local church to serve in the development of the project as hereinafter set forth; *provided* that the Charge Conference may commit to its Board of Trustees the duties of a building committee as here described.

4. The building committee shall:

a) Estimate carefully the building facilities needed to house the church's program of worship, education, and fellowship and/or to provide a residence for present and future pastors and their families.

b) Ascertain the cost of property to be purchased.

c) Develop preliminary architectural plans, complying with local building and fire codes, which shall clearly outline the location on the site of all proposed present and future construction. In all new church building plans and in all major remodeling plans, adequate provisions shall be made to facilitate entrance, seating, exit, parking, and otherwise make accessible facilities for persons with handicapping conditions.

d) Secure an estimate of the cost of the proposed construction.

e) Develop a financial plan for defraying the total cost, including an estimate of the amount the membership can contribute in cash and pledges and the amount the local church can borrow if necessary.

5. The building committee shall submit to the district Board of Church Location and Building, for its consideration and

approval, a statement of the need for the proposed facilities, and the architectural plans and financial estimates and plans.

6. The building committee shall ensure that adequate steps are taken to obtain the services of minority (nonwhite) and female skilled persons in the construction of any United Methodist church, parsonage, institution, or agency facility in proportion to the racial/ethnic balance of the metropolitan area in which construction occurs. In nonmetropolitan areas racial and ethnic persons are to be employed in construction where available and in relation to the available work force.

7. The pastor, with the written consent of the district superintendent, shall call a Church Conference, giving not less than ten days' notice (except as local laws may otherwise provide) of the meeting and the proposed action from the pulpit or in the weekly bulletin. At this conference the building committee shall submit, for approval by majority vote of the membership present and voting, its recommendations for the proposed building project, including the data specified herein.

8. After approval of the preliminary plans and estimates the building committee shall develop detailed plans and specifications and secure a reliable and detailed estimate of cost and shall present these for approval to the Charge Conference and to the district Board of Church Location and Building, which shall study the data and report its conclusions.

9. The local church shall acquire a fee simple title to the lot or lots on which the building is to be erected, by deed or conveyance, executed as provided in this chapter.

10. If a loan is needed, the local church shall comply with the provisions of ¶¶ 2539-2540.

11. The local church shall not enter into a building contract or, if using a plan for volunteer labor, incur obligations for materials until it has cash on hand, pledges payable during the construction period, and (if needed) a loan or written commitment therefor which will assure prompt payment of all contractual obligations and other accounts when due.

12. Trustees or other members of a local church shall not be required to guarantee personally any loan made to the church by any board created by or under the authority of the General Conference.

¶ **2544.** *Consecration and Dedication of Local Church Buildings.*—On acquisition or completion of any church building, parsonage, or other church unit, a service of consecration may be held. Before any church building, parsonage, or other church unit is formally dedicated, all indebtedness against the same shall be discharged.

¶ **2545.** *Merger of Local United Methodist Churches.*—Two or more local churches, in order to more effectively fulfill their ministry (¶¶ 201-204), may merge and become a single church by pursuing the following procedure:

1. The merger must be proposed by the Charge Conference of each of the merging churches by a resolution stating the terms and conditions of the proposed merger.

2. The plan of the merger as proposed by the Charge Conference of each of the merging churches must in addition, if a Charge Conference includes two or more local churches, be approved by the Church Local Conference of each local church in accordance with the requirements of ¶ 2526.

3. The merger must be approved by the superintendent or superintendents of the district or districts in which the merging churches are located.

4. The requirements of any and all laws of the state or states in which the merging churches are located affecting or relating to the merger of such churches must be complied with, and in any case where there is a conflict between such laws and the procedure outlined in the Discipline, said laws shall prevail and he procedure outlined in the Discipline shall be modified to the extent necessary to eliminate such conflict.

5. All archives and records of churches involved in a merger shall become the responsibility of the successor church.

¶ **2546.** *Interdenominational Local Church Mergers.*—One or more local United Methodist churches may merge with one or more churches of other denominations and become a single church by pursuing the following procedure:

1. Following appropriate dialogue, which shall include discussions with the United Methodist district superintendent of the district in which the merging churches are located and the corresponding officials of the other judicatories involved, a plan of merger reflecting the nature and ministry of the local church

(¶¶ 201-204) shall be submitted to the Charge Conference of the local United Methodist church and must be approved by a resolution stating the terms and conditions and missional plans of the proposed merger, including the denominational connection of the merger church.

2. The plan of merger as approved by the Charge Conference of the United Methodist church, in a Charge Conference including two or more local churches, must be approved by the Church Local Conference of each local church in accordance with the requirements of ¶ 2526.

3. The merger must be approved in writing by the superintendent of the district, a majority of the district superintendents, and the bishop of the area in which the merging churches are located.

4. The provisions of ¶ 2503 shall be included in the plan of merger where applicable.

5. The requirements of any and all laws of the state or states in which the merging churches are located affecting or relating to the merger of such churches must be complied with, and in any case where there is a conflict between such laws and the procedure outlined in the Discipline, said laws shall prevail and the procedure outlined in the Discipline shall be modified to the extent necessary to eliminate such conflict.

6. Where property is involved, the provisions of ¶ 2547 obtain.

¶ **2547.** *Deeding Church Property to Federated Churches or Other Evangelical Denominations.*—1. With the consent of the presiding bishop and of a majority of the district superintendents and of the district Board of Church Location and Building, and at the request of the Charge Conference or of a meeting of the membership of the church, where required by local law, and in accordance with the said law, the Annual Conference may instruct and direct the Board of Trustees of a local church to deed church property to a federated church.

2. With the consent of the presiding bishop and of a majority of the district superintendents and of the district Board of Church Location and Building and at the request of the Charge Conference or of a meeting of the membership of the local church, where required by local law, and in accordance with said

law, the Annual Conference may instruct and direct the Board of Trustees of a local church to deed church property to one of the other denominations represented in the Commission on Pan-Methodist Cooperation or to another evangelical denomination under an allocation, exchange of property, or comity agreement; *provided* that such agreement shall have been committed to writing and signed and approved by the duly qualified and authorized representatives of both parties concerned.

¶ **2548.** *Discontinuation or Abandonment of Local Church Property.*—1. *Discontinuation.*—*a)* When, in the judgment of the district superintendent in consultation with the appropriate agency assigned the responsibility of the conference parish and community development strategy, a local church should be discontinued, the district superintendent may recommend its discontinuation. Such a recommendation shall include recommendations as to where the membership (¶ 231) and the title to the property of the local church shall be transferred. On such recommendation that a local church no longer serves the purpose for which it was organized and incorporated (¶¶ 201-204), with the consent of the presiding bishop and of a majority of the district superintendents and the district Board of Church Location and Building of the district in which the action is contemplated, the Annual Conference may declare any local church within its bounds discontinued.

b) If a church has been discontinued by the Annual Conference without direction concerning the disposition of property, the property shall be disposed of as if it were abandoned local church property (¶ 2548.2).

2. *Abandonment.*—When a local church property is no longer used, kept, or maintained by its membership as a place of divine worship, the property shall be considered abandoned, and when a local church no longer serves the purpose for which it was organized and incorporated (¶¶ 201-204), with the consent of the presiding bishop, a majority of the district superintendents, and of the district Board of Church Location and Building, the Annual Conference trustees may assume control of the property. If circumstances make immediate action necessary, the conference trustees giving first option to the other denominations

represented in the Commission on Pan-Methodist Cooperation, may sell or lease said property, retain the proceeds in an interest-bearing account, and recommend the disposition of the proceeds in keeping with Annual Conference policy. It shall be the duty of the Annual Conference trustees to remove, insofar as reasonably possible, all Christian and church insignia and symbols from such property. In the event of loss, damage to, or destruction of such local church property, the trustees of the Annual Conference are authorized to collect and receipt for any insurance payable on account thereof, as the duly and legally authorized representative of such local church.[8]

3. All the deeds, records, and other official and legal papers, including the contents of the cornerstone, of a church that is so declared to be abandoned or otherwise discontinued shall be collected by the district superintendent in whose district said church was located and shall be deposited for permanent safekeeping with the Commission on Archives and History of the Annual Conference.

4. Any gift, legacy, devise, annuity, or other benefit to a pastoral charge or local church that accrues or becomes available after said charge or church has been discontinued or abandoned shall become the property of the trustees of the Annual Conference within whose jurisdiction the said discontinued or abandoned church was located.

¶ **2549.** *Board of Trustees Report to the Charge Conference.*— The Board of Trustees shall annually make a written report to the Charge Conference, in which shall be included the following:

1. The legal description and the reasonable valuation of each parcel of real estate owned by the church.

2. The specific name of the grantee in each deed of conveyance of real estate to the local church.

3. An inventory and the reasonable valuation of all personal property owned by the local church.

4. The amount of income received from any income-producing property and a detailed list of expenditures in connection therewith.

---

[8]*See* Judicial Council Decisions 119, 138, 143.

5. The amount received during the year for building, rebuilding, remodeling, and improving real estate, and an itemized statement of expenditures.

6. Outstanding capital debts and how contracted.

7. A detailed statement of the insurance carried on each parcel of real estate, indicating whether restricted by co-insurance or other limiting conditions and whether adequate insurance is carried.

8. The name of the custodian of all legal papers of the local church, and where they are kept.

9. A detailed list of all trusts in which the local church is the beneficiary, specifying where and how the funds are invested, clarifying the manner in which these investments made a positive contribution toward the realization of the goals outlined in the Social Principles of the Church, and in what manner the income therefrom is expended or applied.[9]

¶ **2550.** *Study of Local Church Potential.*—In static and declining population areas, churches of fifty members or less shall study, under the leadership of the district superintendent, the district Board of Church Location and Building, and the appropriate conference agency, their potential in the area to determine how they shall continue to develop programs as organized churches (¶¶ 201-204), develop cooperative patterns with other congregations, or give special attention to relocation.

¶ **2551.** *Exceptions to Requirements of this Chapter.*—The provisions herein written concerning the organization and administration of the local church, including the procedure for acquiring, holding, and transferring real property, shall not be mandatory in Central Conferences, Provisional Central Conferences, Provisional Annual Conferences, or Missions; and in such instances the legislation in ¶¶ 636-646 and 654-664 shall apply.

¶ **2552.** In situations where a local church or churches share a building with another group performing ministries in different languages and/or with different racial and ethnic groups, it shall be in accordance with ¶¶ 202, 206, and 207. The district superintendent must consent to any such action before imple-

---

[9]*See* Judicial Council Decision 420.

mentation. The district Board on Church Location and Building must be informed of such action.

1. If the congregations are United Methodist, the following should apply:

a) By action of the Charge Conference(s) involved, a covenant relationship shall be mutually agreed upon in written form and shall include a statement of purpose for sharing the facility and shall state whether the agreement is seen as temporary, long-term, or permanent. The covenant of relationship may provide for mutual representation on such bodies as Administrative Council, Administrative Board and Council on Ministries, and other committees and work groups. The Board of Trustees of the church which holds title to the property may form a property committee composed of representatives of each congregation. The purpose of this arrangement is to enhance communication between the two or more congregations, to coordinate schedules and building usage, to involve the congregations in building maintenance and care under supervision of the Board of Trustees, and to coordinate cooperative programs.

b) No United Methodist congregation shall pay rent to another United Methodist church. However, each congregation should be expected to pay a mutually agreed share of building expenses.

c) Cooperative programs may be developed that enhance the ministry of both congregations and their witness to the love of Jesus Christ in the community. Such programs may include joint bilingual worship services and Christian education programs, fellowship meals and programs, cooperative community ministry.

2. If a United Methodist church is sharing with a congregation of another denomination, the following should apply:

a) Prior to agreeing to share facilities with a congregation which is not United Methodist and is of a different ethnic or language background, the United Methodist pastor and the district superintendent shall first contact district and conference congregational development agencies and ethnic leadership to explore the possibilities of organizing a new United Methodist congregation with that ethnic or language group.

b) If it is decided that the United Methodist congregation and the congregation of another denomination should share facilities, a property-use agreement shall be negotiated in writing in accordance with ¶ 2503; this agreement shall have the consent of the district superintendent and shall be approved by the United Methodist Charge or Church Local Conference. Shared activities may be entered into to enhance the ministry of both congregations. A liaison committee to both congregations may be appointed to resolve conflicts, clear schedules, and plan cooperative activities.

3. Ninety-day notification of intent to terminate the covenant relationship shall be made to the district superintendent and to the other parties in the covenant relationship. This termination shall require the consent of the district superintendent following consultation with the parties involved.

Section VIII. Requirements—Trustees of Church Institutions.

¶ **2553.** Trustees of schools, colleges, universities, hospitals, homes, orphanages, institutes, and other institutions owned or controlled by any Annual, Jurisdictional, or Central Conference or any agency of The United Methodist Church shall be at least twenty-one years of age. At all times not less than three-fifths of them shall be members of a local church and/or members of an Annual Conference or the Council of Bishops of The United Methodist Church, and all must be nominated, confirmed, or elected by such conference or agency of the Church or by some body or officer thereof to which or to whom this power has been delegated by such conference or agency; *provided* that the number of trustees of any such institution owned or controlled by any Annual Conference or Conferences required to be members of a local church and/or Annual Conference or the Council of Bishops of The United Methodist Church may be reduced to not less than the majority by a three-fourths vote of such Annual Conference or Conferences; and *provided further,* that when an institution is owned and operated jointly with some other religious organization, said requirement that three-fifths of the trustees shall be members of a local church and/or Annual Conference or the Council of Bishops of The United Methodist Church shall apply only to the portion of the trustees selected by the United Methodist agency or Annual, Jurisdictional, or Central Conference. It is recognized that there are numerous educational, health care, and charitable organizations which traditionally have been affiliated with The United Methodist Church and its predecessor denominations, which are neither owned nor controlled by any unit of the denomination.

Chapter Eight

JUDICIAL ADMINISTRATION

Section I. The Judicial Council.

¶ **2601.** *Members.*—The **Judicial Council** shall be composed of nine members, of which at least one-third shall be women. In the year 1984 and each sixteen years thereafter there shall be elected three lay persons and two ordained ministers other than bishops. In 1992 and each sixteen years thereafter there shall be elected three ordained ministers other than bishops and two lay persons. In 1988 and each eight years thereafter there shall be elected two ordained ministers other than bishops and two lay persons. They shall be members of The United Methodist Church. Elections shall be held at each session of the General Conference for only the number of members whose terms expire at such session. A member's term of office shall be eight years; *provided,* however, that a member of the council whose seventieth birthday precedes the first day of the regular session of a General Conference shall be released at the close of that General Conference from membership or responsibility in the council, regardless of the date of expiration of office.

Members of the council shall be nominated and elected in the manner following: At each quadrennial session of the General Conference the Council of Bishops shall nominate by majority vote three times the number of ordained ministers and lay persons to be elected at such session of the General Conference. The number to be elected shall correspond to the number of members whose terms expire at the conclusion of such session. Each of the jurisdictions and the Central Conferences as a group shall be represented by at least one nominee, but it shall not be a requirement that each of the jurisdictions be represented by an elected member. At the same daily session at which the above nominations are announced, nominations of both ministers and lay persons may be made from the floor, but at no other time. The names of all nominees, identified with the conference to which each belongs and a biographical sketch which does not exceed one hundred words, shall be published by the *Daily Christian*

Advocate immediately prior to the day of election, which shall be set by action of the General Conference at the session at which the nominations are made; and from these nominations the General Conference shall elect without discussion, by ballot and by majority vote, the necessary number of ministerial and lay members.[1]

¶ **2602.** *Alternates.*—There shall be six alternates for the clergy members and six alternates for the lay members, and their qualifications shall be the same as for membership on the Judicial Council. The term of the alternates shall be for eight years; *provided,* however, that an alternate whose seventieth birthday precedes the first day of the regular session of a General Conference shall be released at the close of that General Conference from membership or responsibility in the council regardless of the date of expiration of office.

The alternates shall be elected in the manner following: from the clergy and lay nominees remaining on the ballot after the election of the necessary number of members of the Judicial Council to be elected at sessions of the General Conference, the General Conference shall by separate ballot, without discussion and by majority vote, elect the number of clergy and lay alternates to be chosen at such session of the General Conference. An election shall be held at each session of the General Conference for only the number of clergy and lay alternates whose terms expire at such session of the General Conference, or to fill vacancies.

¶ **2603.** *Vacancies.*—1. If a vacancy in the membership of the Judicial Council occurs at the conclusion of a General Conference because of a required retirement of a member because of age, such vacancy shall be filled by General Conference election of an ordained minister to fill a clergy vacancy and a lay person to fill a lay vacancy, such election to be held in the manner hereinbefore provided in this section, and the person so elected shall hold office during the unexpired term of the member whom the newly elected person succeeds.

2. If a vacancy in the membership of the council occurs during the interim between sessions of the General Conference,

---

[1]*See* Judicial Council Decision 540.

a clergy vacancy shall be filled by the first-elected clergy alternate and a lay vacancy by the first-elected lay alternate. The alternate filling such vacancy shall hold office as a member of the Judicial Council for the unexpired term of the member whom the alternate succeeds. In the event of any vacancy, it shall be the duty of the president and secretary of the council to notify the alternate entitled to fill it.

3. In the event of a forced absence of one or more members of the council during a session of the Judicial Council, such temporary vacancy among the clergy members may be filled for that session or the remainder thereof by the first-elected clergy alternate who can be present, and such temporary vacancy among the lay members by the first-elected lay alternate who can be present, but inability or failure to fill a vacancy does not affect the validity of any action of the council so long as a quorum is present.

4. Any permanent vacancy among the alternates shall be filled by election at the next quadrennial session of the General Conference of an ordained minister to fill a clergy vacancy and a lay person to fill a lay vacancy, and the person or persons so elected shall hold office during the unexpired term of the alternate whom each respectively succeeds.

5. If vacancies in the membership of the Judicial Council occur after exhaustion of the list of alternates, the council is authorized to fill such vacancies for the remainder of the quadrennium.

¶ **2604.** The term of office of the members of the council and of the alternates shall expire upon the adjournment of the General Conference at which their successors are elected.

¶ **2605.** Members of the council shall be ineligible for membership in the General Conference or Jurisdictional Conference or in any general or jurisdictional board or for administrative service in any connectional office.[2]

¶ **2606.** The Judicial Council shall provide its own method of organization and procedure, both with respect to hearings on appeals and petitions for declaratory decisions. All parties

---

[2]*See* Judicial Council Decision 196, and Decision 3, Interim Judicial Council.

shall have the privilege of filing briefs and arguments and presenting evidence, under such rules as the council may adopt from time to time. The council shall meet at the time and place of the meeting of the General Conference and shall continue in session until the adjournment of that body, and at least one other time in each calendar year and at such other times as it may deem appropriate, at such places as it may select from time to time. Seven members shall constitute a quorum. An affirmative vote of at least six members of the council shall be necessary to declare any act of the General Conference unconstitutional. On other matters a majority vote of the entire council shall be sufficient. The council may decline to entertain an appeal or a petition for a declaratory decision in any instance in which it determines that it does not have jurisdiction to decide the matter.

¶ **2607.** 1. The Judicial Council shall determine the constitutionality of any act of the General Conference upon an appeal by a majority of the Council of Bishops or one-fifth of the members of the General Conference.

2. The Judicial Council shall have jurisdiction to determine the constitutionality of any proposed legislation when such declaratory decision is requested by the General Conference or by the Council of Bishops.

¶ **2608.** The Judicial Council shall determine the constitutionality of any act of a Jurisdictional or a Central Conference upon an appeal by a majority of the bishops of that Jurisdictional or Central Conference or upon an appeal by one-fifth of the members of that Jurisdictional or Central Conference.[3]

¶ **2609.** The Judicial Council shall hear and determine the legality of any action taken by any General Conference board or body, or Jurisdictional or Central Conference board or body, upon appeal by one third of the members thereof, or upon request of the Council of Bishops or a majority of the bishops of the Jurisdictional or Central Conference wherein the action was taken.

¶ **2610.** The Judicial Council shall hear and determine the legality of any action taken by a General Conference board or

---

[3]*See* Judicial Council Decision 338.

body, or Jurisdictional or Central Conference board or body, on a matter affecting an Annual or a Provisional Annual Conference, upon appeal by two-thirds of the members of the Annual or Provisional Annual Conference present and voting.[4]

¶ **2611.** The Judicial Council shall hear and determine any appeal from a bishop's decision on a question of law made in a Central, District, Annual, or Jurisdictional Conference when said appeal has been made by one-fifth of that conference present and voting.[5]

¶ **2612.** The Judicial Council shall pass upon and affirm, modify, or reverse the decisions of law made by bishops in Central, District, Annual, or Jurisdictional Conferences upon questions of law submitted to them in writing in the regular business of a session; and in order to facilitate such review, each bishop shall report annually in writing to the Judicial Council, on forms provided by the council, all the bishop's decisions of law, with a syllabus of the same. No such episcopal decision shall be authoritative, except in the case pending, until it has been passed upon by the Judicial Council, but thereafter it shall become the law of the Church to the extent that it is affirmed by the council.

¶ **2613.** The Judicial Council shall hear and determine an appeal of a bishop when taken from the decision of the Trial Court in the bishop's case.

¶ **2614.** The Judicial Council shall have power to review an opinion or decision of a Committee on Appeals of a Jurisdictional Conference if it should appear that such opinion or decision is at variance with an opinion or decision of a Committee on Appeals of another Jurisdictional Conference on a question of law. Under such circumstances:

1. Any person, conference, or organization interested therein may appeal the case to the Judicial Council on the ground of such conflict of decisions; or

2. The Committee on Appeals rendering the last of such opinions or decisions may certify the case to, and file it with, the Judicial Council on the ground of such conflict of decisions; or

3. The attention of the president of the Judicial Council

---

[4]*See* Judicial Council Decision 463.
[5]*See* Judicial Council Decision 153.

being directed to such conflict or alleged conflict of decisions, the president may issue an order, in the nature of a writ of certiorari, directing the secretaries of the Committees on Appeals involved to certify a copy of a sufficient portion of the record to disclose the nature of the case, and the entire opinion and decision of the Committee on Appeals in each case, to the Judicial Council for its consideration at its next meeting.

The Judicial Council shall hear and determine the question of law involved but shall not pass upon the facts in either case further than is necessary to decide the question of law involved. After deciding the question of law, the Judicial Council shall cause its decision to be certified to each of the Committees on Appeals involved, and such Committees on Appeals shall take such action, if any, as may be necessary under the law as determined by the Judicial Council.

4. All opinions and decisions of jurisdictional Committees on Appeal which have been decided prior to the 1988 General Conference shall be sent to the secretary of the Judicial Council within ninety days of the close of the 1988 General Conference. All opinions and decisions of jurisdictional Committees on Appeal decided after the 1988 General Conference shall be sent to the secretary of the Judicial Council within thirty days after a decision. These decisions shall be made available to those who are involved in trials when needed and for those preparing for trial but not otherwise.

¶ **2615.** *Declaratory Decisions.*—1. The Judicial Council, on petition as hereinafter provided, shall have jurisdiction to make a ruling in the nature of a declaratory decision as to the constitutionality, meaning, application, or effect of the Discipline or any portion thereof or of any act or legislation of a General Conference; and the decision of the Judicial Council thereon shall be as binding and effectual as a decision made by it on appeal under the law relating to appeals to the Judicial Council.[6]

2. The following bodies in The United Methodist Church are hereby authorized to make such petitions to the Judicial Council for declaratory decisions; *(a)* the General Conference; *(b)* the Council of Bishops; *(c)* any General Conference board or

---

[6]*See* Judicial Council Decisions 106, 172, 301, 434, 443, 454, 463, 474, 566.

body, on matters relating to or affecting the work of such board or body; *(d)* a majority of the bishops assigned to any jurisdiction, on matters relating to or affecting jurisdictions or the work therein; *(e)* a majority of the bishops assigned to any Central Conference, on matters relating to or affecting the Central Conferences or the work therein; *(f)* any Jurisdictional Conference, on matters relating to or affecting jurisdictions or Jurisdictional Conferences or the work therein; *(g)* any Jurisdictional Conference board or body, on matters relating to or affecting the work of such board or body; *(h)* any Central Conference, on matters relating to or affecting Central Conferences, or the work therein; *(i)* any Central Conference board or body, on matters relating to or affecting the work of such board or body; and *(j)* any Annual Conference, on matters relating to Annual Conferences or the work therein.[7]

3. When a declaratory decision is sought, all persons or bodies who have or claim any interest which would be affected by the declaration shall be parties to the proceeding, and the petition shall name such parties. Except for requests filed during the General Conference, any party requesting a declaratory decision shall immediately upon filing such request submit for publication in *The Interpreter* or its successor—which shall in its next edition publish the same without cost—a brief statement of the question involved. The Judicial Council shall not hear and determine any such matter until thirty days after such publication. If the president of the council determines that other parties not named by the petition would be affected by such a decision, such additional parties shall also be added, and the petitioner or petitioners, upon direction of the secretary of the Judicial Council, shall then be required to serve all parties so joined with a copy of the petition within fifteen days after such direction by the secretary of the Judicial Council. In like manner any interested party may, on the party's own motion, intervene and answer, plead, or interplead.[8]

¶ **2616.** The decisions of the Judicial Council of The Methodist Church, heretofore issued, shall have the same

---

[7]*See* Judicial Council Decisions 29, 212, 255, 301, 309, 382, 452, 535.
[8]*See* Judicial Council Decision 437.

authority in The United Methodist Church as they had in The Methodist Church, persuasive as precedents except where their basis has been changed by the terms of the Plan of Union or other revisions of Church law.

¶ **2617.** The Judicial Council shall have other duties and powers as may be conferred upon it by the General Conference.

¶ **2618.** All decisions of the Judicial Council shall be final. However, when the Judicial Council shall declare any act of the General Conference unconstitutional, that decision shall be reported back to that General Conference immediately.

¶ **2619.** The decisions of the Judicial Council on questions of law, with a summary of the facts of the opinion, shall be filed with the secretary of the General Conference and shall be published in the following manner:

1. Within ninety days following each session of the Judicial Council, the digest of decisions of the Judicial Council shall be published in *The Interpreter* or its successor publication.

2. The decisions of the Judicial Council rendered during each year shall be published in the General Minutes.

Section II. Investigations, Trials, and Appeals.

¶ **2620.** *Preliminary Assumptions.*—The following procedures are presented as much for the protection of the rights of individuals guaranteed under Section III, Article IV, of our Constitution as they are for the protection of the Church. The presumption of innocence, including no carrying out of sentence, shall be maintained until the conclusion of the judicial process. At each step in the proceedings listed in ¶¶ 2621 through 2624, efforts for reconciliation shall continue, so long as these efforts are not used to hinder due process.[9]

¶ **2621.** *Chargeable Offenses.*—1. A bishop, clergy member of an Annual Conference (¶ 412), local pastor, or diaconal minister may choose a trial when charged with one or more of the following offenses: *(a)* immorality; *(b)* practices declared by The United Methodist Church to be incompatible with Christian teachings; *(c)* crime; *(d)* failure to perform the work of the ministry; *(e)* indifference; *(f)* disobedience to the Order and

---

[9]*See* Judicial Council Decision 557.

Discipline of The United Methodist Church; *(g)* dissemination of doctrines contrary to the established standards of doctrine of the Church; *(h)* relationships and/or behavior which undermines the ministry of another pastor; *(i)* racial harassment; sexual harassment.

2. A bishop, clergy member of an Annual Conference, or diaconal minister may choose a trial when the appropriate body (¶¶ 317, 453, 513) recommends involuntary termination.

3. A lay member may choose a trial when charged with the following offenses: *(a)* immorality; *(b)* crime; *(c)* disobedience to the Order and Discipline of The United Methodist Church; *(d)* dissemination of doctrines contrary to the established standards of doctrine of the Church.

¶ **2622.** *Charges.*—Charges against bishops, clergy members, local pastors, diaconal ministers, and lay members shall be subject to the following guidelines:

1. A charge shall not allege more than one offense; several charges against the same person, however, with the specifications under each one of them, may be presented at one and the same time and tried together. When several charges are tried at the same time, a vote on each specification and charge must be taken separately.

2. Amendments may be made to a bill of charges at the discretion of the presiding officer; *provided* that they relate to the form of statement only and do not change the nature of the alleged offense and do not introduce new matter of which the accused has not had due notice. When an amendment or amendments to a bill of charges is or are denied by the presiding officer, it or they shall not be introduced in the form of testimony in the Trial Court. Charges or accusations previously dropped by the Committee on Investigation shall not be brought up in the Trial Court in the form of evidence or otherwise.

3. Charges and specifications for all trials shall define the offense in keeping with the provisions of ¶ 2621 and shall state in substance the facts upon which said charges are based.

¶ **2623.** *Investigation Procedures.*—1. *General.*—a) All charges shall be submitted in writing and signed by the chairperson of the Board of Ordained Ministry, and a copy sent to the person charged, the Cabinet, or immediate family members of any of the above.

b) No charge shall be considered for any alleged offense which shall not have been committed within two years immediately preceding the filing of the initial grievance (¶ 453.1*b*). The introduction of any material relating to events happening before the two-year time period as evidence, as preface to evidence, or as build-up for evidence in the procedures of the Committee on Investigation or the trial proceedings shall be permitted when the presiding officer, after consultation with counsel for both parties, rules that such material is relevant and competent.

c) If possible, the person charged and the person(s) bringing the initial grievance shall be brought face to face, but the inability to do this shall not invalidate an investigation. Other supporting witnesses shall not be permitted at the investigation.

d) The Committee on Investigation may call such persons as it deems necessary to establish whether or not there are reasonable grounds for the charge or charges.

e) The parties may be represented by counsel at an investigation. Basic procedural decisions shall be made in a preliminary meeting with the person charged and his/her counsel having the right to argue procedural points before the decision is made by the chair. All advance procedural decisions and such unanticipated decisions as may come in the course of the meeting of the Committee on Investigation shall be rendered in writing so as to be available for consideration in all further possible stages of the case.

f) Proceedings in the investigation shall be informal. No oaths shall be taken. All procedural decisions shall be made by the chairperson and shall be final.

g) The appropriate **Committee on Investigation** (¶¶ 2623.2, .3, .4) shall conduct the investigation, and if in the judgment of a majority of the committee there is reasonable ground for such charges, they shall sign and certify the charges as proper for a trial (the general offense or offenses under ¶ 2621) and the specifications (the time, place, and specifics of events alleged to have taken place). They shall then forward a copy to the person charged and to appropriate church officials (¶¶ 2623.2*d*, .3*d*, and .4*b*).

2. *Investigation of a Bishop.—a)* There shall be a Committee on Investigation consisting of seven elders in full connection elected by each Jurisdictional or Central Conference, with not more than one elder from each Annual Conference, if possible. Three reserves shall also be elected. The committee and its chairperson shall be elected on nomination of the College of Bishops.

b) If a bishop shall be charged in writing of any of the offenses in ¶ 2621, the president of the College of Bishops (or, if the charged is the president, the secretary) shall convene the Committee on Investigation within sixty days of receiving such charges.

c) In the best interests of the bishop and the episcopal area, in exceptional circumstances the College of Bishops may suspend the bishop pending investigation.

d) Any charges and specifications adopted shall be sent to the person charged, to the secretary of the Jurisdictional or Central Conference, and to the President and Secretary of the College of Bishops.

e) If five or more of the committee so recommend, the College of Bishops may suspend the bishop pending trial.

f) For the purpose of this paragraph the United Methodist bishops of the Central Conferences shall constitute one College of Bishops.

3. *Investigation of a Clergy Member of an Annual Conference or a Local Pastor.—a)* There shall be a Committee on Investigation consisting of seven elders in full connection nominated by the presiding bishop and elected by the Annual Conference. Three reserve members shall also be elected. None of the members or reserve members shall be members of the Joint Review Committee or the Board of Ordained Ministry, the Cabinet, or immediate family members of the above. Should a member of the Committee on Investigation have been a party to any of the prior proceedings in a case which finally comes before the committee, he/she shall be disqualified from sitting on the committee during its consideration of that case, and his/her place shall be taken by a reserve member.

b) If a clergy member of an Annual Conference or a local pastor shall be charged in writing of any of the offenses in ¶ 2621, the charged person's district superintendent shall within sixty days of receiving such charges convene the Committee on Investigation (¶ 453.2). (If the charged person is a district superintendent, the bishop shall appoint another district superintendent as convener.) The convenor shall deliver the written charges to the committee and leave without comment. The convenor may be called back to the committee to give testimony in the presence of the person charged (¶¶ 453.1c and 2622.1).[10]

c) Any charges and specifications adopted (¶ 2623.1f) shall be sent to the person charged, the secretary of the Annual Conference, the charged person's district superintendent, and the presiding bishop.

d) If five or more of the Committee on Investigation so recommend, the bishop may suspend the person charged from all clergy responsibilities pending trial.[11] The person charged retains all rights and privileges as stated in ¶ 443.

4. *Investigation of a Diaconal Minister.*

a) There shall be a Committee on Investigation consisting of not less than three diaconal ministers nominated by the presiding bishop and elected by the Annual Conference. Two diaconal minister reserve members shall be elected.

b) When a conference does not have sufficient diaconal ministers to elect the required minimum committee, and an investigation is needed, the bishop, in consultation with the College of Bishops, shall request members of Diaconal Committees on Investigation from other conferences in the jurisdiction in sufficient number to provide the required minimum committee (¶ 2623.4a) for conducting the investigation.

c) If a diaconal minister shall be charged in writing of any of the offenses in ¶ 2621, the charged person's district superintendent shall within sixty days of receiving such charges convene the Committee on Investigation.

d) Any charges and specifications adopted (¶ 2621.1) shall be sent to the person charged, the secretary of the Annual Conference, the charged person's district superintendent, and the presiding bishop.

---

[10]*See* Judicial Council Decision 557.
[11]*See* Judicial Council Decision 498.

e) If at least two-thirds of the Committee on Investigation so recommend, the bishop may suspend the person charged from all professional responsibilities pending trial.

5. *Investigation of a Lay Member of a Local Church.—a)* If charges of offenses under ¶ 2621 are made in writing to the pastor in charge against a member of the Church, the pastor in charge shall appoint a Committee on Investigation, consisting of seven lay members of the church in good standing, of which at least three shall be women. The pastor shall preside at the investigation, and the district superintendent shall be informed of the investigation and have the right to be present.

b) Any charges and specifications adopted shall be sent to the person charged, to the recording secretary of the Charge Conference, the pastor, and the district superintendent.

c) If five or more of the committee so recommend, the pastor may suspend the charged lay person from exercising any church office pending trial.

¶ **2624.** *Trial Procedures.—1. General.—a)* Church trials are to be regarded as an expedient of last resort.[12] Only after every reasonable effort has been made to correct any wrong and adjust any existing difficulty should steps be taken to institute a trial. No such trial as herein provided shall be construed to deprive the accused or the Church of legal civil rights. All trials shall be conducted according to the Book of Discipline in a consistent Christian manner by a properly constituted court, after due investigation. The administration of oaths shall not be required. At the beginning of the trial the presiding officer shall remind all parties of the duties and responsibilities of church membership (¶ 213) and/or the ordained ministerial covenant (¶¶404.4*e* and 421).

b) Officers of the Trial Court.—Officers shall consist of a presiding officer (¶¶ 2624.2*b*, .3*b*, .4*b*) who shall be another bishop, designated by the resident bishop for the trial of a clergy member, local pastor, or diaconal minister, and a secretary appointed by the presiding officer. The presiding officer may have the conference chancellor or other counsel present for the sole purpose of advice to the presiding officer during the trial.

---

[12]*See* Judicial Council Decision 534.

c) *Convening of the Court.*—The official charged with convening the court (*see* ¶¶ 2624.2a, .3a, and .4a) shall, within twenty days after receiving a copy of the charges and specifications, appoint counsel for the Church and notify the person charged in writing to appear at a fixed time and place no less than ten days after service of such notice and within a reasonable time thereafter to select the members of the Trial Court. No person shall be appointed counsel for the Church or serve as clergy counsel for the person charged or any of the persons bringing charges in a case, who was a member of the Joint Review Committee, Board of Ordained Ministry, or Committee on Investigation who earlier considered the case now before the Trial Court. At the appointed time in the presence of the person charged, counsel for the person charged, counsel for the Church, and the presiding officer, thirteen persons shall be selected as a Trial Court out of a pool of twenty-one persons selected according to ¶¶ 2624.2c, .3c, and .4c. Special consideration shall be given so that the pool reflects the race and gender of the person charged. No person shall serve as a member of the Trial Court who was a member of the Joint Review Committee, Board of Ordained Ministry, or Committee on Investigation who considered the case in the process of coming before the Trial Court. The counsel for the Church and the person charged shall each have up to four peremptory challenges and challenges for cause without limit. If by reason of challenges for cause being sustained the number is reduced to below thirteen, additional appropriate persons shall be nominated, in like manner as was the original panel to take the places of the numbers challenged, who likewise shall be subject to challenge for cause. This method of procedure shall be followed until a Trial Court of thirteen members and two reserve members has been selected. The two reserve members shall sit as observers of the trial and shall be seated as members of the Trial Court, in the event one of the thirteen is not able to continue.

d) *Time and Place of Trial.*—The official charged with convening the Trial Court (¶¶ 2624.2a, .3a, and .4a) shall also fix the time and place for the trial, which may immediately follow the convening of the Trial Court, if notice of the convening is so specified. If such notice was not provided, then the presiding officer shall fix the time and place for the trial not less than ten days following the convening of the Trial Court, unless all parties consent to an earlier trial. Announcement of this trial date may be made at the time of the original convening of the Trial Court.

The person charged may request a change of venue. This shall be a written request to the officers of the court, within ten days of receipt of notice to appear for trial. The presiding officer shall rule upon the request after hearing arguments by the defense and the Church. If the motion is approved, the presiding officer shall name the Annual Conference outside the episcopal area wherein the trial shall be held and shall notify the resident bishop of that conference who shall convene the court. The cost of prosecution shall be borne by the conference where the case originated.

e) Notice.—(1) All notices required or provided for in the chapter shall be in writing, signed by or on behalf of the person or body giving or required to give such notice, and shall be addressed to the person or body to whom it is required to be given. Such notices shall be served by delivering a copy thereof to the party or chief officer of the body to whom it is addressed in person or by registered mail addressed to the last-known residence or address of such party. The fact of the giving of the notice shall affirmatively appear over the signature of the party required to give such notice and becomes a part of the record of the case.

(2) In all cases wherein it is provided that notice shall be given to a bishop or district superintendent and the charges are against that particular person, then such notice (in addition to being given to the accused) shall be given, in the case of a bishop, to another bishop within the same jurisdiction and, in the case of a district superintendent, to the bishop in charge.

f) Counsel.—In all cases a charged person shall be entitled to appear and to select and be represented by counsel, a clergy member of The United Methodist Church if the person charged is a bishop, a clergy member, a local pastor, or a diaconal minister, and a lay member of the said Church if the person charged is a lay member. A charged person shall be entitled to have counsel heard in oral or written argument or both. The interest of the Church shall be represented by a clergy member selected by the bishop. In all cases of trial where counsel has not been provided, such counsel shall be appointed by the presiding officer. The counsel for the Church and for the person charged each shall be entitled to choose one assistant counsel who may be an attorney who shall not have voice in the trial and whose sole responsibility is to advise upon request.

g) Witnesses.—Notice to appear shall be given to such witnesses as either party may name and shall be issued in the name of the Church and be signed by the presiding officer of the Trial Court. It shall be the duty of an ordained minister or a member of the Church to appear and testify when summoned. Refusal to appear or to answer questions ruled by the presiding officer to be relevant may be considered as disobedience to the Order and Discipline of The United Methodist Church.

h) Power of the Trial Court.—The court thus constituted shall have full power as a first action to try the person charged and as a second action upon conviction by a vote of nine or more thereof shall have power to suspend the person charged from the exercise of the functions of office, to remove the person charged from office or the ministry or both, to expel the person charged from the Church, or in case of conviction of minor offenses to fix a lesser penalty. The Trial Court shall present to the court a decision on each charge but not on each individual specification under each charge. Its findings shall be final, subject to appeal to the Court of Appeals of the Jurisdictional Conference or the Central Conference, as the case may be, and shall not take effect until the judicial process is ended, including all appeals.

The penalty fixed by the Trial Court is subject to ratification, but not amendment, in the clergy executive session of the Annual Conference to the extent that the penalty changes the ministerial relationship of the ordained minister. Counsel for the Church will make the required motions to the clergy executive session.

i) If the person charged is found guilty by the Trial Court and appeals his/her case, the sentence imposed by the Trial Court shall not take effect until his/her guilt is sustained at the end of the judicial process, when the Disciplinary appeals process has been exhausted. The resident bishop may, with the unanimous concurrence of the district superintendents, suspend the person charged from all clergy responsibilities but not the related benefits, such as annuity and conference group medical and hospital insurance, pending the outcome of the appeals process. If the person charged should be found innocent at the end of the judicial process, he/she shall be financially recompensed by his/her Annual Conference for the time lost under said suspension. Equitable recompense shall be determined by the conference Council on Finance and Administration, taking into account service years, the loss of income during suspension, and loss of parsonage use, if any. In no case shall the recompense be less than the minimum salary. Time on a suspension imposed by the resident bishop shall be applied to lessen the time of suspension fixed by the Trial Court and sustained or modified by the appeals process.

j) Trial Guidelines.—(1) As soon as the trial has convened, the person charged shall be called upon by the presiding officer to plead to the charge, and the pleas shall be recorded. If the person charged pleads "guilty" to the charges preferred, no trial shall be necessary, but evidence may be taken with respect to the appropriate penalty, which shall thereupon be imposed. If the person charged pleads "not guilty" or if the person charged should neglect or refuse to plead, the plea of "not guilty" shall be entered, and the trial shall proceed. The court may adjourn from time to time as convenience or necessity may require. During the time of recess or adjournment the members of the Trial Court shall be instructed that under no circumstance will they speak to others about the trial or observe media reports regarding the case. When, in consultation with counsel for both parties, the presiding officer finds it advisable, the members and reserves shall be sequestered. Threatening or tampering with the Trial Court or officers of the Trial Court shall be considered disobedience to the Order and Discipline of The United Methodist Church. The person charged shall, at all times during the trial except as hereinafter mentioned, have the right to produce testimony and that of witnesses and to make defense.[13]

(2) If in any case the person charged, after due notice (ten days) has been given, shall refuse or neglect to appear at the time and place set forth for the hearing, the trial may proceed in the

---

[13]*See* Judicial Council Decision 504.

charged person's absence. However, if, in the judgment of the presiding officer, there is good and sufficient reason for the absence of the person charged, the presiding officer may reschedule the trial to a later date.

(3) In all cases sufficient time shall be allowed for the person to appear at the given place and time and for the person charged to prepare for the trial. The presiding officer shall decide what constitutes "sufficient time."

(4) The court shall be a continuing body until the final disposition of the charge. If any member of the court shall be unable to attend all the sessions, that person shall not vote upon the final determination of the case, but the rest of the court may proceed to judgment. It shall require a vote of at least nine members of the court to sustain the charges.

(5) All objections to the regularity of the proceedings and the form and substance of charges and specifications shall be made at the first session of the trial. The presiding officer, upon the filing of such objections, shall, or by motion may, determine all such preliminary objections and may dismiss the case or in furtherance of truth and justice permit amendments to the specifications or charges not changing the general nature of the same. But after the Trial Court is selected as provided for in ¶ 2624.1*d* and convened for the trial, the authority of the presiding officer shall include the right to set reasonable time limits, after consultation with counsel for the Church and counsel for the person charged, for the presentation of the case, provided such time is equal for both. The authority of the presiding officer shall be limited to ruling upon proper representation of the Church and the person charged, admissibility of evidence, recessing, adjourning, and reconvening sessions of the trial, charging the members of the Trial Court as to the Church law involved in the case at the beginning of the trial and just before they retire to make up their verdict, and such other authority as is normally vested in a civil court judge sitting with a jury, but he/she shall not have authority to pronounce any judgment in favor of or against the person charged other than such verdict as may be returned by the Trial Court, which body shall have the exclusive right to determine the innocence or guilt of the person charged.

(6) Objections of any part to the proceedings shall be entered on the record.

(7) No witness afterward to be examined shall be present during the examination of another witness if the opposing party objects. Witnesses shall be examined first by the party producing them, then cross-examined by the opposite party. The presiding officer of the court shall determine all questions of relevancy and competency of evidence.

(8) The presiding officer shall not deliver a charge reviewing or explaining the evidence or setting forth the merits of the case. The presiding officer shall express no opinion on the law or the facts while the court is deliberating unless at the request of the jury and with the consent of both the counsels, the presiding officer may offer interpretation of the provisions of the Book of Discipline, the parties in interest be present. The presiding officer shall remain and preside until the decision is rendered and the findings are completed and shall thereupon sign and certify them.

(9) The testimony shall be taken by a stenographer, if convenient, or recorded by other appropriate means and reduced to writing and certified by the presiding officer and secretary. The record, including all exhibits, papers, and evidence in the case, shall be the basis of any appeal which may be taken.

(10) A witness to be qualified need not be a member of The United Methodist Church.

(11) The presiding officer of any court before which a case may be pending shall have power, whenever the necessity of the parties or of witnesses shall require, to appoint, on the application of either party, a commissioner or commissioners, either an ordained minister or a lay person or both, to examine the witnesses; *provided* that three days notice of the time and place of taking such testimony shall have been given to the adverse party. Counsel for both parties shall be permitted to examine and cross-examine the witness or witnesses whose testimony is thus taken. The commissioners so appointed shall take such testimony in writing as may be offered by either party. The testimony properly certified by the signature of the commissioner or commissioners shall be transmitted to the presiding officer of the court before which the case is pending.

(12) All sessions of the trial shall be closed. However, upon written request of the person charged to the presiding officer, the trial shall be open to any member of The United Methodist Church. Also, the trial may be opened by the presiding officer upon written request of either the counsel for the Church or the counsel for the person charged to family of the person charged or family of people who brought charges to the Church and/or to other personally significant people who are not United Methodist. This does not include, however, the deliberations of the Trial Court, which shall be closed. In addition, the presiding officer may, in his/her judgment on motion of counsel for either party, or on the presiding officer's own motion, declare a particular session of the court to be closed. At all times, however, in the hearing portion of the trial, the presiding officer, the members of the Trial Court, the person representing the Church as well as counsel for the Church, the person charged, and counsel for the person charged shall have a right to be present.

2. *Trial of a Bishop.—a)* The president of the College of Bishops of the Jurisdictional or Central Conference, or in case the person charged is the president, the secretary of the college, shall proceed to convene the court under the provisions of ¶ 2624.1*d*.

b) The president of the College of Bishops (or in the case the person charged is the president, the secretary) may preside or designate another bishop to serve as presiding officer.

c) The Trial Court shall be convened as provided in ¶ 2624.1*c*, with the twenty-one member pool to consist of twenty-one elders in full connection, named by the College of Bishops in approximately equal numbers from each episcopal area within the Jurisdictional or Central Conference. Special consideration shall be given so that the pool reflects the race and gender of the person charged.

d) Counsel for the Church shall be a bishop or another elder in full connection.

e) The Trial Court shall, at the conclusion of the proceedings, send all trial documents to the secretary of the Jurisdictional or Central Conference who shall keep them in custody. If an appeal is taken, the secretary shall forward the materials forthwith to the secretary of the Judicial Council. After the appeal has been heard, the records shall be returned to the secretary of the Jurisdictional or Central Conference.

f) A bishop suspended from office shall have claim on the Episcopal Fund for salary, dwelling, pension, and other related benefits. A bishop removed from office shall have no claim upon the Episcopal Fund for salary, dwelling, pension and other related benefits from the date of such removal.

g) For the purpose of this paragraph the United Methodist bishops in Europe shall constitute one College of Bishops.

3. *Trial of a Clergy Member of an Annual Conference, Local Pastor, or Diaconal Minister.—a)* The bishop of the person charged shall proceed to convene the court under the provisions of ¶ 2624.1c.

b) The bishop shall designate another bishop to be presiding officer.

c) (1) The Trial Court for a clergy member shall be convened as provided in ¶ 2624.1c, with the twenty-one-member pool to consist of elders in full connection. If there are not enough persons in appropriate categories in an Annual Conference to complete the pool, additional persons may be appointed from other Annual Conferences. All appointments to the pool shall be made by the district superintendents. Special consideration shall be given so that the pool reflects the race and gender of the person charged.

(2) The Trial Court for a local pastor shall be convened as provided in ¶ 2624.1c and shall consist of a twenty-one-member pool who shall be local pastors or, when necessary, members of the church. All appointments to the pool shall be made by the district superintendents.

(3) The Trial Court for a diaconal minister shall be convened as provided in ¶ 2624.1c and shall consist of a twenty-one-member pool who shall be diaconal ministers or, when necessary, members of the church.

d) Counsel for the Church shall be an elder in full connection, as provided in ¶ 2624.1c.

e) The Trial Court shall, at the conclusion of the proceedings, send all trial documents to the secretary of the Annual Conference who shall keep them in custody. Such documents are to be held in a confidential file and shall not be released for other than appeal or new trial purposes without a signed release from both the clergy member charged and the presiding officer of the Trial Court which tried the case. If an appeal is taken, the secretary shall forward the materials forthwith to the president of the Court of Appeals of the Jurisdictional or Central Conference. If a president has not been elected, the secretary shall send the materials to such members of the Court of Appeals as the president of the College of Bishops shall designate. After the appeal has been heard, the records shall be returned to the secretary of the Annual Conference, unless a further appeal on a question of law has been made to the Judicial Council, in which case the relevant documents shall be forwarded to the president of that body.

4. *Trial of Lay Member of a Local Church.—a)* The district superintendent of the person charged shall proceed to convene the court under the provisions of ¶ 2624.1c.

b) The district superintendent may be the presiding officer or may designate another elder in full connection to preside.

c) The Trial Court shall be convened as provided in ¶ 2624.1c, with the twenty-one-member pool to consist of lay members in good standing of the charged person's local church, or, when necessary, members of other churches in the same district. Appointments to the pool shall be made by the district lay leader, or, if the district lay leader feels not in a position to be completely impartial, the district lay leader may designate a lay leader of an adjoining district to make such appointments. Special consideration shall be given so that the pool reflects the race and gender of the person charged.

d) Counsel for the Church shall be a lay person who is a member in good standing.

e) The person charged may request a change of venue. This shall be a written request to the officers of the court, within ten days of receipt of notice to appear for trial. The presiding officer shall rule upon the request after hearing argument for the defense and the Church. If the motion is approved, the presiding officer shall name another district wherein the trial shall be held and shall notify the district superintendent who shall convene the court. The twenty-one-member pool shall consist of lay members in good standing from that district. The cost of prosecution shall be borne by the Annual Conference.

f) The Trial Court shall, at the conclusion of the proceeding, deposit all trial documents with the secretary of the Charge Conference. If an appeal is taken, the secretary shall deliver all documents to the district superintendent. After the appeal has been heard, the records shall be returned to the custody of the secretary of the Charge Conference.

¶ **2625.** *Appeal Procedures.*—1. *General.*—*a)* In all cases of appeal the appellant shall within thirty days give written notice of appeal and at the same time shall furnish to the officer receiving such notice, and to the counsel for the Church, a written statement of the grounds of the appeal, and the hearing in the appellate court shall be limited to the grounds set forth in such statement.

b) When any appellate court shall reverse, in whole or in part, the findings of a Committee on Investigation or a Trial Court or remand the case for a new hearing or trial or change the penalty imposed by that committee or court, it shall return to the convening officer of the Committee on Investigation or Trial Court a statement of the grounds of its action.

c) An appeal shall not be allowed in any case in which the person charged has failed or refused to be present in person or by counsel at the investigation and the trial. Appeals, regularly taken, shall be heard by the proper appellate court, unless it shall appear to the said court that the appellant has forfeited the right to appeal by misconduct, such as refusal to abide by the findings of the Committee on Investigation or Trial Court; or by withdrawal from the Church; or by failure to appear in person or by counsel to prosecute the appeal; or prior to the final decision on appeal from conviction, by resorting to suit in the civil courts against the complainant or any of the parties connected with the ecclesiastical court in which the appellant was tried.[14]

d) The right of appeal, when once forfeited by neglect or otherwise, cannot be revived by any subsequent appellate court.

e) The right to take and to prosecute an appeal shall not be affected by the death of the person entitled to such right. Heirs or legal representatives may prosecute such appeal as the appellant would be entitled to do if living.

---

[14]*See* Judicial Council Decision 3.

f) The records and documents of the trial, including the evidence, and these only, shall be used in the hearing of any appeal.

g) The appellate court shall determine two questions only: (1) Does the weight of the evidence sustain the charge or charges? (2) Were there such errors of law as to vitiate the verdict and/or the penalty? These questions shall be determined by the records of the trial and the argument of counsel for the Church and for the person charged. The court shall in no case hear witnesses.

h) In all cases where an appeal is made and admitted by the appellate court, after the charges, findings, and evidence have been read and the arguments conclude, the parties shall withdraw, and the appellate court shall consider and decide the case. It may reverse, in whole or in part, the findings of the Committee on Investigation or the Trial Court, or it may remand the case for a new trial to determine verdict and/or penalty. It may determine what penalty, not higher than that affixed at the hearing or trial, may be imposed. If it neither reverses, in whole or in part, the judgment of the Trial Court, nor remands the case for a new trial, nor modifies the penalty, that judgment shall stand. The appellate court shall not reverse the judgment nor remand the case for a new hearing or trial on account of errors plainly not affecting the result. All decisions of the appellate court shall require a majority vote.

i) In all cases the right to present evidence shall be exhausted when the case has been heard once on its merits in the proper court, but questions of law may be carried on appeal, step by step, to the Judicial Council, according to the provisions of the Book of Discipline.

j) Errors of defects in judicial proceedings shall be duly considered when present on appeal. (1) In regard to cases where there is an investigation under ¶ 2621 but no trial is held as a result thereof, errors of law or administration committed by those in charge of the investigation are to be corrected by the presiding officer of the next conference on request in open session, and in such event the conference may also order just and suitable remedies if injury resulted from such errors. (2) Errors of law or defects in judicial proceedings which are discovered on appeal are to be corrected by the presiding officer or the next conference upon request in open session, and in such event the conference may also order just and suitable remedies if injury has resulted from such errors.

2. *Appeal of a Bishop.—a)* A bishop shall have the right of appeal to the Judicial Council in case of an adverse decision by the Trial Court; *provided* that within thirty days after the conviction the bishop notify the secretary of the Jurisdictional or Central Conference in writing of intention to appeal.

b) It shall be the duty of the secretary of the Jurisdictional or Central Conference, on receiving notice of such appeal, to notify the secretary of the Judicial Council, and the council shall fix the time and place for the hearing of the appeal and shall give due notice of the same to the appellant and to the secretary of the Jurisdictional or Central Conference, who in turn shall notify the counsel for the Church.

3. *Appeal of a Clergy Member of an Annual Conference, Local Pastor, or Diaconal Minister.—a)* Each Jurisdictional and Central Conference, upon nomination of the College of Bishops, shall elect a Court of Appeals, composed of nine itinerant elders, who have been at least six years successively members of The United Methodist Church, and an equal number of alternates. In addition, two local pastors and two alternates shall be elected in the same manner, to serve as members of the Court of Appeals in the event, and only in the event, that the appellant is a local pastor. In addition, the Court of Appeals shall have two diaconal ministers and two reserves elected in the same manner who will serve in the event, and only in the event, that the appellant is a diaconal minister. This court shall serve until its successors have been confirmed. This court shall have full power to hear and determine appeals of clergy members taken from any Annual Conference within the jurisdiction. The court shall elect its own president and secretary and shall adopt its own rules of procedure, and its decisions shall be final, except that an appeal may be taken to the Judicial Council only upon questions of law related to procedures of the Jurisdictional Court of Appeals, or under the provisions of ¶ 2614.

b) In case of conviction in a Trial Court a clergy member, local pastor, or diaconal minister shall have the right of appeal to the Jurisdictional or Central Conference Court of Appeals above constituted; *provided* that within thirty days after the conviction the appellant shall notify the president of the conference and the presiding officer of the Trial Court in writing of the intention to appeal.

c) When notice of an appeal has been given to the president of the Trial Court, the president shall give notice of the same to the secretary of the Court of Appeals of the Jurisdictional or Central Conference and submit the documents in the case, or in case the documents have been sent to the secretary of the Annual Conference, instruct the secretary to send the documents to the president of the Court of Appeals. The Jurisdictional or Central Conference Court of Appeals shall give notice to the president of the conference from which the appeal is taken and to the appellant of the time and place where the appeal will be heard. Both the Annual Conference and the appellant may be represented by counsel as specified in ¶ 2624.1*f*. The president of the conference shall appoint counsel for the Church.

d) All necessary traveling and sustenance expense incurred by the Court of Appeals, the counsel for the Church, and the counsel for the defendant, in the hearing of an appeal case coming from an Annual Conference and appearing before any Jurisdictional or Central Conference Court of Appeals, shall be paid out of the administration fund of the Central or Jurisdictional Conference in which the proceedings arise. Financial assistance may be sought from the General Council on Finance and Administration according to guidelines established by that agency. The president of the Court of Appeals shall approve all expenses.

4. *Appeal of a Lay Member.*—*a)* A lay member convicted in a Trial Court shall have the right of appeal and shall serve written notice of appeal with the pastor and the district superintendent within thirty days of conviction.

b) The district superintendent shall, on receipt of notice of appeal, give written notice to all concerned of the time and place of the convening of a Court of Appeals, not less than ten or more than thirty days after such notice has been delivered.

c) The Court of Appeals shall be constituted in the following manner: the district superintendent shall appoint eleven lay persons who are members of local United Methodist churches other than the appellant's, and who hold office either as lay leader or lay member of the Annual Conference. At the convening of the Court of Appeals, from seven to eleven of these shall be selected to serve on the Court. The counsel for appellant and the counsel for the Church shall have the right to challenge for cause, and the decisions on the validity of such challenges shall be made by the presiding officer, who shall be the district superintendent.

d) The findings of the Court of Appeals shall be certified by the district superintendent, to the pastor of the church of which the accused is a member.

5. *Other Appeals.—a)* The order of appeals on questions of law shall be as follows: from the decision of the district superintendent presiding in the Charge or District Conference to the bishop presiding in the Annual Conference, and from the decision of the bishop presiding in the Annual Conference to the Judicial Council, and from a Central Conference to the Judicial Council.

b) When an appeal is taken on a question of law, written notice of the same shall be served on the secretary of the body in which the decision has been rendered. It shall be the secretary's duty to see that an exact statement of the question submitted and the ruling of the chair thereon shall be entered on the journal. The secretary shall then make and certify a copy of the question and ruling and transmit the same to the secretary of the body to which the appeal is taken. The secretary who thus receives said certified copy shall present the same in open conference and as soon as practicable lay it before the presiding officer for a ruling hereon, which ruling must be rendered before the final adjournment of that body, that said ruling together with the original question and ruling may be entered on the journal of that conference. The same course shall be followed in all subsequent appeals.

¶ **2626.** *Miscellaneous Provisions.—*1. Any clergy members residing beyond the bounds of the conference in which membership is held shall be subject to the procedures of ¶¶ 2620-2625 exercised by the appropriate officers of the conference in which he/she is a member.

2. When a bishop, clergy member, local pastor, or diaconal

minister is charged with an offense under ¶ 2621 and desires to withdraw from the Church, the Jurisdictional or Central Conference in the case of a bishop, the Annual Conference in the case of a clergy member, or the District Conference (where there is no District Conference, the Charge Conference) in the case of a local pastor or diaconal minister, may permit withdrawal, in which case the record shall be "Withdrawn under charges," and that person's status shall be the same as if expelled.

3. When a member of the Church is charged with an offense and desires to withdraw from the Church, the Charge Conference may permit such member to withdraw, in which case the record shall be "Withdrawn under complaints." If formal charges have been presented, such member may be permitted to withdraw, in which case the record shall be "Withdrawn under charges." In either case the status shall be the same as if the member had been expelled.

4. In all matters of judicial administration the rights, duties, and responsibilities of clergy members of Missions, Missionary Conferences, and Provisional Annual Conferences are the same as those in Annual Conferences, and the procedure is the same.

5. Any clergy member or local pastor who shall hold a religious service within the bounds of a pastoral charge other than that to which appointed when requested by the preacher in charge or the district superintendent not to hold such service shall be subject to charges of disobedience to the Order and Discipline of the Church and/or relationships and/or behavior which undermines the ministry of another pastor, and if that ordained minister shall not refrain from such conduct, he/she shall then be liable to the provisions of ¶¶ 453.1 and 2623.

INDEX

The numbers refer to paragraphs (¶¶) and to subparagraphs. Subparagraphs are indicated by the figures following the decimal points.

A

Abandoned church, 523.6*a, d,* 2548.2

Abingdon Press, 1728

Abortion, 71*G*

Absence, leave of
diaconal minister, 313.1
ordained minister, 448, 453.1*d-e*

Accountability
appointee beyond local church, 443.2*a*, .5*a*
conference treasurer, 709.9
deaconess, 1418.7
district superintendent, 529.3
general agencies, 802.2, .6, 803.1, .5-.6, 1303, 1503, 1704, 1803.2
mutual, 112.3*c*
pastor, *footnote, page 213*

Act of Covenanting, 647, 648, 650

Act of Ordination, 432, 434.3, 435.3, 515.4-.5

Administrative Board, 244.2, 253-56
administrative officer, pastor as, 254, 256
amenability, 256.6
Board of Trustees, 256.1, 2524-52. *See* Board of Trustees, local church

Administrative Board, *cont'd:*
chairperson, 249.1, 258, 269.4
character of members, 254
Charge Conference members, 246.2, 251.1*b*
Committee on Finance, 256.1, 269.4. *See* Committee on Finance, local church
Committee on Nominations and Personnel, 256.1, 269.1. *See* Committee on Nominations and Personnel, local church
Committee on Pastor-Parish Relations, 256.1, .3*e-f. See* Committee on Pastor-Parish Relations, local church
in cooperative parish, 206.3
Council on Ministries, 256.1, 257. *See* Council on Ministries, local church
employed staff, 253.4, 269.2*b, f*
lay speaker recommendation, 277.3
meetings, 253.2
membership, 206.3*i*, 227, 247.6, 250.2, 251.1*b*, 254, 269.1-.2, 2552.1*a*
membership rolls, 230.5, 233
membership secretary, 235
minutes, 253.4
officers, 255, 269.1
organization, 255, 269.5
purpose, 253.1
quorum, 253.3
resources, 1218.3
responsibilities, 256

Administrative Board, *cont'd:*
shared facilities representation, 206.3*i*, 2552
special meetings, 253.2

Administrative Council, 244.1, 252
care of church members, 230.1
chairperson, 249.1, 258, 269.4
as lay leader, 252.1*e*
as lay member, Annual Conference, 252.1*e*
Charge Conference members, 246.2, 251.1*b*
Committee on Finance, 256.1, 269.4. *See* Committee on Finance, local church
Committee on Nominations and Personnel, 256.1, 269.1. *See* Committee on Nominations and Personnel, local church
Committee on Pastor-Parish Relations, 256.1, .3*e, f. See* Committee on Pastor-Parish Relations, local church
in cooperative parish, 206.3
meetings, 252.3
membership, 206.3*i*, 227, 247.6, 250.2, 251.1*b*, 252.1, 269.1-.2, 2552.1*a*
membership rolls, 233
organization, 252
quorum, 252.4
responsibilities, 252.1, 256, 257, 262.1*b*
shared facilities representation, 206.3*i*, 2552

Administrative general agencies, 805.6

Administrative location, 453.3. *See also* Readmission to conference membership

Admission into the Church, 216-20. *See* Church membership

Adult ministries, 258.1, 259, 263.3-.4, 265.3

Advance Committee, 1007.5
administering agencies, 914.3*e*, 1007.5*d*

Advance Committee, *cont'd:*
Crusade Scholarships, 1457.3
membership, 1007.5
organization of, 1006.22
participating agencies, 1007.5*a*
projects, 914.1, 1007.5*c*

Advance for Christ and His Church, The, 914.1
Advance Committee, 1007.5
authorized projects, 660.2, 914.3*b*
conditions of giving to, 914.3
conference Advance program, 727
director, 1007.5*a-b*
promotion of, 915, 1411.2*b*, 1906.12
receipts, 914.3*e*, .4
treasurer of, 915.2

Advance special gifts, 914.2
Annual Conference, 726.9*d*, 727.2
health and welfare ministries, 731.4(33)
National Division, 731.4(33), 1415.1*b*
project determination, 727.2, 1007.5*c-d*
United Methodist Committee on Relief, 731.4(33), 1460
World Division, 731.4(33)

Advertising, truth in, 73*D*

Affiliated Autonomous Methodist Church, 648
affiliate/associate member of, 227
becoming, 649
becoming part of The United Methodist Church, 654
Conference of Methodist Bishops, 528
liaison committee, 1436
nonvoting delegates, General Conference, 648.3
restrictions on funding delegates, 2401.2
visitation program to, 648.4

Affiliated United Church, 651
affiliate/associate member of, 227
becoming, 649
becoming part of The United Methodist Church, 654

Affiliated United Church, *cont'd:*
Conference of Methodist Bishops, 528
liaison committee, 1436
nonvoting delegates, General Conference, 648.3
restrictions on funding delegates, 2401.2
visitation program to, 648.4

Affiliate member
Annual Conference, 412.1, 419.4, 1432.5
appointee beyond local church, 443.3*b*, .4
Charge Conference, 443.3*b*
local church, 227, 315.3
Missionary Conference, 660.4*b*

Affiliate Membership Roll, 227, 232.5

Affirmative action, 72*A*, *E-G*

African Methodist Episcopal Church, 2003.6, 2503

African Methodist Episcopal Zion Church, 2003.6, 2503

Age-level and family councils, 265, 726.6, 729.1*d*

Age-level councils, 265
Adult Council, 265.3
Adult/Single Adult/Older Adult Council, 263.4
Adult/Young Adult Council, 263.3
Children's Council, 265.1
Older Adult Council, 265.3
Single Adult Council, 265.3
Young Adult Council, 265.3
Youth Council, 265.2

Age-level, family, specialized-ministries coordinators, 252.1, 259
on Administrative Board, 254
on Administrative Council, 252.1*d*, 263
on Council on Ministries, 258, 263
of disaster response, 731.4(19), 1464

Age-level, *cont'd*
election of, 250.1, 259.1
leaders of age-level councils, 265
See also Coordinator

Agencies, conference, 706-45. *See* Annual Conference agencies

Agencies, general, 801-24. *See* General agencies

Agencies, jurisdictional, 628-35. *See* Jurisdictional agencies

Age
of older adult, 247.6, 249.7, 258, 741.2, 1907
of retirement, 313.2*a*, *c*, 451.1, .2*b-c*, 509.1, .2*b*
of young adult, 247.6, 258, 263.3, 1007.1*a*(4)
of young person, 35
of youth, 224-25, 247.6, 258, 263.2, 905.1, 1007.1*a*(3), 1307.1

Aging
ministry to the, 262.2
rights of the, 72*E*

Air, use of, 70*A*

Alcohol and other drugs, 72*I*, *footnote, page 210*

alive now!, 1202.5

Amenability
of Administrative Board, 256.6
of affiliate member, 412.1, 1431.5
of associate member, 412.1, 419
of bishop, 622
of Boards of Trustees, 244.2, 2512.2, 2528
of church member, 244.2
of clergy appointed beyond local church, 443.2*a*
of conference agencies/staff, 708.5, 726.8-.9*a*, 733.1*a*
of diaconal minister, 308
of general agencies, 802.1, 803.1, .5, 1503

731

Amenability, *cont'd:*
of local church organization, 244.2, 257, 2528
of local pastor, 406.4-.5, 412.1
of member in full connection, 412.1, 422
of ordained minister, 412.1, 422
on honorable location, 452.1*b*
on leave of absence, 448.1
of probationary member, 412.1, 413.4
of student local pastor, 406.7

Amendments to the Constitution, 62-64, *footnotes, pages 20-39*

American Bible Society, 2404

Animal life, 70*C*

Annual Conference, 10, 35-39, 701-45
Advance program, 727, 1007.5*d*
agencies, 706-45, 2512-16. *See* Annual Conference agencies
appeal/petition to Judicial Council, 59.2, 2610, 2615.2*j*
apportionments, 711, 718, 908, 925
archives, 705, 738.1
Association of Retired Ministers, 451.4
attendance at, 406.5, 701.6-.7
basic body in the Church, 10, 36
becoming Affiliated Autonomous Methodist or United Church (outside U.S.A.), 649
boundaries of, 25.4, 29.4, 40-43, 638.11
budgets, 709.1, .4, .6-.7, 710, 711.4
business agenda, 704
camping experiences for handicapped population, 729.1*c*
chancellor, 702.7
Committee on Investigation, 2623.3
Committee on Nominations, 702.8*a*, 726.7*b*(7), 732.4*b*(3)
cooperative parish ministries, 206.2
coordinator
of disaster response, 731.4(19)

Annual Conference, *cont'd*
of youth ministries, 632, 743.3*j*
council director, 529.6, 708.2*b*, 726.7, 730.3, 818, 1006.12
director
of administrative services, 716
of communications, 726.5*b*
Distributing Committee, 1609
episcopal residence, 2514
equal lay-clergy representation, 35
executive session, 704.6. *See* Executive session, Annual Conference
financial obligations, 703.2, 2509
founding date, 824
historian, 631.1, 738.3
incorporation, 702.1
institutions, 709.13, 710.3*c*, 731.4(24)-(26), 732.4*b*, 1515.1*e*, 1901
journal, 705.2-.5. *See* Journal, Annual Conference
lay leader, 702.8*a*. *See* Conference lay leader
lay member, 35, 251.2, 701.3-.5. *See* Lay member, Annual Conference
legal advisor, 702.7
meetings, 702
membership, 35, 249.5, 251.2, 252.1*e*, 701.1, .3
Ministerial Education Fund, 921.2, 1530.2
name, 43
Native American ministries, 274.6*b*
nominations
bishop, 506.1
general agencies, 805.1
nonvoting members, 701.2
number of, 43, 51, 638.11
organization, 702, 706-45
pension responsibilities, 1604.11, 1606-07
Pension Support Fund, 1606.19
place of, 702.3
powers and duties, 36, 703, 704.4
admission/ordination standards, 415, 703.3
annuity rate, 1606.7
apportionment formula, 711
capital fund/special appeals, 709.2, 710.5
central treasury, 709.10

Annual Conference, *cont'd:*
Christian Education Sunday, 273, 276.1, 729.2*c*
clergy member status, 448.1, 703.4
conditions/amount of borrowed funds, 709.8, 1606.8
cooperative parish development, 206.2
diaconal minister's status, 313.1, 734.3*n*
election
of conference agency members, 704.3
of delegates, 14, 37-39
to Central Conference, 637.1
to General Conference, 602, 660.3
to Jurisdictional Conference, 614-15, 620.3, 660.3
equitable salary fund policy, 722.12
examination of clergy members, 453.3, 703.4, 704.6-.7
Golden Cross Sunday, 273, 731.4(33)
minimum salary/supplement, 408.1-.2, 722.3, .5
nomination for bishop, 506.1
ordained/diaconal ministers' personnel records, 705.6, .8
pension credit record, 1606.6
pension funds, 1606.5
personnel policies, 709.11
relationship of institutions, 731.4(24)
Rural Life Sunday, 275.3
sabbatical leave approval, 446
United Methodist Foundation, 709.14, 2513
presiding officer, 702.5
property, 2512-16. *See* Property, conference
racial/ethnic youth caucuses, 1306.1*b*(6)
records, 705.1, .6, .8
reports, 704.4
from Board of Diaconal Ministry, 734.3*l*
from Board of Pensions, 737.5*a*
from Board of Trustees, 2512.6

Annual Conference, *cont'd:*
from Council on Finance and Administration, 713.1
from district Board of Trustees, 2517.2
from district superintendents, 523.9
representation on General Council on Ministries, 1007.1
Retired Ministers Day, 1606.12*e*
secretary, 702.6. *See* Secretary, Annual Conference
special session, 701.4, 702.4
special Sundays, 273
statistician, 702.6
Sustentation Fund, 710.1*f*, 723
time of, 702.2
transfer of local churches into, 44, 271
treasurer, 708.2*b*, .3, 714-16
volunteer-in-mission coordinator, 731.6
voting rights in, 36, 413.2, 419.2, 423, 443.4, 701

Annual Conference agencies, 706-45
additional committees, 706.2
Board of Church and Society, 728
Board of Diaconal Ministry, 734
Board of Discipleship, 729
Board of Global Ministries, 274.6*b*, 658, 731
Board of Higher Education and Campus Ministry, 732
Board of Ordained Ministry, 733
Board of Pensions, 426.1, 737, 1606-09. *See* Pensions, conference Board of
Board of the Laity, 730
Board of Trustees, 2512, 2514, 2548.2
Commission/Committee on Christian Unity and Interreligious Concerns, 739
Commission on Archives and History, 738. *See* Archives and History, conference Commission on
Commission on Equitable Salaries, 722
Commission on Religion and Race, 740

Annual Conference agencies, *cont'd:*
Commission on Status and Role of Women, 741
Committee on Episcopacy, 735
Committee on Ethnic Local Church Concerns, 726.5
Committee on Lay Speaking, 277.3, 278-79
Committee on Ministry to Persons with Handicapping Conditions, 745
Committee on Parish and Community Development, 731.5
Committee on Publishing House Liaison, 726.5*e*
Council on Finance and Administration, 707-16. *See* Finance and Administration, conference Council on
Council on Ministries, 726-27. *See* Council on Ministries, conference
Council on Youth Ministry, 743, 1306.2*a*
Disaster Response Committee, 731.4(19)
general agency members, ex officio, on, 706.5, 739.2, 810.5
Joint Committee on Disability, 744
Joint Review Committee, 453.1*c*
membership, 706.4-.5, 739.2, 810.5
Refugee Resettlement Committee, 731.4(18), 1459.4
study of local church potential, 2550
United Methodist Foundation, 2533.1
United Methodist Women, 742, 1429

Appalachian Development Committee, 1414.11

Appeal, 18, 2625
of bishop, 622, 2625.2
in Central Conference, 638.17
of clergy, 2625.3
Committee on Appeals
Central Conference, 29.7
Jurisdictional Conference, 25.6, 2614

Appeal, *cont'd:*
counsel in, 2625.1*g,* .3*c,* .4
death of appellant, 2625.1*e*
of diaconal minister, 2625.3
errors, consideration/correction of, 2625.1*j*
evidence used in, 2625.1*f*
expenses from, 2625.3*d*
of lay member, local church, 2625.4
penalty determination, 2625.1*h*
questions determined by, 2625.1*g*
on questions of law, 2625.5
restrictions disallowing, 2625.1*c*
reversal of findings, 2625.1*b, h*
right of, 18, 2625.1*c-e*
time limit, 2625.1
vote necessary for decision, 2625.1*h*
witnesses, use of, 2625.1*g*

Appointment, 57, 426, 436-43, 530-34
across conference lines, 426.1, 530.2
of associate member, 419
to attend school, 516.6
beyond local church, 442-43, 516.6. *See* Appointment beyond the local church
of deaconess, 1418.3*b*
of diaconal minister, 310
discontinuance between conference sessions, 452.5
of district superintendent, 517
eligibility, 436
extension ministries, 443.1*b, d*
frequency, 534
full-time service, 408.1, 437.1
itinerant system, 112, 437, 443
less than full-time service, 408.2-.3, 437.2, 533.7
of local pastor, 408
of member in full connection, 422
open itineracy policy, 269.2*f*(1), 530
of ordained minister, 422
on administrative location, 453.3*c*
of another Annual Conference, 426.1
of another denomination, 426.2

Appointment, *cont'd:*
  of another Methodist denomination, 426.1
  on honorable location, 452.1*b*
  retired, 451.6
  prerequisite for, 407
  of probationary member, 413.4, 417
  process for change in, 533
  reappointment, 410.4, 437.2*c*
  of retired bishop, 510.2
  sabbatical leave, 446
  of World Division personnel, 443.1*c*

Appointment beyond the local church, 442-43, 516.6, 1511.1
  accountability, 443.2*a*, .5*a*
  affiliate relationship
    to Annual Conference, 443.4
    to Charge Conference, 443.3*b*
    of missionary, 419.4, 660.4*b*, 1432.5
  Annual Conference attendance, 443.5*d*
  annual meeting of those in, 443.2*b*
  authority to administer church membership vows, 217-18
  baptism of children of military personnel, 218
  categories, 443.1, 1511.1
  Charge Conference, 443.3*b*, 516.4
  endorsement, 1511
  evaluation, 444.2
  General Minutes listing, 443.5*c*
  general provisions, 443.5
  local church relationship, 443.3
  to Missionary Conference, 660.4, .6
  participation in itineracy, 443
  pension credit, 1606.4*h*, 1606.8
  publication of salary, 725
  reports
    to affiliated Charge Conference, 443.3*b*
    to bishop, 443.2*a*
    to conference Board of Ordained Ministry, 443.2*a*
    to district superintendent, 443.2*a*
    to home Charge Conference, 443.3*a*

Appointments beyond the local church, *cont'd:*
  responsibilities, 218, 443.2*a*
  return to pastoral charge, 443
  service on conference agencies, 443.4
  source of annuity claim listing, 443.5*b*
  standards for, 443.1*d*
  voting rights, 443.3*b*, .4, 660.4*b*

Appointment-making, 112, 530-34
  bishop's duties, 57, 426.1, 437.2*e*, 515-17, 530-34, 1418.3*b*
  consultation process, 531-33
  critera, 532
  district superintendent's duties, 57, 519, 521.3, 531-33

Apportionments, 112, 711, 911.5
  for administration, 710.2
  for clergy support, 718-19
  conference treasurer's responsibility, 715.2
  district Board of Stewards responsibility, 711.3
  to districts, 711.3
  for district superintendents' support, 710.1*a*
  for Episcopal Fund, 710.1*b*, 925
  formulas, 709.3, 906.1*c*
  for general church funds, 911.5
  local church promotion, 256.4-.5
  notice to
    Annual Conference, 908
    local church, 247.14
  for other causes, 710.4
  for pension needs, 710.1*d*
  proportional payment of, 737.4
  for World Service and Conference Benevolences, 710.3*d*, 711.4

Approved supply pastor, pension credit for, 1606.3*b-c*, .5*c*

Architectural standards, church facilities, 1202.13

Archival procedures, 705, 1811

Archives and History, conference Commission on, 738
  conference historian, 631.1, 738.3

Archives and History, conference Commission on, *cont'd:*
conference Historical Society, 738.2
designation of historic site, 1812.4
preservation of records/historical data, 738, 1811.3*j*, 2545.5, 2548.3
retention and disposition schedules, 738.1
shrines and landmarks, 738.1

Archives and History, General Commission on, 1801-12
accountability, 802.2, 803.6, 1803.2
administrative and program-related agency, 803.6
amenability, 802.1
archives, 1803, 1811.3
bishop as president, 1806
central archivist, 1811.3*i*
Committee on Historic Shrines and Landmarks, 1812.1
executive committee, 1808
financial support, 1809
general secretary, 1807
Heritage Sunday, 275.2
Historical Convocation, 1810.3
Historical Society, 1810
incorporation, 1802
meetings, 1805
membership, 1804.2
name, 1801
officers, 1804.1, 1806
purpose, 1803
quorum, 1805
representation on Committee on Personnel Policies and Practices, 905.4*d*
staff, 1807
vacancy, 1804.1
voting procedure, 1808

Archives and History, jurisdictional Commission on, 631, 1804.2

Area Committee on Episcopacy, 735.1

Area Episcopal Residence Committee, 710.1*c*, 736

Area expense fund, 710.2*b*, 923

Area/regional Committee/Commission on Higher Education and Campus Ministry, 732.4*d*(14)

Area superintendent, 726.2, 731.5*a*, *h*

Area United Methodist Foundation, 2533.1

Armaments, 75*C*

Articles of Religion, 3, 16, *pages 60-68*

Associate institutions, 1520.4

Associate member, Annual Conference, 419-21
admission requirements, 419-20, 1529.2
amenability, 412.1, 419
from another denomination, 426.2
continuing education, 423.2*b*, *d*, 445, 520.5
disability leave, 450
evaluation of, 423.2*b-c*, 444, 703.4
grievance procedures, 453
honorable location, 452.1
leave of absence, 419.5, 448
as local pastor, 408.1
maternity/paternity leave, 449
minimum salary, 419.5, 437.1, 441.1
ordination as deacon, 419.1, 433.2, 434
pension credit, 419.5, 1606.3*a*
psychological testing, 419
retirement, 419.5, 451
rights, 419, 701.1*c*
sabbatical leave, 419.5, 446
termination, 453.1*f*
transfer, 516.5
See also Clergy; Ordained Minister; Pastor

Associate member, local church, 227, 238

INDEX

Associate Membership Roll, 227, 232.6

Association of Clinical Pastoral Educators, 516.6

Audiovisuals, 1906.7

Audit of accounts
area office, 929
conference treasurer, 713
local church financial officers, 269.4c, 2510
general church funds, 906.4
pension funds, 1608.7b
treasurer, General Council on Finance and Administration, 909

Autonomous Methodist Church, 647
Act of Covenanting, 647.6, 650
becoming, 652
becoming part of The United Methodist Church, 654
concordat agreement, 647.5
cooperation, 647.4
dialogue, 647.4
transfer of clergy, 647.2
visitation program to, 647.3

Autonomous United Church, 647.3, 652

B

Baptism, Sacrament of, *pages 65, 70,* 106
administering, 218, 406, 439.1b, 443.3a
certificate of, 222
of children, 218, 221-22
corporate worship celebration, 1214
prerequisite for church membership, 216.1
register of baptized children, 223

Becoming part of The United Methodist Church, 654

Benevolences, 710.3. *See also* World Service and Conference Benevolences

Bequests
to abandoned church, 2548.4
to Annual Conference, 638.31, 2512.3
encouragement of, 1215.6
to local church, 2528.3, 2532.2, 2548.4
to The United Methodist Church, 906.7
Wills and Estate Planning Task Force, 261.9

Birth control, 72H

Bishop, 52-55, 501-16
absence from general agency meetings, 810.10
amenability, 622
appeal of, 509.3, 622, 2613, 2625.2
assignment, 52, 507, 509.1c, .2e, 932
in Central Conference, 30-34, 512, 638
charges against, 2621-22
consecration of, 49, 506.2c
election of, 15.10, 49, 53, 503, 506, 512, 638.2-.3
episcopal residence, 2514
evaluation of, 735.3f
honoraria, 928
investigation of, 2623.2
leaves, 511, 931
legal advisor to, 702.7
member
College of Bishops, 51. *See* College of Bishops
Committee on District Superintendency, 754.2
conference Board of the Laity, 730.3
conference Council on Ministries, 726.2
conference United Methodist Women/executive committee, 742.4
Council of Bishops, 50, 512.3, 527. *See* Council of Bishops
general agency, 805.2b, .3a, 1412.6
jurisdictional United Methodist Women, 634.4
memoir of, 610.1

Bishop, *cont'd:*
office of, 503-04
as ordained elder, 504
pension, 509, 924, 930-32, 1606.2*c*
powers and responsibilities, 48, 501-02, 514-18
  appointment of district superintendents, 515.4, 517
  appointment-making, 112, 310.4-.6, 426.1-.2, 437.2, 443.1*d*, 515-18, 530-34, 664.3, 733.2*g*, 734.3*p*, 1418.3*b*
  approval
    abandoning local church property, 2548.2
    Central Conference Discipline and Ritual, 638.18, .22
    realignment of pastoral charges, 523.9
    retired clergy member's return to effective relationship, 451.7
  assignment of missionaries/mission traveling preachers, 664.6
  calling extra session of Central Conference, 637.3
  certification of honorable location, 452.1*b*
  as chief pastor, 425
  commissioning of deaconess/missionary, 515.5, 1418.2
  consecration of diaconal minister, 515.5
  consultation on funding conference program, 818
  convening meetings
    of appointees beyond local church and diaconal ministers, 309.2, 443.2*b*
    of Committee on Episcopacy, 735.2
  decisions
    on mission structures, 1415.7*a*
    on questions of law, 54
  deposit of records, 1811.3*b, i, l*
  designation
    of areas of service beyond the local church, 1511.1
    of district of new local church, 270.1

Bishop, *cont'd:*
  of time and place of annual Mission meeting, 664.4
  examination of those entering into associate/full conference membership, 425
  furnishing credentials, 307, 435.4, 515.5
  as general superintendent, 527.1
  granting disability leave, 450.2
  itineracy across conference lines, 530.2
  initiation of grievances, 453.1*a*
  leader of Cabinet, 529.2
  local church transfer, 44.1, 271
  nominations
    for Committee on Investigation, 2623.3*a*
    for conference Board of Diaconal Ministry, 734.1*b*
    for conference Board of Ordained Ministry, 733.1*a-b*
    for Joint Review Committee, 453.1*c*
  ordination of deacons/elders, 432, 435.3, 515.5
  organization of Mission, 270.1, 514.4, 664.3
  overseeing conference/general agencies, 514.1, 515.2, 803.5, 928
  presiding, 32, 54-55, 515.1, 602, 621, 637.3, 664.3-.4, 702.5
  property duties, 2547-48
  providing annual visit to ministry setting of appointee beyond local church, 443.2*b*
  meeting of Committee on Pastor-Parish Relations, 269.2*e*
  Retired Ministers Day, 1606.12*e*
  signing complaint, 453.1*b*
  supervision of territory not in Central Conference, 645
  suspension of person charged, 2623.3*d*, .4*e*
  transfer of clergy members, 427, 516.5, 733.2*m*
  traveling through the connection, 34, 514.2, 637.4
report on clergy supply and demand, 530.2
resignation, 509.4

Bishop, *cont'd:*
retirement, 509-10
salary/expenses, 923-24, 926, 928, 2624.2*f*
special assignment, 507.3, 509.2*e*
suspension/removal, 2624.2*f*
tax-sheltered annuity plan, 930.3
tenure, 53, 512.4, 638.3
transfer of, 52, 612
trial of, 2624.2
under term episcopacy, 512.4
withdrawal under charges, 2626.3
See also Episcopacy; Episcopal leadership

Bishops, list of, *pages 1-6*

Black College Fund, 906, 908, 910, 919
budget, 906.1
disbursement, 906.2
notice of apportioned amount, 908
promotion, 261.5*a*, 732.4*d*(4), 919.3, 1505.20, 1906.12

Black colleges
Black College Fund, 906, 908, 910, 919
Council of Presidents of the, 1523
encouraging endowments for, 1516.3*d*
recognizing needs of, 1514.4
representation on University Senate, 1517.2

Board of Church and Society, conference, 728

Board of Church and Society, General, 1101-16. *See* Church and Society, General Board of

Board of Church Location and Building, district, 2518. *See* Church Location and Building, district Board of

Board of Diaconal Ministry, conference, 304, 734. *See* Diaconal Ministry, conference Board of

Board of Discipleship, conference, 729

Board of Discipleship, General, 1201-28. *See* Discipleship, General Board of

Board of Global Ministries, conference, 274.6*b*, 658, 731. *See* Global Ministries, conference Board of

Board of Global Ministries, General, 1401-67. *See* Global Ministries, General Board of

Board of Higher Education and Campus Ministry, conference, 732

Board of Higher Education and Ministry, General, 1501-32. *See* Higher Education and Ministry, General Board of

Board of Ordained Ministry, conference, 733. *See* Ordained Ministry, conference Board of

Board of Pensions, conference, 426.1, 737, 1606-09. *See* Pensions, conference Board of

Board of Pensions, General, 1601-09. *See* Pensions, General Board of

Board of Publication, General, 1701-44. *See* Publication, General Board of

Board of Stewards, district, 711.3, 2517.2

Board of the Laity
conference, 730
district, 1218.7

Board of Trustees, conference, 2512, 2514, 2548.2

Board of Trustees, district, 2517.2

Board of Trustees, local church, 245, 269.3, 2524-25
abandoned church property, 2548.2
Administrative Board, relationship to, 256.1
amenability, 244.2, 2528
as building committee, 2543.3
chairperson, 254, 2529
Committee on Finance, represented on, 269.4
in cooperative parish, 2527.2
disposition of church building or parsonage, 2541
district superintendent, cooperation with, 523.4
duties, 2527.3, 2532, 2549
election of, 249.4, 2524-25, 2526.1, 2527.1, 2530.3
as guarantor of loans, 2541.12
meetings, 2531
in multiple church charge, 247.17, 2526-27
officers, 2529.2-.3
organization, 2529
powers and limitations, 2532
property committee, 2552.1a
report to Charge Conference, 2549
requirements for membership, 2530.1
shared facilities, 206.3i, 2552
as title holders in unincorporated local church, 2535
vacancy, 2530.3

Bonding
of church officers, 909, 1726, 2510
of conference agency officers, 714, 1608.9b
of officers, United Methodist Publishing House, 1726
of treasurer
conference, 714
General Council on Finance and Administration, 909
local church, 269.4b

Book Editor, 1728-31

Book of Resolutions, 611.2a

Book of Worship, 729.4b, 1214.3

Boundaries, 40-44
of Annual Conference, 25.4, 29.4, 43, 44.3
of Central Conference, 26, 41, 638.11
changes in, 42-43
of episcopal areas, 623.3b
of Jurisdictional Conferences, 40, 42, 44.3
of Provisional Central Conference, 642

Boycott, 247.19, 703.12, 747.5, 802.5

Budget
Annual Conference, 710, 726.10e
general church, 15.9, 906.1
local church, 269.4

Buildings
architectural standards for, 1202.13
Building Committee, local church, 2543.3
consecration of, 2544
dedication of, 2544
program of ministry in, 2543

Burial, authority to perform service of, 406.1, 434

Burial ground, title to, 2527.1

Business administrator, 254, 269.4

Business manager
General Conference, 907.16
local church, 254, 269.4

C

Cabinet, 529
bishop's consultation on new district superintendent, 517
clergy supply and demand report, 530.2
conference council director, 529.6, 726.7a

Cabinet, *cont'd:*
responsibilities
  appointment to less than full-
    time service, 437.2
  appointments, 530-34, 733.2*g*
  counseling elders, 411
  guidelines for accountability
    structures, 443.5*a*
  initiation of complaint, 453.1*b*
  new local church or mission,
    270.1
  nominations to Joint Review
    Committee, 453.1*c*
  planning annual meetings of
    appointees beyond local
    church/diaconal ministers,
    309.2, 443.2*b*
  probationary member under
    special conditions, 416.2
  readmission to conference rela-
    tionship, 454-57
  recruitment, 733.2*a*, 740.3
  reinstatement of local pastor,
    410.4
  retired clergy member's return
    to effective relationship,
    451.7
  review of diaconal minister's
    appointment, 310.5*d*, 734.3*p*
  training for Committees on Pas-
    tor-Parish Relations, 444.1
representation
  on conference Board of Or-
    dained Ministry, 733.1*b*
  on conference Board of the
    Laity, 730.3
  on conference Commission on
    Equitable Salaries, 722.1
  on Joint Committee on Disabili-
    ty, 744
  on Joint Review Committee,
    453.1*c*

Camping and outdoor ministry,
729.1*b-d*
  acquisition/disposition of proper-
    ties for, 729.2*d*
  for persons with handicapping
    conditions, 729.1*c-d*, 1209.5
  standards for, 729.2*d*, 1209.5
  title to campground, 2516

Campus ministry, 1513-16
  advisory relationship of Division of
    Higher Education, 1513.2
  campus pastor, 217
  Higher Education and Campus
    Ministry, conference Board of,
    responsibility, 732
  local church work area, 252.1*a*,
    261.5

Candidacy registrar, 404.2, 733.3

Candidate
  for diaconal ministry, 304-06
    certification of, 304
    Diaconal Ministry, conference
      Board of, responsibility, 734.3
  for ordained ministry, 404-05
    certification of, 747.3, 752.6, .8
    Ordained Ministry, conference
      Board of, responsibility, *foot-
      note, page 212*, 733.2
    Ordained Ministry, district
      Committee on, responsibility,
      footnote, page 212, 752.3-.9
  records of, 733.3

Capital punishment, 74*F*

Central Conference, 26-34, 636-46
  Administrative Board member-
    ship, 254
  admission/ordination standards,
    415
  appeal/petition to Judicial Council,
    59.1, .4, 2610, 2615.2*h-i*
  authorization, 636
  becoming, 637.8
  boundaries of, 26, 41
  Central Conference Affairs, Com-
    mission on, 649, 2301
  College of Bishops, 51, 2623.2*f*
  Committee on Appeals, 29.7
  Committee on Episcopacy, 507.3,
    509.2*d*, .3*a-b*, 511
  Committee on Investigation,
    2623.2*a*
  Committee on Women's Work,
    638.15-.16
  Court of Appeals, 2624.1*h*, 2625.3
  delegates, 27, 636.2
    election of, 37-39, 637.1

Central Conference, *cont'd:*
number of, 636.2
proportionate representation, 637.9
ratio of, 27, 637.1
Discipline, 29.5, 638.21-.22, .33
episcopal administration in, 30-34, 51, 512
General Episcopal Fund, 638.4-.5
Global Ministries, General Board of, relationship to, 637.6, 1431.1, 1436.1
Journal, 637.7
Judicial Court, 29.6, 638.33
listing:
Africa, 636.3*a*
Central and Southern Europe, 636.3*b*, 637.9
Federal Republic of Germany and West Berlin, 636.3*c*
German Democratic Republic, 636.3*d*
Northern Europe, 636.3*e*
Philippines, 636.3*f*
West Africa, 636.3*g*
meetings, 28, 637.2-.3
membership, 27, 636.2, 637.1, .9
number of, 26, 41, 636
organization, 637
powers and duties, 29, 638, 701.3
presiding officers, 515, 637.3, .5
property provisions, 638.27-.31
representation on general agencies, 805.1*c*, 2*b*, 1204.1, 1412.6, 1006.18, 1007.1*a*(2), (7)
secretary of, 515.5, 637.7, 638.7, 2625.2
special session, 637.3
term episcopacy in, 512.4

Certificate
of administrative location, 453.3
of Baptism, 222
of candidacy for ordained ministry, 747.3
of election of delegates, 602.5
of ordination, 435.4
of recognition of orders, 427
of transfer, 220, 240, 270.3

Certification
of candidate for ordained ministry, 404.4, 664.5, 752.6, .8-.9
Diaconal Ministry, conference Board of, duties regarding, 734.4
of honorable location, 452.1*b*
of lay speaker, 278-79
of local pastor, 752.8-.9
of music leaders, 261.10
of transfer of local church, 44.1

Certification Studies in Ministry Careers, 1526.3

Certified Lay Speaker, 277-79, 440.1, 729.7*b*

Chancellor, 702.7

Changes in Annual Conference relationships, 447-51, 734.3*n*

Chaplain
appointment beyond local church, 443.1*b*, 1511.1
authority to administer church membership vows, 217-18
Baptism of children of military personnel, 218
evangelism awareness, 1213.9
pension credit, 1606.4*d*, .8

Chaplains and Related Ministries, Division of, General Board of Higher Education and Ministry, 1510-12
appointee beyond local church, responsibility for, 1511.1
duties, 1511
Endorsing Committee, 1511.2*c*
financial support, 1509.2, 1512
membership, 805, 809, 1508.1
pension administration, 1604.12
standards for special ministry settings, 443.1*d*

Chargeable offenses, 2621-22

Charge Conference, 11, 46-47, 246-50

appointee beyond local church as affiliate member, 443.3*b*, 516.4

Church Local Conference, 2526

convening as Church Conference, 248, 250

date of, 246.4, .7

honorary members, 246.3

Joint Charge Conference, 246.10, 248

meetings, 246

membership, 246.2-.3, 254, 314.1, 406.6-.7, 443.3*a*, 451.5, 452.1*b*, 1418.4

merger of churches, 2545-46

of new local church, 270.7-.8

notice of, 246.8

Permanent Endowment Fund Committee, 2533

place of, 246.4, .8

powers and duties, 11, 46-47, 246.1, 247

election

of Board of Trustees, 249.4, 2525, 2527.1

of building committee, 2543.3

of chairpersons

Administrative Board, 249.1

Administrative Council, 249.1

Council on Ministries, 249.1, 258

work areas, 250.1

of church historian, 247.5*a*, 250.1

of church officers, 47, 249-50

of church treasurer, 249.4

of class leaders, 268.2

of Committee on Finance/chairperson, 249.4

of Committee on Nominations and Personnel, 249.2, 269.1

of Committee on Pastor-Parish Relations/chairperson, 249.3

of financial secretary, 249.4

of foundation trustees/directors/governing board, 2534

of lay leader, 249.5, 251.1

Charge Conference, *cont'd:*

of lay member of Annual Conference, 249.5, 251.2

of members at large of Administrative Council/Administrative Board, 247.6, 250.2

of program support personnel, 258-60, 262

of recording secretary, 247.4, 249.6

of stewards, 250

establishment of foundation, 2534

oversight of lay speaker, 277-79

Permanent Endowment Fund Committee, 2533

property responsibilities, 2528, 2536, 2538-40, 2547

removal of name from membership roll, 230.4, 232.3

salary of pastor/staff, 247.13, 720

shared facilities agreement, 206.3*i*, 2552.1*a*, .2*b*

transfer of local church, 44.1*a*, 271

written ballot to recommend candidate for diaconal/ordained ministry, 304.5, 404.3, *footnote, page 212*

presiding officer, 246.5, 523.1

quorum, 246.6

resources, 1218.3

special session, 246.1, .7-.8

time of meeting, 246.1, .4, .8

translation of proceedings, 246.9

See also Reports to Charge Conference

Charges, 452.4, 2621-23

Chartered Fund, 20, 1605.1

Children

Baptism of, 218, 221-23

confirmation of, 106, 216.2-.4, 225

ministries for, 259

as preparatory members, 216.4, 224

register of baptized, 223

rights of, 72C

Children, *cont'd:*
training of, 225
training for pastors in ministry to, 729.1*g*

Children's Fund for Christian Mission, 263.1*g*, 1210.3*e*

Children's ministries, 258-59, 263.1, 265.1

Christian as Minister, The, 404.1

Christian Education, associate/ director of, 254

Christian Education Sunday (Week), 276.1
Annual Conference offering, 273
conference Board of Discipleship responsibility, 729.2*c*
date of, 276.1
promotion of, 261.3, 1208.7, 1906.12

Christian Educators Fellowship of The United Methodist Church, 1210.5, 1526.12

Christian global concerns, conference coordinator of, 731.3

Christian Methodist Episcopal Church, 2003.6, 2503

Christian Unity and Interreligious Concerns, conference Commission/Committee on, 739

Christian Unity and Interreligious Concerns, General Commission on, 2001-06
accountability, 802.2, 803.5
amenability, 802.1, 803.5
authority and powers, 2004
Ecumenical Staff Officer, 2005.4
executive committee, 2005.2-.3
general secretary, 813-14, 2005.3-.4, .6-.7
Interdenominational Cooperation Fund, 918.1, 2003.14, 2402.2-.3, 2405.2

Christian Unity and Interreligious Concerns, General Commission on, *cont'd:*
meetings, 2005.5
membership, 805-06, 2006
name, 2001
nomination of representatives to World Council of Churches, 2402.3
officers, 2005.1
organization, 2005
oversight of convenantal relationships, 650
program-related agency, 803.5
purpose, 2002
quorum, 2005.5
representation on Committee on Personnel Policies and Practices, 905.4*d*
responsibilities, 261.1, 2003
review of nominations to National Council of the Churches of Christ in the U.S.A., 2402.2*b*
staff, 2005.6
standards/guidelines for local church work area, 261.1
vacancy, 812, 2006.3

Christian Unity and Interreligious Concerns, local church work area on, 252.1*b*, 260, 261.1, 265.1-.3

Christian vocation, 259.1, 261.3, .5*b*

Christian year, 273, 1214.1

Christian Youth Exchange, 1219.3

Church administrator, 254

Church and community ministry, 1414.12

Church and community workers, 254, 731.5*d*, 1414.8, .13

Church and Society, conference Board of, 728

Church and Society, district Committee on, 750

Church and Society, General Board of, 1101-16
accountability, 802.2, 803.5
amenability, 802.1, 803.5
bylaws, 1116
executive committee, 1109
financial support, 1112
general secretary, 813-14, 1114.1
headquarters, 907.2, 1007.25, 1115
incorporation, 1105
meetings, 1111
membership, 805-06
name, 1101
nominating committee, 1110
objectives, 1103
officers, 808, 1108, 1110
organization, 802-10, 1106
Peace with Justice Sunday, 274.5
predecessor boards/corporations/ departments, 1105
program-related agency, 803.5
prupose, 1102
quorum, 1111
representation
Committee on Family Life, 1220.2
Committee on Personnel Policies and Practices, 905.4*d*
National Youth Ministry Organization Steering Committee, 1307.1
responsibilities, 1104
staff, 1114
standards/guidelines for local church work area, 261.2
United Nations Office, 1115, 1422.8
vacancy, 812, 1107, 1109
Youth Offenders Rehabilitation Program, 274.1*c*

Church and Society, local church work area on, 252.1*b*, 260, 261.2; 265.1-.3

Church Conference, 248, 250. *See also* Charge Conference

Church founding date, 824

Church historian, 247.5*a*, 250.1

Church library, 263.1*d*

Church Local Conference, 2526. *See also* Charge Conference

Church Location and Building, district Board of, 2518
abandoned church, 2548.2
building/remodeling plans, 2519-22
building sites, 270, 2519
church building program, 2541.2, .5, .8
church extension, 1415.7(3)
deeding church property, 2547.1
district parsonage, 2517, 2522
district superintendent's cooperation, 523.4
fifty-member-or-less church, 2550
organizing new church, 256.7, 270
sale of church property, 2547.2
shared facilities, 2552
study of local church potential, 2550

Church membership, 208-43, 648.1
admission into, 216-20
affiliate, 227, 304.5
associate, 227, 238
audit of rolls, 233
Baptism as prerequisite for, 216.1, .4, 218, 220-24
care of, 215, 228-31
certificate of transfer, 230.4, 240-41, 270.3
of deaconess, 1418.4
of diaconal minister, 314.1
of discontinued local church, 231, 523.6, .8, 2548.3
eligibility, 208, 216.1
in federated church, 232.7
of former local pastor, 410.1
grouping of, 229, 268
inactive, 230
inclusiveness, 208
instruction in, 216, 220, 225-26
of local pastor, 406.6-.7
meaning of, 211-14, 1901
of military personnel, 218
in new local church, 270
preparation for, 216, 218, 220-26

Church membership, *cont'd:*
  preparatory, 216.4, 223-24, 232.2
  privileges/duties, 211-14, 1901
  reception into, 217-19
  records, 234-35
  removal from, 209, 230
  restoration to, 230.4, 243
  rights/responsibilities, 226, 263.2
  rolls, 209, 219, 232-35, 247.15
  termination of, 236, 242-43
  transfer of, 220, 230.1-.2, .4, 236-43, 270.3, 648.1
  in union church, 232.7
  vows, 211, 217, 230.1
  youth, 226, 263.2

Church name outside U.S.A., 823

Church property, 2501-52. *See* Property; Property, local church

Church-related institutions
  Annual Conference, 709.13, 710.3*c*, 731.4(24)-(26), 732.5, 1447, 1513-14, 1901
  approved by University Senate, 1519-21
  Central Conference, 1901, 2553
  communication responsibility, 1901
  health and welfare, 815-16, 1447, 1741
  educational, 261.5*a*, 709.13, 732.4*b*(2), 815-16, 1513-14, 1741, 1901, 2553
  insurance protection for, 709.13, 907.14
  investment policies, 816
  National Division, 1414.7
  nondiscrimination policies, 815, 2203.9
  printing of materials for, 1741
  trustees of, 816, 2553

Church School Publications, 1728, 1732-39. *See also* Curriculum, church school; Curriculum Resources Committee; Editor, Church School Publications

Church School/Sunday School, 263.1
  Children's Fund for Christian Mission, 263.1*g*, 1210.3*e*
  Commission on Education, 263.1*c*
  curriculum, 263.1*b*, 1223
  curriculum resources secretary, 263.1*e*
  divisions, 261.3, 263.1*a*
  division superintendents, teachers, counselors, officers, 261.3, 263.1*e*
  extension promotion, 729.2*e*, 1211.1
  Fourth Sunday offering, 263.1*f*
  library, 263.1*d*
  mission education, 263.1*g*, 1206.5
  special fund promotion, 1206.5, 1208.8
  standards for, 1209.2
  superintendent, 250.1, 254, 258, 261.3, 262.1, 263.1*c, e*
  teacher recruitment/training, 729.2*f*
  weekday programs, 261.3, 265.1
  See also Church School Publications; Curriculum, church school; Curriculum Resources Committee

Church School superintendent, 262.1
  election of, 250.1, 262.1
  member of
    Administrative Board, 254
    Council on Ministries, 258
  relationship to Commission on Education, 263.1*c*
  selection of teachers/staff, 263.1*e*

Church secretaries, 907.13

Church-State separation, 74*B*

Church, the, 101-03, 107, 201-03
  community of the new covenant, 105, 112.2
  community of true believers, *pages 19, 70,* 201, 203
  congregation of the faithful, *page 64,* 103
  connectional society, 112-13, 203

746

Church, the, *cont'd:*
covenant community, 101-102
members of the Body of Christ, 1901
people of God, 107
reason for existence, 202
strategic base, 202
vessel of mission, 112.3*f*

Churchwide appeal, 274.3, 911.4, 1460, 1463

Churchwide offerings, 273-74. *See also* Special days

Church Women United, 1422.9

Circuit, 205.2

Civil obedience/disobedience, 74*E*

Class meetings, 229, 268

Clergy, 412, 701
appeal of, 2625.3
appointment of, 436-43
change of relationship, 443
chargeable offenses, 2621-22
continuing education, 423.2, 445, 921
counseling elder, 411, 520.4, 733.2*v*
couples, 530.2
delegates
to General Conference, 602
to Jurisdictional Conference, 614.1
ethnic, 530.2, 733.2*a*, 752.1
financial support, 443.1*d*, 710.1, 717-25. *See* Clergy support
investigation of, 2623.3
itineracy of, 112.4
in less than full-time service, 437.2, 660.6
location of, 703.4
marriage of, *page 66*
member of Annual Conference, 412, 701.1
pension, 443.5*b*, 451.2, For detailed listing *see* Pensions, conference Board of
professional responsibilities, 423.2

Clergy, *cont'd:*
publication of compensation, 725
recruitment of, 733.2*a*, 1511.2*a*
representation on
Commission on Pan-Methodist Cooperation, 2403
district agencies, 749.2, 752.1
conference agencies, 706.4, 726.5*a, e*, 734.1
general agencies, 805, 1204.1, 1412.6, 2204.1-.2
jurisdictional agencies, 628
retired, 451
return to pastoral ministry, 443, 451.7
suspension of, 2623.3*c, e*
transfer of, 648.2, 653.4*d*, 703.7
trial, 453.2, 2624.3, 2626.1
withdrawal under complaints or charges, 452.4, 2626.2
women, 530.2
See also Associate member; Full connection, member in; Local pastor; Ordained minister; Ordained Ministry; Pastor; Probationary member

Clergy couples, 530.2

Clergy supply and demand, 530.2

Clergy support, 717-25
Administrative Board's responsibility, 256.5
for appointee beyond local church, 443.1*d*
apportionments for, 718-19
Commission on Equitable Salaries, 441, 710.1*e*, 722, 907.13
determination of salary, 247.13, .20
Equitable Salary Fund, 718-19, 722.5, .7-.8
General Council on Finance and Administration, responsibility for, 710.1
minimum salary, 722.2, .6. *See* Minimum salary
Sustentation Fund, 710.1*f*, 723
unpaid salary, 721

Clinical Pastoral Education, 516.6

Closed session, 821. *See also* Executive session, Annual Conference

Cluster group, 206.3

Collective bargaining, 73*B*

College of Bishops, 51-52
appeal/petition to Judicial Council, 59.1, .4, 2608-09, 2615.2*d-e*
authority to call special Jurisdictional Conference session, 620.2
Mission, relationship to, 664.3
president of
  as convenor of Jurisdictional Committee on Episcopacy, 623
  as convenor of Trial Court, 2624.2
  as signer of Jurisdictional Conference Journal, 627
responsibilities
  appoint Jurisdictional Committee on Entertainment, 24
  arrange plan of episcopal supervision, 51
  determine time/place of Central Conference, 637.3
  fill vacancy on general agency, 812, 2006.3
  name Trial Court, 2624.2*c*
  nominating
    Committee on Investigation/ chairperson, 2623.2*a*
    Court of Appeals, 2625.3*a*
    members of General Council on Finance and Administration, 905.1
  supervise Missionary Conference, 660.1
roles
  appeal process, 2625.3*f*
  assignment process, 507
  bishop's renewal/sabbatical leave, 511.1-.2
  investigations
    of bishop, 2623.2
    of diaconal minister, 2623.4*b*
  involuntary retirement of bishop, 509.3*b*
  special assignments, 52, 507.3
secretary of, 627, 2624.2*a*

Commission/Committee on Christian Unity and Interreligious Concerns, conference, 739

Commission on Archives and History, conference, 738. *See* Archives and History, conference Commission on

Commission on Archives and History, General, 1801-12. *See* Archives and History, General Commission on

Commission on Archives and History, jurisdictional, 631, 1804

Commission on Central Conference Affairs, 649, 652, 2301

Commission on Christian Unity and Interreligious Concerns, General, 2001-06. *See* Christian Unity and Interreligious Concerns, General Commission on

Commission on Communication, General, 1901-08. *See* Communication, General Commission on

Commission on Education, local church, 263.1*c*

Commission on Equitable Salaries, conference, 441, 710.1*e*, 722, 907.13

Commission on Evangelism, local church, 230.3-.5

Commission on Pan-Methodist Cooperation, 2403, 2547.2

Commission on Religion and Race, conference, 740

Commission on Religion and Race, General, 2101-08. *See* Religion and Race, General Commission on

Commission on Stewardship, local church, 261.9*a*, 1215.4

Commission on the General Conference, 605, 907.16

Commission on the Status and Role of Women, conference, 741, 2203.4

Commission on the Status and Role of Women, General, 2201-09. *See* Status and Role of Women, General Commission on

Committee on Appeals
Central Conference, 29.7
jurisdictional, 25.6, 2614

Committee on Audit and Review, 905.4*b*

Committee on Communication
conference council on ministries, 709.4, 726.5*b*, 749.4
district, 749.4
local church, 269.5

Committee on Council Operations, 905.4*a*

Committee on Deaconess Service, 1419

Committee on Diaconal Ministry
district, 304
jurisdictional, 633

Committee on District Superintendency, 754
consultative role, 517, 519.9, 525, 754.5
reconciling role, 453.1*a*

Committee on Episcopacy
Annual Conference, 623.3*f*, 735
area, 735.1
Central Conference, 507.3, 509, 511
Interjurisdictional, 612
jurisdictional, 52-53, 507, 509, 511, 612, 623, 628

Committee on Ethnic Local Church Concerns, conference, 726.5

Committee on Evaluation, 726.5

Committee on Family Life, 1220

Committee on Finance, local church, 269.4
Commission on Stewardship represented on, 261.9*a*
election of, 249.4
lay leader, member of, 251.1*b*
relationships
  to Administrative Board, 256.1
  to Council on Ministries, 257
resources/training for, 907.11, 1215.4

Committee on Health and Welfare Ministries, local church, 262.2, 269.5

Committee on Historic Shrines and Landmarks, 1812.1

Committee on Investigation, 453.1*d*, *f*, .3*b*, 2623, 2624.1*c*

Committee on Lay Speaking
conference, 247.12, 278.1, 279.1, 748.7
district, 247.12, 278.1, 279.1, 753

Committee on Leadership Development, 726.5

Committee on Legal Responsibilities, 905.4*e*

Committee on Memorial Gifts, local church, 269.5

Committee on Ministry to Persons with Handicapping Conditions, conference, 745

Committee on Nominations and Personnel, local church, 245, 269.1
Administrative Board, relationship to, 254, 256.1
election of, 247.17, 249.2, 250
lay leader, member of, 251.1*b*

Committee on Nominations and Personnel, local church, *cont'd:*
responsibilities, 249-50, 257-58, 269.1-.2, 2525
secretary of, 254

Committee on Nominations, conference, 702.8*a*, 726.7*b*(7), 732.4*b*(3)

Committee on Official Forms and Records, 905.4*c*, 1728, 1741

Committee on Ordained Ministry
district, 247.8, 454, 455.4, 752
jurisdictional, 530.2, 633

Committee on Parish and Community Development, conference, 731.5, 1414.12

Committee on Pastor-Parish Relations, local church, 245, 269.2
Administrative Board relationship, 256.1
advisory role, 269.2*f*(8), 531
chairperson of, 249.3, 254
Commission on Equitable Salaries, 722.2
consultative role, 269.2*f*(4), (9), 404.3, 445.4, 449.5, 453.1*a*, 520.3, 531
in cooperative parish, 269.2*d*
district superintendent's relationship, 269.2*f*(8), 520.1, .3, 521.1, 531-33
duties, 269.2*f*
annual evaluation of pastoral ministry, 422.1*b*, 444
to candidates
for diaconal ministry, 304.4
for ordained ministry, 269.2*f*(6), *footnote, page 212,* 733.2*a*
clarifying priorities of pastor/diaconal minister, 520.1
interpreting nature and function of ministry, 269.2*f*(1)
Ministerial Education Fund interpretation, 269.2*f*(7)
to lay employees, 269.2*f*(9)
pastoral/staff appointments, 269.2*f*(1), (5), (8), (9), 1533.1

Committee on Pastor-Parish Relations, local church, *cont'd:*
election of, 249.3, 269.2
in multiple-church charges, 247.17, 269.2*c, e*
Personnel Committee, 269.2*f*(10)
resources/training for, 444, 733.2*n,* 1218.3
as Staff-Parish Relations Committee, 269.2*b*

Committee on Personnel Policies and Practices, 905.4*d*, 907.7*b*

Committee on Planning and Research, 726.5*c*

Committee on Professional Ministry, district, 304

Committee on Publishing House Liaison, conference, 726.5*e*

Committee on Records and History, local church, 247.5*b*, 269.5

Committee on Rules and Regulations, 1603.3

Committee on Trial, 29.7

Committee to Nominate Additional Members, 806

Communication, General Commission on, 1901-08
accountability, 802.2, 803.6, 1904
administrative/program-related agency, 803.6
amenability, 802.1, 1904
budgets, 1906.12, 1908
consultative relationships, 1449.6, .8, 1455.3, 1905, 1909
Division of Program and Benevolence Promotion, 915.4, 919.3, 1007.5*a*, 1907.1
executive committee, 1907.3
financial support, 1908
general secretary, 1007.1*a*(8), 1907.5
incorporation, 1903
meetings, 1907.2

Communication, General Commission on, *cont'd:*
membership, 805.1, .3, 1907.1
name, 1902-03
officers, 1907.3
organization, 1907
purpose, 1905
quorum, 1907.2
represented on Committee on Personnel Policies and Practices, 905.4*d*
responsibilities, 1901, 1905-06
World Communion Sunday appeal, 274.3, 916.4, 1906.12
nomination of United Methodist representatives to Religion in American Life Board of Directors, 1909
One Great Hour of Sharing, 274.2, 916.2
promotion
of Crusade Scholarships, 1455.3
of special day offerings, 274, 916, 1906.12
of United Methodist Committee on Relief, 1460
staff, 1907.5
vacancy, 812, 2006.3

Communications, conference director of, 726.5*b*

Communications, coordinator of
district, 749.4
local church, 250.1, 254, 258, 262.3, 1901, 1906.9-.10

Communities in transition, 207, 731.5*h*, 2550

Communities, other Christian, 71*B*

Community Developers Program, 274.1*a*

Complaints, 453.1, 513.4-.5. *See also* Charges; Grievance Procedures

Comprehensive communication system, 1906.8

Comprehensive Protection Plan, 1604.12, 1606.2*c*
disability leave, 450, 931, 1606
for full-time service, 407.4, 1606.5

Concordat agreements, 647, 653

Concordat church, 12.3, 602.1*b*, 647.5, 653.4

Conference-approved evangelist, 440.1, 729.3*f*, 1213.8, 1606.3*a*

Conference Board of the Laity, 730

Conference coordinator of Christian global concerns, 731.3

Conference council director, 726
Cabinet meeting attendance, 529.6
election of, 726.7
general agency funding of conference program, 818
member conference Board of the Laity, 730.3
nonvoting member of conference Council on Finance and Administration, 708.2*b*
responsibilities, 726.7*b*
training, 1006.12

Conference Council on Youth Ministry, 743. *See* Youth Ministry, conference Council on

Conference Historical Society, 738.2

Conference journal. *See* Journal, Annual Conference; Journal, Central Conference; Journal, General Conference; Journal, Jurisdictional Conference

Conference lay leader, 702.8
coordinating committee on lay work, 702.8*b*
as member
of Annual Conference, 35
of conference Board of the Laity, 730.3

Conference lay leader, *cont'd:*
  of conference Council on Ministries/executive committee, 726.2, .4
  of conference Council on Youth Ministries, 743.2
  resources for, 1218.7
  "State of the Laity" address, 704.5

Conference of Methodist Bishops, 528

Conference Racial/Ethnic Youth Caucuses, 1306.1*b*(6)

Conferences
  Annual Conference, 36-39, 701-45
  Central Conference, 636-38
  Charge Conference, 246-50
  Church Conference, 248
  Church Local Conference, 2526
  Constituting Church Conference, 270.5-.7
  District Conference, 746-56
  General Conference, 12-20, 601-11
  Jurisdictional Conference, 21-25, 612-35
  Missionary Conference, 659-62
  Provisional Annual Conference, 655-58
  Provisional Central Conference, 639-46

Conference superintendent, 657.1
  as member
    of conference Committee on Parish and Community Development, 731.5*a, h*
    of conference Council on Ministries, 726.2
  in Missionary Conference, 660.1
  pension, 1606.3*a*(2)
  in Provisional Annual Conference, 657.1

Conference treasurer, 715
  accountability, 709.9
  bonding of, 714.1
  as director of administrative services, 716

Conference treasurer, *cont'd:*
  nonvoting member of conference Council on Finance and Administration, 708.2*b*
  responsibilities, 715
  treasurer, conference Council on Finance and Administration, 708.3

Conference United Methodist Foundation, 2533.1

Conference United Methodist Women, 741.2, 1429

Conference youth coordinator, 743.3*j*, 1306.2*a*

Confession of Faith, 3, 16, *pages 68-74*

Confidentiality, duty concerning, 440.4

Confirmation, 106, 216.2-.4, 225

Conformity with local law, 638.27, .29, 2506-07

Congregational development, 731.5

Congregational meeting, 44

Connectional People, Journey of a, 112

Connectional principle, 112.3-.5, 530

Connectional structure, 112-113, 203, 530, *page 297*, 732.4*a*(2), 2501

Conscientious objectors, 74*G*

Consecration
  of bishop, 49, 506.2*c*, 515.5
  of diaconal minister, 307, 515.5
  of lay speaker, 278.3
  of local church, 2544

Constituency Roll, 232.4

Constituting Church Conference, 270.5-.7

Constitution, *pages 19-39,* 1-64

Consultation and appointment-making, 269.2, 530-34

Consultation on Church Union, 261.1, 739.4*f,* 2003.4

Consumption, 73*D*

Continuing education, 445
for appointee beyond local church, 443.3*a,* 445.6
for clergy, 423.2, 445, 921, 1529.7
for diaconal minister, 313.1*c,* 315.1, 921, 1515.9
pastor's annual report on, 445.5, 520.5
as remedial action for minister facing complaints, 453.1*e*
support of, 733.2*n,* 734.3*u,* 921

Contribution base, 1606.18, .21

Cooperation, Commission on Pan-Methodist, 2403, 2547.2

Cooperative parish, 205.2
appointment to, 438
Board of Trustees, 2527.2
Committee on Pastor-Parish Relations, 269.2*d*
development, 206.2, 731.6
ministries, 206, 731.6*h*
types, 206.3

Coordination of age-level and family ministries, 252.1*d,* 258, 259, 743.3*j*

Coordinator
adult ministries, 258-59
children's ministries, 258-59
Christian global concerns, 731.3
communications, 250.1, 254, 258, 262.3, 749.4, 1906.9-.10
disaster response, 731.4(19), 1464
family ministries, 258-59
older adult ministries, 258-59

Coordinator, *cont'd:*
persons with handicapping conditions, 258-59
scouting ministries, 258
single adult ministries, 258-59
volunteer-in-mission, 731.6
young adult ministries, 258-59
youth ministries, 258-59, 632, 743.3*j,* 1306.2*a*

Council of Bishops, 50, 527
authorization, 50
financial support, 924
liaison role, 2405
meetings, 50, 527.3
membership, 527.1, 638.22
powers and responsibilities, 527.3, 803.5
acts of covenanting, 650
altering The Advance, 915.6
annual inquiry about consultation in appointment-making, 531.2
appeal/petition Judicial Council, 59.1, .4, 2607, 2609, 2615.2*b*
appointments
to general agencies, 905.4*c,* 1007.1*a*(2), 1307.1, 1702, 1907.1, 2006.1, 2103, 2204.4
to National Youth Ministry Organization Steering Committee, 1307.1
to University Senate, 1517.2
arranging visitations
Affiliated Autonomous Methodist Churches, 648.4
Autonomous Methodist Churches, 647.3
Central Conferences, 637.4
concordat churches, 653.4*c*
bishop's sabbatical leave, 511.2
calling special session of General Conference, 13
churchwide appeals, 911.4, 1006.6, 1463
concordat agreement, 653
Conference of Methodist Bishops, 528
consultation on special days, 906.11, 1006.6

Council of Bishops, *cont'd:*

date of Jurisdictional Conferences, 24

designation of interim bishop, 507.3, 511.2

election of Central Conference representatives to general agencies, 1007.1*a*(2), 1204.1, 1412.6, 1507

filling vacancies, 508, 812, 905.1, 2406

missional priorities/special programs, 1006.1

naming

Commission on Central Conference Affairs, 2301.2

Commission on Pan-Methodist Cooperation, 2403

representatives to World Council of Churches Assembly and agencies, 2402.3

nomination

of Central Conference representatives on General Council on Ministries, 1007.1*a*(7)

of episcopal members of general agencies, 805.2*b*

of General Board of Pensions, 1602.1*a*

of General Commission on Archives and History, 1804.2

of General Council on Finance and Administration, 905.1

of Judicial Council, 2601

of secretary-designate of General Conference, 604

of University Senate, 1517.2

of World Methodist Council, 2401.1

oversight of covenantal relationship, 650

planning cooperation

Affiliated Autonomous Methodist Church, 648.6

Autonomous Methodist Church, 647.4

providing episcopal visitation of mission fields not in Central Conferences, 646

Council of Bishops, *cont'd:*

report/recommendations from General Commission on Christian Unity and Interreligious Concerns, 2003.17-.18, .20

selecting representatives/proxies to National Council of the Churches of Christ in the U.S.A. Governing Board, 2402.2*b*

special assignment of bishop, 52, 507.2-.3, 508

training district superintendents, 1006.12

president of, 649.5, 653.3*b*, 806.2, 807.1, 1007.2

Committees to Nominate Additional Members, 806.2

concordat agreement/proclamation of affiliated autonomous status, 649.5, 653.3*b*

general agency organizational meetings, 807.1, 1007.2, 1412.1

Interjurisdictional Committee on Episcopacy, 612.1

representation

on general agencies, 805.2*b*, 905.4*c*, 1307.1, 1702, 1907.1, 2006.1, 2103, 2204.4

on National Youth Ministry Organization Steering Committee, 1307.1

secretary of

funding of office, 914

as member

of General Commission on Christian Unity and Interreligious Concerns, 2006.1

of National Council of the Churches of Christ in the U.S.A. Governing Board, 2402.2*b*

receiving notification

bishop retiring, 509.3*b*

general agency vacancy, 812

responsible for ecumenical relations, 2405

signing

consecration papers of bishop who resigns, 509.4

Council of Bishops, *cont'd:*
concordat agreement, 653.3*b*
proclamation of affiliated autonomous status, 649.5
See also Bishop; College of Bishops; Episcopacy; Episcopal leadership

Council of Presidents of the Black Colleges, 919, 1523.1

Council on Finance and Administration, conference, 707-16. *See* Finance and Administration, conference Council on

Council on Finance and Administration, General, 901-32. *See* Finance and Administration, General Council on

Council on Ministries, conference, 726-27
Advance special giving, 726.9*d*
age-level/family councils, 726.6
budget responsibilities, 708.6*a*, 710.3*b-c*, 726.10*e*
Committee on Communication, 726.5*b*
Committee on Evaluation, 726.5*d*
Committee on Leadership Development, 726.5
Committee on Planning and Research, 726.5
committees, task forces, consultations, 726.5
conference coordinator of Christian global concerns, 731.3
conference council director, 708.2*b*, 726.7, 730.3, 818, 1006.12
executive committee, 726.4
general agency funding of conference program, 818
membership, 524.2, 702.8*a*, 726.2, 749.4*n*
officers, 726.3
Personnel Committee, 726.4, .8
purpose, 726.1
relationships, 726.9
responsibilities, 726.10
staff, 726.5*b*, .8, 749.2

Council on Ministries, district, 524.1, 749

Council on Ministries, General, 1001-07
accountability, 803.1
Advance Committee, 1006.22, 1007.5
amenability, 802.1, 803.1, 1003
Annual Conference Journals sent to, 705.2
general secretary, 814.5, 1007.7
incorporation, 1002
meetings, 1007.2
membership, 632.8, 805-06, 1007.1
name, 1001
objectives, 1005
officers, 1007.3
organization, 806-07, 810, 1007
as program-related agency, 803.5
purpose, 1004
representation
Committee on Official Forms and Records, 905.4*c*
Committee on Personnel Policies and Practices, 905.4*d*
General Commission on Communication, 1907.1
National Youth Ministry Organization Steering Committee, 1307.1
responsibilities, 1006
budget preparation and allocation, 906.1*b*, 912.1, 1006.2, 1908
date of Native American Awareness Sunday, 274.6
election of general secretaries, 813, 1006.15
evaluation of general agency program services, 802.3, 1006.13, 1904, 1907
missional priorities/special programs, 1005.1, 1006.1
prevention of duplicate programs, 911.2
review of general agency headquarters, 907.2, 1006.25
special days/offerings, 274, 906.11, 1006.6

Council on Ministries, General, *cont'd:*
    valid resolutions, 611.2*b*, 1006.20
    staff, 1007.7
    World Service Special Gifts Committee, 1006.23, 1007.6

Council on Ministries, jurisdictional, 629

Council on Ministries, local church, 257-68
    Administrative Board, relationship to, 256.1
    Administrative Council, relationship to, 252.1
    age-level ministries, 259-60, 263, 265
    care of members, 228-29, 230.1
    chairperson, 249.1, 254, 260, 269.4
    church school teachers/officers, 257, 261.3, 262.1*b*, 263.1*d*
    class meetings, 268
    evangelism priority, 261.4
    membership, 258, 261.9*a*, 268.4
    officers, 249.1, 258
    organization, 257
    program agencies, 263
    resources for, 1218.3
    responding to community needs, 262.2
    responsibilities, 257
    shared facilities representation, 2552.1*a*
    in small churches, 252.1, 257
    task groups, 267
    work area commissions, 266

Council on Youth Ministry
    conference, 743, 1306.2
    district, 756

Counseling elder, 411, 520.4, 733.2*v*

Course of study, 1529.2
    advanced, 416.2*c*, 424, 1529.2
    for associate members, 420.1
    in Central Conference, 638.20
    for local pastor, 405.2, 406.4, 408-09

Course of study, *cont'd:*
    for ordained ministry, 405.2, 406.4, 408.1*d*, .2, 409.1, .4, 733.2*f*, 1529.2
    for probationary member, 417
    school, 1529.2
    special, 424

Court of Appeals
    Central Conference, 2624.1*h*, 2625.3
    district, 2625.4
    jurisdictional, 2624.1*h*, 2625.3

Covenanting, Act of, 647, 648, 650

Credentials
    from another denomination, 427.5
    for diaconal minister, 307
    of member in full connection, 435.4
    of member uniting with another denomination, 452.2
    restoration of, 454
    surrender of, 410.1, 418, 452.3-.4

Criminal Justice, 74*F*

Crusade Scholarship Committee, 274.3, 916.4*b*

Crusade Scholarships
    administration of, 1454-55
    Board of Global Ministries responsibility, 731.4(11)
    Division of Higher Education responsibility, 1515.3*f*
    Division of Ordained Ministry responsibility, 1529.12
    World Communion Sunday offering, 274.3, 1455.2

Curriculum, church school
    approval of, 1208.6, 1224-25
    biblical basis, 1224
    contents, 263.1*b*
    coordinated system, 1737
    editor of Church School Publications, 1226-28, 1733-34
    evangelism concepts, 1213.13
    general description, 1223
    stewardship concepts, 1215.3
    worship concepts, 1214.10

Curriculum Resources Committee, 1223-28
budget, 1226.1*d*, .2*d*, 1736
bylaws, 1228.2
chairperson, 1226.1*c*, 1227.2, 1228.1*d*
consultation with Annual Conferences, 1228.1*b*
cooperative publication, 1226.2*c*, .3
curriculum general plans, 1223
development of curriculum, 1224
editorial staff, 1224, 1227.1
editor of Church School Publications, 1226-28, 1733-34
General Board of Discipleship relationship, 1223, 1225, 1226.1
membership, 1228
promotion/interpretation, 1226.1*b*, .2*b*
representation on National Youth Ministry Organization Steering Committee, 1307.1
United Methodist Publishing House relationship, 1226.2, 1228.1*c*, 1734, 1736, 1740

Curriculum resources secretary, 263.1*e*

D

Daily Christian Advocate, 608.7-.8, 611.4, 2601

Date legislation effective
close of General Conference, 274.4, 505, 627, 629, 805, 920, 924, 931, 1517.2, 1606.4*i*
January 1, 1989, 609
year after General Conference, 638.22

Date of founding, 824

Day care, 262.2, 265.1

Deacon
associate member as, 419.1
authority of, 434
order of, 434

Deacon, *cont'd:*
ordination, 434.3, *footnote, pages 210-13,* 515.4
probationary member as, 413.1
qualifications for elder, 435.1-.2

Deaconess, 1418.2
accountability, 1418.7
on Administrative Board, 254
Annual Conference relationship, 1418.5-.6
appointment of, 516.3, 1418.3
assignment, 1418.7
Charge Conference member, 1418.4
church membership, 1418.4
commissioning, 515.5, 1418.2
Diaconal Ministry, conference Board of, duties, 734.5
full-time service, 1418.3
listing in Annual Conference journal, 734.5*b*, 1418.3*b-c*
National Division relationship, 1418.2, .3*b*, .7, .9-.10
pension, 1418.8
purpose, 1418.1
records of, 734.5*a*, 1418.3*c*
relinquishing relationship, 1418.9

Deaconess Program Office, 1420

Deaconess Service, Committee on, 1419

Death Benefit Program, 1604.12

Death with dignity, 71*H*

Dedication of local church building, 2541

Deeding church property, 2547

Definition
administrative general agency, 803.6
Advance special gifts, 914.2
Advance, The, 914.1
Affiliated Autonomous Methodist Church, 648
archives, 1811.1*a*
assistant general secretary, 803.7*d*

Definition, *cont'd:*
associate general secretary, 803.7*c*
association, 803.12
Autonomous Methodist Church, 647.1
Church, the 107
church year, 820.1
circuit, 205.2
clergy members, 602.2, 701.1
conference benevolences, 710.3*c*
conference institution, 710.3*c*
conference program agency, 710.3*c*
consultation, 531
cooperative parish, 205.2, 206.3
deacon, 433.2
deaconess, 1418.2
department, 802.2*b*
deputy general secretary, 803.7*b*
diaconal minister, 301-02
division, 802.2*a*
documentary record material, 1811.1*b*
elder, 433.1
executive session, 704.6
fellowship, 803.12
fiscal year, 820.1
general agency, 801, 1811.1*c*
general board, 803.2
general church funds, 910
general commission, 803.3
general council, 803.1
general secretary, 803.7*a*
local church, 201
mission, 663
missional priority, 803.9
missionary conference, 659
office, 803.2*d*
open itineracy, 530.1
pastor, 438
pastoral charge, 205.1
program, 803.11
program-related general agency, 803.5
quadrennial emphasis, 803.10
quadrennium, 820.2
section, 803.2*c*
small membership church, 252.1
special program, 803.10
study committee, 803.4
theme, 803.8
treasurer, 803.7*e*

Definition, *cont'd:*
United Methodist Church, The 113, 2501
University Senate, 1517.1

Delegates, 37-39
Central Conference, 27, 636.2, 637.1
General Conference, 12-13, 22, 443.4, 602, 653.4*a*, 660.3, .4*b*
Jurisdictional Conference, 22-23, 443.4, 614-15, 620.3, 625, 653.4*a*, 660.3, .4*b*
voting rights in election of, 413.2, 419.2, 423, 701.1

Depositories for funds, 269.4*d*, 712

Deserts, spread of, 70*A*

Diaconal minister, 301-18
on Administrative Board, 254
affiliate member as, 304.5
amenability, 308
Annual Conference
attendance at, 309.1
lay member of, 35, 309.1, 701.3
appeal, 2625.3
appointment, 310, 516.3
candidate for, 303-06, 734.3*m*
in Central Conference, 701.3
Charge Conference, relationship to, 304.5, 314
charges against, 2621-22
church membership, 304.2, 314.1
commissioned, 306.3*b*(4)
consecration, 307, 734.3*k*
continuing education, 313.1*c*, 315.1, 921, 1525.9
credentials and records, 307, 311
educational requirements, 306.3
employing agency, relationship to, 310.5*a*, 315-18
evaluation of, 734.3*l*
investigation of, 2623.4
leave, 734.3*n*
of absence, 313.1
disability, 313.1*a*
extended, 313.1*d-e*
maternity/paternity, 313.1*b*
personal, 313.1*d*
study/sabbatical, 313.1*c*

Diaconal minister, *cont'd:*

listing in Annual Conference journal, 734.3*g*

recognition, 1526.9

reinstatement, 313.1*e*, .3*c*

representation on General Commission on the Status and Role of Women, 2204.5*c*

requirements, 306

retirement, 313.2

rights, 309

salary and benefits, 315, 734.3*t*

service record, 705.6, .8

support for, 734.3*s-w*

suspension, 2623.4*e*

termination, 313.3

transfer of, 305.3, 312, 313, 734.3*o*

trial, 2624.3

withdrawal under charges, 2626.2

Diaconal ministry, 109, 301-18

candidacy for, 303-06, 734.3*m*

educational requirements, 306.3

employment requirements, 306.2

examination for, 306.5

nature of, 302

psychological assessment, 304.7

recommendation for, 303

relation to other forms of ministry, 301

Diaconal Ministry, conference Board of, 734

annual meeting of diaconal ministers, 309.2

appointment role, 310.5*c*, .6*a*

change in status, role in, 313

candidacy role, 304-06

developing evaluation criteria, 269.2*f*(3)

interpreting diaconal ministry, 734.3*b*

membership, 734.1*b*

promotion of Ministry Sunday, 734.3*b*

records and credentials maintenance, 311, 705.6, .8, 734.3*n*

resources and training, 1525.10-.11

responsibilities transfer, 734.3*i, o*

Diaconal Ministry, Division of, General Board of Higher Education and Ministry, 1524-26

associate general secretary, 1517.2

financial support, 1509.1

membership, 805, 809, 1508.1

Ministerial Education Fund, 921.2, 1509.1

purpose, 1525

responsibilities, 1524, 1526

consecration guidelines/standards, 734.3*j*, 1526.1

continuing education guidelines/resources, 1525.9

criteria for psychological assessment, 304.7

educational/professional standards, 1525.3-.4, .8

resources/training for conference Boards of Diaconal Ministry, 1525.10-.11, 1526.7-.11

Director of administrative services, conference, 709.9, 716

Director of communications, conference, 726.5*b*

Director of evangelism, 1213.7

Director of parish development, 206.2, 726.2, 731.5*a*

Director of The Advance, 1007.5*a-b*

Disability, Joint Committee on, 450.1-.2, 744

Disability leave

for bishop, 511.3

for diaconal minister, 312.1*a*

for ordained minister, 450

pension credit for, 1606.3*a*

Disaster Response Coordinator, conference, 731.4(19), 1464

Discipleship, conference Board of, 729

Discipleship, General Board of, 1201-28

INDEX

Discipleship, General Board of, *cont'd:*
accountability, 802.2, 803.5
amenability, 802.1, 803.5
bylaws, 1204.4
Committee on Family Life, 1220
consultative relationships, 1308.5, 1449.6, 1905
cooperation with other agencies, 1202.13-.14, 1210, 1511.3, 1906.14
Curriculum Resources Committee, 1223-28. *See* Curriculum Resources Committee
division of assets, 1203, 1502
educational standards, 1209
executive committee, 1204.2, .5, 1226.1*c*, 1228.1*b*
financial support, 1206
funds for mission education, 1206.5
general secretary, 813-14, 1203, 1226.1*d*, 1228.1*c*
headquarters, 907.2, 1007.25
incorporation, 1203
International Christian Youth Exchange, 1219.3
Joint Committee on Congregational Development, 1414.13
membership, 805-06, 1204.1
National Association of Conference Presidents of United Methodist Men, 1222
officers, 808, 1204.1
organization, 802-10, 1204-05
predecessor boards, corporations, divisions, 1203
program-related agency, 803.5
purpose, 1201
representation
on Committee on Personnel Policies and Practices, 905.4*d*
on National Youth Ministry Organization Steering Committee, 1307.1
responsibilities, 1202
age-level and family ministries, 1219
chartering/recertifying United Methodist Men units, 264, 1222.1*c*
church school extension, 1211

Discipleship, General Board of, *cont'd:*
devotional life, 1216
education, 1207-09
evaluation National Youth Ministry Organization, 1303
evangelism, 1212-13
General Military Roll, 218, 1213.9
Laity Sunday (Day), 273, 275.2, 1218.5
lay speaker program, 277-79, 1218.6
leadership and ministry development, 1218
men's work, 1222
ministry of the laity, 1217-21
resources
for Committees on Finance, 907.11
for United Methodist Men units, 264.1, 1222
for Wills and Estate Planning Task Forces, 261.9*b*
scouting, 1219.3
staff, National Youth Ministry Organization Steering Committee, 1208.2
standards/guidelines
for church school, 263.1*a*, 1209.2
for local church work areas, 261.3-.4, .10
stewardship, 1215
worship, 1214
special missions, 1206.4
staff, 1205.5
treasurer, 1203
United Methodist Men's Division, 1222
Upper Room, The, 1202.3, 1206.3, 1216.3

Discipline
Affiliated Autonomous Methodist or United Church, 649.3
Central Conference, 29.6, 638.21, .33

Disciplined life, 112.3*d*

INDEX

Discontinuance from probationary membership, 418. *See also* Withdrawal from conference membership

Discontinued local church, 231, 2548.1

Disposition of church building/parsonage, 2541

Distributing Committee, conference, 1609

District Board of Church Location and Building. *See* Church Location and Building, district Board of

District Board of Stewards, 711.3-.4, 2517.2

District Board of the Laity, 1218.7

District Board of Trustees, 2517.2

District Committee on Church and Society, 750

District Committee on Communication, 749.4

District Committee on Lay Speaking, 752

District Committee on Ordained Ministry. *See* Ordained Ministry, district Committee on

District Committee on Professional Ministry, 304

District Committee on Religion and Race, 751

District Conference, 45, 746-56
appeal to Judicial Council, 2611-12
Board of Church Location and Building, 2518
certificates of candidacy for ordained ministry, 747.3
District Union, 747.4, 2517.2

District Conference, *cont'd:*
election
of associate district lay leaders, 748.2
of Committee on District Superintendency, 754
of district Board of Trustees, 2517.2
of district lay leader, 730, 748
membership, 747.1
order of business, 747.1
parsonage, 2517.1, .2
property, 2517-23
secretary, 747.2

District Coordinator of Communications, 749.4

District Council on Ministries, 749. *See* Council on Ministries, District

District Council on Youth Ministry, 756

District director of Church and society, 750

District director of religion and race, 740.2, 751

District Lay Leader, 730.3, 748

District Missionary Society, 727.4

District Nominating Committee, 2517.2, 2518

District parsonage, 2517, 2522

District property, 2517-23. *See* Property, district

District Stewards, 250.1, 711.1

District Strategy Committee for Parish Development, 2519.2

District superintendent, 501-03, 517-26
accountability, 529.3
Annual Conference inquiry, 704.6

761

District superintendent, *cont'd:*
appeal of lay member, 2625.4*b-d*
appointment of, 515.4, 517-18, 660.1
authority to call Church Conference/Joint Church Conference, 248
bishop, relationship to, 521.5, 529
Cabinet relationship of, 529
Charge Conference affiliation, 443.3*a*
financial support, 710.1*a*, 715.2*c*
general guidelines, 502
limit on years of service, 518, 660.1
member
conference Council on Ministries, 524.2, 726.2
district United Methodist Women/executive committee, 755.4
parsonage, 2517, 2522
pension credit, 1606.3*a*
renewal/study leave, 525
responsibilities, 519-24
appointment-making, 57, 519, 521.3, 531-33
approval of pastor's actions
discontinuing services, 444.2
engaging evangelist, 444.1
candidacy role, 404, 417, 520.4, 521.1-.2
chairperson, district Board of Stewards, 711.3
Charge Conferences, 246.4, 249, 313.1*c*, 523.1
Committees on Pastor-Parish Relations, 269.2*e*, 520.3, 521.1, 531
convening Committee on Investigation, 2623.3*b*
executive oversight, district Council on Ministries, 749.3
long-range planning, 524.3, 2550
merger of churches, 2545.3, 2546.1, .3
mission structure determination, 1415.7*a*
new local church, 270.1-.3
nomination district Board of Trustees, 2517.2
pool for Trial Court, 2624.3*c*(1)

District superintendent, *cont'd:*
property, 523.4-.5, 2536, 2538-41, 2543.1, 2547.1-.2, 2548
records of abandoned/discontinued churches, 523.6, .8, 2548.3
shared facilities agreement, 206.3*i*, 2552.2*b*, .3
signing of complaint, 453.1*b*
study of local church potential, 2550
supervision, 519-20, 733.2*e*
task of, 501
training for, 1006.12
transfer of members of discontinued church, 231, 523.8
trial of lay member, 2625.4
See also Cabinet; Property, district; Superintendency

District Union, 747.4

District United Methodist Women, 755, 1429

Division of Chaplains and Related Ministries, 1510-12. *See* Chaplains and Related Ministries, Division of, General Board of Higher Education and Ministry

Division of Diaconal Ministry, 1524-26. *See* Diaconal Ministry, Division of, General Board of Higher Education and Ministry

Division of Higher Education, 1513-21. *See* Higher Education, Division of, General Board of Higher Education and Ministry

Division of Ordained Ministry, 1527-29. *See* Ordained Ministry, Division of, General Board of Higher Education and Ministry

Division of Program and Benevolence Interpretation, 1007.5*a*

Division, United Methodist Men's, 1222

Divorce, 71*D*

Doctrinal heritage, 66

Doctrinal history, 67

Doctrinal standards, *pages 60-77*

Domestic surveillance, 74*A*

Drugs, 72*I*

E

Early retirement, 451.2, 453.1*e*, 509.2, 1606.4*i*

Eastertide, 275.1

Ecumenical relations
Christian Unity and Interreligious Concerns
conference Commission/Committee on, 739
General Commission on, 2001-06
local church work area on, 252.1*b*, 256.8, 261.1
Commission on Pan-Methodist Cooperation, 2403
Consultation on Church Union, 2402.1
Council of Bishops, role in, 2405-06
Ecumenical Staff Officer, 2005.4
National Council of the Churches of Christ in the U.S.A., 2402.2
World Council of Churches, 2402.3
World Methodist Council, 2401

Ecumenical Staff Officer, 2005.4

Editor, Church School Publications, 1226-1228, 1732-33, 1735-36, 1739

Education, 72*C*, 74*D*, 1207.2-.3
Commission on, 263.1*c*
conference Board of Discipleship responsibility, 729.2

Education, *cont'd:*
General Board of Discipleship responsibility, 1207-09
local church work area on, 252.1*a*, 260, 261.3, 262.1*b*
See also Continuing education; Higher Education, Division of, General Board of Higher Education and Ministry

Educational assistant, 254

Educational leave, 445.3

Educational requirements
associate member, 420
candidacy, 306.3, 405.1-.2
diaconal minister, 306.3
local pastor, 407.2, 408-09
member in full connection, 424
probationary member, 415

Effective date of General Conference legislation, 609, 629, 638.22, 805, 807, 920, 924, 931, 1517.2, 1606

Effective immediately legislation, 274.4, 505, 627, 629, 805, 907.7*a*, 920, 924, 931, 1517.2, 1606.4*i*

Effect of Union, 2504

Eight-year rule, 810.3

Elder, 433.1
certification, 435.4
conference-approved evangelist, 1213.8
counseling, 406.4, 411, 520.4, 733.2*v*
course of study for, 1529.2
deacon qualifying for, 435.1-.2
in less than full-time appointment, 660.6
order of, 435
ordination, *footnote, pages 210-13,* 429-32, 433.1, 435.3, 515.5, 638.10
presiding officer at Charge Conference, 246.5, 523.1

Elder, *cont'd:*
supervising pastor, 520.4, 733.2*e*
See also Clergy; Ordained Ministry;
Pastor

Electronic information system, 234

Emergency appeals, 710.5, 911.4,
1906.12

Employment policies, 814.9, 815

Energy, 70*B*

Enlarged charge, 206.3

Environment, 70, 73*D*

Epiphany, 274.1

Episcopacy, 17, 48-57
authority, 15.5
Committee on
area, 735.1
conference, 623.3*f*, 735
Central Conference, 507.3, 509,
511
Interjurisdictional, 612
Jurisdictional, 52, 507.1, .3,
509.2*d*, .3*a-b*, .4, 511.1-.2,
612.2, 620.2, 623, 628
Council of Bishops as collegial
expression of, 527
election to, 49, 53, 506, 512
general guidelines, 502
support of, 25.2, 29.2, 923-32
vacancy in, 508, 620.2
See also Bishop; College of Bishops;
Council of Bishops; Episcopal
Fund

Episcopal areas
area expense fund, 710.2*b*, 924
boundaries, 623.3*b*, 638.6
specifications for, 505

Episcopal Fund, 923-32
allowance for surviving spouse/
children, 924, 926
Annual Conference payment,
710.1*b*, 718
apportionment for, 908, 925

Episcopal Fund, *cont'd:*
area expense fund, 924
budget, 906.1
disability leave support, 511.3,
931
disbursement, 906.2
office expense, 924, 926, 929
payment to resigned bishop,
509.4
pensions, 509, 924, 930-32
promotion of, 1906.12
retired bishop's assignment,
509.1*c*, .2*e*
salaries, 923-26
suspended/removed bishop,
509.3*b*, 931, 2624.2*f*
travel reimbursement, 924, 928
treasurer of, 509.3*b*

Episcopal leadership, 52, 112, 526-
27, 802.6

Episcopal residence, 736.3-.5, 927,
2514

Episcopal Residence Committee,
736, 929

Equal employment opportunity,
740.3*n*, 815, 907.7*b*, 911.1

**Equitable Salaries, conference
Commission on,** 441, 710.1*e*, 722,
907.14

Equitable Salary Fund, 441, 718-19,
722.5, .7-.8

Equitable salary, pastor's right to,
441, 717

**Ethnic In-Service Training Pro-
gram,** 274.3, 916.4*b*

**Ethnic Local Church Concerns, con-
ference Committee on,** 726.5

Ethnic rights, racial and, 72*A*. *See
also* Racial/ethnic concerns

Ethnic Scholarship Program, 274.3,
916.4*b*

Evaluation
of bishop, 735.3*f*
of clergy appointed beyond local church, 444.2
of conference program, 726.5*d*
of diaconal minister, 734.3*l*
of district superintendent, 754.4*e*, .5
of general agencies, 802.3, 1006.13
of ordained minister, 704.6, 733.2*o*
of pastor, 269.2*f*(3), 423.2*c*, 444.1

Evangelism
Commission on, 230.3-.5
conference Board of Discipleship responsibility, 729.3
director/associate of, 254, 1213.7
General Board of Discipleship responsibility, 1212-13
local church work area on, 230, 235, 252.1, 260, 261.4, 264

Evangelist
conference-approved, 440.1, 729.3*f*
pastor's hiring of, 440.1
pension credit for, 1606.3*a*
standards for, 1213.8

Examination, 733.2*g*, 734.3*f*
for associate membership, 414.8, 425
for candidacy for ordained ministry, 403, 404.3-.4
of diaconal minister, 306.5
for membership in full connection, 424-25, 704.7
of ordained ministers at Annual Conference, 704.6-.7
for probationary membership, 414.8
Wesley's historic questions, 425

Executive session, Annual Conference, *footnote, page 212,* 704.6
admit/discontinue probationary member, 416, 418
admit into full connection, 424
allow surrender of ordained ministerial office, 452.3
confirm less than full-time service, 437.2*b-c*

Executive session, Annual Conference, *cont'd:*
elect to associate membership, 420.1
grant disability leave, 450
grant extended leave of absence, 448.1
grant certificates of honorable location, 452.1
grant reappointment to less than full-time service, 437.2
permit withdrawal, 452.3-.5
place in retired relation, 451
receive affiliate member, 443.4
recognize orders from other denominations, 427.3
response to request for trial, 453.3*b*
See also Annual Conference; Closed sessions

Explanatory Notes upon the New Testament, *page 74*

Extended/shared ministry, 206.3

Extension ministries, 443.1*b*, 733.2*g*, 1511.1

F

Family, 71*a*

Family Council, 265.4

Family Life, Committee on, 1220

Family ministries, 252.1, 258-59, 265, 1219

Farming, 72*M*

Farm workers, 72*M*, 73*F*

Fellowship of United Methodists in Worship, Music, and Other Arts, 729.4*c*, 1214.4, 1526.12

Filling vacancy on general agency
by Council of Bishops, 812, 1507, 2006.3
by General Board of Pensions, 1602.1*e*

Filling vacancy on general agency, *cont'd:*
by General Board of Publication, 1702
by General Commission on Archives and History, 1804.1
by General Commission on Christian Unity and Interreligious Concerns, 2006.3
by General Commission on the Status and Role of Women, 2204.6
by nomination from College of Bishops, 812, 905.1, 2006.3
by nomination from Council of Bishops, 905.1
due to absence, 810.9
due to change of residence, 810.8
See also Vacancy

Finance and Administration, conference Council on, 707-16
amenability, 708.5
bylaws, 708.4*b*
conference treasurer, 709.9, 715
depository for funds, 712
director of administrative services, 709.9, 716
district superintendent's salary, 719.1*a*
Episcopal Fund responsibility, 710.1*b*
executive committee, 726.4
fiscal management, 708.6*b*
handling of conference funds, 715.2
incorporation, 708.4*c*
membership, 706.4, 708.2
officers, 708.3
official forms and records use, 715.4*b*
organization, 708.4
pension responsibilities, 710.1*d*, 1606.19, 1607.2, 1608.7*b*
purpose, 708.1
raising mission funds, 1415.7*c*(8)
relationships, 708.6
represented on conference Council on Ministries, 726.2
responsibilities, 709
apportionments, 709.3, 711
audits, 713

Finance and Administration, conference Council on, *cont'd:*
bonding, 714
budgets, 708.6*a*, 709.1, 710
clergy support, 710.1
special appeals, 709.2, 710.5
standardizing local church financial systems, 709.12, 715.6
staff, 726.8, 749.2

Finance and Administration, General Council on, 901-32
accountability, 803.1, 906
amenability, 802.1, 803.1, 904
Annual Conference journals sent to, 705.2
audits, 906.4, 909
business manager of the General Conference, 907.16
Committee on Audit and Review, 905.4*b*
Committee on Council Operations, 905.4*a*
Committee on Legal Responsibilities, 905.4*e*
Committee on Official Forms and Records, 905.4*c*
Committee on Personnel Policies and Practices, 905.4*d*, 907.7*b*
conference Councils on Ministries relationship, 1006.7
consultative responsibilities, 1906.11
Department of Statistics, 905.4*c*
executive committee, 905.3, .4*a*, 917.2
General Episcopal Fund, 638.4-.5
general funds, 910-32. *See* General church funds
general secretary, 814.5, 905.3, .5
incorporation, 903
meetings, 905.2
membership, 905.1
Methodist Corporation successor, 2511
name, 902
National Association of Commissions on Equitable Salaries, 907.14
National Association of United Methodist Foundations, 906.8, 1215.11

Finance and Administration, General Council on, *cont'd:*

National Council of the Churches of Christ in the U.S.A., 916.2*b*, 918.2, 2402.2

officers, 905.3

organization, 905

responsibilities, 906-07

  annuity rate schedule, 1608.6

  budget preparation and allocation, 906.1*b*, 912.1, 1006.1, .2, 1908, 2107

  compensation for retired bishop on special assignment, 509.2*e*

  forms

    Annual Conference records, 705.7

    appointees beyond the local church, 443.2*a*

    church membership records, 234.1-.2

    general agency accounting, 804

    general agency borrowing funds, 911.3

  Judicial Council budget, 917.3

  long-range investments for higher education, 1506.10

  pension responsibilities, 509.4, 930-32, 1606.15

  prevention of duplicate programs, 911.2, 1006.10

  resources for local church administration, 907.12, 1215.4

  review general agency headquarters, 907.2, 1006.25

  special appeals, 911.4, 912.3, 1006.6, 1460, 1463, 1906.12

  special days/offerings, 274, 906.11, 916, 1006.6

staff, 905.5

statement on church finance, 901

as successor corporation, 822, 903, 2511

treasurer, 905.3, 908-09, 914.4, 915.2, 916, 917.2

vacancy, 812, 905.1

World Methodist Council, 2401

World Service Special Gifts Committee, 1006.23, 1007.6

Finance, Committee on, local church, 269.4. *See* Committee on Finance

Financial obligations, 638.31, 703.2, 2509

Financial secretary, 249.4, 254, 269.4

Foundational Studies for Diaconal Ministers, 1526.3

Foundations, 1215.11, 1514.3, 2513, 2533-34. *See also* United Methodist Foundations; Wesley Foundations

Founding date, 824

Fourth Sunday offering, 263.1*f*

Freedom of information, 74*C*

Full connection, member in, 422-25

  admission requirements, 424-25, 1529.2

  amenability, 412.1, 422

  from another denomination, 426.2

  appointment to Missionary Conference, 660.4*b*

  continuing education, 423.2*b*, *d*, 445, 520.5

  disability leave, 450

  evaluation of, 423.1*b-c*, 444, 703.4

  grievance procedures, 453

  honorable location, 452.1

  leave of absence, 448

  maternity/paternity leave, 449

  minimum salary, 437.1, 441.1

  ordination as elder, 433.1

  pension credit, 1606.3*a*

  questions for examination of, 424-25

  responsibilities, 423.1-.2, 701.1*a*

  retirement, 451

  rights, 422-23, 701.1*a*

  sabbatical leave, 446

  service record, 705.6, .8, 1604.10

  termination, 453.1*f*

  transfer, 516.5

  See also Clergy; Ordained Minister; Pastor

Full Membership Roll, 232.1

Full-time service, 408.1, 420.2, 424, 437

Funds, general church. *See* General church funds

G

Gambling, 73*G*

General Administration Fund, 917
budget, 906.1
delegates to World Methodist Council, 2401.2
disbursement, 906.2
notice of apportioned amount, 908
nonvoting delegates to General Conference, 648.3, 651, 2401.2
promotion, 1906.12

General agencies, 801-18, 821
absence from meetings, 810.9-.10
accountability, 802.2, .6, 803.1, .5-.6, 804, 821
administrative, 803.6
Advance administering, 1007.5*d*
Advance participating, 1007.5*a*
amenability, 802.1, 803.1, .5
annual report, 804
appeal/petition to Judicial Council, 59.4, 2609, 2615.2*c*
borrowing funds, 911.3
boycott guidelines, 802.5
budget, 15.9, 906.1*b*(7)
closed session, 821
committee to nominate additional members, 806, 1412.1
communication responsibility, 1901
coordination of nomination/election of, 805
distribution of materials, 1742
documentary records, 1811.2.-3
employment policies, 814-15, 905.4*d*, 907.7*b*, 911.1
evaluation of, 802.3, 1006.13
financial obligations, 2509
funds for Annual Conference projects, 818

General agencies, *cont'd:*
general secretaries, 803.7*a*, 813, 814.5, 905.3, .5, 1006.15, 1603.1, 1807, 1907.5
headquarters location, 907.2, 1006.25
Heritage Sunday theme, 275.1
honoraria for staff, 814.2
ineligibility for voting membership on, 810.3-.4, .6-.9, 1007.1*b*
information from, 802.3-.4, 817
Laity Sunday theme, 275.2
membership, 805-06, 810, 905.1, 1007.1, 1602.1, 1702, 1804.2, 1907.1, 2006, 2103, 2204, 2605
national conferences/convocations, 906.10, 907.8
nondiscrimination policies, 815
officers, 808, 905.3, 1603.1, 1706, 1806, 1907.3, 2005.1, 2105, 2205
organizational meetings, 807
organization, 803, 808-09, 905, 1702, 1907
pensions, 814.3
personnel policies, 814-15, 907.7, 911.1
policy statement, 610.1
power and authority, 811
prevention of duplicate programs, 911.2, 1006.10
printing of materials, 1741
program accountability, 802.2-.3, 803.5, 1006.13
program-related, 803.5
promotional periodical, 1906.15
property, 907.1-.3, 1112.2, 1203, 1502
qualification for general church funds, 911
record of advocacy role, 817
representation on Annual Conference agencies, 706.5, 810.5
review valid resolutions, 610.2*b*, 1006.20
Rural Life Sunday theme, 275.3
socially responsible investment policy, 816
special appeals, 911.4, 912.3, 1460, 1463, 1906.12
staff, 803.7, 814

General agencies, *cont'd:*
Staff Pension Plan, 814.4
vacancy on, 812. *See* Filling vacancy
on general agency
World Service Fund, 912

General Board, 15.8, 803.2
of Church and Society, 1101-16
of Discipleship, 1201-28
of Global Ministries, 1401-67
of Higher Education and Ministry,
1501-32
of Publication, 1701-44
For detailed listings *see* Church and
Society, General Board of; Discipleship, General Board of;
Global Ministries, General
Board of; Higher Education and
Ministry, General Board of;
Publication, General Board of

General church funds, 910-32
Advance, The, 914-15, 1007.5*a*
Black College Fund, 906.2*f*, 908,
910, 919
Episcopal Fund, 923-32. For de-
tailed listing *see* Episcopal Fund
General Administration Fund,
906.2*b*, 908, 910, 917
Human Relations Day Fund,
906.2*j*, 910, 916.1
Interdenominational Cooperation
Fund, 906.2*d*, 908, 910, 918,
2003.14
Ministerial Education Fund,
906.2*e*, 908, 910, 921
Missional Priority Fund, 906.2*g*,
910, 922
One Great Hour of Sharing Fund,
906.2*l*, 910, 915.1-.2, .5, 916.2
Peace with Justice Sunday Fund,
906.2*m*, 910, 916.5
policies, 911
Temporary General Aid Fund,
906.2*h*, 908, 910, 920
United Methodist Student Day
Fund, 906.2*k*, 910, 916.3
World Communion Fund, 906.2*i*,
910, 916.4
World Service Fund, 906.1*b*, .2*a*,
908, 912
World Service Special gifts, 913

General church funds, *cont'd:*
Youth Service Fund, 743.3*g-i*,
906.2*n*, 908, 910, 1310

General Commission, 15.13, 803.3
on Archives and History, 1801-12
on Christian Unity and Interreligious Concerns, 2001-06
on Communication, 1901-09
on Religion and Race, 2101-08
on Status and Role of Women,
2201-09
For detailed listings *see* Archives
and History, General Commission on; Christian Unity and
Interreligious Concerns, General Commission on; Communication, General Commission on;
Religion and Race, General
Commission on; Status and Role
of Women, General Commission
on the

General Conference, 12-20, 601-12
amendments to the Constitution,
62-64, *footnotes, pages 20-39*
business manager of, 907.16
Commission on the, 605, 907.16
composition, 12-14, 602
date of, 13
delegates, 12, 14, 37-39
certification/credentials, 602.5-
.6
election, 12.2-.3, 37-39, 443.4,
602.1*b*, .4, 653.4*a*, 660.3, .4*b*
formula for delegations, 12.3,
602.3, 653.4*a*, 660.3
ineligibility, 413.3, 419.3, 2605
minimum number, 602.3*d*
nonvoting, 648.3, 651, 2401.2
ratio of, 12.1, 22, 602.1*a*
special session, 13
effective date of legislation, 609,
638.22, 820. *See also* Date legislation effective
expenses of, 917
journal, 605-06, 611.1, For detailed listing *see* Journal, General
Conference
meetings, 13
membership, 12, 14, 37-39, 602.1-
.3

General Conference, *cont'd:*
numerical designation of, 824
permanent record of, 611
petitions to, 63-64, 608, 2301.3
place of, 13
Plan of Organization and Rules of Order, 606
power and authority, 15, 601
  Act of Covenanting, 650
  appeal/petition to Judicial Council, 59.1, 2615.2*a*, 2618
  authorization for real estate transactions of The United Methodist Publishing House, 1743
  boundaries
    Central Conference, 26, 41
    Jurisdictional Conference, 40, 42
    Provisional Central Conference, 642
  budget, 15.9, 906.1
  church union, 638.26
  concordat agreement, 653.3
  creation of agencies for special function, 801.2, 917
  determination of number
    Annual Conferences in Central Conference, 638.11
    bishops, 15.10, 29.2, 638.2
  election
    of Interjurisdictional Committee on Episcopacy, 612
    of Judicial Council, 58, 2601-02, 2603.1, .4
    of members of general agencies, 15.8, .14, 805.2*b*
    General Board of Pensions, 1602.1*a-b*
    General Commission on Archives and History, 1804.2
    General Council on Finance and Administration, 905.1
    secretary-designate, 604
    University Senate, 1517.2
  examination of Central Conference journals, 637.7
  granting of autonomy, 649.4, 652.4

General Conference, *cont'd:*
initiate/empower/join boycott, 247.19, 703.12, 745.5, 802.5
organizing conferences outside the U.S.A., 26, 636.1
providing episcopal supervision, 15.4-.5
Provisional Central Conference power, 641
purpose of churchwide offerings, 274
resolutions, 611.2
speaking for The United Methodist Church, 610
use of Methodist Corporation fund, 2511.3
presiding officers, 15.11, 515, 603
quorum, 607
Rules of Order, 606
secretary, 605. *See* Secretary of the General Conference
special session, 13
worship services during, 1214.12

General Council on Finance and Administration, 901-32. *See* Finance and Administration, General Council on

General Council on Ministries, 1001-07. *See* Council on Ministries, General

General Endowment Fund for Conference Claimants, 1605.2

General Episcopal Fund, 638.4-.5

General Military Roll, 218, 1213.9

General Minutes, 443.5*c*, 907.10, 1604.10, 2629.2

General Rules, *pages 74-77*

Genetic technology, 72*L*

Global Ministries, conference Board of, 638, 731
Advance special gifts, 727.2-.3, 915.5

Global Ministries, conference Board of, *cont'd:*
conference coordinator of Christian global concerns, 731.3
mortgage from local church, 2542.2
Native American Awareness Sunday offering, 274.6*b*
One Great Hour of Sharing, 915.5

Global Ministries, General Board of, 1401-67
accountability, 802.2, 803.5
administrative committee, 1407
amenability, 802.1, 803.5
authority, 1404-05
bylaws, 1404-05
Committee on Deaconess Service, 1419
consultative relationships, 637.6, 1403.1*l*, 1449.6, 1905
Crusade Scholarship Program, 1454-55
Deaconess Program Office, 1420
executive committees, 1408.2, 1409.3
financial support, 1411
funds for mission education, 1206.5
general secretary, 813-14, 1409.1*a*, 1412.7, 1517.2
headquarters, 907.2, 1007.25
Health and Welfare Ministries Department, 1439-47. *See* Health and Welfare Ministries Department, General Board of Global Ministries
incorporation, 1406
Joint Committee on Congregational Development, 1414.13
membership, 634.4*a*, 805-06, 1412
Missionary Conference, relationship to, 659-661, 1403.1*l*
Mission and Education Cultivation Department, 1448-52. *See* Mission and Education Cultivation Department, General Board of Global Ministries
Mission Personnel Resources Department, 1453-57. *See* Mission Personnel Resources Depart-

Global Ministries, General Board of, *cont'd:*
ment, General Board of Global Ministries
National Division, 1413-17. *See* National Division, General Board of Global Ministries
objectives, 1403
officers, 1408
ombudsperson, 1409.1*b*
organization, 802-10, 1403.1*b*, 1412
predecessor boards, divisions, departments, 1406.2, 1411
program-related agency, 803.5
purpose, 1401
representation
Committee on Family Life, 1220.2
Committee on Personnel Policies and Practices, 905.4*d*
National Youth Ministry Organization Steering Committee, 1307.1
University Senate, 1517.2
responsibilities, 1402
architectural standards, 1202.13
commissioning diaconal minister, 306.3*b*(4)
cooperation with Affiliated Autonomous Methodist Church, 648.6
determining need/boundaries of Mission, 664.1
ecumenical cooperation, 1403.2, 1404
Native American Awareness Sunday, 274.6
Native Americans ministries, 274.6*b*, 1403.1*m*
property, 907.3, 1403-04, 1411
Rural Life Sunday, 275.3
standards/guidelines for local church work areas, 261.6
support of Provisional Annual Conference, 656.2, 657.3
short-term volunteers-in-mission, 731.6, 1402.14, 1454.7, 1465.1*c*, .3
staff, 1403.1*f*, 1409-10
treasurer, 1409.3, 1412.7

Global Ministries, General Board of,
cont'd:
United Methodist Committee on
Relief Department, 1458-67. For
detailed listing *see* United Meth-
odist Committee on Relief De-
partment, General Board of
Global Ministries
vacancy, 812, 1408.2
Women's Division, 1421-29. *See*
Women's Division, General
Board of Global Ministries
World Division, 1430-38. *See*
World Division, General Board
of Global Ministries

Golden Cross Sunday, 273, 276.2,
731.4(11), (33), 1441, 1906.12

**Great Britain, The Methodist
Church of,** 12.3, 653.3

Grievance procedures, 453

Group ministry, 206.3

H

**Handicapping conditions, persons
with**
camping experiences for, 729.1*c-
d*
conference Committee on Ministry
to, 745
eligibility
diaconal ministry, 306.4
ordained ministry, 414.4
ministries for, 258-59, 262.2-.3,
729.1*d*
nondiscriminatory policy, 815
representation
conference agencies, 706.4
district Council on Ministries,
749.2
general agencies, 805.1*b*, .2*a*
jurisdictional agencies, 628
local church offices, 249.7,
250.4
rights of, 72*G*
training for persons in ministry to,
729.1

**Health and Welfare Ministries De-
partment, General Board of Global Ministries,** 1439-47
associate general secretary, 1444
as corporate successor, 1406.1
executive committee, 1444
financial support, 1445
Golden Cross promotion, 1441
limitation of responsibility, 1447
meetings, 1443
membership, 1412.3, 1446
purpose, 1439
quorum, 1443
responsibilities, 1440
treasurer, 1444
United Methodist Association of
Health and Welfare Ministries,
1442

**Health and welfare ministries, local
church,** 252.1*b*

Health and welfare representative,
250.1, 254, 262.2

Heritage Sunday, 273, 275.2

**Higher Education and Campus
Ministry, area/regional Commis-
sion/Committee on,** 732.4*d*(14)

**Higher Education and Campus
Ministry, conference Board of,**
633, 732

**Higher Education and Campus
Ministry, local church,** 252.1*a*,
260, 261.5

**Higher Education and Ministry,
General Board of,** 1501-32
accountability, 802.2, 803.5, 1503
amenability, 802.1, 803.5, 1503
consultative relationships, 1526.2,
1905
cooperation with other agencies,
1209.3-.4, 1210.1-.2, 1213.8,
1215.13, .15, 1511.3
Council of Presidents of the Black
Colleges, 1523
division of assets, 1203, 1502

Higher Education and Ministry, General Board of, *cont'd:*
Division of Chaplains and Related Ministries, 1510-12. *See* Chaplains and Related Ministries, Division of, General Board of Higher Education and Ministry
Division of Diaconal Ministry, 1524-26. *See* Diaconal Ministry, Division of, General Board of Higher Education and Ministry
Division of Higher Education, 1513-16. *See* Higher Education, Division of, General Board of Higher Education and Ministry
Division of Ordained Ministry, 1527-29. *See* Ordained Ministry, Division of, General Board of Higher Education and Ministry
financial support, 1509
general secretary, 813-14, 921.2*b*, 1517.2
headquarters, 907.2, 1007.25
incorporation, 1502
membership, 805-06, 1507
name, 1501
National Methodist Foundation for Christian Higher Education, 1522
Nominating Committee, 1513.3, 1528
objectives, 1505
Office of Interpretation, 1508.2
Office of Loans and Scholarships, 1508.2
officers, 808
organization, 802-10, 1507-08
program-related agency, 803.5
purpose, 1504
representation
Committee on Family Life, 1220.2
Committee on Personnel Policies and Practices, 905.4*d*
Curriculum Resources Committee, 1228.1*c*
National Youth Ministry Organization Steering Committee, 1307.1
responsibilities, 1505-06
campus ministries, 1504

Higher Education and Ministry, General Board of, *cont'd:*
Ethnic In-Service Training Program, 274.3, 916.4*b*
Ethnic Scholarship Program, 274.3, 916.4*b*
Native American scholarships, 274.6*c*
United Methodist Student Day, 274.4, 916.3, 1515.3*g*, 1906.12
schools of theology, 1530-32
University Senate, 1517-21. *See* University Senate
vacancy, 812, 1507
World Community Day offering, 274.3, 916.4*b*

Higher Education and Ministry, jurisdictional Board of, 633

Higher Education, Division of, General Board of Higher Education and Ministry, 1513-22
assistant general secretary
campus ministry, 1513.5
schools, colleges, and universities, 1513.5
associate general secretary, 1509.2, 1517.2-.3
Council of Presidents of the Black Colleges, 1523
financial support, 1509.2
membership, 805, 809, 1508.1, 1513.3
National Methodist Foundation for Christian Higher Education, 1522
nominating committee, 1513.3
objectives, 1513.4
organization, 1508.1, 1513.5
responsibilities, 1513-15
Black College Fund, 919
black colleges, 1514.4, 1516.3*d*, 1517.2, 1523.1
campus ministry, 1513.2, 1514.1*b*, .2, 1515.2, 1516.3
Crusade Scholarship program, 1515.3*f*
development of corporations, 1516.2*c*
educational institutions, 1513.2, 1514.1*b*, .2, .4, 1515, 1516.3

Higher Education, Division of, General Board of Higher Education and Ministry, *cont'd:*
fiscal matters, 1516.3
higher education, 1513.1, 1514.1a, 1515.3, 1516
United Methodist Student Day, 1515.3g, 1906.12
University Senate, 1515.1, 1516.2b, 1517.4, 1521.3. *See* University Senate
Wesley Foundations, 1513.2, 1515.2, 1516.3b-c

Hispanic, Asian, Native American Educational Ministries, 732.4d(4)

Historian
conference, 631.1, 738.3
local church, 247.5a, 250.1

Historical Convocation, 1810.3

Historical Society, 738.2, 1810.1-.2

Historical Statement, *pages 7-18*

Historic Examination, 425

Historic landmarks, 738.1, 1812.1, .3

Historic shrines, 738.1, 1812.2

Historic sites, 738.1, 1812.4

Home missionary, 254, 516.3, 734.5, 1414.8

Homosexuality, 71F, 402.2, *footnote, pages 210-13*, 906.12

Honorable location, 452.1, .2b, 453.1e, 455

Housing allowance, 269.2f(4), 907.4

Human Relations Day, 274.1, 906.1-.2, 916.1, 1906.12

Human rights, 72, 74A

Human sexuality, 71F

Hunger, 1459.5

Hymnal, 15.6
of The United Methodist Church: The Book of Hymns, 1214.3
The Evangelical United Brethren Church hymnal, 1214.3
promoting use of, 729.4b

I

Inclusiveness, 439.2c, 524.3
appraisal of, 735.3f
on conference agencies, 740.3
in employment of church staff, 815, 911.1
in life of the church, 254, 256.9, 502.3, 519 (3)
violation of, 2108.6

Institutions, United-Methodist affiliated, 306.3, 1516.2b, 1520.1, 2553. *See also* Church-related institutions

Insurance protection, 709.13, 907.14

Interdenominational agencies, 2401-04
American Bible Society, 2404
Commission on Pan-Methodist Cooperation, 2403
Consultation on Church Union, 2402.1
National Council of the Churches of Christ in the U.S.A., 2402.2
World Council of Churches, 2402.3
World Methodist Council, 2401

Interdenominational Cooperation Fund, 906.1, 908, 918, 1806.12, 2003.14

Interjurisdictional Committee on Episcopacy, 612

International Christian Youth Exchange, 1219.3

International Court of Justice, 75D

Interpretation, Office of, 1508.2

Interpreter, The, 2615.3, 2619.1

Investigation, Committee on, 453.1*d*, 638.17, 2623, 2625.1*b-c*

Investment policy, 709.5, 715.5, 816, 2512.3

Investments
Annual Conference Board of Trustees, 2512.3
General Board of Global Ministries, 1411
General Board of Higher Education and Ministry, 1506.10
General Board of Pensions, 1604.3-.4
General Council on Finance and Administration, 906.6

Involuntary retirement, 451.3, 509.3

Itinerant system, 437
in appointment-making, 530
clergy itinerancy, 112.4
Committee on Pastor-Parish Relations responsibility, 269.2*f*(1)
of general superintendency, 17
inability to perform duties in, 453.3*a*
open itinerancy, 269.2*f*(1), 530
racial/ethnic ordained ministers in, 740.3*e*
See also Traveling preacher

J

Joint Charge Conference, 246.10

Joint Church Conference, 248

Joint Committee on Congregational Development, 1414.14

Joint Committee on Diaconal and Ordained Ministry, jurisdictional, 633

Joint Committee on Disability, conference, 450, 744

Joint Distributing Committee, 1609

Joint Review Committee, 453

Journal, Annual Conference, 705.1-.5
contents, 705.3
appointments, 515.6, 705.3*e*
bishop's decision on question of law, 54
Disciplinary questions, 703.11, 705.3*d*, 1604.10
investment policy, 709.5
listings
clergy, 443.5*e*, 450
deaconesses/missionaries, 704.4, 734.5*b*
diaconal ministers, 313.1, .2*c*, 705.5, 734.3*g*
located ordained ministers, 452.1*b*
pension investments, 1608.7*a*
persons certified in professional careers, 734.4*e*
securities, 715.5
pastors' total compensation, 724-25
pension credit for appointees beyond the local church, 1606.4*h*
record of consecration of diaconal ministers, 515.6
reports, 709.3*f*
of conference treasurer, 715.4*b*
of Joint Distributing Committee, 1609.3*d*
salaries of appointees beyond the local church, 725
sources of annuity claim, clergy members, 443.5*b*
depository for, 1811.3*j*
distribution of, 705.1-.2
examination of, 705.1

Journal, Central Conference, 515.5, 637.7

Journal, General Conference
contents
concordat agreements, 653.3*b*
memoirs of bishops, 611.1

Journal, General Conference, *cont'd:*
plan of organization and Rules of Order, 606
depository for, 1811.3*b*

Journal, Jurisdictional Conference, 515.5, 627, 1811.3*j*

Journey of a Connectional People, 112

Judicial Council, 58-60, 1601-19
alternate member, 2602, 2604
appeal to, 2607-14
of bishop, 509.3, 622, 2613, 2625.2
on questions of law, 59.2-.3, 637.5, 2611-12, 2614, 2625.1*i*, .3, .5
authority, 59-60, 2616-18
to determine constitutionality of act, 59.1
of Central Conference, 2608
of General Conference, 2607
of Jurisdictional Conference, 2608
to determine legality of act, 59.4
of Central Conference agency, 2609-10
of General Conference agency, 2609-10
of Jurisdictional Conference agency, 2609-10
to review opinion/decision of jurisdictional Committee on Appeals, 2614
authorization, 58, 803.1
availability of decisions, 2614.4
declaratory decisions, 60, 2615-16, 2618
episcopal decisions, 54
expenses, 917.3
filing decisions with secretary of the General Conference, 2619
finality of decisions, 60, 2618
fixing time/place of bishop's appeal, 2625.2*b*
meetings, 2606
members, 58, 2601, 2604-05
notification of appeal, 2625.2*b*
organization, 59.6, 2606
petitions to, 2615.2

Judicial Council, *cont'd:*
preparation for declaratory decision, 2615.3
publication of decisions, 2619
quorum, 2606
vacancy, 58, 2603

Judicial Court, Central Conference, 29.6, 638.33

Jurisdictional agencies, 25.3, 628-35
appeal/petition to Judicial Council, 59.4, 2615.2*g*
Board of Higher Education and Ministry, 633
Commission on Archives and History, 631
Committee on Diaconal Ministry, 633
Committee on Entertainment, 24
Committee on Episcopacy, 52, 507, 509, 511, 612.2, 620.2, 623, 628
Committee on Ordained Ministry, 530.2, 633
Committee on United Methodist Men, 635, 1204.1
Council on Ministries, 629
Joint Committee on Diaconal and Ordained Ministry, 633
membership policy, 628, 2605
program agencies, 630
short-term Volunteer-in-Mission agency, 731.6
United Methodist Women, 634, 1428-29
Youth Ministry Organization Convocation, 632

Jurisdictional Conference, 21-25, 613-35
agencies, 628-35
amenability of bishop to, 622
appeal/petition to Judicial Council, 59.1, 2608-11, 2615.2*f*
assignment of bishops, 507, 623.3*b*
boundaries, 15.12, 40, 42
College of Bishops, 51
Committee on Appeals, 25.6, 2614
Committees to Nominate Additional Members, 806.1
Court of Appeals, 2624.1*h*, 2625.3-.4

Jurisdictional Conference, *cont'd:*
delegates, 22-23
election, 37-39, 443.4, 615, 625, 660.3, .4*b*
formula for delegations, 614, 660.3
ineligibility, 413.3, 419.3, 2605
minimum number, 614.3
ratio of, 12.1, 23
special session, 620.3
election
of bishop, 25.2, 49, 505-06, 622
of Committee on Investigation, 2623.2
of general agency members, 805.2-.3, 1007.1*a*, 1204.1, 1428, 1602.1*a*, 1702, 1907.1, 2006.1, 2103, 2204.1
episcopal areas, 505, 623.3*b*
examination Annual Conference journals, 626, 705.1
expenses, 619
journal, 627, 1811.3*j*
meetings, 24, 616
National Council of the Churches of Christ in the U.S.A., panel of names for, 2402.2*b*
Nominating Committee, 805.1*a*
nominations
for bishops, 506.1
for general agency members, 805.2*a*, .3*a*
place of, 617
plan of organization and rules of order, 618
powers and duties, 25, 624
presiding officers, 54, 515, 621
quorum, 618
secretary, 1702, 1811.3*j*
special session, 508, 620
time of, 24, 616
Youth Coordinator, 632
Youth Ministry Organization Convocation, 632, 743.3*f*, 1307.2*a*

Jurisdictional Historical Society, 631.2

Jurisdictional Racial/Ethnic Youth Caucuses, 1306.1*b*(6)

Jurisdictional United Methodist Women, 634

Jurisdictional Youth Ministry Organization Convocation, 632, 743.3*f*, 1307.2*a*

Justice, 74*F*, 75*D*

L

Laity Sunday (Day), 273, 275.2, 729.7*b*, 1218.5

Land use, 72*M*

Language used in conferences/services, *page 64,* 246.9

Larger parish, 206.3

Law, 74*E, G,* 75*D*

Laying on of hands, 435.3

Lay leader, conference, 702.8. For detailed listing *see* Conference lay leader

Lay leader, district, 730.3, 748

Lay leader, local church, 251
associate, 251.1
election of, 249.5
interpreter of apportionments/benevolences, 247.14, 251.1*c*
member
Administrative Board, 251.1*b*, 254
Administrative Council, 251.1*b*
Charge Conference, 251.1*b*
Committee on Finance, 251.1*b*, 269.4
Committee on Nominations and Personnel, 251.1*b*
Council on Ministries, 258
district Committee on the Laity, 251.1*b*
in multiple church charge, 251.1
report actions of Annual Conference, 251.1*c*
resources for, 1218.3
in small member church, 252.1*e*

Lay member, Annual Conference, 35, 251.2, 701.4

Lay member, Annual Conference,
cont'd:
election, 249.5, 251.2
interpreter of apportionments/be-
nevolences, 251, 247.14
member
Administrative Board, 254
Administrative Council, 252.1e
Committee on Finance, 269.4
Committee on Pastor-Parish Relations, 269.2
Council on Ministries, 258
report actions of Annual Conference, 251
resources for, 1218.3
seating of alternate, 701.3, .5
in small member church, 252.1e
vacancy, 701.3
voting rights, 36, 701.4

Lay member, local church
appeal, 2625.4
chargeable offenses, 2621.2, 2622
investigation, 2623.5
as local pastor, 406.1, .6-.7
suspension, 2623.5c
trial, 2624.4
withdrawal under complaints/
charges, 2624.4
See also Church membership

Lay missionary, 238, 701.2

Lay speaker, 277-79, 440.1, 729.7b.
See also Certified lay speaker

Leave
for bishop, 511
for diaconal minister, 313.1
listing of:
absence, 313.1, 448.1, 453.1e
disability, 313.1a, 450, 511.3
educational, 445.3
extended, 313.1d-e
maternity/paternity, 313.1b, 449
personal, 313.1d
renewal, 511.1, 525
sabbatical, 313.1c, 453.1e, 446,
511.2
study, 313.1c, 525
for ordained minister, 445-46,
448-50, 453.1e

Leave, *cont'd:*
as remedial action for ordained
minister facing complaints,
453.1e

**Legislative Assembly, National
Youth Ministry Organization,**
1306.2

Leisure, 73C

Lent, 274.2

Less than full-time service, 437.1,
441.2, 442.2, 660.6

Librarian, local church, 263.1e

Library, local church, 263.1d

License, local pastor's, 407, 1529.2

Living will/trust, 2533.4

Loans and Scholarships, Office of,
1508.2

Local church, 201-79
abandoned, 523.6a, d, 2548.2
Administrative Board, 244.2, 253-
56. *See* Administrative Board
Administrative Council, 244.1,
252. *See* Administrative Council
age-level/family councils, 265. *See*
Age-level councils
aid from mission organization,
1415.7i
appointee beyond local church
relationship to, 443.3
apportionments, 711
audit accounts of financial officers,
269.4c, 2510
audit of membership rolls, 233
basic organization, 244-46
Board of Trustees, 245, 249.5,
269.3, 2524-51. *See* Board of
Trustees, local church
bonding of treasurer(s), 269.4b
boycott, 247.19
building committee, 2543.3
building new facility, 2519.3, 2520,
2543

Local church, *cont'd:*

building sites/plans, 2519
building use, 2532.1
care of members, 228-31
Charge Conference, 11, 46-47, 246-50. *See* Charge Conference
Christian Education Sunday (Week), 261.2, 273, 276.1, 729.2c
Church Conference, 248
Church Local Conference, 2526
Church School/Sunday School, 263.1. *See* Church School/Sunday School
circuit, 205.2
class meetings, 229, 268
Commission on Stewardship, 261.9a, 1215.4
Committee on Communication, 269.5
Committee on Finance, 269.4. *See* Committee on Finance, local church
Committee on Health and Welfare, 262.2, 269.5
Committee on Memorial Gifts, 269.5
Committee on Nominations and Personnel, 245, 269.1. *See* Committee on Nominations and Personnel, local church
Committee on Pastor-Parish Relations (Staff-Parish Relations), 245, 269.2. *See* Committee on Pastor-Parish Relations, local church
Committee on Records and History, 247.5b, 269.5
congregational meeting, 44
connectional society, 203
consecration of, 2544
in cooperative parish, 205.2, 206
coordinator of communications, 250.1, 254, 258, 262.3, 749.4, 1906.9-.10
coordinators of age-level/family ministries, 250.1, 252.1d, 254, 258-259, 263, 265
Council on Ministries, 257-68. *See* Council on Ministries, local church
covenant of relationship, 2552.1a

Local church, *cont'd:*

dedication of, 2544
discontinued, 231, 523.8, 2548.1
financial obligations, 2509
financial secretary, 249.4
financial status, Annual Conference inquiry into, 703.8
foundation, 2534
Golden Cross Sunday, 273, 276.2, 731.4(11), (33)
grouping of members, 229, 268
health and welfare ministries representative, 250.1, 254, 262.2
Heritage Sunday, 273, 275.1
historian, 247.5a, 250.1
Human Relations Day, 274.1
incorporation, 270.8, 2528.1, 2529.3
Joint Charge Conference, 246.10
Laity Sunday (Day), 273, 275.2, 729.7b, 1218.5
lay leader, 251. *See* Lay leader, local church
lay member of Annual Conference, 35, 251.2, 701.4, *See* Lay member, Annual Conference
lay speaker, 247.12, 277-79
membership, 208-43, 648.1. *See* Church membership; Lay member, local church
membership secretary, 222, 230.1-.3, 235-36, 250.1, 254
merger of, 2545-46
ministerial support, 256.5. *See also* Clergy support
mortgaging, 2542.1-.2
in multiple church charge, 47, 205.2, 247.16, .18, 269.2c, e, 2527
new church construction, 2519.3, 2520, 2543
new church encouragement, 256.7
offerings, 269.4a
officers, 47, 247-49, 729.7d
One Great Hour of Sharing, 273, 274.2
organization and administration, 244-69
organizing new, 270, 703.10
parsonage, 256.3f, 269.2f(4), 2503.2-.4, 2507, 2527, 2543
pastoral charge, 205, 2526

Local church, *cont'd:*
Peace with Justice Sunday, 274.3
Personnel Committee, 269.2*f*(10)
program agencies, 263-66
program support personnel, 262
property, 2524-52. *See* Property, local church
proportional payment for clergy support, 737.4
purchase of new building, 2520, 2543
records, rolls, 232-35, 244, 247.15. *See* Records; Rolls
remodeling plans, 2520-21, 2543
responsibilities, 204, 1901
rights of congregation, 272
salaries, 247.13, 256.3*e*, 720
sale of property, 2539-41
shared facilities, 206.3*i*, 270, 2552
special Sundays, 273-76. *See* Special days (Sundays)
stewards, 250
task groups, 267
transfer of, 44, 271
in transitional community, 207
treasurer, 249.4, 254, 269.4, 715.2*a*, 737.4*b*
United Methodist Men, 264, 1222
United Methodist Youth Fellowship, 263.2
United Methodist Student Day, 274.4
United Methodist Women, 263.6, 1429
work areas, 252.1-.2, 260-61
World Communion Sunday, 274.3
worship services open to all, 2506
See also Church, the

Local pastor
amenability, 404.4-.5, 412.1
authority of, 406.1, .6, 409.2
from another denomination, 408.4
appeal of, 2625.3
appointment rights, 436
as associate member, 409.1, .5, 419
authority, 406
categories, 408
charges against, 2622, 2626.6
church membership, 406.6-.7
clergy member of Annual Conference, 412.1, 701.1

Local pastor, *cont'd:*
Comprehensive Protection Plan, 407.4
counseling elder's responsibility for, 406.4, 411
course of study, 405.2, 406.4, 408-09, 1529.2
as deacon, 434
discontinuance, 410.1, .4
educational requirements, 407.2, 408-09
eligibility on conference agencies, 408.5, 706.3
full-time, 408.1, .5, 409.3, 701.1
health certificate, 407.4
ineligible as lay member of Annual Conference, 251.2
investigation of, 2623.3
licensing, 406.1, 407.4, 410.4
nonstudent, 405.2, 408.1
part-time, 408.2
pension credit, 1606.2*a-c*, .4*f-g*, .5*a*, .7
as probationary member, 409.1
of promise, 409.5
psychological/psychiatric testing, 407.4
readmission, 410.4, 455.4, 456
requirements, 407-09
retirement, 410.5
salary, 408
as student, 408.3, 409.1-.3
supervision of, 406.4, 411, 520.4
surrender of credentials, 410.1
suspension of, 2623.3*c, e*
trial of, 410.3, 2624.3
voting rights, 701.1*d*, .2
withdrawal under charges, 410.2, 2626.2

Local pastor's license, 405.2, 407, 409.1

Location
administrative, 453.1*d*, .3
Annual Conference right to place on, 703.4
of associate member, 419.5
honorable, 452.1, 733.2*k*

Lord's Supper, Sacrament of the, *pages 64-65, 70*

Lord's Supper, Sacrament of the,
cont'd:
administering, 406, 439.1*b*, 443.3*a*
corporate worship celebration,
1214
World Communion Sunday,
274.3, 739.4*f*

M

Mandatory retirement
of bishop, 509.1
of diaconal minister, 313.2*b-c*
of ordained minister, 451.1

Marijuana, 72*I*

Marriage, 71*C*
local pastor's right to perform, 406
pastor's performance of, 439.5,
638.19

Maternity/paternity leave, 313.1*b*,
449

Medical experimentation, 72*K*

Member in full connection, 422-28.
See Full connection, member in

Membership secretary, 235
accurate records of membership
rolls, 232, 235-36
effort to locate member, 230.3
election of, 250.1
member Administrative Board,
254
member work area on evangelism,
235
preparatory membership roll responsibility, 222
report to Administrative Council/
Council on Ministries, 230.1
report to Charge Conference, 236

**Members removed by Charge Con-
ference action,** 230.4, 232.3

Men
nondiscriminatory policies, 815,
2203.8
representation

Men, *cont'd:*
Annual Conference, 35
Commission on Pan-Methodist
Cooperation, 2403
conference agencies, 706.4, 726,
730.3, .5, 735.1, 741.2
district agencies, 749.2
general agencies, 805, 905.1,
1007.1*a*, 1204.1, 1412.6,
2204.1-.2
jurisdictional agencies, 628
local church leadership, 249.7,
250.4, 254, 258, 265.3
National Division executive
committee, 1416
United Methodist Men, 264, 1222.
See United Methodist Men

Merger of local churches, 1606,
2545-46

Methodist Corporation, 2511

Methodist, use of as trademark, 2502

Metropolitan Commission, 731.5*i*,
1415.7*j*

Migrant workers, 73*F*

Military personnel families, 218,
1505.11

Military Service, 74*G*

Minerals, use of, 70*A*

Minimum salary, 722.3, .6
for associate member, 418.5
full-time pastor's right to, 441.1
of part-time local pastor, 408.2
for retired ordained minister
under appointment, 451.6
Temporary General Aid Fund,
920
waiver of claim to, 660.4*d*
See also Clergy support; Equitable
Salary Fund; Salary

Ministerial Education Fund, 921
Annual Conference share, 921.1
budget, 906.1

Ministerial Education Fund, *cont'd:*
diaconal minister's use of, 734.3*w*
disbursement, 906.2
distribution, 921.1
Divisions of Diaconal and Ordained Ministry use of, 1509.1
notice of apportioned amount, 908
priority status of, 921.3, 1530.2
promotion of, 269.2*f*(7), 733.2*s*, 1505.17, 1906.12
support of schools of theology, 1530.1-.2

Ministerial Pension Plan, 509.2, 1604.12, 1606.2*c*, .18, .20-.21

Ministry
of all Christians, 101-13
diaconal, 108-09
general, 105-07
nature of, 103-04
ordained, 108, 110
representative, 108-10
of the Church, 101-13
of the laity, 1217-22
See also Diaconal ministry; Ordained ministry

Ministry Sunday, 733.2*s*, 734.3*b*

Minority Group Self-Determination Fund, 2108.7

Mission, 663-64
administration of, 663
boundaries, 663.1
establishment of, 663
examination of local pastor/traveling preacher, 663.5
General Board of Global Ministries relationship, 663, 664.1, .3
judicial administration, 2626.4
local church, 270.1
meeting, 663.4
membership, 664.2, .4
National Division relationship, 664.7
presiding officer, 664.3-.4
as Provisional Annual Conference, 656
purpose, 663

Mission, *cont'd:*
representatives to Central Conference, 637.1
superintendent, 664.3-.4
traveling preacher, 663.5-.6, 703.6
World Division relationship, 664.7

Missional involvement, 103
Children's Fund for Christian Mission, 263.1*g*, 1210.3*e*
church extension, 731.5*e*, 1215.14, 1414.13, 1415.7*a*
in church school, 1210.3
connectional principle, 112.3
Mission Education and Cultivation Department, 1448-52. *See* Mission Education and Cultivation Department, General Board of Global Ministries
Mission Personnel Resources Department, 1453-57. *See* Mission Personnel Resources Department, General Board of Global Ministries
National Division, 1414-15. *See* National Division, General Board of Global Ministries
resources for, 1215.14
rural area development, 731.5*f*, *h*, 1414.5
short-term volunteers-in-mission, 731.6, 1402.14, 1454.7
World Division, 1430-31. *See* World Division, General Board of Global Ministries
See also Church, the

Missional priority, 1006.1, .4, .17

Missional Priority Fund, 906.2, 922, 1906.12

Missionary
affiliate conference member, 419.4, 443.4, 660.4*b*, 701.1, 1431.5*a*
assignment of, 663.6, 1431.5
commissioning of, 515.5
lay missionary, 701.2
listing in Annual Conference journal, 705.4

Missionary, *cont'd:*
recruitment/enlistment of, 1454.4-.5
seating, Annual Conference, 701.2

Missionary Conference, 12, 659-62
Advance projects, 660.2
affiliate member, 660.4*b*
as Annual Conference, 12, 602.1*a*
appointment to, 660.4, .6
budget, 660.2
building project, 660.2
change of status, 661
conference superintendent/district superintendent, 660.1
delegates
Central Conference, 27, 37-39, 637.1
General, 12-13, 22, 37-39, 443.4, 602.1*a*, .3-.4, 660.3, .4*b*
Jurisdictional Conference, 22-23, 37-39, 443.4, 614-15, 620.3, 625, 660.3, .4*b*
episcopal supervision, 660.1
judicial administration, 2626.4
membership, 660.4-.5
National Division relationship, 1414.11
nominations to general agencies, 805.1
organization, 660
pension responsibility, 1606.15
as Provisional Annual Conference, 656
representation on General Council on Ministries, 1007.1
rights, 662
waiver of minimum salary claim, 660.4*d*

Mission Education and Cultivation Department, General Board of Global Ministries, 1448-52
Advance, participating agency in, 1007.5*a*
Advance special gifts cultivation, 1449.4, 1450
authority, 1450
bylaws, 1450, 1452
cooperation with Curriculum Resources Committee, 1449.7

Mission Education and Cultivation Department, General Board of Global Ministries, *cont'd:*
cooperation with Health and Welfare Ministries Department, 1441.5
as corporate successor, 1406.1
Crusade Scholarship promotion, 1455.3
executive committee, 1451
financial support, 1450
membership, 1412.3, 1424, 1452
purpose, 1448
responsibilities, 1449
United Methodist Committee on Relief Department relationship, 1449.4, 1450, 1460

Mission Personnel Resources Department, General Board of Global Ministries, 1453-57
authority, 1455
bylaws, 1455.1
Committee on Deaconess Service, 1419
as corporate successor, 1406.1
Crusade Scholarship administration and promotion, 1454.1-.2, .9, 1455.3
deaconess' relationship to, 1418
executive committee, 1456
membership, 1412.3, 1457
purpose, 1453
responsibilities, 1454
short-term volunteers-in-mission, 731.6, 1402.14, 1454.7, 1465.1*c*
United Methodist Committee on Relief Department relationship, 1449.4, 1450, 1460, 1465.1*c*

Missions, local church work area on, 252.1*b*, 260, 261.6, 264

Mission structures, 1415.7*a*

Mission traveling preacher, 663.5-.6

Monopolies, 73*C*

Moving expenses, 710.1*f*

Multiple-charge parish, 206.3

Multiple-church charge, 205.2
Board of Trustees, 2527.1
Charge Conference, 247.18
chargewide organization, 247.16-
.18
Church Local Conference, 2526
Committee on Pastor-Parish Relations, 247.17, 269.2*c, e*
election of officers, 47
lay leaders, 251.1*e*
parsonage, 2527.4
pastoral advisory committee,
269.2*c*
property, 2526-27

Music personnel, 254, 261.10

N

Name, church, outside U.S.A., 823

**National Association of Annual
Conference Lay Leaders,** 1218.7

**National Association of Commis-
sions on Equitable Salaries,**
907.14

**National Association of Conference
Council Directors,** 1006.24

**National Association of Conference
Presidents of United Methodist
Men,** 1222.1*b*

**National Association of Health and
Welfare Ministries,** 1442

**National Association of Schools and
Colleges of The United Methodist
Church,** 1517.2

**National Association of Steward-
ship Leaders,** 1215.11

**National Association of United
Methodist Foundations,** 1215.11

**National Council of the Churches of
Christ in the U.S.A.,** 2402.2
Commission on Communication,
1906.4

**National Council of the Churches of
Christ in the U.S.A.,** *cont'd:*
Commission on Family Ministries
and Human Sexuality, 1220.1*e*
local church interpretation of,
261.1
One Great Hour of Sharing, 274.2,
916.2*b*

**National Division, General Board of
Global Ministries,** 1413-17
Advance administering agency,
1007.5*d*
Advance, participating agency,
1007.5*a*
Appalachian Development Committee, 1414.1
authority, 1415
church and community workers,
254, 1414.8, .13
Committee on Deaconess Service,
1419
Community Developers Program,
274.1*a*
cooperation with Health and Welfare Ministries Department,
1415.5
as corporate successor, 1406.1
Deaconess Program Office,
1418.3*a*, 1420
deaconess' relationship to, 1418
executive committee, 1416
fund administration, 1415.1
Joint Committee on Congregational Development, 1414.1
membership, 1417, 1424
Mission administration, 663.6-.7
organization, 1415
pensions, 1606.15
property, 1415.2
purpose, 1413
responsibilities, 1414
United Methodist Development
Fund, 1414.10
United Methodist Voluntary Services Program, 274.1*b*

**National Methodist Foundation for
Christian Higher Education,** 1522

**National Youth Ministry Organiza-
tion,** 1301-11

784

National Youth Ministry Organization, *cont'd:*
accountability, 1303
Convocation, 1304.1, 1305
 expenses, 1305.4
 meetings, 1305.3
 objectives and responsibilities, 1305.1
 participants, 1305.2
funding, 1309
Legislative Assembly, 1304.2, 1306
 expenses, 1306.3
 nonvoting members, 1305.2*b*
 voting members, 1305.2*a*
purpose, 1302
staff, 1308
Steering Committee, 1304.3, 1307
 election, 632, 1307.2
 membership, 1307.1
 Project Review Committee, 1311
 responsibilities, 1307.4
 term, 1307.3
Youth Service Fund, 1310

Native American Awareness Sunday, 274.6

Native Americans, ministry to, 274.6*b*, 1403.1*m*

New local church
certificate of organization, 703.10
Constituting Church Conference, 270.5, .7
construction of, 2520, 2543
encouragement of, 256.7
incorporation, 270
membership, 270
organization, 270
recognition, 703.10

Nominating Committee
district, 2518
General Board of Higher Education and Ministry, 1528
jurisdictional, 805.1

Nominations and Personnel, local church Committee on, 269.1. For detailed listing *see* Committee on Nominations and Personnel, local church

Nominations, conference Committee on, 726.7*b*(7)

Nominations
Annual Conference agencies, 453.1*c*, 733.1*a-b*, 734.1*b*, 2623.3*a*
bishop, 506.1
Central Conference agencies, 2623.2*a*, 2625.3*a*
district agencies, 2517.2, 2518
Judicial Council, 2601
jurisdictional agencies, 2623.2*a*, 2625.3*a*
general agencies, 805, 905.1, 1007.1*a*(7), 1428, 1602.1*a*, 1702, 1804.2
local church leadership, 257, 269.1
National Council of the Churches of Christ in the U.S.A. Governing Board, 2402.2*b*
Religion in American Life Board of Directors, 1909
secretary-designate of General Conference, 604
University Senate, 1517.2
World Council of Churches Assembly, 2402.3*b*
World Methodist Council, 2401.1

Nondiscrimination, 703.1, 815, 907.7*a*, 911.1

Nuclear weapons, 75*C*

Nurture, local church work area on, 252.1*a*

O

Offering, handling of, 269.4*a*

Older adults
Adult/Single Adult/Older Adult Council, 265.3
age of, 247.6, 249.7, 258, 741.2, 1907
coordinator of ministries to, 258, 259
ministries to, 263.5
representation
 conference agencies, 706.4, 735.1, 740.2, 741.2

Older adults, *cont'd:*
  district agencies, 749.2
  general agencies, 805.1*b*, .2*a*,
    1907
  local church officers and organi-
    zations, 247.6, 249.7, 250.4,
    258

One Great Hour of Sharing, 273,
  274.2
  administration, 916
  budget, 906.1
  disbursement, 906.2
  promotion, 915, 1906.12
  treasurer of, 915.2

Open itinerancy, 269.2*f*(1), 530

Ordained minister, 402
  amenability, 412.1
  appointment of, 426, 436-43,
    450.3
  authority, 217, 406, 439.1*b*, 443.3*a*
  change of relationship, 437.2*d*
  complaint against, 453.1*b, d*
  confidentiality, maintenance of,
    440.4
  continuing education, 1529.7
  course of study for, 1529.2
  as deacon, 434.3, 515.4
  as elder, 429-32, 433.1, 435.3,
    515.5
  evaluation of, 704.6, 773.2*o*
  financial support, 441, 733.2*n*
  grievance, 453
  leave of absence, 448
  location of, 452.1*b*, 453.1*e*
  maternity/paternity leave, 449
  moral/social responsibility, *footnote,*
    pages 210-13
  pension, 1606. *See* Pensions, con-
    ference Board of
  racial/ethnic, 740.3
  relation to ministry of all Chris-
    tians, 401-02
  retirement, 451
  return to pastoral ministry, 457.2*d*
  right to trial, 18
  sabbatical leave, 446
  surrender of office, 452.3
  transfer of, 427
  trial of, 18, 638.17

Ordained minister, *cont'd:*
  use of tobacco/beverage alcohol,
    footnote, page 210
  See also Associate member; Clergy;
    Full connection, member in;
    Local pastor; Ordination; Pastor

Ordained ministry, 108, 110, 401-57
  admission/continuance in confer-
    ence membership, 412-28
  appointments to various minis-
    tries, 436-43
  candidacy for, 404-05
  changes of conference relation-
    ship, 447-51
  entrance procedures into, 403-411
  evaluation/continuing education,
    444-46
  ordination, 429-35. *See* Ordination
  readmission to conference mem-
    bership, 454-57
  relation to ministry of all Chris-
    tians, 401-02
  review of conference membership,
    452-53
  standards for, 430
  See also Associate member; Clergy;
    Full connection, member in;
    Local pastor; Pastor

**Ordained Ministry, conference
  Board of,** 733
  annual meeting with appointees
    beyond local church, 443.2*b*
  clergy supply and demand report,
    530.2
  conference Board of Diaconal
    Ministry cooperation, 733.2*r*,
    734.2, .3*w*
  Division of Ordained Ministry co-
    operation, 426.2*c*, 733.2*a, d,*
    1527.1, 1529.2-.3
  duties, 733.2
    approval
      of less than full-time service,
        437.2
      of sabbatical leave, 446
    classifying local pastors, 408
    evaluation criteria, 269.2*f*(3),
      444
    examination of candidates,
      414.7-.8, 733.2*g*

Ordained Ministry, conference Board of, *cont'd:*

Ministerial Education Fund administration, 921.1

pre-retirement counseling, 453.4

recommendations

administrative location, 455.1*d-e*, .3

appointment of minister of another denomination, 426.2

candidates, *footnote, page 212,* 414, 416

changes of conference relationship, 418, 447-51, 733.2*k*

conference membership, 414, 416, 420, 423-24

extension of time limit for completion of studies, 409.3, 417

extension ministries, 443.1*d*, 733.2*g*, 1511.1

local pastor from another denomination, 408.4

readmission/reinstatement, 410.4, 454

recognition of orders, 427.3

response to complaints, 453.1*d*

training Committees on Pastor-Parish Relations Committees, 444, 733.2*n*

financial support, 733.1*a*

Joint Review Committee relationship, 453.1*b-c*

lay observers, 733.1

meetings, 733.2*c, e*

membership, 733.2*a-b*

officers, 733.1*c*, .3

records, 410.1, 705.8, 733.3

registrar, 404.2, 733.3

represented on Joint Committee on Disability, 744

transfers, 427.2, 515.5, 733.2*m*

vacancy, 733.1*b*

Ordained Ministry, district Committee on, *footnote, page 212,* 752

annual approval of local pastors, 406.1, 407, 410.4, 752.8-.9

Ordained Ministry, district Committee on, *cont'd:*

candidacy process role, 404-05, 747.3-.6

Conference Board of Ordained Ministry cooperation, 752.10

counseling elder reports, 411

district superintendent's relation to, 521.2

membership, 752.1

officers, 752.2

readmission role, 454-57

recommendation of probationary member, 414.3

records, 752.7

Ordained Ministry, Division of, General Board of Higher Education and Ministry, 1527-29

areas of concern, 1527.2, 1528

associate general secretary, 1509.2, 1517.2

financial support, 1509

membership, 805, 809, 1508.1, 1528

responsibilities, 1527.1, .3, 1529

advanced course of study, 416.2*c*, 424, 1529.2

course of study for ordained ministry, 405.2, 733.2*f*, 1529.2

course of study schools, 408.1*d*, .2, 1529.2

credit for course of study, 417

special course of study, 424

studies for local pastor's license, 407.2

use of Ministerial Education Fund, 921.2, 1530.2

schools of theology, 1530-32

Ordained Ministry, jurisdictional Committee on, 530.2, .6, 633, 921.2*a*

Order of St. Luke, 1214.14

Ordination, *footnote, pages 210-13,* 429-35

act of, 432, 434.3, 435.3, 515.4-.5

apostolic ministry, 429

Central Conference's right to change provisions, 638.10

Ordination, *cont'd:*
as deacon, 433.2, 434
as elder, 433.1, 435
laying on of hands, 435.3
meaning of, 432
Missionary Conference's right to change provisions, 662
participation of laity, 435.3
purpose, 430
qualifications, 431
recognition of orders, 426.2-.3, 427.3

Our Doctrinal Heritage, 66

Our Doctrinal History, 67

Our Doctrinal Standards and General Rules, 68

Our Theological Task, 69, 306.5*f*, 414.8

Outreach, local church work area on, 252.1*b*

P

Packaging, truth in, 73*D*

Pan-Methodist Cooperation, Commission on, 2403, 2547.2

Parenting, 71*A*, 449

Parish and Community Development, conference Committee on, 206.2, 731.5, 1414.12

Parish development, 206.2

Parsonage
Administrative Board responsibility, 256.3*f*
annual review of, 269.2*f*(4)
building, 2543
consecration of, 2544
dedication of, 2544
deeds and conveyances, 2503.2-.4, 2507
district, 2517, 2522
in multiple-church charge, 2527.4
title to, 2527.1

Pastor, 438
accountability, *footnote, page 213*
as administrative officer, 254, 256, 439.3
appointment-making process, 269.2*f*(8), 438, 531-33
authority
administer Sacraments, 218, 406, 439.1*b*, 443.3*a*
call special meeting of Administrative Board, 253.2
decide on use of church property, 2534
perform marriages, 437.5, 439.1*g*
suspend member, 2623.5*c*
campus, 217
in charge, 205.1, 256, 2623.5*a*
Committee on Pastor-Parish Relations, 269.2
co-pastor, 205.1
as counseling elder, 411
evaluation of, 269.2*f*(3), 423.2*c*, 444.1
as ex officio member
all church agencies, 254
Committee on Finance, 269.4
United Methodist Women/executive committee, 263.6
work area commissions, 266
financial support, 247.13, 441, 737.4*f*
moral standards, *footnote, pages 210-13*
moving expenses, 710.1*f*
parsonage, 256.3*f*, 269.2*f*(4), 2527.4, 2543
pension default, 737.4
publication of compensation, 724
responsibilities and duties, 439
care of members, 220-23, 227-30, 236-37, 239-43
for children, 221-25
Committee on Investigation of lay member, 2623.5*a*
communication, 1901
confidentiality, 440.4
confirmation, 216, 225, 406.1
continuing education, 445, 520.5, 523.3
diaconal ministry candidate, 304.4

Pastor, *cont'd:*
  instruction in church member-
    ship, 216.1, 439.1*f*
  lay speaker, 278.1*a*, 279.1*c*
  notice of church member's
    move, 237
  property matters, 2536, 2539.3,
    2540.3, 2543.1, .7
  report of gifts/bequests, 2512.5
  report to Charge Conference,
    233, 236, 242, 247.14-.15,
    439.3*c*, 445.5
  teach youth, 226
  transfer membership, 237, 239-
    43
 restrictions, 440
 rights, 441
 sabbatical leave, 446
 on staff, 438
 as supervising pastor, 404.2, 733.3
 See also Clergy; Associate member;
   Elder; Local pastor; Ordained
   Minister; Probationary member

Pastoral Advisory Committee,
269.2*c*

Pastoral charge, 205.1
 appointment to, 438
 as circuit or cooperative parish,
   205.2
 multiple-church charge, 247.16-
   .18
 realignment of, 523.9

**Pastor-Parish Relations, Committee
on,** 245, 269.2, *See* Committee on
Pastor-Parish Relations, local
church

Peace, war and, 75*C*

Peace with Justice Sunday, 273,
274.5

Pension, 1606
 actuarially reduced, 451.2*b*,
   1606.4*i*
 administration of funds, 20,
   1604.2, 1605
 for agency service, 1604.15
 for associate member, 419.5

Pension, *cont'd:*
 for bishops, 509, 924, 930-32,
   1606.2*c*
 changes in benefits, 1604.1
 for clergy member, 443.5*b*, 451.2
 Comprehensive Protection Plan,
   407.4, 450, 931, 1604.12, 1606
 contribution base for, 1606.18
 for deaconess, 1418.8
 for diaconal minister, 315.1, 734.3*t*
 for general agency staff, 814.3
 Joint Distributing Committee,
   1609
 for lay employees, local church,
   269.2*f*(9)
 in merged conferences, 1606.9,
   1609.3*d*
 Ministerial Pension Plan, 509.2,
   1604.12, 1606
 for past service, 1606
 Temporary General Aid Fund,
   920

Pension, conference Board of,
426.1, 737, 1606-09
 accumulation of funds, 1607.4
 audit, 1608.7*b*
 authorization, 737.1
 disbursement of funds, 1606.12*b-c*,
   1607.3
 Distributing Committee, 1609
 executive committee, 737.3
 financing pension/benefit programs, 1607
 investment policies, 1608.1-.2, .4,
   .7*a*
 Joint Committee on Disability, 450,
   744
 membership, 737.2
 officers, 737.3
 organization, 737.3
 powers, duties, and responsibilities, 1606
   bonding, 1609.9*b*
   depositories, 1608.9
   enrollment, 426.1, 1606.20
   journal pension listings,
     1604.10, 1606.4*h*
   pension information and census
     data, 1604.10
   permanent record of propor-
     tional payment defaults, 737.4

Pension, conference Board of,
cont'd:
  pre-retirement counseling,
    451.4
  recommendation for disability
    leave, 450.1-.2, 1606.3*a*
  reports, 737.5
  special meetings, 737.7
  vacancy, 737.2

Pensions, General Board of, 1601-
05
  administrative agency, 803.6
  amenability, 802.1
  authopizations, 1604
  bishops' pensions, 930-31
  Boards of Directors, corporations,
    1602.1*f*, .2
  Chartered Fund, 20, 1605.1
  Committee on Rules and Regula-
    tions, 1603.3
  disability benefit payments, 450.1
  discontinuance of payments, 451.7
  equitable plan Publishing House
    net income distribution, 20, 657,
    1604.9, 1715-16
  executive committee, 1603.2
  General Endowment Fund for
    Conference Claimants, 1605.2
  general secretary, 1602.1*c*, 1603.1,
    1609.2, .3*d*
  headquarters, 1601
  incorporation, 1601.1
  Joint Distributing Committee,
    1609
  location of offices, 1601.3
  maintenance of service records,
    516.5, 1604.10
  meetings, 1602.2
  membership, 805-06, 1602.1
  name, 1601.1
  officers, 1603.1
  pensions for prior service, 1606.15
  permanent funds, 1605
  predecessor boards, corporations,
    1601.1, 1602.1*f*, .2
  quorum, 1602.3
  Temporary General Aid Fund,
    920
  vacancy, 1602.1*e*

Pension Support Fund, 1606.19

Pentecost, 274.5

Pentecost Sunday, 739.4*f*

**Permanent Endowment Fund Com-
mittee, local church,** 2533

Personal leave, 313.1*d*

Personnel Committee, local church,
269.2*f*(10)

Pesticides, 70*A*

Petitions
  General Conference, 608
  Judicial Council, 2615

**Plan of Organization and Rules of
Order,** 606

Plants, protection of, 70*A*

**Policy on socially responsible in-
vestments,** 816

Population, 72*I*

Poverty, 73*E*

Prayer in public schools, 74*D*

Preparatory member, 216.4, 222-24

Preparatory Membership Roll,
216.4, 222-24, 232.2

Pre-retirement counseling, 451.4

Presiding elder, 1606.3*a*

Probationary member, *footnote, pages
210-13,* 413
  admission, 413-16
  amenability, 412.1, 413.4
  annual review, 423
  appointment of, 413.5
  autobiographical statement, 414.5
  continuance as, 417
  counseling elder, 411
  course of study, 415, 417, 1529.2
  as deacon, 413.1, 433.2, 434

Probationary member, *cont'd:*
disability leave, 450
discontinuance, 417 (5), 418
educational requirements, 415
eligibility, 413
examination of, 424
grievance procedures, 453
health certification, 414.4
leave of absence, 448
maternity/paternity leave, 449
ordination eligibility, 413.1, 433.2, 434
pension, 1606.3*a*
psychiatric/psychological testing, 414.4
qualifications for election, 414
rights, 413
service on conference agencies, 413.3
special conditions for becoming, 416
supervision of, 411, 417, 520.4
theological education discontinuance, 417 (5)
voting rights, 413.2, 701.1*b*

Probe staff, 206.3

Program journal, 1906.15

Program-related general agencies, 805.5

Program year, 820.1

Project Review Committee, 743.3*i*, 1311

Property, *page 73*, 73A, 2501-53
Annual Conference, 2512-16. *See* Property, conference
compliance with law, 2506-09
damaged by disaster, 1464
deeds and conveyances, 2507
district, 2517-23. *See* Property, district
Division of Higher Education responsibilities, 1513.4*g*, 1516.3*c*
exceptions to requirements, 2551
general agency, 907.1-.3, 1112.2, 1203, 1502

Property, *cont'd:*
General Board of Church and Society right to hold, 1112.2
General Board of Global Ministries to administer, 1403.1*h*, 1404, 1411.1
General Board of Higher Education and Ministry responsibilities, 1505.18
General Council on Finance and Administration responsibilities, 907.1-.3
instituting/defending civil action, 2508
local church, 2524-52. For detailed listing *see* Property, local church
Methodist Corporation, 2511
National Division to administer, 1415.2
oil, gas and mineral leases, 2505
titles in trust, 6, 272, 2501-05, 2517.2, 2541
United Methodist Publishing House, 1719, 1743-44
Women's Division, 1423.1

Property, conference, 2512-16
Board of Trustees, 2512, 2514, 2548.2
camps, conference grounds, retreat centers, 2516
damaged by disaster, 1464
episcopal residence, 736.3-.5, 927, 2514
gifts, 2512.3
sale, transfer, lease or mortgage, 2515
titles in trust, 6, 272, 2501-05

Property, district, 2517-23
Board of Church Location and Building, 2518. *See* Church Location and Building, district Board of
Board of Trustees, 2517.2
damaged by disaster, 1464
district superintendent's duties, 523, 2536, 2538-41, 2543.1, 2547-48, 2552.2
District Union, 747.4
parsonage, 2517, 2522

Property, district, *cont'd:*
  sale, transfer, lease or mortgage, 2523
  titles in trust, 6, 272, 2501-05, 2517.2

Property, local church, 2524-52
  abandoned, 2548.2
  Board of Trustees, 245, 269.3, 2524-27, 2529. *See* Board of Trustees, local church
  building new facility, 2519.3, 2520, 2543
  building site/plans, 2519
  Charge Conference authority, 2528, 2532
  Church Local Conference authority, 2526
  consecration of building, 2544
  damaged by disaster, 1464
  dedication of building, 2544
  deeding, 2547
  disposition of buildings, 2541, 2548
  gifts, 2512.3, .5
  incorporated, 2537, 2540
  investigation before sale, 2539.3
  merger, 2545-46
  mortgaging for budget expense, 2542
  parsonage, 256.3*f*, 269.2*f*(4), 2527
  pastor's reporting duties, 2512.5
  planning/financing requirements, 2543
  purchase of, 2536, 2538, 2543
  remodeling, 2520-22, 2543
  restrictions on proceeds of mortgage/sale, 2542
  sale of, 2539-40
  shared facilities, 206.3*i*, 270, 2552
  titles in trust, 6, 272, 2501-05, 2535, 2537, 2541
  unincorporated, 2536
  use for other than religious purposes, 2534

Provisional Annual Conference, 9-10, 655-58
  Board of Global Ministries, 658
  delegates to General/Central/Jurisdictional Conferences, 14, 38-39, 637.1, 657.4

Provisional Annual Conference, *cont'd:*
  Distributing Committee, 1609
  financial support, 656.2, 657.3
  judicial administration, 2626.4
  meetings, 657.2
  minimum membership, 656.1
  Mission as, 656
  Missionary Conference as, 656
  National Division relationship, 1414.11
  organization, 657
  pension responsibility, 1606.15
  presiding officer, 657.2
  qualifications for lay members, 643
  superintendent, 657.1

Provisional Central Conference, 639-46
  authorization, 636.1
  becoming Central Conference, 637.8
  boundaries, 642
  composition, 639
  organization, 640
  powers, 641-42
  restriction on electing bishop, 641

Psychological/psychiatric testing, 407.4, 414.4, 419

Publication, General Board of, 1701-44
  accountability, 802.6, 803.1, 1704, 1712, 1723
  administrative agency, 803.6
  amenability, 802.1, 803.1
  authority
    decline publication, 1738
    remove officers/book editor, 1727, 1731
  book editor/editorial director of general publishing, 1728-31
  conference Committee on Publishing House Liaison, 726.5*e*
  corporation officers, 1721-27
  corporations, 1709-11, 1717-20
  curriculum resources, 1226.2*b*, 1736
  editor of Church School Publications, 1227.2, 1732

Publication, General Board of, *cont'd:*

examination of Publishing House affairs, 1712, 1714-15, 1718

executive committee, 1706-07, 1724

executive officer (president, publisher), 905.1, 1007.1a(8), 1702, 1714, 1717, 1722, 1724-27, 1734, 1738

Illinois corporation, 1718.3, 1719

meetings, 1703

membership, 805, 1702, 1705, 1739

name, 1701

officers, 1705-06

organization, 1702, 1706

predecessor boards, corporations, 1708, 1717, 1719

property, 907.3, 1718-19, 1743-44

Quarterly Review, 1729

quorum, 1703

represented on General Council on Ministries, 1007.1a(8)

salaries, 1723, 1730, 1735

supervision of publishing/printing, 1701

as The United Methodist Publishing House, 1701, 1709-44, For detailed listing *see* United Methodist Publishing House

vacancy, 1702

Public education, 74D

Public relations, 726.10i, 1905, 1906.2, .6

Publishing House Liaison, conference Committee on, 726.5e

Q

Quarterly Review, 1729

Questions, Wesley's historic, 403, 425

R

Racial/ethnic concerns

career development for ordained ministry, 1527.2

Racial/ethnic concerns, *cont'd:*

conference Commission on Religion and Race responsibilities, 740.3

conference Committee on Ethnic Local Church Concerns, 726.5

continuing education, 1529.7

equal employment opportunity, 740.3n, 815, 911.1

ethnic clergy, 530.2, 752.1

Ethnic In-Service Training Program, 274.3, 916.4b

Ethnic Scholarship Program, 274.3, 916.4b

General Board of Higher Education and Ministry responsibilities, 1505.7, .26

General Commission on Religion and Race responsibilities, 2102, 2108

Hispanic, Asian, Native American Educational Ministries, 732.4d(4)

inclusiveness, 4, 439.2c, 735.3f, 740.3n, 815, 911.1, 2108.20

itineracy, 740.3e

language ministries, 1414.5

Minority Group Self-Determination Fund, 2108.7

multiracial/multicultural groups, 1529.7

Native American Awareness Sunday, 274.6

Native American scholarships, 274.6c

Native Americans, ministry to, 274.6b, 1403.1m

nondiscrimination, 703.1, 815, 907.7a, 911.1

recruitment, 733.2a, 740.3e, 1529.11

representation

conference agencies, 706.4, 735.1, 740.2, 741.2, 743.2

Curriculum Resources Committee, 1228.1b

district Council on Ministries, 749.2

general agencies, 805, 905.1, .4a, 1007.1c, 1444, 1804.2, 1907.1, 2103, 2204.1-.2, .5b

jurisdictional agencies, 628, 632

Racial/ethnic concern, *cont'd:*
local church offices, 249.7, 250.4
National Youth Ministry Organization Legislative Assembly/ Steering Committee, 1306.2*a*, 1307.1-.2*a*
University Senate, 1517.2
rights, 72*A*
Southwest Border Committee, 1414.11
violation of inclusiveness, 2108.6
youth caucuses, 1306.1*b*(6)

Readmission to conference relationship, 454-57

Recording secretary, local church, 247.4

Records, 232-35, 1811.1*b*, .2
advocacy roles/coalitions, 817
card index, 234
church membership, 232-35
of conference members, 1604.10
depositing of, 1811.3
of discontinuance
as local pastor, 410.1
from probationary membership, 418
electronic information system, 234
of local church, 232-35, 247.4-.5
loose-leaf book, 234
permanent church register, 234
personnel, 705.8, 733.3
service records, 705.6, 1604.10

Records and History, local church Committee on, 247.5*b*, 269.5

Recruitment
Cabinet's responsibility, 733.2*a*
of clergy for appointment beyond local church, 1511.1-.2*a*
conference Board of Ordained Ministry responsibility, 733.2*a*
of deaconess, 1454.4
Division of Chaplains and Related Ministries responsibility, 1511.2
Division of Ordained Ministry responsibility, 733.2*a*, 1529.11
of missionary, 1454.4

Recuitment, *cont'd:*
Mission Personnel Resources Department responsibility, 1454.4
racial/ethnic ordained ministers, 733.2*a*, 740.3*e*, 1529.11

Reformation Sunday, 739.4*f*

Refugee Resettlement Committee, conference, 731.4(18), 1459.4

Registrar, conference Board of Ordained Ministry, 404.2, 733.3

Rehabilitation of offenders, 74*F*

Reinstatement of local pastor, 410.4

Religion and Race, conference Commission on, 740

Religion and Race, district director of, 740.7, 751

Religion and Race, local church work area on, 252.1*b*, 260, 261.7, 265

Religion and Race, General Commission on, 2101-08
accountability, 802.2, 803.5, 2101.1, 2108.20
amenability, 802.1, 803.5
financial support, 2107
general secretary, 813, 2106-07
membership, 805-06, 2103
Minority Group Self-Determination Fund, 2108.7
name, 2101
nondiscrimination policies, 815, 907.7*a*, 911.1
officers, 2105
purpose, 2102
representation
Committee on Personnel Policies and Practices, 905.4*d*
National Youth Ministry Organization Steering Committee, 1307.1
responsibilities, 2108
staff, 2106

Religion and Race, General Commission on, *cont'd:*
standards/guidelines for local church work area, 261.9
Temporary General Aid Fund, 920, 1604.12, 2108.16
vacancy, 812, 2104

Religion in American Life, Inc., 1909

Religious minorities, rights of, 72B

Removal
of book editor, 1731
of church member from roll, 230, 232.3
of general agency member/officer/employee, 811, 1727

Renewal leave, 511.1, 525

Reports
Administrative Council, 252.2b
Annual Conference, 704.4
conference Board of Trustees, 2512.5
General Conference, 804, 906-07, 1604.12, 1704, 1712, 1723, 2108.20
treasurer, General Council on Finance and Administration, 715.4

Reports to Charge Conference
appointee beyond local church, 433.3a
apportionments for World Service and Conference Benevolences, 247.14
audit, 249.4c
Board of Trustees, 2549
church historian, 247.5a
Committee on Finance, 269.4c
Committee on Nominations and Personnel, 249-50, 258
diaconal minister, 314.5
district Board of Church Location and Building, 2518
lay leader, 247.14
lay speaker, 279b
membership, 233, 236, 242, 247.15

Reports to Charge Conference, *cont'd:*
ordained minister
on honorable location, 452.1b
on leave of absence, 448.1
retired, 451.5
pastor, 233, 236, 242, 247.14-.15, 439.3c, 445.5
study committee, 2543

Retirement
age at, 313.2c, 451.1-.2b-c, 509.1, 814.3
appointment after, 451.6, 510.2
associate member, 419.5
bishop, 509-10
Charge Conference membership after, 246.2, 451.5
counseling before, 451.4
diaconal minister, 313.2
early retirement, 451.2, 453.1e, 509.2, 1606.4i
effective date of, 451.2d, 509.1
general agency staff, 814.3
involuntary, 451.3, 509.3
local pastor, 410.5
mandatory, 451.1, 509.1
ordained minister, 451
return to effective relationship, 451.7
voluntary, 451.2, 509.2
after years of service, 451.2

Review of full and associate conference membership, 452-53

Review process for complaints, 453.1b, d

Rights
the aging, 72E
associate member, 419
children, 72C
full clergy members, 423
people, 74A
persons with handicapping conditions, 72G
probationary member, 413
racial/ethnic persons, 72A
religious minorities, 72B
women, 72F
youth/young adults, 72D

Ritual, the, 15.6
General Board of Discipleship responsibilities, 1214.4
revision of, 15.6, 1214.4
of The United Methodist Church:
Book of Ritual of The Evangelical United Brethren Church, 1959, 1214.3
"The General Services of the Church" in The Book of Worship for Church and Home of The Methodist Church, 1214.3
"The General Services of the Church 1984" (English and Spanish versions), 1214.3
The Ordinal 1981, 1214.3
translation of, 638.18
use of, 219

Rolls, 209, 232-35
Affiliate Membership Roll, 227, 232.5
Associate Membership Roll, 227, 232.6
church membership, 209, 219, 232-25, 247.15
Constituency Roll, 232.4
Full Membership Roll, 209, 219, 232.1
General Roll of Military Service, 218
of local church, 230.4-.5, 232-35
Members Removed by Charge Conference Action, 230.4-.5, 232.3
Preparatory Membership Roll, 216.4, 222-24, 232.2
register of baptized children, 223

Rural areas, mission development in, 731.5*f, h,* 1414.5

Rural life, 72*M*

Rural Life Sunday, 275.3

S

Sabbatical leave
associate member, 419.5, 446
bishop, 511.2

Sabbatical leave, *cont'd:*
diaconal minister, 313.1*c*
ordained minister, 446
pension credit for, 1606.3*a*
as remedial action for ordained minister facing complaints, 453.1*e*
salary for, 446

Sacrament, *pages 65, 70*
of Baptism, *pages 65, 70,* 106
of the Lord's Supper, *pages 65, 70,* 274.3
right to administer, 218, 406, 439.1*b,* 443.3*a*

Salary
Administrative Board recommendation, 256.3*e*
Charge Conference setting of, 247.13, 720
Committee on Pastor-Parish Relations recommendation, 256.3*e,* 269.2*f*(4)
conference Commission on Equitable Salaries, 441, 710.1*e,* 722, 907.14
of district superintendent, 710.1*a,* 715.2*c*
equitable, 414, 717
Equitable Salary Fund, 441, 718-19, 722
of local pastor, 408.1-.2
for maternity/paternity leave, 313.1*b,* 449.4
minimum, 722.2, .6. *See* Minimum salary
of ordained minister appointed to pastoral charge, 441
of retired minister under appointment, 451.6
for sabbatical leave, 446
See also Clergy support

Scholarships
Crusade, 274.3, 731.4(11), 1454-55, 1515.3*f,* 1529.12
Crusade Scholarship Committee, 274.3, 916.4*b*
Ethnic Scholarship Program, 274.3, 916.4*b*

Scholarships, *cont'd:*
Native American scholarships, 274.6*c*
Office of Loans and Scholarships, 1508.2
United Methodist, 261.5*a*, 274.4, 916.3

Schools of theology, 1530-32
candidate for ordained ministry enrolled in, 405.1, 424
Division of Ordained Ministry responsibility for, 1527.1
financial support, 921.2, 1530.1-.2
non–United Methodist certification, 1529.10
scholarships for Native Americans, 274.6*c*
University Senate responsibilities, 405.1, 424, 1517-18

Scouting ministries, 258, 1219.3

Sea, use of, 70*A*

Secretary, Annual Conference, 702.6
certificate of organization to new local church, 703.10
certification of local church transfer, 44.1
charges/specifications against clergy member/local pastor, 2623.3*d*
custodian of trial documents, 2624.3*e*
deposit of journals in archives, 1811.3*j*
diaconal minister's credentials, 307
documents to president of Court of Appeals, 2624.3*e*, 2625.3*c*
journal responsibilities, 705.3. *See* Journal, Annual Conference
maintenance of permanent records, 418, 705.1, 733.2*k*, 1418.3*c*(1)
number of General Conference delegates to be elected, 602.4
ordination certificates, 435.5
reports
to General Council on Finance and Administration, 703.11

Secretary, Annual Conference, *cont'd:*
to secretary of the General Conference, 602.5
signs/distributes delegate credentials, 602.6
surrendered license/credentials, 410.1, 418, 452.3-.4
transfer of information, 516.5
written report for clergy member's absence at Annual Conference, 701.6

Secretary, Central Conference, 515.5, 637.7, 638.7, 2625.2

Secretary, Charge Conference, 2624.4*f*

Secretary, Jurisdictional Conference
edits/deposits journal, 515.5, 627, 1811.3*j*
notifies counsel and secretary of Judicial Council, 2625.2*b*
receives:
notice of bishop's appeal, 2625.2*a*
number to be elected to General Board of Publication, 1702
sends pool of names to general agencies, 805.1*d*

Secretary of the General Conference, 604
adjusts delegate formula, 602.3*a*
calculates number
of delegates, 602.3
to be elected to General Board of Publication, 1702
consults:
central archivist, 1811.3*i, l*
Council of Bishops, 605
General Commission on Christian Unity and Interreligious Concerns, 605
coordinates nomination/election process, 805
deposits materials in central archives, 1811.3*b*
edits journal, 611.1

Secretary of the General Conference, *cont'd:*
files original documents, 611.4, 1811
informs:
Annual Conference secretaries, 602.4
jurisdictional conference secretaries, 1702
issues invitations to ecumenical representatives, 605
keeps:
file of Judicial Council decisions, 2619
permanent record, 611
receives:
Central Conference journals, 637.7
Jurisdictional Conference journals, 627
petitions, 608.1
reports of assignments of Central Conference bishops, 638.7
signs:
act of covenanting, 650
affiliated autonomous status, 649.5
autonomous status, 652.5
concordat status, 653.3*b*
supplies certificate of election forms, 602.5
transfers responsibility, 605

Separation of Church and State, 74*B*

Services of worship open to all, 2506

Sex education, 71*F*, 72*C*

Sexuality, human, 71*F*

Shared facilities, 206.3*i*, 270, 2552

Shared ministry, 206.3

Short-term Volunteer-in-Mission ministries, 731.6, 1402.14, 1454.7, 1465.1*c*, .3

Sick leave. *See* Disability leave

Single adult ministries, 258, 259, 263.4, 265.3

Single persons, 71*E*

Sixteen-year rule, 810.3

Slavery, 74*A*

Small membership churches, 252.1, 805.2*c*(1)

Social Creed, 76

Social Principles, *pages 91-92,* 70-76
Administrative Board member's responsibility, 254
church member's responsibility, 214
diaconal ministry candidate's dedication to, 304.1, *footnote, page 213*
in investment policies, 2512.3
ordained ministry candidate's dedication to, 404.4*e*, *footnote, page 213*
program-related agencies concurrence, 1006.14

Soil, use of, 70*A*

Southwest Border Committee, 1414.11

Space exploration, 70*D*

Speaking for The United Methodist Church, 610

Special appeal
churchwide, 274.3, 911.4, 1460, 1463
conference-wide, 709.2, 710.5, 715.2*a*

Special appointment. *See* Appointment beyond the local church

Special days (Sundays), 273-76
as ecumenical observances, 273, 274.2-.3, .5, 739.4*f*
listing:
Christian Education Sunday, 273, 276.1
Golden Cross Sunday, 273, 276.2

INDEX

Special days (Sundays), *cont'd:*
Heritage Sunday, 273, 275.1
Human Relations Day, 273-
274.1
Laity Sunday (Day), 273, 275.2
Native American Awareness
Sunday, 274.6
One Great Hour of Sharing,
273, 274.2
Peace with Justice Sunday, 273,
274.5
Pentecost Sunday, 273, 739.4*f*
Reformation Sunday, 273,
739.4*f*
Rural Life Sunday, 275.3
United Methodist Student Day,
273, 274.4
World Communion Sunday,
273, 274.3, 739.4*f*, 1505.20
See also individual days
offerings, 273-74, 276, 916
promotion, 256.4, 261.3, 274,
731.4(33), 732.4*d*(4), 1906.12
responsibilities
Administrative Board, 256.4
Annual Conference, 273, 275.3,
276
chairperson of education, 261.3
conference agencies, 729.7*b*,
731.4(11), (33), 732.4*d*(4),
739.4*f*
Council of Bishops, 275
General Board of Church and
Society, 274.5
General Board of Discipleship,
275.2, 1218.5
General Board of Global Ministries, 274.6, 275.3
General Board of Higher Education and Ministry, 1505.20
General Commission on Ar-
chives and History, 275.1
General Commission on Com-
munication, 274, 1441,
1906.12
General Council on Finance and
Administration, 274, 906,
915-16, 1006.6
General Council on Ministries,
274, 906.11, 916, 1006.6
Health and Welfare Ministries
Department, 1441

Special days (Sundays), *cont'd:*
Mission Education and Cultivation Department, 1441
themes for Heritage, Laity, and
Rural Life Sundays, 275
without offerings, 273, 275-76

Spiritual formation, 261.4

Staff
Administrative Board member,
253.4
Committee on Personnel Policies
and Practices, 905.4*d*, 907.7*b*
conference Council on Ministries,
314.2, 726.8, 749.2
continuing education, 269.2*f*(5)
diaconal minister as, 310.1*a*, 314-
18
general agencies, 803.7, 814,
907.7*b*
nondiscrimination policy, 815
pastor as, 438
Personnel Committee, 269.2*f*(10)
Staff-Parish Relations Committee,
269.2*b*
Staff Pension Plan, 814.4

Staff-Parish Relations Committee,
269.2*b*. *See* Committee on Pastor-
Parish Relations, local church

Standard Sermons of Wesley, *page*
74

Statistician, Annual Conference,
702.6

**Status and Role of Women, confer-
ence Commission on,** 741, 2203.4

**Status and Role of Women, General
Commission on,** 2201-09
accountability, 802.2, 803.5
amenability, 802.1, 803.5
authority, 2203.1
financial support, 2207
general secretariat/secretary, 813,
2208
meetings, 2206
membership, 805-06, 2204
name, 2201

799

Status and Role of Women, General Commission on, *cont'd:*
nondiscrimination policies, 815, 907.7*a*, 911.1
officers, 2205
purpose, 2202
relationships, 2209
representation
Committee on Personnel Policies and Practices, 905.4*d*
National Youth Ministry Organization Steering Committee, 1307.1
responsibility, 2203
staff, 2208
vacancy, 2204.6

Status and Role of Women, local church work area on the, 261.8

Sterilization, 72*H*

Stewards, district, 250.1, 711.3

Stewards, district Board of, 711.3-.4, 2517.2

Stewardship
Commission on, local church, 261.9*a*, 1215.4
conference Board of Discipleship responsibilities, 729.5
General Board of Discipleship responsibilities, 1215
work area on, 252.1*a*, 260, 261.9, 265, 269.4

Stewards, local church, 250

Student
as candidate for ministry, 405.1
financial aid obligations, 733.2*t*
as local pastor, 408.3-.4, 409, 701.2
pension credit for, 1606.3*a*, .4*a*, *e*
relationship to local church, 261.5*c*
theological, 274.6*c*, 1531
United Methodist Student Day, 261.5*a*, 273, 274.4, 732.4*d*(4), 916.3, 1505.20
United Methodist Student Loan Fund, 261.5*a*, 274.4, 916.3, 1508.2
See also Scholarships

Study leave, 445.2. *See also* Renewal leave; Sabbatical leave

Study of local church potential, 2550

Subdistrict, 732.4*b*(5)

Superintendency, 17, 501-34
appointment-making, 530-34
bishop, 503-16
expressions of, 526-29
district superintendent, 503-04, 517-25
nature of, 501-02
task, 501
See also Appointment-making; Bishop; College of Bishops; Council of Bishops; District Superintendent; Episcopacy

Superintendent, Church School/ Sunday School, 250.1. *See* Church School superintendent

Superintendent, Mission, 664.3-.4

Superintendent, Provisional Annual Conference, 657.1

Supervising pastor, 404.2, 733.3

Surrender of credentials, 410.1, 418, 452.2-.5. *See also* Discontinuance from probationary membership; Readmission to conference relationship; Termination of conference membership; Withdrawal from conference membership

Surrender of ordained ministerial office, 452.3, .5, 453.1*e*(6)

Sustentation Fund, 710.1*f*, 723

T

Task groups, local church, 267

Tax-exempt status of The United Methodist Church, 907.4

Television, 1906.3

800

Temporary General Aid Fund, 920
administration of, 1604.12
apportionments, 908
disbursement of, 906.2
General Commission on Religion
and Race responsibility, 2108.16
promotion of, 1906.12

**Termination of conference member-
ship,** 418, 448.4, 452-53

**Termination of local church mem-
bership,** 230, 236-43

Testifying before legislative body,
610.2

Theme, 803.8
determination of need for,
1006.17
for Heritage Sunday, 275.1
implementation of, 1006.4
for Laity Sunday, 275.2
for Rural Life Sunday, 275.3

Theological schools. *See* Schools of
theology

Theological Task, 69, 306.5*f*, 414.8

Title to properties, 2501. *See also*
Property; Property, local church

Tobacco, 72*J*, *footnote, page 210*

Town and country ministries, 206.2,
731.5*f, h*, 1210.6, 1414.13

**Trademark, "Methodist" or "United
Methodist" as,** 2502

Transfer
Annual Conference membership,
427, 516.5, 703.6-.7
to another denomination, 241-42,
647.2, 648.2, 653.4*d*
of bishops, 612
certificate of, 220, 240, 270.3
church membership, 220, 230.4,
231, 236-43, 270.3
of local church, 44, 271
reimbursement of financial aid,
733.2*t*
voting rights, 703.6

Transitional community, 207,
731.5*h*

Translation, *page 64*
Charge Conference proceedings,
246.9
General Conference legislation,
638.22
name of church, 2
Ritual, 638.18

Traveling preacher, 38, 663.5-.6,
703.6. *See also* Itinerant system

Treasurer, Annual Conference, 715.
For detailed listing *see* Conference
treasurer

**Treasurer, General Council on Fi-
nance and Administration,** 905.3
disbursement of funds, 917.2
general Advance special remittance, 914.4
as general secretary, 905.3
responsibilities, 908-09
as treasurer of The Advance/One
Great Hour of Sharing, 915.2
Youth Service Fund, 1310

Treasurer, local church, 249.4
member:
Administrative Board, 254
Committee on Finance, 269.4
proportional payment responsibility, 737.4*b*
responsibilities, 715.2*a*, 1310

Trial, 18, 61, 2624
amendment to charges, 2622.2
appeal, 2624-25. *See* Appeal
of bishop, 453.2, 638.17, 2624.2
chargeable offenses, 2621
charges, filing of, 2622
of clergy member, 453.2, 2624.3,
2626.1
commissioner, 2624.1*j*(11)
convening of the court, 2624.1*c*
counsel, 2624.1
custody of records, 2624.4*f*
guidelines, 2624.1*j*
investigation procedures, 2623
of lay member, 638.17, 2624.4

Trial, *cont'd:*
of local pastor, 410.3, 2623-24
notice of, 453.3, 2624.1*e*, *j*(2), .4*e*
officers of Trial Court, 2624.1*c*
of ordained minister, 18, 61, 638.17
place of, 2624.1*d*
power of Trial Court, 2624.1*h*
presence of person charged, 2624.1*j*(2), 2625.1*c*
procedures, 2424
reversal of verdict, 2625.1*b*, *h*
right to, 18, 61, 453.2
time of, 2624.1*d*
Trial Court selection, 2624.1*c*
venue, change of, 2624.4*e*
vote necessary to convict, 2624.1*h*, *j*(4)
witnesses, 2624.1*g*, *j*(7), (10), (11)

Trustees, conference Board of, 2512, 2514, 2548.2

Trustees, district Board of, 2517.2

Trustees, local church Board of, 245, 269.3, 2524-25. *See* Board of Trustees, local church

Trustees of church institutions, 2553

Truth in advertising, 73*D*

U

United Church, Affiliated Autonomous, 651. *See* Affiliated Autonomous United Church

United Church, Autonomous, 647.3, 652

United Methodist–affiliated institutions, 306.3, 710.3*c*, 731.4(24)-(26), 1516.2*b*, 1520.1, 2553. *See also* Church-related institutions

United Methodist Children's Fund for Christian Mission, 263.1*g*

United Methodist Church, The, *pages 16-18,* 2, 113, 2501
becoming part of, 654
Constitution, *pages 19-20,* 1-64
continuance of episcopacy, 48
Council of Bishops in, 50
doctrinal history of, *page 50*
doctrinal standards in, *pages 59-60*
ecumenical relations, 5
fulfillment of ministry through, 113
history of concern for social justice, *page 91*
limitation of responsibility, 1447, 2509
name, 2
organization, 8, 40
Restrictive Rules, 16-20, *page 60*
self-understanding, 113, 2501
speaking for, 610
use of name as trademark, 2502

United Methodist Committee on Relief Department, General Board of Global Ministries, 1458-67
Advance administering agency, 1007.5*d*
Advance, participating agency, 1007.5*a*
associate general secretary, 1466
churchwide appeals, 1463
conference Refugee Resettlement Committee, 731.4(18), 1459.4
as corporate successor, 1406.1
disaster response, 1464, 1465.1*a*
executive committee, 1466
financial support, 1460-63
funds for property damaged by disaster, 1464
membership, 1467
objectives and responsibilities, 1459
One Great Hour of Sharing, 916.2*c*, 1459.7
organization, 1465
purpose, 1458
relationship to ecumenical bodies, 1465.2-.3
relationship to World Division, 1465.1*b*

United Methodist Committee on Relief Department, General Board of Global Ministries, *cont'd:*
short-term Volunteers-in-Mission, 731.6, 1402.14, 1454.7, 1465.1c, .3
treasurer, 1466-67

United Methodist Communications (UMCom), 1902-03. For all other references *see* Communication, General Commission on

United Methodist Development Fund, 1414.10

United Methodist Foundations, 906.8, 1215.11, 2513, 2533

United Methodist Men, 1222
conference Board of Discipleship support, 729.7b
conference lay leader, 702.8b-c
Division of, 1222
Jurisdictional Committee on, 635, 1204.1
local church unit, 264
National Association of Conference Presidents of, 1222.1b
national officers, 1222.1e
president of
conference, as member
of Annual Conference, 35
of conference Council on Ministries, 726.2
local church, as member
of Administrative Board, 254
of Council on Ministries, 258
representation
Adult Council, 265.3
conference Board of the Laity, 730.3, .5
conference Council on Ministries, 726.2
Metropolitan Commission, 731.5i, 1415.7j
resources, 1222

United Methodist Men, jurisdictional Committee on, 635, 1204.1

United Methodist Men's Division, 1222

United Methodist Publishing House, 1701, 1709-44
authority of General Board of Publication, 1709-12, 1714-16, 1718-19, 1724-26, 1743-44
bonding of officers, 1726
book editor, 1728-31
conference Committee on Publishing House Liaison, 726.5e
corporations, 1709-11
curriculum promotion/interpretation, 1226.2b
direction and control, 1714
distributor for church agencies, 1742
duties of, 1724-25, 1738
Book of Resolutions, 611.2
cooperative publication, 1740
Jurisdictional Conference journals, 627
net income distribution, 20, 657, 1715
permanent church register, 234.1
publishing/distributing
curriculum resources, 1226.2b, 1736
General Conference journal, 611.1
worship materials, 1214
Illinois corporation, 1718.3, 1719
name, 1701
objectives, 1713, 1718
printer for church agencies, 1741
property, 907.3, 1718-19, 1743-44
publisher (executive officer, president), 905.1, 1007.1a(8), 1702, 1714, 1717, 1722, 1724-27, 1734, 1738
representation
Committee on Official Forms and Records, 905.4c, 1728
Curriculum Resources Committee, 1226.2, 1228.1c, 1734, 1736, 1740
reserve funds, 1715
See also Publication, General Board of

United Methodist scholarships, 261.5a, 274.4, 916.3, 1508.2

INDEX

United Methodist Student Day, 273, 274.4, 916.3
budget, 906.1
disbursement, 906.2
offering, 273, 274.4, 916.3
promotion, 261.5a, 732.4d(4), 1505.20, 1906.12

United Methodist Student Loan Fund, 261.5a, 274.4, 916.3, 1508.2

United Methodist, use of, as trademark, 2502

United Methodist Voluntary Services Program, 274.1b

United Methodist Women, 1421-29
Assembly, 1426
conference Board of Global Ministries, cooperate with, 731.4(8)
conference coordinator of Christian global concerns, 731.3
conference lay leader, work with, 702.8c
Constitution, 1429
conference, 742
district, 755
jurisdiction, 634
local church, 263.6
financial support of Women's Division, 1422.4, 1423.4c, 1427
national officers, 1423.4d
organizing units, 1423.4a
program/policies set by Women's Division, 1422.1, 1423.4b
president of
conference, as member
of Annual Conference, 35, 742.7
of conference Council on Ministries, 726.2
local church, as member
of Administrative Board, 254
of Council on Ministries, 258
representation
Adult Council, 265.3
conference Board of Church and Society, 728.2
conference Board of the Laity, 730.3, .5

United Methodist Women, cont'd:
conference Council of Ministries, 726.2
Metropolitan Commission, 731.5i, 1415.7j

United Methodist Young Adults, 730.3, .5

United Methodist Youth, 730.5. See also National Youth Ministry Organization

United Methodist Youth Council, 254

United Methodist Youth Fellowship, 263.2

United Methodist Youth Ministry, 258, 263.2

United Nations, 75D

United Nations Office, 1115, 1422.8

University Senate, 1517-21
consultative relationship, 1521
executive secretary, 1517.3
financial support, 1517.4
institutional affiliations, 1519
meetings, 1517.3
membership, 1517.2
objectives, 1518
officers, 1517.3
organization, 1517
purpose, 1518
responsibilities, 1520
schools approved for candidates for ordained ministry, 405.1, 420, 424, 1520.2
United Methodist affiliated institutions, 306.3, 1516.2b, 1520.1
vacancy, 1517.2

Upper Room, The, 261.4, 1202.5, 1206.3, 1216.3

Urban ministries, 731.5g-i, 1414.5, 1415.7

Urban-suburban life, 72N

804

V

Vacancy, 812
conference Board of Ordained Ministry, 733.1*b*
conference Board of Pensions, 737.2
conference treasurer, 715.1
episcopacy, 508, 620.2
general agency, 810.8-.9, 812, 905.1, 1507, 1602.1*e*, 1702, 1804.1, 2006.3, 2204.6
general agency staff, 1109
Judicial Council, 58, 2603
local church Board of Trustees, 2530.3
National Youth Ministry Organization Steering Committee, 1307.2*b*
University Senate, 1517.2

Voluntary retirement
of bishop, 509.2
of ordained minister, 451.2

Volunteer-in-mission, short-term, 731.6, 1402.14, 1454.7, 1465.1*c*, .3

Voting rights
affiliate member
Annual Conference, 443.4, 701.1*c*
local church, 443.3*b*
Missionary Conference, 660.4*b*
associate member, 419.2, 701.1*c*
clergy member, Annual Conference, 423, 701.1
concordat delegates to General Conference, 12.3, 602.1*b*
delegates to General Conference
Affiliated Autonomous Methodist Church, 648.3
Affiliated United Church, 651
diaconal minister, 36, 314
elected general agency staff, 814.7-.8
employed staff, local church, 254
full-time local pastor, 701.1*d*, .2
honorary member, Charge Conference, 246.3
lay member, Annual Conference, 36, 701.5

Voting rights, *cont'd:*
lay missionary, 701.2
Mission representative to Central Conference, 637.1
Missionary Conference representative to Central Conference, 637.1
part-time local pastor, 701.1*e*, .2
probationary member, 413.2, 701.1*b*
retired bishop, 510.1-.2
student local pastor, 701.1*e*, .2
traveling preacher, 703.6
youth, 263.2

Vows of church membership, 211, 217, 230.1

W

War, 75*C*

Water, use of, 70*A*

Weapons, 75*C*

Week of Prayer for Christian Unity, 739.4*f*

Wesley Foundation, 732.5, 1513.2, 1515.2, 1516.3*b-c*

Wesley's questions, *footnote, pages 210-11,* 403, 425

Wills and Estate Planning Task Force, 261.9*b*

Withdrawal of membership
Annual Conference, 452.2, .4-.5, 2626.2
local church, 230.1*d*, 242-243, 2626.2-.3
See also Surrender of credentials; Surrender of ordained ministerial office

Women
Church Women United, 1422.9
in ordained ministry, 412.2, 530.2, 1527.3

Women, *cont'd:*
nondiscriminatory policies, 815, 2203.8
representation
Annual Conference, 35
Commission on Pan-Methodist Cooperation, 2403
conference agencies, 706.4, 726, 730.3, .5, 735.1, 740.2, 741.2-.3
conference staff, 726.8
district agencies, 749.2
general agencies, 805, 905.1, 1007.1a, 1204.1, 1412.3, .6, 1804.2, 2103, 2204.1-.2
General Conference delegation from large Affiliated Autonomous Methodist Church, 648.3
jurisdictional agencies, 628
liaison committees, 1436
local church leadership, 249.7, 250.4, 254, 258, 265.3
National Division executive committee, 1416
University Senate, 1517.2
rights of, 72F
United Methodist Women, 1421-29. *See* United Methodist Women
Women's Work, Central Conference Committee on, 638.15-.16
women's work subcommittee, 1436.2
World Federation of Methodist Women, 638.15

Women's Division, General Board of Global Ministries, 1421-29
authority, 1423
bylaws, 1423.1
Church Women United, 1422.9
as corporate successor, 1406.1
deputy general secretary, 1409.2, 1424, 1428
executive committee, 1424
financial support, 1422.4, 1423.4c, 1427
meetings, 1423.2
membership, 634.4, 1428
officers, 1423.4d
organization, 1425

Women's Division, General Board of Global Ministries, *cont'd:*
predecessor groups, 1423.3a
property rights, 1423.1
purpose, 1421
representation
Committee on Deaconess Service, 1419.2
General Commission on the Status and Role of Women, 2204.3
Mission Education and Cultivation Department, 1424
National Division, 1424
World Division, 1424
responsibilities, 1422, 1423.3
treasurer, 1414, 1428
United Nations Office, 1115, 1428.8
See also United Methodist Women

Women's Work, Central Conference Committee on, 638.15-.16

Work, 73C

Work area commissions, 266

Work areas, local church, 260-61
chairperson, 250.1, 252.1, 254, 258, 260, 261, 263.1f-g
listing:
Christian unity and interreligious concerns, 261.1
Church and society, 261.2
education, 261.3, 263.1e-g
evangelism, 252.1c, 261.4
higher education and campus ministry, 261.5
missions, 261.6
nurture, 252.1a
outreach, 252.1b, 261.7
religion and race, 261.7
status and role of women, 261.8
stewardship, 261.9
worship, 261.10

World Communion Sunday, 273, 274.3
budget, 906.1
Crusade Scholarships, 274.3, 1455.2

World Communion Sunday, *cont'd:*
offering, 273, 274.3, 916.4, 1455.2
promotion, 739.4*f*, 1505.20,
1906.12

World Council of Churches, 2402.3
General Commission on Christian
Unity and Interreligious Concerns, interpreter of relationship, 2003.4
Interdenominational Cooperation
Fund, 918.2
local church interpretation, 261.1
promotion of, 739.4*f*

**World Division, General Board of
Global Ministriest,** 1430-38
administration of new commitments, 1437
Advance administering agency,
1007.5*d*
Advance, participating agency,
1007.5*a*
appointment of personnel, 443.1*c*
authority, 1432
coordination of programs outside
U.S.A., 1403.3
as corporate successor, 1406.1
deputy general secretary, 1409.2,
1438
executive committee, 1409.3, 1435
financial support, 1411.2
lay missionaries, 238, 701.2
liaison committee, 1436
meetings, 1434
membership, 805, 1409.3, 1412.3,
1438
Mission administration, 663.7
prohibit use of personnel for intelligence purposes, 1433
purpose, 1430
responsibilities, 1431
treasurer, 1438

**World Federation of Methodist
Women,** 638.15, 1422.9

World Methodist Council, 2401
Committee on Family Life, 1220.1*e*
General Commission on Archives
and History, cooperation with,
1803.1

World Methodist Council, *cont'd:*
General Commission on Christian
Unity and Interreligious Concerns, interpreter of relationship, 2003.4

World Methodist Historical Society,
1803.1

**World Service and Conference Be-
nevolences,** 710.3*d*
Administrative Board promotion,
256.4-.5
apportionment, 711.4
budget, 710.3
monthly remittance to conference
treasurer, 269.4*b*, 715.2*a*

World Service Fund, 910, 912
allocation of, 906.1, 1006.2, 1445,
1512, 1604.8
budget, 904, 906.1, 911.4
contingency funds, 906.1*b*(6),
1006.2*e*
disbursement, 906.2*a*
Fourth Sunday offering, 263.1*f*

World Service Special Gifts, 913,
1906.12

Worship
conference Board of Discipleship
responsibility for, 729.4
General Board of Discipleship responsibility for, 1214

Worship, local church work area on,
252.1*a*, 260, 261.10, 265

Y

Young adult ministries, 258, 259,
263.3, 265.3

Young adults
Adult/Young Adult Council, 265.3
age of, 258, 247.6, 263.3,
1007.1*a*(4)
coordinator of ministries to, 258,
259
ministries to, 263.5
representation

Young adults, *cont'd:*
Annual Conference agencies, 706.4, 726.2, 730.3, .5, 735.1, 740.2
Commission on Pan-Methodist Cooperation, 2403
district agencies, 749.2
general agencies, 805.1*b*, .2*a*, 1702, 1804.2, 1907, 2103
jurisdictional agencies, 628
local church officers and organizations, 247.6, 249.7, 250.4, 258, 269.1-.2
rights of, 72*D*
United Methodist Young Adults, 730.3, .5
Young Adult Council, 265.3

Young person, member of Annual Conference, 35

Youth
adult workers, 1305.2*b*, 1306
age of, 224-25, 258, 247.6, 258, 263.2, 905.1, 1007.1*a*(4)
church membership rights, 226, 263.2
conference coordinator of, 632, 743.3*j*, 1306.2*a*
conference Council on Youth Ministry, 743. For detailed listing *see* Youth Ministry, conference Council on
Jurisdictional Youth Coordinator, 632
Jursidictional Youth Ministry Organization Convocation, 632, 743.3*f*, 1307.2*a*
local church coordinator of ministries to, 258, 259, 263.2
members of general agencies, 1305.2*c*, 1306.2*b*(1)
ministry to, 729.1*h*, 1202.11
National Youth Ministry Organization, 1301-11. *See* National Youth Ministry Organization
participation in National Youth Ministry Convocation, 1305.2
racial/ethnic youth caucuses, 1306.1*b*(6)
representation
Administrative Board, 254

Youth, *cont'd:*
Annual Conference, 35
Annual Conference agencies, 706.4, 726.2, 730.3, .5, 735.1, 740.2, 741.2
district agencies, 749.2
general agencies, 805.1*b*, .2*a*, 1007.1*a*(3), 1702, 1804.2, 1907, 2103
jurisdictional agencies, 628, 632
local church officers and organizations, 247.6, 249.7, 250.4, 254, 258, 269.1-.2
rights of, 72*D*
United Methodist Youth, 730.5
United Methodist Youth Council, 254
United Methodist Youth Fellowship, 263.2
United Methodist Youth Ministry, 258, 263.2
voting rights, 263.2
Youth Council, 247.6, 263.2, 265.2, .4
Youth Service Fund, 743.3*g-i*, 906.2*n*, 908, 910, 1310

Youth Council, local church, 247.6, 263.2, 265.2, .4

Youth ministries, 258, 263.2
conference Board of Discipleship responsibility, 729.1*h*
General Board of Discipleship responsibility, 1202.11
Jurisdictional Youth Ministry Organization, 632
United Methodist Youth Fellowship, 263.2
Youth Council, 247.6, 265.2, .4

Youth Ministry, conference Council on, 743
conference coordinator, 632, 743.3*j*, 1306.2*a*
financial support, 1310
membership, 743.2
promotion of Youth Service Fund, 1307.4
purpose, 742.1
representation

Youth Ministry, conference Council on, *cont'd:*
    conference Board of the Laity, 730.3
    conference Council on Ministries, 726.2
    Jurisdictional Youth Ministry Organization Convocation, 632
    National Youth Ministry Organization Legislative Assembly, 1306.2*a*
    scholarships, 1305.4

Youth Ministry, district Council on, 756

Youth Offenders Rehabilitation Program, 274.1*c*

Youth Service Fund, 910, 1310
    administration of, 1307.4*a*
    allotment of, 1306.1*b*(2), 1309-10
    Annual Conference share, 743.3*g*, 1310
    disbursement, 906.2
    goal-setting, 1306.1*b*(1)
    Project Review Committee, 743.3*g*, 1311
    project selection, 743.3*g*, 1307.4*a*, 1311
    promotion of, 263.2, 743.3*h*, 1307.4*b*, 1906.12